ARCHITECTURE, MEN, WOMEN AND MONEY

ARCHITECTURE, MEN, WOMEN AND MONEY IN AMERICA

1600–1860

BY *Roger·G·Kennedy*

RANDOM HOUSE · *New York*

Library of Congress Cataloging in Publication Data

Kennedy, Roger G.
Architecture, men, women and money in America, 1600–1860.

Bibliography: p.
Includes index.
1. Architecture—United States.   2. Architecture,
Colonial—United States.   3. Architecture, Modern—19th
century—United States.   4. Architects and patrons
—United States.   I. Title.
NA707.K38   1985   720'.973   84-2054
ISBN 0-394-53579-0

Designed by Anita Karl

Manufactured in the United States of America

2 4 6 8 9 7 5 3

FIRST EDITION

for Elisabeth Dean Kennedy

Preface

ONCE, NEARLY TWENTY YEARS AGO, a very old, very frail, yet relentless man, William Gray Purcell, extracted a promise from me that I would try to write a book like this, a book he never had the strength to pull together. This is my belated response.

In the early 1960's I had done twenty-six half hours of television about the architecture of the upper Mississippi Valley. The final broadcast described the rapid growth and subsequent collapse of the system of small country banks in the region around the turn of the twentieth century. That system had nourished a class of independent, intelligent and bold people who became clients for architects like Louis Sullivan, Frank Lloyd Wright, George Elmslie and William Gray Purcell. In the elegiac conclusion of the broadcast and the book that went with the series, I reported the bankruptcy of some of those banks and bankers, the death of Sullivan, the exile of Wright and Purcell's departure for California in 1917, "dying of tuberculosis."

Soon thereafter I opened a letter postmarked Pasadena.

The salutation was "Dear Friend of Good Will." At the end there was no signature, just a caricature of an old man, smiling, and this scrawl: "1900 blues . . . not very blue." The stationery was that of William Gray Purcell.

"I am grateful for your favorable opinion of us," he said. It was as if I had reviewed the Gettysburg Address and been rewarded by an appreciative note from Abraham Lincoln.

"There are several diverse matters I should like to lay before you," he continued. I responded, asking him when and where we could meet. I arranged a banker's trip to Pasadena (I was a banker at the time). We met. We talked—or, to be truthful, I should say he talked. We became friends and avid correspondents. Though Purcell was old and tired, he gave me a year of intense architectural education before he died. He was a persistent writer and demanded immediate response. "Diverse matters" were, indeed, pressing upon him. He knew that this time he really was dying.

When we began our correspondence I was afraid, of course, that an anachronistic wonder would disappear before I could find out what I had done to please him. I did find out, and the answer was a surprise: he thought I had done well in eschewing another thesis on style or another catalogue of buildings—even if the subject of the catalogue were to be his own underappreciated achievements. He was interested less in further attention to himself and his architectural colleagues than in the economic context of their work. In letter after letter he belabored me not to sink into stylistic analysis. Over and over, as I read his injunctions, I could imagine that gentle baritone voice rising to insist that there were plenty of people to write about objects as objects, but few to write about how the economic circumstances of a building's purchaser would determine not only its magnitude but often its shape and function.

I think, in retrospect, that he was amused by the prospect of urging a banker to go "back to the numbers" and not be intimidated by the aesthetics. He was certainly aware that others could do the aesthetics better than I, anyway. Yet it was not an easy charge he gave me. He did not want our inquiry limited to the Midwest, nor to the twentieth century. He wanted all American architecture put in its context, from its beginnings. Doing that would take platoons of writers working full-time, not just one writing part-time. But I felt the weight of his injunction to "get at it!"

I was, in those years, struggling to learn to be a better banker. Still, I did the best I could to comply with his urgings to write, producing another book and a dozen or so magazine pieces during the rest of the 1960's. At the end of the decade I became the chief financial officer of a university and then of the Ford Foundation; my profession took me out of my native Midwest. Later, I had some European clients, as an adviser on investment matters, and others nicely distributed in the United States, so it was possible for me to see quite a few buildings and to burrow through quite a few archives. I was able, again, to think about how structures—houses, especially—might be examined in accordance with Purcell's injunction to do justice to architects by doing justice to their clients. And now that I have become a museum director at the Smithsonian, managing a large staff of historians, there is a double incentive to return to the task Purcell set before me: his insistence and their assumption that each of us should try to add something peculiar to our experience and training to the "increase and diffusion of knowledge among mankind," as our charter reads. So I return to asking questions about architecture and money, architects and clients, architecture in context.

In writing this book, I have imagined myself standing before each work and trying to answer such questions as these:

How was the client (individual or community) able to pay for it?

Were the building funds acquired in ways that led the client to choose its form for disguise or for celebration?

What was the use to which this house was put in the economy? Was it, for example, a "folly"? A reliquary? A rallying-point? A prospectus? A unit of production? Was it just what it seems to be, a shell built around a person or a family? Was it a monument to accomplishment or a proclamation of intention?

What was the mood that surrounded the deployment of the money to lay up this work of art? Were its builders anxious? smug? indifferent to their surroundings? setting up a warning sign? Did they mean to impress, overawe, invite? arouse wonder, fear or admiration? Did they intend to insinuate a degree of gentility they wished to be thought to possess? Or were they so secure in their status that such notions would never have occurred to them?

How important was the personality of the client to the nature of the building? How did the client feel about the architect? How did the architect feel about the client? How did they both feel about their child, the building?

Of course, we never know enough to answer all these queries, but they all follow from the first: Who paid for it?

As I reflected on my conversations with my friend Purcell, it came to seem right to me to begin this story at that juncture in history when European architecture was beginning to force its way into the New World. This was four centuries before Purcell's own time, but he was interested in the persistence of certain interconnections between economics and architecture and their effects, effects dating from the time when the economy of Europe first intruded upon this continent. So I have begun a little before America began, because this nation is the child of mixed parentage—of Europe, of Africa and, earlier, of Asia; out of its childhood it carried in its memory certain ideas of what a building should be.

At the outset, then, we go upstream in this history. We explore the European sources of architectural influence and find that we are also going up a stream of initial capital investment. We go in the direction of subsequent colonial remittances. The first buildings within the continental limits of the United States (those buildings whose economic origins we know well enough to write about) were formed as they were because they were at the extremities of a colonial interchange of investment and remittance. One of the symbols of the colonial status of these ultimate provinces was that their architecture was, despite its novel context, not invented here.

An undertaking like this book, while not unprecedented, is unusual. It cannot be read as traditional architectural history, nor is it economic history illustrated with buildings. It attempts to make available information about the economic context of a number of buildings that are familiar to many Americans, or should become so. It does not attempt to be comprehensive.

This is not said in apology but in rejoicing. The terrain is marvelous, and this book leaves plenty of it unexplored. For example, out of a reluctance to repeat what has already been done well by others, and to avoid contributing to what I feel is an imbalance in available literature, I have gone very light on the material beloved of the Plymouth Rock school of historians. Boston and New York have many competent chroniclers. Bulfinch needs no help from me. If my omissions are provocative, I shall be delighted.

Acknowledgments

IT WAS WITH an awed sense of the generosity of friends and colleagues, and especially of people whom I have never met but who have been willing to help, that I carried a file box of correspondence toward my desk and commenced this listing of those who have assisted this book. I have dedicated it to my mother because of the enthusiasm she has expressed for anything to which I seriously set my hand for fifty-eight years.

Thank you, all.

And Corona Machemer, miraculous intercessor, thank you for justifying my faith in editors. I had been told, prematurely, that the great editors were gone. Wrong. She remains. Thanks, as well, to Jason Epstein, friend and publisher, and to the following scholars:

Michael Zuckerman, Jack P. Green and Brooke Hindle not only read the whole thing but made detailed, specific and helpful suggestions. Gene Waddell read nearly all and, as I reread our correspondence, seems to have made a hundred good suggestions and corrected a hundred errors. Alan Gowans pressed me onward, despite my trepidations about poaching on specialized territory. Robert Post read most of the text with wry wisdom; Gary Kulik and Marcus Cunliffe helped head off trouble at the start. James Ackerman straightened me out, with kindness, on many matters related to Venice and Palladio; Henry Lewis kept me from some common errors about Berry Hill and his special acquaintance, the mysterious John Johnson; C. Vann Woodward emboldened me about the cult of Greek democracy; David Buisseret went to considerable trouble to aid my understanding of the West Indies; David Watkin saved me from gaffes about Grange Park and the Cockerells. I offer thanks to Hanna Lerski, the expert on William Jay; to John Gilpin, of Sycamore Shoals, and to James Hoobler, whose Tennessee knowledge and willingness to discourse helped me traverse perilous territory; to the courtly Douglas Kent of Hyde Hall, whose long, painstaking and good-humored letters are better reading than most history; to the Reverend Raymond E. Davis of Savannah, expert

xi

on William Scarbrough; to John T. Windle and Robert Gerling of Madison, Indiana, and to Emory Kemp, who established the right connections between the West Virginia salt trust and the Ohio River traffic; to Mary Ellen Gadski of the Indiana Historic Preservation Commission; to the staffs of the Indiana State Department of Natural Resources and the Indiana State Library; to Brian Horrigan for many leads and excellent scholarship pointing the way to such people as the redoubtable Harold Cooledge, expert on Samuel Sloan, whom I also wish to thank for his extensive help, and to Charles (Monty) Harris, expert on Dr. Thornton. I am grateful to John Walker and Margaret Davis for drafts of chapters from their own works on Maria Cosway and George Hadfield; to Howard Morrison and Margaret Klapthor and their friends of the National Park Service responsible for the care and understanding of Arlington House; to Ralph Brill for leads to the actual life of Andrew Jackson Downing in the Hudson Highlands; to Ina May Ogletree McAdams, who saved Longwood and first made available the Nutt correspondence and the Nutt portraits.

I wish to thank Kenneth Cook of Halifax County, Virginia, for taking pains to help me about the Whigs, and Ronald Miller for hospitality and welcome stimuli to rethink the qualities of the Natchez Junto. S. Frederick Starr, president of Oberlin College, and master of the clarinet, required that I rethink much from Leningrad to Morgan City, and shared his amazing store of Creole lore. Scott Berger of the Smithsonian Libraries found esoterica and suggested ways through the maze of computerized bibliography. The members of the Historic Christ Church Foundation of Irvington, Virginia, were willing to answer any question about Carters, living, presumptive or dead. I thank them all, among them the late Mrs. Florence Carlton and her successor, Mrs. Conrad Goodwin. Denys Peter Myers acted as resident sage at the Historic American Building Survey, Kym Rice researched Tayloe connections and John Hackett diligently and intelligently worked his way through further Carter archives.

John White, William Withuhn and John Stine answered cheerfully many questions about railroad construction and finance. John Harris of the Royal Institute of British Architects responded with good grace to inquiries about British architects and architecture. Many owners of houses described herein permitted me to visit them; I think especially gratefully of Mr. and Mrs. William Reeve Clark of Milford. Arthur Scully, Jr., read critically and helpfully my chapter on Mobile and the Dakins.

Peter Blake permitted me to offer an unconventional set of seminars to his colleagues and students at Catholic University, and thus got the whole thing started, and my old friends Wayne Andrews and Leonard Eaton showed the way long ago to asking impertinent questions about who paid for architecture.

Russell Fridley and his colleagues at the Minnesota Historical Society sent me all the material one could covet on William G. LeDuc.

William H. Harvey, Jr., and Shelley Harlan helped with the early stages of architectural research. Carol Frost and C. P. Hollins Braestrup made all things possible by meticulous, painstaking and ingenious note-checking, source-checking, bibliography-checking, suggestion-making and good questions. Nancy Long and Joyce Ramey went through more revisions than any of us can count, keeping things straight, correcting my innumerable errors and remaining cheerful. Naomi Glass kept my life in some order and this book in some order, and made it possible for me to do other things, too. I shall thank her properly when all the books she makes possible for me to write are written.

And always, there has been Frances, helping.

Contents

xvi

ARCHITECTURE, MEN, WOMEN AND MONEY

Part I

THE ATLANTIC PROGRESSION

*I*N MODERN FACTORIES *the moment is announced with a whistle or a bell. It is chosen, we are told, under "the watchful eye of a skilled engineer" who knows when the chemical signs are right to drop into the boiling mash of sugar what is called the "strike," a mixture of molasses and sugar crystal. The strike "seeds the solution," and it begins, under that watchful eye, to produce more crystals, thousands, millions more, delicious crystals for afternoon tea, for morning coffee, for rich meals, for the insatiable appetites of Europe.*

In the most famous passage in the history of sugarmaking in the United States, Charles Gayarré told of the "stillness of death" that came among those watching for this moment when, he asserted, it first occurred in Louisiana, in 1794. Each of the watching, waiting throng was "holding his breath, and feeling that it was a matter of ruin or prosperity for them all. Suddenly the sugar-maker cried out with exultation: 'It granulates!' "

The sugar maker, the cuttings from which grew that cane, and much of the capital that had gone into the planting and refining came from the West Indies. There the process had developed from a crudeness that would scarcely have been recognized by today's "skilled engineer." A shed was built, into which the chopped cane was conveyed. Four or five copper kettles, graduating downward in size, decanted successively a boiling brew of sugar and water. As it flowed, it was distilled, hotter and hotter, while impurities were vaporized or skimmed off.

The boiler, predecessor of the skilled engineer, was the most important laborer on the plantation. He, too, determined the moment for the strike, but not from a control booth above a boiler room of stainless steel. His environment was heat and sickening stench.

The great Barbadian planter Edward Littleton reported that "If a Boyler get any part

3

into the scalding sugar, it sticks like Glew, or Birdlime, and 'tis hard to save either Limb or Life." Littleton was a humane man. All his counterparts were not so solicitous of life or limb; slaves were cheap. It was reported that on the island of Nevis, John Pinney "made his boiler test the sugar by dipping thumb and forefinger" into the cauldron, to find out if the sugar "that stuck between the two fingers spun into a thread of the right consistency."

The moment to strike was just one of a series of crucial decisions of timing which made harvesttime on the plantations desperately anxious. It was believed that once the cane was cut in the field, it had to be crushed by sundown in the mill or it would lose much of its sweetness, and in fact, its sugar content did depreciate very rapidly. Once it was milled, and the juice squeezed out, the boiling process had to commence soon or the juice would ferment. Slaves worked around the clock. Planters kept fires burning in the mills so the workers there could see in the darkness. Lighting was no problem, of course, in the boiling house.

I have imagined a hovering space visitor, watching these fires as they illuminated the shorelines of the island empires that Europe kept to supply its sugar. In space time, which I imagine to be more capacious than our own, the watcher might observe the fires of the fourteenth century upon Cyprus, kept aflame by black slaves from Africa and by white slaves from the shores of the Black Sea. New flames would flicker forth around sugar cauldrons on Sicily, then would draw the eye to one island after another across the Atlantic—the Madeiras, Canaries, Azores—and after a great patch of mid-Atlantic darkness, a bright constellation of fires would appear in the West Indies.

By the third decade of the nineteenth century, the watching visitor would see the banks of the Mississippi River glowing with cauldron-fires, while those upon Barbados, Jamaica, Nevis and innumerable small islands were still defying the darkness of the night all through the harvest season. Those fires marked the extremities of the empire of sugar.

In the seventeenth and eighteenth centuries fires used in sugar-refining burned so hot that the West Indies itself became a cauldron, a glowing maelstrom that lit the shores of our own continent. It drew into its powerful motions the energies of European settlers on our shores, whatever may have been their first motives for coming here, and it had a profound effect on the development of American history and architecture in the Colonial period.

If, when looking on a "great house" of that period, you wish to know who paid for it, then, in most cases, no adequate answer can be given without reference to the Mediterranean slave and plantation system, and to the West Indies.

4

Stepping Ashore

THE VILLAS OF ANDREA PALLADIO, rehabilitated in the well-tamed Italian countryside near Vicenza and in the Po Delta, like their colonial offspring in the quiet suburbs of Dublin or along the leisurely rivers of Virginia and South Carolina, seem settled into the centuries. Nostalgic caravans of admirers troop to their gates and, if carrying the right credentials, are admitted to wonder at the tranquil sobriety of their interiors, given gracious docentage by hosts who seem to have been there from the very beginning

If they are to tell us much about the people who built them, these buildings must be seen in the light of their history, not in the light of ours. By this I do not mean their subsequent history, after they were completed; I mean the conditions of their creation. They have affected us, in a multitude of ways this book will examine. We owe at least a chapter to an effort to ascertain what affected them—how these enormously influential buildings came to be.

Palladio's villas, built between 1530 and 1570, have been admired and emulated by architects for three chief qualities: coherence, serenity and grandeur. Clients who admired these qualities, and had accumulated the resources to build largely, were drawn to his work, in Britain and America after 1600.

An American who travels this country will find Palladian buildings wherever the formal European tradition expresses itself. Palladio showed scores of architects how to demonstrate coherence, serenity and grandeur in architecture. Some, like Inigo Jones in the seventeenth century and Lord Burlington in the eighteenth, he showed directly. Many more, and much later, from St. Petersburg, Florida, to Portland, Oregon, he showed indirectly, in the ways in which primary architectural lessons are generally transmitted, through illustrated books and even by word-of-mouth description. Americans worked their way to him through rings of buildings influenced by those influenced by those influenced by him, ever closer to the original, until, in the nineteenth century, some Americans actually confronted his work directly. Scholars who assume that there is no other way to learn

5

Villa Barbaro at Maser, by Palladio

about an architect except through travel grants are sometimes scornful of the thought that Americans could learn much about Palladio through books. But that, as we shall see, is precisely what Palladio intended.

Palladian architecture was borne to this continent by the transfer of an economic system out of the Mediterranean, across the central Atlantic, into the West Indies and finally to the American mainland. That system organized large numbers of black slaves into the production of staple crops for world markets.

At first the chief crop of the slave and plantation system was sugar. Later it was cotton. Palladio's clients did not successfully raise sugar on their Italian plantations, for which he designed the headquarters, nor were they served there by black agricultural slaves. But an important source of their wealth was the island of Cyprus, the first of the Mediterranean islands where the plantation system, dependent on battalions of black slaves, was installed. For three hundred years thereafter, sugar islands worked by blacks were way stations on a Palladian progress from Cyprus to Texas.

Other islands and other plantations served that progress as well. (Ireland, the first of Britain's colonies, was chief among them.) Plantation Palladianism was the proudest expression of the taste of plantation proprietors. And the plantation system was the most powerful impulse behind the European settlement of North America. Thereafter, plantation Palladianism was the characteristic formal architecture of the southern portion of colonial America and continued to be during this nation's first fifty years of independence. Urban Palladianism appeared in the North, and there were a few remarkable instances of the plantation form in the North as well.

So Americans have every reason to seek to discern the economic origins of the plantation system in the eastern Mediterranean, before the fifteenth century, and to follow it as it moved, island by island, westward through that narrow sea, skipping to the islands of the central Atlantic, then to the West Indies in the sixteenth and finally to the mainland Old South in the seventeenth.

While it was still in the West Indies, before it came ashore on the American mainland, that system drew forth supplies of rice from the South, wheat from the Middle Colonies and fish from New England to feed its workers. It demanded that the forests of New Hampshire, Maine and North Carolina supply shipbuilding materials to carry its products. Without the example of that island system, the development of the slave-and-staple system of the cotton South and the sugar South might have been quite different. Without the capital it generated, the West Indians would have been much slower to set their stamp on the Carolinas and Louisiana. Without it, the middlemen of New York and Philadelphia would have been unable to skim the margin of factoring and transshipment from the West Indies trade, and later the southern cotton trade, that was one of the most important bases for their wealth.

A historical phenomenon as powerful as this seldom pauses to accommodate Art.* Palladio was only unintentionally served by the plantation system. Its cross-Atlantic movement happened to get under way at the moment when the great architect was taking advantage of the multitude of economic, social and psychological factors necessary to the creation of a new "style." The plantation system carried Palladio's influence with it, like a balsa-wood model carried on a flood.

It would be conventional to commence a linear demonstration of that point by describing the economic context of the villas designed by Palladio himself, and indeed, we will come to that. But for the moment we have had enough general statements. We need a few human figures to animate the sweep of events. After all, history is an accumulation of biographies.

So let us pause on our journey to Vicenza to observe one or two unprepossessing carriers of history whose experiences show how it happened that great plantation owners were able to become Palladians. Let us spy on the founders of two families, one of which built the most famous Palladian house in Britain, the other in America. In this way we may be better able to see Mount Vernon and Lord Burlington's villa at Chiswick as they were when new, not as they are now, amid their ancient trees, almost as hallowed by time and scholarly attention as their Italian originals. We need to reach those originals in easy stages, so we may arrive before their gates clear-eyed, to see them, too, in their fresh, brash youth, in the midst of their own turbulent beginnings.

---

* *Attila, for example, did not carry architecture in his baggage train, and there was no Louis Kahn with the Mongols.*

Burlingtonian Beginnings

ANDREA PALLADIO had been dead for eight years when, in 1588, a threadbare young lawyer from Canterbury arrived in Ireland with twenty-seven pounds, three shillings, a diamond ring, a gold bracelet and the clothes on his back. He was Richard Boyle. By shrewdness and daring in the law and land-trading he grew powerful enough to pounce on the dispirited Sir Walter Raleigh when that great gambler failed in the last throw of the dice. Raleigh's explorations for gold in America had come to nothing, and his buccaneering had fallen from the favor of Queen Elizabeth. In the 1590's Raleigh was in such a weakened state that he could not resist Boyle's offer to purchase 42,000 acres of his widespread, untended Irish estates for a mere 1,500 pounds.

Richard Boyle,
First Earl of Cork
*From the National
Portrait Gallery, London*

Boyle knew the value of those acres. He proceeded to colonize them with tough Protestant frontiersmen (of the sort who later emigrated to America, like the Lincolns, Calhouns and Jacksons). By ditching, draining, road-building and squeezing rents from his tenants, Boyle made Raleigh's estates, and more land he acquired with their revenues, immensely remunerative. In the process he became the "most powerful subject in Ireland," authenticated by the title Earl of Cork and appointment as lord treasurer in 1631.

Things in Ireland were not, of course, entirely tranquil. Plantation life seldom was. Boyle's seat, Lismore (which means "great fort" in Gaelic), was besieged in various risings, and to protect his other lands Boyle garrisoned thirteen castles with a private army. Just before his death, he and four soldier sons put down the rising in Munster, bloodily and effectively. Another son was Robert Boyle, the chemist and philosopher, but it was not to any theoretician that the chief titles of Richard Boyle, the Great Earl, passed. Soldier-colonizer followed soldier-colonizer in the succession. One of them added English estates in Yorkshire, and the Earls of Cork acquired a second title, Earls of Burlington.

By the end of the seventeenth century, the office of lord high treasurer of Ireland had become almost hereditary, and the Fourth Earl of Cork and Third Earl of Burlington, born in 1694, was invested with that title at the age of twenty-one. But this Richard Boyle spent little time in the "great fort," preferring the serenity of Surrey and smiling Norfolk to gloomy, battered Lismore. Having enjoyed a triumphant and munificent youth touring Italy with his retinue, including his architects and designers, he drained his Irish estates for funds to purchase many of Palladio's drawings, and, then, magnificent villas in the Palladian style in the English countryside for himself and his friends.

The Earl of Burlington made Palladianism the strongest impulse in the eighteenth-century architecture of Britain. He was patron of Colen Campbell and William Kent, and an amateur Palladian architect of no mean skill himself. Architects sponsored by him exerted enormous influence in Ireland as well as England, in the West Indies and in the possessions on the American mainland, which were just then becoming stable and rich enough to be the site of large plantation houses.

Richard Boyle,
Third Earl of Burlington
(painting attributed
to J. Richardson)
*From the National Portrait
Gallery, London*

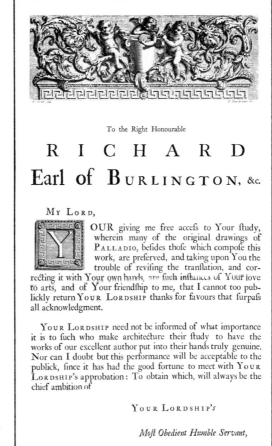

To the Right Honourable

R I C H A R D
Earl of Burlington, &c.

My Lord,

Y OUR giving me free acce∫s to Your ∫tudy, wherein many of the original drawings of Palladio, be∫ides tho∫e which compo∫e this work, are pre∫erved, and taking upon You the trouble of revi∫ing the tran∫lation, and cor-recting it with Your own hands, are ∫uch in∫tances of Your love to arts, and of Your friend∫hip to me, that I cannot too pub-lickly return Your Lordship thanks for favours that ∫urpa∫s all acknowledgment.

Your Lordship need not be informed of what importance it is to ∫uch who make architecture their ∫tudy to have the works of our excellent author put into their hands truly genuine. Nor can I doubt but this performance will be acceptable to the publick, ∫ince it has had the good fortune to meet with Your Lordship's approbation: To obtain which, will always be the chief ambition of

Your Lordship's

Mo∫t Obedient Humble Servant,

Isaac Ware.

Title page and dedication of the first English-language edition of Andrea Palladio's *Four Books of Architecture*, published in 1738

From the Dover Pictorial Archive Series edition, with an Introduction by Adolf K. Placzek, Copyright © 1965 by Dover Publications, Inc.

This association of New World plantations with Ireland is not so strange. When we turn to the *Oxford English Dictionary*, we are reminded that plantation meant "the establishment of Englishmen as landowners in Ireland, the extermina-tion of native proprietors, and the reduction of the inhabitants at large to slavery." Ireland was England's first plantation, her first colony, the training ground for generations of English colonial plantation entrepreneurs.

Away from the green island they sailed, away to the south. In the West Indies they muscled their way into the plantation system of the Spaniards and Portu-guese, a system for which the Dutch and Genoese had been the middlemen. This occurred at about the time another great entrepreneur forced himself into our story, upon a shoreline of neither a British Isle nor a Caribbean one, but in Virginia. There we find a second brash and resourceful founder of a Palladian house, somewhat bedraggled but apparently as irresistible as was Ulysses when damp.

The Foundation of Mount Vernon

THE GREAT EARL OF CORK had been dead fourteen years when John Washington was shipwrecked upon the coast of Virginia in the 1650's. The trading ketch *Sea Horse*, whose mate he had been, had run aground and sunk.

Washington had fled from England, where he had led an embarrassing childhood as the son of a clergyman who had been called a drunkard and tavern-idler by the Puritans. He had gone to sea to seek his fortune, and there, close by that Virginia beach, he found it. He was given shelter by a farmer, who had a daughter, who was wooed and won by John. After the daughter and the sailor were

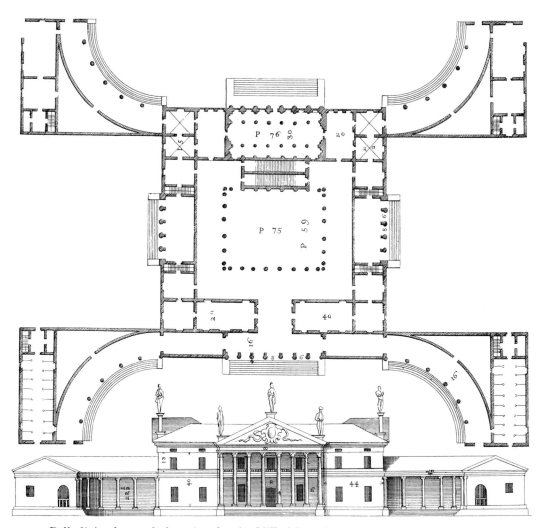

Palladio's plan and elevation for the Villa Mocenigo

From the Dover Pictorial Archive Series edition, with an Introduction by Adolf K. Placzek, Copyright © 1965 by Dover Publications, Inc.

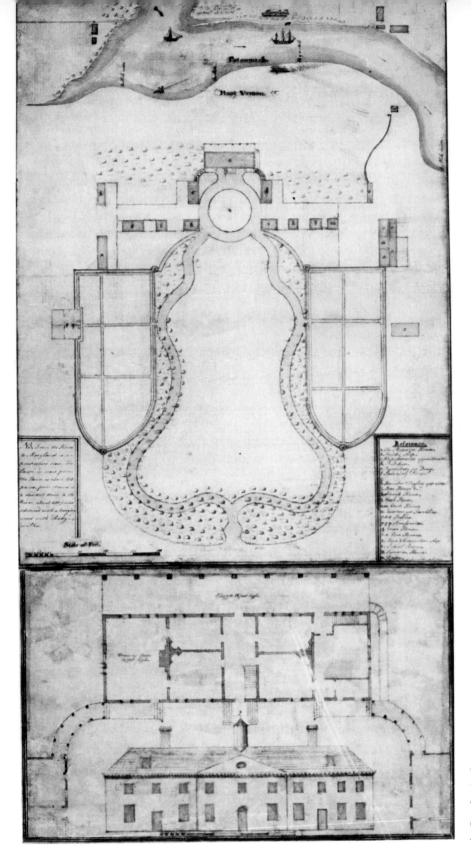

Watercolor plan of Mount
Vernon showing the Palladian
"wings" and the original house
*Courtesy of the Mount Vernon Ladies'
Association*

married, the farmer gave his son-in-law seven hundred acres, the first increment of what were to become the Washington estates. Though his first wife died young, John Washington progressed by dint of qualities that we can only imagine. (His second wife, who brought him more property, had been accused of operating a bawdy house, and his third, herself married three times before, was asserted to have been the mistress of the royal governor.) By 1674, three years before his death, John Washington owned more than five thousand acres.

His great-grandson, George, the most eminent of American soldier-colonizers, amassed more than seventy thousand acres and laid up Mount Vernon. The house manifested the strong and original architectural talents of the Washingtons, but the curve of the arms that reached out from the central mass of Mount Vernon toward its outbuildings was of Palladian derivation. On a Virginia hilltop beside the Potomac, as in the marshes of the Po Delta, this reaching-out, in measured, symmetrical colonnades, provided shelter and order.

Only one of Palladio's own compositions with such curving wings was actually completed, for he sent forth his architectural experiments into an extremely unstable economy. But his unfinished projects were as important as those which were completed, because his fame was largely due not to his actual buildings but to his published designs (and derivations from them published as a result of the sponsorship of eager devotees like Robert Boyle). To American colonists, including the descendants of John Washington, Italy was as distant as the other side of the moon. For them the distinction was trivial between what was built and what was merely an architect's intention. What mattered was the combination of those formal qualities to which we have referred: coherence, serenity and grandeur— and, of course, utility.

Colonials were intensely practical people. To them fitness was of equal importance to delight. They found in Palladio a boldness of formal invention and a satisfaction in solving practical problems. His respect for antiquity was no more than an appropriate recognition that all architectural problems are not new, nor need all solutions be. That is why, perhaps, his example was so persuasive to innovators like George Washington.

CHAPTER 2

Palladio and the Plantations

THE "REAL" PALLADIO, Rutilius Taurus Aemilianus Palladius, was an obscure Roman who wrote about aristocratic country life. Perhaps one reason he was obscure was that for a thousand years after his death, literacy was so rare in Europe that writing about architecture was of very little importance to one's reputation. The invention of movable type, about 1450, meant that thereafter reputations could be built on the written word and on good illustrations, as well as on buildings. The age of publicity had begun.

In the age of publicity, names are of great importance, and it is fitting that the most famous of the originators of that age, known to us as Gutenberg and Palladio, should have recognized this fact. The art of printing had been rapidly advanced by a number of craftsmen, among them a man who called himself Gutenberg, which had a more patrician sound than his patronymic Gensfleisch ("gooseflesh" in German). Similarly, if one wished to elevate the stonemason son of a hatter into a classical architect and writer, might it not be wise to cease calling the young artisan di Pietro, son of Peter, and entitle him—why not?—Palladio? And so it was that one of history's great clients, intending immortality for his protégé, set out to create a career for him which would last long beyond his lifetime through the use of books, and named him accordingly. As Gensfleish became Gutenberg, di Pietro became Palladio, architectural writer by nomination, in Vicenza in 1540.

Palladio's sponsor was Giangiorgio Trissino, poet, playwright and scholar of the classics. Trissino intended to make Vicenza the Academy of Italy. One of its earliest graduates was to be the young man he had found at work with a chisel upon the new loggia for his villa, and whom he gave an education. He took the boy on three long trips to Rome, and arranged for him intensive training in all aspects of architecture, engineering, fortification and topography. He introduced him to the most eminent architects of the day and to scores of potential clients. But Trissino understood something of even greater importance: an architect cannot become widely known solely by virtue of his buildings. They are not portable. Books are.

Palladio came to manhood at precisely the right time. Two groups of clients suddenly appeared in the neighborhood of Vicenza—clients whose needs we will examine in a moment. With equal suddenness movable type and bookmaking appeared, as if to make his splendid plans accessible to distant readers, to make Vicenza famous—poor Vicenza, trampled by its greater neighbors—famous with Palladio. More fortunate still, though Trissino could not have known it, the culture and economy of the Mediterranean were about to spread out across the globe. The plantation system and the Italian architectural style would move together across unknown oceans to unknown continents.

Though the book became the means of propagation of the designs of this reborn Palladio, before the book came the architecture, and before the architecture came the clients. Trissino's own responses to the young di Pietro were powerful signs that he had discovered a man who possessed the qualities that would bring other clients: great skill, of course, great diligence, great personal beauty. He had that capacity simultaneously to flatter and to communicate one's own genuine enthusiasm which is essential to an architectural career. With Trissino's help, Palladio added appropriate packaging. When the model was complete, the mentor described the combination of man and artifact in these words: "Face dark. Eyes fiery. Dress rich. His appearance that of a noble genius."

The great portraitist Veronese also felt the power of those eyes and understood, as a man of the theater, the importance of rich dress. The proper accoutrements of genius clothed skill with elegance, for the person. It was the counterpart to clothing fitness with delight, for the building. Here is how Veronese saw the mature Palladio:

> The fire in the man's eyes I have caught, I believe . . . His arrival was that of an emperor, attended by his apprentices and sons. His dress of magnificent velvets and gold galloon, was quickly doffed for a more dégagé suit of satin, in which he works.*

There is nothing lovelier than a well-balanced house of soft colors amid its gardens, seen from the water. That is the way to see the Palladian houses of the Carolina low country, like Drayton Hall, and of the Virginia Tidewater, like

---

* No architect before Palladio lived so prosperously as did he, in the flood tide of his success. He wrote one of his clients, the very grand Daniello Barbaro: "I leave for Asolo surrounded by a retinue Worthy of Yourself. My New Liveries have arrived, such Display will entrance all along My Route." (James Reynolds, Andrea Palladio and the Winged Device, p. 107.) The liveries were of yellow and black silk, and the retinue joined him as he lounged amid cushions of cut velvet under a canopy of yellow and black linen, aboard his barca osservare. There he could watch the progress of the villas he was constructing—and, of course, be observed by entranced potential clients "all along" the shores of the slow-meandering streams which served as the route of his travel and the reflecting mirrors of his progress as an architect.

Andrea Palladio, in an engraving by
Picart after a lost original
by Veronese

Mount Airy or Mount Vernon, or Maryland's proudly porticoed Whitehall, on its
hill above the bay outside Annapolis. One can imagine Palladio, transported three
hundred years and three thousand miles, on his barge upon these American rivers,
looking up at these villas and rejoicing in their deference to his lessons, commend-
ing their builders on their discretion and giving thanks, perhaps, that through
them he had provided Trissino some of that immortality he sought. He had never
been able to keep another promise he had given his mentor: "Soon I shall quit
Venice and build you the Vitruvian Palace you want."

Many of Palladio's promises, to himself and to his clients, could not be kept.
He, and they, had an enormous but very brief opportunity. And thereby hangs
the tale of the Venetian economy of his time.

The Economic Context of the Palladian Villa

THE VENETIAN ECONOMY in the sixteenth century was managed by men of whom
the patrons of Palladio were typical. We can scarcely picture those men in the heat
and bustle of everyday business; we have no painted images of them so. We have
them, instead, grandly costumed, posing for posterity in the portraits of Veronese

17

Villa Foscari, by F. Costa
Courtesy of the Museo Correr, Venice

and Titian. Architectural history places them, posing once again, in the grandest costumes of all: houses designed by Palladio. This is how they wanted to be remembered, leisured and serene, in ancient halls, amid acres long accustomed to their prudent husbandry. This is not how they were.

Palladio called for soft pastel colors to mellow the spanking-new stucco of the plantation-headquarters he designed for these men. He used materials that, while sturdy, would quickly acquire the appearance of age, and the forms he chose were intended to convey the impression that they were anciently established, undisturbed for centuries. But the appearance of rural repose should not beguile us into mistaking Palladio's patrons for country gentry.

Some were professional soldiers, come to architecture with saddlebags full of loot and the accumulated savings of expensive soldiering, come desiring to purchase respectability, come to rest upon the land before resting longer within it.

Some were merchants, turned through policy to farming. Some had been

Benedetto Pesaro is presented to the Virgin by St. Peter in honor of his conquest of Cephalonia and Santa Maura from the Turks. Altarpiece by Titian conveying at once patriotic achievement and piety, and immortalizing portraiture.

Photo: Mansell Collection

Palladio's Villa Rotonda near Vicenza
Photo by Wayne Andrews

both farmers and merchants, but were newly persuaded to build grandly for their own habitation upon estates of which they had been absentee landlords. They seem very fine and very prosperous. But they were not likely to be so sure of themselves, nor so indifferent to appearances, as people who have lived long upon their land and who are comfortable in their rent rolls tend to be. They were, in short, ideal architectural clients.

Merchants do not easily withdraw huge sums from commerce and recommit that capital to housekeeping amid swarming insects beside drainage ditches upon soggy reclaimed land. The iron-fisted Venetian traders (and occasional humanists) had no nostalgia for the mainland to induce them to transfer their affections to agriculture. They did so only because their investment alternatives had become unpromising. The opportunity-lost cost of diverting their capital to the country-side had diminished as trading opportunities in the eastern Mediterranean diminished, and the price of both farmland and farm products seemed likely to rise.

Some patrician families had owned land on the mainland for centuries, but it was new to think of building on that property a primary residence, signaling an intention to take personal charge of agricultural investment. In the center of the sixteenth century, Venetians became, for the first time, country gentlemen, living palatially like Roman latifundists.

Venice had been a great commercial empire, which had fattened as the eastern Roman Empire had weakened; Constantinople, the capital of that empire for a thousand years and more, had fallen to the Turks in 1453, and a period of constant warfare with the Turks followed. Though there was general prosperity, these wars drained the resources of the Venetian oligarchs. They lost in battle the crown of their empire, Cyprus, with its sugar plantations. Their Levantine trade was increasingly perilous.

The volume of Venetian-registered shipping fell by half during Palladio's career. The exhaustion of mast-building timbers in Illyria led to a state monopoly over the remaining trees (see Chapter Seven for an American analogue). The crew-providing classes were diminished—perhaps by a third—by a plague in 1575–77. Turkish control of the Bosporus cut the Venetians off from the traditional sources of white slave-crews on the north coast of the Black Sea. Piracy, even in the Adriatic itself, was on the rise, and the new Atlantic powers, Britain, Holland and Portugal, were cutting into the old Venetian markets beyond the Mediterranean. The central European export trade in goods of Mediterranean origin began to fall into the hands of central European merchants.

These changes so destabilized the Venetians that, though they responded with remarkable ingenuity to challenges near at hand, they recoiled from distant opportunities on the high seas. When, in 1585, Philip II of Spain offered Venice the monopoly of the spice trade in Lisbon and Antwerp, Venice declined.

The Venetian oligarchs had grown rich in the old Mediterranean trade, in manufacturing luxury goods and in raising sugar on their Cyprian plantations. They were in no sense feudal, though by the middle of the sixteenth century some had assumed the demeanor of landed gentry. Some of them, it is true, bought ancient fiefs and the titles that went with them, but the benison of sod is a British social sacrament, unknown to Venice. Like the contemporary Florentines, Venetian patricians were proud of being merchants. It was with pride, for example, that Girolamo Priuli, great-nephew of two doges, recorded in his diary: "My father . . . did not spare himself day or night in finding ways of making money." He was not impressed by the recent appearance of younger men "devoting themselves to pleasure, delight and the country life, meanwhile abandoning navigation and maritime activities." Palaces ashore might consume large sums of money, "but it was from the sea that all benefits came."

These families became, and remained, rich through quickness, intelligence, a ruthless concentration on business and a willingness, when necessary, to fight to protect their commercial interests. They were, in these ways, like the oligarchs of Charleston, South Carolina, whose eighteenth-century houses, like the Venetian villas of the sixteenth century, can, in their mellow repose of the twentieth century, convey a false impression of the people who built them. They were not

21

reposeful; their times were violent. The Palladian villas of Carolina were built upon land their owners wrested from the Indians. The Palladian villas on the Venetian mainland stood upon land torn from other Italians, lost and then regained in a bitter struggle with the league of Pope Julius II, Louis XII of France, Ferdinand of Aragon (husband of Isabella of Castile, and co-sponsor of Columbus' voyages) and the Holy Roman Emperor Maximilian.

The Venetian beneficiaries of that contest presented to Palladio the commissions that brought him to the attention of his other class of clients: the Vicenzan aristocrats who became the professional soldiers who actually led the troops in that war. Some of them, enriched by booty, became eager clients for architecture. They were not trained in the slow and subtle modes of keeping wealth in times of peace, however, and most of them ran short of money while their residences were still under construction. As a consequence, Vicenza has the husks or a module or two of ten Palladio façades, with barely enough rooms behind them to make a single large house.

If we see these buildings only as magnificent designs in Palladio's books, we will miss the truth about the nervous merchants and overreaching mercenaries

Barto Colleoni, mercenary captain of the Venetian Republic, as a triumphant caesar
Photo: Mansell Collection

Villa Trissino at Meledo—all that was built

who were his clients. Oh, there were gracious and unhurried humanists among them, like Trissino, and there were men who could be truly clothed in the velvet adjectives of the time, "magnificent," "serene" and "noble." But the aborted palaces of Vicenza and the husks of villas in the Venetian delta are records of a social history not very dissimilar from that which we learn from the Palladian ruins of Ireland, Jamaica and America. The ruined walls of Rosewell in Virginia, or of a score of blackened and gutted Palladian houses in Ireland, lead us back not so much to the book-architecture of Palladio as to the real history of Venice and Vicenza.

The Extroverted Villa

LET US TURN NOW to that architecture itself, to see what Palladio designed for his most important clients, the traders recycling mercantile profits into land. He gave them what they desired, buildings that had a classical pedigree. Part of the wealth

23

to build them had come from picking the bones of that vestige of the classical world, Byzantium, in its last extremity. Part had been squeezed from plantations that carried into the modern world the worst features of the ancient slave-driven agricultural system.

There is some propriety, therefore, in Palladio's use of Roman architecture. But the urban Roman villas that one can see depicted in frescoes, and whose outlines appear in excavations, were introverted. One might say that Palladio turned them inside out; like a surgeon, he snipped one side of the closed, hollow rectangle of the villa-compound and bent back the sides, revealing long colonnades centering on a portico with a pediment supported by columns. There was, of course, another kind of Roman villa, like those described in Pliny's letters, rambling assemblages of loggias, porticoes and courts, built where the countryside was safe. Palladio pulled all these elements into a balanced, coherent design, including the necessary functions of a large farmyard. Repose was felt in the symmetry of the placement of the house, revealed at the center, in meticulously measured relation to the whole extended pattern. The wings often terminated in

THE ATLANTIC
PROGRESSION

Plan and elevation for the Villa Trissino at Meledo, by Palladio

From the Dover Pictorial Archive Series edition, with an Introduction by Adolf K. Placzek, Copyright © 1965 by Dover Publications, Inc.

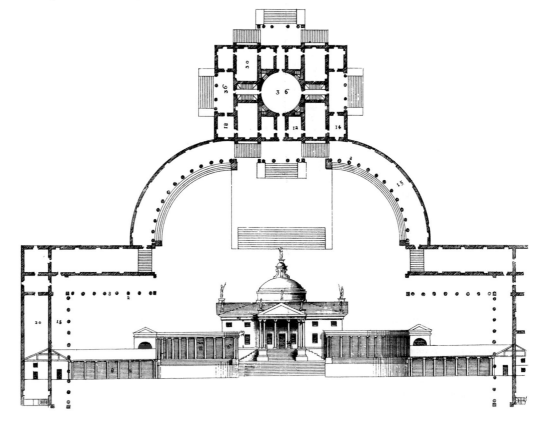

service buildings which in the Roman prototype had been merely service areas on one side of the interior court.

Grandeur, in the Palladian scheme, was imparted by that central portico. The opening-out made the statement that it had become safe to be open. The object revealed made a second statement: that Palladio and his clients were the cultural heirs of the ancients.

The portico is a crucial symbol for all the rest of our story. As a form, it was reserved by the Romans exclusively for religious and civic architecture. Even Augustus thought it wise to receive from the Senate permission to place a portico on the exterior of his house. Palladio was bolder; he used porticoes as ceremonial faces for the houses of private citizens.*

This is probably the place to file away in the memory of the reader two images, both derived from the work of Palladio, though they will not come into this discussion again until ten or more chapters have passed.

Two forms of Palladian portico were used in America. The first was what I call the biloggial form, two "porches" (in the American use of porch), one on top of the other. In Palladio's idiom, each of the two loggias employs a different order of columns. The first, supporting the floor of the second-story porch, uses the Ionic. The second, supporting a triangular pedimented gable, uses the Corinthian.†

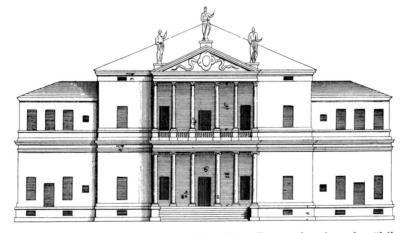

Elevation for the Villa Cornaro at Piombino Dese, showing the "biloggial" portico

From the Dover Pictorial Archive Series edition, with an Introduction by Adolf K. Placzek, Copyright © 1965 by Dover Publications, Inc.

* *Palladio had the benefit of earlier experiments in the residential use of the portico, but even in the hands of a great architect like Sangallo, it had only been awkwardly and somewhat timidly placed on a solid façade, never as the centerpiece of a long extroverted façade like those Palladio produced.*

† *The biloggial form under a pedimented gable was probably original to Palladio, though I have found one German reconstruction drawing, of the temple of Athena at Pergamum, which might have given Palladio a precedent had he been familiar with it.*

Elevation for the Villa Ragona, showing the "porticular" form

*From the Dover Pictorial Archive Series edition, with an Introduction by Adolf K. Placzek, Copyright © 1965
by Dover Publications, Inc.*

The second type of portico was the full temple form, its columns rising
unbroken from base to pediment; a familiar model would be the Parthenon. Because the emphasis is on the portico—the gable end of the temple—we can call
this the porticular form.

A portico is a grand place—a place to stand or to be announced. A loggia is
cozier, a place for strolling or lounging about to watch the sun set across the
marshes.

Palladio was quite explicit about why he used these forms. He was creating
temples for the imagination of his clients, for their fantasies of, as he put it,
"grandeur and magnificence." "Besides," he said, "the portico being thus made
more conspicuous . . . accommodates well the ensigns or arms of the owners."
What stage-management: a coat of arms! upon a classic pediment!*

Palladio's success in manipulating these powerful symbols was but one of the
triumphs of a career that provided the brightest glow of the long, long lingering
sunset of Venice. That glow, however, falls within an attendant shadow, a darkness of human misery so intense, and so vast in its scope and consequences, as to
be without equal in all the chronicles of man. Palladio's architecture is ineradicably
associated with the plantation system, and the plantation system with slavery.

Sugar, Slaves and Plantations

PLANTATIONS WORKED by black slaves were the source of the wealth of many
Venetian patricians. The Cornaro family had been proprietors of great sugar plantations on Cyprus, worked by black slaves. Among Palladio's clients were the

---

* *A coat of arms, it should be recalled, was a shield bearing the visual identification of the knight who
carried it, so his retainers could find him, support him and maintain their discipline in battle. It was like a
banner, or a trumpet call, in a largely illiterate age, and served the same military function as the walkie-talkie
of later times. It had not been the escutcheon of tradesmen grown rich, nor of hired captains. Neither tribesmen
nor these hired warriors had roles in society like those of feudal knights, any more than did the subsequent owners
of plantations worked by slaves, in the least feudal of all social organizations.*

Badoer family, chief suppliers to Cyprus of black slaves from Africa and white slaves from the shores of the Black Sea. On Cyprus in the tenth century, sugarcane and slaves commenced their long westward progress from island to island, plantation to plantation: to Sicily in the eleventh century, to the Madeiras, first sugar islands of the Atlantic, to the Canaries, to the Cape Verde Islands and finally, in the sixteenth and seventeenth centuries, to the Americas, farthest of the Antilles, farthest extension of the plantation system.

The tragedy of sugarcane was one of comparative advantage, with fatal consequences. Wherever it was grown it prevented the growing of other crops in rotation and restricted the space available for food crops. Food was imported to feed the planters and their slaves; it was uneconomic to leave land to grow food for anyone else. Woe to the native populations. Fernand Braudel, the *magister* of French oceanic historians, tells us that in the Canaries, "sugar was almost certainly as responsible as the brutalities of the first conquerors for the disappearance of the indigenous natives, the Guanches," and the same story was repeated on island after island in the Caribbean. Braudel goes on:

> It was the sugar plantations which generalized the use of slave labor, leading to the enslavement of the Berbers of the African Coast whom Christian pirates from the Canaries would carry off in their raids, and particularly to the slave trade on Negroes from Guinea and Angola which in the middle of the [sixteenth] century, again because of sugar, reached the shores of the American continent.

It was Genoa, not Venice, that accelerated the transfer of the slave and sugar economy to the West Indies, seizing on the infirmities of Venice and profiting by its failure of nerve in the face of the vastness of the Atlantic. The Genoese supplied the capital that moved the sugar plantation system from Sicily to the Canaries and Madeira. It was the Genoese mariner Christopher Columbus who conveyed sugarcane for planting in the islands of the Caribbean, transporting it from the Canaries to his satrapy of Hispaniola. And yet, until we come to the revivals of the late nineteenth century (in Newport, Rhode Island, for example), it is difficult to find a shard of Genoese artistic influence anywhere in the New World.*

The Venetians, looking eastward, cut off from the western Mediterranean by the Apennines, immobilized their capital close to home. Their spendid Palladian estates turned out to be relatively poorer investments than the investment the Genoese made in the Atlantic sugar business. Nevertheless, it was Venice that was, through Palladio, the most powerful architectural influence on America in its Colonial period, except for the vernacular traditions of the groups who settled there.

---

* The third great city-state of the Italian Renaissance, Florence, like Venice, did not venture into the New World. The Florentines tied up capital in paintings, sculpture and urban palaces, and then compounded their infirmities by lending huge sums for long terms during a period of such rapid inflation that it has been called a "price revolution." They lent "long" in inflationary times and thereupon fell short in purchasing power.

An Addendum

As THIS BOOK is being edited for the last time before going to the typesetter, I pause on this assertion, which still seems to me to be true, and would be agreed to be so by most architectural historians. Yet someday a book needs to be written giving more credit to the influence of Sebastiano Serlio (1475–1554), the Bolognese master who worked in Rome until the sack of that city in 1527 and lived in France for the last thirteen years of his life. Serlio's books of architecture were not only the first really practical carpenter's guides, competing quite successfully with Palladio's somewhat later volumes. Serlio did more: his mansion for the cardinal of Ferrara in Paris was the prototype of the French townhouse, the descendants of which can be seen today in New York. His corner-turreted design for a château at Ancy-le-Franc showed how to effect the transition between a medieval castle and a peaceful country house which we discuss in Chapters Three through Five. The H-plan house of which Stratford, in Virginia, is America's most magnificent example (Chapter Six), carries on this tradition, and may itself have been suggested by one of Serlio's illustrations. And I have before me, as I write, his Design IV, which one could argue had as much influence on Dutch and English brick houses of the seventeenth and eighteenth centuries as those Palladian precedents suggested in Chapter Seven. But the major point made here, that there was a tie between the plantation system and the progress of the Palladian form across the Atlantic, will not be much affected by a later book that readjusts the balance between Serlio and Palladio in America.

CHAPTER 3

Sugar, Slaves and Architecture

IF WE ATTEND only to the full-scale Palladian buildings created by the plantation system as it moved across the Atlantic, we will miss that part of the story which shows how architecture evolves, and how it is likely to evolve in similar ways in contexts evolving similarly. If seeds from the same plant are placed in two pots containing the same earth, and then the climate about each experiment is adjusted to change in the same way, it is likely that the eventuating plants will be similar. So it is sometimes with architecture. And so it was with Palladianism in Italy and in the successive outposts of the plantation system, especially in the West Indies.

The evolution of that style in the Po Delta was recapitulated to a remarkable extent in Jamaica and Barbados, and even in South Carolina. This parallelism tells us some unexpected things about the culture, in the biological sense, into which the seeds of Palladian taste were set in all these places.

Observe the kind of work Palladio did at the outset of his career, in the 1540's, before he pried open the fortified farmhouse and made it into a classical villa. He found in the countryside around Venice examples of buildings within which interloping Venetian clients felt safe: stout, compact farmhouses, constrained and prudent, not much removed in spirit from the little castles that had been built there earlier. It is easy in Italy to see how this form evolved, force-fed by the genius of Palladio, into something more open, more confident and therefore more vulnerable. There remain plenty of examples of each stage of the progression. The evidence of the similar process that occurred in the West Indies and in mainland America has been ruined and battered and uglified by subsequent remodelers; to identify that evidence more easily we should look again at the prototypes, not just at the famous buildings of Palladio's maturity but also at those on which he learned his trade, at the military farmhouses he first designed.

Palladio's Villa Godi, in Lonedo
Photo by Phyllis Dearborn Massar

The Architecture of Fear

FORTIFIED, OR FORTIFIABLE, these blocky buildings with pavilions or turrets at the corners, clearly derived from the forms of medieval castles, could be called pre-Palladian (in Italy) or proto-Georgian (in America). (We need not trouble ourselves with fine distinctions among the periods of the architecture that might be called Georgian, Palladian or otherwise, as yet.) Wherever they were built there was reason to fear. Fear had been a dominant influence on the residential building of the Middle Ages. It was the alleviation of fear that permitted Palladio to open out the villa on the Venetian shore. Before he turned the villa inside out, it, too, had been defensible. The land upon which all his early clients built their villas was near one dangerous border or another; it was only later that things were so serene that the villa could drop its guard.

The open-villa Palladianism of Venice or of the plantations of the Western Hemisphere implied control of the landscape. Its entrances could become ostentatiously, ceremonially exposed. Its embracing colonnades extended a proclamation of confident control across the skyline, from one extremity of the field of vision to the other.

Palladio's followers, such as Thomas Jefferson, often intended their buildings to be seen amid an entire sculptured terrain. Jefferson's Rotunda, at the University of Virginia, is the culmination of a carefully modulated series of terraces. Jefferson played land-shaper on a vast scale, as well, at Monticello, where even the name is Italianate. These places are no longer defensive; their colonnades are exposed to an environment because they do not seem to doubt their control of that environment.

In Palladio's lifetime his clients moved from a level of insecurity of which a corner-turreted house is a fitting expression to what an American might call a Jeffersonian level, anxious but not fearful. In the colonies that sequence was repeated. When in the seventeenth and early eighteenth centuries a European moved out of recently pacified Britain or France to the colonies, he moved backward from residual anxiety into fear. The perpetual civic violence of the late Middle Ages was not yet out of mind, and it was easy to slip back from the architectural forms of the Renaissance when circumstances returned to something like medieval conditions.

Villa Trissino at Cricoli, home of Palladio's first patron,
the count Giangiorgio Trissino

Photo by Ferrini, Vicenza

This is what happened in the West Indies, where society reverted to a system —slavery—based on violence. The forms of living, in architecture, reverted as well. One quite appropriate form of retrograde architecture was the fortified farmhouse, which in its larger instances had the demeanor of a border fortress grudgingly accepting the possibility of peace, bristling with turrets at the corners. At the extremities of the plantation system there are a remarkable number of surviving ruins of such buildings, some in their primitive, genuinely military form and some in their later modifications, which reduced the turrets to ornamental corner pavilions.

Life on the Islands

THE CONDITIONS THAT produced these recapitulations were those associated with the growing of sugar on tropical plantations served by slaves. The Spaniards had been cultivating sugar for more than a century on Hispaniola when the British finally established themselves on Barbados. That colony was a rough contemporary with Plymouth (1620) and Massachusetts Bay (1630). Its first export crop was tobacco, but some experiments with sugar demonstrated that an acre in cane produced three to ten times as much revenue as an acre of tobacco. Soon sugar forced out tobacco and stimulated a growth of wealth and population that was much more rapid than on the mainland. In the seventeenth century, Barbados had a population equal to that of either Massachusetts or Virginia.

In none of the three was life for the Europeans peaceful or secure, but on Barbados wealth was much more concentrated, and architecture, as a consequence, was more explicit in its purpose. Today one can read that purpose more easily there than one can in Massachusetts or Virginia, because some Barbadian houses of the late seventeenth and early eighteenth centuries were larger in scale and more massively built of more permanent materials than the few remaining contemporary buildings on the mainland. As with them, their style was retrograde. They were not like architecture of the same scale at the same time in England, where the peace resulting from the end of the civil wars and the subsequent accession of William III, in 1688, brought forth in a generation that flowering of porticoed villas which we associate with Lord Burlington.

Though the sugar planters in the West Indies had ample wealth to build in the new Palladian style by the end of the seventeenth century, they did not do so quickly. As late as the 1730's they surrounded themselves with the defensive architecture that would have been anachronistic in the British Isles, except in equally fearful Ireland. And, as in Ireland, there was ample justification for this hesitation to open arms in a Palladian gesture. Even during the tobacco-growing period, when most of the land was still owned and worked by small holders, the larger plantations made use of an underclass of indentured servants. Many were slaves for a term, and unhappy about it. Some had been shanghaied—or, to use the contemporary term, barbadosed. Fear of this restive class of white agricultural laborers was enough to induce planters who were rich enough to make use of forced labor to fortify their residences.*

With the coming of more and more black slaves, the large plantations grew larger; poorer whites were forced out, and reciprocal hatred between master and worker increased. Workers ceased to have claims of consanguinity on masters, and freed of such claims, masters became more and more brutal. The results of their actions appear in the following statistics: 170,000 blacks were brought to Barbados in the half century after 1650. Of these, and their progeny, only 40,000 were still alive in 1700. Six blacks died each year for every birth on the Codrington plantation. The average life expectancy for a black on the Littleton plantation was seventeen years. Barbadian planters came to be surrounded by enemies they themselves had brought to work for them, to die for them. The air was full of hatred.†

Knowing this, we should not be surprised to find that the first large plantation houses in the islands were fortresses. Here is a description of Colbeck Castle, in Jamaica, the largest seventeenth-century residential building in any British colony in the New World:

> A grand, gloomy pile of gray limestone . . . The three story central block is almost square, ninety-four by eighty-four feet, with walls three feet thick and thirty-six feet high. There are four massive corner towers, with distinctive round port-hole windows at ground level. These towers are joined by . . . double arcades . . . The kitchen, bakery and other service rooms are far removed, placed in four symmetrically arranged outbuildings situated at the castle's two-acre compound.

Colbeck was rivaled in size by a similar Jamaican great house. The ruins of Stokes Hall show that it also had four towers loopholed so each could "receive supporting fire from its neighbors." The most ambitious of these early fortress-plantations, known to us only from drawings and a few scattered stones, was the tall red-brick and cut-stone château, in the style of Louis XIII, built behind two rings of walls by the French governor of St. Kitts. The original Holborn, residence

---

*Richard Ligon, a diarist, reported in 1647 that "the planters' houses were built in the manner of fortifications" to resist attack by the servant-workers with "bulwarks and bastions from which they could pour scalding water upon the attacking servants and slaves." Twenty years earlier the defection of English indentured servants had made it easy for the Spanish to capture the island, and only two years later a revolution of indentured servants nearly succeeded in taking control of the entire island. (Richard S. Dunn, Sugar and Slaves, pp. 69, 256.)

† As early as 1661, when blacks and whites were still probably about equally numerous on Barbados, the government of the island passed a slave act "requiring plantation overseers to keep slave cabins under close surveillance, searching twice a month for stolen goods, clubs, and wooden swords." An act of 1688 spoke of the "Disorder, Rapines and Inhumanities to which they [the slaves] are naturally prone." How much disorder could they achieve? It is characteristic of all masters of slaves that they are loath to keep records of slave revolts. Yet there is documentary evidence of seven violent slave outbreaks in Barbados between 1640 and 1713. (Dunn, op. cit., pp. 239, 256.)

Colbeck Castle
Courtesy of the Jamaica Tourist Board

of the British governors of Barbados, stood behind walls ramping up to a gateway flanked by sentry houses with gun slots. In 1774 this building was "thought to be the noblest and best edifice of its kind either in North America or any of the British Colonies in the West Indies." Indeed it was: two hundred feet of Palladian elegance about a grand portico—yet at the corners were residual turrets to remind us of Colbeck.*

The builders of Colbeck or Stokes Hall were, like the early clients of Palladio, on a border, though this was a border of uncertain location—without? within? who? where? Colbeck was on the frontier between classes, between masters and workers. It was like Richard Boyle's Lismore and many other houses in Ireland, John Bull's first, distressful colonial island.

The parallels between the lives of British colonials in Ireland and in the West Indies are remarkable when one looks beneath the skin color of the servile class. On Barbados, or Jamaica, and in County Wexford, into the eighteenth century, plantation houses had gun-ports on the upper stories. Many were raised on high basements to leave only barred and bolted windows easily accessible from the ground. Palladian principles appropriate to the damp earth of the Po Delta called

* It was a reconstruction in the 1830's that gave Holborn its present battlements and crenellations.

for such elevation, but so also did a social environment that required massive locks and chains behind the most polished of front doors.

Uncomfortable Anachronism

A REVERSION TO turreted fortress-farmhouses was an appropriate response to the political environment of the West Indies. Within its walled compound, between its bellicose towers, Colbeck had a central mass that was lightened by loggias, places where the breeze could be caught, and where even the wary soldier-planter could pause to enjoy the tropics. These pre-Palladian buildings were at least Mediterranean in their derivation, adapted, to some extent, to a hot climate. In the West Indies at about the same time, however, there appeared another architectural expression of insecurity which could not be called appropriate either to the physical or to the political environment, though it must have suited the psychological needs of those who built it. Like the dinner jacket, tight collar and black bow tie worn in the tropics by British colonials in our own time, the gabled medieval houses that appeared in the West Indies were psychologically ordained anachronisms.

Anachronism, when it is still rooted in recollection, can be very reassuring. We know that, but we also know that sometimes reassurance is purchased at a high price in discomfort. So it was in the West Indies. Many of its great houses were built by very rich men constantly traveling to England and Holland. These planters were not, like their contemporaries in New England, pressed for money. Yet they persisted in cold-climate medievalism in hot-climate colonies.

It is one thing for cold-climate medievalism to persist in cold climates. One can attribute certain New England or Virginia houses to nostalgia or to cultural lag. Bacon's Castle in Virginia (c. 1655) or its wooden cousin, the Iron Monger's House at Saugus, Massachusetts, the first Harvard College (1638–42) or the First Town House in Boston (1657) were *retardataire* but not irrational. Tradition and adaptation were not, in them, incompatible.

But what are we to make of the fact that the most ambitious Gothic houses in the New World are to be found where no such compatibility existed? What about those who insisted on cold-climate buildings in Barbados and Jamaica? What psychological imperatives required them to flout, so strenuously, their surroundings? Does not their architecture intimate a point of view that was expressed again, somewhat more subtly, in the houses of their spiritual progeny, the mainland planters? I think West Indian anachronism helps us understand, for example, why the white-columned, porticoed mansions of the 1840's were so vehemently white, so unyielding in their linearity, so anxious to impose their suzerainty on the green abundance of the southern plains (see Chapter Twenty-two).

Two great seventeenth-century houses of Barbados are especially eloquent as

35

Drax Hall
Courtesy of the Barbados Board of Tourism

psychological statements. They were expensive, artificial and tight, three or four stories tall, with high-pitched, many-gabled roofs. The eminent historian Thomas Waterman calls Drax Hall and St. Nicholas Abbey "the finest British Colonial dwellings of the period in America." He dates these buildings from the reign of Charles II or of William III. Others think they are considerably younger, but all would agree they appear to be considerably older. As Waterman says, their "exteriors are so typically Jacobean that except for the tropical setting it is hard to realize that they stand five thousand miles from London."

These houses of sun-absorbing red brick, compressed verticality and steep roofs ready to repel snow that never comes, of pursed little windows, are unwilling to acknowledge their environment. Within such houses two or even three generations of owners wore clothing as little adapted to that setting.

The plans of these large houses tell us more than their façades. As has been said in another context, they are not defensible except in a strictly military sense.

They were dense, airless cubes, covered by gable roofs running side by side, leaving deep intervening valleys.*

What one seeks in the tropics is shade from the sun and openness to the breeze. One gets as far off the ground as possible. If one cannot afford a loggia, a hammock will do. But these colonials ignored the lessons of the natives and of their Spanish competitors. They piled low-ceilinged rooms one behind another, making cross-ventilation difficult, and placed their primary living quarters on the ground floor! Did these seventeenth-century sucrigarchs live this way solely because their houses had to serve as fortresses? Surely not, for the Spanish distinguished between tropical fortresses and tropical "bungalows structured of wood and plaster, with tile floors, shuttered windows, tiled or thatched roofs, and great

St. Nicholas Abbey
Courtesy of the Barbados Board of Tourism

* *The earliest remaining mansion of Portsmouth, New Hampshire, the MacPhaedris-Warner house, had a simplified form of this roof, a single valley between two ridges, forming an M, but it was soon covered with a new roof: presumably New Hampshire snow, beyond the expectations of old Hampshire, collected in that trough, and adaptable New Englanders preferred dry heads to sentimental associations.*

37

double doors opening into the street or interior courtyards . . . designed for maximum coolness and able to withstand tropical storms." The explanation cannot be purely military. Economic history suggests a supplementary explanation—that the price of exploitation is alienation.

The Architecture of Alienation

IN THE WEST INDIES, as the large sugar plantations worked by blacks replaced smaller holdings, the magnates grew further and further apart from the poorer whites, and there was little sense of community. Nevertheless, the architectural forms the great planters chose implied an anachronistic and wholly artificial squirearchy. Many of the early plantation houses were in the form of small English country houses of the late medieval period—forms quite contrary to West Indian social and climatic realities.

Samuel Long, with 11,183 acres in six sugar-producing parishes, had a principal room in his house "large enough to hold sixty chairs and seven tables." In such halls in England, squires would entertain their neighbors. One need not romanticize feudalism unduly to recall that such rooms at least implied a relationship of knights and vassals, united in a skein of protection, support and reciprocal reinforcement.

On Barbados feudal reciprocity had no greater part in life than it had on Cyprus, or on the later slave plantations of the southern mainland. The lords of the sugarlands worked their retainers to death. Then they bought new ones.* On Barbados, too, the irony became most poignant: in settings and even in costumes derived from the romances of Sir Walter Scott, the direct economic successors to Barbadian sugar planters fell to jousting.

Here is West Indian feudalism:

> It was the custom in Jamaica, at least, for the plantation slaves to assemble once a week in this room and patiently squat on the floor to receive their doles of rum. In 1683, Colonel William Ivey, a member of the Jamaica Council, was tipped off by a faithful slave that the other blacks on his plantation were plotting a revolt. Ivey quietly gathered as many armed white men as he could and secreted them in the lower rooms of his house; then he summoned his 180 Negroes for their rum ration. The blacks came into Ivey's hall and sat down unsuspectingly, whereupon the whites rushed in, nabbed the ring leaders, and took them off to be whipped, maimed, or killed. This grim story tells us, among other things, that Colonel Ivey had a very large hall in his house.

This grim story also tells us why some English planters stayed confined and,

---

* One should bear this lack of reciprocity in mind when one comes to scrutinize the great halls of such houses as Stratford in Virginia, and especially of Gothic Revival plantations in the Old South.

for nearly a century, refused to accommodate the climate. Their houses were "neither cool nor able to endure the shock of Earth quakes." In a climate that cries out for tall and airy rooms, those of the sugar nabobs were said by a visitor in the 1650's to be "so low . . . I could hardly stand upright with my hat on." As a result, "in the afternoons, when the Sun came to the West, those little low roofed rooms were like Stoves or heated Ovens." The planters "not only shut out the night breezes believing them to be unhealthy but slept in beds enveloped by curtains, as at home."

They themselves were enveloped as well. They desired not to look dark, like their Negroes, nor red, like the remaining "white" farmers who still struggled in the leavings of the great plantations. They shunned the sun, wearing "broad brimmed hats, neckcloths stockings and gloves." They made some concessions to the climate in the fabrics they used, but for the most part continued to dress as their Britishness required: inventories of the 1670's show half the suits to be of wool; hats were worn atop periwigs. A visitor thought it noteworthy that "coming from a cold country they should continue here to clothe themselves after the same manner as in England."

The rich overdressed, overdrank and overate, even by seventeenth-century standards. Despite good medical advice to the contrary, they persisted in eating their main meal when the sun was hottest, at two o'clock in the afternoon. They seldom washed, believing sea bathing (like night breezes) to be unhealthy. They slept fitfully because of their propensity to drink themselves into a stupor before retiring. As a consequence of these habits, they died young. Richard Dunn, one of the best of the historians of the West Indies, puts it neatly that life there, in the seventeenth century, was a "race between quick riches and quick death."

The pretentious houses of these planters were disguises, falsely representing their proprietors as country gentry. Their own bodies supplied images more expressive of the truth: they got little exercise and were carried about in litters, and their sports were predominantly passive and indoor. Their gluttonous diet and vast intake of alcohol fitted them with an appearance to match their style of life: when they visited the mainland they were seen to have "carbuncled faces, slender legs and thighs, and large prominent bellies." Drax Hall or St. Nicholas Abbey might invoke Olde England, but their owners looked what they were, debauched colonials.

The Harvest Is Gathered

YET THEY WERE very rich, the richest men by far in any British colony in the Western Hemisphere. The first surge of sugar wealth came between 1640 and 1680, a period during which the Virginia planters were still struggling amid the stumpage to establish a bare courtesy of circumstance. The sugar planters of the

West Indies became richer than colonial Virginians or South Carolinians ever did, and became so more quickly.* Wealth on this scale opened its customary way to power in Whitehall. It bought admission to English upper-class life, to which many of these planters repaired as soon as they could. Five had been made knights or baronets by 1665, and a dozen more gained knighthood in the eighteenth century.

They were often resented: it was not always an admiring observation for fashionable Londoners to use the current cliché "as rich as a West Indian." But time, talent and money bring respectability—William Beckford of Jamaica became alderman and then lord mayor of London. In 1770 he gave a dinner at the Guild-hall "attended by 6 dukes, 2 marquises, 23 earls, 4 viscounts, 14 barons and 18 baronets." The political power of men like Beckford was formidable; by the nineteenth century their intermarriages and their cross-investments had made them, according to Bishop Wilberforce, especially formidable in the House of Lords. There was representation of the aristocracy, the gentry and the great merchant houses in the lists of slave owners who were compensated after the passage of the Emancipation Act of 1833. The mainland colonials during the same period made no similar record of entry into the peerage, plutocracy or political power. Only a few sparse knighthoods were granted here and there for loyal service as royal governors. None went to anyone for getting "as rich as a West Indian."

West Indian money made it possible for the Lascelles family to engage the services of Robert Adam to create their palace at Harewood, for the Countess of Home to pay his commission for her house on Portman Square and for Lord Mayor Beckford's son to engage James Wyatt to lay up his Gothic fantasy, Fonthill Abbey. Doddington, the great Palladian pile near Oxford, was built of Barbados sugar revenues, brought home by men returned from the colonies to set up Country House–keeping.

The collapse of the sham-Gothic tower of Fonthill anticipated the ultimate state of many of the houses of those sucritots who remained behind in the islands. The sugar plantations of Cyprus, Madeira, Barbados, Jamaica and Louisiana are strewn with ruins. Only in Britain itself do the survivors of the West Indian system remain stately and sedate. In their grand serenity some sugar profits have lost their bitterness with time. Harewood and Doddington hide their Caribbean past beneath Palladian elegance. Like the American mansions of a little later, these great British Palladian-Revival houses of the middle of the eighteenth century were derived from a new and direct examination of ancient architecture on the part of

* After the first sugar boom, in 1646, a five-hundred-acre plantation on Barbados was worth more than the entire island a few years before. A century later, Jamaica was making vast fortunes for planters like the Beckfords and the Prices. William Beckford and his relatives owned nearly 60,000 acres, much of it actually producing sugar. A sense of how rich he was can be gained when we recall that it is probable that no colonial Virginia planter ever had more than a few hundred acres actually in slave-worked tobacco production, and that an acre in sugar could be valued at three to ten times more than an acre in tobacco.

Harewood House, north front (*above*) and south front (*below*)
Photos printed with the kind permission of the Earl and Countess of Harewood

men like Robert Adam. The development might be called a second Renaissance, though the continuity with the Renaissance was still powerful.* In any case, the houses retain the Palladian forms that had come to Britain a century earlier, at the same time the first great rush of colonial wealth made it possible for hundreds of newly enriched people to build on such a scale.

Relaxation and Neo-Palladianism

IN THE CARIBBEAN islands themselves, the Palladian progression into the open-villa form did not begin until the mid- to late eighteenth century, when the form was being "revived" in England, but fortified houses like Colbeck and somber medieval buildings like Drax Hall were eventually joined by some that took a more cheerful view of the prospects of survival amid a restive slave population. The reasons for this relaxation from the architecture of fear and from the architecture of alienation are not presented to us neatly in building "programmes" or correspondence between architects and clients. These clients were not notably articulate about such things, and time, insurrection and hurricanes have dealt brutally with what few records they kept in the islands. We may surmise that the process of intimidation of slaves, known as "seasoning," had had some effect; the most rebellious, on Jamaica at least, may have fled to their own mountain communities, leaving the more docile on the plantations. Perhaps fear had been around so long that, like the possibility of atomic war today, it simply became part of the atmosphere in which life went on. The records are so poor that we cannot tell with any precision whether or not life for the white plantation owners and managers actually became safer or not. All we can tell from the architectural record is that they built as if they felt safer.

In 1774 it was observed that "it is but of late that planters have paid much attention to elegance in their habitations." The transition had begun with first things first: the planters commenced to erect extraordinarily elaborate Classical factories (sugar refineries) and mills. (Ruins of grandiose examples can be seen at Kenilworth, Good Hope and Orange Valley, on Jamaica.) They put their attention on the buildings that made money, not where they lived. Edward Long, in the 1770's, observed that it was "not unusual to see a plantation adorned with a very expensive set of works, of brick or stone, well executed, the owner residing in a miserable thatched hovel, hastily put together."

First, perhaps, came an opening-out into a forecourt, protected by guard-houses at the corners and a high wall: Brievengat, from the middle of the eighteenth century, on Curaçao, is a Dutch version of such an intermediate form. Later

42   * See Chapter Twelve for the relationship of the Renaissance to Cooperstown, New York.

The Mill House at Kenilworth

Copyright © 1982 by Pamela Gosner, reprinted with permission of Three Continents Press

on that island, full-scale Palladianism appeared along the streets of Willemstad, and it made its appearance also in the prosperous French islands of Martinique and Guadeloupe, and even produced a full-scale villa on Marie Galante, the Château Murat.

Brievengat

Copyright © 1982 by Pamela Gosner, reprinted with permission of Three Continents Press

Jamaica offers another transition form at Halse Hall, about contemporary to Brievengat, where the basement is of masonry and the corner towers have shrunk into pavilions of frame. Later came full, triumphant plantation Palladianism. Rose Hall, a large Palladian villa of the 1770's, has recently been restored; Marlborough,

43

Halse Hall

Copyright © 1982 by Pamela Gosner, reprinted with permission of Three Continents Press

of the 1790's, looks much like one of Thomas Jefferson's essays of the same time, with a portico of the same shape as the last version of Monticello. To those who do not expect Palladian grandeur in the islands and forget how rich those islands were in the colonial economy, the assemblage of government buildings in Spanish Town comes as a dazzling surprise: from 1760 through 1820 there were built the Old King's House, the House of Assembly, the Government Archives and Record Office, the Armoury and the Rodney Memorial. Together they are the most

Rose Hall

Courtesy of the Jamaica Tourist Board

complete statement of the Palladian civic ideal in the Western Hemisphere. There was nothing in Virginia or the Carolinas to match them.*

The fact that the most important Palladian buildings in the West Indies are not residential reminds us of the planters' priorities, which were expressed, as well, in the order in which they applied the classical style to the buildings on their

Marlborough
Courtesy of the Jamaica Tourist Board

own plantations. The big money went home, home to Britain, to build great houses there. The successors of the West Indians, the first generation of planters in the Carolina low country, also included many who raced homeward to Britain with their winnings. But there, as the eighteenth century unfolded, a different pattern began to emerge, equally absentee but on a shorter leash. Low-country planters remained in America, but not on their plantations. They created a little London in Charleston, from which they paid state visits to the overseers of their rice, indigo and cotton plantations.

* *As a poignant reminder of the role of the mid-Atlantic islands in transmitting the system to the New World, there was also a Palladian Revival in the Canary Islands in the middle of the eighteenth century.*

Old King's House
Courtesy of the Jamaica Tourist Board

The visitor to either the islands or the low country is thus often disappointed in the expectation that great wealth must have produced large and elegant country houses in the fashionable styles of England or Holland. The exceptions, like Jamaica's Rose Hall and South Carolina's Drayton Hall, are wonderful. Yet it is generally true that the plantation economy south of Virginia did not produce architecture as ambitious as that built by owner-managers of the great houses of the Virginia and Maryland Tidewater.

CHAPTER 4

Dutch Colonial

HIGH-GABLED, STEEP-ROOFED houses like those we observed in the West Indies were also built on the mainland. These pre-Palladian forms developed in the late Middle Ages, over centuries, to accommodate cramped urban sites in northern Europe. They were so strangely inappropriate to living on plantations in the tropics that they suggest an architecture of alienation. In urban settings, more like those in which they originated, they were straightforward evidence of trading communities extending over great stretches of time and huge expanses of ocean.

In this chapter we leave, for a while, the Palladian progression, to examine in a little greater detail the origins and expression of this medieval urban form, which we saw in the last chapter in Drax Hall and St. Nicholas Abbey. In doing so, we have to adjust our focus from the continental perspective of most history-writing to an oceanic one.

I have never understood what art critics mean by the term "painterly." Its meaning, however, is quite clear to me when applied to the writing of history. It refers to schoolbook graphics that instruct us that British culture oozed across the North American landmass as if a can of red paint had been upset in Boston. A more sophisticated version adds blue paint oozing westward from Quebec, and a green puddle around New Amsterdam, amid a variety of candy stripes where the paints interpenetrate. Painterly graphics suggest that the story begins in these oozing enclaves. Architectural history, however, teaches us to look at maritime communities first, and only then at continental communities.

Fernand Braudel has shown us the way, once again. He has made it impossible for future historians to think of the Mediterranean as a watery void. Thanks to him, we know it as a basin composed of shoreline societies, which until very recently had more in common with each other than with their hinterlands.

The North Sea was such a matrix. So was the Caribbean, which by trade, investment and architecture expanded to the mainland shore as far north as Rhode

Island. The first agents of this extension were the Dutch. On their heels came the British. By the end of the seventeenth century a new Anglo-Dutch community was created in the New World.

Two hundred years ago it would have been easy to see the architectural lineaments of that community: New York, Charleston, Bridgetown on Barbados and Port Royal on Jamaica looked remarkably alike and, to our eyes, remarkably Dutch. They were actually Anglo-Dutch, like ports of similar aspect in East Anglia and the Low Countries, which stood around shallow estuaries, crowded with steep-roofed houses. In the attics under those roofs were warehouses. The external signboard for the trade goods within was curved or stepped gables. In England and Zeeland little gabled ports can still be seen today, much as they were when built three or four hundred years ago. In America they have been sadly treated by time. What New York lost to progress, Port Royal lost to earthquake and tidal wave. Yet here and there, on the Charleston waterfront, for example, one can still see a group of pastel-colored, stuccoed Anglo-Dutch houses. (We do not know, of course, whether or not they were pastel-colored in their youth; it

Watercolor known as the "Prototype View" of New Amsterdam, 1650–53
Courtesy of the Museum of the City of New York

was twentieth-century artists, led by Alice Ravenel Huger Smith, who thought they would be prettier so, and painted over the intervening drab.)

The Gable Goes West

THE FLEMISH GABLE is so important a trace element of the Anglo-Dutch community that we now step back into the late Middle Ages to consider how it became so.

In Holland and in the marshy extremities of East Anglia, dry land was too scarce to be lavished on warehouses, and goods were stored far off the ground, in an attic, above a merchant's house. To permit access to this upper story, winches and pullies lifted trade goods into an attic door like that of a haymow, right from a barge on a canal.

As a merchant waxed prosperous, his attic-warehouse was enlarged. It acquired ornamental devices. In the North an ornamented gable was as important to a merchant's sense of achievement as the pediment above a classic doorway provided by Palladio for a coat of arms. A gable could be given patterned brickwork, stepped and curved edges and spiky finials. In its full panoply it became a symbolic statement of a social shift; the merchant was asserting his independence from the old nobility of the land. Our contemporary Alan Gowans describes the process:

> Medieval towns had heretofore been communities of feudal peasants, who went out in the morning to work surrounding fields, returning to the protection of the walls at night. But the Dutch city was created by merchants, middlemen whose homes and places of business were one and the same . . . In situation and function these houses were different from those of farmers, or of the "working class"; and the difference in appearance soon became symbolic of class status as well.

Sparks of irony often fly up from the brushing of aesthetic against economic history. One of these is how arriviste merchant symbols were adopted by arriviste landed gentry, after a sea change. In the late sixteenth and seventeenth centuries ornamented gables moved from town to country, from Holland and Flanders to England. There they were adopted by newly rich and newly ennobled Tudor magnates. The booty of the Spanish Main, the squeezings of Ireland, the spoils of confiscated monasteries and of defeated rivals went to pay for gabled country houses so huge that they were called "prodigy houses."

Amid the sculptured greenery of vast private parks, these country houses displayed, as pure ornament, forms that had served a functional purpose in the crowded streets of towns in the Low Countries. Elizabethan and Jacobean courtiers, recently grown rich, ornamented their gables with brick- and stonework as gorgeously extraneous as the false fronts of saloons in Virginia City and Butte. Symbols of a merchant triumph over landed aristocracy became the favored form of architectural display of the landed class.

49

Old Stone House (Cortelyou House)
Courtesy of the New-York Historical Society, New York City

In the New World another irony was added: though the ornamented gable arose as an urban form, the replacement of the housing stock of seventeenth- and early-eighteenth-century cities has left only one or two gabled survivors. The Leendert Bronck House in West Coxsackie, New York; the Old Stone House at Gowanus, in Brooklyn; and Fort Crailo, up the Hudson, are the most ambitious and interesting of the lot. Our best examples are urban types marooned in the countryside, like Chekhovian heroines waiting to get to Moscow.

What were these houses like inside when they were young, in the colonies settled by the Dutch? Though frontier conditions decreed a parsimony with space as severe as that of crowded cities, we can imagine interiors enriched by pictures, furs and fabrics, manifesting a love of polished surfaces, mirrors, tiles, jewels and glass like that which produced the soundless, motionless plenitude we see in the paintings of Vermeer.

Outside, these Dutch houses presented a hard face to the world. They were built of stone and brick. Contemporary Yankee houses were most often of wood, though they were placed in the same natural settings, with the same kinds of trees standing about, upon the same rock shelves, in the same climate. Few Dutch houses stood broadside to the street. They offered to the world an elbow, their narrow side to the front, as do the Charleston houses which, to this day, represent the same tradition. Like their ancestors along the North Sea—like their cousins in the West Indies or at Charleston—they were not just residential in origin. The door on the narrow, street side was for commercial entry. The master of the house did his business in the reception rooms on the ground floor, and family rooms were often a story above.

Constantly in the Anglo-Dutch community of trade and architecture, we are reminded of the mercantile origins of the Founding Fathers, a point to which we will have frequent occasion to return. We are also reminded of the uneasy alliances and frequent violence that marked Anglo-Dutch bickering over division of the profits of those alliances.

Nichols House,
Bridgetown, Barbados
Photo by David Buisseret

Trade and Violence

THE DUTCH AND THE BRITISH in the seventeenth century extended into the Atlantic their oscillations of alliance and warfare, and the periods of violence between the two came more often as time went on. At the end of the previous century British assistance to the Dutch in their struggles with Spain had exasperated Philip II, who sent his Grand Armada to chastise the meddling Protestants. The defeat of his fleet proclaimed Britain to be a world power, in partnership with the Dutch. British and Dutch vessels set sail westward in common predatory attacks on the Iberians. The British made free to establish bridgeheads on the American shore, which was claimed by Spain but patrolled by the Dutch.

In 1609, while the British were poking about the Virginia underbrush, Henry Hudson, a British captain in the service of the Dutch, explored the coast farther north and penetrated deep into the interior, upon the river that was later named after him. A year earlier the Pilgrims had begun their twelve-year incumbency in Holland. When they came to depart, they considered a plan to emigrate under Dutch protection to New Amsterdam. They set out instead for Virginia, and settled in the end for their landfall on Massachusetts Bay. It was one of the small explosive accidents that tilt whole continents. The Pilgrims reinforced a very fragile British colonial effort.

This event, so easy to ignore at the time, occurred shortly before the first bloody confrontation between the Pilgrims' recent, patient hosts and their countrymen, a war fought in the 1650's between the Dutch and Cromwell's Commonwealth. In the next decade a new alliance of Holland, Denmark and France beat the British down and secured important commercial concessions, the Dutch penetrating deep into the enemies' waterways, burning British shipping upon the Thames and the Medway and, across the Atlantic, the James. Then the tides of war turned in favor of the British; New Amsterdam fell in 1664, was retaken in 1673 and was finally ceded in 1674. Meanwhile these two Protestant powers enjoyed another round of privateering against the Spaniards, culminating with the British fleet's greatest prize of all, the treasure fleet from the West Indies, taken off Cádiz.

These were not wars of principle; they were wars for trade. As one English captain put it, "The trade of the world is too little for us two, therefore one must down."

Until the end of the seventeenth century, the Dutch were more active traders along the Atlantic coasts of Europe and North America than were the British. While Britain was convulsed by its civil wars, the Dutch turned their energies from the East Indies to the West Indies and made the Caribbean a Dutch lake. Spanish warships were swept from the sea. The great Dutch admiral Piet Heyn captured the Spanish treasure fleet off Matanzas, with booty worth fifteen million guilders. After their destruction of the Spanish maritime power, the Dutch replaced the Genoese and Portuguese to become the supreme carriers of New World trade. They were responsible for what may have been the most important event in American history: in 1619 they brought Africans in servitude to the mainland.

New Amsterdam

TO SUSTAIN THEIR SUPREMACY, the Dutch established New Amsterdam as their northern base. They not only introduced the sugar and slaves system to the eager colonists of the West Indies and the coastal South, but supplied "technical assistance" as well—credit, technology and manufactured goods. Then they stood by to carry off the sugar when it was produced. Later they offered the same services to the tobacco planters of the Chesapeake, dominating the carrying trade there until the mercantilist policies of the Restoration drove them out. Edward Winslow said in 1655 that the West Indian planters "doted on the Dutch commerce." So did the Virginia planters, whose assembly invited the Dutch to bring in their "wares and merchandise," including slaves, and buy tobacco. The Dutch, cruising offshore and dominating the life of the trading towns, were "good merchants but ill planters," said the governor of Barbados, while the British planter class concluded that "planting is a happy and convenient way of thriving."

Before Newport, Rhode Island, acquired that dubious distinction in the eighteenth century, New Amsterdam was the home port for more slave ships than any other city in North America. In 1665 New Netherland as a whole had a higher proportion of slaves than either Virginia or Maryland, much higher than North Carolina or any of the British northern colonies. As late as the end of the Colonial period there were as many slaves in New York as in Georgia. In some of New York's rural counties, like Dutchess, the percentage of blacks was as high as in rural North Carolina.* In New Amsterdam, and in no other colonial town except Newport, slave trading was a civic, not merely an individual, enterprise. The chief slaveholders were also the chief urban magistrates. The great patroons owned many slaves. The Dutch, having introduced Negro slaves to Virginia, waxed wealthy in the slave trade throughout their mid-Atlantic trading territory. Their success was a demonstration and thus an invitation to competitors.

Beginning in the middle of the seventeenth century, the British, in response, turned the old program of Elizabeth I, Drake and Hawkins, once directed against the Spaniards, on the Dutch. That program was still a public-private partnership in slaving, but in the seventeenth century it was on a much larger scale. No longer was it merely a sovereign's individual complicity in a voyage or two; now it required a fleet, sustained by a bureaucracy. No longer was the prize a flotilla of a few galleons bearing slaves and precious metals; now it was the dominance of continents and a commerce in millions—literally millions—of slaves. The Spanish

---

An inconspicuous outbuilding at Hyde Park, home of Franklin Delano Roosevelt, housed the slaves kept by the great-grandfather of the President.

were much weakened by 1660; the British no longer were forced to seek Dutch assistance against them. Parliament prohibited its American colonists from trading with the Dutch and interposed a fleet to police its prohibition. Many colonials (the Virginians in particular) resented this interposition and evaded it when they could.

To replace the Dutch control of the slave trade, the African Company was organized. To enlarge opportunities for that company, a group of "Proprietors" was encouraged to open a new market for slaves by colonizing the shores of the Carolinas. In 1664 New Amsterdam was seized, at the orders of the Duke of York, though Britain and Holland were not formally at war.

The Dutch monopoly of the Caribbean trade, and of the slave and tobacco traffic with Virginia, was broken. But the Dutch commercial system survived, and it remained a powerful influence on architecture into the next century, in the villages in the Hudson Valley and northern New Jersey, in the little port cities of Jamaica and Barbados, and in the first set of South Carolina plantations. A Barbadian architectural historian, George Hunte, tells us that the Dutch brought the tools required by "carpenters, joiners, smiths, masons, mill-wrights, wheel-wrights, tinkers and coopers . . . the Dutch were the mentors of the English plantation owners." They were mentors of a style the planters themselves desired, for reasons suggested in the last chapter. A cold-country architecture, ill-adapted to subtropical islands, was built by Dutch artisans for British planters because they wanted their houses to look and feel familiar. All the Dutch modeling and all the Dutch tools and all the Dutch artisans in the Indies would not have prevailed against another psychology.

Two twentieth-century reviewers of Barbadian history, Carl and Roberta Bridenbaugh, reported that Dutch influence was predominant in the rebuilding of the Bridgetown waterfront at the dawn of the eighteenth century. Drax Hall and especially St. Nicholas Abbey, the greatest houses of this period to survive, with their curvilinear gables and large chimneys, reflect the pervasive Dutch architectural influence.

They reflect that influence as it shaped architecture not once but twice: Dutch commercial power and Dutch artisanship in America in the seventeenth century reinforced their cultural penetration of Britain itself a hundred years earlier, when the gables of prodigy houses had become symbols of Olde England itself. Caribbean great houses like Drax Hall and St. Nicholas Abbey, probably built between 1675 and 1700, echo greater houses in England, like Kirby Hall (1575), Montecute (1599), Holland House (1607), Charleton (1612) and Blicking (1626). Anglo-Barbadian nabobs, full of nostalgia for the old country, were comforted to look up at masons and carpenters at work on the skylines of their plantation houses and see them forming reminiscences of fashionable houses laid up at home in the time of their youth. Design ideas from the Low Countries had been a part of British practice for generations; it merely took the reinforcement of Dutch architects, trading partners and workmen for these ideas to come again to the surface.

One of the oldest houses in South Carolina is Medway, about twelve miles

Medway

Courtesy of the Library of Congress

northeast of Charleston, at the fringe of what was once the Barbadian subcolony along Goose Creek. A house at Medway was built in 1686 by Jan van Arssens, Seigneur de Weirnhoudt, leader of a group of Dutch settlers. It was burnt early in the eighteenth century, but it seems probable that it was rebuilt in something like its original form, that the stepped gables on the chimney ends added grace to a story-and-a-half rice plantation headquarters which could be entered either down a long double alley of trees from the city road, or from its own landing on the river.* Then it was remodeled, but with every extension and addition its gables were borne aloft, like an Olympic flame or a knightly banner. Van Arssens' spirit remained strong, even after his wife's innumerable descendants made engulfing accretions to the house of soft brick from the clay beds along the Medway River (now prosaically renamed the Back).

---

* A long run of South Carolina architectural historians fixed Medway as the original van Arssens house, but an unpublished study by Agnes Baldwin, now at the South Carolina Historical Society, contains portions of letters indicating that it was burnt early, as reported.

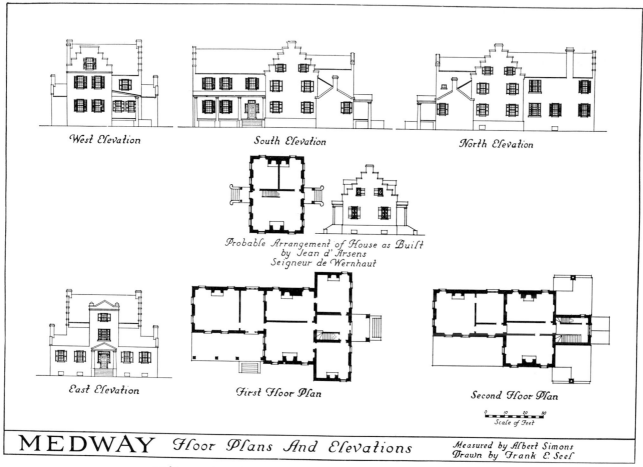

West Elevation South Elevation North Elevation

Probable Arrangement of House as Built
by Jean d' Arsens
Seigneur de Wernhaut

East Elevation First Floor Plan Second Floor Plan

Scale of Feet

MEDWAY *Floor Plans And Elevations* Measured by Albert Simons
Drawn by Frank E. Seel

Medway elevations

Courtesy of the South Carolina Art Association

Van Arssens' widow married Thomas Smith and brought him enough accumulated properties to merit a group of post-feudal titles invented by the British regime to impart some of that instant antiquity which the merchant-patroons were then also purchasing in New York. In South Carolina holders of vast unexplored areas of pine barren could call themselves "cacique" and "landgrave." Landgrave, with its Rhineland associations, is a wonderful title for the owner of Medway. The architectural historian Samuel Gaillard Stoney, seeing the place in its low-country setting, felt the house "had as good right to be standing over a canal in the Low Countries of Holland as beside rice fields in the Low Country of South Carolina."

The oldest surviving house in Virginia, Bacon's Castle, could with as good a right stand along a canal in the Anglo-Dutch fenland of East Anglia, near a town like Great Yarmouth. It stands, instead, amid the flat, rich fields of the delta of the James, near Smithfield. It was built about 1655 by Arthur Allen, of a similar configuration to the original Medway but much larger. It was always of two and a half stories, with a "porch" or vestibule in front and a stair-tower across the main hall at the back, where Medway had only steps (perhaps a *stoep*, covered in the Dutch manner). The Allen house has more elaborate gables, too, with curves and steps that terminate in tall, clustered Tudor-Gothic chimneys. In this house Nathaniel Bacon's rebels holed up, in 1676, to withstand a siege from the relentless governor, Sir William Berkeley. A price had been set on Bacon's head for leading a campaign against the Indians and against Berkeley's express command: the Indians had been raiding the plantations of Bacon and his friends, but were the Governor's fur-trading partners. Bacon's Castle has suffered some interior remodeling, but its great beams, whitewashed plaster walls and deep-set window seats in thick masonry could have accommodated Vermeer's porcelain ladies.

St. Luke's Church, in nearby Smithfield, is one of a small group of churches on the mainland to survive almost intact as a representative of the late medieval North Sea architectural community. It, too, has a stepped gable, and the classic pediment over its doorway, like the similar pediment at Bacon's Castle, shows the print of the fingertip of the Renaissance.

The late medieval tradition lasted in South Carolina for another hundred

Restored south façade of Bacon's Castle
From H. C. Forman, Architecture of the Old South, *Harvard University Press*

57

years. Flemish gables were still used at the stables of North Chacan plantation about 1760 and at St. Stephen's Church seven years later.*

These buildings demonstrate the interplay of the Dutch and the British around the North Sea, then in the West Indies and finally along the coast of the mainland. Samuel Stoney saw Medway, his South Carolina house, as Dutch. He saw its parish church, St. James, Goose Creek, as so West Indian that it would be appropriate in either Antigua or Barbados. It is sometimes very hard to sort out what is Dutch from what is Carolinian, or Antiguan or Barbadian, especially since the same man might have built a church or house in any of those places.

All design ideas within the North Sea trading territory, as it extended itself into the Caribbean, did not originate with the Dutch, at least not directly. Nor were all stiff, high-gabled houses confined to the tight rows required by the scarce land along the wharves of Amsterdam or Bridgetown. The ancestors of the doughty seaman John Washington (see Chapter One) had built such a hall at Sulgrave, not far from Northampton, in central England. In a relatively brief period of prosperity, which did not carry through to subsidize the founder of the Virginia branch of the family, the Washingtons of Sulgrave showed how the successful woolen merchants of such a town might build when they strove to settle into the countryside and assume the lineaments of squires. The façade indicates the traditional cross-plan of the smaller squirearchy of the late Tudor period, with a gable presented to the world atop a forward-thrust short wing at the center. Many of these houses matched the front projection with another at the rear, sometimes containing a stairhall.

Americans unwilling to make the pilgrimage to Sulgrave can see this form at Bacon's Castle, at the Iron Monger's House at Saugus, or in the shape of the original Medway. They can see it, as well, in a sort of museum copy, at Bremo Recess, on the upper James River in Virginia, where John Hartwell Cocke pointedly created an anachronism in 1805, "copied from . . . the well-remembered old six-chimney house in Williamsburg, once the property of the Custis family, and Bacon's Castle." Cocke was staking his claim as the squire of a new domain at the extremity of the Tidewater, staking it in a way common in the West Indies and on the mainland, with a squire's house.

These tall cross-plan buildings can be found in many places where colonists tried to include the shores of the New World within their old community of customs and symbols. Some remain on Bermuda: Walsingham, Tankfield, Inwood and Norwood are good examples. On Curaçao the gables are more fanciful, and the houses larger.

* *Hugh Morrison has suggested that the famous reconstruction of Bruton Parish Church, in Williamsburg, Virginia, may have omitted similar gables, which it may have borne in 1683. But, on the other hand, recently discovered drawings demonstrate that the equally famous reconstruction of a flanker of Middleton Place, near Charleston, which does have curved gables, is a tribute to nineteenth-century romantic imagination. Other churches that are similar to St. Luke's are St. Peter's, New Kent (also much restored), and the pointed gables at Yeocomico and Merchant's Hope Church in Virginia.*

Bremo Recess
Photo by Wayne Andrews

In South Carolina the form persisted into the eighteenth century, where the projected stair-tower appeared at Middleton Place and at the Ashley Hall plantation of Stephen Bull, Anthony Ashley-Cooper's deputy in the first government of the province of Carolina. Staircases need not be enclosed in the South; many are not, even in this climate-conditioned age. The persistence of such cold-climate forms in a hot climate can be explained rather simply as the reuse in America of architectural habits acquired in Europe. Or, somewhat more ambitiously, one could explain that when people can, they will strive to assert their role and station, and their possession of place, by the devices they feel express ownership. Territoriality, anthropologists have called it. As we have seen, something yet subtler is expressed when the architectural devices chosen to establish territoriality are extremely, indeed unreasonably, uncomfortable.

CHAPTER 5

The Caribbean Cottage

TIME MELLOWS ALL; stains and scratches become patina; edges soften in the twilight; harsh, hustling young men become avuncular elders. The brick and stone Dutch houses of the Hudson Valley have acquired quaintness. Quaintness, in fact, is a Hudson River quality, in literary history as well as in architectural history. During the nineteenth century, Bostonians were preeminent in chronicling history on a continental scale. This left cozy kills, cloves and wicks to the Hudson River school of historians. The very continental sweep of the Yankees forfeited to the Hudson River chroniclers-of-the-quaint much of the contest for readers who need a picture—a specific local picture—of the scenes of history.

Washington Irving and James Fenimore Cooper have done as much, or more, to fill the American imagination with images of the Colonial period as Francis Parkman or John Fiske or Samuel Eliot Morison. We owe to them a ready store of imaginary architecture, much of it Dutch. If we, in our turn, place this Dutch Colonial architecture in its economic context, it can provide stimuli to imaginary scenes that neither Irving nor Cooper fancied very much. Such stimuli can redress the heavy weight of nostalgia that fills the Hudson Valley with legend. Cooper and Irving told marvelous stories, but they did not try to give any sense of what life was like for most people in that region. The Hudson Valley had a class structure more like that into which the British Caribbean colonies degenerated than that of their other mainland settlements. If we associate the West Indies with the verandah-girt houses of the Hudson Valley, we can more easily read their meaning.

Verandah-girt? What happened to the high-gabled, masonry Dutch cottage? When it went to the country it was, like the people who built it, remarkably adaptable. Dutch traders (often, after 1700, flying the English flag and looking to New York as their home port), plying the sea lanes between the West Indies and the Atlantic Coast of the mainland, observed, in the vernacular traditions of the New World, structures that suggested ways of living comfortably in such a world.

Those suggestions, accepted by supremely practical seafarers, led in time to the sensible idea of surrounding the traditional North European cottage with a verandah. So was born the structure that is often called Dutch Colonial. It is a term that pays decent deference to the role of the Dutch in the commerce of the region, knitting it together into a community within which such ideas could circulate, but we will not use it very much because these houses were not limited to former Dutch colonies, nor is it at all likely that only Dutch seafarers carried this style in their architectural baggage.

The verandah-girt cottage was, however, the most important article of architectural commerce of the Anglo-Dutch trading area in the New World, exchanged between the West Indies and the mainland. It was informal and indigenous. Except in the predominantly Dutch-settled areas, with their strong masonry tradition, and along the upper reaches of Delaware Bay, where German masons shared that kind of tradition, the cottage was most often constructed very lightly of wood and surrounded by verandahs, or piazzas or, to say much the same thing, exterior balconies. To call these felicitous appendages loggias would be to offer too stately a suggestion; to call them porches is to use a twentieth-century word though it meant something quite different (an enclosed vestibule) in the period we are discussing.

In the most primitive form of porch, extended eaves were suspended upon stilts above water, or above the ground. A high-pitched roof was composed of thatch or straw or reeds or shingles. Sometimes, in the Caribbean, walls made of posts were covered with planks; some were thickened to assume the appearance of masonry by a covering of tabby, a compound of shells, shell lime and sand, the composition of which was probably a Spanish or North African contribution, carried along the trade routes to South America and the West Indies.

The origins of this familiar structure have been endlessly debated. Though it has some similarities to the East Asian bungalow, and ingenious scholars have found precedents for its verandahs in the balconies of medieval houses in the north of France, in North America it seems to have sprouted wherever the sun was hot and there was plentiful rain. The verandah is probably an indigenous American contribution to architectural history. It is likely that Europeans tried it out where they first came and had to adapt to such a climate: in the West Indies. It may owe something to memories of Africa, and something to the architecture Europeans and Africans found when they came to the West Indies. One does not need to be too strenuous about seeking a single source for such a natural means of shelter; it is enough to say that it had appeared on all the shores touched by the Anglo-Dutch trading continuum by the end of the eighteenth century.

I have called it the Caribbean cottage, but I am not prepared to fight very hard to defend the hypothesis that it began there: the evidence, archaeological, literary or pictorial, just doesn't exist. In fact, one of the pleasures of history is the inexplicable. The coincident first appearances of cottages with sitting porches throughout maritime North America, about 1740, is a delectable mystery.

An effort to unravel that mystery will be made at the end of this chapter, but in order to introduce some real people into the tale, we might look first at the sort of households that added verandahs to their country houses along the Hudson during the last half of the eighteenth century. Some of those houses had been there a century and more, and stood in stone, acting as fortresses, compact and defiant. They were not large enough, nor were the plantations of which they were head-quarters rich enough, to support the creation of the corner turrets or the walled forecourts of the Caribbean. There were no Colbecks on the Hudson. But in scale these fierce little Dutch outposts served much the same function as Colbeck. Their circumstances were more similar to Jamaica than one might easily observe in the haze of nostalgia blown about them by Irving and Cooper.

Van Cortlandt

OLOFF VAN CORTLANDT, trained in Dutch law, in turn trained his son Stephanus, the first man born in the colonies to become mayor of New York. His manor house was one of the first to be remodeled into the verandahed style.* In 1697 the son's service to a succession of English governors of New York was rewarded by a license to buy land from the Indians, and he acquired 87,000 acres, a few for farming and the bulk for trading purposes and for leasing to tenants. His house at Croton (now separated from the Hudson by the Croton railroad station) was originally a stone fort, like those of the early European planters in the West Indies. When times became more pacific, in the mid-eighteenth century, it, like its Carib-bean cousins, spread out and up, to become a raised cottage with verandahs all around. It is the most perfect manifestation of the West Indian–Dutch plantation house on the mainland. Appropriately, it was probably built by slaves. Among the owners of slaves listed in New Amsterdam as early as 1656 were not only the original Oloff van Cortlandt but also his brother-in-law, Govert Lookermans.

Accumulation of wealth generally means sharing in the growth of an econ-omy. Rapid accumulation often means being careful not to share that share too widely with others. In New Netherland and then in New York this was accom-plished by restricting the number of sharers in an economy whose benefits were increasing very rapidly—possibly more rapidly than anywhere else in the northern colonies in the eighteenth century. Fur trading, land trading and the carrying trade created a class of merchants supported by slaves, indentured servants and tenants who were kept in a state close to peonage. Denied access to capital, they had little share in the growth of the economy; the social structure of New Neth-erland and New York was, in this way, very reminiscent of that in the West Indies.

Sometimes a social and economic affinity induces an aesthetic affinity. Archi-tecture along the Hudson had a distinctly Caribbean look.

It looks remarkably similar to the country house built outside Nassau by the British governor of the Bahamas, Lord Dunmore.

The Van Cortlandt Manor house in Croton-on-Hudson, New York

Photo by Langdon Clay

Verplanck

MANY DUTCH-BUILT HOUSES acquired verandahs. Some, it seems, were built with them, a completed amalgam, though we can never be entirely sure. One that seems to have originated as a raised cottage with a verandah was Mount Gulian, near Beacon, New York. It was built about 1737 by Gulian Verplanck, upon a portion of the lands accumulated by an ancestor of the same name, who emigrated to New Netherland about 1645. The founding Verplanck had been a supercargo on a trading vessel; after he came ashore he quickly prospered as a shopkeeper and built a "substantial stone house" on Broadway. He made a smooth transition to British rule, succeeding Stephanus van Cortlandt as mayor of New York. In 1682 Gulian Verplanck and a partner (Francis Rambout, a Protestant refugee from the region of Antwerp) received a license to negotiate with the Indians for land extending from Fishkill to Poughkeepsie. It is said they first struck a bargain for all the land they could see, and then climbed to the top of Mount Beacon, from which, indeed, they could see almost twenty miles to the north. This splendid example of colonial surveying was confirmed by King James II in 1685, after van Cortlandt, who stood in well with the British governor, was sagaciously let into the partnership.

The successor and namesake of the first Gulian Verplanck laid up Mount Gulian "by the labor of his own slaves." In a ground-floor room, overlooking the Hudson, on May 13, 1783, former officers of the Revolutionary Army organized

63

Mount Gulian (destroyed by fire in 1931)
Courtesy of the New-York Historical Society, New York City

the Society of the Cincinnati.* There is a certain irony in this location: the behavior of the Verplancks had been sufficiently ambiguous during the preceding hostilities to gain them another kind of decoration, a set of paintings by Angelica Kauffmann, whose medallions add elegant muted color to so many Adam ceilings in Britain. They were bestowed by the British commander in New York, Lord Howe, to commemorate the profuse hospitality offered him by Mount Gulian's owners in their town house, where, one must assume, the Cincinnati might not simultaneously have found a welcome.

Landlords and Tenants

SLAVERY AND INDENTURED SERVITUDE, as devices that served to concentrate the winnings, were very common in all the colonies. Tenantry akin to peonage, however, appeared uniquely in the Dutch colony and persisted along the Hudson for eighty years after the British assumed political control.

* *The most interesting records of Mount Gulian's constant stream of celebrated visitors after the peace were kept in the seven-volume diary of the slave James Brown, who was the chief gardener of the estate and a sharp social critic.*

Tenants came to New Netherland as early as the shipload of brick, stone and tile that the patroon Kiliaen van Rensselaer sent from Holland for the construction of a headquarters building for his plantations on the eastern shore of the Hudson. It was named Fort Crailo, after an estate he had bought outside Amsterdam with the profits of his diamond business. A block in Fort Crailo's cellar carries the date 1642; the brick house above may have grown around a small stone fort of that date. The surviving brick residence is of the Dutch urban type, with a steep roof terminating in a gabled parapet, ornamented with bricks laid parallel to the roof-line and forming a sawtooth pattern, with a shoulder at the bottom. It stands today in a Victorian neighborhood in Rensselaer, New York, where its gun-ports and narrow, deep-set windows covered with heavy shutters set on wrought-iron hinges seem as out of place and time as a man in a breastplate and helmet. Fort Crailo was at the outset a traders' refuge from the Indians, and later an overseers' refuge from unruly tenants. Like a diminutive Colbeck Castle, it was a fortress against enemies without and within.

Neither Kiliaen van Rensselaer nor the son who succeeded him ever saw his New World possessions, but his grandson exchanged his claims to the family business in Amsterdam for his relatives' shares in what was by then New York. The decision by the sellers to stay focused on the diamond and pearl business was akin to that of Venetian merchants to stay in the Mediterranean trade. Old Kiliaen had induced the family to take a ride with the West India Company. They had supplied guilders to fit out privateers, to raid Spanish shipping and to build ships to contend against the Portuguese dominance of the slave trade between Africa and the Caribbean. For that sort of work, a base in New Netherland was a convenience and could also serve as a collection point for furs and timber.

Though Kiliaen van Rensselaer and a few others heeded Henry Hudson's

Fort Crailo, as rehabilitated in the 1930's

From the New York State Office of Parks, Recreation and Historic Preservation, Bureau of Historic Sites, [Fort] Crailo State Historic Site

glowing reports of the agricultural possibilities of the land, most Dutch investors kept their attention on more familiar lines of business. This left a great opportunity for a few intrepid spirits who in 1629 received a Charter of Freedom and Exemptions, under which any promoter who induced fifty adults to settle on his land could claim feudal dues in perpetuity from them and from all subsequent settlers. Each barony (patroonship) was four leagues long, on one side of a river, or two leagues along both banks, extending as far inland as one could go without butting into another patroon. This was the feudal format employed by van Rensselaer and van Cortlandt to organize their lands and their tenants. Kiliaen van Rensselaer's descendants came to control twenty-four miles along both sides of the Hudson, and thousands of tenants.

From Delaware to Connecticut five vast patroonships were created, of which only van Rensselaer's remained long in the original family's hands. They were not, at the outset, successful economically, because they attracted few tenants. Not even the very poor of Holland or Britain found appetizing the prospect of departing societies where the grip of the landed aristocracy was weakening, to come to a raw New World and submit to peonage under hard-fisted merchants turned for profit to the land. So, on a symbolic level, Fort Crailo was a stronghold of anachronistic land tenure, holding out against that transforming tide of immigration which elsewhere in America was creating, for good or ill, a new pattern of settlement and a new attitude toward land (see Part Two).

British landowners, like the Livingstons, who replaced, and intermarried with, the Dutch, decked out the old patroonships with a full array of marvelously anachronistic feudal devices: landlords became lords of manors, holding courts-leet and courts-baron. Recent scholarship has shown that the dues they extracted were not much more onerous than those required of other tenants in the colonies. But because manor owners would not sell the huge tracts they preempted, the agriculture of the Hudson Valley developed less rapidly than that of the Middle Colonies, and the best frontiersmen in the central colonies, the Scotch-Irish, chose in their tough, cranky, independent way to move west and southwest through Pennsylvania and the great valley of Virginia. They might otherwise have landed at Manhattan or at the deep-water ports up the Hudson and headed west from there. The Germans, who were, as a group, among the best farmers* in colonial America, also were rebuffed when they tried the Hudson Valley; their unhappy reports sent their cousins to Pennsylvania.

But for the landlords' efforts to behave like real patroons, agricultural New York might have benefited from the Pennsylvania Dutch and its frontier might have advanced at the pace of the long-legged Scotch-Irish. The owners were in the way. They held their ground at places like Fort Crailo, which was occupied successively by van Rensselaers, Schuylers, Livingstons, van Rensselaers again, Schuylers again, and van Rensselaers yet again. The patroon system, and its successor, the form of landlord control peculiar to New York, kept the Hudson

* *There is scholarly dispute about the likely winners of any colonial "best farmer" contest.*

Valley an enclave of seventeenth-century society; Dutch Colonial houses and the social structure of a Dutch colony persisted there until the region was swept into the nineteenth century by the Erie Canal.

In the great estates, tenants remained in desperate peonage unless they could accumulate enough capital to become landowners. Many lived no better than slaves and some worse. Lord Bellomont, after touring New York in 1700, reported to the Lords of Trade: "Mr. Livingston has on his great grant of 16 miles long and 24 broad but 4 or 5 cottages as I am told, men that live in vassalage under him and work for him and are too poor to be farmers—have not wherewithal to buy Cattle or stock a farm. Colonel Cortland has also on his great grants 4 or 5 of those poor families. Old Frederick Phillips is said to have about 20 families."

The sparsely settled landholdings were dangerously exposed to the French and the Indians. In the eighteenth century, British colonial policy attempted to fill the void by revising the system to permit a new class of speculators, like van Cortlandt and Frederick Philipse (see Chapter Seven), to move in and sell outright much of the acreage recovered from expired patroonships. One of New York's chroniclers wrote that thereupon "groups of men who possessed capital bought enormous areas in the river-counties and sold farms as vigorously as a modern promoter develops new plots—there were scandals, occasioned by political graft, fraudulent grants and overlapping boundaries, but the situation gradually cleared, and even at its worst, the lot of the smaller buyers, on the land covered by the patents of the actual homesteaders, was better than that of the tenants on the manors."

It is impossible to measure such matters, but it seems probable that no other ruling class of Colonial times, except that of the West Indian planters, was as exploitive as the Dutch, so blandly indifferent to the condition of the poor. Peter Stuyvesant spoke of the workers of New Amsterdam as "the scrapings of nationalities"; he and his peers saw little need to provide for their educational or religious needs. As Alan Gowans has pointed out, this attitude "in the long run . . . meant the inevitable extinction of Dutch culture. Churches, schools, and public institutions are the essential agencies for transmitting a national heritage from one generation to another . . . The mercantile spirit was set against providing them . . . but, to survive, colonies need something more . . . so it was that the future in the New World belonged to others than the Dutch." But that future was tinctured by the past: the Dutch passed on to the British a system of combined slavery and debased tenantry unique in North America.

Against that system, from the very beginning, there were revolts. The first was led by Jacob Leisler in 1689. The last was the "tin-horn rebellion" under Smith Boughton in 1844. By the early nineteenth century even New York could no longer justify slavery. The states north of the Mason-Dixon line commenced its abolition with the Revolution (states to the south of the line did so also, but their efforts were aborted, one by one). Most had completed that abolition well before New York's gradual process worked its way out in 1827. By then it had become difficult to justify a single family's owning forty square miles of farmland,

67

taking a fourth of the price of any acreage sold by a tenant, requiring rents and menial service of tenants who lived in peonage. The manorial system was finally erased in 1846.

By that time the Dutch Colonial architectural style had expired. It was, therefore, about ready for sentimental revival as a rural cottage, of which many specimens can still be seen, some wearing the ambitious gambrel roofs that mark them as "true Dutch Colonial." (Nineteenth-century revivalists did not choose to reconstruct, as well, the compact, steep-roofed, gabled urban houses that had been built from Albany to Willemstad.) Now let us circle back, having given that bucolic cottage a few inhabitants, and see whether we can unravel any part of the mystery of its origin.

The Mysterious Cottage

THE COTTAGE WITH VERANDAH cannot be proved to have existed anywhere in the Western Hemisphere before 1700, or even before 1725. Yet by 1750 or 1760 it was everywhere! Well, not quite everywhere. Only where the West Indian traders reached, from coastal New England south along the Atlantic Coast, around Florida to Louisiana, up the Mississippi with the French as far as their outpost-garrisons around St. Louis. Later it showed up in the St. Lawrence Valley.

One of architecture's eeriest puzzles is the apparently simultaneous appearance, in many places distant from each other, of verandahs, piazzas and loggias—all forerunners of the sitting porch, as we now call it. They appear in too many places to be explained by diffusionist theory. No coherent explanation can glue them together, except what historians most loathe: coincidence, and multiple coincidence at that.

Today we are accustomed to the rapid spread of technological innovation through mass publication, advertising and military competitiveness. Diffusion by these means responds to an obsession with novelty among things as well as among ideas. We are, therefore, likely to look at the nearly coincident appearance of similar artistic forms in many places and conclude that somebody invented the prototype, and others, elsewhere, rushed to copy it.

Diffusion did occur in earlier ages, but not nearly so rapidly. Coincidences were more likely to be coincidences. Eighteenth-century people could be as delighted as we at a new and good idea, but they had not our means to obtain it. Here, for example, is Chevalier Jean de Pradel writing in Louisiana in 1753: "What a great convenience these galleries are in this country!" He had more than three hundred feet of galleries around his plantation house (six hundred feet, if one counts both the upper and lower tiers)! He enters our discourse because the same delight was being felt in the West Indies, the Carolinas, Maryland, Illinois and Georgia at about the same time.

We cannot prove the appearance of galleries in Louisiana much earlier than 1740. They were not shown in drawings of the 1730's. An architect named Ignace

Middleburg Plantation

Collection of Carolina Art Association, Gibbs Art Gallery, Charleston, S.C.

François Broutin submitted a galleried plan for a public building in 1749, and his grandson built a vast galleried house sometime between 1746 and 1763.

The dates are about the same in the West Indies. Richard Dunn tells us that descriptions of Port Royal as it appeared in 1688 and of Bridgetown in 1695 include no galleries. But four houses in Kingston, drawn about 1740, showed "ample verandahs and arcades."

An act of the South Carolina Assembly of 1700 and a drawing of 1739 indicate that open "piazzas" (what we would call porches or even porticoes) were built to shelter front steps in Charleston.*

There are a number of early South Carolina plantations that have galleries: Middleburg, sometimes said to be the oldest, built about 1699, probably did not acquire its long verandah as early as the core of the building, but it seems likely that the gallery was there by the time Oakland, not far away, was built with a gallery around 1740.

Coastal North Carolina, isolated behind its swamps and deep estuaries from its mainland neighbors, was even more tightly bound to the West Indies than Virginia or South Carolina. Its oldest surviving houses, built in the 1720's, do not have porches, but Clear Spring, constructed about 1740 in Craven County, does. A description of the thriving port of Wilmington in 1757 speaks of brick houses two and three stories high "with double Piazzas which make a good appearance." Wilmington's Smith-Anderson House, built about 1745, apparently already had "an engaged double gallery along the side flank," like a Charleston single house, perhaps. Cottages in Beaufort and New Bern seem to have followed the new fashion in the 1750's and 1760's, and by the Revolution, the sitting porch was a North Carolina institution.

---

* Gene Waddell suggested recently that the great fire of 1740 on the waterfront may have spread more rapidly because of these inflammable structures, which by that time had become larger balconies. (Waddell, unpublished letter, April 28, 1982.)

Sitting porches appeared on the frontiers, too. Even in Georgia, still an experiment in colonization without slaves, still apart from the main trading network in the 1730's and 1740's, a long verandah like Middleburg's appeared upon Savannah's Orphan House by 1740. In Maryland the blacksmith and Indian trader Jonathan Hager may have had his verandah as early as 1740, when he built his stone house in the outpost that bears his name.

In Cahokia, on the central Mississippi, Jean-Baptiste Saucier, another trader, built a house of vertical logs chinked with broken rocks held by lime mortar about 1737 and surrounded it with a widely extended roof held up by posts, providing a Mississippi Valley sitting porch.

The south coastal cottage, "Caribbean," for convenience, is akin to another indigenous building which we can call the St. Lawrence Valley cottage. In the cold Canadian climate, cottages were often built into hillsides, snuggling into the earth, rather than holding themselves above it. We do not know when French traders first built balconies or verandahs on the exposed, or down-hill, sides of their stone cottages in the St. Lawrence Valley. But we do know that by the early nineteenth century this St. Lawrence Valley cottage was firmly established on the cold hillside of Canada.

The Mississippi Valley type, of which Saucier's was an early example, was neither partly buried in a hillside, as in Canada, nor built on stilts, as in the South. It stood upon the earth with its main living quarters at ground level. The French built many such houses in temperate areas up and down the Mississippi Valley. Sometimes they grew into three-story stone mansions in urban centers like St. Louis, but most of the time they were simple wooden cottages of one level.

The farther south one goes in that valley, the higher off the ground does the cottage rise, until, in Louisiana itself, a whole house, as much as three stories high, is suspended upon a high basement to escape the damp and catch the breeze. Since no one really knows, some writers have assumed that the French brought this form from the West Indies to the mainland valley at about the same time they brought sugarcane cuttings, and lowered it to the ground as their settlements progressed northward. There were plenty of mariners bringing trade goods northward out of the Gulf into the Mississippi and the Tombigbee, often the same mariners who penetrated the St. Lawrence and the Hudson. But it is equally likely, as we have suggested, that the "porch" developed almost simultaneously in many places in the mid-Atlantic trading territory, probably about 1730.

Verandahs were sometimes extravagantly set about all four sides (which tends to be the case in rural areas along the Gulf Coast and the Mississippi), sometimes along just one (as in densely settled regions of the South or where the winter is fierce and one only wants to leave one façade fully exposed). In the nineteenth century, verandahed cottages appeared as fur-trading outposts within the Arctic Circle, as whaling stations on the Monterey coast of California, among the earliest houses in Minnesota, very commonly along the central Mississippi, on the chill cliffs of the Gaspé and beside bayous half-hidden by tropical foliage.

It is useful to contrast this cottage with the buildings of the Spanish possessions, where the Mediterranean tradition ordained quite different forms. Perhaps the distinction between hot-and-dry and hot-and-humid explains the coexistence of two tropical traditions, of which the Caribbean cottage represents the humid variety and the Spanish hacienda the dry. Large haciendas were built around courts, with walls to the street, emphasizing privacy and implying the need for defense. It is a format derived from millennia of practice from Greece to Iberia, and it is absolutely different in feeling from a cottage, which is vulnerable, expansive and, one might say, extroverted.

That word recalls the Palladian villa, with which ambitious cottages first competed and later mated. Like the Palladian villa, the cottage is a Mediterranean house turned inside out. The cottage has no grand entranceway, no pedimented gable, no colonnaded hyphens reaching out to dependencies. Nearly always, the cottage is the size of a dependency. Porticoes were added to the cottages after the merger of the two forms in the nineteenth century, when such amalgams became fairly common—for example, in Nassau.

Like the Palladian villa, the Caribbean cottage, except in Canada and along the Mississippi, is associated with the plantation system. Even in New York it retained a remarkably close association with the slave system—not only along the Hudson but even inland, near Cooperstown (see Chapter Twelve). The Dutch and the British, always trading in things and ideas, were the carriers of this form, together with slaves.

So, behold the first American architectural style, simple, forthright, practical! By 1750 buildings like these could be seen at many of the ports of call in the

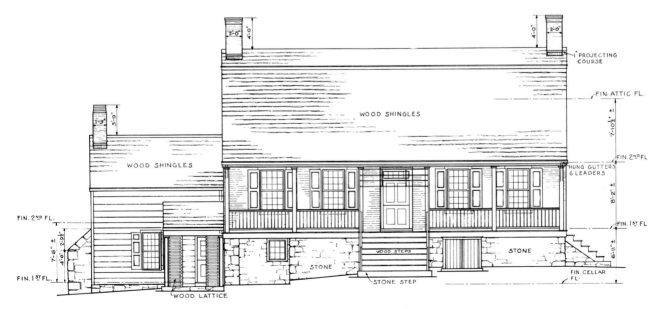

HABS elevation of the Dyckman House, a surviving example of a Dutch cottage in Manhattan
Courtesy of the Library of Congress

Anglo-Dutch skein of trade. They were, in a way, the country cousins of the descendants of the gabled low-country townhouse. New Netherland, and its capital, New Amsterdam, had been operated only briefly by the United New Netherland Company (1614–21). Thereafter it became a mainland subsidiary of the West India Company. The West Indian focus was only accentuated by the British capture of the colony in 1664; a full century thereafter, most of New York's shipping was still engaged in the West Indian trade. And after the American Revolution there was yet another upsurge of that trade, still captained by many seafarers with old Dutch names.

Another Addendum

SINCE THIS CHAPTER was written, I have seen two unrelated bodies of research that add to our uncertainties about the origins of the cottage form.

The first is an Italian reconstruction of a Villanovan herdsman's house of about 900 B.C., based on an urn, for ashes, which survives. It has a front porch, composed of posts supporting overhanging thatched eaves. Obviously these ideas have long commended themselves to people living in hot climates.

The second is a remarkably detailed account of the archaeological evidence of the forms of domestic construction that were probably more common in seventeenth-century Virginia than the masonry or frame houses that have survived to us. It appears that many British settlers lived in thinly constructed impermanent houses, walled by twisting brush among posts stuck in the ground, under roofs composed of thatchlike materials. I imagine them to have a very Villanovan appearance. Could some of them not, too, have extended their eaves, impermanently, of course, to provide shade, supported the overhang with posts, and anticipated the Caribbean versions? Or are other scholars right in thinking the Native Americans who preceded the Europeans into that region had already devised the cottage form? Nobody really knows!

Part II

Going Ashore
to Stay Ashore

T<small>HE PLANTATION SYSTEM</small>, *ravenous and implacable, had forced its way out of the Mediterranean and across the Atlantic. Then it was ready to assault the mainland, to seize the coastline from the Chesapeake to Florida, and later, from a base in Louisiana, to take control of the shores of the Gulf of Mexico. Finally, having consolidated its bridgeheads, it was ready for a campaign to organize the interior. It did not succeed in this final effort, though it thrust out salients as far north as the Ohio and as far west as the Brazos.*

The Dutch had been the carriers of slaves to the mainland, of gold to finance planting, of seeds and barrels and food to supply the islands which had been given over so much to sugar that they could not feed themselves. In our last two chapters the Dutch have occupied the stage because they carried, along with all the other commerce, a traffic in architectural ideas throughout their vast oceanic trading territory. They were not alone. In this commerce, ranging from slaves to architecture, they had partners and competitors—the Scots, the English, the Danes, the French and, later, the Yankees. But the role of the Dutch was so essential to the process that they have deserved center stage.

In the last chapter we observed the relaxation of the tight, grim little North European cottage as it acquired verandahs and breathed more easily. Chapter Three described two other openings-out: the pre-Palladian turreted fortress-farmhouse spread and became a porticoed villa in its home country, the Venetian mainland; then it did so again in the West Indies.

At the end of the eighteenth century a traveler in Italy could see porticoed country villas 250 years old, often with dependencies planned to impart a serene and orderly sense of the dominance of the landscape. Smaller but similar buildings could be seen in the West Indies and the Canary Islands, only fifty years old, or younger. Also in the West Indies and along the mainland coast of North America, the same traveler could see verandahed cottages which had evolved in a more informal way from small, defensible farmhouses.

The clenching and unclenching of architecture once again took place as the plantation system, still well served by the Dutch, spread to the shores of the southern mainland from the West Indies. The process started later there. To observe it, we need not go all the way back to the sixteenth century, as in Italy, nor quite so far as the middle of the seventeenth, as in the West Indies or along the Hudson, but only to the end of the seventeenth and the beginning of the eighteenth.

As planters tried a succession of crops in the coastal areas of Virginia and South Carolina, they began with fortified houses, some of them quite like the turreted buildings seen among Palladio's early work and in the West Indies at Colbeck or Stokes Hall. This form later expanded either into the formal, open villas suggested by Palladio's mature designs or, more informally, into Caribbean cottages (or, by 1800, into various combinations of the two).

In order to see where we are heading, it may be useful to call to mind now the scenes of the finished process of unclenching: the dozing cottages of the Carolina shore, or the relaxed red-brick manor houses along the James. But we are not there yet. Life in most places around 1700 is still too unsettled, too raw, too dangerous. We are amid the harsh beginnings of the mainland plantations.

CHAPTER 6

Transitional Architecture Ashore

BEFORE SETTLING INTO what seems to us, in the haze of romantic recollection, Georgian serenity, the English colonies of the Atlantic seaboard kept their guard up. Among the architectural relics of that time are a number of houses that provided a greater degree of domestic tranquility than blockhouses or stone forts, but were not ready to aver that the neighborhood was entirely safe. Their demeanor is more pacific than that of fortified houses like Colbeck Castle or Stokes Hall, yet more bellicose than the later red-brick symbols of a settled border.

These transitional houses retain the martial air of the borderlands, like the Italian houses we have called pre-Palladian, which had been guarded by towers at the corners. In the presence of increasing civil concord, the towers shrank into mere reminiscences: only a turret might remain after a period of peace, or a floor plan that put four rooms at the corners, thrust out like the arms of an H.*

The H plan arrived upon the mainland from the islands during the transfer of the plantation system,† a movement of men and capital intended either to create a secondary set of plantations on the West Indian model or to create a source of supplies for the island plantations, always the center of attention during the Colonial period. The focus was on the Caribbean; the planners of British imperial policy glimpsed the mainland only out of the corners of their eyes.

---

* *These little fortlets were still being built on the frontier as late as 1832, in Ohio. The Renick house, Mount Oval Farm, near Circleville, is an example.*

† *Under similar circumstances and at about the same time, the H plan appeared upon Mauritius, in the Indian Ocean, where it remains imbedded in the vernacular tradition. It is also worth noting that the form was used in deliberate anachronism for a Gothic country house by Benjamin Henry Latrobe, as late as 1800—see Chapter Thirty.*

What could be seen was sand-spit and marsh, and beyond, tall pines, which to an economic eye became masts and spars, pitch and resin. As distractions, there was also a bewilderment of native fruits and nuts; the wild strawberries were so profuse they turned crimson the boots of the explorers. The air was boisterously animated. Fleets of birds sailed the skies. The gatherings of carrier pigeons were so dense that when they settled, they could break the branches of trees. Upon the ground, strange animals like bison and elk eddied across savannahs under enormous oaks, crushing windrows of underbrush, and the rivers swarmed with fish. The little animals that lived near these rivers flashed golden pelts to the Europeans' dazzled eyes. Murmurous with life, silent only when the birds quieted before a storm, the fecund continent awaited Economic Man.

For decades the mainland, though rich as Eden, seemed merely the farthest of the Antilles. Whatever might lie behind the scrubby offshore islands was perceived as a barrier between the West and the East Indies, barren of the kind of precious metals the Iberians had found to the south. Later it was found to have some use—as a source of those things which could not compete with sugar for Caribbean acreage—and became differentiated into regions, each one of which could best supply one or another group of needs to the islands.

The Middle Colonies, as we shall see, came to supply cattle and wheat to feed the West Indies; South Carolina and Georgia, rice. The lumbering colonies, especially New Hampshire, North Carolina and what is now Maine, offered barrel staves and marine supplies to carry island products. They were able to develop their own means of organizing production in spite of a continuing shortage of labor, and accepted the immigration from the West Indies of some of the white settlers unable to resist the competition of slaves deployed against them by the sugar oligarchs, who by the late seventeenth century were coming to dominate the islands, changing what had once been a fairly diversified economy of small holders into one concentrated on a single crop in fewer and larger holdings.

Diversification to the mainland was not only useful to the planters of the West Indies; it was a part of an allocation of investment believed to be essential to the British national interest. The British government was persuaded by the West Indian lobby that the economic growth of England could be powered by a sugar-fed engine. It was largely in the hope of replicating the lucrative experience of the West Indies that the southern set of mainland colonies were organized. Mercantilist calculations broadened their appeal and led to subsidies of products, like indigo, tobacco and some marine supplies, intended not just for the West Indies but also for the home market. Yet the mainland economy lagged in an essentially secondary role to the islands through most of the Colonial period.

There is a lively debate on details, but economic historians seem to agree that the economy of Great Britain received an enormous stimulus toward rapid growth and change as a result of the inflow of revenues from the West Indies. The receipts from those islands, spread across the entire population of Britain, were not a huge increment, but they were not spread out. They flowed in a narrow, deep stream into the coffers of a few very rich people, who had, therefore, the capacity to invest their surplus in new industrial processes. New trades grew up, new shipping was built, hundreds of thousands of farmers left the British Isles for the Caribbean isles. Shrewd people with money gained the experience of reaping specialized crops from colonies that were denied the opportunity to process those crops into finished goods, their population being trained in the habits of production of raw materials and consumption of finished goods of British manufacture.

There were, of course, subsistence farmers throughout the European colonies in the New World, but from the perspective of those trying to manage imperial economies, they were of trivial significance. There were also, from the outset, suppliers of tobacco, indigo and a little silk directly to the European metropolis. The tobacco growers, especially in the region of the Chesapeake, developed quite independently of the mid-Atlantic plantation system, commencing their operations with very few black slaves and shipping directly to British ports. But they, too, over time, adopted the organization of plantation life and the deployment of slave labor which had proved itself profitable farther south. So it is appropriate that we continue, for a while, to pursue the slave plantation system as it fixed itself on the mainland in its most conspicuous and powerful form, that which moved from Barbados to the Carolinas.

This movement was much accelerated by the need of Charles II to reward those who had assisted in his restoration in 1660. He found it a great convenience to be able to parcel out new titles of nobility, estates in Ireland and much larger tracts of land in America. His beneficiaries include all the great names of the Restoration; among the Lord Proprietors of the portion of America named after Charles (Carolina) were Albemarle, Shaftesbury, Clarendon, Craven and Carteret.

These great lords did not choose to inspect their distant property. They gave over the governance of vast enterprises, spanning the central Atlantic, to men who they believed had the experience to make it work. Eleven of twenty-three governors of South Carolina between 1669 and 1737 were West Indians or sons of West Indians. Seven were from Barbados. The Proprietors themselves were eager to extend the plantation system. Six of the eight were also investors in the slave trade through the Royal African Company, and planned to increase their revenues not only through land sales but through selling Africans to those who bought the land.

Among the earliest recruits to their mainland properties were offspring of West Indian plantation owners who could assure their children of no appropriate status in the already crowded islands. Cadets of the great West Indian families, Colletons and Middletons and Draytons, went to Carolina to gather fortunes in a new arena, as their grandfathers had done in the West Indies.

The houses built by these men when they came into the Carolinas were also, so to speak, younger sons or grandsons, smaller and simpler versions of Caribbean houses, which were, in their own way, smaller and simpler versions of the great houses of Britain. The first permanent large-scale housing in the mainland colonies south of the Chesapeake took these descendant forms: 1) the Anglo-Dutch urban

77

type, with its prominent gables; 2) the pre-Palladian or proto-Georgian, the main architectural subject of this chapter; 3) somewhat later, the Georgian style, Palladian in origin (or Serlian; see Chapter Two) and most often, in the South, encased in brick; and 4) the verandahed cottage.

Art is often embroidery upon commerce. Sometimes the designs of the embroidery follow the patterns of commerce. Sometimes those patterns are too complex and too intertwined to permit economic history to be read through art history. So it is with this part of our story. We have suggested four architectural forms. It happens that they were used by people who grew—or tried to grow—the four staple crops whose passage to the mainland we have chosen to observe in this chapter. They were used, as well, as we shall see later, by wheat growers and tobacco planters, by sea captains and merchants, by anyone rich enough to accumulate a building fund or skilled enough to build on his own, and in most mainland colonies, not just Carolina. Even among our four and four, unfortunately, there is no pairing up like lovers in a Gilbert and Sullivan finale, and the greatest of the surviving proto-Georgian houses in the Western Hemisphere, Stratford Hall, in Virginia, has, as we shall see, no certain connection with any one of the four "Carolina" crops, nor indeed with West Indies.

Sugar

THE WEST INDIANS WERE disappointed when they found that the soil and temperature of the mainland did not permit a direct transfer of the sort of sugar plantations they had developed in the islands. They tried transplanting island cane to the area around Savannah in the 1740's, and failed. They failed twenty years later in Florida, where from 1763 to 1783 they undertook a series of fascinating utopian ventures with plantations manned with indentured servants. In Florida as on Barbados, white "slaves for a term" did not make good workers in the tropics, nor did enslaved Indians.

Black slaves did raise some sugar in Florida during the second period of Spanish rule, from 1783 to 1819, but it was not until a new wave of West Indians came ashore in the 1830's that Florida sugar production began in earnest. This last gasp of the old Barbadian plantation system was described by Farquhar Macrae in 1835: "Some two years since I came first to Florida, after a residence of some years, as a sugar planter in the British West Indies, from whence I was forced, with a sacrifice of property and prospects, by the mad abolition act of the infatuated English government [the abolition of slavery, in 1834]. My object in selecting Florida as a residence, was to establish, under a secure and honest constitution, a sugar growing estate." Macrae was far from destitute—the abolition of slaves in the British West Indies was compensated abolition, not confiscation. Still, he made it clear that his idea of a "secure constitution" was one free from the agitations either of abolitionists or of temperance movements. He advised sugar planters to become distillers because "it will require a vast increase of Temperance Societies, before that stimulant becomes valueless." Under the lash of men like this, Florida sugar production grew tenfold in the 1840's, especially after Andrew Jackson destroyed the capacity of the Seminole group of tribes to resist the whites and to provide sanctuaries to Negroes.

Hispaniola sugar seed cane was transplanted to the Mississippi Delta very early in the eighteenth century, and the French government and the Jesuits persisted in producing it in the 1730's and 1740's, though it was not yet a commercial crop. Then in 1785 Josef Solis, an emigrant from Hispaniola, led the way to a series of increasingly successful efforts at sugar production on a commercial scale. Thereafter the region of the lower Mississippi became the great mainland source of sugar, particularly during the boom years from 1833 (when the Louisiana crop already supplied a fifteenth of the world's exported supply) through the 1850's (when it produced a fourth of that supply).

Though sugar was not produced on a significant scale in the Carolinas or Georgia or Florida in the Colonial period, some very fine architecture was built there by the heirs and heiresses of sugar fortunes. There was the home of Anne Colleton, for example. The Colletons had been fortunate in turning sugar into money in the West Indies. They reinvested some of that money in South Carolina, in a house that affords us a convenient excuse to let imagination play on architectural history.

The Roman playwright and philosopher Seneca described the place of retirement of the general Scipio Africanus as a turreted farmhouse. We are free, because the site has long ago disappeared, to imagine it as Seneca implies it was, a very early example of the pre-Palladian or proto-Georgian style, having a central mass and four corner turrets, in an H plan. There the victor over Hannibal might have welcomed a kindred spirit, Sir John Colleton, some of whose progeny lived in houses that were the diminutive descendants of the one Seneca described.

Colleton was shrewd, tenacious, ferocious and sickly. His body was so twisted that his surgeons inserted, to facilitate the discharge of "matter" from his liver, a golden tube, but his infirmities did not prevent him from fighting bravely for Charles I against the Commonwealth and Cromwell. He battled to the last on the losing side, spent much of his fortune for the king and suffered exile to Barbados. There he learned what the sugar and slave system could do to make men rich, and saw, too, how it was creating a class of land-hungry but able displaced persons as great planters crowded out the smaller.

After the Stuart Restoration, Colleton brought together, as Proprietors, seven other men who had either been all along of the king's party or (like John Locke's sponsor, Anthony Ashley-Cooper, Lord Shaftesbury) had made a timely switch. It was Locke and Ashley-Cooper who devised the philosopher's delight of feudalesque titles (like landgrave and cacique), religious toleration, land allocation reflecting slaveownership, denial of the right to practice law for money, and other devices that made the Fundamental Constitution of Carolina a sort of crossbreed between Plato's *Laws* and a promoter's prospectus.

John Colleton himself never enjoyed the direct experience of that contrivance, though once, when at odds with Charles II, he threatened to emigrate to one of his baronies in Carolina. His heir, Peter Colleton, succeeded him as Lord Proprietor and was also a member of the Council of Barbados, where he resided. He and his brother Thomas so dominated affairs on the island where lay the chief family interests that a luckless and tactless third brother, James, was fobbed off on their Carolina holdings in 1686. James actually served briefly as governor before being forced out, and back to Barbados.

Another of the Colletons, Anne, married Hugh Butler, a mainlander. They leased the southern portion of the family's Fairlawn barony, northeast of Charleston, in 1726, and built upon it a tiny, pacified version of a fortified farmhouse, called Exeter. It reduced the four towers we have imagined for Scipio's villa into four corner rooms in an H shape. The house was the victim of nineteenth-century remodelers who forced upon it a piazza which it could not carry gracefully, and

Exeter

Collection of Carolina Art Association, Gibbs Art Gallery, Charleston, S.C.

Fenwick Hall before restoration

Collection of Carolina Art Association, Gibbs Art Gallery, Charleston, S.C.

thereby showed how a single object cannot be made handsomely to demonstrate historical progression unless an architectural talent is present to solve the puzzle.

Rice

RICE CULTURE CAME EARLY to the Carolinas. The colony had done well on the frontier crops of hides and furs and livestock, but it was the expanded culture of rice that truly united the West Indian and Carolina communities. As early as 1663 the erosion-enriched marshlands of the Carolina shore seemed attractive to Lord Albemarle, who thought they might be planted to produce a cheap food crop for the growing gangs of plantation workers in the Caribbean, and African rice seed was brought with black slaves to the Carolina coast before 1685.

Those of us who like to think that virtue is only one of the rewards for redeemed sinners find in the tale of the Fenwicks of Fenwick Hall a heartwarming affirmation of our generous views. Robert Fenwick was a pirate, one of those "Red

Sea men" who ranged from Suez to Surinam to the Caribbean and the Carolina coast. The Lord Proprietors were quite indifferent to predators such as he, until the bumper rice crop of 1696 drew enough of them together to imperil the food supply for the West Indies. Then, for the first time, virtue was fully armed. Some pirates went ashore to become planters, others sought easier marks in other seas. Fenwick was admitted ashore from his privateer *Loyal Jamaica* only on good behavior. Having observed the change in the risk/reward ratio for local piracy, he turned to planting rice. About 1730 his brother John replaced a log house with the brick structure that remains today, altered only by the addition of an octagonal wing in 1787. Fenwick Hall was a classic small Palladian house of the type we will explore in the next chapter, a solid cube under a steep roof, flanked by two complementary outbuildings. It looks positively demure beside the Stono River; its interior is elegant but not pretentious, respectably readying the Fenwicks for a return to England. There John became a country squire. His daughter became a duchess.

Freed of the depredations of men like Robert Fenwick (before he changed careers), other rice planters deployed battalions of Negroes to clear the shoreline swamps, to build terraces and canals. They tried upland "dry" cultivation until about 1720, but then found it better to raise rice as a muck crop, requiring rich, renewable soil and plenty of fresh water, and moved upriver. Now the plantation system entered a new phase, as the needs of Caribbean slave battalions, raising sugar for absentee owners, required the organization of ever larger battalions of Carolina slaves to clear, ditch, canal, terrace, plant and harvest rice.

The great swamps thus artificially created, like the old ones along the coast, became, themselves, the cause of a sort of seasonal absenteeism, and an important impetus to the growth of Charleston. We must, therefore, give proper attention to the architectural influence of the mosquito.

The South Carolina historian Samuel Stoney tells us that during most of the eighteenth century, "instead of shunning the country in summer, town people actually went into the swamps for campings and maroonings, to hunt deer and to fish." Something happened after the planters created artificial freshwater swamps. All we know is that sometime just before the Revolution, a new and more virulent strain of malaria appeared in the Carolinas. Planters might not know that mosquitoes bred in the swamps carried the fever, but they knew the swamps were deadly. Those who could afford to do so repaired to Charleston, which was built upon a breezy sand-spit, relatively free of malaria.

These Charleston absentees were not so completely removed from their source of wealth as were the sugar nabobs who went to London and left their West Indian plantations in the hands of overseers. However, absenteeism grew among plantation owners in South Carolina. After 1800 very few great plantation houses were built in the Carolina low country. But in the eighteenth century, before the flight to Charleston, several were built which we will examine in some detail.

Drayton Hall, the South's greatest Palladian house, was among the first products of rice prosperity. After the French and Spanish wars of the mid-century, which interrupted the orderly flow of rice to its markets, a new burst of plantation building occurred. Then came another mansion, Middleton Place. Finally, between the Revolution and the abandonment of the countryside as a primary place of residence by the rich planters, a third surge of rice-plantation building occurred, including the Pinckneys' El Dorado. We will wait until Chapter Eight to describe Middleton Place and Drayton Hall, but El Dorado we shall take up here. It was a sort of hybrid, combining a Palladian core, with spreading wings, and the piazzas of the Caribbean cottage. We can see it most clearly set amid fields growing not rice, but the other of the two crops that built it—indigo.

Indigo

FOLLOWING CYPRIAN SUGAR and African (later Italian) rice came indigo, which like them required large areas worked systematically by battalions of black slaves to be produced on a commercial scale. It originated, as the name implies, in India. The British navy regarded the deep blue dye produced from the plant as essential to the proper garbing of seamen. (Later, English gentlemen ashore came to like it, too.) It was galling to have to buy the coloring for the imperial uniform from the colonies of the imperial enemy, France. Equally galling was the drain on the empire's balance of trade suffered in the acquisition. So the British offered a handsome subsidy for the production of indigo, and when, in the late 1730's, rice went through one of its unprofitable periods, shrewd mainland planters turned their attention to the high-priced tincture.*

The governor of Antigua, George Lucas, placed his ailing wife and their resourceful daughter, Eliza, on a plantation on Wappoo Creek, upriver from Charleston. In a few years, local stories tell us (perhaps a little enthusiastically), Eliza produced a complex system of tidal management and crop placement which made indigo a commercial crop in the Carolinas. Moses Lindo, the most prominent of the Sephardic Jews whose aptitude for trade and broad culture contributed much to Charleston's vitality in the eighteenth century (see Chapter Ten), arranged for the marketing.

Eliza Lucas brought her wealth, her intelligence and her architectural taste to a marriage with Charles Pinckney, a rice planter. One of her sons was a member of the Constitutional Convention of 1787, and another became minister to Spain and Great Britain. It was he who named their plantation El Dorado. As that house took its final form in 1797, it completed the attenuation of the tight, defensible plantation house of the West Indies. To permit the air to flow through each room, wings grew out, and then yet farther out, one room after another reaching for a breeze. Ceiling heights rose, too, and enclosing all were galleries.

---

* *Indigo required that large imperial subsidy for commercial success. When the subsidy was removed as a result of American independence, indigo ceased to be a commercial crop. Its producers were among the clear losers of the Revolution.*

El Dorado

Courtesy of the South Carolina Historical Society

To see how far planters had gone in a century of adaptation, compare Colbeck or Drax Hall with El Dorado, or with Bluefields and Good Hope on Jamaica. Another example would be the Admiral's House on Antigua, an extended, elevated cottage surrounded by double balconies, its windows jalousied in the Spanish style, its interior walls painted a cool white, and its ceilings, finally, high enough to let the hot air circulate and pass out through tall windows. Palladio had cut one side of the old enclosed villa and opened it out into a colonnade. So El Dorado, completely free of such military impedimenta as those old towers at the corners of H-plan houses like Exeter, spreads into the landscape. This is an ingenious building, as ingenious as Eliza Lucas, but not the only contribution of the Pinckneys to the architecture of the warmer sections of America.

The remarkable capacity of Eliza Lucas Pinckney to make fresh use of a combination of other people's ideas appears in her last major work, the remodeling of her daughter's house, Hampton. The name of the place, and its Palladian full temple portico, were bestowed by her after she returned from a trip to London. There she had observed the great actor David Garrick in one of his favorite roles, "Hampton." She had seen Garrick's Thames-side villa, designed by Robert Adam. It had a temple-form portico, quite restrained in its relationship to the house. She made it much more prominent at Hampton. When her work was complete, she was able to welcome George Washington, whose verandah at Mount Vernon was the only shaded space in America of equivalent scale (see Chapter Eight).

Hampton
Courtesy of the Library of Congress

Silk

SILK, LIKE INDIGO, had been a costly drain on the British balance of payments. The hated French had learned to produce it, but the recalcitrant worms would not thrive in the British climate. Perhaps they might in the Carolinas. The experiment was made: mulberry trees grew prodigiously, but the worms did not. Well into the nineteenth century, some Georgia and Carolina families kept mulberry trees and silkworms to make a little silk thread for their own use, but unlike indigo, silk never became a weapon to use against the French. It remained a disappointed hope, memorialized in the names of buildings like Savannah's Filature (silk thread manufactory), where a ball for George Washington was given in 1791.

Silk Hope was the name of the South Carolina plantation of Sir Nathaniel Johnson, who had been governor of Antigua. His daughter emblazoned the em-

Mulberry "Castle"
Courtesy of the Library of Congress

blem of that hope as a sort of coat of arms over her door—a mulberry sprig framed in a horseshoe—and renamed the place Mulberry, though its commercial crop was rice.* Mulberry appears, at first glance, to be a diminutive version of turreted houses like Scipio's (as we imagine it), like a maquette for one of Serlio's designs for a French château like Ancy, or like Colbeck recollected in tranquility and reconstructed in miniature. It is not, strictly speaking, in the shape of an H, because the pavilions, with their turrets, are extensions of an essentially square and quite self-contained little house.† Like quite similar structures on Mauritius, half a world away, it is ready to become something more open, but not quite ready

---

* *Another silk plantation, called Mulberry Hill, was established by Joseph Gibbons, of Barbados, outside Savannah. Gibbons' daughter, Hannah, married Mathew McAllister in 1787. They produced very little silk, but they were the grandparents of the harmless snob Ward McAllister, whose assiduously sustained Georgian accent was one of the devices he employed as Newport's social arbiter in the late nineteenth century.*

† *Halse Hall, on Jamaica, could be described in the same way.*

—and, indeed, this peaceful structure actually became a fort, very briefly. Those ornamental but scarcely functional pavilions were armed to withstand a siege during the Yemassee War (1715–28), and the house itself was then selected to be the center of a fortification, complete with cannon.

Stratford Hall

COLBECK CASTLE AND STOKES HALL were the largest houses in the form of an H in the British colonies in the Western Hemisphere. They are but ruins now. Stratford Hall, though much smaller, has survived them. There may have been others in Virginia—Tuckahoe, a Randolph house, became an H by additions—and certainly there were several in Carolina, though few remain. But Stratford is so elegant an example of the proto-Georgian that it is without challenge as the finest survival of the type in the Western Hemisphere. It came late, around 1730, built upon a Virginia headland by Thomas Lee, of the third generation of that family to be established there. They had been planters of tobacco and wheat, shrewd traders in land and merchandise, keeping their ties to their London merchant cousins and very conservative in their political outlook. Their house seems at first glance as backward-looking as the literary tastes of the scholar of the family, Richard Lee (1647–1714)—whom Louis Wright, a historian of our time, once described as "a belated Elizabethan"—retaining as it does the shape of a border

Stratford Hall
Photo by Wayne Andrews

87

Estate House, Good Hope, Jamaica

Copyright © 1982 by Pamela Gosner, reprinted with permission of Three Continents Press

fortress. Its military theme is established by two sets of truculent chimneys like those Sir John Vanbrugh designed a generation earlier for Blenheim Palace, home and monument to the martial prowess of John, Duke of Marlborough. Once inside, the focus is upon a Vanbrughian great hall, under a coved ceiling, not quite feudal in feeling, not quite Renaissance.*

Stratford is not, however, just a small provincial version of the grandiose palaces Vanbrugh designed for the magnates of England. It is more complex than this, more venturesome—perhaps more American? Not that, surely—the scholar Richard Lee repined for England, and had among his many volumes not one book about America, unless his history of the West Indies might be so called. Yet perhaps that is a clue: perhaps Stratford does stand in the same line as Colbeck and Stokes Hall. It is not like any other structure of the Chesapeake. One feels it really belongs farther south, perhaps in Jamaica or South Carolina. There it would still be an exception, but a step in a process which would be fulfilled at El Dorado.

In Stratford's case that fulfillment is implied in a finish, an elegance with which an old form is presented, a form very subtly adjusted to a new physical and psychological climate. To see how southern Stratford is (how really southern, as the West Indies are southern), we must be willing not only to move it geographically in imagination but to place a hand across its façade to hide its huge chimneys. Imagine it sheathed in stucco rather than brick. Is it not a West Indian raised plantation house?†

* *The hall at Stratford reminds us of Gilling Castle, the Yorkshire home of Virginia's true gentry, the Fairfaxes.*

† *To me, this impression is reinforced by the reconstruction, in the 1930's, of the stairways at its side in accordance with Jamaican precedent. I do not know whether or not this was the intention of the reconstructors, but a half dozen Jamaican antecedents came to mind.*

I am not urging a West Indian tie for Stratford's H plan; semi-medieval buildings like Samuel Carpenter's Slate Roof House, of about 1687 in Philadelphia, and other very early buildings in Boston also took the shape of an H. But they were two-and-a-half-story vertical buildings, not raised cottages with brick shells and grandiose chimneys. Stratford was unique. And despite Richard Lee's literary tastes, this house, built by his progeny, expresses, I believe, a new spirit of commitment to the New World, a new artistic independence from the old, which preceded by nearly a generation the political expression of that independence. By the middle of the eighteenth century, a few mainland planters, among them the Lees, who could afford to send their sons to England or Scotland—if Roman Catholic, to Belgium; if Huguenot, to Geneva—ceased to do so, for a complex of reasons. Chief of these was that they did not like the habits those sons there acquired—too urbane, insufficiently (to use that word they were not quite ready to use) American. And they began to build a different kind of architecture, an architecture of permanence, not of military occupation but of participation in the land. Whatever the sentiments of Richard Lee, Thomas Lee had come ashore to stay.

CHAPTER 7

Anglo-Dutch Provincial

I T IS KNOWN to real-estate advertisers everywhere but in the South as "Southern Colonial." It is, historically, the most widespread of the architectural expressions of the Anglo-Dutch commercial continuum. It appeared on a world stage in the 1650's in Holland. Oliver Cromwell, Protestant lord protector of England, was at war with the Protestant Dutch, who were keeping in comfortable exile Charles Stuart, soon to return to England as King Charles II. Charles was thought by some Puritans to be a crypto-Papist, but never mind, Cromwell's ally against the Dutch was His Catholic Majesty Louis XIV of France, to whom Cromwell sent eight thousand of his best soldiers to wage war against the Dutch and simultaneously against the former blood enemies of the Dutch, the very Catholic Spanish.

It is difficult to sort out the commercial wars of the seventeenth century. It is also difficult, but not impossible, to follow the ways in which the power politics of the period were reflected in its architectural history. In Britain and in Holland during the reign of Charles' father, Charles I, there had been the tentative but elegant appearance of a sort of compact Palladianism. In England it was a court style, initiated by Inigo Jones (1573–1652), who had visited Palladio's work in Italy and conversed with Palladio's pupils.* Jones was a Roman Catholic who suffered persecution and whose practice was destroyed during the Puritan protectorate of Cromwell. He became a revered figure, though he actually built very little—far less than his famous followers, Christopher Wren (1632–1723; how wonderfully long-lived those two great men were!), Hugh May (1622–84) and John Webb (1611–72). In Holland the chief Palladians were Jones's contemporary Jacob van Campen (1575–1657) and Pieter Post (1608–69).

* *Jones, also, certainly knew his Serlio. It would be easy to argue that the Dutch and British architects we discuss in this chapter were as much influenced by Serlio's designs for small houses as they were by Palladio. That argument does not affect our main theme. Serlio's admirers are free to read "Serlio and Palladio" for "Palladio" here. See Chapter Two.*

Political turmoil in the 1640's and 1650's in England kept Inigo Jones from completing any of the largest projects he designed. But it had one beneficial effect on architecture: it drove to Holland, with Charles, Hugh May and other architects who were in a position to benefit from acquaintance with the tidy red-brick and dressed-stone buildings that van Campen and Post were building for the Dutch court and for rich merchants. The appreciative eyes of the British visitors at The Hague fell upon the palace of Prince Maurice of Nassau. It was the ideal form for a compact northern mansion, with all the clarity and symmetry and precision of Palladio, but somehow more cozy. In the Netherlands, land was scarce. In England, Puritan strictures affected even Royalists with an aversion to outward show. Led by Hugh May, the architects of the Restoration found the Dutch experience harmonious with the ideals of Inigo Jones. The compact and cautious houses of the early years of the Restoration set a tone that came to suit the means of provincial gentry in Britain and America throughout the eighteenth century.* The Dutch

Palace of Prince Maurice of Nassau. The wings are a later addition.

Courtesy of the Royal Netherlands Embassy, Washington, D.C.

   * *The Royal Palace in Amsterdam was under construction all during the Dutch exile of Charles and his architects; it showed John Webb how, later in England, the Palladian style could be applied to a very large building. His vast new range for Greenwich Palace (now Greenwich Hospital) shows how well he had learned to set a brave central pediment for sculpture amid the ghosts of four corner towers.*

style, which we may call Dutch-Palladian, was thus already firmly imbedded in England when it was reinforced by the arrival of a Dutch prince to reign as King William III, who brought with him, in 1688, a train of Dutch noblemen and favorites, and an affection for Dutch architecture.*

Sir Peter Lely's self-portrait (left) with architect Hugh May
Courtesy of the Hon. R. H. C. Neville

When buildings like those of May and his circle appeared in America, they were often attributed not to him but to Christopher Wren. This is amusing because, despite some claims to the contrary, Wren cannot be proved to have designed and built any country houses. Culturally anxious American colonials (and

---

* *The appearance of Dutch architecture at the court of the restored Charles was not an expression of any necessary affection for the Dutch themselves. Charles had learned how rich the Dutch had become trading slaves and sugar, and he was hardly ashore before he renewed Cromwell's campaign to wrest control of maritime commerce from his erstwhile hosts. Charles's bread-and-butter letter contained the Black Spot.*

many who have written about them) ascribed the patterns of their houses to a man great enough to be entrusted with the design of St. Paul's Cathedral, rather than to a man named May. Yet Hugh May is the true author of that American architecture known as "the style of Wren" (when it is not called Southern Colonial). Sir Edwin Lutyens, the most proficient twentieth-century British prestidigitator of that style, invented for it the term "Wrenaissance." (Lutyens was the designer of that tour de force, the British Embassy in Washington. The embassy, like Lutyens' term, winks at the graceful but somewhat prissy symmetry that from the time of Hugh May to the time of Edwin Lutyens was often attributed to Wren.)

This style, well known by the end of the Stuart era (1688) and in common currency by the reign of Queen Anne (1702–14), we often tend to call Georgian. We call it so because it had its full impact in our own country during the reign of George II (1727–60) and that portion of the reign of George III when he was still king in the thirteen colonies (1760–76—or was it 1783?). Thus it came to us two or three generations after it arrived in Britain, and four or five generations after it became fashionable in Holland.*

It continues to have powerful influence, though it has been subjected to countless suburban indignities. From the first in America, it contended and blended with the Caribbean cottage, and with the fortified residence of an earlier period. Let us turn now from its appearance to its message, from its style to its psychology.

After the Restoration, and especially when the period of civil wars was finally ended in the 1680's by King William's victories over King James, the Wrenaissance, warm, stable in its massing, comforting in its intention, became the chosen domestic architecture for squires all over Britain. The homeland was finally secure. Wren's brick façade for Hampton Court expressed that security. If such a vast building can be domestic, it was—certainly by comparison to the blaring Baroque of courtly architecture elsewhere in Europe. Domesticity can be smug, but this architecture was more than that. It was, in fact, even more than a visible sigh of relief. It was a prayer—*gratias agimus.*

In America, a little later, it expressed the same feelings, but the relief was from other perturbations. The colonies had been born in violence. The Europeans were opposed by people who, though technologically at a disadvantage, were very competent fighters. In addition, the Europeans had long been engaged in interinvader altercations.† Americans had thus been busy with their own violence. Its ending was gratefully received, and that gratitude was eloquently expressed in Georgian architecture.

---

* We persist in calling it Georgian though the Georges were from Germany, where Palladian architecture did not prosper against the prevailing fashion for the Baroque, and though the Georges did not seem to like the Wrenaissance very much.

† The southernmost English colonies on the continent were initially "marches" (a word that in Europe had given rise to a title for the governor, or captain, of such an exposed frontier region: marquis, marchese,

Nearly all the earliest architecture of the Carolina and Georgia coasts—and of Maine at the other extremity—was composed of fortresses, large and small.* Those settlers who ventured outside them built for themselves little forts, composed of the materials that came to hand, just as their forefathers had in the Middle Ages. Hewn cyprus blockhouses were the true Colonial houses of upland Georgia and the Carolinas. There the Indians were a threat throughout a thirteen-year period (1715–28) and the Spaniards maintained a virtual state of siege until their governor of Florida was beaten back from the doorstep of Savannah in 1742.

Virginia and Maryland, though exposed to occasional Dutch and Spanish forays, worried most about the Indians. An uprising in 1622 killed off a third of the white settlers, and there were Susquehannock raids until 1675. Those tensions led to outbreaks of violence among the settlers themselves, one of which came to an end around the walls of Bacon's Castle (see Chapter Four) in 1675. Seven years later there were other civil disorders called the Tobacco Riots. Peace descended in the 1690's, as it did in England, and with it came domestic, to replace military, architecture.

In 1981 a group of historians at Williamsburg, led by Gary Carson, described that coming as the replacement of what they called "impermanent" architecture with what Robert Beverley called, in 1705, "large Brick Houses." "Homegrown patricians," the builders of these houses "ruled their counties, married their cousins, and founded parochial dynasties that delighted in building architectural monuments to their self-esteem and their belief in a posterity."

Domestic Architecture

THE SHAPE OF THIS architecture is extremely interesting. It generally followed the Anglo-Dutch Palladian form we have called Wrenaissance. We could expect that in public buildings laid up during the reign of the Anglo-Dutch monarchy of William and Mary. At Williamsburg the Governor's Palace is a beautifully rendered obeisance to Dutch patterns, and the Capitol needs only to have a little imagination work on it for it to become a little brick castle. Dig out the sand that surrounds it, replace it with water, weeds, ducks and swans, and you have before you a place like Laarne, near Ghent, a good representative of the moated manor

---

marcensis) *against the Spanish. James Oglethorpe was a "marcher lord," who saw his outpost-colony in the same way the Prussians saw theirs, set amidst the Slavs, at the other end of the expansion of Europe. Georgia and Pomerania had much in common, then and later, and Georgia's colonists, the nineteenth-century planters of Mississippi and Alabama, were the New World's closest equivalents to Junkers.*

* The plans of the coastal towns of that region, including Charleston and Savannah, were those of Roman camps.

house of the late Middle Ages, remodeled and tranquilized in the seventeenth century. There are dozens like it in Holland and northern Belgium.

But for the residences of hard-trading, practical merchant-planters, why not the Caribbean cottage or the gabled urban form that continued in the West Indies? Many Virginians, we have learned, were too poor or too rootless to aspire to more than an architecture of impermanence, but nonetheless, when we look at the buildings that were created by those who could choose to build permanently in the Old or the New World, we find that the leading spirits among them were eager to ornament their landscape with an ambitious architecture, while their West Indian peers were not. Why did these colonial oligarchs not save their money to build on a genuinely grand scale in Britain? They would not have been rich enough to construct Harewood or Fonthill, but by 1776 some, like Ralph Izard, could, in fact, afford a town house in London as well as a house in Charleston and a half dozen plantations. Yet they became not colonials but provincials.

Governor's Palace
Colonial Williamsburg Photograph

This is a crucial distinction: colonial architecture seems to patronize its setting. It treats its environment—the colony in which it is built—as a mere adjunct to an imperial system, created and sustained to supply its needs. Provincial architecture is created by persons who think of themselves as living at a rather greater distance from the metropolis than some, perhaps, but who wish to be considered in all other respects like them. They are not, for example, to be taxed without representation.

Virginians and South Carolinians who took a stake in the land built provincial, not colonial, houses. The Virginians, especially, became genuine country families in the British mold. Though they might speculate elsewhere, their architecture announces that their old plantations were not for sale. Three or four generations of occupancy in a single spot became sufficient to constitute a commitment to that spot. This was not quite the sort of commitment that arose when a British country family spent a thousand years accumulating acreage, but the eighteenth-century Virginia sense of ancestral permanence was also quite different from the impression conveyed by later Americans that all land, even the family graveyard, was real estate, for sale.

The manor house of Frederick Philipse
From the New York State Office of Parks, Recreation and Historic Preservation, Bureau of Historic Sites

Pride and Place

THE DEVELOPMENT of a truly provincial architecture is a large occasion in our history. It marked the appearance of the first American landed aristocracy, proud of place, and of Place. The key to understanding that architecture is that it expressed a new relationship not just of building to land but of builder to land. To put the matter another way, this "architecture of home" expressed a new attitude toward nature, toward land and the natural products of land. A planter committed to land was a new kind of person. Virginia, for example, was not initiated as a plantation but as a factory. Its imperial function was to serve as a trading post, where factors would acquire furs and fish and seek precious metals. It was, in short, to be the same sort of place as New Amsterdam. But between 1675 and 1725 something changed in both places. Virginia became a plantation, and certain artisans and shopkeepers in New Amsterdam itself became rich enough to become landed gentry. The common qualities of the two colonies are often understated, because the new-rich Dutch are somehow seen as different from the new-rich Virginians. We too often begin with the James River plantations, the houses of artisans and merchants who became landed gentry in Virginia, without seeing their similarities to those of the same period from New Hampshire to South Carolina. Therefore let us, instead, first present a splendid example just up the Hudson from New York City.

The Master Ranger of Yonkers

IF IT WERE UPON the James River, instead of jostled by the pizza joints and body shops of downtown Yonkers, the great Georgian mansion of Frederick Philipse would have the care of a ladies' sodality. It might, perhaps, produce a filiopietistic newsletter of its own. It is a forthright stone balustraded structure quite representative of advanced Anglo-Dutch Palladian taste in 1692, the date of the marriage of Philipse to Catharine van Cortlandt. If, as some writers assert, the south façade was built then, it was extraordinarily *à la mode* for the colonies. It would have graced any small English or Dutch country gentleman's estate of the time. If it assumed its present form a quarter-century later (the view of other scholars), it still would be among the earliest of the Georgian mansions of the mainland colonies, a worthy peer of those of Portsmouth, New Hampshire, or along the James.

Philipse was the grandson of a Hussite refugee to the Netherlands. He was a carpenter by trade who learned his craft in Holland during a building boom caused by the need to house religious refugees from Antwerp. He became a general contractor when he reached New Amsterdam, initially as carpenter to the Dutch West Indies Company. The town was short of skilled craftsmen. Efforts to teach "carpentering, bricklaying, blacksmithing . . . to the negroes, as it was formerly

9 7

done in Brazil," were encouraged by the directors, but these skills were kept in white hands after Governor Stuyvesant responded that there were "no able negroes fit to learn a trade." The colonists preferred to use Negroes as common labor rather than share the benefits of a great building boom. They were already branching out into the fur trade, and saw to it that slaves might be purchased for "Beaver or Provisions, such as Beef, Pork, Wheat, or Pease, at Beaver Price."

Philipse garnered enough capital to be received into the commercial elite, acquiring, formally, the "Small Burgher Right." Thereafter he speculated in houses, lots and farms from Albany to the Delaware River. He was a paradigmatic frontier figure. In a fluid and booming economy he pushed upward from artisanship to trade, and ultimately to land speculation. With two partners he bought most of a failed patroonship and filled out his holdings by 1693 to include twenty-two miles of the Hudson River shore.* Finally he reached the golden rung; his diligent accumulations under British rule were described in a royal charter as constituting the Manor of Philipsborough. He, as lord of that manor, was authorized to preside in the "Seat," which is the manor house we see today. After his death, his granddaughter Mary, for whom George Washington had been an unsuccessful suitor, was given in marriage. At the wedding this ascended carpenter could look down from the heavens to see his son, the Second Lord, "wearing the gold chain and jewelled insignia of the ancestral office of Master Ranger of the Royal Forests of Bohemia." The house, the title, the "ancestral office" are all of a piece.†

Fish and Furs

THERE WERE SOME who thought the mainland would become a new Barbados. After they had tried the rocky soil and cruel climate of New England, these would-be Yankee planters turned to commerce, especially to the profession that comes naturally to people who find poor soil but many animals: the trade in skins. Many returned to the ancient way of mariners, fishing. Fishermen from Devon and Cornwall established themselves early from North Carolina to the rocky inlets of New England. From bays and sounds and estuaries they sailed to supply first-class fish to the Catholic peoples of the Mediterranean, second-class fish to the Atlantic islands nearest Europe, the Canaries, Madeira and the Cape Verdes, and the rest to slaves on West Indian plantations.

There is a story told by Cotton Mather, among others, about a clergyman speaking too long on the subject of the Puritan Fathers to a congregation of fisher-

* The original patroon of Yonkers was Jonkheer (Baron) Adriaen van der Donck, whose only lasting imprint upon his barony is his title.

† Since the Philipses were Tories, and most of their property was expropriated after the Revolution, we do not know what would have become of any of these shimmering anachronisms in the nineteenth century.

men and provoking from the back of the hall the comment: "Our ancestors came not here for religion. Their chief aim was to find fish." There is poignancy in the comment—the getting of fish and furs is not a pastoral pursuit, nor do these goods come as the fruits of husbandry. On the first frontier, and later, nature's bounty had to be extracted by men who endured much, suffered much and caused, one must allow, much suffering.*

Scattered here and there in New England were a few villages established by religious groups as self-sufficient communities. Their citizens, whom we might now call subsistence farmers, intended to stay put, from the outset, though some of their numerous progeny might have to find new farms. But it is probably safe to say that there were not many such communities. Our sentimental images of people living out generations in the same village, upon the same homeplace, are probably a false picture of early New England. The first Yankees, like the first farmers in tidewater Virginia, were tough, bustling, hard-bitten and lively people, on the move. Life was not easy for them. They could not have built a new society if they had been as bland as their descendants sometimes like to think.

This was even true of the founders of Charleston, South Carolina, America's most genteel community. It was, in the seventeenth and early eighteenth centuries, a fur trader's rendezvous, like Jackson Hole, Wyoming, or Mendota, Minnesota, or Portsmouth, New Hampshire. The Proprietors, those distant courtiers who ordained Charleston's founding, also owned shares in the Hudson's Bay Company and learned how lucrative could be the supplying of deerskins for gloves and beaver for hats. In a single year (ending in December 1707) Charleston shipped to London 121,355 deerskins and innumerable beaver pelts. Entrepreneurs then introduced cattle, and Charleston made the transition from a fur town to—dare we say?—a cow town. In the later eighteenth century its dusty streets were full of cattle, driven by cowboys on long drives from places like the locality later called Cowpens, in the backcountry. Charleston's ascent to gentility began as it ceased to be the prototype of Jackson Hole and became a prototype of Dodge City.

We will come shortly to some discussion of two great landholding families, the Carters of Virginia and the Wentworths of New Hampshire. But we should note, first, as we catalogue the economic uses of land and its natural products, and the architecture that arose from those economic uses, that these famous landed gentry were "fur people" before they were "land people," a transition typical in the colonies. The MacPhaedris-Warner House, in Portsmouth, New Hampshire, was built on the benefits of the skin trade. MacPhaedris later went into fishing and became a general merchant, but his wealth, like that of his relatives, the Wentworths, came initially from precious hides. Bickering between Dutch and English

---

Later, New England fishermen sought seagoing mammals for their oil and were still called "fishermen" even after they became whalers. The lamps by which a million histories were read, and written, were fueled by the vital juices of one of man's friendliest and largest mammal relatives. Newburyport, New Bedford and Nantucket built great houses from the benefits of whaling, which is, and has been, a civil war among mammals.

traders over competition in fur-gathering in the Connecticut Valley was one reason for the British desire to eliminate the Dutch from New Amsterdam (another reason being Dutch competition in the slave trade). And the Hudson River patroonships were peltries before they were planted in agriculture.

Marine Architecture

MARINE ARCHITECTURE can be studied in the literal sense—the design and construction of ships—and not so literally, as the kind of architecture, on land, built by money accumulated from selling marine supplies. These supplies were essential to the power of Venice, as we have seen, and were equally essential to the kings of England. Royal sheriffs found New Hampshire's private lumbermen less interested in geopolitical necessity than in their very profitable sales of masts to the king's enemies in Spain and Portugal.

Ship supplies also created the first surplus wealth in North Carolina: its vast, sandy low-lying plain produced pines tall and straight enough for masts and oozing resin for caulking. In the beginning of the Colonial period, North Carolina was very thinly populated; life there then was more like that in Maine or New Hampshire than that in tidewater Virginia or South Carolina plantation country. If one knows this, one already knows much of what one needs to know about the early architecture of North Carolina. A marine economy of small entrepreneurs later developed into a plantation system, but even in 1790 the racial composition of that colony was more like that of Virginia than like that of South Carolina. At the end of the Colonial period, when two thirds of the people in coastal South Carolina were black slaves, two thirds of those in North Carolina were white and free.

In New Hampshire and Maine, ship supplies supplemented fish and furs as the primary sources of building funds for the magnificent Georgian houses in Portsmouth and Kittery, and made the Wentworths and Pepperells and Langdons rich even before they began speculating in land. The first English colonial ocean-going vessel, the *Virginia*, was launched at Popham, Maine, the year after Jamestown was settled. (As late as 1870 more than half of all American-launched vessels were built in Maine shipyards.)

Twentieth-century visitors to the little ports at the mouth of the Piscataqua River (pronounced "Pis-cat-away") are preconditioned to expect little white clapboard houses of the sort that look good in the snow or photographed through yellow-green leaves in the manner of Samuel Chamberlain. This is, indeed, *The New England Image*, the title of one of Chamberlain's most sumptuous books. These expectations, however, are insufficient, for Portsmouth, New Hampshire, developed a highly sophisticated urban society, largely dominated by precisely the kind of family alliances that we expect in Virginia, and with very similar architectural consequences.

100   We noted earlier the brick mansion built around 1720 (expert guesses range

The MacPhaedris-Warner House, Portsmouth, New Hampshire
From the Historic Photographic Collection of Strawbery Banke, Inc.

from 1712 through 1723) by the fur trader Archibald MacPhaedris, one of those ubiquitous Scots who ranged the coasts from the West Indies to Nova Scotia. It struck our eye because its original roof was like that of Drax Hall, in Barbados, steeply pitched and shaped to leave a deep trench in the center. This was not a roof for snow country like most of Scotland or New Hampshire. It was a roof for southern England in the Tudor period; it would have been out of fashion by 1720, as well as impractical. After a few years MacPhaedris or his son-in-law, Jonathan Warner, completed the transition of their house into the Anglo-Dutch Palladian mode, superimposing a formal balustraded gambrel, with a cupola riding atop a flattish plane, on the old **M** shape.* The interior is handsomely paneled, and the stairhall is decorated with a series of paintings, probably by Langdon Towne, the

* *Benjamin Franklin himself installed a lightning rod up there in 1762.*

hero of Kenneth Roberts' *Northwest Passage*, including two suitably terrifying portraits of the Indians with whom MacFedris did business, and a lady at a spinning wheel, possibly Mrs. McFedris. (I have now spelled this surname in each of the ways offered by the architectural historians who have written about the house.)

That lady's name was Sarah, and the masts in which she had an interest were probably as important to understanding how this house could be built as were the furs of her husband, or their later joint mercantile ventures. She was a Wentworth, sister of one governor, aunt of another, daughter of a lieutenant governor and granddaughter of a tavernkeeper. This complexity requires a family tree of the Colonial Wentworths, which can also serve as a guide to their surviving houses in Portsmouth.

1. Samuel, the tavernkeeper (1641–90)
     2. Dorothy, m. Henry Sherburne: Sherburne House, c. 1725
         3. Sarah, m. Judge Woodbury Langdon: Governor Langdon House, 1784
     2. John, the lieutenant governor (1671–1730): built the first portion of the Governor Benning Wentworth House at Little Harbor, c. 1695
         3. Governor Benning (1696–1770)
         3. Sarah, m. Archibald MacPhaedris: MacPhaedris House, c. 1720
             4. Mary, m. Jonathan Warner
         3. Mark
             4. Thomas: Wentworth-Gardner House, 1760
             4. Governor John (1737–1820): Governor John Wentworth House (343 Pleasant Street), 1769

There are at least six more extant houses associated with the Wentworths in Portsmouth, but these are the most famous and accessible. How did they come to be built?

Fishermen from the British Isles were prospecting the coast of New Hampshire in the early seventeenth century before Jamestown was founded, and though the lordly Proprietors of this portion of King Charles's possessions were as absentee as those of Carolina, the fishermen were not. They spread out their own livery of seizin,* nets drying in the sun, on the islands of the Piscataqua, and formed communities of structures built of sod and stone and saplings. On Smuttynose Island there was a tavern, on Star a little fort, on Hog a brewery and bowling alley. Soon Scotsmen and natives of Northumberland commenced building log houses (not chinked log cabins, with timbers fitted into notches near the ends— the Scots hewed their timbers square and fitted them close). These blockhouses showed this northern extremity of British settlement to be as much a frontier as

* A legal term meaning the indicia of occupancy and preemptive claim.

Mural in the stairhall of the MacPhaedris-Warner House
Courtesy of Mrs. William F. Harrington

Georgia, and as dangerous. In the 1720's, after a century's bickering, the Indians drove the whites almost completely out of Maine.

Serving the needs of fishermen on Smuttynose was a tavernkeeper named Samuel Wentworth. Those were rugged days; fishing villages were like mining camps; one needs little familiarity with such frontier conditions to imagine that tavernkeeping was a diversified enterprise. Yet during Samuel Wentworth's lifetime his son John was already a member of an elegant circle whose "pomps and vanities and ceremonies," said John Adams, made "that little world, Portsmouth," the closest counterpart in the northern colonies to Charleston, South Carolina. John Wentworth commenced a house at Little Harbor, two miles south of Portsmouth, which grew later into a tangle of more than fifty rooms (cut back by twentieth-century owners to a mere twenty-three). From its windows John Wentworth could watch the harbor for trouble. He could stable the horses of thirty armed men. His house was fitted with a huge door stoutly locked and barred. It was more than a residence; it was a fortress and a country seat in the British fashion.

From that house the Wentworth fortunes expanded. John's son Benning became governor, and so did his grandson John. Benning's elevation seemed inevitable—his feudality, the selectmen of the town of Londonderry, rejoiced that one "sprung from such ancestors" might "come to fill the chief seat in the government" and prayed that "the name of Wentworth" might become hereditary in that office. *103*

Jere Daniel, a twentieth-century commentator, has noted that others did not greet that thought so ecstatically. One opponent said the province was like "a field of battle after the fight is ended; the common people being compared to the carcasses, and those who are the chief in power to the vultures and ravens glutting on the carnage."

In Benning Wentworth's time, those chief in power lived very well indeed. Six intermarried families worshipped in their own Anglican chapel and divided the chief offices of power and profit. The provincial Council met in the council chamber in the great house at Little Harbor, as if Wentworth were lord of the manor. They responded to a summons that read: "Governor Wentworth's compliments, and commands you to come to Little Harbor to drink the King's Health."

That chamber is a wonderful place, dominated by a great chimneypiece displaying two bosomy ladies who might be caryatids from a design by Inigo Jones and might also be figureheads for New Hampshire trading vessels, trading within or without the law. The governor, Benning Wentworth, assured his agent at Whitehall that the king's forests were being well protected from depredation by

The Governor Benning Wentworth House at Little Harbor

From the Historic Photographic Collection of Strawbery Banke, Inc.

Council Chamber of the Governor Wentworth House at Little Harbor
From the Historic Photographic Collection of Strawbery Banke, Inc.

Governor John Wentworth,
by John Singleton Copley

*From the Hood Museum of Art, Dartmouth
College, Hanover, N.H., gift of Mrs. Esther
Lowell Abbott in memory of her husband,
Gordon Abbott*

the surveyor general (his nephew), while his friends were doing a marvelous business in masts. "The place of my residence is within a mile of . . . the harbor . . . and no vessel can come into port without coming within my sight, which . . . has contributed in great measure to the chastity of the port."

In those days the governor's brother, Mark, had "a dock of masts always ready to supply the wants of those . . . in need, at his own price . . . and the countrymen cut what trees they please, making masts of the best" and converting the rest into milled lumber.

Land, fur, fish and masts were profitable commodities for the Wentworths. Their portraits were painted by Blackburn and Copley. Their houses rose in ever-increasing elegance. Their attainments were to have a final statement in a great country house for Governor John Wentworth, built in the wilderness near Wolfeboro, but when Wentworth, a Loyalist, left for England at the outset of the Revolutionary War, that house was left incomplete and it burnt not long afterward.* It was a great wooden building under a gambrel roof, of five bays, more than a hundred feet across the front, larger than Mount Vernon. Wentworth, writing to Joseph Harrison, brother of the architect Peter Harrison, described it as "a Lilliputian Wentworth House," but that would only have been true by comparison to Wentworth Castle or Wentworth Woodhouse, two enormous country houses built by his distant and powerful relatives in England—Wentworth Woodhouse was longer than seven Mount Vernons laid end to end.

Wentworth House at Wolfeboro had a central hall leading into a ballroom forty feet long, an "East India room (probably so named for its wallpaper), a kings and queens chamber," with niches for statues of the governor's sovereigns, a "green room" and a "blue room," a library and a council chamber. Its barn was equally large; the stable and coach house could accommodate the governor's thirty horses; there was a sawmill, a dairy, a smokehouse and a joiner's shop. It was the most ambitious country house in eighteenth-century New England, except, perhaps, for another, also quite possibly designed with help from Harrison, for Wentworth's partner and friend, Governor William Shirley of Massachusetts.

Shirley Place was built in Roxbury and is now being restored. It was begun by Shirley, a great lawyer, spoilsman and governor, soon after he bought the thirty-three-acre estate around it at the end of 1746. His tenure in the service of the crown, and in the service of his friends, was coming to an end. They had prospered mightily in purse and reputation from the Spanish and French wars, especially from victualing expeditions against the French after 1744.

These wars had dislocated the rice trade of South Carolina, as noted in the previous chapter, but were a boon to the expedition-outfitters of New England. First, in 1739, Britain commenced a series of attacks on the Spanish colonies in the West Indies. Admiral Vernon assaulted Cartagena, and so impressed George Washington's half-brother Lawrence that he renamed his Hunting Creek planta-

* Made a baronet for his loyalty to the crown, Wentworth later became governor of Nova Scotia.

William Shirley, by Peter
Pelham after John Smibert
*From the National Portrait Gallery,
Smithsonian Institution, Washington,
D.C.*

tion Mount Vernon. James Oglethorpe repulsed a Spanish riposte against Georgia
in 1742. The French joined in the war against Britain in 1744 and produced a draw
in the Treaty of Aix-la-Chapelle in 1748, under which all sides relinquished their
conquests. (Death did not, of course, relinquish the thousands who had fallen in
battle, and the thousands more who had died of fever off Cartagena or aboard the
French fleet of d'Anville, which appeared off Nova Scotia, terrified the colonies
and was defeated only by pestilence.)

Death and disaster were as much a part of the eighteenth century as Georgian
architecture, but for some, war meant huge profits. Thomas Hancock of Boston
had been a political foe of William Shirley, but as his profits from the West Indies
and Newfoundland trade gave him increasing leverage, he could not be denied an
accommodation. Hancock and his partners, Charles Apthorpe and John Erving,
became the primary outfitters of the expeditions espoused by Shirley against the
Spanish and French. At the war's end, Hancock, Apthorpe and Erving were the
wealthiest men in Boston.

All became mighty patrons of architecture. Hancock had already built a
splendid mansion just before the war, which later passed to his famous and patriotic son, John. Nothing like it had been seen in the northern colonies: it was of

Shirley Place
Courtesy of the Society for the Preservation of New England Antiquities

solid granite, with paneled walls and damask curtains and brilliant carpets. The
Apthorpes extended their building program through two houses around Boston
and one in New York, but Shirley, quite possibly with the aid of his protégé,
Peter Harrison, outdid them all.

The broad façade of Shirley Place was of rusticated wood (chiseled to simulate
stone). Ten giant pilasters emulated the Palladian style of Inigo Jones and John
Webb. The balustraded roof bore a cupola the size of many a Boston house. Inside,
one awaited reception by the great man in an anteroom paved in blue and white
marble. Then, through double doors, one passed into a two-story saloon, paneled
below pale greenish-gray plaster, clean and clear and classical in the high-
eighteenth-century manner. Through a story-and-a-half-high Palladian window,
one could see the harbor, beyond the garden with its maze, its clipped hedges
and ordered flowerbeds.

Sir William Shirley liked order. He lamented that Boston seemed to be taking
a "Mobbish turn." He disapproved of government by town meeting, where "the
meanest inhabitants . . . by their constant attendance . . . generally are the majority and outvote the Gentlemen, Merchants, Substantial Traders and all the
better part of the inhabitants; to whom it is irksome to attend." In these views he
was joined by his architect, Peter Harrison. We wish we knew more about their
relationship. Shirley may have trained Harrison as truly as Trissino trained Palladio.

King's Chapel,
Boston
*Courtesy of the Society for
the Preservation of New
England Antiquities*

Though he has had a biographer, and is often called America's first professional architect (though his profession was that of a merchant and customs official), and though we can still enjoy his buildings—like King's Chapel in Boston; Christ Church in Cambridge; and the Touro Synagogue, the Brick Market and the Redwood Library in Newport—we do not know what we really want to know about Harrison. We are ignorant of how he found his way to patronage and to his art. His papers were burnt by a patriotic mob, and none of his great clients was prone to keeping journals. But Peter Harrison reintroduces, on American shores, the theme of the relationship between architect and client, a theme that will grow in emphasis in this book as we move from the sparse records of the earliest colonies into a fullness of documentation that can tell us something solid about how money and taste and friendship have reinforced each other in this country.

We can be certain that Harrison and Wentworth and Shirley, and William Pepperell of Kittery, Maine, as well, knew one another, and that they were all members of a group of prosperous provincials who remained loyal to the Crown. They were united in a taste for British Palladian principles, and also by ties of commercial interest. Their alliance even extended to like-minded men in Virginia: John Wentworth called on William Byrd at Westover, and his admiration for that house might explain the remarkable similarity of its doorway to that of Portsmouth's Wentworth-Gardner House. Perhaps he carried home with him a copy of the model for them both, in a pattern-book, William Salmon's *Palladio Londinensis.* *

Harrison (1716–75) was a sea captain from Yorkshire who was captured by the French in 1744, taken to their fortress at Louisburg and later released. His architectural skill permitted him to sketch the fortifications well enough to guide the British forces under the command of Pepperell and Shirley to the capture of the place in the next year.† Shirley rewarded him, it seems likely, with an opportunity to work on the design of Shirley Place in 1746. Harrison began collecting architectural books, including Salmon's, Hoppius' *Palladio*, Isaac Ware's *Designs from Inigo Jones and Others*, and William Kent's *Inigo Jones*. Having found his avocation, he married into a merchant family of Newport, to which Shirley was also related.

In 1749 the vestry of the Anglican congregation in no-longer-so-Puritan Boston were given a very substantial sum of money by Shirley to build what we now call King's Chapel, and were persuaded that it should be designed by "Mr. Harrison, of Rhode Island, a gentleman of good judgment in architecture." Later, through his trading connections with the Vassall family, Harrison received the commission for Christ Church, Cambridge. The pastor of that church was one of the Apthorpes. We can see great similarities in the designs made for three members of that family in Boston, Brighton, Massachusetts, and New York, and for Sir William Pepperell's mansion in Kittery, all completed in the 1760's. We do not

* *For more on Salmon, see Chapter Nineteen, on the Carters of Tennessee.*
† *Wentworth had declined the commission.*

Sir William Pepperell,
engraving by H. Wright
Smith after a portrait by
Smibert

*Collection of the Maine Historical
Society, Portland, Me.*

The Lady Pepperell House   *Collection of the Maine Historical Society, Portland, Me.*

need to contend that Harrison had a hand in the design of them, since there were, by that time, plenty of people who could work from plenty of handbooks to do work of that sort. But it would have been strange, given all these associations of political sympathy, trade and taste, if a man of his skill had been avoided by friends when they needed advice about architecture.

Pepperell, Governor John Wentworth's neighbor across the Piscataqua on Kittery Point, was also a Loyalist, who had been made a baronet for his leadership of the Louisburg campaign. The Lady Pepperell Mansion, completed in 1760, after William Pepperell's death, has two giant pilasters set about a doorway that sports playful dolphins almost identical to those upon the mantel of John Wentworth's own mansion, between Pleasant Street and South Pond, in Portsmouth (what a lovely address!). Sir William was proud to be known as the "Piscataqua Trader" and as the richest man in the colonies. The latter accolade was, of course, applied to a number of his contemporaries, but, like the Wentworths, he had benefited hugely from the extrication of furs and lumber from the land. We have benefited from the happenstance that all these men—Shirley, Pepperell and Wentworth—were united by bonds of commerce, by a single martial exploit and by a friendship with a Yorkshire sailor with architectural talent.

CHAPTER 8

Home and Land

THOSE WHO TRADE in the fruits of land as commodities can come to see land itself as a commodity. Land has been the most important article of commerce in American history. Endless land lay upon the horizon, like a vast warehouse full of treasures. First one could remove as much as possible of its portable inventory—fur, fish, naval supplies and precious metals. After it was, so to speak, bare, one would still own it. Then what? Rather than sentence oneself and one's progeny to husbandry—sell it! This was the strategy followed by the founders of most of the first great American fortunes; those who remained fur traders and fishermen were, by comparison, much smaller fry.

In the seventeenth and eighteenth centuries, agents of the crown were expected to enrich themselves in, and from, office. These were not twentieth-century civil servants. Governor Wentworth of New Hampshire, Governor Berkeley of Virginia and Lieutenant Governor Clarke of New York were given huge tracts of land by the king and were expected to get rich by selling them.

Royal largesse had distributed great estates to those who had deserved the gratitude of kings. The estates in America distributed by the Stuart kings were seldom seen by those who received them directly from the Crown. They were parceled out for sale through their agents. Robert "King" Carter of Virginia was such an agent, vending land owned by his employers, Lord Culpeper and his heirs, the Fairfaxes. In New Hampshire the Crown itself was the seller, using the Wentworths as agents. The Wentworths and the Carters retained for themselves choice but very scattered pieces. John Wentworth's formula was to keep five hundred to eight hundred acres of each township for which he, as royal governor, issued a patent.

The Wentworth houses, in Portsmouth, New Hampshire, and the Carter houses, along the James and beside the Blue Ridge, show how profitably could the land hunger of a rising population be accommodated. They also show how these land agents sought to appear before their peers—stable, resolute and securely rich. *113*

The seat of the Clarkes, Hyde Hall in New York, is so magnificent an instance of such a house, physically juxtaposed to an earlier West Indian cottage, so curiously delayed a century after its time, that it deserves much of Chapter Twelve to itself.

We will better understand the importance of fine houses, conveyances and costumes to American landowners if we look beyond the obvious role of this finery in preening and strutting. They were, and are today, a part of an elaborate and subtle process akin to that in chemistry called seeding. A crystal is placed in a saturated solution and seems to attract to itself, out of that solution, more crystals like itself. In the same way the appearance of prosperity, often conveyed by a comfortable house and elegant clothes, attracts to itself prosperity. An appearance of solidity, though false at the time it is manifested, may draw to it the resources whereby it becomes true.

It is difficult to hold in the mind two large ideas that seem in conflict with each other. But we must try to do this if we are to grasp a central paradox in American attitudes toward land. The first of these ideas is that continuity of possession of land and of an ancestral home has the same emotional, and therefore

Westover Plantation
Colonial Williamsburg Photograph

economic, value in America as it does elsewhere. The holders of property gain credit in the eyes of their neighbors by its continuous possession, and by the care they are able to bestow upon it. The second, and seemingly incompatible, idea is that as a nation we have been engaged in Agritrade, the buying and selling of land as a commodity, to a degree that has dazzled and disgusted our own most thoughtful historians, and has delighted those Europeans whose pleasure it is to note our incongruities.

Many of the plantation houses in the Tidewater, for example, have survived as expressions of the continuity of colonial families, on ground hallowed by their ancient names, only because their families were successful in selling land elsewhere, in defiance, therefore, of those social values associated with continuous use.

American economic growth has benefited from high valuations put on the consequences of discontinuity. We display a willingness to keep on moving and buying. We seem less willing than other nations to become attached to the unique qualities of each piece of land, its characteristic smells, sounds and colors. Thorstein Veblen was our most lethal critic of this disrespect for the uniqueness of place: he asserted that it was an essential trait of the "American pioneering spirit to seize upon so much of the country's natural resources as the enterprising pioneer could lay hands on." We have worked the soil of so much of our land as we could easily tend, and "have carried for speculation as much more as we could, and thus we have been cultivators of the main chance as well as of the fertile soil." Veblen was writing of midwestern Americans in the nineteenth century, but he could as well have been writing of planters along the Chesapeake in the eighteenth.

The Power House

FROM THE MOMENT the first of us decided he wished to persuade his neighbors he was a sound fellow, we Americans have set a high value on the outward signs of permanence. In our Colonial period there was still much vitality left in a British tradition that made country houses themselves sources of power. It was not necessary that these houses, while in the country, be the centers of large agricultural estates. The contiguous plantation of Mount Vernon never exceeded a thousand acres, though its owner possessed seventy times that much. Westover proclaimed the fierce intention of the Byrds to occupy its neighboring five hundred or six hundred acres, but several hundred thousand additional acres provided the wherewithal to hold them, and few were ever farmed by the Byrds.

This sort of arrangement was not invented in America. The prodigy houses of many Tudor and Stuart courtiers were not headquarters of self-contained feudal communities. Bishop Goodman remarked of Lord Burghley's Theobalds that it was very large and very stately, but had no feudal function representing lordship, no suzerainty over broad fields, and its woodlands were so skimpy they could not even provide its own fuel. What function did it serve?

Mark Girouard is responsible for the clearest exposition in modern literature of the functions of these places, calling them "Power Houses." The great house was a means to wealth. From clever use of land and house one could gain more land, more wealth and an even larger and more impressive house. Power, as late as 1800, was based on the ownership of land. This does not mean one was required to farm it. In England one leased it to tenants; in America much of the revenue came from land sales, but the principle was the same.

Girouard says that on the whole the great British landowners "did not farm for profit and often did not farm at all. The point of land was the tenants and rent that came with it. A landowner could call on his tenants to fight for him, in the early days of the country house, and to vote for him—or his candidate—in its later ones." Out of his rents the landlord could pay more people "to fight or vote for him, either by hiring them to do so, or by keeping up so handsome and impressive an establishment that they felt it was to their interest to come in on his side." Finally, the marvelously responsive British political system would reward those who manifested large resources and many followers "and displayed them with enough prominence," for such a person "was likely to be offered jobs and perquisites by the central government in return for his support."

In Britain and in America this process was self-reinforcing. The more a land-owner prospered, the more anxious his fellow landowners were to be connected with him. Through good connections and marriages he or his descendants acquired the leverage for still more jobs and perquisites.

But does all this seem rather remote? It is not, after one gives it a little thought. Consider the importance to many modern Americans of a cozy relationship with a banker. An imposing house, well-scrubbed cars and children, and a charming spouse are very important reassurances to potential lenders of credit. And credit is essential to that leveraged ascent to wealth which all architects recognize in the biography of many of their best clients. The basic difference between the pattern Girouard describes and that of the nineteenth and twentieth centuries is that the real-estate developer, or land trader, no longer requires access to the Crown. Instead, he requires access to Credit. The drama is the same, though the costumes differ.

In the eighteenth century the costumes were the same in the American provinces as they were in Yorkshire, or Wiltshire, or in the suburbs of Dublin. Gilded coaches and liveried postilions appeared in Maryland, extensive and exotic gardens in South Carolina; Wrenaissance mansions of brick, stone or, in the North, wood took up their stations. Michael Zuckerman of the University of Pennsylvania has pointed out to me, in conversation, that these symbols were only effective because the actors and the audience were in agreement about their meaning. Certain forms would, I should think, partake in the potency of certain archetypes of permanence and power, but the specific symbols accepted in specific times would vary. It happens that in the period we are discussing, the symbols of power and permanence were those of the Restoration of the British monarchy, especially the Anglo-Dutch forms that came into currency with William III, when the monarch, finally, sat firmly on his throne, and patriarchal authority radiated outward from the sort of palaces chosen by William and his courtiers.

In America fur traders, fish traders and land traders grew rich and held up splendid masks to be seen by travelers passing those relatively few acres they retained from trading. They participated in the deliberate statements of architectural power adopted by their king and aristocracy at home, and in the techniques of power, otherwise known as manners, which were played out in those settings. The profuse hospitality so celebrated in Colonial times had a political and commercial function. It was not lavished on any vagrant; it was bestowed on peers and potential partners, to demonstrate the resources of the host, to ingratiate, inspirit and dazzle. It suggested, in the parlance of our own day, that when a "good deal" was in the offing, here was a "set of deep pockets," and a reliable disposition, to be "cut in."

We must be very clearheaded as we appraise those who became landed gentry. They were no leisured agrarians. They were in trade, pairing off in changing partnerships, seldom committed for life. The correspondence of George Washington and William Carlisle, of William Byrd II, of the Wentworths and their numerous connections, of the Laurenses and the Manigaults, is a constant testing of intention and capacity, of trust and a willingness to join in a gamble. Coaches, houses, gardens, wines and nubile daughters all were important elements in this testing.

Traders and Planters

COLONIAL CHARLESTON CORRECTLY perceived its affinity to Venice, though to call the two "similar" would be imputing a depth and antiquity of civilization to the former which would have seemed ludicrous to any citizen of the latter. Yet they were both cities whose commercial classes were important agricultural entrepreneurs and also important patrons of architecture. The apparent differences between the essentially urban orientation of Charleston and the unbroken emphasis of the Virginia gentry on life in the country on independent plantations should not lead us into the misconception that the Carolinians were, at the outset, very different from the Virginians. A stray Venetian could have found a compatible place among either.

Palladio's merchants-turned-planters would have been at ease on the James as on the Brenta, so long as they retained their willingness to join a syndicate. Their partners might have included William Byrd, the son of a London goldsmith, John Berkeley the ironmaster, John Carter the vintner or William Fitzhugh, son of a woolen draper. The British origins of the Lees and the Jeffersons are not at all easy to descry (despite generations of earnest genealogical inquiry), though we do know that the first Richard Lee came to Virginia to represent his cousins, who were in trade in London. The historian Louis Wright says of the Ludwells, the Spensers, Thomas Stegg, Robert Bolling, Richard Booker, Miles Cary, George Brent and John Chew that they "belonged to trading families distinguished for their industry and shrewdness."

Though many Virginians were dependent on tobacco planting in the Colonial period, many others tried desperately to diversify away from the erratic world prices for tobacco. Tobacco did not occupy as much of Virginia's Colonial landscape as corn. Land speculating was probably the chief source of wealth. The Lees, Thomas Stegg, Robert Carter and Benjamin Harrison were heavily dependent for their income on retailing. Richard Lee moved early into wheat.

Most of these planters sold to their neighbors goods purchased from ships at their wharves, often exchanging these for the tobacco of small planters. They were clothiers, hardware merchants, and some, like Carter Braxton, were dealers in slaves and convicts. As they accumulated wealth and, with it, power in the provincial councils and courts, they emulated the houses being built in Britain itself by other provincials very like them in origin, aspiration and attitude.

Historians have earnestly sought the names of the architects for the houses built by these families around the Chesapeake in the eighteenth century. Their true architects were the providers of the pattern-books imported from England. I find the clients far more interesting than shadowy pattern users like Richard Taliaferro or John Ariss, expecially since no one has proven that these migrant manipulators of post-Palladian architectural clichés had much more influence on the taste of their clients than did their tailors or vintners.

William Byrd and Robert Carter chose their own architectural symbols: red brick to cover rectilinear blocks; steep, emphatic roofs; and trim of white stone. They and lesser men, up and down the coast, welcomed Georgian domesticity quietly into the New World. It was, of course, the architecture of fashion and was used even by those like John Fenwick of Fenwick Hall, who had no intention of settling into colonial life and betook themselves home to England with their winnings.

Some transplanted Barbadians did not choose to depart after the mainland enriched them. The Middletons of Barbados came to South Carolina, prospered and then divided; William Middleton of Crowfield, a mansion of 1730, repaired to England, and his brother Henry became head of the family in Carolina. Barbadian beginnings, two generations of Carolina shrewdness and good fortune, marriage and management provided Henry Middleton with fifty thousand acres of land in twenty or more plantations served by about eight hundred slaves.

The centerpiece of his rice plantation, Middleton Place (1755), was tall, massive and flanked by dependencies, each of them big enough to be residences. It was plundered during the Revolution and burnt during the Civil War, and its ruins finally succumbed to an earthquake in 1886. In its full glory, its great depen-

Sketch of the Middleton Place House, about 1841
Courtesy of the Middleton Place Foundation, Charleston, S.C.

dencies strung out in a straight line with the main house, it provided a complement to Drayton Hall, its near neighbor down the Ashley, built seventeen years earlier.

Middleton's main block was a four-square, almost cubical structure under a hipped roof, which looked as if one of the earlier houses of the Wrenaissance type had been elevated a full story off the ground. This was not all, however, for Middleton Place was one of the first of the mainland's great houses to make a further gesture of adaptation: it never had a Palladian portico—and at some time it acquired a one-story piazza all across the front. This New World appendage to Anglo-Dutch Palladianism was welcome, whether it came from the West Indies or was the fertile invention of local carpenters, for it provided cool outdoor living space.

During these years, other houses, most of them quite small, had been propped farther and farther off the ground. When the Barbadian Draytons were sufficiently settled in South Carolina to create their magnificent mansion, Drayton Hall, they had only a foot or so to go to put their living rooms in the very elevated position of those of some of Palladio's villas of the 1550's (for example, the famous Rotunda, the Villa Emo and the Villa Foscari). But Palladio himself, as far as I can learn, never placed the main floor so high and then also placed on top of it that biloggial portico which appeared on his Villas Pisani and Cornaro (they hugged the ground).

Drayton Hall, combining a high elevation and two superimposed porches, finally brought Palladio and the West Indies together. The two piazzas yield the same amount of outdoor living space as the one, all the way across the front, at Middleton Place, but Palladio had shown how to impart a far more elegant appearance than could be achieved by Middleton's long verandah—consolidate it in the center, double it, give it classical details. Tropical experiences suggested that the whole apparatus be raised as high as possible. The most elegant expression of this

119

Carolina Palladianism was the Miles Brewton House (1767–69), in Charleston.*

In order to appreciate the freshness and boldness of designs like these, it is helpful to compare them with contemporary work elsewhere. Westover, the Virginia mansion of William Byrd II, was an almost exact contemporary of Drayton Hall. Carter's Grove is contemporary with Middleton Place. It was built for Carter Burwell, grandson of Robert "King" Carter, who accumulated even more land for speculation in Virginia than Byrd. Both houses stand in genteel succession to the Governor's Palace at Williamsburg (1706–20) and the matching Wrenaissance buildings that reassure each other across the William and Mary campus, Brafferton Hall of 1723 and the President's House of 1732.

The other great governor's mansion of the southern colonies was designed for Governor Tryon of North Carolina by John Hawks, whom Tryon had brought over from England to do the job. Hugh Morrison assures us that Hawks and

Drayton Hall

Credit: Drayton Hall, Charleston, S.C. A property of the National Trust for Historic Preservation and the State of South Carolina.

* *The double portico would have been seen again at Monticello if Jefferson had finished the house according to his first design (though in it he reverted to the strict Palladian, ground-hugging version, he was building a mountain-top mansion, which was already exposed enough). He did use the biloggial form for a pavilion at the University of Virginia.*

Carter's Grove
Colonial Williamsburg Photograph

Tryon deferred to Morris' *Select Architecture* and "recollections of Lord Harcourt's estate, Newnham, in England."

Miles Brewton was, it seems, of sterner stuff. His and Tryon's houses were built at the same time. He, too, brought over an English architect (Ezra Waite), but there is no English prototype for the use they, together, made of Palladio, though they did have Drayton Hall to show the way to elevate a Palladian house, as did Palladio himself, in a hot climate. It is likely that Brewton was a great deal cooler on muggy midsummer nights than was Tryon, two hundred miles farther north, in his airless Anglo-Dutch pile. Tryon's Palace, with curved colonnades reaching out to dependencies, hugs the ground, making no concession to its terrain. It is textbook Anglo-Dutch Palladian in the way appropriate to the cool climate around the North Sea, but not to North Carolina.

In Virginia, George Washington added curving colonnades like those at Tryon's Palace to Mount Vernon during the period in his life when he was still very much determined to play the British country squire. It was then, too, that he encased his house in wood, painted and sanded to simulate stone blocks, and, in

Tryon's Palace
Courtesy of the State Department of Cultural Resources, Division of Archives and History

an awkward effort to achieve Palladian symmetry, caused false windows to be placed high on the wall encasing the banqueting hall. The hall was added to the house just before he and the colonies declared their independence. When he returned from the war, nearly a decade later, he was a changed man. Then he made two further additions. One was a cupola, bearing upon its apex a weathervane designed to his specifications—a bird carrying an olive branch in its beak. The other was his boldest creation as a designer, and the most familiar architectural form in America: the ninety-four-foot-long portico on the river side.

There is no Palladian precedent for Washington's portico. Nor, for that matter, is there any exact West Indian one, though it is tempting to recall that Washington's only overseas journey was to Barbados. It seems to me that in his old age he knew exactly the effect he wished to achieve. He was the most eminent man in his country. He wanted a stately setting, but he was in need of no exact architectural precedents. He had a sharp eye, as he showed in his earlier designs for his parish church and his constant instructions to his builders. So he may have recalled the one-story verandahs he had seen in the Caribbean and combined them in his mind with the giant pilasters he had seen in Palladian pattern-books—and invented a form that has become his trademark. He used the simplest means to create a breezy, shaded place, away from the afternoon sun. He had earned it.

Much had changed in the half century between the beginning of Drayton Hall and the completion of Mount Vernon. Some of those changes can be per-

Mount Vernon, West Façade
Courtesy of the Mount Vernon Ladies' Association

Sketch of Mount Vernon's verandah, by Benjamin Henry Latrobe
Private collection

ceived in the kind of pedimented gables to which Palladio had pointed long before.
Just before the end of the Colonial period, Washington rebuilt the roofline of
Mount Vernon to set such a gable awkwardly over the doorway. It was in the
position Palladio provided for the coats of arms of his clients. Perhaps Washington
might have placed his there, if his life had taken a different turn. He would have
had plenty of precedents. Drayton Hall's second-floor drawing room uses such a
triangular space for the Drayton arms; St. James Church, Goose Creek, South
Carolina, presents not just the hatchment of the proud donors, the Izard family,
but also a grand, carven royal coat of arms; the Governor's Palace at Williamsburg
(at least as reconstructed) gives us heraldic splendor not only inside the banqueting
room but also over its door; Governor Horatio Sharpe of Maryland placed his arms
over the doorway of Whitehall, his banqueting pavilion near Annapolis; and it
seems likely that Tryon did the same.

Coat of arms in the drawing room, Drayton Hall

*Credit: Drayton Hall, Charleston, S.C. A property of the National Trust for Historic Preservation and the
State of South Carolina.*

At Mount Vernon, named for the British admiral whose exploits in the West
Indies had given the Washingtons their first opportunity at martial glory,* a coat

1 2 4

* *In the same war that made Governor Shirley's Boston friends so rich (see Chapter Seven).*

George Washington as
a young man, by
Charles Willson Peale

*Washington/Custis/Lee
Collection, Washington and Lee
University, Va.*

of arms did not appear. George Washington not only laid a striking, original but
sensible portico across the other side of his house but also used the ceremonial
center of the Palladian pediment for an elliptical window, hinged so that it could
be opened to admit cool air to the attic.

He was a remarkable man, very conscious of images, very attentive to dress,
deportment, carriage, expression, how he was depicted, how he rode a horse, how
his house expressed the mask he wished the world to believe to be the man. He
had survived an unstable childhood. His father, though he made a remunerative
marriage (not nearly so remunerative, however, as George's), still moved his family
three times before George was twelve to accommodate the shifting demands of a
rather marginal iron business. During the future commander-in-chief's adoles-
cence, his models were clearly the Fairfax family, genuine country gentry, who
had inherited Lord Culpeper's Virginia holdings, and into which George's brother
had married. As a young man he aspired to be a British officer and had himself
painted wearing the highest provincial insignia available to one who was not, quite,
a British officer.

125

Washington was a scientific farmer, subsidizing his experiments with his trading activity, his grist mill, marriage to an heiress and land speculations. He made an immense amount of money trading in land over a two-thousand-mile front, constantly outguessing his competitors in both agricultural and urban speculation. All the while he was gaining confidence. Yet, until he entered the service of the Revolutionary Army, he had not fully become the kind of man who could have finished Mount Vernon as he did.

Though Washington and his peers among the planters of Virginia were a robust and sturdy lot, intellectually vigorous and aesthetically sound, they were, by choice, provincials. For true elegance in the eighteenth century, one must look to a city. There was no genuine urban center in the Chesapeake region—nor any south of Philadelphia, all along the Gulf Stream until one reached Cartegena, save Charleston. Charleston, sustaining Drayton and Brewton, was the most elegant city in the northern half of the hemisphere. None other could match the subtle, shimmering, silken grace of Charleston. Perhaps no place could where English was spoken, except London itself. We will approach Charleston, however, not by way of Virginia, with which she had very little intercourse, but instead from the north and then from the south. For bypassing the Chesapeake was one leg of the great triangle of Colonial commerce, which reached from Rhode Island to Charleston. Another ran from the West Indies to Charleston, and the third united the other two, carrying the familiar themes of West Indian influence into the interior of New England through its Narragansett gateway.

CHAPTER 9

Yankees
and West Indians

NOBODY SEEMS TO READ long quotations. An author who makes use of them can be suspected of exhaustion of invention or, worse, of quailing before the authority of a senior faculty mandarin, whose views on tenure may be adjusted somewhat by attribution. Attribution is the chief form of flattery among scholars. The layperson, though blessedly unacquainted with the ticket-booths of scholarship, may be legitimately suspicious when a touching deference to the eloquence of others is set out in smaller type or italics. These devices signal that it is time to skip.

Please resist that impulse here. We require at this stage in our narrative a contrast between Yankee traders and the plantation operators of what we can call the Oldest South. I cannot offer so pithy and trenchant a statement of my own as this by Richard Dunn:

> The contrast in lifestyle between the sugar planters and the Puritans in the 17th Century goes way beyond religion, slavery, and climate. To begin with demography, the early New Englanders were exceptionally healthy and fertile people; in the village of Andover, the average couple died at age 70, having raised 7 children to maturity while in Barbados hardly anyone lived to age 70 and the average white couple raised 1 or 2 children to maturity. The family was the prime instrument for socialization, with parents training their children in habits of restraint and introspection, but the West Indian colonists lacked effective family guidance and were much more undisciplined exhibitionists and free-wheeling. The New England villages were stable, cohesive little communities, where children habitually settled near their parents and few planters moved away, while the West Indian parishes were in constant flux . . . ; few families stayed or survived for more than a generation, and the most successful

planters retired to England. Most of the New Englanders lived in frugal but modest comfort, whereas Jamaican inventories and St. Christopher compensation claims show far more stratification, with ostentatious wealth at the top and desperate poverty at the bottom . . . In New England, the young were deferential to their elders, repressed the adolescent rebelliousness and often waited into their thirties to marry and set up on their own, while in the islands there were no elders, the young were in control, and many a planter made his fortune and died by age 30. In short, the Caribbean and New England planters were polar opposites; they represented the outer limits of English social expression in the 17th Century. In the North American settlements—few were really poor and oppressed. But in the Caribbean settlements, the contrary happened. For all their boisterous pioneer crudity, these island colonies evolved a more extreme pattern of social stratification than in England: rich versus poor, big planter versus small planter, master versus slave, white versus black.

By the nineteenth century, New England was no longer so dependent economically on the West Indies, but the contrast Mr. Dunn sets forth had become descriptive as well of the relationship between the Yankees and the planters of the mainland South. The southern symbiote was no longer in the islands, but had moved ashore. The psychological and economic importance of that transfer was immense; the American South became heir to the psychoses as well as the agronomy—and, perhaps, the architecture—of the Caribbean.

In the seventeenth and eighteenth centuries there arose an intricate, remunerative and addictive triangular relationship. At one vertex were the West Indies; at another were their direct successors, the Carolinas. The colonies about Chesapeake Bay were less dependent on the West Indies trade, but the connections of just one family, the Washingtons, may give a sense that the West Indies were still important. George Washington's only travel outside the thirteen colonies was to Barbados. The island (now called Roosevelt Island) in the Potomac owned, for a time, by his adopted son, George Washington Parke Custis, was once called Barbados; the Parke in Custis' name was taken from his ancestor, a governor of the Leeward Islands; and, of course, Mount Vernon was named to commemorate the leader of a Caribbean campaign.

At the third vertex were New Amsterdam and its natural successors in the trade, the ports of Rhode Island. When West Indian planters created a subsidiary plantation economy in the Carolinas, they simultaneously offered important trading opportunities to New Yorkers and then to the Yankees. New Amsterdam began as an outpost of the West Indies, and Newport became the largest center of the slave trade and sugar traffic in New England.

The Middle, or "bread," Colonies also had their own important relationships with the West Indies. A few examples may give the flavor of the two-way traffic: wheat in huge quantities went from Pennsylvania to feed plantation slaves. From the other direction, from Bridgetown and Port Royal, came commercial families like the Dickinsons, the Norrises and the Carpenters to lead Philadelphia, and there was a slave colony from Barbados on the Hackensack River as early as 1669.

This chapter will focus only on New England. We will have something to say about the Middle Colonies in Part Three, but we will not here repeat the twice- and thrice-told tale of Philadelphia's preeminent role in the eighteenth century, and indeed well into the nineteenth. Others have done that well, and it needs no redoing. We are after parts of the Colonial story which may not be quite so well known.

In the earliest phase of the relationship of the West Indies to New England and the South, Yankee merchants found the West Indies more rewarding than southern mainland ports. This is because it was not until the nineteenth century that the South Carolina merchant-planters eschewed their role as merchants and accepted the West Indian view that trade was beneath them. When they did so, they signaled good news to the Yankees, who had learned in the Caribbean the lesson they later applied toward the mainland South: never discount the value of snobbery. The Barbadians were too busy reaping the quick profits of the sugar culture and too anxious to appear to be gentry to soil their hands with commerce. So much the better for Yankees, who had no agricultural alternative.

The West Indian market was huge: it bought more than two thirds of New England's exports in the Colonial period. Fish went from Massachusetts and all the northern coasts (low-grade fish, to be sure), barrel staves from New Hampshire and Maine, and then wondrously assorted articles of merchandise transshipped by Boston merchants. Though New England was, of course, a great importer of finished goods from old England, more than 20 percent of mainland imports came from the West Indies. Three quarters of this was sugar and sugar products, rum, muscovado and molasses; 90 percent or so of the molasses went to make more rum. There were thirty distilleries in Rhode Island and sixty-three in Massachusetts in 1750. The West Indies were the great bilateral trading partners of New England.

These trade relationships were the training ground for Yankee ingenuity. The balance of trade of the northern colonies ran at a perpetual deficit throughout the Colonial period, so ingenuity was a necessity. Where but by courage and craft could money be found to buy the goods of need and desire? New Englanders led the way to economic independence. Rhode Island emerged from grubbing for subsistence on rocky fields by raising and shipping horses to power Barbadian sugar mills, but it was not these and the other products of agriculture or forestry or fishing that built the large Yankee fortunes of the later Colonial period. It was commerce itself. By 1775 the mainland colonies as a whole earned more from shipping than from any single commodity save tobacco. When we add in profits, insurance and interest arising from the shipping trade, even the tobacco trade was surpassed. The New England colonies produced more than half of all returns from Colonial shipping.

As we have noted, the great families of Barbados and Antigua frequently sent off shoots to settle the Carolinas, and there were close family relationships between the earliest Virginia planters and the West Indians. There was, as well, a skein of kinship between the Yankees and the West Indiamen. John Winthrop, founder and governor of Massachusetts Bay, has been associated in our minds only with New England, but he was, perforce, interested in both that colony and the West Indies. His second son, Henry, was one of the earliest to try his fortune on Barbados, as a tobacco planter. John pronounced Henry's product to be "very ill conditioned, fowle, full of stalkes and evil coloured" and desisted from sending him the full complement of indentured servants he requested. Another son, Samuel, settled in Antigua. John Winthrop was delighted with the possibilities of trade with the unfolding slave and sugar economy: "It pleased the Lord to open to us a trade with Barbados and other islands in the West Indies." Once that trade was open, it stayed open:

> By the 1680's nearly half the ships that served the islands came from New England, and over half the ships entering and clearing Boston were in the West Indian trade . . . A pair of cousins, both named John Turner, from Massachusetts and Barbados, shared ownership in a ketch; in the 1660's the Massachusetts cousin built the House of Seven Gables . . . Samuel Parris brought two Indian slaves—John and Tituba—with him from Barbados to Salem village, and it was John's witch cake and Tituba's incantations that launched the Salem witchcraft frenzy in 1692.

Mr. Dunn tells us that while the Massachusetts cousin was building the House of Seven Gables in Salem for a few hundred pounds, perhaps, the Barbadian cousin was selling a little more than two hundred acres of sugar property for nearly six thousand pounds. With capital like that, he could easily have built a house as big as Drax Hall, which would show what the Salem house aspired to be. Drax Hall had twelve gables, after all, and was of solid masonry, whereas the survival of Salem's wooden seven into Nathaniel Hawthorne's day was something of a miracle of fire avoidance. The high-gabled Anglo-Dutch urban house type, of which he reminded us, was an "economy model" of much grander versions built where the British colonies were genuinely remunerative.

This peaked, compact style was, as we had earlier occasion to observe (see Chapter Four), more apropos to snowy New England than to the West Indies. As compared to old England, the North American colonies suffered from a climate of both extremes: its winters were colder and its summers much hotter. The lessons of West Indian architecture could easily be observed by Yankees trading there, and we can wonder if the undatable verandahs of the coast of Maine may not be considerably older than commonly estimated. There is no need to assume that the sailors of the Piscataqua were less appreciative of shade in summer than those of the Ashley and the Cooper; they may have joined that remarkably widespread rush to build verandahs which we observed in Chapter Five.

There is no need, either, to settle the matter, for the West Indies had enough influence on coastal New England in other ways to justify much more discussion of the Caribbean origins of Yankee architecture than the subject usually receives. Without the West Indies trade there would not have been the money to build

House of Seven Gables

Photo courtesy of House of Seven Gables, Salem, Mass.

many of the early buildings we see along Massachusetts Bay and Cape Ann and
Narragansett Bay, at Portsmouth and Kittery. Without that trade Yankees could
not have developed the merchant class that led the revolt against Britain in the
1770's. After independence exposed them to the buffeting of international competitors (from which the British fleet had hitherto protected them), it was experience
and capital gained in the West Indies trade that from 1787 to 1808 enabled New
Englanders to rise to the occasion. It provided the ships, the stores, the warehouses, the confidence and a primary school for full-scale international mercantile
competition, while the British, Dutch, French and Danes were distracted by the
Napoleonic Wars.

Piracy, Privateering and the Slave Trade

RHODE ISLAND'S PIRATICAL mariners plundered plantation cargoes from the ships
of others; Rhode Island's merchants garnered revenues by selling slaves to plantations to produce more cargoes fit, in turn, for pillage. Piracy, privateering and
slave trading were associated professions in Rhode Island, as they had been in

131

England since the time of Drake and Hawkins. In the seventeenth and eighteenth centuries freebooters were everywhere: the British Council of Trade and Plantations was told in 1700 that the coasts of America and the West Indies were swarming with pirates.

Earlier (in Chapter Six) we saw, beneath the Jolly Roger, the Fenwicks of Fenwick Hall, one of whom became father-in-law to a duke. Under that terrifying banner, or another quite easily mistaken for it, the ensign of the freebooting privateer, there now appear the founders of several great seafaring dynasties in New England. One was Simeon Potter, who terrorized the sea lanes between the slaving stations of West Africa and the West Indies. Potter's home port was Bristol, Rhode Island, where his sister Abigail waited for an appropriate spouse. Simeon Potter produced a young colleague named De Wolf, and from their union sprang one of Bristol's most eminent families.

Their son was, at twenty, the captain of a slave vessel owned by John Brown of Providence. It was Brown who rose from his seat in the Congress of the United States to cry that Americans wanted money and a navy, and ought to use the means to obtain it, otherwise Great Britain would get all the slave trade to itself! Brown was the richest and most powerful man in the colony, farseeing, brazen and brave. He and his brothers had grown rich in the West Indian rum trade, manufacturing iron and spermaceti candles, and in the slave traffic. One of the brothers, Moses, became a Quaker and publicly opposed that trade. Perhaps even more nettlesome, he proclaimed himself to be a pacifist when his brothers were

Moses Brown
Courtesy of the Rhode Island Historical Society

John Brown of Providence
Courtesy of the New-York
Historical Society, New York City

not averse to privateering. Moses focused upon the family's educational interests, which produced Brown University and the school that bears his full name, but even he had a Midas touch: he was largely responsible for bringing Samuel Slater to Pawtucket in 1789 to link together a series of Arkwright water-driven cotton spinning frames into the first American textile mill.

The capital created by the West Indies trade, by rum, by the iron business and by the slave traffic thus directly sponsored the onset of the industrial revolution in Rhode Island, and the beginnings of competition in manufacturing between the United States and Great Britain.

John Brown was the leader of the family. His cry for a United States navy was his third successful exhortation to his countrymen to take to the sea, armed to the teeth. Rhode Island commissioned its own navy in June 1775, and one of its two vessels had formerly been John Brown's slaving brig, the *Katy*. In October of that year the Continental Congress established its navy, and the *Katy* reappeared, now dubbed the *Providence*, the first ship authorized by the congress. She was soon back in her old haunts, capturing Nassau from the British and, more to her taste, providing John Paul Jones with his first command as a sort of congressionally chartered privateer. His status was like that of Drake and Hawkins, let loose on the Spaniards by Queen Elizabeth two centuries earlier. John Brown was also the provider, from his family's ironworks, of many cannons to the cause of independence.

133

While these activities, and a long gamble on the success of the cause of independence itself, left John Brown a very rich man, he is chiefly interesting to us as the patron of another of his brothers, the celebrated Providence architect Joseph Brown. Like most of the other merchants in that seafaring city, John Brown and his brothers had lived above their places of business on Towne Street, keeping an eye on the docks opposite. But as early as 1774, even before the great burst of post-independence prosperity, the Browns were proud of Joseph's three-story brick mansion up the hill on Main Street. As in a Dutch house, its gable is turned to the street and given a bold ogival curve. Its original entrance was on the second floor, with a doorway echoing the curve of the roof, and flights of steps to the street splayed out in the West Indian fashion.

Joseph Brown's house on Main Street in Providence
Courtesy of the Rhode Island Historical Society

Joseph Brown rang a new note in American domestic architecture, a boldness in taking traditional elements and expanding them far beyond traditional scale. He initiated a tradition which persists in an unbroken line through Frank Furness to Bernard Maybeck and Charles Moore. Joseph Brown was perhaps the first of the post-modernists; he was certainly a gifted amateur architect, and he established Rhode Island's slightly manic architectural tradition, which was sustained after him by John Holden Green and Russell Warren.

After independence, John Brown sent his ships into the East India trade and to China in 1787. Those who like to see history as a helix will be pleased to note

John Brown's house on the corner of Power and Benefit Streets, Providence
Photo by Wayne Andrews

that he also sent the first American vessels directly into the old Venetian trade routes of the Levant, just as his brother Joseph was designing an elegant Palladian house for him on the corner of Power and Benefit Streets (a wonderful intersection). It is a full three stories of brick, five bays wide, with a pavilion thrust forward in the center bearing a muscularly overscaled Venetian window in a curved arch. The interior is elegant and opulent, rejoicing in carven woodwork and ceremonial space. John Adams, that shrewd architectural observer, called it the new nation's most magnificent and elegant mansion.

Down the coast at Bristol, Brown's young captain, James De Wolf, was soon to build his own monument to the southern trades. He had learned his lessons well and became the patron of the architect Russell Warren. Bristol was Warren's base, and De Wolf his most munificent client. They were both the beneficiaries of the peculiar opportunities created by the economics of slavery. The international traffic in slaves had been forbidden by national law since 1794, but South Carolina repealed all the state slave laws in 1804. Cotton was spreading upland, carrying the slave system with it and creating an enormous demand for fresh supplies of black labor. In the next four years, 202 slave ships, contraband under national

135

Russell Warren
*Courtesy of the Rhode Island
Historical Society*

law, landed in South Carolina. Fifty-nine were from Bristol, and of these, ten were owned by James De Wolf. Then came the War of 1812. For the Browns and De Wolf it brought another season of privateering. Just one of James De Wolf's ships captured prizes worth, in sum, a million dollars.

De Wolf's mansion, the Mount, built in 1808 (and destroyed in 1904), was the direct, explicit product of those ten voyages to South Carolina. It was appropriate that Russell Warren should have been its architect, for he, too, was making a career at both abutments of the Rhode Island–Carolina association, but nothing he did at the southern end could compare with this strutting three-story assemblage of Palladian windows, Carrara marble mantels, Hispaniola mahogany staircases, French murals and a glazed dome.* Indeed, all his major work for the De Wolf family seems curiously ahead of its time. It looks like the late paroxysm of the Classical Revival as it appeared in the Louisiana plantation houses of the 1850's, or the enormous houses built while the thunderheads of the Civil War were darkening the skies of middle Tennessee. Yet here it was, built in the first decade

* *Unless he had a larger hand than we think he had in the houses of the Hamptons thirty years later—see Chapter Twenty-three.*

of the century, while in the South the Classical tradition of Wren and Gibbs and Hugh May still held such excesses in check.

The Mount, built of the proceeds of the slave trade and of piracy, managed an offensive gesture toward another race, victimized even more closely at hand: upon its roof stood a figure of King Philip, the chief of the native people who had controlled the site before the De Wolfs' compatriots drove them out. Perhaps the sense of dominance was justified to some extent: James De Wolf became, in time, a United States senator. His brother William also grew great as a privateer and slaver, and also obtained from Russell Warren a splendid if somewhat strenuous celebration of the South Carolina trade, called Hey Bonnie Hall.

George De Wolf, the third brother, waited two years more for his Warren extravaganza, Linden Place, which is still the grandest thing in Bristol. It is fortunate he did not wait much longer, for he was a true West Indian, investing heavily in sugar plantations in Cuba, and lost much of his fortune when those plantations failed in 1825. Linden Place has a Palladian door, slightly gothicized at the shafts,

Hey Bonnie Hall (now demolished)
Courtesy of the Rhode Island Historical Society

and a Palladian window, shrunk down from the scale of Joseph Brown's but located in the same place, over the door, and within a now vastly overscaled arch. The house has been remodeled somewhat, but its forest of columns and pilasters was apparently there when it was built in 1810. It has more in common with Henry Howard's Louisiana extravaganzas, or Nashville houses like Belmont (see Chapter Twenty), than anything built within a generation of its own time.

Linden Place
Photo by Wayne Andrews

Warren designs are not resposeful. Warren advertised his wares and expressed his temperament in his own house. Like many architects' residences, it states a point of view. Its quoins are set diagonally, deliberately destabilizing, and the pilasters of its portico are set just far enough away from the wall to deny any structural purpose. Warren was tricky and nervous—perhaps this is why he attracted clients like the De Wolfs. He gave them fashionable houses, the components of which are just a little out of key, one with another. They are a bit noisy, without being so noisy as to draw the scorn of other architects, or to invite his clients to fear the disdain of their neighbors. Each of the De Wolfs was eager to make a mark. Warren provided those marks—indeed, those masks. Like many masks, they revealed more about their wearers than may have been intended.

Southern Exposure

BRISTOL AND NEWPORT were outposts of the Caribbean system, like New Amsterdam—and like Charleston or Savannah. The reciprocity between Rhode Island and the Old South, established in the seventeenth century, has persisted to this

Nathaniel Russell, by Charles Fraser

From the Carolina Art Association, Gibbs Art Gallery, Charleston, S.C.

day. Architecturally, they had as much in common in the eighteenth and early nineteenth centuries as one might expect. Russell Warren, for example, was active as a designer and as a builder at both ends of this axis of affinity. He was the contractor for courthouses designed by William Jay and by Robert Mills (see Chapter Eleven) and of Savannah's old Courthouse. He owned and designed two houses on Ellery Street in Charleston, which have disappeared, but they nonetheless interest architectural historians because their site was owned by Nathaniel Russell.

Russell was a Providence merchant who lived, as did Warren, both in Rhode Island and in South Carolina. The land may have been the medium of exchange

139

whereby Russell paid Warren for some part of the design (or for being the contractor) of his mansion laid up on Meeting Street in that city about 1811. The design cannot be assigned to Warren—it is much too subtle for him—but the property transfer and elements of style suggest that he had an important part in the building.

The mystery of the design of the Russell House may never be solved. It is curiously honest; it makes no effort to disguise its merchant origins, raising its living quarters to the second floor, leaving the ground floor to be entered directly from the street on the short side, like any of the tradesmen's houses abandoned by the Brown brothers, or Russell himself, on the Providence docks. It stretches itself lazily, in curves, away from the street, like a great brick cat, with double stripes of brick along its flanks. Its windows are set back into curved recesses like the most meticulous work of Benjamin Latrobe or Sir John Soane.

Nathaniel Russell's house on Meeting Street
Photo by Charles N. Bayless. Courtesy of the South Carolina Historical Society.

Benjamin Henry Latrobe recurs in these pages, as he does in any history worth its ink of American architecture, engineering, drama, poetry, politics or invention between 1796 and 1822. He was of French descent, English birth, German education and cosmopolitan interests. His best-known works are the basic model of the United States Capitol, the remodeled White House, the Baltimore Cathedral, the Philadelphia Water Works, several pavilions at the University of Virginia, and a famous series of journals, now being published, one handsome volume after another.

Warren could do nothing so sleek as the Russell house, but he did design several houses for merchants engaged in the West Indies trade in Providence and Newport. One of them, for Levi Gale, a sugar merchant, still survives as the chapter house for Peter Harrison's Touro Synagogue.

The Gale House symbolizes one of the dozens of baffling incongruities of religion and commerce in Newport, the nation's most complete museum of architecture from the seventeenth through the nineteenth centuries. Though it provides a remarkable inventory of architectural types, it should not be assumed that Newport was typical of other towns in New England, except its neighbors, Providence and Bristol. These outposts of the South Atlantic maritime system retained the stamp of that system in their economy, psychology and architecture long into the nineteenth century. Their trading patterns and the mix of their revenues were not at all like those of cities engaged in the coastal traffic, or of international ports such as Boston and the Cape Ann group.

Samuel Eliot Morison seems to have been right in assuring us that slaving "had never been an important line of commerce in Massachusetts." (The list of slavers supplying South Carolina, to which we earlier referred, for example, contained just one ship from Massachusetts.) Salem, Morison writes, "had a regular trade with the West African coast, rum and fish for gold dust, palm oil, and ivory; and it would be surprising if an occasional shipmaster did not yield to the temptation to load 'black ivory' as well," but surreptitiously, for "it was forbidden, under heavy penalties, by an act of the General Court in 1788." Newport, on the other hand, was so blatant in its principal activity as to replace New Amsterdam as "the Slave Market of the North."

Newport pirates ravaged the seas from the Red Sea and Madagascar to the South American coastline; Newport slavers patrolled the coasts of Africa as well. When the Peace of Utrecht in 1714 provided the British fleet as a protection for the slave trade, Newport rushed to institutionalize that traffic by assigning half the revenues from slave profits to paving its streets.

It is ironic that Narragansett Bay should have become a slavers' harbor, for in its tolerant shelter there was also a haven for the settlement of Quakers. In the eighteenth century half the population of Newport were members of the Society of Friends, and as Quaker opposition to slavery increased over the course of that century, an uneasy truce of conscience was sustained between those whom Sir Edmund Andros called the "Quaker Grandees of Rhode Island" and many of the town's other grandees.

The Redwood Library in Newport
Courtesy of the Redwood Library and Atheneum

Even the Quaker merchants, who generally eschewed piracy and privateering, were among the trading partners of the West Indies and the mainland South. Peter Harrison, whom we encountered in Chapter Seven, was Newport's first important architect, responsible for the Touro Synagogue, the oldest remaining place of Jewish worship in the United States. This tribute to the religious tolerance of the city was matched by another: Harrison, born a Quaker but become a sometimes intransigent Anglican, found as his great patron the Quaker Abraham Redwood, who came to Newport via Antigua, where his son owned the Casada Garden sugar plantations. Other members of the Redwood family established themselves in Charleston.

There is much architecture in Rhode Island that shows its affinities to the southern plantation system. Washington County, on the western shore of Narragansett Bay (which, incidentally, is customarily called by its natives "South County," for geographic, not sociological or historical, reasons), was organized in the eighteenth century into extensive plantations worked by slave labor, raising grain and cattle for the Caribbean and southern markets. The proprietors of these plantations were the farthest north of the customers for the slave merchants of Newport and Bristol, with whom they had many ties. Kingston was one of the headquarters villages for this group, and its streets, little affected by intrusions of the nineteenth and twentieth centuries, look very much like the villages along Albemarle Sound or around Cape Fear.*

---

* No careful architectural work seems yet to have been done to examine the parallels between the two enclaves of rural slavery in the North, the Hudson Valley and "South County"; there is a great opportunity there for some eager graduate student.

Hearthside

Courtesy of the Providence Public Library: Rhode Island Collection

Perhaps the most sentimental reminder of the association between the South and the Narragansett Bay plantations is the country mansion called Hearthside, which was built in 1810 by Stephen Smith just outside Providence. Smith was another Quaker merchant, who, it is said, won $50,000 of Louisiana sugar money in a lottery and spent it on this large stone house to lure a southern lady to marry him. Its end gables borrow oversized ogees from Joseph Brown's house in Providence, and across the broad side is a great unpedimented Mount Vernon–style portico. The lady, it appears, was unpersuaded, and Smith lived out his bachelor's life botanizing and undertaking a series of daring business ventures like the Blackstone Canal, which was intended to provide water transportation all the way upcountry from Providence to Worcester, Massachusetts.

There is no doubt that the affinity of Newport to the slave system made it a comfortable place for southern patronage well into the nineteenth century, after it had declined commercially and become a resort. Though the slave trade was gone, it welcomed plantation owners from the South who came there to escape the heat and the dangers of the plantations. "Summering at Newport" began in the 1730's for West Indians, and they were soon joined by families of Charleston merchants, so many, indeed, that it became known as "the Carolina Hospital." Comfort was not merely a matter of temperature, but of compatibility as well. Considering their

143

common experiences, it was natural for West Indians and South Carolinians (like Wade Hampton I; see Chapter Twenty-three) to find Newport congenial. Its most handsome early "cottages" were laid up for southerners, like Noble Jones of Savannah, Richard Upjohn's client for the Gothic villa Kingscote.

The architectural traffic flowed both ways along the north-south trade route. In 1774 South Carolina's first native-born architect, Gabriel Manigault, visited Rhode Island. In the other direction went a succession of Rhode Island contractor-architects, led by Russell Warren. After him went Clark Sayles, designer of Georgia plantation houses and contractor for the Burke County Courthouse. Isaiah Davenport, whose house on Columbus Square in Savannah was one of the first products of that city's surge of interest in historic preservation in the 1950's, was another Rhode Island builder.

It is appropriate for us now to follow them as they traveled southward, back to the Carolinas.

CHAPTER 10

Charleston

HERE SHE IS: Charleston, doyenne of cities, mistress of molasses-colored rivers tincturing the sea. Charleston, grand old lady, wearing pearls while she gardens. Azaleas bloom at her touch, as do burning oleanders and icy hydrangeas. Above her ribboned hat the blue sunlight catches the "ample and fragrant blossoms, purple cones and scarlet pendant seeds" of magnolias, like those which delighted the great Proprietor Sir John Colleton when they came to "adorn successively and perfume the woods from May to October" on his Devonshire estate.

Charleston has always been a city of flowers: the magisterial Swede, Linnaeus, named the gardenia for Charleston's own Dr. Alexander Garden; the family of Peter Poinsett, keeper of the Charleston tavern having the "best repute for cooking and good Madeira," gave their name to the poinsettia. We are told that Governor John Drayton himself translated from the Latin Thomas Walter's *Flora Caroliniana*. André Michaux arrived from France in 1786 to collect native plants, and stayed to introduce crepe myrtle, mimosa and tea olive. Tradition says he was responsible for letting loose riotous Japanese camellias on Charleston's gardens. Riots of this kind can be quieted only by the breeze of the sea, which mixes for Charleston a potpourri of scents—wintersweet, daphne, sweet bay, loquat and wisteria, honeysuckle and jessamine.

Charleston once was a town that smelled also of sweating cattle and cowboys, long-unwashed fur traders and the stacks of pelts dumped by Indian bearers. One can imagine the furs piled in front of 39 Church Street, the home and place of business of the trader George Eveleigh, which remains there to remind us of its origins. Charleston, then, smelt of hides of deer, of pirates and of honest seamen; it smelt of black fear when a slave auction was on the docks; it smelt of white fear, too, in the long nights when Charlestonians sat behind high walls built not to keep tourists out but to keep at safe distances that three quarters of the population which had no pearls to wear while gardening.

The George Eveleigh House, Charleston
Courtesy of the South Carolina Historical Society

Ah, Charleston, now most delicate of American cities, beneficiary of two hundred years of nostalgia! How does she feel about her real youth, when "single houses" made use of all three entrances: one from the garden for the family, after the sturdy gate had been opened and then the sturdy door; one at the back for slaves; and one at the front for the master's business? Has she forgotten that there was, indeed, business? Has she forgotten Henry Laurens, son of a saddler, Gabriel Manigault, carpenter, and his brother Pierre, tavernkeeper? They built a city for her, they and their rough brethren.

Two apparently similar groups of tradesmen who arrived at about the same time, one in Virginia and one in Carolina, went in quite different directions. The first families of Virginia, though they lived by trade at the outset, abandoned it after the third and fourth generations, and built no cities equivalent to Charleston or Savannah. They aspired to be country squires. Their Charleston equivalents looked on the country estates as sources of wealth to support city mansions. Their models were no British "country families," shivering in drafty relics of a feudal past upon endless ancestral acres. They longed, instead, for London and lived like Londoners in Charleston.*

This urban affinity is remarkable, because it was not the way of those West Indians whose economic progeny they were. As we have seen, the West Indian planters chose the squire's life, leaving their scraggly towns to the Dutch, the Scots and the Yankees, despised traders.

During its golden age, from 1760 to 1775, Charleston grew to be a genuine urban center. It only began to lose its pace with independence. In 1790 it was still close to Boston in size (sixteen thousand versus eighteen thousand), still showing Baltimore its heels, hardly conscious at all of the village of Savannah. It remained substantially larger than Baltimore until the century was nearly spent. True, it was smaller then New York or Philadelphia, but the spotty evidence available on the subject suggests that some of its oligarchs were wealthier than their counterparts elsewhere. Alice Hanson Jones, surveying the distribution of riches in 1774, found that nine of the fifteen largest estates in her sample were in the South, and eight were in South Carolina alone. The largest of all was Pierre Manigault's. The richest woman in the Jones survey was also a South Carolinian, Abigail Townsend.

Sephardim and Huguenots

MORE IMPORTANT THAN quantities of any kind, even of relative wealth, are indices of the quality of urban life in Charleston. At any time, and certainly in the eighteenth and nineteenth centuries, the best "urbanity indicator" for an American city is the size of its Jewish population. A yet more precise litmus is provided by its number of Sephardic Jews. Eli Evans, the historian, has found that nearly half the total Jewish population in the United States in 1810 was concentrated in Charleston; there were more there than in New York. Many of these were Sephardim, who had gone first to Savannah, known then to be free of religious persecution (though perilously close to the Catholic Spanish from whom their ancestors had fled). Families like the Sheftalls and the Minises presided over cultivated households while Savannah was still a few scattered frame buildings on a sandhill. Philip Minis was the first white child born in Georgia. As that colony faltered, however, many of its Jews moved to the more salubrious trading environment of Charleston.

There they became an even more effervescent factor in the life of the South. As we have seen, Moses Lindo made a commercial crop out of Eliza Lucas' exper-

* *Only Ralph Izard actually kept a house in London, as had Thomas Stegg of Virginia, grandfather of William Byrd I.*

147

imental indigo. A Scottish philanthropist, Sir Alexander Cumming, failed in a scheme to settle 300,000 Jews in a new national home among the Cherokees (the Cherokees gave the idea a better reception that did the Jews), but a steady trickle of highly skilled and energetic Jewish immigrants did settle in Charleston. John Locke sought to protect the rights of Jews in his draft of the constitution of Carolina; though this passage did not make it through to the final version, Jews did vote there on the same basis as other freemen. A recent historian, Charles Reznikoff, asserts that Charleston was "the first community in the modern world to grant Jews that right."

Judah P. Benjamin, who became a United States senator and a financial genius of the Confederacy, was a product of that community, born in the West Indies and given his first commercial experience selling fruit in his parents' shop on King Street. Justice Benjamin Cardozo of the United States Supreme Court, possessed of analytical equipment as fearsome as that of his contemporaries, Oliver Wendell Holmes and Louis Brandeis, was descended from the mulatto child of a Charleston Cardozo. The Sephardim in Charleston, like the Tobiases, generally bestowed their genes on the modern world more conventionally, through intermarriage with the other early trading families of the city. Charleston presented Jews with more opportunity to prosper and mingle easily into the larger community than any other Colonial city. A part of its urbanity is certainly by grace of this Jewish concentration.

Another force offsetting the West Indian influence was a group much more numerous than the Jews: in 1700, one third of South Carolina's legislators spoke French. Most of these were Huguenots from urban areas, skillful artisans who aided the Jews in giving South Carolina a powerful urban culture. The Manigaults and Laurenses, Ravenals and Petigrus, Hugers and Gaillards, St. Juliens and Duprés, unlike the West Indians, had no tradition of squirearchy. I am no expert in the architecture of upward mobility among seventeenth-century Huguenots (and I have found no one who is), but I offer the hypothesis that a Huguenot grown rich would hope to move from one street in La Rochelle to a better street in La Rochelle, not to some chill village in the Dordogne.*

When they fled towns like La Rochelle and came to America, these Huguenots carried with them a different set of aspirations from those which animated their Virginian contemporaries. Among the Virginians, it is sometimes said, there were just enough genuine "scions of country families" to reinforce tradesmen's longings to set up as gentry in country houses (one thinks of the Fairfaxes with their close ties to the Washingtons, or the Randolphs and their Jefferson relations). We know of no stowaway scions among the Huguenots. They were carpenters and coopers, blacksmiths and sailmakers, weavers and workers in gold, silver and leather. Some were shipwrights, and for a generation it seemed that Charleston might be a shipbuilding city. Some, too, were clergymen, advocates and doctors.

---

* I have offered in my book American Churches another and complementary suggestion: that the circular churches of Robert Mills may owe a debt to the circular, or concentric, churches of the Huguenots.

Nearly all aspired to exchange the blue smock of a tradesman for the fine linen of a merchant.

It was because they were skilled craftsmen that they were actively recruited by the Lord Proprietors and the British government. It was first expected that they knew the secret of producing silk; the British hoped one of the Frenchmen would disclose some arcane means to tease the little worms into surviving and multiplying. As it turned out, the mystery was found to lie not in the Gallic temperament but in the climate. Though the exiles had no arcanery to apply to the production of silk, it soon became apparent that they had a sharp instinct for trade.

Louis XIV lost much by his revocation of the Edict of Nantes in 1685, an action that left no doubt that he would deny the French Protestants the practice of their religion. Thus he drove these diligent people into the arms of his Protestant neighbors. Some sense of what was thereby denied to France can be gained by recalling the boldness and sagacity of the Huguenots before 1685, while they still held power close to the French throne. The Huguenot Roberval led the first effort toward French settlement of Canada in 1541, while the British were still barely venturing past Land's End. Admiral Gaspard de Coligny (who was murdered on St. Bartholomew's Eve) had organized the first expedition of Huguenots to settle the Carolinas in 1562. Neither attempt succeeded, but it was Huguenot energy that animated a French colonial policy which, if sustained, might have won a continent.

Once established in Carolina, the Huguenots created upcountry towns like New Bordeaux and Abbeville, but it was a real city, Charleston, that most appealed to them. There they rose so rapidly that "rich as a Huguenot" came to have the same meaning as "rich as a West Indian" in London, or "rich as a Quaker" in Newport. Rich or poor, the French (like the Dutch) found it natural to turn the elbows of their houses to the streets, a traditional and necessary posture in the confined cities from which they had come. Charleston's waterfront to this day retains a strip of row houses (Cabbage Row) which are very like those of some seventeenth-century views of West Indian cities, and cities of the Low Countries and the Atlantic Coast of France.

Like the ports of Holland and of the French Huguenot coast, Charleston and New Amsterdam were shaped by substantial fortifications, and grew within them. They were the only cities in the British colonies to do so—as Wall Street, the Battery (one in each city) and Magazine Street remind us. (Between 1750 and 1770 Savannah, too, spent a term within fortifications, but they were so much larger than the space needed by its tiny population that Savannans were free to indulge in diminutive urban sprawl.)

Portions of Charleston's fortifications were redesigned and rebuilt, it seems, by Gabriel Bernard, tutor, uncle and guardian of Jean Jacques Rousseau. Bernard had served against the Turks with Georgia's Proprietor, James Oglethorpe, under Prince Eugene of Savoy. He then returned to his native Geneva and was kept busy improving its Calvinist fortifications against the threat of an invasion from Catholic

Cabbage Row ("Catfish Row" in *Porgy and Bess*), Charleston
Courtesy of the South Carolina Historical Society

France. He was kept even busier trying to discipline his wayward, willful nephew after Jean Jacques' mother died and his father deserted the scene. In his *Confessions* Rousseau reported that his uncle had supervised the building of the city of Charleston and had died there shortly after designing its plan.

Bernard did work in South Carolina and Georgia for a year or two before his death in 1737, much of the time for his old comrade in arms, Oglethorpe. He may have had a hand in laying out eleven towns for Swiss Huguenots, and it is suggested by several historians that he created the plan of Savannah itself. There is a scholarly wrangle on the point, but all seem agreed that Rousseau was claiming too much when he said that his uncle designed the "plan" for Charleston; that city had been growing in accordance with a plan since 1680.

It is not easy to find a rock, much less a stone quarry, in the Carolina low country, but Dutch and Huguenot masons did the best they could to build something like their old towns in this warm and humid country where even good clay for brick was scarce. Stucco over "tabby" looked like French stucco over rubble or brick. Paul St. Julien, at his plantation, Hanover, laid a stucco band across the largest assemblage of bricks he could gather, and incised thereon the words *peu à peu.* Samuel Gaillard Stoney calls that brickwork "Gallic," which indeed it may be, and sees in "the many stucco enrichments and the high pitched roof of Brick House [on Edisto Island] . . . the air of French work of the time of Henry IV or Louis XIII." The real thing, the grand example of French work in the colonies, was, we may recall, the Governor's House on Grenada. But many of the French did seem to prefer bricks to frame sheathing, and one of them, Zachariah Ville-pontoux, made famous bricks for his plantation, Parnassus, and supplied them for the building of both St. Michael's Church and Pompion Hill Chapel. This affinity for fancy brickwork may have encouraged Thomas Waterman, the grand old man of Colonial Williamsburg, to suggest Huguenot, rather than Dutch, origins for the curvilinear gables of St. Stephen's Church, near North Chacan in French Santee, and he may be right.

Charleston's Golden Age

UNDER THE SPUR of the town-loving and resourceful Jews and Huguenots, Charleston grew rapidly during the Colonial period. As an exporting seaport it became

Brick House on Edisto Island (later destroyed by fire)
Photo by Mills Lane

two and a half times larger than New York and was well ahead of Boston and Philadelphia. It was the quintessential urban center of the South, in part because of its concentration of Jews and Huguenots, in part because of the mosquito, in part because of a consolidation of trading activity in a port city. The malarial consequences of upland rice-planting did force the planters into town after 1780 or so, but their urban preferences were already established by then. Many of them, of course, began in town and acquired plantations outside it.

The coastal Carolinas contrasted sharply with the region about the Chesapeake, where the large plantations, set upon deeper streams, served as their own ports. When Virginians became rich, few showed much desire to live throughout the year with the tradesmen in Alexandria. The Washingtons kept a raised cottage there, and the Lees several townhouses, but aside from the Carlyle House there is not a mansion to match those of Charleston. It is remarkable how quick were the Virginians to abandon Williamsburg for the country after it ceased to be the center of politics. When the capital was moved to Richmond to escape the British in 1780, Williamsburg virtually disappeared, its population declining to less than 1,200 by 1795. Twenty thousand South Carolinians were already committed to Charleston by then, and the removal of their political capital to Columbia in 1790 left them unperturbed.

Portrait of Miles Brewton
by Sir Joshua Reynolds
Private collection

Portrait of the Middletons by Benjamin West
Courtesy of the Middleton Place Foundation and Dr. Henry Middleton Drinker

Charleston grew rich for the first time as the child of the West Indies, favored by imperial preference, nurtured by British mercantilist policies. Rice enjoyed a steady and protected market, indigo and marine supplies had hefty subsidies, and the costs of defense were largely borne by British taxpayers. It is important to recall that, unlike their northern competitors, Charleston's merchants were net creditors, not debtors, in commodity trade balances as the Revolution commenced. They were proud as creditors often are when the credits are good—proud as we see them in Miles Brewton's portrait by Sir Joshua Reynolds, or the Middletons' by Benjamin West, or a whole range of oligarchs painted by Charleston's "court painter," Jeremiah Theus.

This was the time when a visiting Rhode Islander, Elkanah Watson, said Charleston had achieved an "almost Asiatic splendor," and Josiah Quincy, dining with Miles Brewton in 1773, was dazzled by "the grandest hall I ever beheld," with its "azure blue satin window curtains" and "excessive grand and costly look-ing-glasses." Quincy complained of "State, magnificence, and ostentation, the natural attendants of riches," and noted that "the number and subjection of their slaves tend this way." (Except that Portsmouth had fewer slaves, he was echoing the sentiments his kinsman, John Adams, expressed about the elegant city upon the Piscataqua.)

Miles Brewton House

Photo by Frank Haskell, courtesy of Carolina Art Association/Gibbs Art Gallery

Charleston was ruled by a merchant class that owned plantations, and a planter class that, throughout the Colonial period, was also engaged heavily in trade. "They looked to the Augustan London . . . of Queen Anne and the Georges, rather than the older traditions of English country families." Louis Wright, a twentieth-century South Carolinian whose words I have just quoted, is as careful as William Byrd II to tell us of the other side of Augustan urbanity, its shallowness and its cruelty.

Charleston paid a heavy price for its emulation of the Great World. Governor John Drayton lamented that "the citizens of South Carolina were too much prejudiced in favor of British manners, customs, and knowledge, to imagine that anywhere than in England, anything of advantage could be obtained." Obeisance to style became transmuted into deference to greater sophistication in finance, and, finally, to a surrender to British control of commerce. Eugene Genovese and other contemporary historians have pointed out that Charleston's dependence on British traders, especially Scots, explains how she was able to ship a greater volume of goods than New York though she had only half the urban population.

In the first decades of the nineteenth century, Charleston's magnates ceased to work at mercantile life at the hard-driving pace of their fathers and grandfathers. Increasingly they acquired some of the worst qualities of the West Indian planters, including indolence and drunkenness. Though they now lived in the city, most of the time, they became less and less urbane. Many grew proud, and irritable, pretentious and lazy.

Independence?

UNLIKE THE YANKEES and the merchants of Philadelphia, Charleston did not gain economic independence with political independence. She failed to create her own credit system or her own merchant marine. She relied increasingly on others to ship her goods, to finance them and to insure them. As she came to rely on cotton as her staple export, she fell into a worse dependence: others set her prices. She therefore came into a new, subtle economic thralldom, enjoying none of the benefits of the old mercantilism.

The central determining fact of Charleston's life at the end of the Colonial period was that her elegant elite could not, or would not, seize control of her economic destiny.

She was weakened not only by her continuing economic dependence on Britain but also by her special exertions in achieving political freedom. The Revolutionary War was, for the South, its first civil war. It is often the case in such conflicts among brothers that alignments are determined more by antipathy than by interest. The forces seeking independence were led by planter-merchants of the coastal area who resented being treated as colonials rather than provincials. Yet they were well aware that the profitability of their chief crops—indigo, rice and marine supplies—was artificially sustained by the British mercantilist system of subsidies and protected markets. It seems that their pride was at stake to a greater degree than their avarice. Seldom have creditors sought independence from debtors, yet the Charleston nabobs cut themselves loose from the British, with whom they enjoyed a very favorable balance of trade.

Upcountry, in what George Washington later called "the most miserable pine barren," and in the low, red dirt hills of the Piedmont, a long, bloody and confused fraternal struggle lasted more than a decade. It reopened the antipathies between coastal planters and the upcountry farmers, trappers and Indian traders which had already produced pitched battles on the Great Pee Dee and at Alamance. Many upcountry people sided with the British government rather than with the lowlanders, who were familiar and proximate enemies.

155

Intersectional squabbles, according to one South Carolina historian, made "many a man . . . scorn to follow, against a sovereign who had given him his land, the cross-country politicians from whom he felt he had suffered far greater wrongs than any imposed by Parliament or King." The bloodiest battles of the war were fought between Tories and Whigs. British and "Continentals" were relatively respectful antagonists. Their irregular partners became unforgiving and savage enemies. The South was ravaged by regular armies and by roving bands of partisans. After the war, the merchant-planters who owned indigo plantations and those who had sold marine supplies lost their imperial subsidies and were turned away from their old protected markets. Rice producers had to fight to recover their customers and find new ones. Tens of thousands of slaves had been freed, or stolen (depending upon the teller), by the British forces.

The planters and merchants of Charleston won a revolutionary struggle and lost huge quantities of capital. The backcountry, which was heavily Tory in its sentiments, lost less, for its products were not generally sold on world markets. Politically, it gained the substitution of a weak government that had a real interest in protecting whites from Indians for a strong British government that expressed some sympathy with the Indians and showed very little interest in the westward expansion of a scarce white labor force.

The South suffered more from the war than other sections, and came back more slowly. In 1791–92 per capita exports from South Carolina were only half what they had been in 1768–72, and though Georgia was less dependent on export business, it, too, was crippled commercially. This experience contrasted with that of New York, which increased its exports by 30 percent. Massachusetts was also comfortably ahead; it had very little to recover from, relative to South Carolina; the British departed early, and there were excellent profits from privateering.

Philadelphia's wartime situation was equally pleasant but for a reverse reason. During the war itself the British had come early and stayed. There were violins, candlelight, warmth and good business in Philadelphia while Washington's rebels froze at Valley Forge, nearby. After the war, the loss of the huge West Indies market in salt meat and wheat flour, a decline in associated shipbuilding and a regional cost inflation arising from a postwar buying panic to use up accumulated specie (wartime hoarding?) all produced such a severe depression that for three years even a weakened South Carolina exported more than Pennsylvania. But the Napoleonic Wars presented new opportunities for Philadelphia traders who could find their way past the intervening blockades to either France or Britain, and in the late 1790's Philadelphia was able not only to sustain its population race with New York but also to sustain itself as the nation's richest city, as well as its capital.

Thus, while survivors of the War for Independence in Georgia and the Carolinas nursed their wounds and emerged, groggily, from the shelter of a mercantilist system that had been tactless and overbearing but ever so remunerative, elsewhere in the 1790's port cities were full of crowds and bustle. Baltimore, Philadelphia and New York were enjoying new adventures in architecture. Charleston was beginning to lag. She grew at less than the national rate of population increase in the postwar decades.

Charleston's oligarchs, at the outset, did not lament these differences. The merchants of Philadelphia, of Boston, of New York and of brash young Baltimore were dividing a growing pie with many newcomers, some of the fresh waves of immigrants whom the Charlestonians—not so long ago immigrants themselves— now found rather distasteful.

As time passed, Charleston's differences from other American port cities grew more obvious. Concentration of wealth among southerners, generally, was greater than in the North. Esquires, gentlemen, officials and merchants held twice the wealth of their counterparts in New England. A free population of 650,000 in the South owned half the wealth of all the colonies. The other half was distributed among twice as many northerners, 400,000 slaves and a few indentured servants. To look just at the urban contrast, recalling that Charleston was the only city of size in the South at the time, the average southern white citydweller owned assets worth $41,650 in 1980 dollars, in contrast to an average of $12,400 in New England and $18,600 in the Middle Colonies.

Already Charleston was diverging from the somewhat more balanced class structure emerging elsewhere. Her merchants, as we have noted, were wholesalers and jobbers, not shopkeepers, insurers or financiers. Nor were they producers of luxury goods (there are splendid exceptions like Thomas Elfe, but the statement is generally correct). The city ceased to develop a strong middle class that could cross-pollinate with older wealth. Her oligarchs looked to Europe, and to the past, for their standards of behavior and of architecture. Elsewhere, even in Savannah, Americans were beginning to move with greater self-confidence toward cultural independence.

The springtime of the Republic was fertile in artistic invention. Very little of this reached Charleston. In Charleston, Huguenot merchants, now with two generations of wealth and intermarriage behind them, sent their sons to study in Geneva (French-speaking and Protestant) as well as London. They were well aware of French and British architectural ideas and employed them in their town houses, at considerable expense. But they did not seek out those architects, like Joseph Jacques Ramée or Benjamin Henry Latrobe, who used those ideas freshly and with panache.* They do not even seem to have given residential commissions to James Hoban when he lived in their city, though when he later designed the

---

* In the North the new nation was the beneficiary of the skills of an assembly of professionals of rigorous French education. Among those born in France were Ramée, who practiced for five years in New York, Philadelphia and Baltimore (1811–16). Ramée's plan for Union College, in Schenectady, New York, rivals Thomas Jefferson's for the University of Virginia. Maximilian Godefroy was the first professor of architecture in the United States, a church-builder and participant with Benjamin Latrobe in the Baltimore Exchange. Joseph François Mangin is best known for his work on the New York City Hall, and Stephen Hallet for his designs for the National Capitol in Washington. Major Pierre Charles L'Enfant not only laid out the basic design for the city of Washington but commenced a château for Robert Morris in Philadelphia.

Gabriel Manigault
*Courtesy of the
Albert-Knox Gallery*

White House they were proud a man so authenticated had worked in Charleston. Nor did they engage, for residential work, Robert Mills, a native-born genius, though they were willing to entrust to him public commissions, nearly all up-state.*

By 1790 overseers managed most plantations, most of the year, eating a mush of bark to fight off malaria. Many owners spent long holiday seasons, as well as the malaria season, in Charleston. If they were very rich, they traveled north in the hot months; in some cases they spent decades traveling or studying in Europe.

Gabriel Manigault was such a traveler, and he brought back fashionable architectural ideas from his travels abroad. The gifted namesake of the carpenter-

---

* *During this period, however, some of the Charleston oligarchs, like the Pinckneys, were architecturally daring on their remote plantations. The Pinckneys were always exceptions to any rule. As far back as the 1740's, before Peter Harrison experimented with Palladian forms in New England, Charles Pinckney had commissioned the first mansion in the South to demonstrate the idea of a "grand" portico (not two superimposed orders, as at Drayton Hall or the Miles Brewton House). It perished long ago; photographs show that its white plastered pilasters were not quite pillars, but they were boldly set against the red brick of a forward-thrust pavilion under a pediment. The effect was very close to the full temple form, which appeared throughout the South seventy or eighty years later under Jefferson's urging. There was, of course, El Dorado in the 1780's (see Chapter Six).*

founder, he was the beneficiary of intervening generations of rice-planting and wholesale trading. One grandfather was a successful speculator in Charleston's urban growth, and another possessed an excellent architectural library. The progression from carpenter to architect, which occupied a single lifetime in such cases as William Buckland or Thomas McIntyre, took a little longer in the case of the Manigaults, and, as a consequence, Gabriel was accounted an amateur. (By this it was meant, like Thomas Jefferson, Peter Harrison or Dr. William Thornton, first architect of the National Capitol, he need not earn his living by architectural fees.)

Manigault made the pilgrimage of Charleston Huguenot oligarchs to study in Geneva, traveled widely in Europe and read law in London, where his father-in-law, Ralph Izard, kept a house on Berners Street. Though he was a Tory (he swore allegiance to the Crown in 1780, as had many others, including Wade Hampton—see Chapter Twenty-three), the charming traveler was welcomed back among the elite when the war was over and given commissions for two distin-

Joseph Manigault House, Charleston
Courtesy of the South Carolina Historical Society

guished buildings, the Chapel of the Orphan House and the mansion of his brother Joseph.

In Manigault's work one can see, in fully developed form, the curved staircases, oval bays and soft Adamesque ornament, the gentle, almost frail style of Charleston's silver age. One can see it as well in the oval drawing room of the Nathaniel Russell House. Here the opulent alliance of Rhode Island and Charleston expressed itself in its full glitter and sheen. But the South's grande dame was tiring. She was wary. She avoided passion; she even avoided exertion. She was comfortable amid the smooth, the sinuous, the derivative. She approved small-figured ornament, delicate fanlights and languidly drooping plaster swags. Hers was the architecture of autumn; her grapes gathered final sweetness before the frost.

Meanwhile James De Wolf's ships shuttled around the golden triangle between their home port of Bristol, the West Coast of Africa and the convenient wharves of Charleston. The Yankees grew rich and put their winnings into textile mills and iron foundries and new patents. A new power was rising upon the thin soils and the rocky headlands of the North. Commerce was in the ascendant, and the great names of Charleston had turned their proud backs on commerce.

CHAPTER 11

Savannah: William Jay and Robert Mills

G EORGIA, LIKE MAINE, was a frontier province. Like Maine, it was held by Indians of great military skill, and by the end of the eighteenth century had been penetrated by European invaders only at its extremities. Savannah, its cultural capital, was and is very different from Charleston, just up the coast and up the social ladder in the Colonial period. Savannah's plan conforms to the muscular order of a Roman camp; Charleston's streets appear to be whimsical because the city is compiled of a gaggle of tiny suburbs, originally built around swamps and ponds, each laid out according to a different axis.

Charleston was reclining in her silver age while Savannah was booming, and providing commissions for the controlled yet fervent architecture of William Jay, an architecture of a uniquely athletic urbanity.

Jay worked in Savannah a bare five years from 1817 to 1822, while he was still in his twenties. Savannah was young, too. It had only begun to grow after independence.

Georgia had not produced much rice or indigo, and so it had less than South Carolina to lose from the war. There was also less of Georgia to lose anything. The power of its inland Indians was so great that only very slowly were they pushed away from the coast; in truth, until a Yankee tinkerer named Eli Whitney came to Georgia to work on a Rhode Island general's bonus plantation, there was little reason to push them. Whitney tried to find some means of removing the sticky seeds from the fibers of the only kind of cotton that seemed willing to grow on the scrubby, sandy property given General Nathanael Greene by the state of Georgia as recompense for Greene's services in organizing the victory of the independence forces in the South. The gin he eventually invented worked well enough to make that plant a profitable crop for Greene's successors and, as machine and plant were modified, profitable for all the upland South to this day.*

The cotton gin and Eli Whitney began Savannah's boom years; the steamboat, William Pitt and Napoleon Bonaparte accelerated the boom's rise. Pitt and Bonaparte were the protagonists in another round of imperial conflict between Britain and France, which tied up the shipping and sucked up the economic resources of those two countries during the first two decades of American independence.

Skirmishes with the United States sputtered along the horizon of Britain's attention as it dealt with the global threat posed by Napoleon between 1812 and 1815, but except for the expedition against New Orleans which made Andrew Jackson presidential, Britain undertook no serious campaigns against the vulnerable southern states. Meanwhile, the disabilities of both Britain and France opened the way to American merchants and seamen, and when Britain finally put Napoleon away in his second and final island exile in 1815, the steamboat was ready to give the intrepid but financially frail Americans another modest edge.

Brash, tough Savannah was, with New York and Baltimore, among the chief beneficiaries of these machines and these events. After the close of the War of 1812, what had been a cotton boom became a cotton frenzy. The price per bale more than doubled between 1814 and 1818. Production also expanded and, multiplying more by more, produced an extraordinary burst of wealth. This was Savannah's hour; it outstripped Charleston in competing for the cotton business of the interior. Savannah's merchants were not complacent; they were willing to try even such radical innovations as the new technology of steam.

Charleston had done well with her lazy Ashley and her torpid Cooper (which, Charlestonians say, form the Atlantic Ocean when they meet at the Battery) when travelers had to paddle or push their way upstream. But Savannah had been built upon a river that was navigable far into the hinterland after steamboats were able to move against the current.

Savannah grew prosperous with postrevolutionary cotton; its boom years came after 1817, with steam navigation. In the next decade its population increased by 50 percent. No longer did cotton and tobacco come downriver on flatboats, which had to be broken up after unloading. New, shallow draft vessels were devised, which could be reused, chugging upstream and down, up to Augusta and down to Savannah, again and again. Steam navigation permitted Savannah to invade the backcountry constituency of Charleston; the spoils of that invasion accumulated.

Soon Savannah's merchants and factors, men like William Scarbrough,† were rich enough to enter the transatlantic competition with New York, Boston and

---

* Some modifications began immediately—see Chapter Twenty-three; some more important ones waited a generation—see Chapter Twenty-four.

† I am solemnly assured by the Reverend Raymond E. Davis of Savannah, the Scarbrough expert, that this is and was the family's approved spelling, various plaques and histories to the contrary notwithstanding.

Baltimore. Upland cotton producers could set their bales aboard steamships at Augusta, pile them on the wharves of Savannah and see them loaded on ocean-going steamships bound for the British market. No upland planter within reach of the Savannah River needed any longer to slog the slow overland route to Charleston. By 1825 the silver age of coastal South Carolina was over, though she was full of pride. The palm had passed decisively—though briefly—to Savannah.

Let us now move carefully: we are about to enter sacred ground. It was not just money that came into Savannah at this time. Talent and sympathy, boldness and aesthetic sensitivity, economic competence and artistic genius came too. This is the context conducive to art.

In Savannah, for half a decade, there existed the reinforcing relationship of an architect of genuine genius, just into his twenties, and a group of clients who valued his gifts and were able to pay for an expression of those gifts. These clients were, in their way, as amazing as the artist.

I have puzzled much about how this came to be, and have concluded that it must be one of those instances in which things become possible in a province that are not possible in the metropolis. Sometimes energies are drawn to the extremities of a social system, where they arc across the open scene, flash and accomplish miracles. In such places people say, "If we don't do it, nobody will." They can say so because they have already enjoyed such success that they do not doubt they can do it.

The Jay Connection

ONE OF THE REASONS those clients were there, strange to say, was because they were related, in complex ways, to William Jay, father of the architect. The elder Jay had been a young genius too, but at another art, oratory. He was a celebrated boy evangelist, speaking more than a thousand times to large audiences before he came of age. He was no mere showman, however. He was known and respected by John Wesley, Bishop Wilberforce and Hannah More, whose tastes were for the genuine. More important for this story, he was also known to Cornelius Winter and Robert Spear. Winter was a teacher of Negroes. He went to America in the middle of the eighteenth century, determined to help educate the slaves, despite the admonition of another evangelist, George Whitefield, that he would be "whipped off the plantations."

On his travels Winter found, in Savannah, Robert Bolton, a saddler and Georgia's first postmaster, who, it happens, was the grandson of another preacher to Negroes. (Bolton's grandfather had faced down a Pennsylvania grand jury for this activity, proscribed in many colonies by custom if not by law.) Bolton told Winter that he could open a public exposition in his house for blacks and whites. Bolton's brother-in-law, the merchant (and future governor) James Habersham, told Winter, "You shall instruct my negroes whoever else refuses you." Winter's

163

efforts were, however, easy to brush off, despite their sponsorship, because he lacked the full credentials of ordination. So Habersham and Bolton sent him to England to take Holy Orders. There he told the elder Jay of his adventures. The evangelist was now one of England's most celebrated preachers, residing in Bath. When Bolton's son appeared on a cotton-trading expedition, Jay welcomed him into his house. Bolton fell in love with Jay's daughter, Anne, married her and began persuading his brother-in-law, the younger William Jay, to bring his manifest architectural talent to America.

Robert Spear was a Manchester cotton factor who knew the elder Jay and was represented in Savannah by the Boltons. He was an avid searcher after ideas and talent. Having found a strain of cotton in Cádiz that had promise, he shipped it off to the Boltons to try in America; it seems possible that this is how Sea Island cotton found its way to America.* Spear also found a beautiful young woman, fell in love with her and had her taught graces by the accomplished Jay sisters. In the household too, of course, was the young William Jay, and Spear joined Bolton and Winter in coming under the spell of this extremely attractive young man. The painter William Etty remembered the beauty of the younger Jay all his life. Our best guess about how he actually looked is a portrait by Etty in the Museum of York, in England, that may be of him (the subject is listed as "unidentified" in the museum catalogue). We can learn more from what others said of him, and, more important, the testimony of action: he was a man others wanted very much to have near them.

In Savannah a small, self-confident and unconventional community, of which the Boltons and Habershams were leading figures, was waxing rich. Richard Richardson, a West Indian merchant, joined the group when he married Bolton's sister. To their plantation income he added the salary of the presidency of the Savannah branch of the Bank of the United States, and the powerful sponsorship of the Philadelphia financier Stephen Girard. By the marriage of Richardson into the Bolton family, William Jay acquired a third powerful potential client, while he was emerging, in his fifteenth and sixteenth years, as a person of ready wit and talent with a pencil.

He was growing up, as well, in a household sensitive to architecture. Though his father had gained an international reputation through his forensic skills, he had begun life as a stonemason, working on the most stupefying product of West Indian *nouveau richesse* (transplanted to Wiltshire), William Beckford's Fonthill Abbey. After he became a celebrated preacher and removed to Bath, his son grew up in a magnificent townscape created by the architectural genius of two John Woods, father and son. Their clients were eighteenth-century believers in the curative powers of the waters—and of the social life—of that spa. For a boy with an eye for architecture and an instinct for adventure, Bath was the right place to be led into a career of design and building.

* For the introduction of other strains of cotton by other architectural clients, see Chapter Twenty-four.

William Jay (?),
by William Etty
Courtesy of the York City Art Gallery

When he was ready, William Jay the younger went off to London to apprentice himself to an architect. There he became adept in the sort of experiments in the manipulation of classical elements, and in permitting light to enter from unexpected angles into interior space, that the great John Soane was employing to dazzle the English eye.

Though the young Jay secured one important commission, the Albion Chapel, and did very well with it, the economic strains of the Napoleonic period were not kind to architects. Even Soane had much less work than his genius justified. But in Savannah, European troubles were creating American opportunity. When the miscreant Corsican was safely packed off to St. Helena, and British consumers became free to satisfy their own demand for cotton goods, and British manufacturers could resume the marketing of those goods to the "developing world," especially Latin America, raw cotton was called forth from America in exchange for a stream of pounds sterling.

William Jay rode that stream westward to join his sister Anne and her merchant-planter husband in Georgia. He arrived in Savannah on the *Dawn* in Decem-

165

Richardson House
Courtesy of the Library of Congress

ber 1817. Savannah's cotton wealth was piled high upon the docks, ready to be shipped to the ravenous mills. Jay climbed ashore, past the bales, and set to work at once. He had been sketching a mansion for his brother-in-law, Richard Richardson; the foundations had probably already been laid before his arrival.*

Nothing like the splendors he now wrought for this most sympathetic of clients had appeared in Savannah before. Indeed, the curving interior walls, the serpentine portico and the semicircular stairs of the Richardson House were so sophisticated that the best Charleston work of the time seemed a little amateur and provincial by comparison. The columns in its hall bore gilt capitals. Brass glimmered upon inlaid mahogany on the stair. There were tricks and surprises with light. An amber skylight in the hall carried the eye aloft; in the dining room, a Greek key design stood against the light in a strip above the sideboard. The corners of the parlor were deliberately made ambiguous by fanlike plasterwork.

Already, in this house for his sponsor and relative, Jay felt free to play with Classic forms (in the same way Bernard Maybeck used Gothic tags in his work a

* He had also been sketching a church for Savannah, but it was not built to his design.

century later). Jay would take an acanthus leaf and use it to support a balcony, stretch his columns, twist his porticoes, sculpt his staircases, mingle wood and metal and stone in extravagant ways, fearless of what other architects might think, just as Richardson, his client, was fearless of what other merchants might say.

The merchants, of course, were so buoyant in their prosperity that they were little perturbed by novelty. They embraced it. Jay's next client was William Scarbrough, who set his steamship, the *Savannah*, in a race against the world.

Parlor of the Richardson House
Photo by Van Jones Martin. Courtesy of Mills Lane.

William Scarbrough

*Courtesy of the Georgia Department
of Archives and History*

Scarbrough owned cotton land in South Carolina and experimented with new marketing devices and new mechanical devices. Jay gave this buccaneering entrepreneur a vast entrance hall, more than two stories high, with a balcony supported by great Doric columns. It was lit by an outsize fanlight, a muscular manifesto of virtuosity, in which Scarbrough and Jay declared their independence of one of the finicking conventions of the time, those prim little fanlights placed above Federal doorways, which could be seen everywhere along the coast.

At the back of the Scarbrough house is what is now called the ballroom, with marble mantels and with piazzas at either end for the respite of dancers on summer evenings. Flanking the entrance hall are two parlors with curved ends and curved mantels. The house was intended to impress, and it did. Scarbrough was the host there at a reception during the most famous series of social events in Savannah's history, a gala dinner party and dance for President James Monroe in 1819.

Scarbrough has left to us a letter that admits us into the field of emotional force between Jay and his clients. Writing to his wife, he spoke with joy of the new house Jay had provided them and gleefully reported the first sight of a "temporary pavillion of great extent on the Church Square . . . lined with red Baize or flannel with festoons and pilasters of white muslin . . . elegantly done—and by candle light will look most superbly. The President will be pleased by Savannah . . . he may be recd. at costly and splendid rate; but nowhere with such pure and genuine taste,—Jay will begin to attain the prominence, which low jealousy and perverted judgement would not before reward him."

Scarbrough House

Photo by Van Jones Martin. Courtesy of the Historic Savannah Foundation, Inc., Savannah, Ga.

Entrance hall,
Scarbrough House

Photo by Van Jones Martin

Branch Bank of the United States in Savannah
From the collection of the Georgia Historical Society

It may be that Scarbrough and Bolton, Richardson and Habersham were themselves feeling some of that "low jealousy." Perhaps their architect, still not yet thirty, was the lightning rod for "perverted judgement" that resented the sudden affluence paraded in his designs. But Jay had four or five years of splendid opportunity while his clients remained rich. For Richardson he executed plans for the Branch Bank of the United States. When he designed and acted as a contractor for the Savannah Theater, Richardson purchased from him the indenture by which he was to be paid his fees (a "municipal bond" which Richardson, but not Jay, could then afford to hold).

In Savannah Jay had no thoroughly trained architectural competitors in the latest international fashions to whisper admonitions against experiment into the ears of his clients. The neighbors might object, but he was singularly free from what might today be called "professional drag." He could dare—and his clients, confident in their prosperity, could dare with him.

For his next house, built in 1820 for Archibald Bulloch, a young merchant-planter, Jay provided a series of essays in the use of the circle.* The portico was an engaged circular temple of Corinthian columns upon a podium. The entrance hall contained a bizarre inner nest of six columns encasing a circular stairway, and at the rear was a round drawing room under a dome.

There are a number of subsequent houses attributed to Jay that are more cautious experiments with curves. In 1818 Alexander Telfair received another

* *Like his Albion Chapel, the Bulloch House shows Jay's affinity to the geometric Classicism of the architects of the British and French enlightenment.*

**Archibald Bulloch
and his family**
*From the collection of the
Georgia Historical Society*

Archibald Bulloch House
Courtesy of the Georgia Historical Society

1 7 1

Entrance hall of
the Archibald
Bulloch House
*Courtesy of the Georgia
Historical Society*

demonstration of the flexibility of the fanlight form, set in a restrained, clean
façade with only four other windows on the street side. The art collection of the
Telfair Academy is displayed today in two long drawing rooms with elliptical
ends, and in another round room and a matching parlor with Soanian recessed
corner-curves. That academy still serves Savannah, though the theater and the
Bank of the United States Jay designed have gone the way of the Bulloch House
—lost to fire, vandalism and "progress."

   Jay's appearance in South Carolina shortly after 1820 as a migrant architect
seeking work—newspaper advertisements tell us he was forced to turn his hand to
the speculative building of a Gothic seaside villa, and to promoting urban development schemes—suggests that his clients in Savannah were no longer able to

Alexander Telfair House

afford him. And indeed, 1820 was a year of disasters for Savannah. A fire destroyed much of the residential area in January. In September a ship from the West Indies carried into port the yellow-fever virus, and an epidemic wiped out one quarter of the city's population.

Savannah's troubles had actually begun about the time William Jay arrived, though they did not become apparent for a while. The city had grown marvelously rich marvelously fast, but it had only one source for all that wealth; like many small suppliers of great industrial companies in the twentieth century, Savannah found that the slightest dyspepsia on the part of the buyer meant disaster to the dependent seller. And from 1819 onward, the managers of the British financial system felt the need to take measures to alleviate indigestion. All over the world, from the streets of Manchester to the back roads of Georgia, lesser folk found themselves out of credit, out of work or out of food. The clients of William Jay experienced the virulence of the British disease in 1819–22; the clients of Charles and James Dakin were to experience much the same symptoms in 1837–39 (see Chapter Sixteen).

The second war for American independence (also known as the War of 1812) was, from a British point of view, merely an incidental irritation accompanying the world war against Napoleonic France. In 1815 both the main event and the sideshow came to an end. American manufacturers, protected by Jefferson's embargo and by wartime prohibitions on trade, were suddenly confronted with the full force of British competitors, who turned on them and dumped huge quantities of cotton goods, especially, on the American market. This drove out of business many American firms, largely in the central states and the North. British shipping interests, released from wartime service, returned to compete with American shippers in the same regions; freight rates and reshipment profits fell almost as rapidly as manufacturing profits.

Simultaneously, the huge increase in British purchases of raw cotton, needed to supply the mills, drove up prices in the South. Higher prices had their usual effect: commensurate increases in the amount of cotton land going under cultivation. This land was often bought with borrowed money. Southern planters and shippers enjoyed that brief and intoxicating prosperity of which Savannah was the most conspicuous beneficiary, and, within Savannah, it was those who had the closest associations with the British market who were able to commission the works of William Jay. To buy the talent of this brilliant young purveyor of the latest British architectural ideas, they, too, used borrowed money. They borrowed more to furnish their shining new houses expensively and to clothe themselves. A flood of southern indebtedness was presented through the banking system, just as the capacity of northern banks to offset it by receipts from manufacturing and shipping had all but disappeared.

Then the British, concerned at the flow of specie (gold and silver) that had gone out to pay for cotton purchases, sharply reduced their willingness to accept American paper. The result was a catastrophe for Americans in debt, and very hard times even for those who had stayed liquid. Cotton output in 1819 was double that of 1814, and cotton prices were half what they had been in 1818. Freight rates in 1819 were less than a third what they had been in 1815. The directors of the Bank of the United States tightened their lending policy in 1818 to catch up with the British and to save the bank. Not for the last time, the bank took the blame for international conditions beyond the control or the ken of most Americans. "The Bank was saved," William M. Gouge said at the time, "and the people were ruined."

William Scarbrough had sold his plantations to produce cash for his steamship investments; he was dependent on brisk trade with high freight rates to restore his fortunes and was one of the first to go under. The S.S. *Savannah* was the first steamship to cross the Atlantic, but even its maiden voyage, on May 20, 1819, was not profitable. Scarbrough was forced to sell more assets at auction, and a year later he was jailed for debt. The support mechanisms provided the financially fallen by the American mercantile community were demonstrated when he appeared in *Shaw's Directory* in 1822 as the president of a marine and fire insurance company, and his still affluent relatives bought his house at the auction, so, like

Nicholas Biddle (see Chapter Fifteen) some years later, he was not forced onto the street merely because his creditors foreclosed on his house.*

We have some indications that Scarbrough was still dreaming of faster and faster steamboats and larger and larger cotton crops as late as 1836, long after his house had gone on the auction block. By that time nearly all the others who had made up Jay's small circle of clients had gone under as well. As the chronicler of the Bolton family put it, "Men went to bed rich and rose up beggars." There were no purchase orders for cotton. Brokers, like the Boltons, were caught with huge inventories for which there were no customers. That firm alone lost twenty thousand pounds, and went bankrupt.

Archibald Bulloch's mansion became a boardinghouse; it went on the block in 1822. In that year Richard Richardson resigned under pressure as president of the Planter's Bank; he sold his house and disappeared from Savannah in 1828. It is from the Girard papers that we learn he was forced by the collapse of his mainland fortunes to go back to trading in the Caribbean system, and died at sea in 1833.

With Scarbrough, Richardson and Bulloch gone, with the Boltons bankrupt or nearly so, William Jay was without sponsorship in Savannah. He had, apparently, already done some work in Charleston, and became, for a while, the equivalent of a civil servant (not happily and not for the last unhappy time). He was able to secure one final grand commission there, a house for William Mason Smith, on Meeting Street. Smith was another minister's son. His father had been bishop of South Carolina and founder of the College of Charleston. The bishop also married an heiress, Elizabeth Paget, and thus gained, in the words of his biographer, "better advantages of condition than were possessed by the clergy generally." He left to his son six thousand acres of prime rice-growing land, so the cotton panic of 1820 did not afflict the family profoundly.

Architecturally, the Smiths were Anglophile and sophisticated. The senior Smith's Bishop's House on Glebe Street was one of Charleston's great mansions, and he was by marriage rich enough to repair regularly to England for respite from his pastoral chores. Even in 1768, sniffed his Charleston biographer, it was "more common for the inhabitant of this Province to cross the Atlantic . . . than to [go] to the Northern Colonies, where they . . . were less at home." Indeed, during "the misunderstanding between the Parent Country and the Colonies" the Bishop was "a loyal and faithful subject of the British realm, in church and state." These

---

* Anthony F. C. Wallace (an anthropologist who writes history as more historians should write it) tells us how and why the system worked. The mutual insurance company served to spread not only the risk of losing goods but the risk of losing executive jobs as well. It was not only "an underwriting mechanism but also a source of employment for . . . financially embarrassed associates." Businessmen at the time, struggling together to be free of the European imperial system, supported one another. "The failure of a fellow merchant . . . was like the wounding of a fellow officer in combat or the illness of a fellow missionary in a heathen land . . . to let him sink in adversity would only weaken, not strengthen, the survivors." (Anthony F. C. Wallace, Rockdale: The Growth of an American Village in the Early Industrial Revolution, p. 50.)

William Mason Smith
House on Meeting
Street
*Courtesy of the South Carolina
Historical Society*

words, published in 1820, give some sense of Charleston's continuing affinity for things British. They also suggest that William Jay was fortunate in finding a final client for his Regency style, for he was probably running into difficulties not only from a failing economy but also from upcountry resistance to his urbane British manner. Even in Charleston, cotton was replacing the Tidewater crops to become the dominant influence on the life of the region. That meant that the sober Scotch-Irish of the Piedmont were coming into power, replacing the transatlantic elite, which had been Jay's source of clients. The upcountry descendants of displaced crofters could hardly have felt at ease with the youthful Regency wit.*

Jay did secure, perhaps with the help of Smith, the post as chief architect for South Carolina's commission charged with building a group of upcountry jails and courthouses, and he designed several of them (for which the ubiquitous Russell Warren served as contractor). But then a native son appeared to contest his place, a man of humorless steadiness more consonant than Jay's ebullience with Presbyterian preferences in unsteady times. That man was Robert Mills, and he soon replaced Jay, both on the commission and as designer for its buildings.

Jay gave up and returned to England. He found some work, finally, in another boom town, the spa of Cheltenham. There, we have learned from the indefatigable researches of Hanna Lerski—recently published—he designed another large house, Watermoor, and it appears that he was also able to prove his skill at large-scale urban design of the sort John Nash had made fashionable in Regent's Park, in London. He laid out one whole side of the "Parade" in Pittville, at the edge of

* For upcountry taste see Part Four.

Cheltenham. But Jay was a moth always to fly too close to the flame; like Nash himself, like Latrobe, like the Dakins, like Bulfinch, he went bankrupt in his efforts to link architecture to speculation.

In Jay's case the collapse of his Pittville schemes in 1829 seems to have broken his spirit. His father used all his remaining influence to find him work at a safe distance, and he was finally forced to accept what must have seemed to him to be a sinecured exile—an appointment to Mauritius, an island as remote as St. Helena. It had been the home of the dodo bird, and was so removed from civilization that it had served as the setting for *Paul et Virginie*, Bernardin de Saint-Pierre's parable of the simple life. Mauritius was no place for a man whom his apparently dour father described as possessing "a large share of wit and humor, qualities always dangerous and commonly injurious to the possessor." Jay, said the mourning clergyman, had been "led into expense by his admirers and flatterers," and, one suspects, into an addiction to alcohol like that of other architects, Louis Sullivan, Minard Lafever, John Notman, Harvey Ellis and Charles Rennie Mackintosh among them. William Jay died in this place of exile in 1837.

Southern Exertions

TYRONE POWER, the great Irish actor who would have been a boon companion to Jay, visited Georgia in 1834 and reported seeing in Savannah "several very ambitious-looking dwellings, built by a European architect for wealthy merchants during the palmy days of trade . . . They are mostly deserted, or let for boarding-houses, and have that decayed look which is so melancholy, and nowhere arrives sooner than in this climate." How quickly that decay had come! It was only twelve years since the completion of Jay's last work. The efforts of Savannah and Charleston to reverse the course of decline had petered out just a year or two before Power's visit. While those exertions lasted, they provided many more opportunities for architects, though they had come too late for Jay.

In the 1820's Charleston was still very rich, but her responses were slow. She was the chief casualty of a series of blows to the South administered by the scruples of Virginia Presidents. Thomas Jefferson was the first of them to put the South at an economic disadvantage to New England, preferring purity to prosperity. His policy of neutrality in the Napoleonic Wars had led to Acts of Embargo and Nonintercourse, which meant, in effect, that southern cotton and rice could not be sold either to the British or the French, and that southern consumers were without access to the European goods on which they had become dependent.

New England was handed a captive southern market for its manufactured goods. An enormous burst of textile production ensued in the North. Yankee peddlers had a field day along the back roads of the South. Along the coast, vessels from New York entered into a lively competition with those of Liverpool, carrying southern cotton to the mills of the Midlands and the fledgling mills of New England. Southern shipyards had nearly given up the contest. Only a few diehards like William Scarbrough were still keeping up the fight; by 1825 even they had been vanquished. Charleston never really entered the contest; all the pineries of North Carolina were not enough to build a single southern shipyard to slug it out on equal terms with those of Maine.

Then, while the whole country was recovering from the War of 1812, and the South was beginning to gird itself for a race to the new lands of the Mississippi Valley acquired in the Louisiana Purchase, James Madison drove home a second blow. His rejoinder to a plea by the South for federally financed internal improvements was a relapse into his old Jeffersonian orthodoxy. He vetoed legislation for canals and turnpikes that John C. Calhoun had extricated from the Congress. The veto came despite Calhoun's warning that only by such a system could the South be bound into the expanding nation, that the price of Jeffersonian purity (now tarnished by the expediencies of two decades) would be "disunion . . . the greatest of all calamities, next to the loss of liberty, and even to that in its consequences."

Madison's veto opened the West to DeWitt Clinton and the cash-rich investors of New York, who needed no federal financing. They built the Erie Canal and diverted the produce of the Great Lakes region through the Canal and down the Hudson. The Southeast was making other choices, reinvesting in land and slaves, attempting to reproduce itself in the valley of the West, but hesitant, most of the time, to divert capital from an economy it understood into indistinct possibilities.

There was one last spasm of energy left in South Carolina, one final desperate effort to deploy its declining store of disposable capital, not into more slaves and more land and more cotton, but instead into a lively interchange with the West and its diversified agriculture. The state legislature laid on its citizens, and especially on Charlestonians (the tax structure was particularly onerous to the city), a heavy burden of new excises to finance a program of canals, turnpikes and that group of courthouses and educational facilities in the newer upcountry counties which had provided to William Jay his final flicker of opportunity. At the same time they raised the money to defeat Savannah's steamboats with a steam railroad to the Savannah River—a new jump in the checker game—to "land" at Augusta. When that railroad line was completed in the late 1820's, it was the longest in the world. But one railroad to a point near the head of navigation of a short river flowing to the Atlantic was no match for a canal to the Great Lakes, or a railroad to the Ohio River, flowing westward into the richest valley on earth.

The game was over; Charleston could not effectively compete in the race to the West. Her remaining antebellum years degenerated into rancor and false pride, into the bellicosity of the passed-over and the past prime. That final surge of her energy, however, like Savannah's golden years (which preceded and provoked it), provided a splendid set of opportunities for architecture.

Russell Warren, that Yankee peddler of architectural ideas, prospered from the design for a new type of truss he worked out for South Carolina's Great Pee Dee River Bridge. William Jay himself had been an early advocate of cast-iron

Robert Mills and his
wife, daguerreotype by
Jessie H. Whitehurst

From the National Portrait
Gallery, Smithsonian
Institution, Washington, D.C./
Gift of Richard Evans

construction, and he might have built a reputation as an engineer if his erratic disposition had not left him vulnerable to the bulldozer ambition of Robert Mills.

Mills was born in South Carolina in 1781 and went north to learn about canal-building and architecture at the knees of the great Latrobe. He returned to the South and continued his education by observing the work of the Hessian engineer John Christian Senf, who designed the Santee Canal in South Carolina. Past his ceremonial courthouses and jails there soon ran turnpikes and canals, some promoted and some, perhaps, laid out by him, though even he was dogged by the political appointees who were set upon him to supervise these endeavors, "gentlemen not professional men . . . chosen because they enjoy the good opinion of the Legislature."

Mills was the certain author of nine powder magazines on Charleston Neck, a lunatic asylum at Columbia, the De Kalb Monument at Camden, and the marvelous Marine Hospital (a Gothicized West Indian structure still standing on Franklin Street in Charleston). His proposals included canals, swamp reclamation, waterworks, bridges, railroads and lighthouses. He offered a design for a canal between Charleston and Columbia, and thence to the West. He proposed a vast water-supply system for Charleston, and was, he said, the chief proponent of the railroad between Charleston and the Savannah River. He even proposed a monorail system, carrying cars "saddlebags fashion."

179

Martha Laurens, portrait by
Wollaston
Courtesy of the South Carolina Historical Society

Congregational Church, Charleston
Courtesy of the Library of Congress

Two of his buildings, both public and both in Charleston, are good examples of the interplay of architect and patron.* The client for one was the Congregational Church, a leading member of which was Martha Laurens, an admirer of Mills and an understanding amateur of architecture. She and her historian husband, Dr. David Ramsey, may have known James Hoban, for her father, Henry Laurens, is reported to have been the man who recommended Hoban to George Washington as architect for the White House. In any case, her husband reported in his memoirs that she provided Mills with a little sketch for a circular church, from which Mills in 1804 produced the first circular church plan in America.†

Mills's great work in Charleston, however, is the so-called Fireproof Building, finished in 1827. It is a severe, clear, late Palladian building, with a hidden oval hall lit by a skylight. Though its nominal client was the Board of Public Works, its spiritual client, I think, was Thomas Jefferson.

Fiske Kimball wrote in the middle of this century that Jefferson had taken Mills into his household while the young man was working on the White House under Hoban. After observing him and providing access to his great architectural

Fireproof Building
Courtesy of the South Carolina Historical Society

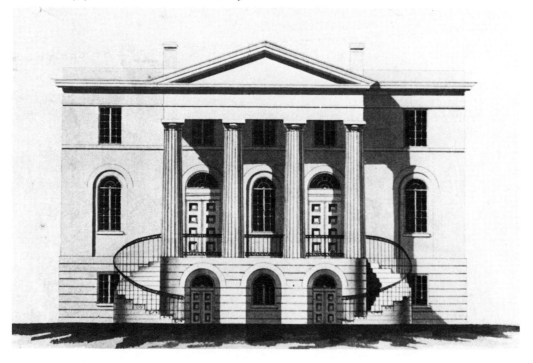

---

* *Better even than his famous works in Washington, D.C., the Washington Monument, the colonnade of the Treasury Department, the Patent Office and the E Street side of the Old Post Office.*

† *I have argued elsewhere that if the source of this idea was not Martha Laurens, it was, in a sense, Maria Cosway.*

library, Jefferson commended him to Latrobe. Latrobe, with Jefferson's encouragement, sustained the education and, even more important, the confidence of this forceful but awkward young man, and launched his career.

Palladio had his Trissino, Peter Harrison his William Shirley, William Jay his Richard Richardson. But Robert Mills had as his sponsors two Presidents of the United States. It was Jefferson who focused Mills's attention on Palladio. Twenty years later, contemplating the problem of the Fireproof Building, Mills turned to his copy of Scamozzi's edition of Palladio, showing a three-story building over a high arcaded basement and presenting a great four-columned portico with a round-arched window to either side. Mills regarded the sides of the building as flanking wings and designed the two pediments to meet in the middle to form a Palladian block.

Others worked from that Palladian prototype, but Mills did not depend upon literal, fussy British Palladianism. His own genius responded better to Latrobe's spare and subtle answer to Palladio's stimuli. Here, in this relatively modest Charleston building, bright and confident in the pale lavender sunlight of the southern summer, stands Mills's cleanest, clearest work. It is the creation of Mills the architect, Jefferson the patron, Latrobe the mentor, and, I suppose, the Board of Public Works.

Stairway, Fireproof Building
Photograph by Gene Waddell, 1979

Rachel Jackson's tomb
Courtesy of the Ladies' Hermitage Association

It is strange that no novelist has yet been drawn to Robert Mills. Not only was this self-possessed, heavy-handed, upright man sufficiently beguiling to catch the eye of Thomas Jefferson, but a generation later he became the court architect for that fiery, contentious but emotionally vulnerable old soldier, Andrew Jackson, for whom Mills redesigned his house, The Hermitage. We will spend some time in its environs in Chapter Twenty. Here we should note that Mills was responsible for its great portico, by which the old house came to look somewhat like Mount Vernon. With this mask the wily Cincinnatus of the West expressed great delight. It is ungainly and theatrical, like a toga worn by an old Indian fighter. In the garden, however, is the tomb of Rachel Jackson, almost certainly designed by Mills and no counterfeit. It is a consummately lovely work of art, well worth the pilgrimage many Americans make to The Hermitage. In it we can see both Mills and Jackson at their best.

A single hand, therefore, delineated the most intimate of masks for Thomas Jefferson, at Monticello, and for Andrew Jackson, in remote Tennessee. We can regret that Robert Mills's autobiography is silent about his relationship with these great clients. It is silent on all matters of feeling.

Perhaps some fortunate researcher in Mauritius will someday come upon an autobiography of William Jay. Now, that would be a find!

183

CHAPTER 12

An Upcountry Boomtown

THE MOST DRAMATIC single event in the story of the state of New York was the opening of the Erie Canal on October 26, 1825. Cannoneers upon successive hilltops sent a chain of explosions crashing across the state to announce the first Erie water to flow into the Hudson. The news took eighty-one minutes to resound from Buffalo to Manhattan. Then a procession of ships began to move eastward through the canal and down the Hudson. As they passed Athens, the town's musketeers fired a welcoming volley, answered by a shot from a brass cannon mounted on the bow of *The Young Lion of the West*, which was bearing to the Atlantic two western eagles and two wolves, a fawn, a fox and four raccoons. Carl Carmer, in one of the great modern setpieces of American maritime history, tells us that upon the Hudson and in New York Harbor there was such a celebration that one observer rejoiced: "After Alexander of Macedon had carried his arms into India he did not descend the Indus with greater triumph or make a prouder display."

DeWitt Clinton had beaten John C. Calhoun in the race to the West: "Clinton's Ditch" began to turn the compass-needle of national commerce from the north-south axis of the Mississippi toward the east-west axis that the great western railroads later made permanent.

Clinton and New York's capitalists, enriched by fees skimmed from the transshipment of southern cotton, had raised the money to build their canal without federal funds. The voices of the captain of the *Young Lion* and his respondent, ashore on the docks at Rochester, drove the point home: "By whose authority and by whom was a work of such magnitude accomplished?" "By the authority and the enterprise of the people of the state of New York!" That enterprise had finally shaken the Hudson Valley out of its Dutch colonial past, and it was booming. The capital of the river province was Albany, which in the 1820's acquired a skyline dominated by the style of a single architect. Here from the pen of Edward Root, a gentleman historian of the early twentieth century, is a picture of Albany in 1825:

> As seen from the river . . . the skyline . . . was crossed by seven buildings: on the right, by the belfry of the Academy and the modest steeples of the First Lutheran Church and St. Mary's; in the centre, by the lofty spire of the Second Presbyterian and the dome of the new City Hall; and on the left, by the steeple of St. Peter's and the circular cupola of the State Capitol and its wooden statue of Themis. Every one of these seven buildings . . . was (with the possible exception of the Second Presbyterian) by Philip Hooker.

By the time Hooker completed his labors, he had designed three banks in Albany, its city hall, its principal school houses, a theater, three municipal markets and the State Capitol. A British visitor in 1822 spoke of the uniformity of style of the city's churches, and said he would not be surprised if one architect had designed them all. One architect had—Philip Hooker.

Albany is a creature of the Hudson, that easy avenue into the continent, that "mighty deep-mouthed river" reported in 1524 by Giovanni da Verrazano, a Florentine serving France. A century later Henry Hudson pushed upstream all the way to the present site of Albany, leading the way for the Dutch to settle there.

Albany dozed for nearly three centuries after Verrazano's first probe. It was a frontier trading post, a base for expeditions against the French or the Indians, or, during the war for independence, against the British in Canada. But it did not rush into the eighteenth century, much less the nineteenth. It was the capital of the past. It was the citadel of those vast landholdings which perpetuated the retrograde social structure we described in Chapter Five. Tenants toiled on the vast estates. Landlords resisted selling to small farmers and thus retarded settlement. And New York sustained pockets of slavery similar to the plantations of the West Indies and the mainland South. In 1790 there were eleven thousand Negro slaves at work in rural New York, most of them owned by rich Dutch farmers in the older settled areas where they had little chance to escape. Ten percent of the population of Ulster County was composed of black slaves.

Ethan Allen of Vermont, though erratic, touchy and miserly (see Chapter Sixteen), was a hero among his neighbors because his attacks against New York landlords like the Clarkes, who held land in Vermont, were directed against those holding their property only for lease. These great Proprietors, Loyalists and advocates of independence alike, were allied in perpetuating forms of peonage unacceptable to Allen's revolutionary generation, and they were very tenacious. As the rocky farms of New England gave up their surplus population to a great migration westward, emigrant sons and daughters of Massachusetts, New Hampshire and Vermont passed through a strange intermediate zone, the Hudson River Valley, which had much the same geography and ecology as New England but was socially and architecturally more like the Dutch West Indies than the villages of the Yankee homeland.

As the nineteenth century opened, Albany was still, according to the New Englanders who streamed through it on the way to the West, "more Dutch than decent." It had no sewers and no water mains. Its inhabitants, living in ancient, peaked-roof Dutch houses, poured their garbage into the street and "resigned the problem of its removal to a little army of wandering pigs."

Finally that dark vale was pried open by itinerant Yankees and enterprising city folk from Manhattan. New buildings began to be built, to replace those of the seventeenth century. Stylistically, however, those around Albany were old new buildings. A laggard sociology was provided with a laggard architecture. Fortunately, the chief provider was Philip Hooker, who made nostalgia into fine art. In 1798, when Albany was visited by Timothy Dwight, the celebrated educator noted that "one of the . . . churches is new, handsome and ornamented with two

North Dutch Church, Albany

From the collection of the McKenney Library, Albany Institute of History and Art

186

towers crowned with cupolas. None of the other . . . buildings claim any particular attention." This was Hooker's North Dutch Church, which still stands.

Hooker and his clients found it quite natural to demonstrate their mercantile prosperity by sweeping away the old Dutch Gothic.* They found it equally natural to replace it with buildings that made Albany in 1830 look like a handsome provincial British town of 1730.† Old churches and houses were exchanged for others. These were younger in age, of course, than those replaced, but they were born old in style, a half-century older than their contemporaries being built across New York's western counties, in Ohio, Michigan or Indiana.

The rest of the country was abandoning the Wrenaissance for a succession of revivals, including the one they called "Greek,"‡ during the Age of Jackson, but Hooker and his patrons clung to the architecture of the eighteenth century. They persisted in following colonial precedent, filtered through forms distantly derived from Palladio, who had himself made rather free use of classical forms. In this way things were not "revived" in Albany; they were continued.

Why was this so? Why would these men take their winnings and invest them in architectural forms that bore no relation to the time in which they were so successful? One can only guess: perhaps these rich men were manifesting some hidden regret. Perhaps they were only winning reluctantly. Perhaps they were being dragged into the world of DeWitt Clinton, and of Aristabulus Bragg and Steadfast Dodge, two of the characters invented to embody the idea of the new order by the novelist laureate of the old, James Fenimore Cooper. Perhaps they turned backward to the eighteenth century at home because they wished no more to enter the nineteenth than did Cooper.

Two buildings designed by Hooker may exemplify this nostalgic spirit. The Chapel at Hamilton College was designed by 1825 and built in 1827. It is, therefore, roughly contemporary to the up-to-date Grecian First Presbyterian Church in nearby Troy. But Hooker's design for the façade comes out of the middle of the eighteenth century. So, too, does his Union College Building in Schenectady. Though it was completed in 1797, it could have been constructed in Britain in 1690, or in Boston or Williamsburg in 1730 or 1740.

That Hooker and his clients desired such an architecture might lead us to think that in this period Albany was, economically, a backwater. Yet, instead, its growth was very rapid, its prosperity warming to a tax assessor's heart, and it was in constant, quick communication with Boston, New York and the rest of the world. It multiplied its size more than tenfold during Hooker's professional career. It tripled in the period from 1790 to 1810 and doubled again in the decade of the

---

* *This was a term used by Hooker's contemporaries to describe any very old architecture. It was also applied to the buildings the Yankees found in Mobile in the 1820's.*

† *American cities generally were laggard behind contemporary British or French taste, but not so laggard as Albany.*

‡ *The "Greek period" will be the subject of Part Three, and then of one or two more chapters before we are finished.*

Erie Canal. Albany chose not to be fashionable. It did not wish to be provincial Dutch any longer. It became provincial British instead.

The Architect

PHILIP HOOKER CAME TO Albany in time to benefit from the enormous growth of central and western New York, so it is fitting that he was one of those who paid for the celebration of the opening of the canal. He had much to celebrate, as we saw in Edward Root's survey of Albany's skyline. Thanks to the researches of

Chapel at Hamilton College, Clifton, New York

Credit: Hamilton College

First Presbyterian Church, Troy, New York
Courtesy of the Rensselaer County Historical Society

Root, we can piece together some of the facts of Hooker's life—though Root, an unworldly member of the very worldly family that produced both Elihu and Orrin Root, was not much interested in the politics and economics that made Hooker's career possible.

Philip Hooker was born in Rutland, Massachusetts. After apprenticeship as a carpenter, he developed an architectural practice by political skill in the service of a very conservative economic elite. He was a devoted member of what was then called the "Albany Regency" and was repeatedly elected to such offices as alderman, assessor, city superintendent (of construction) and city surveyor, as a follower first of Martin Van Buren and then of Thurlow Weed. Van Buren and Weed were elevated to national eminence, the first as President of the United States, the second as boss of New York. Gore Vidal, that cynic's cynic, presented an admiring portrait of Van Buren in his novel *Burr*, which tells us something. George Dangerfield, the last of the Whig historians, said of Weed that "there was not a trace of idealism in his character." Of the Regency in general, Dangerfield concluded that "their efficiency was sometimes impaired, if not altogether devoured, by a consuming greed for office."

One can become very confused by associating the Martin Van Buren of this period with either the young Martin Van Buren, who argued for the interests of the tenants against the landlords, or the old Martin Van Buren, the Free Soil candidate for President in 1848. The Regency of the 1820's was quite content to align itself with the great landowners when it came to important things, like power and money. It was not distracted by theory. Mayor Philip Schuyler van Rensselaer appointed Philip Hooker to survey the course of the canal from Albany to Schenectady, thereby distributing some of the patronage of a project that was, in fact, the creation of the Clintons, rivals to van Rensselaer and patrons of the surveyor Hooker replaced. Hooker designed for the mansion of the mayor's brother, Stephen van Rensselaer III, two stately Palladian flankers (which were dropped overboard when the house was dismantled and moved to become a fraternity house at Williamstown, Massachusetts; the house itself has since been torn down).

Albany, in which Hooker held so many offices over three decades, was (to quote Mr. Dangerfield again) "the grubbiest school of political intrigue in the United States." It was also becoming a world port, thanks to Clinton's canal. In 1824, the collector of the Port of Albany reported 5,374 boats; in 1828, after the canal was opened, 14,478. Two hundred eighteen plied the Hudson regularly between Albany and New York City, and 87 more served ports farther south. Albany and Boston became trading partners; in 1828, 163 vessels, four times as many as in 1821, served the two. In 1828, 12 steamboats docked in Albany each day.

All this activity created, as it generally does, opportunity for an architect who is politically astute. Hooker's appointment as city superintendent was not greeted with enthusiasm by Clinton's Albany *Gazette*, which said his predecessor had "executed his duties with ability and fidelity" and sourly described Hooker as "one of the aldermen of the Fourth Ward." Many were the plums he received from the Regency, and then from Weed. Yet he was, it appears, a little old-fashioned in his own strict ethics: even in that contumacious age, no scandal was attributed to him after he was in office, while he performed a long succession of public projects. When he resigned from public service—and opportunity—in 1825, he was a prominent citizen.

At the end of Hooker's life he moved away from the Van Buren faction toward a more explicit political affiliation with the great landowners. He had been a candidate for Van Buren's National Republican and Working-man's Party as late as 1831, but in 1833 and 1835 he was a Whig.

The Client

To be a Whig in the 1830's in the United States generally meant to be of the party of the merchants and landowners, opposed to the more radical views of Andrew Jackson. (The term "Tory," of course, had described a Loyalist to the Crown during the Revolution, so it was thereafter only useful as an epithet. Men who would have been Tories in England tended to be Whigs in the United States.)

George Hyde Clarke.
Portrait by Samuel F. B.
Morse showing the
verandah on the south
front of Hyde Hall.
*From the St. Louis
Art Museum*

If any man in the state of New York deserved both descriptions, it was Philip Hooker's greatest client, George Hyde Clarke of Hyde Hall. Clarke was the perfect patron for an architect who happened to live in the nineteenth century but was comfortable working in eighteenth-century forms. And Philip Hooker's training in "the grubbiest school of political intrigue in the United States" would have made him quite at home in the kind of life upon which George Clarke's fortune had been based. Like the Wentworths of New Hampshire, the Clarkes had been immensely successful spoilsmen during that period of British Colonial government when fortunes were accumulated by the holders of public office. When Edmund Burke said, "The charge of systematic corruption is less applicable to Sir Robert Walpole than to any other Minister who ever served the Crown for such a length of time," his accolade was only comparative.

As we observed in Chapter Eight, Governor Wentworth of New Hampshire retained a portion for himself of each township of Crown land he allocated for settlement, and thus accumulated nearly 100,000 acres. The great-grandfather of Hooker's patron had adopted the same practice to accumulate even more. This George Clarke (1676–1760) was secretary of the province of New York, and, for a while, its acting governor (the title was lieutenant governor). He was the nephew of Prime Minister Walpole's distributor of patronage, William Blaithwait, and served as deputy for New York to Walpole himself in that great man's role as auditor general of the plantations. These offices, said his biographer demurely, "afforded peculiarly favorable opportunities."

Clarke was described as "of no brilliance of gifts or striking force of character" but capable of "steady attention to the opportunities of his position, coupled with painstaking assiduity in keeping contact with important sources of political and social influence in England." He married, in 1712, Anne Hyde, daughter of the late royal governor of North Carolina, a relative of Queen Anne and of Lord Cornbury, lately the governor of New York.

Mr. Secretary Clarke was a tidy man, who restored order to a province seething under patroonships, slavery and indentured servitude. Twice during his tenure in office the magnates of New York City were reminded of the anger just beneath the surface and responded with violence of their own: after the slave revolt of 1712 was put down, eighteen of the rebels were executed. One was manacled and starved to death, one was broken on the wheel; three were burned at the stake and six others committed suicide in confinement. In 1741 the threat of another outbreak in the city led to rioting and the destruction of some of Clarke's property. After this "Negro Plot" was discovered, thirteen slaves were burned and eighteen hanged. Clarke received parliamentary compensation to cover his losses "and more, according to his enemies."

After nearly forty-two years in the New World, Clarke returned to England to live on his English estates. His second son, Edward, followed the pattern of the time, married a West Indian sugar heiress. His daughter married Ballard Beckford, of the great Jamaican family that had produced William Beckford of Fonthill, and moved to the island to live with her husband on his sugar plantations. Edward Clarke's oldest son was a notorious scapegrace, who lived most of his life abroad; *his* son, another George, our patron, was born during his father's travels, in Dijon, in Burgundy.

Our patron did not inherit the Jamaica plantations that had come into the family through his grandmother until his father's death in 1824, but he lived there when he was not in New York or on his English estates. His sugar income was important. He came to New York while still a minor, and left on the brink of the Revolution, not choosing sides in that struggle. He returned in its aftermath, in 1789, to reinstate his claims to the New York estates, left two years later and returned again in 1806. The timing of these comings and goings had important economic consequences: the New York legislature was predatory about the property of Tory landowners, and 120,000 acres were at stake. Clarke fought his way through lawsuits that took him to the United States Supreme Court (*Jackson* v.

Clarke, 1818) and, in the end, received exemption from expropriation. In the process he apparently became increasingly interested in New York and decreasingly in his wife, whom he had married and left behind in England. When he appeared in Albany in 1806, he was prepared to take up permanent residence.

He rented a house very close to the capitol building, which Hooker was then constructing, and the two men became colleagues as chairmen of committees of the Society for the Promotion of the Useful Arts. In the 1820's Hooker's architecture was making very cautious progress into the last half of the eighteenth century. Clarke was ideologically and temperamentally an English—or West Indian—nabob. Hooker drew a townhouse to Clarke's specifications in 1816. In the following year Clarke was ready to begin establishing an appropriate country seat. His consort was now the vivacious and ambitious widow of James Fenimore Cooper's brother, Richard. Clarke bought for her the most prominent situation above the waters of what had seemed, until then, the Coopers' private lake, and there George Clarke and the former Mrs. Cooper* built Hyde Hall over the years from 1817 until 1836.

We know rather more of Clarke's character than we do of Hooker's because history records violence, and considerable violence came of Clarke's constant efforts to impose his exalted notions of seigneurial right. Throughout the Mohawk and Hudson valleys he moved to raise rents from tenants who had tilled the same soil for decades. In response, they disputed his title on the ground that, despite the technicality of his minority at the time of the Revolution, he was an enemy alien. Since the tenants were numerous, and the property was valued at a million dollars or more, the state legislature was sympathetic, the senate going so far as to authorize the governor to start legal proceedings to clear the titles in favor of the tenants. The governor, however, was not so minded, and though tenants of the Clarkes, Livingstons and van Rensselaers continued to contest those titles, in the 1850's their efforts at legal redress were finally rebuffed by the state supreme court; even so, as late as 1878 they were still in revolt, burning down houses, throwing down fences and exhausting the soil.

The management practices of George Clarke, Jr., (successor to Hooker's client) were learned at his father's knee. When leases ran out, all farms with their improvements reverted, without compensation for the tenants, to the landlord, who often then adopted a policy of issuing annual leases. The perpetual struggle between an unpopular landlord and tenants who could always avail themselves of the option of leaving their homes and trekking to the West led to a steady decline in the quality of the remaining tenants, of the fertility of the soil (for which the tenants felt no obligation or affection) and, ultimately, of the quantity of tenants. *The Freeholder* of May 16, 1849, reported that George Clarke, Jr., was trying to sell

---

* *It is conceivable that she was still Mrs. Cooper. Clarke apparently never bothered to divorce his first wife, and there is no record of a marriage to Mrs. Cooper.*

off his farms. Charleston, New York, the center of disaffection in the Clarke holdings, lost half of its population between 1840 and 1880.

The West Indian Connection and Hyde Hall

GOING
ASHORE TO
STAY ASHORE

WE ARE GETTING ahead of ourselves, however (an error toward which neither George Clarke nor Philip Hooker was prone). In the 1820's and 1830's the means employed by Clarke to exact rents from his tenants were only slightly more unpopular than those of the Livingstons or of the successors to Stephen van Rensselaer. He was neither more nor less severe than the landowners who were his contemporaries in the South or his West Indian relatives.

The oldest portion of his house might have been built by one of those relatives —in the West Indies. Hyde Hall looks down from a knoll on Otsego Lake as if it were looking down on Montego Bay. The house is nearly always photographed to display its fine east front, finished in gray-brown local limestone. An earlier design would have made it more like Hooker's recollections of the mid-Georgian, of brick faced with stucco. In its final form it has a spacious portico about the entrance, and above it, a high gable set upon pilasters.

The east front of Hyde Hall
Courtesy of the New York State Historical Association, Cooperstown

Drawing room at Hyde Hall
Courtesy of The Magazine ANTIQUES

This is curious enough for 1830, but the interior is amazing. Visitors in the 1940's found rows of family portraits decking the walls, solemnly surveying bales of hay stacked in the drawing room. Symbols of pride and decline were familiar enough in those years, but above the portraits and the hay, one's eyes could pick out the magnificent ceilings of the drawing room and dining room. Edward Root called them "two of the finest rooms constructed in a private house in America before 1840," and he may be right.

When in 1893 one of the two ceilings was restored, the workers used an old plaster mold designed by Hooker and thus made it possible for us to see how truly antiquarian were Clarke and Hooker. Root described the ceiling as like that designed by Inigo Jones for the Double Cube Room at Wilton, but "mercifully spared pictorial embellishment by third rate decorators." Wilton is a great British country house near the home of the Clarkes in Wiltshire; its Double Cube Room was completed in 1649, two centuries before the parlor at Hyde Hall.

Nowhere in America does one find an example of longer continuity of taste. Hyde Hall also represents the final expression, north of Louisiana, of another continuous development, the sugar and slaves plantation system. There is much

195

irony in this, for it could not have been built out of that continuity alone. It required additional revenue arising from modern manufacturing and modern steam transportation.

Part of its building costs were actually paid with iron hollowware, from a foundry of which the Clarkes were part owners. The rest of the east front, one could argue, was financed by the unearned increment added to the value of the Clarke lands by the steamboat, which accelerated the pace of western migration and vastly increased commerce on the Hudson and the Great Lakes, and brought much higher values to their properties.

So Hyde Hall, built of a burst of "new money," defies the usual rule that such a burst usually clears the way for new architecture. Instead, Hooker and Clarke used new money to build old architecture, in much the same way that Fenimore Cooper, in his library down the lake, wrote, for the new popular magazines, nostalgic novels about kindly landlords contending against change. Later,

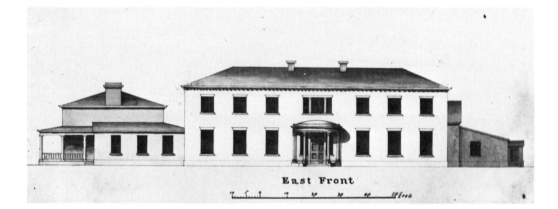

East Front

Philip Hooker's first (1818) design for the east front of Hyde Hall (*top*) and his final design

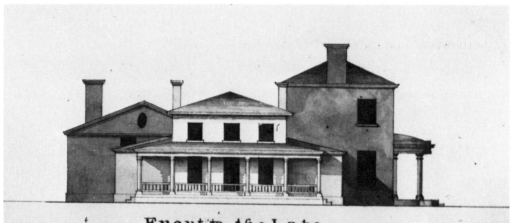

Hooker's rendering of the south front of Hyde Hall in his first design
Courtesy of The Magazine ANTIQUES

greater architects and clients would create, out of the same nostalgia, the Gothic Revival and other Picturesque styles (see Chapter Thirty).

Though Hyde Hall was to some extent a product of "new money," part of it, the oldest part, came from the oldest "big money" in North America—money derived from sugar and slaves. That is what the house tells us.

Tucked away at the end of the often-photographed stone façade is the south front of 1817. It was called "the cottage," a stucco building with a piazza around three sides, looking like a Jamaican overseer's house brought down to the ground —looking, that is, very much like low-country Carolina houses built by the first settlers from the West Indies (see Chapter Eight). This unlikely emigrant sits beached near Cooperstown, New York, hiding in the shadows of a Renaissance plantation house, reminding us of the long, long continuity that stretches from the plantations of the sugar islands to the shores of Otsego Lake.

Hyde Hall is a great house, architecturally, and a social document of the first importance. It was also the last work of Philip Hooker. Both he and George Clarke died during the winter of 1835–36. The sugar and plantation system had only a little longer to go: two years later the British emancipated their slaves in the West Indies, and left the Old South standing virtually alone.

197

Part III

THE CLASSIC PERIOD

Philip Hooker's style was of the eighteenth century, sustaining that courteous, contained way of building we often call Georgian, though it began in England with the Stuarts and lasted in America until the 1830's. It lasted so long here because of the reluctance of architects like Hooker, and their clients, to go even as far into the nineteenth century as the taste of the Age of Jefferson, though they lived in the Age of Jackson.

In Part Two we watched the arrival of that style upon American shores, long after it had come to dominate the tastes of the gentry and of the rising tradesmen in England. Its Palladianism lay in its balance, its symmetry, its success in adapting, in Anglo-Dutch brick or American frame, Palladio's stuccoed cubical classicism.

Thomas Jefferson execrated these red-brick Wrenaissance boxes because he associated them with Williamsburg and British colonialism. He was a genuine radical in architecture; after some extraordinary experiments of his own, he made fresh contributions to the Palladian tradition, even before he went to France and found there an affirmation of his previous preferences. He, and a whole generation of British and French cognoscenti, turned to the books of Palladio directly (or to pattern-book authors who had done so) and found in them a porticoed villa style,* with dependencies set out in enfolding arms around an entrance court.

In the Colonial period there had been built a few examples of the villa style, with a forecourt but without porticoes.† But this neo-Palladian format, or even its major components, did not take root. Until the completion of Monticello, the University of Virginia and

---

* There is scholarly dispute about the breadth one may permit in use of the term "villa." My ample use can be defended, but such a defense would be wearisome here.

† Mount Airy, the Tayloe house in Virginia, is our best-known example, and Tryon's Palace, in North Carolina, another. It happens that another Mount Airy was built in the 1860's overlooking Troy, New York, by a Tayloe descendant. For this information, and for information on Philip Hooker, I am indebted to Douglas Bucher of Albany.

Union College, in Schenectady, New York, Americans had not seen a house, or a group of pavilions, set in a Palladian "campus."

It is convenient to single out the temple form, with a full portico, or its most domestic cousin, the biloggial "frontispiece," as convenient signs of this transition. Before 1783 Classicism in the temple form had appeared only in pavilions for summer parties, like Whitehall, near Annapolis. Biloggial blocks could be seen in the South, at Drayton Hall or the Miles Brewton house, but were not yet composed in a true graduated system of central building and affiliates. Ideological Classicism as "serious architecture" did not appear until after the Revolution.

Ideological Classicism, what we in America often, though lazily, call "Greek Revival," is usually associated with Thomas Jefferson: the White House portico was only added to that essentially Anglo-Irish Colonial mansion when it was redesigned by Benjamin Henry Latrobe at Jefferson's request; and the Capitol, so protracted and so confused in its construction, with its domes and its tall, thin columns, its complex experiments with light and its spatial surprises, was its great monument.

This elder offspring of Ideological classicism was primarily Roman, however, not Greek. The blockier, simpler, more massive Grecian, with thick columns, forthright and rectilinear spaces, eschewing domes, began as a cadet branch, at the home of George Washington Parke Custis, Arlington House, about 1820, and soon outgrew its senior sibling, thanks largely to the patronage not of Jefferson but of a Philadelphia banker, Nicholas Biddle. Architects like George Hadfield and Ithiel Town drew directly upon Greek architecture, as rediscovered by archaeologists whose work was published long after Palladio's death (Palladio, like Jefferson, knew very little of Greece); in the "Grecian" vernacular the basic Palladian form, a porticoed central block with smaller flankers, was reduced to a block with attachments as modest as lean-tos.

People loyal to the eighteenth century, like Philip Hooker and his biographer, Edward Root (who wrote in the twentieth), did not admire the Greek Revival. Root lamented that "beyond" Philip Hooker was "the wilderness, and after him, the Greek Revival and the architectural Babel of modern times." We need not share Root's low opinion of subsequent architecture to consider the possibility that in the architecture of Hooker and George Clarke, "the Renaissance as an exclusive and continuous development came to an end." We cannot yet write an obituary for the architecture of Thomas Jefferson, though one might have seen his death, as well, as the ending of a continuous Renaissance tradition. My own view is that his architecture was fresher and more experimental than a mere continuance, but there is no question that the Greek Revival was something quite different. It was a revival, not a continuance.*

The Greek Revival arrived across the Hudson from Albany around 1830, when the brash, parvenu merchants of Troy commissioned James Dakin to create the First Presbyterian

---

* It is noteworthy that the Greek Revival, though immensely popular in the United States, stopped at the Canadian border. There are a few exceptions to this rule, along Lake Erie in Ontario, but they are adscititious to the Canadian architecture of the time, which was like that of Philip Hooker.

Church and John Colegrove the Rensselaer County Courthouse, both handsomely Hellenic, if rather stiff. These were not merely fashionable architecture. They were political statements. The times were full of talk about the Greek struggle for independence from the Turks. In Athens, Troy and hundreds of other towns given Hellenic names, Greek embellishments were displayed upon thousands of white-painted buildings. The First Presbyterian Church in Troy was, in its region, a prototype for many other buildings, courthouses, churches, schools, stores and houses that adhered to the rather squatty, forthright proportions of the Greek—not the Roman—temple form, and was as well one of the forerunners of the Government Street Church in Mobile (see Chapter Sixteen). By the time the Mobile church was built, Ideological Classicism was well under way in its campaign across the South and the middle states, advancing in two armies, the Roman and the Greek (which we could also describe as the Palladian and the Revived—the Jeffersonian and the . . . we shall see).

CHAPTER 13

Speculators,
Stagecraft and Statecraft

THE CAPITAL CITY of the United States was laid out in the 1790's, in an arbitrary ten-mile square imposed on a swampy and bedraggled landscape at the head of navigation on the Potomac River. The first bidder for the honor had been Kingston, New York. Even Lancaster and Reading, Pennsylvania, and poor, passed-over Williamsburg, Virginia, had hoped to gain the prize. But after a seven-year wrangle, Thomas Jefferson obtained Alexander Hamilton's support for the Potomac site in exchange for his promise to lobby for the assumption by the nation of the states' Revolutionary War debts.

The Virginians hoped that the location of the nation's capital would fertilize their exhausted soils with the compost of bureaucracy, and draw to the Potomac Valley the sort of commercial and manufacturing activity that was enlivening and enriching the valleys of the Delaware, the Hudson and the Merrimack. George Washington expected to see there the "greatest commercial emporium in the country."

Washington's friend William Thornton, the architect and physician, shared the dream. He was heir to a West Indian sugar fortune not as great as William Beckford's (see Chapter Three) but large enough to subsidize first an apprenticeship in architecture in Philadelphia and then a distinguished amateur practice. He surpassed all amateur expectations by overcoming a number of designers who earned their living by architecture in the competition for the best design for the Capitol Building. Standing on the hilltop upon which it was to be built, Thornton predicted a population of 160,000 for the city within a few years.

Alas, so great were the distances to other urban centers, so uninviting to commercial traders was the dispirited tobacco economy of the area, and so meager was the soil in comparison to rich agricultural districts farther north and west that even the promise of an expanding government did not induce many to flock thither. Ten years after it was founded, the capital had only 3,200 people. It had only 23,000 in 1840, though the President of the United States himself had sponsored the digging of the Chesapeake and Ohio Canal, which opened in 1828, and the city had joined the Baltimore and Ohio Railroad system in 1835. By that time, however, so many other canals had been promoted and failed, so many other links to other urban centers had been tried, tested and snapped, that there were few who had much faith in the Federal City. Efforts to build its connection to industrial centers and major seaports were the sump of energy and fortune for more than one great architect, Benjamin Henry Latrobe among them.

Even before the British burnt the only impressive buildings in the generally squalid place in 1814, it was a scene of desolation, described thus by James Sterling Young, the city's best historian: "Two unfinished stark white citadels [the Capitol and the Executive Mansion] towered above the terrain from hilltops on opposite shores of a dismal swamp, more like ruins amid the fallen fragments of their own stone than new and rising edifices. Where monuments had been planned, brush piles moldered and rubbish heaps accumulated."

The Irish poet Thomas Moore put it in verse: "This embryo capital, where Fancy sees / Squares in morasses, obelisques in trees."*

Fancy was not easily brought to earth, however, nor was Fancy's consort, real-estate speculation. The Duc de La Rochefoucauld-Liancourt asserted that "in America . . . more than anywhere else the desire for wealth is the dominant passion, there are few operations that fail to fall into the hands of speculators," and this was especially true of "the establishment of the Federal City."

The duke's friend, the Philadelphia capitalist Robert Morris, bought six thousand lots in all; though his holdings in the District rose to include 745 prime acres, he was a small holder by comparison to the Washington family. The capital city nestled against an array of Washington lands: there was Mount Vernon itself, and next door, Woodlawn Plantation and River Farm. Closer to the Federal City were four thousand acres along Four Mile Run, and two thousand more within the District, though on the Virginia side of the Potomac. They had been accumulated during the Revolutionary War by Martha Washington's son "Jacky" Custis, with the encouragement of his stepfather, General Washington. Later the general himself apparently acquired many acres within the District, on the Maryland side. The chief beneficiary of these Washington and Custis acquisitions was Jacky's son, George Washington Parke Custis.

Perhaps "beneficiary" is the wrong word. "Victim" might be more appropriate, for Custis carried the burden of these enormous holdings, together with the greater burdens of a guilty youth and of the Washington name. As the Tidewater economy languished, he was tethered to Arlington and could not follow other Washington heirs who staked out their futures in the rich Shenandoah Valley.

* *Moore later regretted his nastiness.*

United States Capitol before it was burned in 1814.
Watercolor by William Birch.

Courtesy of the Library of Congress

Nor could he free himself to consider the wilder dream of the Mississippi Valley, beyond the Blue Ridge. He was enormously rich in land, yet all his life he wondered how one so amply endowed could be so perpetually short of cash. He lived out an unfulfilled life, in an unfinished house, always promised a golden future, always the custodian of a golden past.

He was not alone among those whose fortunes declined as the Federal city failed their hopes. Robert Morris was joined in partnership by the Nicholsons, also of Philadelphia, whose wealth had come from Barbados and the West Indies trade, and John Greenleaf, of Massachusetts. This group sold 1,500 lots of five acres or more to Custis' brother-in-law, Thomas Law, and William Mayne Dickinson.

Law and Dickinson had built up fortunes in India and came to America full of the intoxicating expectations of men like Morris, Washington and Thornton.

Law started his American career in a fine house, where he served as host to La Rochefoucauld-Liancourt. He was congratulated upon his beautiful and energetic wife, George Washington Parke Custis' sister, Eliza. The duke thought her wise and honest, though he was not so sure about Law's speculative ventures, noting that Law had once had a large fortune but appeared to be losing it. There was no land-rush to the Federal City; most of these Anglo-Indian and West Indian gains were sunk in its mosquito-ridden swamps. Dickinson and Law thereby reversed the rhythm of the career of Lord Cornwallis, who after his defeat at Yorktown went on to be gloriously successful in India. By July 1797 Greenleaf was in jail, and Morris and Nicholson were in hiding from their creditors.

All the Custis family, one after another, fell into the same morass in the decades after General Washington's death. Kindly Thomas Law, who had rejoiced in the respect of his friends in England and was said by them to have been adored by natives of India, was deserted by his spoiled and beautiful wife as he sank into a series of failed speculations. Law might have been a poet, as his brother-in-law, George Washington Parke Custis, might have been a painter or a playwright. They both failed as artists, as speculators and as public men, though Custis' decline was agonizingly slow.

Arlington House

ARLINGTON HOUSE—also called the Custis-Lee Mansion—is the most conspicuous private residence in America. It is ironic that Robert E. Lee, an essentially modest man who came to live there, should have been the one to tell us that it was intended to be "a house that any one might see with half an eye." It would be easy to mistake its design as self-advertisement on the part of Custis, who certainly loved the limelight (in the literal sense). He was by far the greatest landowner in the District (its Virginia portion, largely owned by Custis, was not returned to Virginia until well into the nineteenth century), and he had built a mansion in the midst of his vast estate, high on what he called Mount Washington. But to read Arlington House as self-promotion would be to miss the complexity of Custis' character. In a sense, the very conspicuousness of his house was an act of deference.

Few visitors saw it as anything but a theatrical gesture, especially if they are British. In 1832 one English visitor, Godfrey Vigne, said Arlington House was "visible for many miles, and in the distance has the appearance of a superior English country residence." But, he went on, "as I came close to it, I was woefully disappointed." Frances Trollope judged it "a noble looking place . . . which . . . forms a beautiful object in the landscape." They thought of it as performing the functions of Greek Revival country houses in their own country, and like many British critics ever since, they missed the point. The "object" was intended to be "noble looking"—primarily from one direction, almost like a stage flat. It was

205

meant to be seen along the axis that begins with the National Capitol, proceeds past the Washington Monument (one might say the other Washington Monument) along the Mall, and crosses the Potomac where now the Lincoln Memorial reposes in its neo-Attic splendor. In 1985 that axis must be adjusted somewhat by the Memorial Bridge (which replaces a bridge lower down the Potomac, put there against the advice of the proprietor of Arlington House by the perverse Jeffersonians).

The house itself huddles behind a portico with huge Doric columns, five feet thick at the base. Custis was building for effect—a distant effect. He and his architect omitted, therefore, the details of the "correct" Greek orders (the relationship of column, capital and entablature). All was in the grand impression. The porticoed façade was covered by a simulated stone invented by David Randolph, who called it "hydraulic cement"—it was compounded of fossil shells found near Jamestown—scored and streaked to simulate marble blocks; the hollow brick columns were given the same treatment. The steps of the portico, which could not be seen at a distance, were of wood, though the highly visible balustrade was also of simulated stone. The west, or back, side was, apparently, left as exposed brick.

What was it intended to mean? For what purpose was this eye-catching? Why

Arlington House. Pencil sketch, made in 1824.
Courtesy of the Virginia Historical Society

was this house used as a dramatic device? It was to be a residential symbol. Custis lived there, but he lived as a priest lives in a temple, a temple dedicated to George Washington. In Washington's lifetime Custis had been no source of pride to the Great Man. After Washington's death all his own pride was in that exalted memory. He served George Washington in death far better than he ever served him in life. And his chief service was in architecture.

From his grandiose portico, he looked out on a capital that was a squalid embarrassment of the general's expectations. For much of Custis' life, the embarrassment was compounded by the control of the city by the Jeffersonians, whom he detested. Jeffersonians and speculators possessed it all. His own fortunes, received from the hands of the First Virginian and First President, steadily declined, despite desperate efforts, including repeated forays into the speculation he loathed and which had ruined his brother-in-law. Upon his hilltop he lived amid Washington relics and Washington memories, spending his modest talent, his declining endowment and his whole precious life drawing attention to the Founding Father of the Capital City and of the Grateful Nation. Arlington House is George Washington's monument as truly as Robert Mills's latter-day obelisk, a monument sustained by steady incursions on George Washington's own fortune and the fortune of Martha Washington, as they had been transmitted to Custis.

Arlington House was America's first house to be more Greek than Roman. That the city about it should be classical had seemed obvious to Washington and Jefferson, who were intent on importing dignity to both the capital and the new country, and on replacing the frame shanties and red-brick eighteenth-century houses that Jefferson, especially, associated with British colonial rule. But that the house should be Greek, not Roman, was not so obvious. Mr. Jefferson had strong views about architecture, and he "abominated" Greek architecture, according to Benjamin Henry Latrobe, his favorite architect, who should have known. Yet the most evident residence in the city, except for the President's mansion, was Greek. And the author of that aberration, quite deliberately, was George Washington Parke Custis.

George Washington Parke Custis

GEORGE WASHINGTON PARKE CUSTIS saw himself as the curator of a great collection of mementos of the Father of His Country, who had adopted him* and from whom he took his name. Arlington House was his museum. He lived for a while in one of its two side pavilions, which he had built in 1804, but as he inherited or purchased more and more Washington memorabilia there was less and less room for him and his family. After the great porticoed central section was constructed

---

He was the grandson of Washington's wife, Martha. His father, Jacky Custis, was her son by her first husband. Washington adopted father and son, as sons, in succession.

between 1817 and 1821, he lived there, still surrounded by Washingtoniana; Arlington House became the Washington shrine, and he its sacristan. The nephews of the great man, who actually bore the Washington name and who inherited Mount Vernon, regarded that estate primarily as their home, not as a public facility. It fell to Custis to compensate for his unprepossessing youth by playing the role of "the child of Mount Vernon," a title he delightedly assumed.

He assumed, as well, the role of political heir to Washington, not that he ever showed a sign of thinking himself a large enough figure to succeed to a commensurate national role. He tried to keep pure the political legacy of Washington; one of the functions of the architecture of Arlington House was to manifest that the Washington tradition was not the same as the Jefferson tradition.

This other Washington monument must not, therefore, be another Roman or Palladian temple, in the mode of Jefferson's Governor's Palace, or Jefferson's Rotunda for the University of Virginia, or Jefferson's approved designs for the Capitol or the White House. Jefferson! Jefferson! Jefferson! There was the rub! Washington Custis was a passionate Federalist, and later a Whig. He abominated Jefferson. So did his adored grandmother, Martha Washington, who said that next to her husband's death the most painful experience of her old age was having to

George Washington Parke
Custis, an engraving by
J. C. Buttre after a lost
portrait by Gilbert Stuart
*From the Arlington House Collection/
National Park Service*

receive Jefferson at Mount Vernon. So, too, had his father, Jacky Custis, who during his brief political career had opposed Governor Jefferson, boycotted the session of the Virginia Chamber of Deputies over which the governor presided, and retired from that chamber rather than work with him.

Custis continued that antagonism. He ran, to rather ignominious defeat, as an anti-Jeffersonian candidate for the Virginia Assembly in 1802, having charged the President's party with fostering the seditious notions of the French Revolution. Two years later he was hammering at the same theme, proclaiming that French revolutionary ideas had led to the rule of Napoleon, "the Corsican Caesar," implying that Jefferson might be headed in the same direction. (Napoleon's endorsement of Roman architecture may have added to Custis' aversion, but Jefferson was a bogeyman closer to home.) Jefferson's embargo against British goods, which was deeply injurious to most southern planters, offered Custis an opportunity to advocate the Hamiltonian doctrine of domestic manufactures, even to the extent of giving President Jefferson a homespun waistcoat of what he called "Arlington cloth."

Custis was the first of a line of southern-born figures in these pages whose loyalties were national, and whose architecture showed it. He did not resent the fact that the embargo enriched New England, though it was at the expense of the South: "We enrich a friend, not support an enemy," he said in 1808. He called for an American heraldry of "the plough and the loom," and he espoused a national uniform of homespun gray coat and trousers ("not discernible in the woods at any distance"), calfskin cap and hunting knife, and offered a prize for the best example. He tried repeatedly to encourage southern industry, bemoaning the decline of his section and the low level of education to be found among Jefferson's vaunted yeomanry.

By 1812 Custis began to hold sheep-shearing contests near his home at Arlington, offering prizes for cloth and sheep, espousing native breeds against the imported merinos favored in the North. These were little Federalist rallies, out of date and place, for which he composed elaborate orations and pageants and painted huge canvases depicting the glories of Washington and the early Republic. He was an eloquent speaker, possessed of a powerful and pleasant voice, but he was not taken seriously as a political leader. His instincts, perhaps, were too theatrical: he disposed his canvases behind him as "flats." At the end of one oration he said: "This may be the last time my old canvas may shade this work of Peace." Actually the real shade was provided by George Washington's old campaign tents, which Custis fitted out for his pageants.

He was not a fool, and he was not without courage. Rejected by James Madison for service as an officer in the War of 1812 (perhaps to prevent Custis' becoming a more effective political threat), he volunteered as an artilleryman and participated in another ignominious defeat, the disastrous Bladensburg campaign, in which the British thrust aside a hastily assembled American force and proceeded to burn some buildings in Washington.

In an angry interlude in the nation's political life, when a Jeffersonian mob killed one Federalist, General Lingan, and badly wounded another, "Light-Horse Harry" Lee, Custis refused to heed President Madison's order forbidding public ceremonies and delivered a passionate speech for "the right of opinion, the liberty of speech, and the liberty of the press . . . prostrated at the feet of lawless power." Jefferson's Alien and Sedition Acts were a decade past; now the "feet of lawless power" were Madison's feet.

Custis abandoned his Federalist-Whig sympathies only when his patrifamilial responses were stirred. To him, Andrew Jackson seemed almost a reincarnation of George Washington. He took the "Hero of New Orleans" to Mount Vernon and excoriated Jackson's enemies, "the little men, the mad men" who were preaching disunion in Jackson's native South Carolina. "Call me a Yankee while I live," he proclaimed, "let it be graven on my headstone!" He and the South should stand with Jackson for Union and the Constitution. "I love Virginia much, but I love my WHOLE COUNTRY more!" No wonder it was difficult for Robert E. Lee, his son-in-law, to make his decision to stand with Virginia in 1860, a decision made in George Washington Parke Custis' own bedroom, which Lee inherited.

Custis blamed slavery, "the unhappy error of our forefathers," for the South's retarded pace in industrializing. Lavasseur, the Marquis de Lafayette's* secretary, noted that Custis could offer good, cool reasons for his aversion: "If Mr. Custis, instead of a great number of indolent slaves, who devour his produce . . . would employ a dozen free laborers, I am sure he would triple his revenues." But Custis had deeper feelings about slavery than that. He called it "the mightiest serpent that ever infested the world" and thought it an evil that had an ill effect on southern whites as well as blacks, contrasting the lethargy of the South to the vigor of the developing West. He supported the African colonization scheme and offered one of his prize plantations, on Smith Island, Virginia, as a "refuge for the poor Africans until a real colony" could be made for them. At one time he hired Irish laborers to work alongside his black slaves in an experiment anticipating some scholarly controversies about the relative profitability of free and black labor. He was pleased when Lafayette established a colony of free Negroes and freed all the slaves in his West Indian plantations who would go there.

Internationally, Custis was always for the underdog: he led many a St. Patrick's Day parade, clad in a green Irish coat. He sympathized with the Russians when attacked by Napoleon, and with the Poles when attacked by the Russians. In domestic politics he stood in the Washington tradition; he was a Federalist/Unionist/Whig, except, of course, when Andrew Jackson assumed the mantle of his foster-father. When he supported Zachary Taylor for President in 1848, he was still able to campaign in "rich, full-toned voice." As late as 1860 it was to Custis that Robert E. Lee found it appropriate to complain of the "selfish, dicta-

---

The son of the marquis, George Washington Lafayette, and many other friends of G. W. P. Custis shared his first two names; another was George Washington Craik. It must have been a little oppressive.

torial bearing of the 'cotton states,' as they term themselves." After Custis' death, on the brink of the War Between the States, Lee still wrote in 1861 to his own son as Custis might have written to him: "I can anticipate no greater calamity for the country than the dissolution of the Union . . . Secession is nothing but revolution." In the same letter he stated his own dreadful dilemma: he would "sacrifice everything but honor for its [the Union's] preservation." Honor led him to leave Arlington House and ride southward toward Richmond and the Confederacy.

Custis and, after him, Lee could support their independent views because they were heirs to a very large though steadily declining inheritance. Custis' wealth was a combination of Parke, Custis and Washington lands. From his father he inherited two plantations northeast of Richmond on the Pamunkey River: White House, with eight thousand acres, and Romancock, with four thousand. The old Custis family seat had been Arlington, and the eastern shore, and this also came to him, along with Smith Island and the Washington and Custis holdings around the edges of the capital city.

All his life Custis struggled to keep these properties productive, refusing to be stuck with the erratic and declining tobacco market. But diversification was expensive, and he was constantly in debt. His experiments with sheep were his most famous means of escaping the decline of tobacco. He purchased the best of the Mount Vernon flock, and was one of the most consistent advocates of what became, ultimately, the experimental husbandry of the U.S. Department of Agriculture. He was moderately successful in conversion of tobacco lands to corn and wheat. When European or West Indian prices were good he was quite prosperous. But he never seemed to get his timing right; he described himself as always unlucky in hitting prices, though by the end of the 1840's he was doing better than many other planters, selling ships' masts from his Pamunkey plantation and grazing nearly two thousand head of cattle on his land above Mount Vernon. He was a better agriculturalist than real-estate speculator, though no one living so close to the edge of the maelstrom could avoid being dragged in, and despite the disastrous example of Thomas Law he embarked on two grand land-development schemes. The first, called Washington Forest, on his land along Four Mile Run between Arlington and Alexandria, was to include a village named Mount Vernon. It died aborning in 1807, and his losses might have taken him under but for the ironic arrival of a belated legacy from the general, the court settlement of one of that shrewder speculator's better investments, his extensive lands in western Virginia. Custis' second venture, in 1835 above Alexandria, was called Jackson Village. It also failed.

The Character of Custis

LYDIA SIGOURNEY, the New England bluestocking, dismissed Custis as "an oddity, an eccentric." He was certainly not "clever" by her standards, though that is the

George Washington Parke Custis and his sister Nellie. Portraits by Robert
Edge Pine.

*Credits: (G. W. P. Custis) Washington/Custis/Lee Collection, Washington and Lee University, Virginia;
(Nellie) Courtesy of the Mount Vernon Ladies' Association*

term his doting grandmother, Martha Washington, used to describe him. "Grandmother always spoiled Washington," said his sister Nellie. The general had
thought him promising and vowed to give him a liberal education. The old gentleman's heavy hand, however, pressed Custis into a textbook case of childish passive
aggression. His grandfather expected "ready submission" and got "an almost unconquerable disposition to indolence." At Princeton he rebelled "in various ways
to lessen the authority and influence of the faculty" and was dismissed. Princeton
was only one of a series of schools that found him intractable. The general knew
the pattern: Custis would go silent, "would not . . . make a candid disclosure of
his sentiments," would "forget what he does know, so inert is his mind." He
possessed "competent talents . . . but they are counteracted by an indolence of
mind." Custis' dogged refusal to be educated "astonished" Washington, though he
had "ample fortune, good education . . . and good disposition."

Instead Custis became an acolyte to the Washington myth, serving memories
of the past, and built Arlington House as a sort of repository of memory, re-
freshed, if necessary, by pageants, plays and paintings. He welcomed thousands

of people to the shrine, offering free ice, boat rides and dances. Even after his oratorical days were over he was willing to play his violin, to orate or to appear in his antique clothing to tell stories about the General.

It was easy to lampoon a man who was always ready to rise at a public dinner for another Washington speech, to lead a parade, to compose a historical drama or to paint an allegorical painting of his foster father. When he refused to be intimidated by the Jeffersonian mobs, he was called "that ridiculous figure Custis . . . the standing laughing-stock of the district" by the newspapers. His plays were dismissed as "absolutely destitute of plot, incident, character and stage effect." When he described himself as "a poor farmer" to his banker, he seemed undignified, and visitors to Arlington remembered "a shabby old man with angular features and thin grey hair, who would come down from the mansion, violin in hand, and amuse the children by the hour." At his death, most newspapers ignored him. A few were kind, but the Chicago *Tribune* gave him the bitter obituary it reserved for southern planters, saying his propensity for postprandial oratory made him "known in gastronomic circles as the Inevitable Custis."

Yet disappointing as he may have been to Washington, and to himself, a just estimate of him may be found in a letter written after his death by a clergyman to

Sketch by Benjamin Henry Latrobe of George Washington Parke Custis
and Martha Washington with a classical muse

Courtesy of the Maryland Historical Society, Baltimore

Mrs. Robert E. Lee: "Your father was distinguished by talents which would have made him envied in any profession . . . but his ample Fortune, extensive and generous hospitality, and the care of his large estates led him rather to Agricultural pursuits, general literature, and the indulgence of his tastes for the fine Arts."

He served his endowing foster father. He served his estates. He served his need to find himself a stage, any stage, for oratory, for parading, for pageant, for historical drama. He would paint the flats, put up the tent, provide the music, buy the boats to carry the audience to his performance, offer the refreshments. He even offered the tickets, in his ruffled cuffs and old-fashioned waistcoat, while Mrs. Sigourney noted with disdain that an old plow rusted in the front yard.

His dramatic performances were, in a way, a tribute to George Washington, too. The Father of His Country had himself refined a youthful love of dramatic performance into a steely and calculated deployment of face, figure and voice for public effect. His manner and bearing were important elements of his statecraft. His recorded utterances and his letters are full of references to the stage.* As a young man he spoke of the "scenes" of life, of "a perfect, unvarying constancy of character to the very last act." He hoped, at the end of his career, "to close the drama with applause . . . to retire from the theater with the approbation of angels and men." He wrote to one of his nephews that it was "absolutely necessary, if you mean to make any figure upon the stage, that you should take the first steps right," and though neither of his adopted sons (George Washington Parke Custis and his father before him) nor any of his nephews became a large "figure upon the stage" of national life, he was still content if his family performed creditably "the parts assigned to us."

George Washington Parke Custis loved the drama of his role, and played it in his motley, the costume worn in the days of his glorious youth and his foster father's glorious age. His stage was Arlington Heights, the central set his house, the first Washington Monument in the nation's capital. That house is still there, still visible from most of the official city "with half an eye." It was intended to be so, both by Custis and by his architect, George Hadfield, who had learned stage-craft as a student of James Wyatt, the most brilliant of Britain's designers of buildings as giant props. Hadfield was the perfect architect for a client like Custis.

George Hadfield

MANY NEWSPAPER ACCOUNTS at the time of George Hadfield's death stated that he had been the designer of Arlington House. His obituary in the favorite newspaper of George Washington Parke Custis made the same assertion. Since Custis was

---

* I am indebted to Howard Morrison and Margaret Klapthor for these references to Washington's stage-craft. They skillfully employed Washington's metaphors of the stage as the framework for the most comprehensive museum exhibition about his life attempted in America.

very much alive, jealous of his reputation, and had something to say on every subject, it is inconceivable that he would have left a misattribution of that sort uncontested. Yet it is very strange that no correspondence between Custis and Hadfield has been found.

Hadfield was a brilliant youth in a brilliant time, but a time that broke most of its promises. He and his sister Maria were the children of Charles Hadfield, originally of Manchester, the proprietor of a chain of inns in Italy. They were born in Florence, where their parents kept an especially elegant establishment near the Pitti, serving many of the rich young Englishmen on the Grand Tour. Surviving letters from these clients indicate that Charles was charming and politically shrewd, and all the evidence demonstrates that his wife was as socially ambitious as an innkeeper's wife can be. Consider for a moment what it was like for a genteel lady to be at the service of a spoiled and dissolute clientele, and it is easy to understand the beguiling, accomplished, shrewd juggernaut her daughter became.

The youth of George and Maria Hadfield was exposed not only to the capricious winds of what we now sweetly call the "personal service industry" but also to genuine trauma. Four of their brothers and sisters were murdered by a lunatic nurse, and Charles died soon after, leaving his wife and four remaining children to fend for themselves.

As their parents' children, Maria and George Hadfield had both met innumerable powerful people, including the best artists of Florence and Rome, and they themselves were endowed with great skill in drawing, though few material gifts. After her father's death, Maria was removed from her convent school and plunged into society, "ambitious, proud and restless." She found sponsorship to study painting under the famous Zoffany in Florence and with the Roman masters of the day. She also studied other crafts of the salon, and "with a form extremely delicate . . . a pleasing manner of the utmost simplicity . . . knowledge of . . . five or six languages" she entered the great world of Rome.

Next she conquered London, coached and prodded all the way by her mother. Her sponsors there included the painter Angelica Kauffmann, who persuaded her to reject the suits of artists and composers until marriage was proposed by Richard Cosway, seventeen years her senior. Cosway was growing rich as an art dealer and (to a much lesser degree) as a skillful painter of miniatures of members of the raffish circle about the Prince of Wales (the future George IV); he provided entry into that circle, and into the affections of the prince. After the Cosways' marriage in 1781, the prince and his friends were frequent guests, at all hours, in their house, which still stands in Pall Mall.

1781 was the year in which Maria's brother George commenced a different sort of education, entering the Royal Academy as a student. During the next decade he, too, manifested his charm by becoming the protégé of the Queen Consort and Lady Chesterfield.

While George studied, the Cosways opened an establishment in Paris "for Maria's health." There she sustained her friendship with John Trumbull, the

Maria Cosway
*From the Thomas Jefferson
Memorial Foundation*

American painter, who introduced her to Thomas Jefferson. Jefferson, it could be said, was the love of her life, and by Jefferson's own account, he loved her.*

The relationship between Maria and Jefferson has drawn the attention of generations of scholars; George Hadfield's biography is known to us largely because parts of it can be seen illuminated by the blaze of that scholarly fire. He seems to have been sponsored for a four-year tour of Italy to study architecture, and we know he was regarded by his peers as possessing a knowledge of architec-

---

* *She must not be thought to have been so detached from the mores of her time, and especially of the friends of the Prince of Wales, as to have confined her attentions to Jefferson. It seems likely that she was simultaneously carrying on a more intensely physical relationship with the Corsican general di Paoli, who was very probably the father of her daughter, Louisa Paolina, born in 1789 She kept an enormous collection of di Paoli's letters. What else she kept we do not know, for her papers are locked in the archives of the Vatican.*

tural theory superior to that of any of his contemporaries. He won the silver and gold medals from the Academy, the first student to do so in a generation, and was invited to join the atelier of James Wyatt, one of the most successful architects of his time, master of both the Classic and the playful Gothic, and beloved of the aristocracy of his day. Hadfield acquired a splendid education in the profession.

In 1791 the construction of the new capitol building of the United States had become embroiled in a series of squabbles among the largely amateur architects available and the politicians and contractors who swarmed about the ugly, swampy, desolate and raw village on the Potomac. The commissioners wrote Trumbull, asking him to send them a young architect who could straighten things out. He, Benjamin West, the president of the Royal Academy, and Wyatt recommended Hadfield, though it seems unlikely that they really thought he would go or, if he went, would stay beyond the period needed to finish the job. After all, he had just been nominated for membership in the Architects' Club by Wyatt and the august Henry Holland.

Then to the disgust of them all, Hadfield was blackballed, probably, thought Wyatt, by one of Wyatt's professional enemies, John Soane or Mathew Brettingham. The snub was bitter to a man who had grown up as a hotelkeeper's son and who, though a survivor of a long and anxious rise of derivative respectability, in large part through the exertions of his sister, was always at the mercy of the

Thomas Jefferson, attributed to Rembrandt Peale
White House Collection

opinions of others. Hadfield never referred to these events in his few autobiographical writings. When asked what had led him to be drawn from a bright career among the glitterati of London to the mudflats and malarial swamps of Washington, he said only that there had been a premium of five hundred dollars and a building lot in the new city. Having been blackballed by one of his professional peers, he may have thought things would be better in a new country, where architects were scarce.

He was to encounter a virulence of professional jealousy in Washington that would make the rejection by the Architects' Club seem a mere bagatelle. At the outset he drew the ire of the local practitioners by commenting on the conditions he found when he accepted the appointment. The lack of professionals was "plainly to be seen from the pile of trash presented as designs for said building." So much for Dr. Thornton's winning design. Thornton's enemies had "represented to General Washington unfavorable reports" of his plan and submitted to the President a substitute. Washington had magisterially ordered the new plan given the old appearance—though, as a man of considerable experience in architecture, he should have known a plan and an elevation have to relate to each other. He tried compromise and asked an able designer but inexperienced architect, Hadfield, to make it all work, somehow. If instead, as Hadfield later complained, he had "offered an adequate sum" to any "eminent architect in any of the great cities of Europe" to do the whole job, the building would "long ago" have been completed for "half the sum that has been expended on the present wreck."

It was Washington's refusal to support Hadfield's proposed third plan that led to his resignation from the job. He might have gone with a grand gesture and taken a ship to England. There he would have been welcomed by West, Wyatt and Trumbull, who had been his friend for more than a decade. Trumbull later said, "This most admirable artist and excellent friend" had "connections—who had some influence with the late King George IV," who in turn might have secured him "the execution of the extensive and splendid works" that were given, instead, to John Nash.* But he had not his sister's resilience nor her iron will. Beaten down, he simply retired from the field, no more successful in surviving the tong wars of the Washington architects than he had been in London. The principal subject of the next chapter, Benjamin Henry Latrobe, while engaged in his own battles to complete the Capitol, accused Thornton, a very skillful infighter, of "driving to ruin" both Hadfield and his predecessor, Stephen Hallet. Hadfield ruefully commented later, "I have long since learned that it is possible to be deprived of one's own, for the advantage and reputation of others."

He had been deprived of even the symbols of his youthful reputation; in 1812 Latrobe, in settling his own accounts with the city superintendent, bought and returned to Hadfield the Royal Academy's gold medal, which had been given to that tough old contractor as security for a loan and left in pawn for nearly fourteen

---

* It was Nash who showed the full extravagant grandeur to which the stage-management of architecture could be carried, in the vast ranges of buildings along Regent's Park and Regent Street.

years. Latrobe wrote to Hadfield: "In losing the prospect of an independence arising from your professional talents, it would be too much were you also to part with the honors you have so deservedly obtained." He was sure their common enemies had brought Hadfield's career to an end.

Latrobe's requiem was a little premature. Hadfield remained in Washington and eked out a living with a few commissions and by teaching architecture. He neither returned to England nor even went to Philadelphia, the center of the nation's economic, social and political life. Having as a youth fallen under the shadow of his brilliant sister, he later retreated before his more energetic rivals. In fact, his disposition seems a perfect match for the indolent and unfocused Custis. Trumbull, in 1795, spoke of Hadfield's modesty, the same term that was used by his friend Ferdinando Fairfax in recommending him to President Monroe to fill the post of architect of public buildings, which Latrobe had resigned. Later, Thomas Jefferson in a letter to Maria Hadfield Cosway put the matter more strongly. Her brother, though "much respected in Washington, and, since the death of Latrobe, our first architect," did not "push himself" enough. Maria responded, perhaps with gentle irony, in the light of her own aggressive youth: Hadfield's not putting himself forward, she said, was a "family fault." *

After he lost the superintendency of the Capitol, Hadfield tinkered with a brick-and-tile-making machine, for which he received a patent in 1800. In 1803 Jefferson, then President, assured Maria that Hadfield had completed with great success the commission for a city jail which the President had encouraged as an experimental center for his theories of solitary confinement. Hadfield also designed the first Treasury Department building, which was burned by the British in 1814. He was elected to the city council of Washington in 1802 as a Jeffersonian, and

Elevation by George Hadfield for the first executive office
of the Treasury Department
Courtesy of the Massachusetts Historical Society

* *Latrobe, after Hadfield refused to join him in his war on Thornton, spoke of him as a man who "loiters here, ruined in fortune, temper, and reputation, nor will his irritable pride and neglected study permit him to*

Washington City Hall by George Hadfield, now the District Court House
Courtesy of Douglas Evelyn

through Jefferson's intercession he was granted the commission for the city arsenal. Though Latrobe was chosen to design the mansion of John Van Ness, Hadfield built a theater for Van Ness, and the family mausoleum, a freely composed Neoclassic monument.

Commodore David Porter, another Washington speculator and civic leader, chose Hadfield to design his mansion on Meridian Hill, and Hadfield received as well commissions for speculative houses, a hotel, the Branch Bank of the United States and finally the Washington City Hall. The last of these is the only one of these buildings that remains, now serving as the District Court House.*

The City Hall is Hadfield's best surviving work, but Arlington House is his most famous. Today it stands unchallenged as America's most remarkable example of residential architecture conceived as memorial. It was so, long before the nation's armed forces built our national cemetery around it.

---

take the station in art which his elegant taste and excellent talent might have obtained" (Talbot Faulkner Hamlin, Benjamin Henry Latrobe, p. 286). Others did not find Hadfield irritable so much, it seems, as diffident and perhaps a little distant. Latrobe, passionate in friendship and in antagonism, always at odds with somebody, may have found Hadfield's bachelor coolness irritating.

* Hadfield wrote wryly to Jefferson in 1822 that he was "much obliged" for the ex-President's desire to assure Maria that he was "in good health and doing well," asserting that he enjoyed the former but "as to the latter I cannot say much." The city was suffering from a "scarcity of money" but he had "for the two preceding seasons been occupied in the building of the City Hall." (Hadfield to Jefferson, Jefferson Papers, volume 222, op. 39775, Library of Congress.)

Custis had his reasons for choosing a Greek form, solid and heavy and unambiguous. Hadfield would have been at ease in Jeffersonian Roman as well as Federalist Greek, though we have no reason to think he had any special fondness for his sister's friend Mr. Jefferson. After all, he had been brought to America by George Washington—everyone seems agreed upon that—and his most consistent client was Custis.* The letters that passed between Hadfield and Jefferson have no coziness of tone, and Hadfield was conspicuous in his absence from the group of architects whom Jefferson consulted about the University of Virginia.

It is likely that Hadfield turned to the Greek with the ease of one who had studied the Greek originals in their ruined state in Italy, and who knew from his master, Wyatt, how to make a villa out of a temple. If that was what Custis wanted, then that would be what Custis would get! But there may be more to it than that. Hadfield's generation of architects contained many theorists who believed the Grecian to be the appropriate style for republican heroes, and Hadfield was designing a residential reliquary for such a hero.

* *It may seem odd that so little is said here of Mrs. G. W. P. Custis. That is because so little is known of her. And George Hadfield—son and brother of driving women—remained a bachelor.*

CHAPTER 14

Classic in Context

THE SYMBOLIC QUALITIES of the work of George Hadfield and of the famous designs of Benjamin Henry Latrobe, to which we will turn shortly, are difficult to understand unless we step back at this point to see them in their transatlantic context. There were more complex ideas available to architects of the 1790's than the stagy and shallow intellectual basis of most of what was done in the Grecian style in Britain. Ideological Classicism provided a clear franchise for Hadfield to adopt the "primitive" Greek forms he chose for Arlington House. It was to be a porticoed temple, with simple Doric columns, appropriate to a building that was at once a residence and a shrine.

In explaining why he used porticoes upon houses, Palladio had suggested that temples had evolved out of houses, and that, therefore, people proud of their achievements might exhibit glory by occupying houses once again become temples. Palladio was a great authority when George Hadfield studied in Rome; Palladio's guide to that city was still the standard for travelers. French writers at the end of the eighteenth century had added to the Palladian theory the concept that all residential architecture had developed out of little porticoed huts, little wooden temples. Work by archaeologists had provided celebrated examples of the "real Greece," both in Greece itself and in its ancient colonies in Italy.

Even in remote Sweden, eighteenth-century nobles built such huts rather solemnly upon their estates to remind themselves of the Nobility of Man, and so did French and British noblemen, right up to the time of the French Revolution, when such notions (and some of these properties) fell into other hands.

American hero-statesmen provided perfect opportunities for the celebration of that "simplicity of the ancients" which, all through the eighteenth century, had been proclaimed as an architectural objective in western Europe. There, of course, it was often engulfed in the luxuries demanded by clients. "Noble simplicity" was the term used by the great propagandist for Greek architecture Johann Joachim Winckelmann, an abbot without an abbey but never at a loss for an epithet.

The English theoretician Richard Payne Knight gave a perfect description of an imaginary Greece, which could be transferred without alteration to an imaginary America: "In the fine age of the arts of Greece, civilization had just arrived at that state, in which the manners of men are polished, but yet natural." He might have been describing the manners consciously displayed by Benjamin Franklin, or George Washington. For such men, the appropriate temple-house would be simple, stripped, Grecian-noble, of republican simplicity. It would be noble and massive, like Washington himself.

The work of European intellectuals who emigrated to America, and of the generation of native-born architects they trained, has not been very well understood by European critics. Perhaps that is why the American Greek Revival received these widely disparate assessments from a great British historian and an equally distinguished American.

According to Sir John Summerson,

> The Greek Revival, which started in England . . . quickly spread to America . . . I do not think anybody would consider it one of the more glorious episodes in architectural history. The Greek orders always remained curiosities—specimens brought out of a museum. Since the Greeks never evolved the daring mechanics of style which the Romans had done . . . the revived Greek elements tended to be used as cumbersome and costly appendages to modern buildings of otherwise rather negative character . . . cultural luggage carried by buildings they screen . . . a very dead deadend.

Latrobe's biographer, Talbot Hamlin, saw not a very dead deadend but instead a time when "man in America, around 1820, had rediscovered his five senses." Was it not a "glorious episode"? "Never before or since, I believe, has there been a period when the general level of excellence was so high in American architecture, when the idea was so constant and its varying expressions so harmonious, when towns and villages, large and small, had in them so much of unostentatious unity and loveliness . . ."

The explanation of these two apparently diverse responses to the Greek Revival is that the two observers were not, in fact, looking at the same things. Though Latrobe had a hand in the origins of residential Greek Revival architecture in Britain in the early 1790's and of the American institutional Greek Revival a few years later, the two revivals were quite different in character. Ours was not as impoverished of symbolism as the British; the British was not as unscholarly as ours.

American Greek Revivalists were often quite serious about symbolic architecture, but seldom about antiquarianism. They made use of Grecian forms very freely, without the anxiety about precise replication of the antique that obsessed the British Revivalists. The British were pleased when their architects "got it right" in reproducing ancient orders and ornament accurately. They often lapsed into a somewhat finicking and deferential nostalgia. The American mood was one of confident fellowship with the ancients, to whom they felt an affinity of statecraft. Statesmen on both sides of the Atlantic took upon themselves figuratively (and occasionally literally) classical garb, but there were differences in mood. The gentler spirits among the British dilettanti were looking backward, with a tear and a gentle gesture of regret. The American classicists had no time for nostalgia. They were looking forward, with a cheer and a wave of recognition. The British watchword was *Ave atque vale*; the American was *Excelsior!*

From 1750 onward, while most of America was still a raw materials economy, as rural as the region around the Baltic Sea, with virtually no sign of industrialism, Britain's "dark Satanic mills" already were employing a large population. America did have small regions of intrepid and resourceful industry around Philadelphia, later around Oswego, New York, and in New England, led by entrepreneurs quite as ingenious and sophisticated as any in Britain. But we had no industrial cities like Manchester, no region to compare with the British Midlands, where a half dozen places that had begun as iron manufactures or as cotton-milling centers were spreading their sooty fingers across the countryside.

And in Britain, in response, perhaps, little decorative white temples began to appear beside artificial lakes in the carefully shaped landscapes set about English country houses. They were built by the chief beneficiaries of industrial growth, of colonial expansion, and of the systematization of agriculture. Especially they were built by the bankers who grew rich on the financial transactions that flowed from British imperialism. Somewhat later, huge Greek Revival houses and, especially in Scotland, huge Grecian public buildings were built as well, but, unlike many American counterparts, very little British Classic architecture (excepting that of the fiercely pedagogical Scots) seems to have been built by people intending to instruct rather than merely to please.

There are no equivalents to these monuments to Arcadian reaction in America. We did have a few large houses that made a gesture toward Parthenonic grandeur, but our revival was genuinely popular, widespread and consciously freighted with symbolism. The social differences between the two countries, cloaked as always by their similar languages, gave rise to wide differences in the connotations of similar buildings. By 1815 only 40 percent of the population of England was still working the land. In the United States that proportion was about 95 percent. If one were to contrast rapidly-urbanizing Britain to the American South or West, the difference is even more striking: as late as 1860 only one city in the South had a population of over 100,000; in 1840 only four cities west of the coastal states had more than 10,000 people!

In America the Greek Revival was an expression of the pre-industrial age, a little anxious about the onset of the new. It was not already nostalgic, as it was in Britain, about the departure of the old. In Britain there was no popular Greek Revival, no little residential temple for the average man. The British Greek Revival was, from its outset, an expensive enterprise. In the 1750's the elegant Society of Dilettanti financed the travels of James Stuart and others, who found remnants of Attic purity amid the squalor, poverty, infectious diseases and capricious despotism of the Turkish administration of prostrate Greece. By the end of the decade, green British parklands disclosed playful Parthenons (as well as diminutive cathedrals for piquancy). Though the scale of British Greek Revival buildings later became enormous, they never became entirely credible as habitations nor escaped their role as amusements.

The largest of Britain's Greek Revival houses, in fact the largest Greek Revival private house built anywhere, was Grange Park, the palace of an heir to a banking fortune, Henry Drummond (1786–1860). Grange Park was commenced in 1809, after Drummond's return from a Grand Tour of Greece.

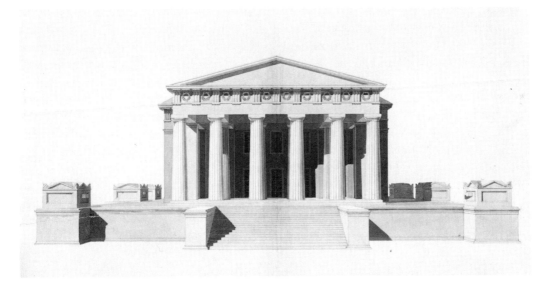

Elevation by William Wilkins for Grange Park, Hampshire
Courtesy of the British Architectural Library/RIBA

Like William Beckford, the builder of Fonthill, Drummond was one of a coruscating lot of Regency dandies and eccentrics. Thomas Carlyle described him as a saint, wit and philosopher, but he was too soft to be any of these. He was a dandy.*

His architect, William Wilkins, was only eight years his senior. Together they remodeled an older house into a Grecian fantasy to rival Beckford's equally grandiose essay in Gothicism at Fonthill (see Chapter Three). Wilkins and Drummond became related by marriage. They were already united by memories of travels through Greece, and by a determination to turn their backs on the indus-

---

* *Drummond was brought up by the great prime minister Lord Melville, who contended ineffectually with the spendthrift habits of his youth. Then suddenly in 1817, tired of the fashionable world, he sold his properties and embarked for the Holy Land, where he began a new career as mystic, professor of political economy at Oxford, member of Parliament and founder of the Catholic Apostolic Church.*

trial transformation of Britain, and toward the glories of a pristine Classic past in the English countryside.

Grange Park became a huge place, nearly four hundred feet long and two hundred deep (including the later additions by C. R. Cockerell). Even as Drummond left it, after his interest and purse thinned, it seemed rather stagy. Mallet, the diarist, said that "a good family house" had been turned "into a very bad one . . . a Temple instead of a house."

That was really beside the point, as Beckford demonstrated when he turned to temples. These buildings might be houses, and temples, but essentially they were stagecraft. James Wyatt, Beckford's architect for Fonthill, was perfectly capable of props for either a Classic or a Gothic performance. After the tower of Fonthill ignominiously collapsed, however, he was discharged by Beckford and thereby lost the opportunity to design his erstwhile patron's next fantasy, which was to be in the best Classic style. Beckford sought out a new designer and repaired to Bath to lay up his new vision, with a tower almost as tall as that of Fonthill, this time capped not with a cathedral spire but with a cast-iron and much enlarged replica of the Choragic Monument of Lysicrates. It was "Classic vertical," as Grange Park is "Classic horizontal." (Since Beckford never occupied the building in Bath as a house, it is probable that its first residential use occurred in the 1970's, when new owners made a house of it.)

William Beckford,
by Sir Joshua Reynolds
From the National Portrait Gallery, London

William Beckford's
Folly in Bath, the
Lansdown Tower.
*Courtesy of the British
Architectural Library/RIBA*

It was C. R. Cockerell, the next architect to take a hand in classicizing Grange Park, who understood best the nature of Classic stagecraft. On a brilliant summer day he saw the "sunshine on the buildings . . . the lights and shades and reflections as in Greece. The rooks and jackdaws in the lime tree avenue sailing and cawing in the air brought home the recollections of the Acropolis." He would not insist on the real Acropolis. A stage flat of the Acropolis, or a landscape of classical Italy, would do. These houses, however massive, were scenery, vast enlargements of garden tempietti. "Nothing," said Cockerell, could be "finer, more classical or like the finest Poussins. It realizes the most fanciful representations of the painter's fancy or the poet's description . . . There is nothing like it this side of Arcadia."

227

C. R. Cockerell. Portrait
attributed to Chalon.
*From the National Portrait Gallery,
London*

Classical Baggage

ARLINGTON HOUSE WAS commenced in 1804, earlier than Grange Park, and was as theatrical as any British Grecian house. Yet it was the opposite of a folly. It was theater, but theater conceived in deadly earnest. The drama of its form, and the drama of its setting, were intended to draw to it not the delectation of dilettanti but the reverence of the citizenry for a fellow citizen, George Washington, one of their own but of a lofty, unbending spirit.

We know so little of Hadfield's own character that it is intriguing to read the words of the eulogy offered for him at the Columbian Institute. They suggest that the Doric style might have been appropriate for him, as well as for Washington: "The ruling temper of his mind was a lofty, unbending spirit of independence. He preferred the simplicity of republican institutions . . ."

Simplicity and modesty. Loftiness as well! These are surely the ideal qualities for the architect of a monument, in Grecian form, to Washington. Poor Hadfield, celebrating Republican virtue. He had so little else to celebrate. For him, and for so many others drawn to the brave experiment, America was the wreck of fortunes. Some of the lucky ones, like the Frenchmen J. J. Ramée and Maximilian Godefroy, got away in time to salvage something of a European practice. Some, like William Jay, exhausted themselves in a spurt of productivity before decamping, but never resumed a fully fruitful artistic life. Some, like Latrobe, fiercely fought back, and built a career against all odds. But together they transferred the highest standards of European architectural rationalism, elegance and precision to America. They were the insects of cultural pollination, their careers dying as they did nature's job for her.

Hadfield"s life abounded in ironies; architectural historians persist in supplying them when they touch the materials that were left to them by his life. He died on February 5, 1826. The most powerful figure in American architecture, Ithiel Town,* attended the funeral, and wrote his daughter of the passing of "an Architect of respectable standing sent to this country at the instance of General Washington some twenty-five years ago." We know so little of Hadfield's social life in America that it is tantalizing to read Town's statement, in the same letter, that they had been acquainted—especially tantalizing because Town's biographer, the erudite Roger Hale Newton, points out that at this time Town produced a "trio of domestic buildings that may easily have introduced the strictly Grecian set of proportions into central New England," and lists among them the Bowers House, in Northampton, Massachusetts, the massing of which borrows from that of Arlington House, and which is generally credited with setting a style that swept westward with New England migration (see Chapter Twenty-seven for its later adventures).

Newton calls Town's letter "puzzling." He wonders about this unnamed architect. "Who can he be—Stephen Hallet?" So easily was George Hadfield forgotten! The architect for the most conspicuous private house in America!

His other prominent work, like the Porter House and his Washington Bank, has gone. But we can see what he could do on a monumental scale in the Washington District Court Building, as good a building as anything in the city. It came just at the end of his life. It may have been some satisfaction to him to be reminded, suddenly, in the 1820's, of the world he had left behind: a legacy of 1,500 pounds was willed to him by the Countess of Chesterfield. He had known grand

---

* *We will catch many glimpses of Town in these pages, though he did not enter into the kind of charged interaction with a client that more interests us than tales of artists alone, so he does not appear as a central figure. His career and Hadfield's had very different trajectories. He was a farmer's son from Connecticut, with the Yankee skills that Mark Twain admired. His architectural and engineering practice included the state capitols of Illinois, Indiana and North Carolina, custom houses and scores of private houses, athenaeums, churches, cathedrals and collegiate buildings. His patent truss made him rich; his architectural library, the largest in the Western Hemisphere, helped to make him famous. He was a shrewd businessman, a welcome partner, a patron of others and a man who has had no lack of attention, in his own lifetime and thereafter. He died in 1844, full of honors, affluent, a great man and much beloved.*

dukes and crown princes, queens and countesses, known them as affectionate patrons and friends. In Washington he had known the best America could offer, and the client for which he is best remembered was, in his sometimes pathetic way, a kind of royalty. If Custis was a Louis Philippe with bad luck, so, perhaps, was George Hadfield a John Nash with bad luck.

Benjamin Henry Latrobe

ON OCTOBER 1, 1795, George Hadfield assumed his impossible assignment as superintendent of the building of the Capitol of the United States of America. He had left behind a great success in England. Disaster was ahead. On November 25 of that year, Benjamin Henry Latrobe, bankrupt and mourning the death of his wife, set forth to America to recoup his fortunes. He, like Hadfield, who was almost exactly his age, had made the choice for the New World against the advice of many of his friends. But Latrobe was hard to persuade. Then and throughout his life, he was his own man.

One result of this independence was that he seldom found a sympathetic client, so he will always appear in these pages looking in on somebody else's story, not as the hero of any of our chronicles. But he is the greatest figure in the first three generations of American architecture (I do not see anyone before Henry Hobson Richardson standing even chest-high to Latrobe), and if he looms too large for us to treat fully here—he would overweight this book, and he has received his due in Talbot Hamlin's elegant biography—nevertheless we cannot proceed in this history without a page or two of Latrobiana.

He was another engineer-architect, trained in the same atelier as C. R. Cockerell of Grange Park, married and then a young widower, prosperous at first like William Jay because of the influence of his clergyman father, then, in hard times, bankrupt. He came to America, established a considerable practice in Philadelphia, was recognized as a genius by Thomas Jefferson, was given the chore of completing the "botch" of the Capitol after Hadfield was driven off the job, and left his mark on the White House as well, and on the designs for the University of Virginia. His masterpiece is the Roman Catholic Cathedral in Baltimore (for which he did have a great client, but his relationship to Bishop John Carroll is already too often told to require retelling here). He fought with everybody except Carroll, designed many wonderful works of residential architecture, canals and waterworks, and died in New Orleans of yellow fever in 1817.

That is the sum. Now, here are a few details—glimpses of the man, which may tell us something of his character and the part he played in the Greek Revival in America.

"From the days of our grand old Uncle Boneval, Pasha of Belgrade," he once wrote to his brother, "we have been an eccentric breed." It is to the *Memoirs* of Casanova that we owe the fullest—perhaps one should say the most fulsome—

Benjamin Henry Latrobe,
by Charles Willson Peale
White House Collection

account of the "large harem on the Bosphorus" kept by this uncle, a Catholic turned Muslim, a French count who was, indeed, created a pasha by the sultan of Turkey. (It is a pity that this is not a book that has space for an Ottoman detour; but duty calls, and we must pursue the Protestant brother instead.) Jean de la Trobe emigrated to England and then to Ireland, where he fought and bled for William III at the Boyne, settled in Dublin and became a linen merchant. His grandson Benjamin, now called Latrobe, was a Moravian preacher, a friend of Dr. Samuel Johnson.*

The architect Benjamin Henry Latrobe was the son of that Moravian and Margaret Antes, who came from Pennsylvania, where her father had donated to the Moravians the land on which they founded the city of Bethlehem. Her grandfather had been an abbot and carried the German hereditary title Baron von Blume; he had become a Protestant, married an abbess and found asylum in tolerant Pennsylvania. The former clerics were not, apparently, penniless, for when their great-grandson, the architect, was bankrupted in London in 1796, their Pennsylvania lands offered to him a strong inducement to commence a new life in

---

* *Dr. Samuel Johnson was congratulated by James Boswell for the breadth of his religious tolerance in a friendship with a Moravian. The Moravian was the senior Latrobe. The West Indian connection seems inescapable in this history, for Latrobe's career was launched under the patronage of the West Indian Middletons. One of the family had been so appalled by the condition of the slaves on his plantations, to which he paid a state visit, that he sought the assistance of Latrobe's father, and other Moravian clergymen, in alleviating those conditions.*

231

America. (These lands were much more attractive than the town lot and five hundred dollars that persuaded poor George Hadfield to come to America!)

Pennsylvania was a haven for many gifted people, not all the descendants of pashas, counts, barons, abbots or abbesses. It was also a forcing-bed for the seeds of the Neoclassical architecture these people brought with them, ideas developed in France, Germany and England during the last half of the eighteenth century, a time of vigorous experimentation in jurisprudence, social policy, welfare reforms and architecture. But the wars of the French Revolutionaries against their neighbors and their neighbors against them, the imperial wars of Napoleon and of the older empires against Napoleon, and the economic warfare waged by all these parties against each other exploded and wasted resources that might have gone into architecture. So, many talented people emigrated, to escape political persecution or merely to find work.

We have seen what happened to George Hadfield in the District of Columbia and then a few years later to William Jay in Savannah. But these were little peripheral communities, offering opportunities to architects only to the extent that a few—really very few—public buildings were created during the first decades of the Republic. (As we have seen, commissions for these buildings were not always tickets to Serendip.) Philadelphia was conceded to be the pineal gland of the thirteen original states. Charleston's day was spent, William Penn's city had become the metropolis of the mainland, and the mainland itself was no longer on the horizon of the economic world, glimpsed out of the corner of eyes looking toward the West Indies. America was rising, as the ravaged islands sank into that exhaustion from which they have not yet recovered. Philadelphia was now in center stage. Its vitality illuminated the whole slope of the continent east of the Appalachians, quite dazzling the envious eyes of the Yankees and the crafty merchants of Manhattan and the planters of the South, who now turned to that new light almost as readily as they had to London.

It was not unchallenged. New York was fast catching up, and would soon pass Philadelphia in the population race. The Pennsylvania legislature, dominated by Old Jeffersonians and therefore averse to governmental funding of internal improvements, was not willing to compete forcefully with New York or Baltimore, despite the hectoring of young Nicholas Biddle. Philadelphia architecture was dominated by the very conservative Carpenters Company, which fixed prices, controlled access to all levels of the construction industry and met in secret, a guild and secret society in one. It was as resistant to change as the legislature, despite the hectoring of Benjamin Henry Latrobe.

By the 1820's, brash Manhattan was exploiting its relatively easy though lengthy access to the West, while Pennsylvania remained divided by the wrinkled ranges of the Appalachians. After the completion of the Erie Canal in 1825, New York could supply Pittsburgh more readily than could Philadelphia. The force of commerce, as usual, drew with it the energies of the intellect and the arts. Yet Philadelphia, in second place, was still first to any other city on the continent, and its influence was enormous, particularly in the expanding South, as it spent off the endowment of genius left by Latrobe and his students. Though his tone was querulous (he was complaining of the larceny of his ideas by the Carpenters Company), Latrobe was not exaggerating much when he said, in 1812: "I have changed the taste of a whole city. My very follies and faults and whims have been mimicked." A large part of this legacy of taste to Philadelphia was a capacity to work ingeniously and freely in Grecian forms.

Latrobe disclosed his dexterity in Classicism early in the 1790's, while he was still in England, when he placed Doric porticoes upon the flanking pavilions of the Middletons' Hammerwood Lodge, which was probably his first independent commission. Grange Park may have been the largest of the Grecian residential houses in Britain, but it came nearly a decade after Hammerwood (and actually a year later than another essay in the Doric, which had been designed by George Dance the Younger for another banker, Sir Francis Baring). Despite the sponsorship of the Middletons, Latrobe's English practice languished during the resumption of the French wars; his great opportunities, Greek or not, came in Philadelphia, close to those Pennsylvania lands of his mother. Philadelphia was as well the home of his second wife, who brought him a modest dowry, clients and consolation.

Neither in Britain nor in America did Latrobe permit his Grecian "bigotry" to deny him the pleasures of working Roman forms (or forms of his own invention, like corn-cob capitals) into buildings others now call Greek. He was not much interested in ascriptive purism, and in deference to him, we need not be either, so long as we deal with certain ideological confusions arising from the promiscuous use of the term "Greek Revival" (in Chapter Twenty-two).

The association of bankers with Greek forms that commenced in Britain with Drummond and Wilkins, Baring and Dance, continued in America as soon as Latrobe secured the commission for the Bank of Pennsylvania, which was built between 1798 and 1800.* It was dominated, internally and externally, by its great domed central space, the vaulting of which was thought wonderful at the time, since it was beyond the ken not only of the Greeks but also of the Carpenters Company.† (Latrobe had been in London, where Sir John Soane showed many architects and bankers how to admit light into domes from concealed sources in his designs for the Bank of England.)

It may be noted that Latrobe did not complete a single building that could be fairly described as in the Parthenonic, or Grecian temple, form, except when associated with a most un-Grecian dome.

† If surrounding a dome with two Ionic porticoes makes the Pennsylvania Bank "the country's first Greek revival structure," then Talbot Hamlin is justified in saying so, and adding that Latrobe was "the initiator of the Greek revival." Hamlin is at pains to point out, in a magnificent book bearing the name Greek Revival Architecture in America, *that "the term 'Revival' used in connection with 'Greek' is a misnomer." We can be easy about all this, now, bearing in mind that the "new American Greek Revival, which thus received in Latrobe's work such a distinguished start, is not truly a revival at all. Greek details are used, but imitation of Greek building forms is conspicuously absent." (Talbot Hamlin,* Greek Revival Architecture in America, *pp. 35, 43 and 88.)*

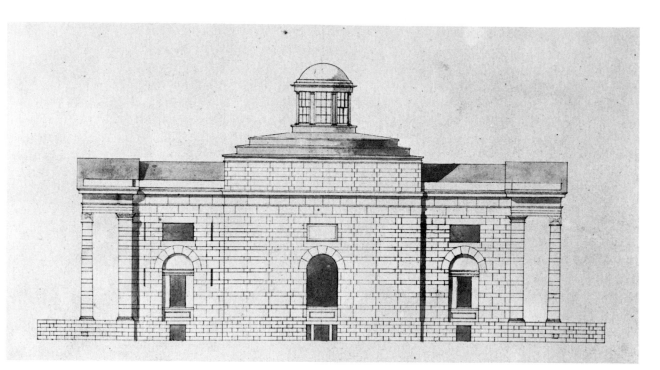

Elevation by Latrobe of the Bank of Pennsylvania
Courtesy of the Historical Society of Pennsylvania

Latrobe's Philadelphia houses, cubical and classic but not discernibly Greek, were the models for a whole succession built across the middle of the United States, especially in the Ohio River towns like Madison, Indiana, which we will explore in Chapter Twenty-eight. It was his bank designs, in the porticoed temple form, and those of his student William Strickland, that gave the Classic Revival, in general, its formative impulse—an impulse that Nicholas Biddle and other bankers welcomed.* After them, other financial people, and clients of financial people, followed.

Latrobe often returned to Grecian form for banks and bankers, but never mechanically. At the end of his life he proposed a grand temple-form building for the Second Bank of the United States in Philadelphia. He was defeated in the competition by his pupil, Strickland, whose design was tighter, more "correct." Latrobe was impatient with correctness; he was, as he had pointed out to his brother earlier, of "an eccentric breed." His favored mode was Neoclassic, but in 1807 he wrote to his brother again, saying playfully (I assume): "Your fondness for Gothic architecture has induced me to erect a little Gothic building in this city,

* *Jefferson had proposed a remodeling of the decrepit Governor's Mansion at Williamsburg into a temple-form house "with a pediment front the full width of the roof"—without a dome—when he assumed the governorship way back in 1779. Nothing came of it, however, and much came of Latrobe's Pennsylvania Bank.*

the Philadelphia Bank. Externally it will not be ugly." The exterior *was* ugly. But the interior was jubilantly eccentric, with a fan-vaulted banking room centering on a large cast-iron pendant. The bankers were bemused, but not for long. Soon they longed for his Classical style, and got it, once again, from Strickland. The "little" Gothic bank went down; a secondhand essay in Latrobian Classical replaced it. Strickland in those days was winning many commissions for "Grecian" buildings. Strickland, unlike Latrobe, was a friend of Nicholas Biddle (see Chapter Fifteen). It is often said that the American Greek Revival began in Philadelphia in 1798 with Benjamin Latrobe's Bank of Pennsylvania. Certainly Classicism, including a Grecian strain, first flourished there—but only after Latrobe's death.

It is true that without his example, and without the services of men whose talents he had nurtured, the soil would not have supported Nicholas Biddle's exertions to make the Grecian the "official" style of financial Whiggery. Yet in the 1830's and 1840's it was a great client, more than any individual architect, who was most responsible for the rapid diffusion of the Greek Revival. That client was Nicholas Biddle. Latrobe claimed to have "changed the taste of an entire city"; Nicholas Biddle never made such a claim. Yet he might have asserted with almost the same degree of truth that he had changed the taste of an entire country. He, as much as Latrobe, was the true founder of the Greek Revival in the United States.

It may be just as well to note here that those who accept Andrew Jackson's image of Nicholas Biddle as an antidemocratic figure in the great political morality play of the 1830's may find it hard to square Biddle's advocacy of the Greek with my description of it as an architecture carrying a heavy load of democratic symbolism. Biddle himself, of course, did not see anything incongruous in the use of Greek forms for branches of the Bank of the United States and for courthouses, or, for that matter, for the houses of proud citizens of a republic. He did not consider himself any less an embodiment of the triumph of republican virtues than Jackson, who seemed to him no more republican than the emperor Augustus. From its first appearances in Latrobe's bank at Philadelphia and Hadfield's residential reliquary for G. W. P. Custis, the Grecian style did celebrate republican institutions, though somewhat more Federalist or Whiggish than Jeffersonian or Jacksonian.*

* I am indebted to S. Frederick Starr for pointing out that Classicism in Russia and Germany was seized by the ruling party of each for its own purposes, just as there was a peculiarly Tory classicism in Britain. Georg Wilhelm Hegel, the German philosopher, systematized these matters for those who like systems.

CHAPTER 15

Nicholas Biddle

On September 2, 1804, Nicholas Biddle, barely nineteen years old, set out on the first voyage (as far as we know) taken by an American citizen to Greece. His passport described him as standing five feet seven, with chestnut hair about a high forehead, chestnut eyes, "a middling nose" and "a middling mouth." He was of more than middling intelligence. He had taken a degree in the classics from Princeton at the age of fifteen, and then gone off to learn the law, despite the efforts of his parents to slow him down, to keep him from treading on the heels of his elder brother.

Though he was very handsome and very, very bright, he was not content. All his life he needed approbation. Accomplishment was not enough for Nicholas Biddle; accomplishment was without sweetness until it was recognized. An important part of his self-perception was what he saw in the eyes of others. That is why he was so careful about his posture, his tailoring and his architecture. He was, one can guess, a quiet extrovert. When Biddle was young, his bookishness made him lonely. He was not playful. He recalled that his boyhood "was not I think happy." Later, his biographer tells us, he was "sensitive about his too youthful appearance and tried to make himself seem older by assuming a grave and serious manner. And, whenever he was questioned about his age, he would add four or five years in order to gain the respect to which he felt entitled."

At Princeton he embarked on Latin and Greek as languages needed by "those who intend to move in a higher sphere," and he decided to make the dangerous journey to Greece in order to set himself still higher. It was not merely education he sought, but invidious education; "knowledge," he said, "is doubly valuable when it is exclusive . . . we must be contented sometimes to build our reputation on the ignorance of our neighbor."

Though he was, as his friend and client Aaron Burr remarked, "a very extraordinary youth," he could not have dawdled into eminence with that unperspiring grace which is possible to the handsome and intelligent when they are also very rich. His parents were respectable, but not notably affluent. They came of good stock, with a typically American, spotty financial past.

The first American Biddle was one of the Quaker Proprietors of West Jersey, who settled at a place called Mount Hope in 1681. (Nicholas was born in "the Northern Liberties"; place names, like places, were incandescent with meaning around that Quaker settlement.) The Proprietor's son was a prosperous farmer, but his son's son failed as a poet and as a merchant. This was the Nicholas after whom our hero was named. The son of the failed poet went to sea and returned to become a successful merchant and banker, having married in New Bern the daughter of an obscure upcountry North Carolina merchant (see Chapter Seventeen). It was this substantial couple who were the parents of Nicholas Biddle, the celebrated banker. They started him on his way. He went further by his industriousness and his intelligence. His equity and first working capital came by his marriage into the Craig family, Philadelphia merchants and much more affluent than the Biddles, after which "his personal contribution, whatever its size, would only add to each year's surplus."

His ambition was nourished by his study of the classics, which led to his trip to Greece. That trip, in turn, gave his ambition new vehemence. Perhaps one could say that it gave it an ideology for which Classical architecture provided a set of symbols. For Nicholas Biddle, architecture was not a casual study. It made tangible the metaphors that defined his reality.

After a stay in Paris, serving as secretary to the American minister, he set off to Greece aboard the brig *Themistocles*. His mind was full of images of classical Greece, drawn from his studies. When he arrived on its shores, he was appalled by the degeneracy of the people, fallen "from a civilized nation to a barbarous posterity." He had not yet seen Athens.

He relied on his knowledge of ancient geography to find his way across the plains of Elis and finally stood before the buildings of which he had read so avidly. They were defiled by the presence of contemporary Greeks, "these wretches, little superior to the beasts whom they drive heedlessly over the ruins." How low they had fallen! How much they needed men like him to raise them up! Biddle was as handsome as Byron. He was a good amateur poet. But in 1806 the Greeks were not yet providing romantic foreign poets an opportunity to lead them in revolt.

Following another destiny, Biddle knew he must return to Philadelphia. He had been trained to think that "every good citizen owes himself to his country and his family." His country, too, was led by people of whom he—like Washington Custis—disapproved. Much as Greece, it needed him. He would not be content now, he wrote his brother, merely to be an attorney . . . he would be an "Orator, in the classical style," and "devote himself wholly to the world and politics and building a . . . name as a statesman." Shocked into statesmanship by the sight of those dirty men and animals among the broken remnants of his romantic classical dreams, Nicholas Biddle walked amid the ruins. At "every step of my path," he said, "I become a better citizen."

237

Nicholas Biddle as a young man,
by John Sartain
after Thomas Sully
*Courtesy of the Historical Society of
Pennsylvania, Gratz Collection*

Biddle and the Arts

THE AESTHETIC IDEALS of Nicholas Biddle were developing compatibly with his political ideals. For him, architecture aspired to the Grecian, sculpture to the Roman. Biddle studied classic sculpture in the Louvre, guided by Houdon, the creator of famous busts of Washington and Franklin. In Florence and Rome he was given a sense of the classical landscape by the painter John Vanderlyn. He made careful sketches and measured drawings of the Greek buildings he visited. When he returned to London to dine with James Monroe, the American minister there, and some rather patronizing British scholars, he scored "a kind of American triumph" which "overjoyed" Monroe and established the basis of an intense friendship.

Soon after he returned to Philadelphia, in 1807, he began courting Jane Craig, by the approved method of courting her mother first. He proposed a Grecian garden house for the Craig estate, which was called Andalusia, and twenty years later, when he and Jane were established in the main house, he instructed the youthful architect Thomas U. Walter to encase that pleasant Georgian building in a complete Grecian peripteral colonnade derived from the Temple of Theseus.

Biddle in his temple was far more successful than George Washington Parke Custis in his, in diversifying his agricultural holdings. Unlike Custis, he had other income to pour into agriculture—fertilizer, new strains of seed and new farming technology were oppressively expensive. Biddle the banker is famous; Biddle the agronomist should be better known. The lands he acquired were by the end of his life producing wheat, corn, barley, oats, buckwheat, rye and vegetables for city markets and supporting both dairy cows and beef cattle. He made money as a farmer. At the same time he became the most powerful banker in America, edited the papers of the Lewis and Clark expedition, wrote and translated poetry, edited the *Portfolio*, a magazine of opinion and criticism, practiced law and sustained a very active interest in politics.

He energetically promoted the use of Grecian forms for other buildings in his own city and, through his growing financial influence, in many other cities from Louisiana to Maine. His friend Strickland won the competition for the Bank of the United States in Philadelphia in 1818 by adhering to the building committee's instructions that it be "a chaste imitation of Grecian architecture in its simplest and least expensive form." Biddle was intensely interested in the outcome, and his father sent a special messenger to Andalusia to announce it. Nicholas served as chairman of the building committee, which saw to it that the structure was completed as chastely designed.

Andalusia
Courtesy of The Magazine ANTIQUES

William Strickland's Second Bank of the United States in Philadelphia
Courtesy of the Historical Society of Pennsylvania

Biddle's greatest contribution to architecture (aside from making it certain that Americans thought of bankers as grand figures worthy of inhabiting temples) was his suborning of the clear intentions of another majestic Philadelphia client, Stephen Girard. Girard was a French émigré, who began as a seaman and became master of a trading vessel and then a merchant and banker whose prosperity waxed so great that only John Jacob Astor rivaled him among the capitalists of the early Republic. (One really cannot compare wealth in liquid assets, like those of Girard, with urban real estate like John Jacob Astor's or with vast agricultural holdings like those of Wade Hampton I; one can only say they were all very rich indeed.) When he died in 1831 he left an enormous sum to endow Girard College for the education of orphan boys like himself. Nicholas Biddle was one of the trustees of his estate.

240

Girard College for Orphans at Philadelphia, engraving by A. W. Graham
From the I. N. Phelps Stokes Collection/The New York Public Library/Astor, Lenox and Tilden Foundations

The campus of Girard College in Philadelphia is dominated by a magnificent marble peristyle Grecian temple, quite "correct" archaeologically, and four smaller temples, apparently independent but subtly related in placement (quite unlike the intertwinings of buildings and walkways in Roman palaces or Jefferson's University of Virginia). Neither Girard nor Thomas U. Walter, the architect selected for the work, had originally had anything like it in mind.

Girard was establishing a school for orphans and stipulated "simplicity and purity . . . avoiding needless ornament," giving rigid specifications for interior dimensions and means of construction. He "did not recommend the Greek and Latin languages," and his feeling for Greek and Latin architecture was made clear by his referring to the Corinthian moldings of the steps of the First Bank of the United States as "those Kick-Toes."

Walter was the son of a bricklayer, and left to his own devices (though Biddle admitted that he might have learned some Classicism from Mr. Strickland), he would probably have preferred academic buildings like those he designed for Bucknell University (then the University at Lewisburg). They were "plain brick . . . and simple white entablatures." Biddle determined "to wean Mr. Walter from his plan," which was also the plan approved by the other trustees. Walter, an

241

aspiring architect, bent to the will of the most powerful client in town. "He behaved perfectly well about it," said Biddle.

Walter was no match for Biddle; few men were. He heard the headstrong banker's injunction that he abandon the perfectly sound concept that conformed to the testator's instructions ("to which the natural self-love of a young artist, of course, attached him") and seize, instead, "this rare opportunity of immortalizing himself by a perfect chaste specimen of Grecian architecture." He also heard the drum-roll of power behind the words.

A Grecian casing was fitted around a remarkably skillful deployment of the fireproof devices and vaulting, which Walter, a quick study, had learned from both Strickland and Robert Mills (see Chapters Ten and Eleven). Biddle's reward was the commission to remodel Andalusia, and to launch Walter on a career. (He was only twenty-eight when he won the Girard competition.) He went on to build a large and eclectic practice, succeeding Mills as U.S. government architect in 1861. He extended the National Capitol and replaced its low dome with its present neo-Baroque contour. Thereby he showed the way to his full acceptance of mid-century architectural megalomania in the Philadelphia City Hall, for which he shared the responsibility with his partner John McArthur, Jr., in the years after the Civil War. Walter lived until 1887. (This pliant, adept and courteous man, always *au courant*, lived from the time of Thomas Jefferson to that of Grover Cleveland.)

Thomas U. Walter
*From the Historical
Society of Pennsylvania*

Girard College and Andalusia set a pattern. But they also were the high-water marks of the power of Nicholas Biddle. A few years later, when the college was still uncompleted after the expenditure of $1.3 million (perhaps, comparing wage rates only, twenty times that much in 1985), the Bank of the United States was slain by Andrew Jackson, and Biddle lost his own fortune. The trustees of Girard's estate dismissed him as chairman. His friend Charles J. Ingersoll used a Grecian metaphor to compare him with Acteon, torn to pieces by dogs who had once "licked his hands and fawned on his footsteps."

Nicholas Biddle was the first American banker to be first citizen. His life was a long, proud struggle for eminence, for service and for power. He began by seeking a political career. He did not seek it hard enough to abandon Aaron Burr, who had been a friend of his father, though friendship for Burr meant the animosity of Thomas Jefferson. Nor was he quick enough in jettisoning the Federalist party, which he had joined in his student days. He remained a Federalist until that dying enterprise affronted his nationalist convictions by its flirtations with the secession of the New England states during the War of 1812.

At Princeton his roommate had been Arthur Rose Fitzhugh, a kinsman of George Washington Parke Custis. Like Custis, Biddle began his political career with an address on the character of George Washington. He attacked the Jeffersonians, viewing with alarm their French affinities and the decline of France into Napoleonic tyranny. He and his father were both elected as Federalists to the state senate, where he served two separate terms. But after the expiration of the Federalist party he failed to secure either election to the United States Congress or selection as governor or senator. The local Jeffersonians probably stood in his way as much because of his friendship for Burr as for his laggard departure from Federalism.

There is some irony, under these circumstances, in the fact that it was President Jefferson's Embargo of 1807 that gave the strongest boost to Biddle's financial career. The embargo not only encouraged domestic manufactures (and thereby appealed to unregenerate Federalists like Custis) but also encouraged the law business in Philadelphia. It provided, said Biddle's friend Horace Binney, an unparalleled harvest to lawyers, largely from insurance claims. Biddle had been well trained in this sort of thing when he served in London and Paris, where he also learned about international finance while arranging for the money to complete part of another unorthodox Jeffersonian transaction, the Louisiana Purchase.

It was through his scholarly interests that Biddle first came to the attention of men like James Monroe, Jefferson's Minister to Paris. Monroe gave him some access to the Virginia dynasty, and Biddle, in turn, despite his Federalist sympathies, received in friendship a succession of Jefferson's young intellectual colleagues from Virginia, like William Short and Edward Coles, with the architectural consequences to be seen in Chapter Seventeen. These associations, however, were not enough to gain him either an ambassadorship or electoral advancement. In 1818 a friend in Washington wrote him that the reason Monroe, who had become President the year before, did not give him a post abroad was because "You are a great favorite with the Chief Magistrate. I mean personally. He has the sort of personal affection for you he fears to indulge."

By 1822, however, the embarassment had, apparently, diminished sufficiently for Monroe to approve Biddle's elevation to the presidency of that Hamiltonian institution which had finally commended itself to the Jeffersonians, the Bank of the United States. Biddle had commenced his ascent to that eminence back in 1811, when on his twenty-fifth birthday he arose in the state senate to give an impassioned defense of the concept of such a bank, but he turned to banking only after he was denied eminence as a statesman; when Monroe first appointed him as a government director to its board, in 1819, he owned no stock in the Bank.

Biddle's association of national institutions, especially banks, with Classical architecture, aesthetics and citizenship was demonstrated in his selection of George Tucker, a political economist and the first professor of moral philosophy at the University of Virginia, to write a powerful panegyric for the Greek Revival in the *Portfolio* as early as 1812. Biddle himself translated French and Greek poetry for the magazine, and thereby made John Jacob Astor apprehensive. Astor expressed doubt that such a man, whose classical learning "overjoyed" James Monroe, might be too addicted to "elegant literature" to make a good banker. Biddle responded with characteristic bravado, in verse:

> *I prefer my last letter from Barings or Hope*
> *To the finest epistles of Pliny or Pope . . .*
> *One lot of good bills from Prime, Bell or the Biddles*
> *To whole volumes of epics or satire or idylls.*

It is doubtful that this satisfied Astor, but Biddle was satisfactory both to Monroe and to the Philadelphia merchants, and had no obvious competitors. Thereafter he had his way in banking and most other things for more than a decade. The bank moved into its chaste Grecian building in 1824, on a day of intense pride to its president. That building was headquarters for eighteen branches, from New Hampshire to New Orleans and west to Louisville, each of them housed then, or soon thereafter, in architecture of which Nicholas Biddle approved.

In the same year, William Jay produced his Grecian design and won the commission for the branch Bank of the United States in Savannah.

James Dakin made a marvelous little temple-bank in Louisville, which was so flexible it now serves as a theater. He and his brother Charles whipped up a larger and wilder variation for Henry Hitchcock's bank in Mobile, at which we will glance in the next chapter. One hundred years later, the Prairie School master George Maher took up the form again in Winona, Minnesota. There Maher showed how lively and beautiful could be made a Classic container for the town banker, who was still, in Winona, the first citizen of the town.

The history of first citizen Biddle's battle with Andrew Jackson, who brooked no competition, has been told from every conceivable point of view except that of a mouse in the gold vault. (One thinks of Robert Benchley's dissertation on the Treaties of the Newfoundland Banks, from the point of view of the fish.) We need not do that again here. Biddle was beaten, and retired behind his peristyle at Andalusia.

He knew he was beaten—though still rich—by 1835, when he concluded "that the promise is good for 'winding up' " the bank. The national charter expired; Old Hickory triumphed. In 1836, though the Bank of England and the private British banks were pulling in their gold, Biddle and a group of partners paid $6 million—much too much, it turned out—for a state charter for the Philadelphia branch. As cotton prices plummeted, Biddle tried to corner the market to sustain them as if he still had his old power. He failed, was forced out as president in 1841 and was sued by the same stockholders who had earlier given him a set of

James Dakin's Branch Bank of the United States in Louisville, now the Actors Theatre
Photo by Richard Trigg

245

George W. Maher's Winona Savings Bank (now Winona National Savings Bank)
Photograph courtesy of Winona County Historical Society

gold plate for his services. Hailed into court for criminal conspiracy and for "vulgar misdemeanors by a secret conclave of greasy householders" (in the words of the diarist Philip Hone), he was found innocent, but his fortune was gone; he had committed it to his last proud gesture of imperial finance.

During this time he put himself further at risk, as men are wont to do when stretched beyond their powers, by falling in love with a black-eyed, well-formed Italian lady named Ameriga Vespucci. She had been the mistress of a Polish nobleman who had died in Italian revolutionary broils—she said she had fought in men's clothes at his side, and had a scar to prove it—and she had come to America to seek her fortune. After a brief and (his biographer asserts) chaste flirtation with Biddle, she moved on to Washington, while Biddle served as treasurer of a fund she sought to raise. Such a role was, quite naturally, thought to be undignified by those who knew of their liaison. By that time she had become the mistress of John Van Buren, son of the President, who lost her as the final stake in a card game with George Parish. Parish kept her thereafter isolated in his mansion in Ogdensburg, New York.*

* *The house was probably designed for him by Ramée. The Parishes were an amazing merchant family of Hamburg and New York, and Ramée did work for them, it seems, on both sides of the Atlantic. That relationship will have to wait for discussion in another book.*

Biddle hated President Van Buren, whom he called "unfit to lead a great nation," and particularly resented the effects upon his foreign banking friends of Van Buren's financial policies, which, like Jackson's before him, acted to "plunder the strangers who have confided in us." In 1840 he hoped that the country might recover from the panic caused by the intense politicizing of the banking system, as well as from international monetary disruptions (which were so complex as to offer, even a century later, raw material for hundreds of thesis writers). The New York banks had not followed Biddle's lead into the support of credit and cotton prices; they had contracted their loans and kept themselves solidly based on gold and silver. The elimination of Biddle's central bank in Philadelphia played into their hands; so did his subsequent flailings about. He was ready to abandon the competition with New York and the battle with the Jacksonians in 1841, seeking from the Whig administration of William Henry Harrison the ambassadorship to Austria. His old friend, stockholder and debtor Daniel Webster, now Secretary of State, was unwilling to assume the political risks of appointing a discredited man.

Nicholas Biddle died amid such disappointments in 1844. The Philadelphia *Inquirer* said of him that he had passed a "busy, active, and anxious life." William Cullen Bryant spoke for the Jacksonians (as the Chicago *Tribune* had once spoken of Custis, for the Republicans): Biddle had died, he said, "at his country seat, where he had passed the last of his days in elegant retirement, which, if justice had taken place, would have been spent in the penitentiary." He was able, in fact, to live on at Andalusia because his wife and son bought the place out of foreclosure, after his own fortune had gone.

The other great Greek Revival building in Biddle's life, the bank, was visited by Charles Dickens after Biddle's death. Dickens saw in the moonlight "a handsome building of white marble, which had a mournful ghost-like aspect, dreary to behold . . . It was the tomb of many fortunes; the great catacomb of investment; the memorable United States Bank."

It was also a building into which the aspirations of a great man had been poured. He had aspired to be a statesman of Periclean grandeur. Once those aspirations had been associated with the columned splendors of his imaginary Greece. Once they might have been satisfied with the role in his nation's affairs to which his manifest talents seemed to entitle him. Then he might have found his proper setting in the temples of government in Washington.

After his political hopes were dashed, he transferred his ambitions to the world of finance and gave them their own Classic setting. The Bank of the United States was, at its climax of power, a rival to the government itself, and the bank's president had his own set of columned temples in every major city in his country. But what, one can ask, might have happened if Nicholas Biddle had not befriended Aaron Burr? What might have happened if he had pursued his friendship with James Monroe more avidly, or had solicited the favors of the Old Jeffersonians of Pennsylvania? Might he have had a political career? And would banks, then, have been built to look like temples?

CHAPTER 16

Mobile and Yankee Classicism

NICHOLAS BIDDLE, and the British bankers for whom he often was the arm, had a very long reach. He was influential in architecture, and essential to large-scale credit, as far as Mobile, Alabama, and beyond.

The first map to give this continent the name "America" showed Mobile Bay very clearly, indicating that the Spanish had explored that coast by 1507. They actually tried settling the area by 1559, and succeeded in the seventeenth century. Then the villages of the Gulf Coast dozed in the heat until they, and their little strip of hinterland, became the only prize won by the United States in the War of 1812. Samuel Haines, an early traveler who visited Mobile under the Spanish, said its five hundred inhabitants were predominantly composed of "people of color . . . who are generally free and possessed of real estate." It appears that Mobile at the end of the eighteenth century was a typical Caribbean town, largely composed of West Indian cottages. Colonel Peter Hamilton said of it that "as a traveler walked about Spanish Mobile, he would see little of American energy," but by 1810 "there began to be seen an occasional wide-awake Yankee come to make his fortune."

Though much of the energy behind the commercial expansion of Mobile did come from wide-awake Yankees, the real power was elsewhere. It was Liverpool and Manchester that sent most of the steamboats up the rivers after cotton, and it was cotton profits that drew the Americans westward. While the drama onstage was an American drama, the puppeteers were far away, setting the prices, providing the ultimate financing (or refusing to do so) and determining the pace of growth. On the very day in 1813 that the United States flag was hoisted for the first time over Mobile, *Niles' Weekly Register* reported a ship from Liverpool in the harbor.

Mobile and all of Alabama lay under the shadow of the masts of that tall ship, yet Americans at the time were far more conscious of the power of their own steamboats than of the power of steam-driven looms in the Midlands. Like Savannah before it, Mobile was a steamboat town. The steamboat upon broad, slow rivers was the South's answer to mule-drawn vessels on the North's canals. John C. Calhoun had prophesied that his region would need federal help. He failed to obtain it, for in 1826 President Monroe vetoed his improvement scheme. In the same year, after the Erie Canal was finished, Mobile received the first of a series of federal subsidies to widen and deepen the channel from her docks on the Tombigbee River to the Gulf. For the next fourteen years the work went on while steamboats scoured the hinterlands for cotton. This was the bonanza decade for Mobile. Powered by steamboats and Yankees, Mobile's population multiplied by four. Her greatest entrepreneur, Henry Hitchcock, asserted that "our city may be said to have been built during the ten year period." He could have gone on to assert, with justice, that the buildings to mark that growth were largely his handiwork, and bore the stamp of his architectural partners, Charles and James Dakin.

James Dakin was born in 1806 and his brother Charles in 1811, near the intersection of Massachusetts, Connecticut and New York. They began as carpenters and became prodigious builders. Though the career of Charles Dakin was very short, by the time he died he and his partners had transformed Mobile from a Caribbean village into a Classic Revival city. The Dakin brothers did not indulge in sibling rivalry for credit for design, and it is fruitless to try to do so in retrospect, though the evidence suggests that James was the better draftsman of the two. It is enough to know that they and Hitchcock had only half the booming decade of the 1830's together, and what an adventure they had!

Henry Hitchcock

HENRY HITCHCOCK was born on a farm near Burlington, Vermont, in 1792. His grandfather was Ethan Allen, the leader of the Green Mountain Boys, who seized Fort Ticonderoga from the British early in the Revolutionary War. Allen went on to become a contentious local chieftain who warred on landlords from New York, negotiated with the British for the incorporation of Vermont into Canada, and grew very rich and very miserly.

To his numerous progeny, however, Ethan Allen made his indelible mark as a religious heretic, whose tract, *Reason the Only Oracle of Man*, offended the proprieties of New England and led to his being ostracized by the God-fearing (perhaps the clergy-fearing) people of the province. The Hitchcocks took public service and religion seriously. Henry Hitchcock's brother, General Ethan Allen Hitchcock, another phenomenon, is famous for salvaging Zachary Taylor's Mexican campaign of 1846. He did so while annotating Swedenborg and Spinoza, and corresponding with Longfellow about Rossetti's translations of the mystics.*

Henry Hitchcock was haunted in a different way by the ghost of his grandfather. His life might be said to be a long commentary on, or dialogue with, the miserly old deist. When General Lafayette made a personal call on Hitchcock during his visit to Mobile, explaining that he did so in deference to his old friend Ethan Allen, Hitchcock remarked drily to a friend that "this is the only fruit of my inheritance from that quarter." Yet his inheritance did include his grandfather's doctrine, with which he had to contend in some way, just as did his brother, in his less conventional and more severely intellectual fashion.

Henry Hitchcock responded to the death of his first two sons, to the narcotics addiction of his mother and to his early financial strains by taking pride in "stoic fortitude." He "did his duty," erecting cottages for destitute widows, and was accounted a "benevolent man" but one "strongly opposed to warm-hearted piety

Henry Hitchcock
*From the Library,
Alabama Department of
Archives and History*

* *The pedant who wrote General Hitchcock's biography for the* Dictionary of American Biography, *and who obviously would have been equally impatient with Carl Jung, dismissed as "literary curiosities" Hitchcock's pioneering inquiries into the work of the alchemists, which "endeavored to prove that the leading alchemists were . . . devoted to symbolic presentation of a liberal pantheistic philosophy."*

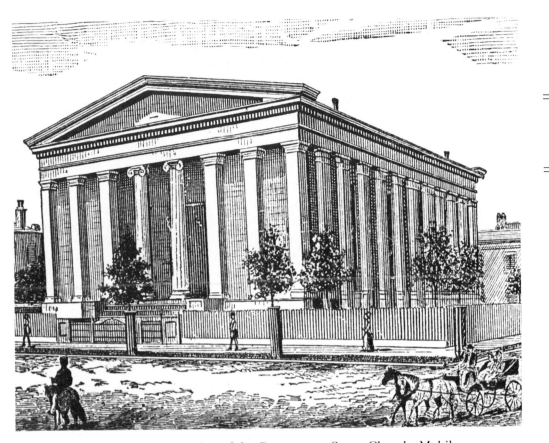

Nineteenth-century engraving of the Government Street Church, Mobile

*Courtesy of the Local History Division of the Mobile Public Library and the University of South Alabama
Photographic Archives*

. . . especially to all religious excitement." He said of himself in this period that it
was "too much my pride to act with scrupulous honor," without acknowledging
his frailties, believing he had "nothing to confess to man."

The Government Street Church in Mobile, which is among the most beautiful
Classic Revival buildings in the South, is not a testament to the pride of ennobled
yeomen, as are many residential temples in America. It is, instead, a monument
built to acknowledge excess pride. Hitchcock recognized that he had been "too
proud to be saved," too proud sometimes, in his hurry in business, to acknowledge
others on the street. But one morning, when he was still in the full flush of success,
he entered the little local Presbyterian church, "fell on his knees . . . and spoke
. . . of conscious guilt, of long cherished pride, of agonising struggle and of comfort and joy resulting from . . . accepting salvation bought with blood." That
comfort and joy resound in the interior of the new church he caused to be built,
drawing forth the Dakins' architectural genius.

Like any great architectural space, the Government Street Church has to be   *251*

Interior of the Government Street Church
Copyright © Thigpen Photography

experienced to be appreciated: one could fill paragraphs of unavailing description of its clear white light, the originality of its use of Egyptian and Greek forms, its sense of antiquity, of intelligence and, most of all, of passionate belief. Henry Hitchcock was its prime mover; it was one of two great monuments to his conviction that learning and religious fervor both required containers to shield and protect them, and that these containers should be sufficiently grand to be set at the center and summit of the community. The other was the domed Barton Academy. Hitchcock brought Charles Dakin to Mobile early in 1836 to help him create the church, the academy and fifteen other commissions in that single year. How he accumulated the resources to do so is an American story of talent, energy and good fortune on a frontier.

His father died while Henry was attending the University of Vermont. Since his grandfather Allen was disinclined to help, he supported his mother and five younger sisters and brothers, working on a farm and studying law. In 1816, at the age of twenty-four, he set out for the West, on borrowed money, rowing a flatboat to pay for transportation. He found a place to live in St. Stephens, upriver from Mobile, brought his mother and siblings to join him and hung out his shingle as a lawyer. He must have been competent and charming, for two years later he was appointed the first secretary of the Alabama territory by its governor, and participated, with his partner, in the founding of the Tombeckbe Bank. When statehood came, just one year after that, he was elected to the convention and drafted the final form of the state constitution, in his twenty-seventh year. Shortly thereafter he was elected the state's first attorney general.

That was also the year in which he went north to contend, in a lawsuit, against an old enemy of Andrew Jackson's, Colonel Andrew Erwin, of Bedford, Tennessee. Jackson had killed a member of the Erwin clan in a duel, and his friend John Eaton had fought a duel with Andrew Erwin himself. Erwin's son had married the daughter of Jackson's deadly foe, Henry Clay. Jackson treated the enemies of his enemies as his friends, and invited young Hitchcock to stay at his home near Nashville, Tennessee, The Hermitage. Hitchcock, like most people, was impressed by the general, whom he described as of "wonderful energy, strong intellect, and great decision of character." Hitchcock's assessment of Jackson was, however, adjusted by the virtues he found in Colonel Erwin and, especially, in Erwin's sixteen-year-old daughter, Ann. By the time he married the lady, two years later, he had become disaffected from Jackson and wholeheartedly adopted the politics of the Clay-Erwin clan.

Clay's influence brought him appointment as United States district attorney for the Mobile region after he announced his view that "General Jackson could not be supported with any propriety for President."

Hitchcock's Whiggish views were those of most of his clients, who were cotton planters and bankers. The financial system of Alabama—unlike that of Natchez, for example—was like that of the West Indies. It never accumulated much liquid capital, nor did it diversify very much. It relied almost entirely on a single crop for collateral and on British discounters (operating through New York and Philadelphia intermediaries) for liquidity. It was, as Hitchcock and his friends discovered, very fragile.

Alabama had great expectations, among them continuing in a beatific state of tax exemption. The Spanish and French had not bothered to levy taxes during their occupation, and in the early 1830's Alabama's citizens were persuaded that revenues derived from chartered state banks would be so great that state taxes were abolished by the legislature! Private citizens shared this enthusiasm: in 1836, at an assembly to bid for shares in Hitchcock's principal bank, the Planters and Merchants of Mobile (for which the Dakins were the architects), there was such a throng that one G. W. Brown mislaid his bamboo stick, gold mounted, with an ivory head, in the shared enthusiasm and later had to offer a reward and no questions asked.

Engraving of the 1839 fire in Mobile, Alabama. The Planters and Merchants Bank is on the left, the United States Hotel on the right.

Courtesy of the University of South Alabama Photographic Archives

Henry Hitchcock was by this time not only an eminent lawyer but a hugely successful businessman as well. He was thought to be the richest man in the state, with assets appraised at more than two million dollars in 1837. He could afford to give up the private practice of law and take a seat on the Alabama Supreme Court. In 1836 he became its chief justice.

During these ascending years he was an architectural client of extraordinary boldness and munificence. Charles Dakin, sometimes in partnership with James Gallier and sometimes with his brother James, delivered design after design that made Mobile into a gleaming white Classic Revival city.* Aside from the Government Street Church, the Barton Academy and the Planters and Merchants Bank, there were sixteen large brick buildings and the United States Hotel, which, when designed, was among the three largest in the country (the largest was the St. Charles Hotel in New Orleans, also by Gallier and Dakin).

* *Millie McGehee has discovered the earlier contribution of Classical ideas to Natchez by a Yankee architect, Levi Weeks, who designed Auburn, for a Yankee client, Lyman Harding, in 1812. (McGehee, "Auburn in Natchez.")*

The Dakins also designed for Hitchcock a smaller hotel, a headquarters building for an ambitious steam-powered cotton press, store buildings and warehouses —but, curiously, no residence. Perhaps the Government Street Church was the face Hitchcock wanted to present to the world, or perhaps he felt the town to be his mansion. Though he and his family lived very well in an old but fine house, it seems probable that his abandonment of pride led him to eschew a mansion for himself. In any case, there was no Hitchcock-Dakin house to match Andalusia, or the Scarbrough-Jay house of a decade earlier in Savannah. Alabama's greatest residence to display the elements of a Dakin design is Gaineswood, built one hundred miles upriver at Demopolis in the 1850's by General Nathan Whitfield, who had come to Alabama while the Hitchcock-Dakin partnership was in full swing. Whitfield, it is said, was his own architect, but he certainly knew the Dakins' work, and perhaps combined ideas from a variety of Dakin buildings in the somewhat sprawling mansion; certainly some of its ornament was orderd "by the yard" from suppliers in New York who warehoused such material, designed by an old associate of the Dakin brothers, Minard Lafever.

Charles Dakin

WE KNOW VERY LITTLE of the personality of Mrs. Henry Hitchcock, or of Charles Dakin. Like Henry Hitchcock, Dakin grew up supporting a widowed mother, for his father died when he was thirteen. He learned the carpenter's trade. In 1833, at the age of twenty-two, he was apprenticed to James, who had entered the firm of Town and Davis, in New York City. There he met a cranky, egocentric, self-

James Dakin's business card   *Photo by Arthur Scully, Jr.*

J. M. DAKIN
ARCHITECT,
Clinton Hall,
NEW YORK.

255

assertive Irishman, James Gallier, and the three men helped another carpenter of genius, Minard Lafever, to develop a book of patterns that, more than any other, influenced the construction of Classic Revival buildings in America. In 1834 Gallier and Charles Dakin embarked for the Old Southwest despite their fears of yellow fever, that sudden and murderous disease which had aborted the promising career of Benjamin Latrobe's gifted son and then had struck down the great man himself as he was directing work on the New Orleans water system.

Gallier and Dakin were partners in both Mobile and New Orleans, where James Dakin joined them at the end of 1835. Sorting out which buildings can be attributed to which of the three is impossible, though it was apparently Charles who worked most closely with Hitchcock in Mobile. That association was built on credit, and the shrewd men in London and Manchester who were the powers behind the throne of King Cotton were preparing in 1836 to reduce their exposure in cotton credits—as they had done before, in 1819, to the ruination of William Jay's clients in Savannah.

The Panic

THE FINANCIAL HISTORY of the Panic of 1837 is most often recounted to Americans either by admirers of Andrew Jackson or by admirers of his opponent, Nicholas Biddle. But there would have been no Biddle in this contest without his British backing, and no collapse of credit if his reductions of the money supply had not been merely spasms within far more significant constrictions in London and Manchester. As early as July 1836 the British began boosting their discount rate, and subsequently refused to buy most American bills. Their actions proceeded from a cool determination that the flow of credit to the United States, especially in payment for cotton, had been "excessive."

News traveled slowly; it was not until January 1837 that a letter reached Mobile reporting that the British had expressed the view that so much gold and silver had flowed to the United States that Britain was having difficulty with her own currency. There was a run for gold; Alabama state bonds failed to sell in England. Cotton prices began to fall; what had brought seventeen cents in 1835 was down to eight cents by March 1837. The Rothschilds refused to extend further credit to a cotton bank in New York, and it failed. The Barings announced they were restricting lending to the United States. All four banks in Mobile, so bravely begun, closed their doors, offering the explanation that they were forced to do so by the collapse of cotton prices and the ensuing panic for specie.

A Mobile paper, *Niles' Weekly Register*, reported "no sales of cotton yesterday . . . everything is dull . . . The lawyers and the sheriffs are the only busy men in town." Slave prices fell, following cotton prices; a newspaper reported that those recently sold for $1,200 to $1,500 could now be had for $250 to $300. A group of state legislators met in the court house, and a resolution was offered, sustained by

Judge Henry Hitchcock, that called on the banks to explain themselves and on the public to refrain from violence.

Hitchcock himself had good cause to question the behavior of banks. While he had huge assets, worth perhaps between fifteen million and eighteen million in 1985 dollars, he was also deeply in debt. General Ethan Allen Hitchcock stated that Nicholas Biddle's bank was asking 18 to 24 percent in annual interest from his brother. In the teeth of the panic, Henry sought to refinance his debt, mortgaging his assets for $800,000 (perhaps six million 1985 dollars). In a frenzy of activity he struggled to recoup his fortunes, building a new cotton press, new business properties, a livery stable and warehouses, and hurrying to complete his great hotel.

He did so in reliance on what he believed to be the personal assurances of Nicholas Biddle. He was mistaken. Biddle, refusing to respond personally, ordered a Third Cashier to demand accelerated payment (according to Hitchcock's recollections). Hitchcock responded with his last great scheme: he commenced raising silkworms and mulberry trees on a grand scale.

This must have seemed madness to his friends; for two years he had been standing off his creditors, negotiating with the banks, proudly keeping six or seven hundred people employed. Now he had succumbed to "silk hope," as had other desperate southerners before him (see Chapter Six). There was no more architecture to be made. Charles Dakin's own financial affairs were in such disarray that James was only able to stave off the bankruptcy of the firm a little longer by finding work in New Orleans. Charles, seeking business, or perhaps seeking escape, went off alone to Europe. Two months after he returned, in the spring of 1839, he suddenly became ill and died. He was twenty-eight years old. He was buried obscurely, in a section of a Louisiana cemetery for fever victims, at the end of July 1839.

Hitchcock was still struggling. The citizens of Mobile had come to see him as a hero in a desperate fight against "the monster Bank." Without solicitation on his part he was elected to the Alabama House of Representatives, but on the day of his election, in August 1839, he, too, was struck by yellow fever, and died six days later. He was followed to his grave by "the largest concourse of sorrowing citizens that we ever witnessed," reported the Mobile *Advertiser*. The epitaph on the tombstone of Charles Dakin can serve for them both:

> *Tis ever thus, with all,*
> *Always the first to go,*
> *The dearest, noblest, loveliest are.*
> *He went amid these glorious things of earth*
> *Transient as glorious.*

CHAPTER 17

The Halifax Whigs

THE POWER OF NICHOLAS BIDDLE was often deployed in the service of those British cotton-buyers and advancers of credit whose interest it was to keep the American South, like Ireland and India, a commodity-producer rather than a manufacturer. But he also supplied credit to the manufacturers of the neighboring Brandywine Valley, who were tooling up to compete with British manufacturers. Furthermore, through his example and his influence, southern retailing and southern speculations in real estate outside the cotton belt were sufficiently encouraged so that in a few places southern entrepreneurs began to develop, as he had, a kind of independent financial base. This permitted a few of them to escape the plantation system almost as effectively as did the rising Brandywine manufacturers.

Among these diversifying southerners were a group among whom he might have grown up, had the sexes of his parents been reversed. They are the subject of this chapter. Another set, whose financial independence developed later, was financed by Biddle's agent, Levin Marshall, in Natchez (see Chapter Twenty-four).

Biddle had ties of kinship, friendship and economic interest with the upcountry people who lived in his maternal grandfather's trade territory, the Piedmont area centering in Halifax County, North Carolina, and the adjacent "southside" region of Virginia, which also contains a Halifax County. This is a pleasant coincidence, for given their political views, we are free to call these magnates the "Halifax Whigs." Biddle's affinities to merchant-planters of the Piedmont were typical of a major Philadelphia financier in his time, but in his case they were intensified by common political and aesthetic ideals.

These great planters, whose holdings straddled the North Carolina–Virginia line, were separated from the seaboard by swamps and slow-moving tobacco-colored rivers. Amid their thousands of acres and hundreds of slaves they grew comfortably richer, acquired more land by intermarriage, raced fine horses and built elegant houses, using Philadelphia craftsmen, Philadelphia furniture and Philadelphia styles. Though they were uncontested rulers of their own domains, they looked to Norfolk, Richmond and especially to Philadelphia for their models.

This picture, which is the traditional one, is good as far as it goes, but it presents the upcountry planter-merchants too much as provincials. They refused to be penned in by their circumstances. They were not backwoodsmen. They were entrepreneurs whose retail operations spread across the Piedmont, and their real-estate investments extended as far west as the Great Plains and as far north as Lake Superior. Like their friend Nicholas Biddle, they were national in the scope of their ideas and of their transactions.

They built some splendid Greek Revival houses. Chief among these was Berry Hill, situated where the Coles family had purchased lands that had been one of the upcountry farms of William Byrd II. James Coles Bruce enlarged the property to five thousand acres. The buildings were within twenty landscaped acres surrounded by a stone wall, and today are presented in their full Grecian grandeur after the visitor travels a half-mile avenue of mature ailanthus trees, which were quite rare in 1850. Cedar hedges segregate flowers from vegetables, park from farm, farm from orchard.

The interior of the main house presents two drawing rooms on either side of a Virginia center hall. Out of that hall rises a superb double staircase, which meets at a landing and then proceeds upward in a single unified flight, quite as daring as William Jay's fanciful staircases of twenty years earlier in Savannah. The plaster cornices probably were drawn from Philadelphia pattern-books. James Coles

Berry Hill
From the Virginia Museum of Fine Arts

259

Stairway and parlor at Berry Hill in 1890   *Cook Collection/Valentine Museum, Richmond, Va.*

Bruce heavily influenced the design of Berry Hill, working with the assistance of an architect, John Johnson, and of a squad of Philadelphia craftsmen, like those Thomas Jefferson had to import to work at Monticello. Bruce and Johnson also imported from Philadelphia woodwork, marble and other fine materials, which had to be brought by water to Albemarle Sound and then up the Roanoke and Staunton Rivers.*

Much more important than imported materials, however, was the grand imported concept of an Acropolis with a cluster of carefully composed residential temples upon it, which also came from Philadelphia. Girard College was such a group, but the main house and outbuildings at Berry Hill improved on the college. They are set apart, above the landscape, and the two small outbuildings—temples, too—face each other, completing a kind of Palladian arrangement, though the units are Grecian, not Roman, in origin. One can see, at Berry Hill, the way the South might have been, if Biddle's Hellenism had been crossed successfully with Jefferson's Palladian planning at the University of Virginia. But the old tidewater South was too exhausted for this, and the new transmontane South lacked such subtleties of taste—as we shall see in Part Four.

The Coles Connection

HOW CAME BERRY HILL to be there? At the end of the eighteenth century, John Coles, a Richmond merchant, bought land in the Piedmont, in Halifax County, and began distributing it among his sons and grandsons. His progeny, who remained merchants and became planters as well, laid up a series of solid Jeffersonian houses, culminating in 1830 with Estouteville, the mansion of his grandson John Coles III. The builder of Estouteville was James Dinsmore of Philadelphia, who had been trained by Jefferson as a carpenter and elevated by him to be the contractor for the University of Virginia.

In one of these houses were born Isaac and Edward Coles, brothers of John III. Isaac became secretary to Thomas Jefferson, and Edward to James Madison. Edward recuperated from a long illness at Andalusia, where, according to Nicholas Biddle's biographer, he "virtually became a member of the family group." It was not his destiny to remain in Philadelphia, or to settle tranquilly in Virginia, or to build a house to commemorate his stay with the Biddles. His life was too frenetic for that. Andalusia had to wait for its Virginia offspring to appear in the 1840's, at Berry Hill, the house Edward Coles's cousin, James Coles Bruce, constructed (or remodeled; the evidence is not clear as to whether or not an earlier house is

* Charles Bruce, brother of James Coles Bruce, built a Gothic mansion at Staunton Hill upon his five thousand acres, not far away, about eight years after the remodeling of Berry Hill. Tarover, another, smaller, Gothic house, was built by Thomas Bruce, son of James Coles Bruce, to replace the first residence of his father, which burned in 1853. They are all still there.

261

submerged in its fabric) on land that had been owned by Isaac Coles. Fiske Kimball tells us that James Coles Bruce as well "spent some time in Philadelphia, just before inheriting the estate and undertaking the new house, and was influenced by Andalusia in his choice of a type."

It is a pity Edward Coles did not turn to architecture, for he was a man of intense conviction and energy. In 1814 he tried to induce his neighbor and mentor, Thomas Jefferson (to whom he bore an eerie similarity in frame and face), to lead an antislavery crusade in Virginia, but the Sage of Monticello was too old and weary, and, perhaps, too reduced in circumstance, to be able to consider liberating those slaves who were his only remaining capital. Coles thereupon took action that went far beyond the regretful, embarrassed or merely frustrated antislavery speeches of many of his Virginia peers: he actually departed for Illinois, freed his slaves and staked many of them to 160-acre farms in the new territory. He was elected governor of Illinois in 1822, and as governor, despite a strong pro-slavery legislature, defeated a serious attempt by other emigrants from the South to make Illinois a slave state.

Some writers have been disposed to see Jefferson as a tired hypocrite, and Coles as an unblemished young romantic. But admirable as Coles was, he suffered

Edward Coles
*From the Historical
Society of Pennsylvania*

from the same stiffness and invidious pride that made other Whigs so uningratiating. He was heavily righteous, and without humor. It is unlikely, but barely possible, that someone more subtly endearing might actually have persuaded Jefferson to remember his youth and engage again the problem of slavery. Such a person might have deployed the same qualities to build a larger political career, having won election and mobilized the moral fervor of frontier Illinois to defeat slavery. Coles was too pious, too righteous, too proud. He may have irritated Jefferson; he certainly irritated the amiable Hooper Warren, who shared both his antislavery views and, for several months, his living quarters. He was, said Warren, an "extremely obnoxious man" who made no secret of his "unconquerable prejudice against 'Yankees.' " The historian Theodore Calvin Pease summed him up as a "stiff little Virginia aristocrat." His stiffness led him into lawsuits and encouraged an almost successful coup by his lieutenant governor, who contended in 1825 that by making a trip out of the state, Coles had in effect resigned. His obnoxiousness made his reelection out of the question. He tried for election to the Congress in 1831, ran a bad third and departed in disgust for Philadelphia, once again to recuperate. He did not return to live in either Virginia or Illinois. Instead he joined William Short, another young Virginian who had served as secretary to Jefferson, and chose Philadelphia as home.

Edward Coles was not Nicholas Biddle's only friend among his contemporaries in Virginia—at Princeton, Biddle's closest associates, beginning with Arthur Fitzhugh, had been from Virginia, and these friendships were kept green by mutual interests, including the raising of racehorses and common ownership in business enterprises. The shadowy architect of Berry Hill, John Johnson, of whom we know very little except that he was a planter in the locality and was the son of Colonel William Ransome Johnson, a horse-trainer and -breeder, also had connections to Biddle.

The Whig Grandees

THE GROUP OF MERCHANT-PLANTERS who were Nicholas Biddle's natural allies, and whom I have chosen to call the "Halifax Whigs," had much in common with the antisecession Whigs of Natchez and of Mobile, the Unionists of South Carolina and the old Federalists like George Washington Parke Custis. They are not easily described by stereotypes drawn from either northern or southern propaganda; they were moderate men; some might call them (though not, certainly, Edward Coles) "trimmers." Remarkably unconstricted by their section, they were national in sympathy and in economic activity, willing to seek compromise and intelligently averse to violence.

Calling them "Halifax Whigs" encourages us to associate them with the most famous of compromisers, or trimmers, George Savile, Marquis of Halifax, the British statesman after whom all those New World courthouses and counties were named. George Savile (unlike his unfortunate descendant, another Lord Halifax, the compromiser of the 1930's) was a heroic figure. As leader of the moderates of England, he welcomed William III to the throne in 1688, and did so with such skill that the "revolution" of that date was nearly bloodless.

Halifax, said Winston Churchill, was "one of those rare beings in whom cool moderation and width of judgment are combined with resolute action. He could defend the middle course with a constancy usually granted only to extremists . . . He never shrank from the blasts of public frenzy, and rose above all taunts." This is, as well, a good description of the southern moderates of the 1850's, including the Halifax Whigs of North Carolina and Virginia, and men like Haller Nutt of Natchez (see Chapter Twenty-four).

The circle of southern friends to which Arthur Fitzhugh introduced Nicholas Biddle at Princeton in 1800 was similar to that which surrounded James Coles Bruce at the Harvard Law School twenty-five years later; one of its members was the son of Biddle's predecessor as president of the Bank of the United States, Langdon Cheves. Cheves was born in a log fort in frontier South Carolina, where his mother had gone for refuge during the Revolution. He was poor, but he clawed his way upward in the South Carolina Bar, was elected to Congress and in 1814 became speaker of the house. In 1819 he took the Bank of the United States from the hands of a Jeffersonian hack, who had mismanaged it hopelessly, and steered it back to solvency.

After resigning from the bank, Cheves returned as a lawyer-planter to South Carolina, where he was a near neighbor, geographically though seldom politically, to James Henry Hammond (see Chapter Twenty-three). He led the opposition to nullification in 1829 and headed off an early movement for secession in 1850. His ties to Philadelphia were close. He had practiced law there and sent his daughter to school in the city. (He insisted she study both the Greek and the Latin classics; she once composed a drama called "Caius Gracchus.") He also commissioned William Strickland to design his town house in Philadelphia, and probably was responsible for Strickland's selection as architect for the Classic Revival façade of the College of Charleston.

The son of this formidable man "sat often at table" with young James Coles Bruce at Harvard, reported another member of the group, Edward Carrington Marshall, son of the Chief Justice, to his mother. "Mr. Bruce," he went on, was "a hopeful son of . . . a very rich merchant in Halifax county . . . We have a large table, confined to Southerners and what are called gentlemen yankees."

James Coles Bruce was married in 1829 and, politically ambitious, was elected to the Virginia Assembly in 1831, the year of Nat Turner's rebellion. Caught up in the fever of the moment, he made speeches defending slavery. After he returned to his constituency he was "astonished to learn" that many of his peers did not agree; these squires were opposed to slavery on principle and were seeking, though without success, some means to its gradual abolition.

After he matured, Bruce often expressed regret for his youthful transgression,

James Coles Bruce,
portrait now at Westover

*Credit: Ronald H. Jennings,
Photographer*

both moral and political. He never again sought public office, except for local posts of honor such as justice of the peace. He was, like his neighbors, a man caught in a hopeless dilemma. He had not the extraordinary courage to break out, as his cousin Edward Coles had done; he held hundreds of slaves. But he deplored the effects of the slave system on whites and blacks, and was a consistent public opponent of the South's "Peculiar Institution," which Edward Coles called "our great national sin." One sympathetic biographer said of Bruce that unlike many of his contemporaries, he did not engage in slave-trading or -breeding. (Andrew Jackson for a time made his living at the former, and Thomas Jefferson sustained his standard of living by the latter.)

Bruce was an active supporter of the Whig Party. Like Cheves and George Washington Parke Custis, he opposed nullification. Disregarding the "blasts of public frenzy," he and his business partner, James S. Easley, were Union supporters in 1860 and 1861, hoping that "the disturbances now existing between the two sections of our glorious country may again be settled without bloodshed." As late as April 1861 Easley planned a trip to Iowa. When the Civil War broke out, he wrote his agent there to ask: "Do you think a Virginian . . . could pass through your country with safety and without annoyance?"

Bruce continued to oppose the secession of Virginia even as a delegate to the state's Secession Convention of 1861, though he finally joined the majority after

Lincoln's call for southern troops. Thereafter he equipped two companies of Confederate volunteers. His son Charles was killed at Malvern Hill. Two weeks before the surrender of Robert E. Lee at Appomattox, James Coles Bruce died of tuberculosis, at the age of sixty.

Diversifying Northwestward

THESE MERCHANT-PLANTERS of the middle of the nineteenth century, like the Carters and Byrds before them, lacked neither courage nor intelligence. Nor did they lack means. It is frequently forgotten that between 1780 and 1880, some southerners negotiated with Philadelphia as financial equals, with "deep pockets," as a current expression goes, meaning with adequate cash reserves. Contrary to the impression conveyed by some historians, all southern planters did not lock up their entire capital in slaves and land.

In 1810 there was as much of America's small stock of manufacturing equipment in Virginia and southward as in New England and the Middle Colonies. Southerners in 1820 owned more than half the stock in the Second Bank of the United States held by United States citizens. South Carolinians were second only to Pennsylvanians in holdings in "Biddle's Bank" and, with Marylanders, owned more than a third of the shares privately held in the United States. Southerners were not satisfied merely with stock ownership; in 1850 banks from Virginia to South Carolina held more silver and gold coins than those of New York and Pennsylvania combined.

Nor were the real-estate investments of southerners limited to the South. Wade Hampton II (see Chapter Twenty-three) bought 2,080 acres at the Green Bay, Wisconsin, land sales of 1836. It was not an act of self-exile that took Edward Coles to Illinois: in four years, from 1833 to 1837, southerners bought nearly 53,000 acres of rich Illinois prairie from the Springfield Land Office alone. The Wilsons of Elizabeth City, North Carolina, reinvested their winnings from the West Indies trade in 175,000 acres of Iowa land. A Louisiana planter, E. E. Malhiot, colonized with Cajuns a domain of 22,000 acres in central Illinois.

An indefatigable researcher of the 1930's, Paul Wallace Gates, dug through land-office records and reported that "the largest land business in the South and one of the most significant in the entire country was operated by James S. Easley and William Willingham of Halifax Court House, Virginia."

James Easley had been spotted by James Coles Bruce as he was working on Pannill's Bridge, near Brookneal, Virginia, in 1837. We are told by Pocahontas Edmunds, the chronicler of Halifax County, that from then on, "Easley was his favorite partner." Bruce, we know, left Easley five hundred dollars in his will, no small sum in those days. Mrs. Edmunds also reports that by the late 1850's Easley owned "more than 400,000 acres, most of it in Iowa," acquired after a reconnaissance of Iowa and Illinois in 1852, while his more silent partner, Willingham, "scouted Texas in 1853 and then other states."

Easley and Willingham, together with their partners, including the Bruces, "entered" (meaning brought title to) a total of 350,000 acres in Iowa, Missouri, Minnesota, Wisconsin, Kansas and Nebraska. The Cabells of Virginia, related by marriage to the Bruces, focused on Indiana. In the same year that Wade Hampton was in Green Bay, Wisconsin, Landon Rose Cabell and a partner bought 22,500 acres at an auction sale at La Porte, Indiana. It is entirely likely that one of Edward Coles's activities as registrar of the land office at Edwardsville, Illinois, before he became governor, was to keep an eye out for good parcels for his Virginia relatives.

Some of these northern land investments were enormously profitable. Stock in the Bank of the United States was, for nearly a decade, a very good thing as well. When its charter was snuffed out by Andrew Jackson, southern capitalists diversified into other securities. James Easley reinvested the rents from his land-holdings in Wisconsin and elsewhere in the Northwest, and in the stock of the La Crosse and Milwaukee Railroad. The firm of Winslow and Lanier, headed by James F. D. Lanier, initially of North Carolina and later of Madison, Indiana, was one of the agents for these transfers. Lanier had family connections with the Cabells, and in a sense, the story of his rise to financial power is also a tale of southern diversification, an investment of North Carolina brains in Indiana (see Chapter Twenty-nine).

Even the South Carolina gentry, so often described as bitterly sectional in their political and economic interests, joined in the national diversification of southern investments. Some of them shared almost commensurately, for a period, in the Unionist political views these investments implied. Encouraged by William Wilson Corcoran, the patron of the arts and banker of Washington, D.C., South Carolina congressmen William W. Boyce and William Aiken joined Senators John Breckinridge of Kentucky and Robert Hunter of Virginia in buying portions of the town projected at Superior, Wisconsin. Corcoran and his partner, George Riggs (of the Riggs Bank), entered nearly ten thousand acres in the St. Croix River Valley and huge acreages across the upper Mississippi Valley. Thomas Edmonston and five other South Carolinians followed Wade Hampton II into the Green Bay district with entries of more than one thousand acres each. William J. Grayson, who invested ten thousand dollars in Indiana lands in that period, spoke of a southern "mania" for northern land, involving "men, women and children, clergy and laity."

Mr. Gates estimated that southerners owned a total of 1,500,000 acres in the northwestern states and territories, counting just those purchases of one thousand acres or more! Eight hundred thousand of those acres were bought after the country began coming apart during the Kansas-Nebraska debates of 1850. As late as 1858 to 1860, the capital migration from the South accounted for purchases of 170,000 acres.

The leaders in this migration, or, to speak more accurately, this diversification of southern capital, were the Halifax Whigs: the Bruces, Easley and Willingham. The latter two lived in Halifax town, around the Court House Square (though Easley, the senior partner, also owned a farm called Woodbourne, which he purchased in 1846 from the second wife—Elvira Cabell Bruce—and children of James Bruce), and the houses they built, smaller than Berry Hill, were of the compact, cubical Philadelphia form of the 1840's with a severity, and some ornamental detail, borrowed from the Greek Revival.

Through the Fire

AFTER THE DEATH OF James Coles Bruce, Bishop Randolph of Virginia called him the most brilliant man he ever knew. Brilliance was not enough to lead a man through the political and moral dilemmas of his time, but Bruce was certainly capable of finding his way through the intricacies of business. He was said to be worth six million dollars at the onset of the War Between the States, some of it—not all, by any means—inherited. On his own he had spread his holdings into railroad securities and bank stock, and he had joined Easley and Willingham in their western land investments. He had also looked southward. While Easley was covering the upper Mississippi Valley and Willingham the edges of the Staked Plains of Texas, Bruce was looking into possibilities in Cuba.

These men were resilient. During the Civil War Easley and Willingham managed to salvage some of their western lands, and to collect rents enough to keep up the taxes. A month after Generals Lee and Grant silenced the guns at Appomattox, just thirty-five miles north of the Halifax courthouse, Easley and Willingham were writing Hoyt Sherman, their agent in Des Moines and brother of General William Tecumseh Sherman, that they were ready to move back onto the western scene.

We must assume the answer to their earlier inquiry about the safety of southerners in wartime had been negative, but now: "We are truly happy to be able again to resume our former pleasant correspondence" and to "resume our usual annual pleasant visits to your beautiful country."

The Halifax partners were in the West immediately, to collect back payments. By 1875 Easley had bought 160,000 acres more in tax sales in Iowa, and substantial parts of the towns of Council Bluffs and Sioux City. He was not sentimental about land. He sold off 154,000 acres during the same period, as prices swelled from six dollars an acre to twelve dollars. He operated in the postwar years in Kansas, Missouri, Illinois, Nebraska and Wisconsin, as well as in his main fiefdom, Iowa. Even on his deathbed he clung to his belief in the appreciation of prairie lands: "Hold on to my western lands," he told his wife. "They will be worth something." Worth something!

What were they worth? Recent scholars have helped us dig a little below the mythology about "landsharks" to give us a clearer idea of how mortgage-holders like these operated. Easley and Willingham, and their partners the Bruces, made most of their money on interest (on "paper"), not on appreciation in land—though they got rich enough on both. Their interest earnings could compound, because they had few loan losses, and this was true because the land they used as security increased in value. Its productivity was increased by those to whom they lent money. They seldom had to collect through foreclosure.

Contrary to some historical clichés, these absentee investors were well served by their local agents, like Hoyt Sherman, with whom they apparently enjoyed good relations over decades. Even more surprising, they did not seek to create tenancy, much less peonage, for they had no economic incentive to do so. They wanted to earn high rates of return on safe loans, to go on to buy more land, sell it on more contracts and collect more interest. In a sense they were not in agritrade after all. True, the commodity that passed through their hands was land. But they were no more traders, perhaps, than is a local banker who makes car loans. (Actually, most automobiles depreciate in value; land in the Middle West during the period from 1850 to 1878 did not.)

Thus did the Halifax group diversify out of a failing tobacco economy into a rising wheat and corn economy. Though they described themselves as planters, they were really bankers; in economic terms their diversification was not into land but into paper. Nicholas Biddle had made Philadelphia the leader of the Greek Revival and of banking. The Halifax Whigs followed Biddle's lead. They looked to Philadelphia for leadership in architecture and finance, even after the Greek Revival fell from fashion and Nicholas Biddle fell from power.

The North Carolina Magnates

A CLUSTER OF GREAT houses was once the pride of counties just across the border from Virginia in North Carolina. The best of these houses have been desecrated in the twentieth century, treated like old automobiles, stripped of their valuable parts for house museums, and the carcasses left to rot. Some were already derelict when the spoliation was done, exposed to the weather and to vandals, so those who salvaged some of their "working parts" felt they did well by posterity. There is always, however, the possibility that these houses might have survived intact through those Depression years into North Carolina's new industrial age. Then they might have been restored by corporate middle managers from the new cities not far away.*

Fate decreed otherwise, and as we examine the remnants of these houses, at Winterthur and elsewhere, we can only try to imagine them as they were built, a little earlier than Berry Hill. Tall, thin-columned, almost spidery, they were richly ornamented by North Carolina merchant-planters who, as the Coleses and

---

* A recent scholar tells us that the "great mansions have been carried off to be installed not far from the northeastern cities that inspired them. Descendants of the slaves who made the culture possible are tenants in many of the great houses, but leave when the places fall further into decay, to be replaced by stores of the other great resource that built these houses—tobacco." (Doug Swaim, ed., Carolina Dwelling, p. 87.)

269

Bruces did, looked to Philadelphia for leadership in taste, but who were, on the evidence we have before us, more willing than the Virginians to add their own stylistic idiosyncrasies.

One of the most famous artifacts collected by Henry Du Pont for his anthology of rooms at Winterthur was the staircase from Montmorenci, a house built above Shocco Creek in Warren County, North Carolina. Accounts vary as to whether the staircase now in Winterthur is the real one or not; some of the men who in 1935 worked to remove a staircase from the house and transport it to Delaware claimed that it fell off the truck on the way and was smashed. Others asserted that it got there safely but was too frail to reinstall. Photographs of it *in situ* show that it was elegant enough to justify the effort to return it to the Delaware Valley, from which, after all, its original inspiration came. It was the centerpiece of a house in which Philadelphia proportions and Philadelphia "composition" (prefabricated) ornament were amplified by exuberant local craftsmen, who invented gougings, and reedings and carvings of their own. From Philadelphia came plaster and a substance like molded papier-mâché, which could be attached to mantels and entablatures. Throughout the burgeoning cotton and tobacco states, from the North Carolina uplands to Natchez and Mobile, the craftsmanship of Philadelphia found its way into remote places, where it added elegance-by-the-foot, elegance from catalogues and from pattern-books, to enrich the lives of hundreds of lonely planters and their families.

Montmorenci (now destroyed)
Courtesy of the Henry Francis du Pont Winterthur Museum, Winterthur Archives

Stairhall at Montmorenci
*Courtesy of the Henry Francis du Pont
Winterthur Museum*

Montmorenci was one of a half dozen North Carolina houses of this type, built by slave-owning landowners for whom, according to one of their descendants, "the omphalos was Philadelphia. Even after the war . . . my Grandmother somehow managed to make the trek to Philadelphia." William Williams, the owner of Montmorenci, looked to Philadelphia as his financial center, his architectural guide, and as another place where the "breeding and racing of thoroughbred horses was the focus of community social and recreational life." Known as "Pretty Billy," he owned nearly six thousand acres in Warren County alone, plus his father's plantation in Halifax County. Montmorenci was probably built about 1820, and was furnished by Williams on his frequent trips to Philadelphia. By the time that diner-out, Lafayette, visited North Carolina in 1825, the house displayed a portrait of Williams' niece by Charles Willson Peale, and a collection of Pennsylvania furniture. We do not know very much about Williams as an individual, but we do know that his mother and the first two of his four wives were all named Elizabeth Alston! He was a general in the militia in the War of 1812, and died in 1832.

The mansions built by Williams and his peers in North Carolina in the 1820's

271

"Pretty Billy" Williams
*Courtesy of the Henry Francis du Pont
Winterthur Museum*

show just the first touch of the Greek Revival in their ornamental detail. They also carry the marks of their makers' nostalgia for that earlier period which in our scheme belongs to Jeffersonian Neoclassicism, though they are certainly not trapped in a kind of leaden nostalgia, like the "Jeffersonian" houses of the transmontane New South we shall see in Part Four. Why, one may ask, however, do they not, like Berry Hill, embrace the new? Their owners' conservatism did not come of ignorance of the latest in architecture, or an inability to afford it. The group of oligarchs who built them were rich, and they were not isolated provincials. They were regularly in Philadelphia, Roanoke and New York, where they had ready access to the new Hellenic fashions. But the riches of the North Carolinians came from the accumulation of the benefits of old circumstances, not from a burst of anything new—and life about them was changing rapidly. We can imagine them, like the West Indians of the eighteenth century, not to be very confident they could dominate a new age. So they used the forms of the old, perhaps as a shield against the new.

Part IV

ACROSS
THE MOUNTAINS

T HROUGH THE CUMBERLAND GAP, *in the last quarter of the eighteenth century, the emigrants straggled on foot, in carts and on mounted animals. They were driven by necessity and led onward by hope. Armed with the latest and most efficient implements of European military technology, their system of belief did not require them to be very remorseful about the consequences of their invasion to the natives of the region. And they were fortunate in their timing.*

Control of the central valley of the North American continent was achieved by Americans despite the best efforts of a number of other contenders. Among these others were the Native Americans, the French, the British and the Spanish.

Advance parties of the Spanish Latin American empire had explored Tennessee in the 1540's and again in the 1560's, but neither the Spanish nor the French occupied it. They were content merely to dominate its trade, the Spanish from settlements at Pensacola and Mobile, the French from a series of towns along the Mississippi. When the first British-American "explorers" reached the valley of the Cumberland, they found that their way was made a little easier by the dissatisfaction of the Indians with the terms of trade offered them.

During the middle and late eighteenth century, the settlement line shows a bulge, arising from a vast seepage across Kentucky and Tennessee, where settlers from the East broke through the membrane of interests that had attempted to hold them behind the Appalachians. That membrane, composed of the coincident purposes of the great Iroquois Confederacy in the north, the Cherokees (another confederacy), Creeks, Choctaws, Chickasaws and smaller tribes in the South, the French, the Spanish, (who wished a comfortable buffer in front of their possessions in Mexico) and those members of the British aristocracy who were not themselves speculating   *273 in western lands, might have been enough to delay for a long time the invasion of the West by British colonials soon to call themselves "Americans." But for one brief but crucial period, the French, British and Spanish were distracted by a succession of wars over what seemed far richer spoils, the West Indies and India, and the Shawnees temporarily abandoned their posts as guardians of the passes and the bluegrass plains (the Shawnees went foraging about north of the Ohio). While the door was unlocked, between 1770 and 1800, the Americans poured through the Cumberland Gap and spilled out into the plains on the other side. The population of Tennessee tripled in the decade before 1800, more than doubled again by 1810, and by 1840 was eight times greater than at the beginning of the century.*

Neither politically nor architecturally did the "hardy pioneers" who came over the Cumberland Gap with Daniel Boone come into a virgin land. Politically, they felt themselves released from one field of force and drawn into another, as they made clear in their repeated flirtations with the authorities at the magnet closest them, New Orleans—there were a series of ventures exploring the possibilities of detachment from the United States and attachment to the Spanish Empire—and these political forces were expressed in architecture, as they usually are. Though the settlers who came into Tennessee from the East carried with them their own traditions of housing, the region had an architecture well before they arrived. There were, of course, substantial buildings in the villages of its settled agricultural Indian tribes. And there was the architecture of the Spanish and French—and of the British traders among them—who had for nearly two centuries inhabited settlements along the fringes of the Indian empires. Long before the Cumberland passage was opened, Mobile and Pensacola appeared to be West Indian villages; as late as 1800 travelers were much struck by the similarity of Natchez to towns in the West Indies, particularly St. Johns, Antigua (see Chapter Twenty-four).

"Houses all with balconies and piazzas" were common by 1775 in the villages of the Mississippi Valley and the Gulf Coast, which ringed the rich lands of the interior. These cottages were familiar to seafarers who had traded with the West Indies, but they were a revelation to visitors from the highlands of the East, and they supplied a whole new repertory of ideas to people who were now to accommodate themselves to the hot, humid land along the banks of western rivers. In 1814 and 1815 Wade Hampton I became the first eastern entrepreneur to invest heavily in Louisiana plantations (see Chapter Twenty-three). After him came many others; the constant travels of these investors between their East Coast and their Mississippi Valley holdings were a necessary preliminary to the crossbreeding of the Caribbean cottage (our convenience term for a complex phenomenon) and the now somewhat tired tradition of columnar architecture that was brought by the emigrants across the Piedmont into the river valleys of Tennessee, Kentucky, Indiana and Ohio.

This is not the place for an extended stylistic recapitulation—we have larger game afoot —but it may be worth noting simply that that columnar architecture itself was a crossbreed of the two overlapping Classicisms discussed in Part Three, one of which we can call, for short, Jeffersonian and Palladian, and the other Greek, Arlingtonian or Andalusian.

The larger game is putting the consequences of all these interconnections in context. The architecture of the first British-American settlements beyond the Appalachians, and, after it, that of the whole inland South, was for the most part a backwater architecture—the artifactual evidence of the display and then the exhaustion of the last great energies of the plantation system. As it progressed into the valley in the middle of the North American continent, that system, which we first descried at the eastern extremity of the Mediterranean, was coming to the end of its long history of conquest, still directed from the metropolis, from Europe. But from the 1830's men like Nicholas Biddle, in cities like Philadelphia, New York and Boston, were contending against that metropolis for control of the continental mass. There were new powers rising, new financiers having their own agendas—and new sources of architectural influence.

Any unsentimental survey of the region between the Fall Line in the seaboard South and the Mississippi River—that is, the inland region settled by emigrants from the oldest South—will yield the conclusion that in the nineteenth century, in that vast domain, there were no great clients for architecture who can be included between a discussion of Henry Hitchcock (Chapter Sixteen) and Haller Nutt (Chapters Twenty-four through Twenty-six). The son and daughters of Wade Hampton I, and their spouses, come to mind as exceptions, but they are about all. There was a profusion of wealth, suddenly acquired and concentrated in the hands of people avid for display. But men of means and of taste were not there to the degree that they were in Savannah, in Philadelphia, in Halifax, Virginia, or, of course, in New Orleans and its cultural dependencies, including Mobile.* The frontier magnates of the Middle South showed their ambitions in houses that were large but that were not architecturally very bold—less bold, for example, than those of frontiersmen building smaller houses in western New York, Michigan, Indiana or Ohio, as we will observe in Part Five.

Natchez was always the great exception among southern interior cities. In Natchez arose a class of literate, cosmopolitan clients—many of them doctors of medicine as well as planters—whose architecture represents a unique accomplishment in the new South. We complete this part of the book with a group of chapters devoted to the greatest of these, Haller Nutt, who sustained the Classical tradition of geometry and reasoned order under the most unlikely of surfaces.

The story of Haller Nutt (and that of Wade Hampton II) offers another occasion to test a hypothesis underlying the writing of this book. It has been stated earlier, and was frequently expressed by those Prairie School architects to whose point of view I was introduced by William Gray Purcell, that bold and successful architecture is likely to be produced when an economy has enlarged itself quickly, when the energy of the newly rich has not been wholly spent in that enlargement and when there is a group of these potential clients interested in architecture.

Patronage of positive change in art is likely to occur among the new rich who care about

---

* New Orleans was always, from the 1790's until 1860, a place where wealth and taste and talent could be found in fruitful conversation. But the New Orleans of the Dakin brothers and the Latrobes, father and son, of James Gallier and of Henry Howard—in his disciplined youth—has been as thoroughly presented to American readers as Bulfinch's Boston, so we will leave that splendid, exotic city to its own eloquent chroniclers, as we turn up the rivers from the Gulf.

art. This matter is important; let me put it yet another way: boldness in architectural form is likeliest to be patronized when there is energy left among clients to whom success has come quite quickly, and easily enough to permit them a sufficient largeness of vision and vigor to take an interest in aesthetics.

Now let us see how well these ideas are supported by the evidence adduced in the final two parts of this volume.

CHAPTER 18

Orpheus Observed

ORPHEUS DOES NOT instantly come to mind when one thinks of Nashville. But one does not need to reach conclusions, nor discover parables, instantly. So Orpheus it is, Orpheus and what he lost in looking backward. That is a myth for all times and places, including Nashville in its first fifty years.

We are, and have always been, a nation of migrants. From time to time there has seemed to be a pause in our wanderings, a taking of breath, a gathering of ourselves to lay some wreaths, touch hands, exchange reminiscences. But soon we are off again.* We have, from time to time, deceived ourselves about our past, thinking that in some remote time there was a true serenity, a golden extended Indian summer, when the sunlight shone upon us, we surveyed the harvest and were in no hurry to go. We nourish our self-deceptions with elegiac artifacts and family myths. We collect antiques: we put milking stools in front of fireplaces; we hang the instruments of obsolete agricultural technology on our recreation-room walls; the Du Ponts collect rooms for Winterthur; the Rockefellers collect houses for Williamsburg.

It is as if we are trying to buy a tranquil past. Sometimes we merely attempt to rent one. We take a house, or a room, in places "time has passed by." Actually, we are just visiting places we have, ourselves, passed by, in a rush. We hanker for summer places in backwaters of stability and continuity, white-painted New England villages, red-brick southern villages.

Chief among our symbols of stability is the southern mansion, sleeping away the centuries, its white columns composing a kind of cage to keep what lies within from being touched by time. When Amos Kendall, a member of Andrew Jackson's cabinet, looked upon The Hermitage, he saw its new portico across the front and wrote: "Everything . . . looks perennial, perpetual."

---

* I make no claim for our being uniquely restless; comparability in such matters is beyond the range even of cliometricians.

The Hermitage
Courtesy of the Ladies' Hermitage Association

That is exactly how Old Hickory hoped it would look. But we should not be so easily deceived. The white columns of The Hermitage, and of thousands of houses marking the great southern migration between 1820 and 1860, were intended, perhaps, to look perennial, but they were the outgrowth not of stability or of continuity, but of change, flux and motion. Very few were built in old communities. They mark the migration routes, rows upon rows of columns. They remain along the trails of the American hegira, from the first, almost imperceptible rising of the Fall Line, up the tilted Piedmont, to the little towns where we readied ourselves for the assault on the ridges of the Appalachians. They appear again, back somewhat from the highway, marking the fertile fields of central Kentucky and Tennessee, at the way stations of our transmontane wanderings.

White columns were built to reassure, as symbols of the kind of conditions their builders hoped to achieve. We have accepted them as symbols of an order already achieved, whereas they are, actually, signs (in the Jungian sense) of the conditions that made that reassurance so desperately necessary. One can read such signs more easily in the state of Tennessee, in the light of its peculiar history, than anywhere else in America.

The first generation of conquerors of the region, who staked their claims in the 1770's and 1780's, did not do the staking with columns. The columnar Neo-classical style (as we have seen) was the product of the transfer of taste from Britain during the 1790's and the first years of the next century, given a symbolic vehemence by the garbled impression of ancient history among the Founding Fathers, who associated Greek, and even imperial Roman, architecture with Republican virtue. The men of the revolutionary years expressed themselves in the West in very unrevolutionary rhetoric, desiring to be thought like "the best members of society," not a "lawless mob." They were embarrassed by the impression of them conveyed to the settled folk of the seaboard by their somewhat more lively conditions. The rhetoric of their architecture, like the rhetoric of their petitions (which we will read at greater length in the next chapter), was conservative, using the architectural vocabulary of the middle of the eighteenth century.

They went to considerable trouble to give themselves the appearance of being like the best of the previous generation, not only building very oldfashioned façades but even importing rooms from older houses to reinstall in new shells. They carried the physical expressions of tradition in their wagons and saddlebags. In the next chapter we will glance at the Washington family's transfer to the West of their containers for culture, including a parlor transplanted from Alexandria to what is now West Virginia, and the even more peculiar reinstallation of a paneled interior by the Carter family in Tennessee, where they also reinstalled the names of children and of houses.

Politics and Architecture

IN TENNESSEE THE INSTINCT to recoil into the architecture of the immediate past was very strong. Perhaps this was because Tennessee's leading spirits did not have excess energy for the art of architecture; perhaps it was because they were not very confident in their taste, however they may have blustered. It was not because they lacked the means.

Once the emigrants from the eastern seacoast and the Piedmont had forced their way through the Cumberland Gap into Kentucky and Tennessee, an empire was given into their hands, and some of them became rich very quickly. With their new economic power they sought high positions in the nation's political life with astonishing success, taking shrewd advantage of their very marginality to move to power in the narrow range left them between the great, almost evenly poised Democratic and Whig parties of the older states, producing a cluster of Presidents and presidential candidates who succeeded the "Virginia dynasty."

Andrew Jackson carried the Ark of the American Covenant through the Cumberland Gap. In the West it remained. From the transmontane domain came Henry Clay and James K. Polk, Abraham Lincoln and Stephen Douglas. There military reputations were made by William Henry Harrison, Zachary Taylor, John C. Frémont and Winfield Scott. As many Presidents were born or nurtured in Kentucky and Tennessee (Jackson, Polk, Lincoln and Andrew Johnson) as in Virginia (Washington, Jefferson, Madison and Monroe). Kentucky's Henry Clay almost scaled that eminence, which he so passionately desired; only good fortune in finding military success and a new political base in the West made Virginia-born William Henry Harrison a serious contender for the presidency.

The political success of these men was not, it must be noted, the result of any doctrinal boldness. In politics as in art, they were remarkably conservative and chary of change; Andrew Jackson was a slave-trader and slave owner of the eighteenth century, who resisted to the end the changes in American capitalism that created modern industrial and urban society. The Democratic party in his hands, though it had a huge popular following among the "new classes," the rising mechanics and small farmers, was profoundly unenergetic in generating novel doctrines. Jackson, unlike his contemporary Napoleon Bonaparte, whom he so much admired, did not crush an old order to make room for a new. He strove to crush the finance-capitalist new order before it could crush the world of his youth.

It is not outrageous to suggest that there was a poverty of aesthetic invention in Tennessee equivalent to its impoverished intellectual life in the Age of Jackson. (Before the sharp outcries become deafening, let me add that this is passing strange, because there is usually an outpouring of ideas and of new forms when there is an outpouring of economic wealth as there was in the inland, upland South.)

Why should this have been so? It seems to me likely that some part of the answer may lie in the abrupt transition between the southern leadership exemplified by Thomas Jefferson and that of men like Andrew Jackson and John C. Calhoun, a transition the more difficult to observe because none of the three was what he seemed.

Certainly Jackson was not the prototype of Franklin D. Roosevelt, a radical aristocrat. He was neither radical nor an aristocrat. (It can be argued that FDR was not truly radical either, but that is another argument. He certainly seemed so to many at the time.) Let us look at the other two:

Jefferson was not a Tidewater aristocrat; he was a son of the Piedmont. Had he been a true Tidewater participant in the international commodity economy, his politics, and, I suggest, his architecture, might have been less innovative* and his politics less independent. The Tidewater had served an international economy with tobacco and wheat; though many of its eighteenth-century inhabitants probably would have survived without selling commodities abroad, its aristocratic minority could not have done so very grandly. In the Piedmont, however, the voice of the international system was more muted; there were more subsistence farmers, more actual prototypes of the Jeffersonian ideal of independent yeomen.

Jefferson, in fact, attempted to establish plantation life free of international

---

* *Doubters about the radical quality of Jefferson's architecture may wish to review Buford Pickens' splendid article, "Mr. Jefferson as Revolutionary Architect."*

Andrew Jackson,
engraving
by Longacre
after Sully

*Courtesy of the National
Portrait Gallery,
Smithsonian Institution,
Washington, D.C.*

markets and free of centralized industrial organization, which he anticipated would require cities and centralized political organization, both of which he feared. But the plantation system was an international system. Inevitably he was drawn into selling tobacco and wheat into it, and just as inevitably into selling slaves to keep it going. That was not his desire, and it ran against his earlier principles, but he was by then defeated, himself a transition figure; the South had fallen into the hands of John C. Calhoun and Andrew Jackson.

Mr. Jefferson did not wish to be the last word in architecture. He wished to be the first word, to establish a vigorous independence of mind that would nourish fresh, new art. Instead, when the creative energy went out of his portion of the South, his influence became what he most feared: deadening, suffocating, like the intellectual world of Calhoun.

Calhoun, like Andrew Jackson, took upon himself the toga of a Roman aristocrat and turned his back on his own past as a frontiersman. He embraced the past, not his own experience. He was an upcountry farmer's son. His father had no slaves. Yet the upcountry men he led became the great absentee slaveholders who entered into a sort of implicit compact with the international plantation system and its ancient ways. Calhoun, and the class of planters who followed him, became dependent and neocolonial, not in their intentions but in their effects. Their splenetics in the 1850's were mere parodies of his harshly rational apologia for the slave and plantation system.

When there is such a quick turning from the making of money to an embrace of the past, when there is fear, not delight in risks run and joyfully bested, then architecture, great, fresh architecture, loses its moment. That there could be such a moment, even in the South, we shall observe when we return to the main line of American architectural and economic development in Chapter Twenty-four. In Natchcz, we shall see, a few people reared themselves out of the plantation system and looked beyond it. There they found the energy that is required to break through deferential patterns, to trust one's taste and to make something new and better.

Roundheads and Cavaliers

LET US LOOK MORE closely at the architectural record of some of the newcomers. In the spring of 1779 John Donelson, abroad the *Adventure*, led a flotilla of forty or more emigrant boats out of Virginia and North Carolina, down the Tennessee River and up the Cumberland to Big Salt Lick, which later was called Nashville. They survived Muscle Shoals, an Indian attack and casualties among the women and children. Donelson cleared some land at Clover Bottom and laid in the first cotton grown in middle Tennessee. Donelson's daughter Rachel was to become the wife of Andrew Jackson—The Hermitage would be built and rebuilt near Clover Bottom—but in the next five years Nashville contained "only two houses, which . . . merit that name; the rest . . . only huts." It acquired a brick structure in 1791, and the Methodist evangelist Bishop Francis Asbury found "not less than one thousand people were in and out of" the unfinished stone church that awaited him when he arrived that same year. There were perhaps forty thousand people in the territory. Five years later, after Tennessee was admitted as a state, Nashville was still so crude that the Duke of Orléans, later King Louis Philippe of France, could not find a bed to share with less than two others.

Who were the people who came into Tennessee? Lying along the western frontier of the British colonies was a mountain kingdom occupied largely by Scotch Presbyterians who, as we become acquainted with them, sometimes seem to have hated almost everybody, and for good reason. They had left their huts in Scotland to serve in Ireland as cheap labor on estates owned by Anglicans. They had been ground between those landlords and the Catholic Irishmen whom they were driving into starvation. In the eighteenth century their rents were raised, their woolen industry squeezed out, their religious inclinations frustrated. Their cousins were defeated by the brutal Duke of Cumberland after a last rising against what many of them regarded as the Hanoverian usurpers of the British crown, which was rightfully to be held by its only Scottish dynasty, the deposed Stuarts. It was a bitter thing, indeed, that the most important single place in the highland empire they came to occupy, after they escaped to America, was Cumberland Gap, named after the man who defeated their hopes at Culloden.

Had the ancestors of Andrew Jackson been English rather than Scottish, they would not have ridden with Rupert; they would have walked with Cromwell. The visages even in their nineteenth-century descendants appear flinty, humorless. They seem to be driven by terrible internal guilt and passion, violent, restless and

James K. Polk (*left*)
From the National Portrait Gallery,
Smithsonian Institution, Washington, D.C.

John C. Calhoun (*below*)
From the Yale University Art Gallery/Gift of John Hill Morgan

Henry Clay (*above*)
From the National Portrait Gallery,
Smithsonian Institution, Washington, D.C.

283

intolerant. Among these Scotch-Irish Roundheads and non-conforming Ulstermen there must have been sunny spirits, full of dance and song, ready to embrace, to laugh and love, but if there were, they have left us little to remember them by. We see instead, perhaps unfairly, a people fiercely coming ashore in America, fiercely settling in western valleys, fiercely taking the land of the middle South and planting it with cotton.

The Scotch-Irish were indomitable and skillful frontiersmen. In the mountains they were joined by Germans who had come down from Pennsylvania (over a third of the population of that state was German-born in 1776), a group that gave some stability to the fractious and cranky Scotch-Irish. In Pennsylvania the Germans had preferred to build of stone, and decorated their houses with paint and their wooden surfaces, in architecture and furniture, with carving. This ornamental "Pennsylvania Dutch" style did not travel well. Perhaps it implied a determination to stay in a place long enough to enjoy the benefits of such laborious craftsmanship. For emigrants, the simpler traditions of south German timber construction were more serviceable, and the Pennsylvania Dutch were early adepts of the log cabin. They instructed the Scotch-Irish, and the notched-log, corner-jointed cabin became so common as to be the characteristic folk architecture of the region.

What of the myth commonly associated with that cabin, the myth of the free and independent yeoman? The elements of this myth were articulated by a representative of the frontier area, Charles Faulkner, during the Virginia slavery debates of 1832. He spoke of the people of western Virginia as "substantial, independent yeomanry—no population upon the face of the Globe," he asserted, "is more distinguished for an elevated love of freedom—for morality, virtue, frugality and independence, than the Virginia peasantry west of the Blue Ridge."

When these "peasants" moved south and west, and through bravery and hard driving made themselves into planters, when they began expanding their dog-trot log cabins into plantation houses and finally added columned porticoes, they no longer would happily have accepted the appellation "peasant." Now they were "gentlemen."

They chose their architecture to make that point. It was, in the first generation, retrospective, implying an association between themselves and the Virginia gentry. Jeffersonian Palladianism had its last, somewhat rickety moment in Tennessee and Kentucky. Like the freebooters who made themselves into West Indian sugar-planters, these trans-Appalachian rural new rich built themselves into the past, in an effort to give themselves pedigrees through architecture. In this they were unlike their urban new-rich contemporaries in Savannah, perhaps because there happened to be an amazingly daring group of clients in Savannah, and an architect, William Jay, with the training to build in the very latest fashion, fresh from England, and the genius to add to what was fashionable the fruits of his own invention.

The yeomen-become-slaveowners in Tennessee were not lucky enough, or, it seems, very eager, to find a William Jay—and Robert Mills was only available for a façade and a tomb (see Chapter Eleven). They turned to the prototypes offered by Tidewater slaveowners, both architecturally and socially. Nor were they on much better terms than had been those Tidewater gentry with the yeomen who stayed yeomen, up on the hillsides about them. These poorer farmers had no slaves and kept large areas of the rougher, more mountainous western territories free of both blacks and slavery to the extent they could. They lived in equal hostility to slaves and to slaveowners.

The new class of aristocrats had every reason to relapse into an architecture that set them apart from the grubby present and said distinctly that they were no longer yeomen. Their wealth and their status depended on the ownership of other persons who were not free, were not independent and were not ever going to be yeomen.

We should romanticize neither Jeffersonian reality nor Jacksonian reality. We tend to forget that in the slave states, planters very quickly accepted the view of their intellectual laureate, George Fitzhugh, that "agricultural labor is the most arduous, least respectable, and worst paid of all labor. Nature and philosophy teach all who can to avoid and escape from it and to pursue less laborious, more

Andrew Jackson, lithograph
after a daguerreotype by Brady
*From the National Portrait Gallery,
Smithsonian Institution, Washington, D.C.*

respectable and more lucrative employments. None work in the field who can help it. Hence free society is in great measure dependent for its food and clothing on slave society."

Fitzhugh's formulation of a slave owner's view of yeomanry is important, because it reminds us that there was a fundamental difference between the stream of migration that went west along the Great Lakes and the stream that poured out of the southern highlands into Kentucky and Tennessee. Among those who went the southern route were a few non-yeomen, scions of planter families who were forced westward, who acted as seeds of the old plantation system, ready for planting in new soil. When those seeds germinated, it was found that they had retained much of the psychology and the architecture of the Tidewater. It is foolish to believe that the roads to the West were clogged with Cavalier families traveling in long lines of wagons full of family portraits and silver, but there were enough of these transplants to require us to see what effect they had on the West.

We do not speak of the Jacksons and Polks and Lincolns and Hamptons and Clays. They never could have been thought to have ridden with Rupert. There were, though, a few Carters, a colony of Washingtons, a Randolph or two—not many, but enough to give the Scotch-Irish lessons in deportment.*

The Decline of the East

THERE IS NO MYSTERY about what motivated the highlanders to keep moving; their log cabins became crowded, their cornfields became tired and they heard plenty of stories about rich land, for the taking, in the West. For the aristocrats the story is different. The admixture of the frontiersmen with people of some education and polished manners occurred because the latter had a different but equally powerful impulse to move westward. What can be called "tobacco push" pressed them out of the Tidewater.

This formulation is, of course, too simple, except as an encouragement to reflection on the fact that something pushed the Virginians and Carolinians long before the depredations of Generals Grant and Sherman. They were pushed as much by the failures of their wheat crops as by the failure of the tobacco with which our nostalgia surrounds them. Moreover, they were always ready to diversify and speculate in western lands. But after the Revolution, especially after 1790, they not only diversified, they moved. They were driven to do so and they were drawn to do so. The failure of old fields propelled them, and then they, like the others, were caught up and pulled faster and farther by "cotton pull."

---

* For some, the lessons were not ennobling. The nephews of Thomas Jefferson, for example, were a degenerate lot, like some other cadets of "the best of society." As their chronicler, the novelist William A. Carothers, lamented, they were "cursed and condemned to earn . . . bread by the sweat of the brow." (William Robert Taylor, Cavalier and Yankee, p. 223.)

During their heyday, at the end of the eighteenth century, the great families of Virginia were in a powerful position to support the Virginia presidential dynasty. Their chief products for export were tobacco and wheat; tobacco seemed to be the most important. "Seemed" is, and must be, a straddle word, because the relative economic importance of wheat and tobacco is very difficult for historians to disentangle from the prickly thicket of export prices. Tobacco, as Michael Zuckerman and other scholars have pointed out, may have occupied the minds of many planters, but it had very little multiplier effect, whereas bread crops, especially wheat, created a web of artisan-based subeconomies that increasingly supported the resilient and resourceful Middle Colonies and the growth points of industrialism along the Delaware. The founder of the Virginia dynasty, George Washington, had no illusions about the tobacco economy and tried every means of diversifying out of it, impressing the importance of doing so on his adopted son, George Washington Parke Custis, as we have seen.

Though it lived in part on the revenues of wheat, Virginia did not succeed in creating as lively an economic base as Pennsylvania, and slowly lost ground. For a while, however, she and the other great tobacco producer, North Carolina, seemed to dominate the economic life of the colonies. They stood equal to the concentration of great wealth in a few hands in South Carolina; in the 1790's Virginia had a larger white population than Massachusetts or Pennsylvania. The total population of North Carolina was greater than that of New York. Virginia owned twice as many slaves as South Carolina. Tobacco ranged from a third to as much as half the value of all exports toward the end of the Colonial period, and this in the face of those British taxes which multiplied the cost of tobacco to consumers by a factor of five or more, and against which so much Virginia wrath was directed. When the interruptions in navigation produced by the worldwide Napoleonic conflicts required Europeans to begin growing their own tobacco, and the British did all they could to diminish imports from the United States, Virginia had the capital as well as the necessity to speculate in western lands.

By the early nineteenth century tobacco exports had ceased to grow at all, despite huge increases in the number of potential tobacco consumers. Tobacco made up less than half the percentage of exports it represented earlier. It fell to one thirteenth of the value of American exports by 1850; cotton assumed the role tobacco had had in Colonial times.

With these facts in mind, let us listen to the voice of Thomas Jefferson as he described failure. Tobacco, he said, was a "culture productive of infinite wretchedness. Those employed in it are in a continued state of exertion beyond the powers of nature to support. Little is raised by them; so that the men and animals on those farms are badly fed, and the earth is rapidly impoverished." Larger and larger tracts were required to provide virgin land to be ravished by the tobacco plant, since every planting after the first produced a more bitter leaf. Small cultivators were driven out, and even the large planters were unable to sustain production near their homes.

Those who turned to wheat did not turn to better practices, so that John H. Craven, a neighbor of Jefferson's, reported that after the old methods of tobacco and wheat culture had moved all the way to the Blue Ridge, the land of Albemarle County was "worn out, washed and gullied, so scarcely an acre could be found in a place fit for cultivation." A British traveler through the same region, Charles Anbury, said that the land was so denuded of cover that the rains "washed away the earth, which being of a red cast, appeared like a torrent of blood." Jefferson spoke of these conditions as "the tragedy by which we have . . . lost so much," and watched his young relatives and friends packing up to head west.

Nearly a third of the white children born in Virginia and Maryland around 1800 chose to emigrate westward, or were forced to do so, by 1830. In the 1930's, a hundred years later, Virginia still had not recovered from the decline of the tobacco economy and the plantation system built on it. The WPA *Guide to Virginia* reflected in these words upon the antebellum period:

> Tobacco planters gave up their impoverished farms to briars and broomsedge and moved to the western frontiers or into the new cotton states. Fairfax county by 1833 had become a ruin; Norfolk . . . had lost half its commerce in 25 years. In much of the piedmont and the tidewater, plantations were so run down that they could support only their owners; land values fell from $206,000,000 to $90,000,000 from 1817 to 1830.

To planters dependent on slave labor to work their remaining fields, that decline in the economy meant that they were forced to sell slaves to buy food for those they kept and to sustain their own ruinously profuse standards of hospitality. All the major figures in eighteenth-century Virginia—Jefferson, Madison and John Marshall among them—believed slavery to be a moral evil, somewhat palliated by long-term commitments by masters to sustain slaves through infirmities and old age. It was galling that even this thin veil of moral assurance was now wrenched away, but wrenched away it was.

As the West received free whites like those we have described, it also consumed unfree blacks, sold to pay the debts of Virginia and North Carolina. In those states, in the words of John Randolph of Roanoke, "men are raised for the market, like oxen for the shambles." During the great years of western migration, Virginia sold more than 300,000 slaves, most of them to work the new cotton fields of the West. At the bottom of the Panic of 1819, Jefferson lamented that the export price of slaves had so far declined that "beyond the mountains we have good slaves selling for one hundred dollars, good horses for five dollars."

Prices were up the next year, and Jefferson's voice was heard to utter these words: "I consider a woman who brings a child every two years as more profitable than the best man on the farm, what she produces is an addition to the capital, while his labors disappear in mere consumption."

So far had Virginia fallen. And we must remember from what a pinnacle of pride and prosperity! The fortunes of the great planters had been founded in the fecund second part of the seventeenth century and first part of the eighteenth, when tobacco was cheap to grow and could be sold for high prices. There were disappointments along the way—one whole generation of Virginians had been brought down by the tobacco depression of the seventeenth century, when prices fell from twenty-seven pence sterling per pound to seven-tenths of a pence—but the great planters were able to pounce when those more vulnerable to ebb-time markets had to sell. Thus they engrossed the lands of the small farmers. With much fluctuation, the trend of tobacco prices was upward after 1700, and they rose to a level about four times as high at the end of the century as at their nadir.

By that time the Carters, Byrds, Washingtons, Lees and Berkeleys had tens of thousands of western acres to give to their sons and into which to shift their slaves. Robert "King" Carter, from the Tidewater, could set up his son George on forty thousand Piedmont acres in Loudoun County, Virginia, centering about Oatlands. In the next chapter we will look more closely at the western investments of other sons of Robert: John Carter of Corotoman, and Landon of Sabine Hall. Carter Burwell could build Carter's Grove and also endow his progeny with six thousand acres in Clarke County whereon to build Carter Hall. The Beverleys, decended from the iconoclastic historian of Beverley Park, in Middlesex County, shared that great gentleman's very early feeling that Virginia, not England, was "my country," and a dislike of selling off any of their fifty thousand acres on the Tidewater side of the mountains. In the 1730's they acquired nearly 120,000 more in the Shenandoah, a tract called Beverley Manor.

The historian was the brother-in-law of William Byrd of Westover. The descendants of the former sold off their valley land to support their great house, Blandfield; the descendants of the latter found the Shenandoah a refuge to which they could repair after they had squandered their inheritance, chosen the losing side in the Revolution and lost Westover to their creditors.

The Washingtons were the great house-builders of the proximate West up the Potomac, in the farthest corner of Virginia (now within West Virginia). In that area alone, George Washington controlled 35,000 acres, and his brothers, nephews and their children built Harewood, Happy Retreat, Cedar Lawn, Claymont Court, Locust Hill, Bellair and Blakeley, while his cousins laid up Fairfield and Audley.

These Washington houses are quite conservative architecturally; Harewood and Fairfield were probably designed by the shadowy John Ariss, who helped George Washington with his remodeling of Mount Vernon. Harewood is a four-square stone mansion of English-Palladian design, with two flankers on line. As early as 1760, George Washington had visited its forerunner, "Bro. Sam'l's Quarters." After Lafayette visited the place he sent "Bro. Sam'l" a mantel to match the one he had given to Mount Vernon. Lafayette was followed by Louis Philippe and two other displaced Orleanist noblemen. In the drawing room of Harewood, Dolly and James Madison were married.

Claymont is very large, perhaps three times the length of Mount Vernon, and

Blakeley

Blakeley and Claymont Court

Engravings by William D. Eubank from The Washington Homes of Jefferson County, West Virginia *by Charlotte Judd Fairbairn, published by Whitney & White, Ranson, W.V.*

Claymont Court

is the farthest upland of any of the houses that carry the superimposed galleries of what we have, despite some qualms, called the Caribbean style. Like the Pinckneys' El Dorado, built twenty years earlier, Claymont is a cottage extended to catch the breeze, but it looks westward, toward the blue, beckoning mountains. It has left the shore and has become a way station on the road to the west.

The decline of King Tobacco and the rise of King Cotton do not quite parallel the decline of the Virginia planters and the rise of the Tennessee planters. Virginia is no perfect proxy for the Old South, and Tennessee is no perfect proxy for the New South west of the Appalachians. But there is sometimes a virtue in biography in giving human scale to themes so vast that we may otherwise recoil before them, and so complex that we may despair of trying to bring them within any net of words. The next chapter presents the story of a Virginian named Carter as he was drawn westward, to attempt, beyond the mountains, to make his mark in architecture and to create a dynasty, a hundred years after a Virginian named Carter had done so on the Atlantic shore.

CHAPTER 19

The Carter Mansion

I N ELIZABETHTON, TENNESSEE, is an ungainly frame farmhouse, ill at ease in what appears to be an unplanted suburban lot next to a busy highway, a kind of disconsolate appendage to Sycamore Shoals State Park. This house, called locally the Carter Mansion, was built between 1775 and 1800. It is a major document of the westering migration, and a conundrum besides.

Talbot Hamlin, a path-breaker in architectural history, sought forty years ago to induce others to follow him to the Carter Mansion by telling his readers that they would find within it an "extraordinary great hall" and a "lavish Baroque fireplace." But even with Hamlin's advertisement, the place has not attracted much further attention, though millions of Americans pass it on their way to the Great Smoky Mountains National Park. Some curiosity, one would think, would have been provoked by his remark that the "interior finish is said to have been made originally in 1749–50."

What could Hamlin have meant by that? Who said so? On what authority? The architectural evidence supports the idea, but then suggests more questions; the first thing one sees in that interior is a hall, fully paneled, with an oddly off-kilter chimneypiece. The staircase beyond is much too stately for the room; it comes forward awkwardly from a landing that impinges on a window. That hall could, with some generosity, be called "great," but the fireplace—"Baroque?" We need not be too fussy about the way Hamlin used this term; he could have meant by it what we now might call "early Georgian." Or he might simply have meant "elaborate beyond any legitimate expectation." The great hall in Elizabethton is certainly that. Who would expect to find in a Tennessee farmhouse a paneled room with fireplace drawn from Plates XXIII and XXVI in William Salmon's *Palladio Londinensis*? Salmon's pattern-book was published in London about 1700, and provided designs for many Colonial houses in the next fifty years, but was very seldom used after 1765. Crude though its execution may be, this Tennessee interior might easily have been found in a Tidewater mansion of 1749–50.

The Carter Mansion
Photo by Timeless Images

That last sentence can be read quite literally. The great hall in Elizabethton may, in fact, have been found in such a mansion, or what was left of such a mansion, and shipped, much later, to Tennessee to give an appearance of Tidewater respectability to a house, and thereby to a person, of rather mysterious antecedents. Salmon's book provided sketches from which were executed details in buildings constructed by Robert "King" Carter of Virginia (see Chapter Eight) and his descendants between 1700 and 1760. Salmon's derivations from Palladio (and Lord Burlington's British Palladians) appeared in 1732 at Christ Church in Lancaster County, Robert Carter's most important commission after his own mansion, Corotoman, nearby. They could be seen again and again in the houses built by his heirs: Rosewell, Sabine Hall, Nomini Hall, Shirley, Cleve and Carter's Grove. And now, again, on the Tennessee frontier, fifty years later.

There is no documentation for the exact date of the Carter Mansion in Elizabethton. In 1775 one John Carter owned the 640-acre tract upon which it was built. A fort was there in 1777, and Carter was in residence—some residence—on "the plantation" in 1778. There are references in records of that time to "Carter's office." John Carter died in 1781, leaving furniture and cutlery inventoried to be appropriate for such an establishment. His son Landon inherited the place, which was still fortlike enough to commend itself as a "public Magazine" for "Gunpowder & 1,000 lbs of Lead" in 1782. The house is unusual in the region in having lower

Hall, stairway, and great
chimneypiece, the Carter
Mansion

Photo by Timeless Images

walls of heavy timber filled with brick nogging, the sort of thing one might expect to find in a house that could also serve occasionally as a fort. The basement could have served as the magazine.

Yet Carter was not maintaining a primitive frontier post; the exterior was weatherboarded very early, and in the great hall that elaborate paneling was installed to hide the timbers and brick. Across the great hall from the fireplace are the entrances to two small rooms, not much larger than closets. One enters and discovers another surprise: both are fully paneled. Next to the front door is a perfect small Virginia room of about 1750, with none of the awkwardness of the installation in the great hall. Murals were recently discovered over the fireplaces of another small ground-floor room and of a large fully paneled ballroom upstairs. If one ascends the staircase to the ballroom, one finds that the stairhall and staircase maintain their monumental scale as they proceed upward. They are far out of the scale of this frontiersman's cottage. They were implying, one feels, that its owner had been born to grander things.

By 1796 that owner's son, Landon Carter, was living on a scale that almost justified the interior and made the exterior seem somewhat demure. There were

A "perfect small Virginia room" of 1750
Photo by Timeless Images

Robert "King" Carter

*From the National Portrait
Gallery, Smithsonian
Institution, Washington, D.C.*

two or more water-powered mills near his house, and he was entertaining on a grand scale in the ballroom. The French botanist André Michaux and his son were visitors in that year, and Governor John Sevier, a partner in real-estate speculation with Landon Carter,* attended a ball at the house in May 1800.

What can we learn from other, better-documented houses about the habits of great Virginia families who wished to transplant their pattern of life to the West? Let us assume that the Carter Mansion was built after 1775 and before 1781. The Washingtons' Harewood, in what is now West Virginia, would then be its contemporary. The drawing room for Harewood was brought by wagon all the way from Alexandria, on the Potomac, over the Vestal Gap road. Was the lower, well-proportioned room of the Carter Mansion also carried westward? Had it been first installed somewhere else, perhaps in a house built by King Carter himself?

We do not know the appearance of the first Carter mansion, the family seat, Corotoman, because that house was severely damaged by fire in 1729. The Mary-

* *And with Andrew Jackson and Wade Hampton as well.*

land *Gazette* of February 4, 1729, reported the burning of "the fine large house of Col. Carter," and the inventory of Carter's estate, made after his death three years later, shows household possessions for only a relatively small house. Yet—the old buccaneer had been intensely interested in architecture, in houses especially, and his diary makes strangely little mention of the fire, lamenting only the total destruction of his wine cellar.

Perhaps Corotoman was not completely destroyed. Some of the interior might have been salvaged, or one of the dependencies, perhaps an office, might have been only partially burnt. For those last three years of his life, Robert Carter might have continued to live amid salvaged furniture in the dependencies of the "fine large house." He, or his eldest son, John of Corotoman, seems to have built another small house nearby, where John lived for his remaining ten years. These two relatively modest places may no longer have seemed grand enough to merit maintenance after John's death in 1742, especially since it is probable that he and his principal heir, Charles, had by then finished work on the dependencies and commenced work on the main structure of a much bigger house at Shirley.

There is a painted panel over a fireplace, now re-erected in the Du Ponts' museum of rooms at Winterthur, which was once in a Virginia house called Morattico, built around 1711. The panel depicts a very large country house with pilasters on the sides and what appear to be three tiers of pilasters or verandahs on the front. It is surrounded by a fence with curiously domed pavilions at the corners. There is a theory that it may depict Corotoman. There is another theory that it depicts, instead, an English mansion from which came the ancestors of Mrs. Carter—which may have lent some elements to Corotoman. There is no way to prove these matters, one way or the other, but it is eerie that the painted panel upstairs in Tennessee's Carter Mansion, though very much in need of careful cleaning, seems to show an archaic mansion behind a fence with a curiously domed pavilion at the corner.

Now for the central enigma: the identity of John Carter of Tennessee. If he was, in fact, what that paneling, and his conduct, implied him to be, one of King Carter's descendants, there may be an easy explanation for the use of the *Palladio Londinensis* in Tennessee, for the architecture of the time of Handel in the time of Beethoven. Or, on the other hand, we may have only a good example of the use of a borrowed identity within an architectural persona.

John Carter of Tennessee

JOHN CARTER OF TENNESSEE, though prominent and rich, was remarkably vague about his origins. Among the headstones of the Tennessee Carters in the ancestral graveyard near the mansion, his alone carries no place or date of birth. Whatever records may have existed at the time of his death in 1781 were lost in a fire in the

1820's. There is a persistent tradition that, as the *Dictionary of American Biography* puts it, "he was a kinsman of Robert (or 'King') Carter." Tennessee historians sixty years ago reported "an earnest effort to trace the lineage of John Carter," without

Morattico overmantel painting
Courtesy of the Henry Francis du Pont Winterthur Museum

Painted panel, the Carter Mansion
Photo by Timeless Images

298

"satisfactory results," but in the 1920's they were sufficiently confident of the family tradition of kinship to assert that John "owed his prominence to superior education and to the social position of his family."*

John Carter emerges into history as an Indian trader at a spot marked by a highway sign west of Kingsport, Tennessee, which says he was there in 1769. He had come from Amherst County, on the upper reaches of the James River, in Virginia, where he had been a merchant and trader associated with the firm of Carter and Trent. One of the principals in that firm was Edward Carter (1733–92), younger brother of Charles Carter of Shirley, son of John Carter of Corotoman, grandson of King Carter. Edward Carter and Alexander Trent were also in partnership in an iron business, the Albemarle Iron Works. Other partners in that venture were William Cabell and Thomas Walker, and the whole group commenced speculations in western lands, which extended, in the case of the Cabells, into the post–Civil War period.

Edward was one of those great planters' younger sons to whom were distributed portions—sometimes tens of thousands of acres—from among the acquisitions of the founders. They were generally given, as well, some capital, sometimes a house, and a battalion of slaves. With these assets, often at the fringes of settlement, they were expected to establish a new colony of the old way of life. On the death of his father, Edward was bequeathed 9,500 acres in Albemarle County, just north of the James River. At a place called Carter's Bridge, on a hilltop overlooking the Hardware River, John Carter of Corotoman had built a small frame headquarters for some of his Piedmont holdings, a place he called Blenheim. There Edward went to live, and there he remained until his death in 1792.

These western Carters were counted with the Coles, Cabells and Randolphs among the oligarchs of piedmont Virginia. When John Carter appeared in Tennessee he was, apparently, trailing clouds of their glory with him. The *Dictionary of American Biography* tells us blandly that "by reason of his eminence he became the most prominent member of the community which included such distinguished pioneers as John Sevier."

Like Robert "King" Carter a century earlier, John of Tennessee was a planter, merchant and Indian trader. In 1769 he was in partnership with Edward Carter and the Trents "on the James River"; sometime in that year he went over the mountains. It is easy enough to pursue his career after he arrived in Tennessee; the puzzle is where he came from, how he conveyed to others the sense that, wherever that was, it was "eminent."

To understand the house he built, perhaps we should move out in concentric circles, from what we have now established toward what we can only guess. We can begin in his trading post on the James, a river that runs from Amherst County,

---

* *Others referred specifically to the line "of several Landon Carters of Virginia" (descended from King Carter's son Landon I).*

past the holdings of the Carters of Albemarle, past Jamestown, port for Williamsburg, and then to the sea.

Can we follow him all the way back from Tennessee to salt water, and thereby search out his origin? Perhaps. Early records of western Virginia show the purchase in 1774, by one "John Carter, merchant of Williamsburg," of two hundred acres owned by a French and Indian War veteran in what is now Tennessee.

This was apparently a decisive move. The James River partnership of Carter and Trent was wound up by February 1775. From that date onward, John Carter was committed to life over the mountains, sometimes in that distant part of Tennessee which came to be called Carter's Valley and sometimes in the Watauga settlements, a little farther east. His places of business soon became the chief enterprises of the colony, and bridgeheads for settlement. The Cherokee chiefs protested in 1772 that "Virginia people" were "insisting for Plantations" on Indian lands. Other men who thought they had a monopoly of the trade and, said the chiefs, "supply'd us for many years," resented the competition of men like "Mr. Carter," whose trading was so brisk that "if he comes into our Towns to deal with us its what he will." As early as December 1769 Virginia's governor was informed that "such men as Carter" were attracting the younger Indians away from their chiefs and their old trading patterns.

Breaking into somebody else's territory, on that frontier, was a risky business. Perhaps as a warning, Carter's store was pillaged in 1772, but Carter was unabashed. He stayed on, and apparently earned enough goodwill among the Indians to justify his being named by the Virginia government to try to persuade the Cherokees not to go to war on the settlements in 1774. Three years later he wrote the revolutionary governor of Virginia that the great Chief Little Carpenter had offered to provide five hundred Cherokee warriers "to fight the English or any Indians." By this time the trader had become a leader of the revolutionary frontiersmen, and his trading post had become a fort. In the same letter, Carter notified the governor that he was himself something of a border chieftain. He said he would do everything in his power to regulate the militia, to defend the frontier "and for the benefit of the United States," but he would brook no interference with his command. "If my dignity is to be sported," said this Tennessee Hotspur, "I have no need for your commission as commanding officer."

Independence was risky but potentially profitable. We cannot be sure that the "John Carter . . . of Williamsburg" who bought a Virginia warrant for two hundred acres of Tennessee in 1774 was the same John Carter of Amherst and Watauga who registered a 640-acre squatter's claim in the next year (and registered it again, this time with North Carolina, in 1778). We do know quite a lot about the relationship of politics to the accumulation of large tracts of land. John Carter's methods in achieving such accumulation are a bridge between those of King Carter (see Chapter Eight) a century earlier and those of Wade Hampton I, beginning in the 1770's and continuing over the next half century (to be described in some detail in Chapter Twenty-three).

In recompense for the loss of his trade goods in 1772, John Carter received from the Indians the huge tract later known as Carter's Valley and so commenced the acquisitions that led his peers to believe him, at his death, one of the largest landowners west of the Allegheny Mountains. He was a partner in other speculations with the future governor of Tennessee John Sevier and James Robertson, which almost certainly means with Andrew Jackson and Wade Hampton I as well, for they were members of many of the same syndicates.

Carter was one of the founders of a series of proto-states by which the settlers of the West organized themselves for protection from the Indians, from horse thieves, from swindlers and from governments unsympathetic to their hunger for plantations on Indian lands. One of the pleasures of reading the history of Kentucky and Tennessee is the fertility of invention displayed by these men and their friends in the nomenclature of speculation. Like all real-estate operators, they learned how to dignify their "developments."

Raw, muddy villages, with hogs and children running about the stumps, were given grand names, to attract others to join the first settlers—and to relieve them of their excess landholdings at a good price. In the same way, aggregates of millions of acres were frequently renamed; the general territory in which Sevier and Carter were operating was called, from time to time, Vandalia (1769), Transylvania (1775), Polypotamia (by Thomas Jefferson in 1784), Westsylvania, Watauga and Franklin (in stages during the early years of the republic).

John Carter was selected in 1772 to be chairman of the Board of Thirteen, which was the governing body of the Watauga Association, and was also in effect its chief justice. That association was described by the historian of the frontier Frederick Merck as "an irregular squatters association . . . a conspiracy to resist the law." Theodore Roosevelt in his *Winning of the West* exalted its charter as the first written constitution adopted west of the Appalachians. Two years before the Declaration of Independence, Lord Dunmore, the last British governor of Virginia, told Whitehall it was "a dangerous example to the people of America, of forming governments distinct from and independent of his majesty's authority."

That purchase by John Carter of Williamsburg of two hundred acres he had good reason to believe to be in the western reaches of Virginia (now within the borders of the state of Tennessee) is instructive. It helps us understand the fervor of the famous petition of the Wataugans in 1776. The settlers were asking North Carolina to annex them, shortly after independence from Britain had been declared. In language drafted under John Carter's chairmanship, they referred to their having squatted on North Carolina land, believing themselves to have been in Virginia all the while, because the lines (originally surveyed by Peter Jefferson, father of Thomas) were not clear and "many persons of distinction were making purchases." Others, they said, had followed these distinguished persons, "supposing many of them who were gentlemen of the law, to be better judges of the constitution."

The petitioners were most desirous not to be thought to be "as we have . . . been many times represented . . . a lawless mob." They described themselves instead as eager for help in dealing with "murderers, horse-thieves and robbers" *301* and those who have "endeavoured to defraud their creditors." They wished to become "in every respect . . . the best members of society."

A treaty with the Cherokees, signed the next year, showed that the Wataugans had another set of fears and wishes in common with the "best members of society" on the Tidewater. They were already trading in slaves, already growing cotton, and they knew that an alliance of the Indians and runaway Negroes had exploded in the faces of the Spanish near Natchez in 1729. Anticipating the program of Andrew Jackson and his generals in the Seminole War, they asked: "And should any runaway Negroes get into the Overhill [Indian] Towns, the Cherokee are to secure such slaves" for a suitable reward.

Carter was the leader of the delegation sent by the Wataugans to the North Carolina Provincial Congress. He secured a commission as colonel, important to his "dignity," and helped marshal the scanty forces of the frontier against the British, the Indians rallied by the British and, most dangerous of all, the local Tories. By 1780 civil war was being waged on the frontier, with Indians and whites on both sides of the general War for Independence.

The civil and revolutionary war in Tennessee had commercial possibilities for John Carter, as it did for Wade Hampton in South Carolina: "The property of the Tories on the Western Waters . . . was declared confiscated . . . Col. Sevier and Col. Carter and their friends entered [claimed] a good deal of these lands; and the Tories still hovering in the country, got wind of it." First these British sympathizers tried to get possession of the entry-books, where titles to land were recorded by the entry-taker, who was, it happened, John Carter himself. Carter responded by hiding "the bonafide records in the woods." The Tories "then . . . resolved upon killing both Sevier and Carter," but the wife of one of the Tories was friendly with Sevier, warned him, and the two record-keepers followed the records into the woods. Solemnly the local historian tells us that "the records were never found, but the Tories were soon subdued, and the titles of those who entered these confiscated lands were deemed valid." John Carter died a very rich man in 1781.

He endowed a dynasty. It was minor, of course, by comparison to that established by King Carter, but he could provide his sons with three thousand pounds in cash and thousands of acres. In 1799 two of his sons owned nearly a quarter of all the slaves in Tennessee.

Landon, one of those sons, was born in Virginia in 1760 and emigrated to Tennessee with his father. He was educated at Liberty Hall (now Davidson College) and fought the Cherokees in 1780 and the British in 1781 and 1782. He, too, rose to the rank of colonel and, after the war was ended, succeeded his father as one of the leaders of feisty frontier assemblies: he was secretary of the Jonesboro Convention of 1784, which organized the state of Franklin, and served as speaker of its shadowy senate, member of its first council of state, and its secretary of state. Then, as Tennessee absorbed Franklin, he attended the convention that drew its first constitution. (His son later was the draftsman of the present state constitution.) The county of his residence was named for him, and the town where he lived, Elizabethton, was named for his wife.

The mystery deepens. We now know that when John Carter appeared in Tennessee in 1769 with his acknowleged son Landon, he was also accompanied by two other sons, John and Emmanuel. There are many clear legal references to these men in their relationship to the elder John in the early records of Tennessee. John Carter, Jr., did respectable duty as a registrar of deeds after his father's death. But the *Dictionary of American Biography*'s entries for his father and his brother ignore him, and the subsequent Tennessee Carters did not acknowledge his existence. Why not? What was embarrassing about him? And what about this note in the Tennessee files from one Tennessee historian to another (undated but probably from the 1870's): "Have [you] any knowledge of Col. John Carter, the brother of Col. Landon Carter? The son of the latter and the Hon. Wm. B. Carter promised me near three years ago some sketches of these two brothers, but for some reason has never done so, though more than once kindly reminded of it"?

We must ask again, who was the first John Carter of Tennessee?

Why did his children omit date and place of birth from his headstone? What was the basis for their belief, repeated to historians of the family, that he was a

Landon Carter
Courtesy of the Tennessee Department of Conservation

kinsman of King Carter? What might that kinship tell us about the origin of that fine "Baroque" paneling?

King Carter died in 1732, leaving as his principal heir his eldest son, John Carter of Corotoman (1689/90–1742), who became secretary of the colony of Virginia. Burrowing through the Carter wills and records has thrown up a series of leads—some of them false*—but none suggests a likelier hypothesis than this:

After the death of his first-born, legitimate son, John of Corotoman sired, possibly during his Williamsburg years, an illegitimate son who was also given the name John. This child grew up in Williamsburg and was given a good education and perhaps some capital to join in the family trading company of Carter and Trent, under the tutelage of his older half-brother, Edward. (John of Corotoman was often in Williamsburg in 1736–7, the period during which John of Tennessee —John of Williamsburg?—was conceived.)

The wisps of evidence about the character of John of Tennessee confirm such a hypothesis: he had the Carter entrepreneurship, hardness and courage. He was certainly received as a gentleman, one of those "persons of distinction" who impressed his neighbors in Tennessee. He was very prickly about precedence and his "dignity" but at the same time unwilling to be explicit about his birth and youth, though he left to his children the sense that he had some mysterious kinship to the great Carter family of the Tidewater.

The daughter of Landon of Tennessee, soon after she married General Nathaniel Taylor, named their house, completed in 1816, Sabine Hill. Was she teasing her progeny to recall that Landon Carter of Virginia, son of King Carter, brother of John of Corotoman, uncle of Edward of Blenheim and quite possibly, like Edward, a partner of her grandfather's (and his half-uncle to boot), had built a mansion named Sabine Hall in 1730? Maybe she knew him to have been especially kind to her grandfather. Maybe that was why her father bore the name he did.

---

* *Among the false leads:*

1) The first-born of John of Corotoman was a son named John, born about 1726, which would do all right for John of Tennessee. But the child apparently died before 1730 (his name appeared in codicils to wills listing Robert Carter's heirs only between those two dates).

2) The name "Landon" comes into the Carter family through King Carter's marriage to Betty Landon. Their son, known to us as Landon I (1710–78), had a son John, known as John of Sudley, after a house he built in Prince William County. This John's birthdate is not firmly established, but was about 1739, which makes him a contemporary of John of Tennessee. He, like John of Tennessee, had sons named Landon and John, apparently contemporaries of Landon and John, Jr., of Tennessee. We know very little about what happened to John of Sudley after he married Janet Hamilton, built his house and produced at least nine children. He is said to have lived until 1789. We do know that his son Landon is associated with a house called Woodland, in Loudoun County, Virginia, and his son John with Number Six in Fauquier County. These facts do not tie to the well-recorded events of the life of Landon of Tennessee from his arrival there with his father, in his tenth year, through his marriage in 1784 and his death in 1800, nor to the few recorded incidents of the life of his apparently older brother John, who was still extant in Tennessee as late as 1812, and appears in the records there in 1796, 1797, 1802 and 1812, known as "Major." (See the Carter Archives, Christ Church, Irvington, Virginia.)

Genealogical scholars may find more clues to the Carters of Tennessee. Architectural scholars may unravel the mystery of the origin of that "Baroque" paneling in the mansion in Elizabethton. Until they do, we are free to let our imaginations fill the gaps in our knowlege.

I like to think John Carter of Tennessee was a "real" Carter, and that his paneling was "real" as well, that it came from Corotoman. I imagine that John Carter of Corotoman salvaged a small room from a dependency of that house—perhaps even a portion of a stair and part of the paneling of a larger room—and bequeathed them to an illegitimate son, also named John, of whom he was fond. That son could have kept them and shipped them, in the manner of the Washingtons of Harewood, to form the core of his plantation at Sycamore Shoals. He might have asked frontier carpenters to finish up the house in that archaic (Baroque?) style, with the aid of a Palladian pattern-book, a book he may also have inherited.*

We need to know all the story. As it stands, the record of these frontier Carters tells us how the patterns of behavior on one frontier, in economics and in architecture, sometimes repeated themselves on another, as much as a century later. And we know for certain that it was very much in the interest of a family named Carter, in Sycamore Shoals, Tennessee, to give themselves a stage set that immediately implied to a visitor, as soon as their door was opened, that they were set apart, and above, the rest of the jostling, striving freebooters of the frontier. Sometimes it is not the façade that counts. Sometimes a persona can be a mask worn on the inside.

* It was probably not until 1816 (the date written on the upstairs wall) that an itinerant painter could be found to give Tidewater dignity by marbleizing the lower paneling at the mansion and to do similar work at Sabine Hill. That leaves unexplained the murals. Perhaps we will never know what they represent, but I like to think they tell us something more about Corotoman.

CHAPTER 20

The Legitimate Succession

Some gentlemen of the Old South, like James Easley, Wade Hampton II and John Manning, traveled and invested widely in the West but remained firmly rooted in the East. Some went west to stay, like the Randolphs of Louisiana, the Laniers of Indiana and Thomas Jefferson's unfortunate nephews in Kentucky. Then there were apparent gentlemen, like John Carter of Tennessee, who were remarkably silent about where, and when, they were born and who their parents were.

Much more common, however, were men who wished to become gentlemen, who came from rough beginnings and took big gambles and, by hard dealing and good luck, came to possess land and houses and people to do their rough work for them. Gambling for high stakes, for horses and women and land, gambling with big winnings and big losses, in wild alternation of exultation and prostration—this was the life of the leaders of the American colonization of the trans-Appalachian South.

Their chieftain was Andrew Jackson. It took fifty years as a gambler for Jackson to achieve that eminence from which he could inveigh, as President of the United States, against gamblers and speculators.

Jackson early aspired to the quality of a Tidewater aristocrat, though he was born on the frontier. When he inherited a small fortune from his Scotch-Irish grandfather, he squandered it on horseracing, cockfighting, drink and women in Charleston, South Carolina. When the money ran out he turned to studying law in North Carolina, but his cantankerous nature took him into one duel too many, and it was wise to leave town. In 1788, when he was twenty-one, he purchased a Negro girl and took off with her across the mountains to Nashville.

Gamblers on a large scale had already preempted huge portions of the region in which Jackson was about to try his hand. For example, 400,000 acres were claimed by the family of Chief Justice John Marshall. Yet there was still plenty to make his eyes glisten, especially when he learned from his elders how to combine politics and speculation. Jackson's mentor was his father-in-law, John Carter's partner, John Donelson. Donelson had lost his first fortune in a manufacturing scheme and then joined in the lobbying and speculating of another colleague of Carter's, Richard Henderson, who claimed a million acres or more, but was finally reduced to a mere 200,000.*

When Donelson became surveyor for North Carolina's interests in west Tennessee, a small group of promoters and legislators entered claims for two thirds of six million acres released by North Carolina statute in a scheme that became known as the Yazoo Land Fraud. Stockley Donelson, his son, who entered twenty thousand acres near Chattanooga, was one of the beneficiaries; Andrew Jackson was another, receiving one thousand acres.†

Jackson, as we have noted, was Donelson's son-in-law. In Tennessee, clans were as important as in the Scottish highlands: one of Jackson's business partners, John Hutchings, was Donelson's grandson; the other, John Coffee, married Donelson's granddaughter. As lawyer for his wife and other Donelson heirs, Jackson later won five thousand acres more when the United States settled more Yazoo claims. With John Overton, Jackson speculated in five thousand acres, which later became the city of Memphis, and made good on the property by negotiating its release to white settlement from the Chickasaws. It was his practice to take fees for his legal services in land, and he later said he had acquired enough in that way "to make a country."

The very uncertainty in titles that first enriched Jackson as a land lawyer later was his undoing. Nothing was settled, and the trick was not to put one's personal credit behind a claim. A French traveler reported in 1802 that the occupant of every house at which he stopped "expressed doubts as to the soundness of his neighbor's title."

Aside from the insecurity of tenure for those who were actually settled upon the land, Jackson's own example showed how ephemeral could be speculative profits. In 1795 he became engaged in an elaborate effort to sell in Philadelphia not only much of 130,000 acres he and Overton owned in Tennessee, but also a large parcel, on commission, for Joel Rice. He disposed of some of the land, but slipped: he guaranteed Rice's title. It seemed worth the risk to get twenty-five cents an acre for what cost ten cents an acre in Tennessee. The buyer gave notes, which Jackson endorsed to buy merchandise and a store. But the maker of the notes went into bankruptcy, and even worse, Rice's title was found to be defective. Jackson was forced to sell his store, merchandise and land. Though he eked out enough money to build and rebuild The Hermitage, he was never thereafter free of financial

---

* *Jackson's neighbor and associate William Blount was called by the Creek Indians the "dirt king" because of his insatiable appetite for land.*

† *The widow and children of John Carter received ten thousand acres from the state of North Carolina when, after his death, his part of this transaction was distributed. The principal beneficiary was Wade Hampton I (see Chapter Twenty-three).*

worries, and lived debt-ridden in old age, amid anxiety and fragile elegance, like Jefferson, Madison and Monroe.

Jackson had plenty of reason for his hatred of banks and bankers. His biographer, James Parton, said of him that it began with his hatred of debt. As President, the old speculator spoke, with the heat of the painfully converted, of "ruinous" expansions and contractions of credit, of "rash speculation, idleness, extravagance, and a deterioration of morals," of bank credit which "engenders a spirit of speculation injurious to the habits and character of the people" and creates an "eager desire to gain wealth without labor." This is an exact description of the way of life to which the westerners aspired: they gambled to get rich without labor, to acquire great tracts of land, some which they would sell, and some of which they intended to have worked by slaves. Since "none work in the field who can help it," they hoped for a life of "wealth without labor."

It was a measure of the adaptability of ideas to interest that slaveowners could see themselves as freed by the labor of others to "pursue more respectable employments" and simultaneously as yeomen whose government "shall not take from the mouth of labor the bread it has earned." The language is Jefferson's, in his First Inaugural Address.

The Architecture of Middle Tennessee

JEFFERSON, JACKSON and James K. Polk: that was the sequence some westerners believed to be the legitimate succession of Democratic politics. The architecture of this succession of slave-owning "yeomen" pivots around The Hermitage.

These men were beyond the reach of the Tidewater, no longer much prodded by "tobacco push" emigration, and were instead chiefly affected by what we will describe in the next chapter as "cotton pull." They deployed Jeffersonian political rhetoric and further extended its extension of the ideal of free and independent yeomanry to accommodate slaveocracy. They adjusted Jefferson's architectural rhetoric even more radically, until a bloated and distorted Palladiosoid became the architecture of a cotton plutocracy. Its late Roman appearance expressed the taste of men whose oratory was full of Roman images: Jacksonian orators, like Robert Rantoul, Jr., developed a whole range of "old Roman" images for Old Hickory. The affinity for the frontier Roman in architecture, little constrained by Palladian coherence and serenity, was very strong in the Tennessee of Jackson and Polk, and passed from Tennessee in the 1840's and 1850's throughout Louisiana, Mississippi and Alabama.*

---

* Guidebooks to these areas are prone to describe anything with columns as either "pure" or "purest" Greek Revival. But the purest Grecian to be found in America is very impure indeed, and what there is in the South is more likely to be there because of Nicholas Biddle than because of Andrew Jackson.

We can see a weakening of Tidewater restraint and the growth of bullying Romanism in the development of The Hermitage itself. Jackson's house, quite naturally, set the style. It was, of course, the very opposite of a hermitage: it was a political clubhouse and a military headquarters and the capital of a vast speculative empire all at once. It was, as a consequence, the most influential building west of the Appalachians.

Andrew and Rachel Jackson first inhabited not so much a house as an assemblage. There was a central frame section amid a litter of log cabins, like a hound amid pups. That was in 1804. When they could, they gave it a façade modeled on a small Palladian-Jeffersonian house, Linden, which they had seen on their honeymoon in Natchez. Linden had been built about 1790. It had a delicate biloggial portico like that Palladio had given the Cornaro and Pisano families.

The chief influence on Jackson, of course, was not Venice but Jefferson: this biloggial form had so delighted the great Virginian (as he found it in his pattern-books) that he had used it for his first design for Monticello, left unfinished when he was called to his French embassy in 1784. After his return he completed the building in another style, but he encouraged others to employ carefully modulated double porticoes: one of them appeared about 1800 at Annfield in the Carter-Washington colony up the Potomac in Clarke County, built for his cousin Ann Randolph Meade and his friend Matthew Page. Along the edges of the "howling wilderness," inhabited by the Indians and by frontiersmen like Andrew Jackson, double porticoes were the emblems of taste still constrained by Tidewater Classicism. Some of the western planters had actually begun to send their sons to Jefferson's University of Virginia, where examples of his scheme could be found by the 1830's. In Tennessee, after Jackson added the weight of his prestige to this graceful, controlled and unpretentious design, it became the badge of an established planter.

Jackson's friend and ally at the frontier bar, Randal McGavock, was said to have traded a pony and a second-hand shotgun for his Harpeth River holdings; it is probable that his Indian trades were never "open covenants, openly arrived at." They were, however, very large in scale, giving McGavock the prestige to become mayor of Nashville before he moved to Franklin, Tennessee, to keep an eye on his prime cotton and wheat land in Williamson County. His wife and Rachel Jackson were close friends and helped each other plan their gardens. The McGavocks' Carnton, allegedly named after the family estate in County Antrim, Ireland, was built at the same time as the first Hermitage, along similar lines, with a verandah all across the back and a biloggial portico at the front.*

---

* After Carnton, in the environs of Nashville, came Hamilton Place in 1832, the first of the great houses of the Polk family; Fairmont, in 1837, built by a former resident of Natchez, John Smiser; Belair, in 1838, on land presented by the seigneur of Belle Meade, John Harding, to his daughter when she married a scion of the Clays of Kentucky; and Old Town, in 1842, built on some of John Donelson's land by Thomas Brown of Virginia. See Chapter Thirty-one for Harding, the Civil War and Angora goats.

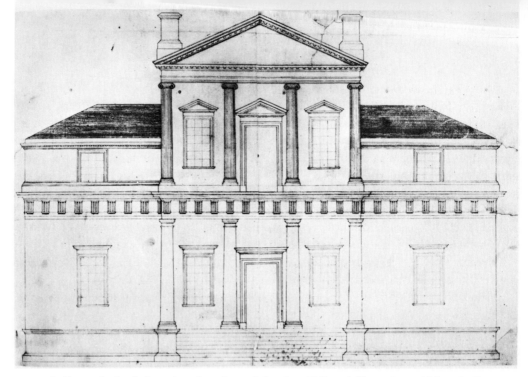

Jefferson's final elevation drawing of the first "biloggial" version of Monticello
Courtesy of the Massachusetts Historical Society

Carnton

Photograph by David Seiberling, the Carleton Association, Inc.

In 1834, however, the relatively demure biloggial portico at The Hermitage burnt, and Robert Mills accommodated the wish of the old hero of Tennessee to replace one façade of the house with a properly presidential portico modeled on Mount Vernon's. Thus was set in motion a new Tennessee tradition for an attenuated clustering of huge pillars at the front of the house. When their work at The Hermitage was done, the master carpenters who executed Mills's design crossed the road to commence construction of Tulip Grove, a gift from "Old Hickory" to his nephew and namesake, Andrew Jackson Donelson. It retained the dignity and finesse of Mills's instruction; its central white-columned portico was still in scale, on a front of red brick. But it gave another push toward a hankering after higher and higher style, which ultimately was parodied in the houses of the Mississippi cotton lands just before the War Between the States.

The Polks

AROUND NASHVILLE THERE are scores of large houses with clustered white columns, which grew taller and taller as the cotton years unfolded. There are a hundred or more elsewhere in Tennessee, and in its dependencies across the border of Mississippi and Alabama. They mark the most intense concentration of rural population in the antebellum South.*

Sometimes the great tall columns went all the way across the façades of these houses, in a sort of apotheosis of the verandah, which had been growing grand in Louisiana and Natchez in the 1820's. More often the columns stood in a central cluster, taller (in proportion to the width of the building) than any Greek would have permitted, taller even than the Romans' emphatic style. Occasionally they appeared supporting a pavilion placed in front of another row of equally large columns across the front of the house which bore behind all these yet a third plane of giant pilasters. This was the façade presented by George Polk, a cousin of James K. Polk, Tennessee's second successful contender for the presidency.

Rattle and Snap, the largest of the Polk mansions, was built in 1845. Its ten great columns were said to have been brought by river from Cincinnati and then overland by ox-team, to be placed with four in the center and three set back at each side. George Polk's house transcended the already ambitious proportions of the second Hermitage; it was, in spirit, like the work of a late Roman provincial. One of its recent admirers, Joseph Frazer Smith, wrote that it was intended to provide "housing of a very proud and important family with a domain of almost feudal extent."

What a long way the Polks had come! After the Revolution, Ezekiel Polk and his son Samuel had struggled westward from North Carolina. With them came

* *The bluegrass region of Kentucky was a competitor for that honor; it was settled earlier, and white, vertical symbols of rural wealth began to appear there, as well, in the 1840's.*

Rattle and Snap
Photo by Wayne Andrews

Ezekiel's cousin William and his four sons, George, Andrew, Lucius and Leonidas. Leonidas became a bishop and a Confederate general.* All became rich. Ezekiel had not been, it seems, ecclesiastical in his sympathies. He was, instead, a splendid and uninhibited example of the frontier spirit. The tombstone at his plantation near Bolivar, Tennessee, carries these verses:

> *Here lies the dust of old E. P.*
> *One instance of mortality*
> *Pennsylvania born, Car'lina bred*
> *In Tennessee died on his bed*
> *His youthful years he spent in pleasure*
> *His latter days in gathering treasure;*
> *From superstition liv'd quite free*
> *And practiced strict morality,*
> *To Holy cheats was never willing*
> *To give one solitary shilling.*

James K. Polk, the most prominent of this "proud and important family," was born to the Samuel Polks of Columbia, Tennessee. It is said that he walked six miles a day to meals while at the University of North Carolina rather than mix

312

* *He reappears as a client for architecture, briefly, in Chapter Twenty-six.*

with the hoi polloi in the Commons. His sister was not so proud: she reported that Rattle and Snap got its name from the high-stakes game in which her grandfather won the land. It is handy that the name remains, to remind us of its origins in frontier speculation, rather than the title Oakwood Hall, which it acquired during the surge of genteelification that overcame portions of the South after the War Between the States.

Adelicia H. F. A. Cheatham

ON A SIMILAR SCALE, and with similar origins, is Belmont, the mansion Mrs. Isaac Franklin created in Nashville to provide a facility for entertaining on a grand scale. It has two immense columns in front, within a sheltered central hollow surrounded by pilasters, a device simple Tennessee houses a generation earlier had employed

Landscape of Belmont, unknown artist
Copyright © 1981, Bob Schatz. Courtesy of the Historic Belmont Association.

to evidence a little Classicism without extravagance. Here it is done on a Brobdingnagian scale. Even today, encrusted with additions to perform its subsequent role as a ladies' college, Belmont is eminently worth seeing, though on the grounds, only its one-hundred-foot brick watertower remains; the orangery and the bowling alley, the octagonal teahouse and the art gallery, the summer pavilion, the zoo, gardener's house, propagating house, bear house, large and small stables, deer park, lake and "endless gardens" have all gone.

Its proprietress, Adelicia Hayes Franklin Acklen Cheatham, could have eaten Scarlett O'Hara for breakfast. She was the sister of a very handsome young man who had been killed in a typical Tennessee brawl by James K. Polk's brother William. She had grown to become a beauty, and when she was twenty-one she set her cap for the richest bachelor in the state. Isaac Franklin was a shifty-eyed (judging from his surviving portrait) slave-trader, then forty-nine. Adelicia Hayes announced that she liked his house, which was called Fairview, set in the middle of two thousand profitable acres. It was large and imposing enough in a Jeffersonian way, but as soon as they were married, she commenced improving it. She doubled its size and began learning his business. Founded on the slave trade, his fortune extended into seven plantations in Tennessee and Louisiana and ten thousand acres in Texas. When he died, eight years after the wedding, she broke his will, which had contemplated a comfortable living for her but, to her dismay, diverted the bulk of the estate to endow an academy to be built at Fairview.

Three years later Adelicia married Joseph Acklen. She later told her children she married him for love, but she was not carried away. Shrewdly, she required

Adelicia Hayes
Franklin Acklen
Cheatham,
artist unknown
*Copyright © 1981,
Bob Schatz*

314

Front hall of Belmont, with portrait of Adelicia Acklen and child by Bush.
Photograph by Giers in the period after the Civil War.
Collection of Deborah F. Cooney

Grand Salon, or "ballroom," after the Civil War. Photograph by Giers.
Collection of Deborah F. Cooney

him to sign an agreement that her property should remain hers and her heirs'.
Together they vastly extended her holdings, investing in Nashville real estate and
an array of Louisiana plantations. In 1860 they reported assets of two million
dollars in real estate and another million in personal property. They had enlarged
a summer villa called Belmont, on a hill near Nashville, and added the outbuildings *315*

Isaac Franklin
*Courtesy of the Historic
Belmont Association*

described earlier. Though there was an architect, Prussian-born Adolphus Hei-
man, who could produce designs in the Gothic, the Greek and the ceremonial
Italianate, the house is not his but hers. It seems doubtful that he did much more
than give that strong-willed woman what she asked, including the enclosure of the
West Indian double-stairs and galleries at the back to create a huge double-height
ballroom under a coved ceiling. A double range of Corinthian columns run down
one side, and upon the cornice, imperial eagles perch.

The villa had been of wood. The house that encased it was of brick. That still
did not seem grand enough, so in 1860 Adelicia had it stuccoed to appear as stone
colored in a reddish ocher.

The Acklens did not have long to bask in this glory. The Civil War was upon
them. Adelicia guarded her Tennessee properties while her husband tended the
Louisiana plantations, repenting his oath of allegiance to the Confederacy as he
was asked to destroy his cotton. In 1863 he died there, leaving a huge crop to spoil.
Adelicia, who kept on good terms with both sides, went into the teeth of the
fighting, above New Orleans, to rescue it. She arranged with the Confederates to
spare her cotton, and with the Federals not only to let her pass through the lines
but, it is said, to transport part of it in army wagons. She personally escorted two
thousand bales to Liverpool and was paid $960,000, probably in gold.

Joseph Acklen
Courtesy of the Historic
Belmont Association

William A. Cheatham
Courtesy of the Historic
Belmont Association

Like its mistress, Belmont survived the war, and so did its contents. During the fighting, Adelicia carried paintings, silver and jewelry to sanctuary at the house of Mrs. James K. Polk, who was on good terms with the triumphant federal forces. Apparently all was forgiven the Polks by the Hayes family, especially under wartime conditions when precious material was at stake.

After the war our heroine married William A. Cheatham, a widower somewhat younger than she, "aristocratic in bearing"; again she made sure by means of a nuptial compact that her property remained in her hands. With Cheatham she reigned as Nashville's queen. Old Randal McGavock noted in his diary that her diamonds were "the largest single stones I have ever seen," and one visitor to her last wedding asserted that he could not tell whether she was still beautiful or not because "neck, brow, arms, hands and waist were blinding with a glitter of diamonds." The harness for her horses was silver-mounted; her coachmen wore her livery.

Some of the neighbors were not impressed. One of the daughters of Lucius Polk, told that after Acklen's death Adelicia had designs upon her father, wrote a friend that the family felt the splendid lady was a "complete woman of the world and very fond of making a display of her wealth which is very parvenuish I think." Some foreign visitors were even more severe: Thérèse Yelverton wrote of Belmont in 1875, "The marbles and pictures were said to be in the style of the Borghese Palace. . . . or the Doria Pamphile, or the Corso. But compared with these . . . the place I had been visiting was a mere burlesque. Yet wherever I went in Tennessee, I was to hear of this beau ideal of splendor."

Adelicia Hayes, etc., etc., was no burlesque. She was the real thing: a frontier woman who made good in a big way. She seemed to enjoy herself. The very respectable Dr. Cheatham apparently came to bore her as she approached seventy. She left him and moved to Washington, D.C. There she began building another mansion, on Massachusetts Avenue, far removed from Rokeby, her father's house in Tennessee, which had been one of those early, rather diffident biloggial houses, built when Tennessee was still a colony of Mr. Jefferson's Virginia and not very sure of itself.

CHAPTER 21

Cotton Pull

WHEN THE SUN DECLINES, the southern summer comes awake. The heat relents a little; men move easier, freed of some of the burden that heat lays upon the shoulders. Cattle switch their tails more rapidly and pull themselves up out of the shadow of the thorn trees to head along the track toward the barn. Birds commence their evening flights, no longer having to struggle so hard against the thick air. Screen doors slam; people call to each other. Men come home from the fields; women wipe their faces as they prepare eternal southern variations on the basic themes of pig flesh, root crops and corn.

After the birds complete their twilight rounds, out of innumerable hiding places arise insistent buzzing and chittering and whining. Darkness fills with proclamations that the insect hours have come.

An hour or so later, the insects, too, having made their position clear, settle in for a night of quiet consumption, decomposing houses and vegetables, hayricks and ancestral records, libraries and portraits and barrels full of apples, turning all into compost.

In the 1830's and 1840's, sometimes when there was no wind, when the night was truly silent of all local noises, there was heard another sound. The moon rose and surveyed the half-globe beneath it, and an attentive southerner of those antebellum years could hear the sound of the looms.

Alabama had been in bed four hours. Across the Atlantic, Manchester was already at work. From the east there came the rackety-clacketing of the looms, the insatiable looms that held the South in bondage, unrelenting, monotonous, imperious.

Yoked to the looms, though they were bound insensibly and invisibly, were the rich and poor, black and white, in the largest labor camp ever constructed, from the James to the Brazos, from the Gulf of Mexico to the Ohio River. It was organized into a multitude of units of production to serve the mills. Manchester, of course, was not quite a monopsonist—the brothers Brown and their partners in

Rhode Island had been joined by other domestic textile manufacturers.* But as late as 1860, less than a third of the cotton produced in the South went to all its customers, combined, outside the British Midlands; the power of Manchester declined only very slowly in the years after it ordered to its liking the economy of the South.

The central reality of antebellum southern life was its neocolonial dependence on the cotton manufacturers of the British Midlands. The central myth of the antebellum South was independence, especially the independence of each plantation. The free and independent yeoman of the Jeffersonian ideal became a poverty-stricken subsistence farmer, perhaps with a black slave or two poorer and more miserable only than he was, while the planter, enthralled to the cotton economy, became a breeder and driver of black slaves, managing hundreds or thousands of acres of cotton, living in a columned citadel surrounded by the cabins of his work force.

He would have been and done some of these things anyway, because of the exhaustion of eastern soils and the artificiality of the Jeffersonian ideal. But when the complex of pressures we have encapsulated as tobacco push was followed by cotton pull, most planters acquiesced in becoming at once the victims and the beneficiaries of world markets. They thought themselves free amid the unfree all about them—though they depended on crops whose pricing, distribution and credit system was almost wholly in the hands of others.† Alone and powerless to defend themselves against the vagaries of the international market, they persuaded themselves that they were, instead, living in a self-sufficient community, insulated from the world outside.

The architecture they chose was a proclamation of this myth. It was rectilinear, blanched out of any of the colors found in nature, and it flaunted its openness. White columns stood about broad varandahs. Great windows admitted the breeze, and any other intruder who made it so far down the oak alley to the house. Obviously this was quite a different sort of architecture from the fortress-houses built by West Indian planters when they were at the same early stages of fixing their rule on new land, with new gangs of slaves. The difference is important; a myth had been created, which is still powerful in the popular mind to this day, and which created an architecture to suit.

In order to study that architecture, let us set forth that myth in its classic statement, by its most articulate apologist, John C. Calhoun:

> The Southern states are an aggregate, in fact, of communities, not of individuals. Every plantation is a little community, with the master at its head, who

---

* *As we have noted, one of the principal effects of Jeffersonian isolationism was to strengthen the capacity of northern manufacturers.*

† *Just as "tobacco" in "tobacco push" is a convenient catch-all for a number of money crops produced in the Tidewater and the Piedmont, including wheat, so "cotton" in this context can be read to include sugar, of which the same general statements can be made.*

The model for the movie version of Tara, actually D'Evereaux, near Natchez
Courtesy of the Mississippi Department of Economic Development

concentrates in himself the united interests of capital and labor, of which he is the common representative . . . equally represented and perfectly harmonised. Hence the harmony, the union, the stability of that section.

Louis Wright, in his history of South Carolina, adds the familiar embellishments:

white-columned plantation houses, ladies in silks and crinolines, chivalrous men . . . an eagerness for glory (military if possible) and a disdain for lowly money-grubbing in trade. Labor . . . was all performed by happy black slaves, singing and dancing in the dusk in front of their quarters. In the great house, servants were always smiling with polished politeness.

And proceeds to comment:

With some exceptions this picture is false.

The key elements in Calhoun's description are stability, harmony and union. His central image is an independent "little community." His words still powerfully condition our fantasy of the Old South, largely because architecture came to the service of myth and gave it solid and dramatic form. The South's persona was the white-columned plantation house. Its mask became accepted as its reality. In its own time and thereafter, the white-columned façade has protected from analysis several attendant concepts, especially the "cult of Athenian democracy." Some quite respectable historians have offered us the theory that this cult served a systematic ideology, supporting the Greek Revival they tell us is the prevailing architecture of these plantations. We will deal with each of these elements—the mask, the alleged ideology and its alleged Hellenic antecedents.

Independence

WHEN TOBACCO PUSH and cotton pull had done their work, there was scant independence left for Calhoun's little communities.

Political independence had been sought to secure certain inalienable rights and certain hard economic realities, among them freedom from price-fixing by European powers. The Founding Fathers had thrown off British mercantilism; they had suffered enough, they felt, from what George Washington called, in his Farewell Address, the "insidious wiles of foreign influence."

Foreign influence was, as it turned out, wilier still. Though the British Empire was shattered by the American Revolution, and the relatively clumsy devices of its mercantilism destroyed, the shrewdest of British statesmen were unperturbed. They perceived that the essentials were still in place; economic dependence would do just as well as political subservience. The Earl of Sheffield was confident that "Great Britain will lose few of the advantages she possessed before these States became independent, and with prudent management she will have as much of their trade as it will be her interest to wish for, without any expense for civil establishment or protection."

The means by which British colonialism was reimposed on the mainland South were subtle, but as effective as they had been in the West Indies. A diversified economy with a multitude of small holders, operating with a fair degree of self-sufficiency, came to be consolidated into large plantations. Most plantations became obsessed with the production of a single cash crop for a world market. The appetite of that market for cotton, especially, was irresistible. Even before the cotton gin brought the upland South completely into the British neo-imperial system, the former colonies were deeply dependent on the British market and becoming more so: they shipped 50 percent more to England in 1790 then in 1784. In the decade after the gin began its miraculous transformation of the southern economy, exports to Britain nearly quadrupled.

The old Colonial commerce had been a mere "peddling traffic," rejoiced Herman Merivale, the British economist, in 1839, "compared to that vast international intercourse, the greatest the world has ever known," which grew up thereafter. One of his peers, William Huskisson, was sure Britain had suffered no injury from what he called the "disseverence of the United States . . . viewed as a mere question of commerce." That commerce was largely composed of a single slave-produced crop. By 1850 cotton made up more than half of United States exports to Britain, more than ten times its next competitor, wheat and its products. Cotton-dominated traffic constituted four fifths of British imports. Calhoun's "independent" plantation was a febrile outpost of the empire of cotton. A web of power, knit in the British midlands, far more tenacious than had been the suzerainty of the tobacco brokers a century earlier, stretched out over the American South.

American economic independence eventually was secured through urbanization, specialization and mechanization. (It is arguable that we would be better off now with cottage industries and subsistence agriculture, but those choices were made by 1860, and made for us, for better or worse, by the North, not the South.) Most planters reposed in proud ignorance of complex machines (except a few steam-powered gins),* yet it was the steam engine that ruled the South, steam in the service of the empire of Manchester.†

Insatiably, Britain's mills devoured the cotton of the American South. At the start of Washington's first term, exports were worth less than 180,000 pounds sterling; in the middle of Jefferson's they were two hundred times greater; by 1860 they had multiplied in value twenty times again. The mills consumed new cotton and spewed forth a stream of cheap cotton goods, which made mill owners immensely rich and immensely powerful. In 1785 cotton exports brought to Britain about a million pounds in revenue—thirty-nine million in 1830. The millers needed cheap raw cotton and Whitney's gin provided it, yes, and the rich black southern soil provided it, and sweating black labor provided it. Manchester commanded and the South answered.

The architectural consequences of the South's continuing cultural and economic reliance on Great Britain were much the same as those which can be observed in Canada. Neither of these cultural dependencies developed the vigorous independent architectural life that was emerging between them, in the northern states, under the leadership of the second generation of architects after independence. Virginia, Maryland and Delaware went dead, architecturally, after the death of Thomas Jefferson and the departure of Benjamin Latrobe, and stayed comatose for the rest of the century. We will give some focused attention shortly to events in the Mississippi Delta, but it is fair to anticipate that discussion by asserting here that the only work of major importance in that region was performed by architects from the North—and by one from Paris. The unhappy statement true for New Orleans is true, as we have seen, for Mobile. Economic dependence was reflected in artistic dependence.

Other, subtler factors deepened that dependence. Among them were the consequences for the South's artistic self-confidence of the falsity of each of Cal-

---

There were, of course, a few remarkable exceptions among the planters, like Rush and Haller Nutt in Natchez. See Chapter Twenty-four.

† Steam power appeared in the year of Yorktown, the year of Watt's patent for rotary motion, which converted the little chugging steam engine of the mines into a source of industrial power for the Midlands. Manchester's first steam spinning mill went into operation in the inaugural year of the American presidency; the first steam loom factory opened in 1806. Thirty years later there were almost 120,000 power looms in Great Britain, nearly all in the cotton industry.

Judge Daniel R. Tucker
House (Lockerly),
Milledgeville, Georgia,
about 1839
Courtesy of the Library of Congress

houn's premises, or, to put the matter in reverse, the truth of the opposite to each of his assertions about the nature of the protypical southern antebellum communities.

Stability

As COTTON PRICES moved wildly up and down, each little community of the South was exposed to intoxicating riches and desperate disappointment. Payments for luxury goods, mules, vacations, and interest on loans were made by southern planters from very erratic revenues. They did not receive the balanced blessings that come to better-diversified farmers; it was a bonanza at best, bust at worst, and volatile prices all the while.*

Manchester was buyer and banker, too. The planter who borrowed money to lay in a crop, on one set of expectations, often found when reaping-time came that

* *Early in the nineteenth century, the Napoleonic Wars and their sideshow, which we call the War of 1812, produced interruptions in international cotton markets beyond the control of either producers or consumers: American cotton exports multiplied sixty times between 1790 and 1806, fell by three quarters during the embargo*

Manchester—distant, imperturbable Manchester—had created quite another set. The same financial intermediaries set the price of money and the price of the cotton that had to be converted into the money for repayment. The result was described by the Mobile *Register* during one fairly typical deflationary episode:

> The British . . . demand payment in cotton at 7 to 12 cents a pound, for merchandise which was measured when sold by the same cotton from 14 to 19 cents. They have thus a right to require two bales of Cotton where only one was originally contemplated.*

As independence had a special meaning for American planters, so does risk have a special meaning to economists. It means uncertainty of future outcomes, either good or bad. Investors seek to diminish their risks by diminishing the covariance of their sources of income (the degree to which they all go up or down together). The antebellum South was, in this sense, far more exposed to risk than other sections, not only because it was more specialized in agriculture and, within agriculture, more specialized in a single staple crop with a very few customers, but because it did not diversify into urban trades, except in New Orleans (which was in some ways an international rather than a typically southern city). In 1790 two of the five largest cities in the Union had been in the South. In 1860 only New Orleans was among the first fifteen.

The planters' successive invasions of the West led to their being more and more exposed to volatile and destabilizing international markets, for the South responded to every increase in prices with increased purchases of new western lands to commit to cotton. William Cullen Bryant described "long trains of cars heaped with bales, steamer after steamer loaded high with bales coming down the rivers, acres of bales on the wharves, acres of bales at the railway stations." The southern horizon would expand whenever demand pushed up prices.

Cotton prices seemed to regulate migration. Answering the calls given by each burst of higher prices, the slave and cotton culture surged, in spasms, westward. The pull of prices could be seen at work all through the antebellum years, sucking emigrants out to plant and reap and wear out new lands, to move on, plant and reap and wear out land again. British industry pulled the cotton off the

---

years of 1807 and 1808, multiplied by six to the brink of war in 1810, fell as far again during the war and regained their volume at its end.

Then came the years of peace. Manchester drove the chariot; the American cotton planter was dragged in its dust as it careened from price to price. From a price-relative of nearly 300 in 1816, cotton fell steadily to 92 in 1831, rose to 170 in 1835, fell to 87 in 1840, rose to 103 in the next year and fell to 60 in the next three years. Two years later prices were at 102 again, but fell in the next two back to 66, doubled in the next year, fell to 82 the next and were back to 100 the next. Is this a picture of stability?

* The complaint of debtor-producers of crops for world markets was heard a half century later from the wheat farmers in the Midwest. The Register *was the spokesman of the proud proprietors of great plantations. They would have been most uncomfortable in the entourage of later leaders like Robert La Follette or Ignatius Donnelly. Yet their circumstances were the same as those of the Greenbackers and Populists at the end of the century: they were net borrowers in a long deflationary period.*

uplands and down the rivers, sucked the white fluffy stuff out of the South in an endless flow of raw fiber. The rivers were white with cotton, and the Gulf of Mexico bore white currents from Mobile and New Orleans eastward past the Keys and on, almost unbroken, across the Atlantic into the Irish Sea, to Liverpool and Manchester.*

The huge suction pump of the mills acted on the American brain to cause what one traveler to Georgia diagnosed as "a kind of cotton insanity." The agents of the mania were the men from Manchester and then from New England. John Davis observed its effects early. He found a party of "cotton manufacturers from Manchester" one evening at Dillon's boardinghouse in Savannah: "Cotton! Cotton! Cotton! was their never-ceasing topic." Fredrika Bremer, the Swedish novelist, passed the same spot on a steamer fifty years later, and the madness was still abroad in the land: "On deck, a few gentlemen, planters, who were polite and wished to talk, but talked only of cotton, cotton, cotton." Mesmerized and destabilized, the South became not an assemblage of communities but a vast flux.

It is said that nearly half the white population of South Carolina had moved westward by 1860. In a time of rapid population growth and large families, so small a proportion of those born in that state remained that it grew at only a twelfth the rate of most northern seaboard states. Its young people headed west. Along the Carolina coast the extinct indigo plantations and the old, expiring cotton lands fell to briars and broom sedge, like the leached-out tobacco land of Virginia.

The pace of the cotton migration into the Old Southwest was astonishing. There were 9,000 whites and blacks in Alabama in 1810. There were 128,000 in 1820, when Mississippi already had 75,000. In 1830 there were 310,000 in Alabama and 137,000 in Mississippi; in 1840, 591,000 in Alabama and 376,000 in Mississippi; in 1850, 772,000 in Alabama and 607,000 in Mississippi. By 1860 Mississippi, which a generation earlier had been Indian territory, an open land of hunters and a few corn planters, was producing more cotton than Georgia and South Carolina combined.

We must be wary of impressions conveyed by these statistics taken in the large, for they can convey an illusion of a simple two-step progression from east to west. Such a progression would have been disorienting and destructive enough of the continuities of community life. The real experience was worse.

The practice of working soil to death and slaves to exhaustion was repeated over and over. Many families moved more than twice in a generation, each time sinking a few tentative roots into the ground, each time planting a few flowers at the doorstep, each time learning how to find a church, a store, a compatible neighbor. Small wonder the isolated plantations nurtured one of the least educated white populations of any section in the nation, small wonder that from the outset of the southern diaspora, southern health and literacy fell behind the rest of the nation.

* As we noted earlier, cotton mills in the North of the United States offered increasing competition to the British, but these metaphors still suggest the aggregate effects described.

The desolating army of King Cotton moved on a broad front across the South, drawing people away from homes but lately started, leaving blighted hopes and exhausted soil behind. By 1847 the first generation of cotton lands planted in Georgia had been worn out. Everywhere Eli Baxter saw "worn-out, sad, exhausted plantations . . . barrenness and exhaustion . . . dreary desolation." Emily Burke observed "deserted plantations where slaves had cultivated the soil as long as it will produce anything, then left for another to be used in the same way." Adam Hodgeson moved west out of Georgia amid "many gangs of slaves whom their masters were transporting to Alabama and Mississippi . . . Often a light carriage, of a sallow planter and his lady, would bring up the rear of a long cavalcade, and indicate the removal of a family of some wealth, who, allured by the rich lands of Alabama . . . had bidden adieu to the scenes of their youth and undertaken a long and painful pilgrimage through the wilderness." In Georgia the number of white farmers in Wilkes County fell by half in twenty years. By 1850 there were nearly 60,000 Georgians in Alabama and 17,000 in Mississippi. John Lamar of Macon, Georgia, wrote in 1847 to his cousin Howell Cobb:

> Lord, Lord, Howell, you and I have been too used to poor land to know what crops people are making in the rich lands of the new counties. I am just getting my eyes open to the golden view . . . Buy we must.

The South was a place of "men in constant motion." The westering migrant became one who "clutches everything, he holds nothing fast, but soon loosens his grasp to pursue fresh gratifications." De Tocqueville's description proceeds to tell of planters who rode westward followed by their household goods and their slaves, seeking a cotton bonanza that "perpetually retires from before them, yet without hiding itself from their sight, and retiring draws them on. At every moment they think they are about to grasp it; it escapes at every moment from their hold. They are near enough to see its charms, but too far off to enjoy them; and before they have fully tasted its delights, they die."*

Those who made the trek west often built, there, white houses, whose columns clung anxiously to the earth. The three-story portico standing before the residence of the Virginia-born novelist William Alexander Carothers, near Lexington, Kentucky, has fallen to ruin, like the fortunes of its owner, who for six years tried to live there the life he described in his romances. He spent his patrimony and that of his cotton-heiress wife, and went bankrupt in 1829. It was in those western counties of Kentucky that the nephews of Thomas Jefferson, who had emigrated with their slaves and household goods, declined into murder, suicide and alcoholism. Jefferson's glimpse of an Eden of yeomen appears in Carothers' novel _The Knights of the Horseshoe_, which set a fashion for thinking of the westering of young Virginians as a romantic adventure. But occasionally in its pages one

---

* We remember Richard Dunn's description of the prototypes of nineteenth-century cotton planters, the sugar planters of the West Indies two centuries earlier, in a "race between quick riches and quick death."

catches sight, instead, of another sort of migration, lonely and anguished, into exile. "We are just allowed to peep into the Garden . . . and then banished forever amid the dark byways."

Living in an unstable and dependent economy produced in the South a natural aversion to accepting change in politics, and an architectural preference for symbols of stasis. This "conservatism" (really resistance to change and aversion to aesthetic risk) of southern architecture seemed, until 1850 or so, to present a tranquil face to the world. Then the artificial repose exploded in the disordered and frenetic buildings of the years immediately before the War Between the States. Was this, possibly, because for the first time the great planters felt relatively— only relatively—stable in their fortunes? The best cotton lands had been consolidated, the land was tamed, prices seemed to be steadying, while in the North the depression of 1857 struck down many who had speculated too much in western lands and railroads. Perhaps all that had happened was the passage of two generations in the West. The first had completed its anxious striving, within a shell of borrowed and *retardataire* respectability, and the second, rich and proud, could be more expansive. What it produced was not great architecture; that is seldom the product of a second generation, and almost never the product of a sealed and fearful society. These southern arrivistes made large architecture, which is something else again.

Dr. Marcus A. Franklin House, Athens, Georgia, 1847
Courtesy of the Library of Congress

Harmony and Union

JOHN C. CALHOUN would have us accept a pretty picture of the "little communities" of the cotton South. There we would find "harmony" and "union." At the center of each plantation would be the planter, and, to Calhoun's picture, subsequent writers have added a white-columned house, of which Tara, of *Gone with the Wind*, is the most indelibly fixed in our imagination.*

It is no difficult trick to demolish this edifice, but it needs to be done with the care of a restoration architect collecting a museum specimen. Each element is precious; each is instructive.

Now, for example, how often was there in fact a white-columned house at the center of a planter's holdings, or amid them? How often, indeed, were the larger planters themselves to be seen amid those holdings? The easy answer is that the planters were in the nineteenth century increasingly as absent as they could afford to be. As a result, the architecture of plantation life changed. This was in major part because life on those plantations was not very pleasant even for their owners, not nearly so harmonious or so united as white-columned architecture, and John Calhoun, implied.

Thomas Jefferson had lived in the midst of his chief plantations. Did it matter that he was succeeded as the leader of democracy by Andrew Jackson, the frontier lawyer and speculator to whom it would not have occurred to limit his living to what he might glean as a planter? Eliza Lucas Pinckney may have lived upon her lands, during the healthy season at least, but by the Age of Jackson she no longer set the tone—instead, we see before us Adelicia Cheatham.

The aridity in architectural invention that we have observed among these great absentee landlords of the immediately antebellum decades cannot be explained only by noting that they were, in fact, absentee, and that their overseers lived in small houses. Small houses in the North were being built by local carpenter-builders like Jonathan Goldsmith, in Ohio, whose designs were of equal refinement to the larger and elegant buildings freshly designed by architects like Francis Costigan of Indiana (see Chapter Twenty-nine).

Some other hypothesis is needed. I suggest, for the sake of debate, that absenteeism tends to create an estrangement from the land, and that a respect for the land is as necessary as (in my general theory) are new wealth and a sympathy

---

* *It is indeed our imagination that sees Tara as a white-columned house. Margaret Mitchell, the author of* Gone with the Wind, *described Tara in her book as a "whitewashed brick plantation house . . . a clumsy, sprawling building . . . built according to no architectural plan whatsoever." In letters written after her book's publication, she explained, " 'Tara' was very definitely not a white-columned mansion," and noted, "Since my novel was published, I have been embarrassed on many occasions by finding myself included among writers who pictured the South as a land of white-columned mansions . . ." (Richard Harwell, ed.,* Margaret Mitchell's "Gone with the Wind" Letters 1936–1949 *[New York: Macmillan, 1976], pp. 255, 359; I am grateful to Laurie Stearns for bringing this information to my attention.)*

329

with first-rate talent in design for the creation of very good architecture. Such architecture is an art in sympathy with its setting.

America in the early part of the nineteenth century was not yet much clotted into cities. So we have been discussing country architecture. My hypothesis works fairly well in cities, however, for good urban architecture must be especially respectful of its surroundings: there is no such thing as an ill-mannered urban masterpiece. The precondition for good architecture anywhere is respect; when respect becomes sympathy, one can expect more; when sympathy becomes affection, it is legitimate to expect something very good indeed.

Much of the wealth of the first New South was derived from speculating at a distance, not from the locality in which it was displayed. Houses were built out of remittances from overseers who drove crews of slaves their owners may have never seen, on lands in new states and territories in which the owners had interest but for which they could hardly have affection.

The great houses of the second generation of the Hampton family, to be visited in Chapter Twenty-three, were built out of absentee remittances, it is true, but they were also built out of huge commitments to local agriculture on the part of an extraordinarily responsible group of mutually reinforcing people who were like the best of the British Whig families. They were national in their breadth of view, in their taste and in their economic interests but they took very active and effective part in the affairs of the locality in which their largest holdings were located. As we will see, they were as exceptional as the little band of Unionists in Natchez—see Chapter Twenty-four—or the Halifax Whigs of Virginia.

Elsewhere across the South, the "new men" diversified into western lands, took their winnings and returned home to live in their colonnaded compounds* in the way of West Indian sugar nabobs returning in triumph to England. Like Beckfords, Lascelleses or Codringtons, they drew their revenues from overseer-managed agricultural enterprises, with respect to which such words as "harmony" and "union" have no meaning. It is a shock to discover from the architectural evidence how little meaning they had to the many smaller planters who did not rely on western revenues but still left their lands under the direction of their overseers. Very few of these "middling" planters chose to live on their plantations. They congregated instead in towns like Athens or Washington, Macon or Jackson, Columbia or Milledgeville, or on suburban estates like the great houses of Natchez.†

---

* *Carolina Hall, near Florence, is South Carolina's only cage-form peripterally colonnaded mansion. It was built by an investor in western lands.*

† *Wilbur Zelinsky's researches into the location of white-columned houses in Georgia still extant in the 1950's led him to the conclusion that there were hundreds of what he called Greek Revival houses in the principal towns of the South. There were relatively few on its plantations. "In the course of almost a thousand miles of systematic . . . traverses along the dirt roads of rural Georgia, exactly one mansion that could qualify as Greek Revival was encountered. Eighteen additional rural types were met with along the principal old highways of the state (now entirely paved)." Ralph Flanders, reviewing the evidence twenty years earlier, had concluded that*

In these smiling villages, in the evening, on their verandahs, these planters could forget for an hour or so the unruly prices for cotton and sugar. If they stayed away from their croplands they could forget, as well, their equally unruly slave labor force. Unlike their West Indian predecessors of the first striving generations, they could no longer build fortress-houses; times had changed, and open houses were the vogue; they repaired instead to the mutual reassurance of clusters of architectural symbols of stability, harmony and order.

Until the researches of recent scholars raked away the compost of a century's myth-making, we were unable to see how desperate was the need for order. We now know that the circumstances of the planters were very trying indeed. Thomas Jefferson once anticipated Calhoun by describing Monticello as a place "where all is peace and harmony, where we love and are loved by every object we see." But he and his contemporaries knew better. They could not be very sure of the love of some of those "objects." Jefferson himself, late in an anxious life, admitted that, if the slaves were freed, "all the whites south of the Potomac and Ohio must evacuate their States." John Randolph said that talk of Negro equality was advising them to cut their masters' throats. John Marshall believed "nothing portends more calamity and mischief to the Southern States than their slave population." And the Jeffersonian floor leader in the House of Representatives, Albert Gallatin, feared freeing the slaves would "throw so many wild Tigers on Society." Until the 1820's and 1830's, men like these not only feared but abhorred slavery: John Randolph of Roanoke, John Taylor of Caroline, George Washington and John Marshall all "lamented and detested" it; very few planters would defend it except as an ugly, pernicious economic necessity.

Some did defend slavery on economic grounds; the "positive good" position did gain strength in the South in the 1840's. But not many planters actually believed that little communities like theirs, built on slave labor, were models of harmony and union anywhere. They were in close touch with the West Indies and the rest of the slave empire of the South Atlantic. Every ship brought news or rumor of slave revolt, and the history of revolts was as old as slavery; the events of their own lifetime had been bloody and convulsive enough to fill their nights with terror.

No complete chronicle of these revolts can be constructed, because every effort was made by slaveowners throughout the system to prevent contagion by suppressing the news. Nonetheless, that information was shared, and the fear that came of it and of the rumors that oozed out from the suppression of it. This had long been true.

There had been slave revolts in Columbia in 1530, 1548 and 1550, and in

---

planters on a large scale (the exception rather than the rule) "had their residences in the city usually, leaving the management of the plantation to an overseer." (Wilbur Zelinsky, "The Greek Revival House in Georgia," pp. 9ff.)

Venezuela in 1608 and 1670. After a massacre of their masters, slaves in Brazil established their own nation, which remained independent from 1605 to 1695.

In the eighteenth century a great revolt in Venezuela annihilated a Spanish force, and there was a widespread belief that by 1800 thirty thousand rebellious Negroes were living in the jungles. It is probable that there were similar but much smaller Negro communities in the Blue Ridge and the Dismal Swamp. British authorities negotiated treaties with Negroes holding portions of Jamaica and barely put down the kind of revolt that was successful against the French on Santo Domingo under Toussaint L'Ouverture.

Large islands, like Jamaica, and areas with open frontiers, like Guiana, saw constant revolts and incursions of free blacks from the jungle. Racial violence broke out in Jamaica in 1669, 1672, 1673, twice in 1678, 1682, 1685, 1690, 1734, 1760, 1765, 1766, 1795, 1807, 1815, 1824 and 1831. The great outbreaks in Jamaica were the "Maroon War" of 1795 and the "Christmas Rising" of 1831. Eugene Genovese, who has collated these events, says that "Guiana averaged about one significant revolt, not to mention serious conspiracies, occurring every two years from 1731 to 1823."

In New York, the northern terminus of the slave plantation system (before Newport and Bristol assumed that distinction), one revolt of blacks occurred in 1712 and another in 1741. In South Carolina a conspiracy to revolt was discovered in 1720, and violence broke out at Stono in 1739. Denmark Vesey organized another revolt, which barely failed, in Charleston in 1822.

In Louisiana there were revolts at Pointe Coupee in 1795, and that described by Genovese as the "biggest in American history" was put down by Wade Hampton I in 1811 (see Chapter Twenty-three). In Virginia, Gabriel Prosser's conspiracy in Richmond in 1800 anticipated Nat Turner's rebellion in 1831, and Tennessee was threatened by risings throughout the 1850's.

White southerners, then, had reason to fear, and their response to fear took two forms: first, violent repression (often accompanied by profound guilt); and second, that only partial effort at self-deception (only partially successful) expressed in the myth of the happy, harmonious plantation and the white-columned architecture that symbolized it.

The Foreign Policy of Fear

FEAR BRINGS REPRESSION at home; that is an old story. But in the first half of the nineteenth century, fear, thickening the atmosphere of the Mississippi Valley, led to violence among nations. This was no new thing within the American experience of the plantation system. Thomas Paine had played on the same fear in *Common Sense*, indicting England for having stirred up the Indians and the Negroes against the colonists. Jefferson echoed the device and charged George III with having imposed slavery on the colonies and then with "exciting these very people to rise in arms among us."*

The generation of Paine and Jefferson had heard that as early as the 1720's blacks and Indians had banded together to rise against European settlers in Natchez. As we saw in Chapter Nineteen, the whites who had invaded Tennessee in the 1770's feared other risings, and the Watauga Petitions spoke of that anxiety.

From 1800 onward, along the Gulf Coast, the policy of the United States was as much influenced by fear of alliances of blacks and Indians, chiefly among the group of tribes we call Seminoles, as by covetousness for escaped slaves and land. One mixed village was destroyed by Andrew Jackson on the Apalachicola River soon after his victory at New Orleans. Jackson offered his Indian allies the blacks and the Indians he defeated as slaves, and threatened other Indians in the neighborhood that they, too, would suffer unless they returned escaped blacks to the white forces.†

American forces, led by Jackson and General Edmund Gaines, invaded Spanish territory to recover slaves and chastise Indians, in 1816 and 1817. In 1821 the United States took possession of Florida from Spain, and Jackson became governor at Pensacola. Charging two British traders with "acting as chiefs of the negroes and Indians," Jackson had them executed. They were the most conspicuous European casualties of a struggle that was not, in this sector, primarily between white Americans and either the British or the Spanish. It was described by one of Jackson's subordinates, General Philip Jesup, as "a Negro, not an Indian War." Jesup warned: "If it be not speedily put down, the south will feel the effects of it on their slave population."

Jackson's wars were a continuation of the slaveholders' efforts to minimize outside agitators by driving real or imagined enemies from their frontiers, in a pattern familiar to observers of other totalitarian systems, and they flickered and flamed along the southern frontier from 1812 until the end of the last Seminole resistance in 1837. They focused successively on the British and the Spanish, but always, without surcease, on the Negroes and Indians. Secretary of War Lewis

---

*Though there is no evidence whatever that the king was guilty of the first charge, it is true that after the proclamation by the Fourth Virginia Convention that Virginians stood ready to resist "every species of despotism," the royal governor, Lord Dunmore, responded with the fine irony of his breeding by emancipating the colony's slaves. Dunmore's writ ran only to the gunwales of the warship to which he had hastily repaired, but a generation later, during the War of 1812, Admiral Sir Alexander Cochrane, commanding the British fleet, solicited "the cordial support of the Black population." Cochrane was "confident that Maddison [sic] will be hurled from his throne" by the British army supported by a corps of Negro "cossacks." "The Blacks are all good horsemen," he told Lord Bathurst. Ludicrous as may seem the notion of squadrons of black Cossacks sweeping across the steppes of Maryland, white slave owners had good cause to be relieved when few of their slaves did, in fact, choose to exchange one set of masters for another, and take up arms for the British. (Walter Lord, The Dawn's Early Light, pp. 44–45.)

† In the next year his nephew and his business partners commenced speculation in cotton lands in the area, which still belonged to Spain.

Aaron A. Cleveland House, Washington, Georgia, early nineteenth century;
enlarged 1841–46
Courtesy of the Library of Congress

Cass stated a consistent objective when in 1835 he directed General Winfield Scott
to "allow no terms to the Indians until every living slave in their possession,
belonging to a white man, is given up."

The story of the acquisition of cotton lands from the Indians, through fraud,
warfare and starvation, is too familiar to need recounting here. We should note
that it began as cotton prices doubled during the last years of the War of 1812,
that it was compounded by the fear of planters that remaining Indians would offer
asylum to escaping blacks, and that it is generally true to say that every Alabama,
Mississippi and Tennessee "big house" was built on land extricated from its previous Indian occupants by force or fraud.

Finally, in the 1840's, after the southeastern Indians had been removed, new
threats and new opportunities were perceived along our southern and western
frontiers. Andrew Jackson, in retirement at The Hermitage, joined President John
Tyler and Secretary of State Calhoun in fanning the fear that Mexico's emancipation of its slaves in 1829 would be followed by the abolition of slavery in Texas.

In 1843 Jackson was eager that the United States should absorb independent Texas lest the British come to control it, free its slaves and encourage slave insurrections in the United States from that base. Heading off that threat was one of the primary reasons for the annexation of Texas as a slave state.

There is no reason to doubt the sincerity of the fears expressed by these men; by the 1840's the capacity of southern planters to distinguish real threats from midnight visions had grown very precarious. They had a need for an architecture that implied cool, classic reason. They were not blind to the absence of independence, serenity, harmony and unity in their lives. It would have been easier for them to bear the reality if they had not also been fully aware of the price they were paying to seek these qualities through repression and violence.

The effort of the South to find reassurance in white columns—those classical symbols of order and stability—became even more strenuous as the opinions of mankind increasingly failed to give it moral assurance. Classic Revival plantation architecture was created in America at a time when an extraordinarily rapid change of opinion about slavery swept across the western world. A system that had gone almost entirely unquestioned throughout human history became, in a mere century and a half, not only morally repugnant but also forbidden by law over nearly all its previous imperium. Kings and popes had exchanged slaves as late as the sixteenth century; British royalty, from good Queen Bess to Queen Victoria's uncle, had participated in the slave trade. But starting in 1775, one after another of the bastions of slavery fell. The colleagues of the American southern planters disappeared. One after another, those who could have shared the burden of defending the system toppled over, and, in the end, the American planters were left almost alone to face the opprobrium of the world.*

The noose drew tighter around the southern conscience as slavery was abolished in the British colonies—even in the West Indies—in 1838, and in all Danish and French colonies as part of the revolutionary actions of 1848. One planter spoke for many southerners who feared they would "like the weak, the dependent, and the unfortunate colonists of the West-Indies . . . drag on a miserable state of political existence, constantly vibrating between our hopes and our fears." They entered the War Between the States knowing that the "peculiar institution," on

---

* One of the old stepping-stones of the sugar and slaves plantation system, Madeira, abolished slavery in 1775; two years later it was joined by Vermont; other New England states followed in the early 1780's. Though the French National Convention abolished slavery in 1794, the year the slaves of Haiti led by Toussaint L'Ouverture and Henri Christophe abolished it by Revolution, Napoleon repealed abolition in 1802—too late to restore slavery to Haiti. American slave owners recalled that of the 3,600 French troops who fought for American independence at Savannah in the 1780's, 545 were blacks, most from Haiti, and one of these was Christophe. Charleston, thereafter, sought to prevent Haitian sailors from mixing with mainland Negroes on its wharves, for fear of another Christophe, closer to home.

New Jersey, New York and Pennsylvania followed the New England states in abolishing slavery; then Latin American nations joined the procession: Argentina in 1813, Colombia in 1814, Chile in 1823, Central America in 1824, Mexico in 1829, Bolivia in 1831, Uruguay in 1842, Ecuador in 1851, and Peru and Venezuela in 1854.

which their peculiar architecture was based, had been repudiated by all civilized nations of the western world except Brazil, and in Puerto Rico, Cuba and the Dutch colonies. Even the Dutch gave way in 1863.

Southern slave owners knew of armed resistance of blacks throughout the plantation world. They knew that their own position was under moral attack throughout that European and American intellectual and civil society of which they believed themselves to be a part. And, finally, they were unremittingly at war with blacks and Indians on their own frontiers. Such were their circumstances, and with them in mind we can now engage with their architecture itself in a little greater detail. For the shaping of architecture is never unrelated to the psychology of the people who build it, and that psychology arises from circumstance.

Form follows feeling. When clients are quite comfortable with their role, and sure of the way they are perceived by others, they seem likely to build houses—masks—that represent them, cheerfully, as they are. I think of the Whig aristocrats of Britain in the early eighteenth century, and the twentieth-century suburbanites of Oak Park and River Forest, Illinois, as examples of this straightforward mask-making. When the opposite is true, architecture becomes the art of dissembling. The antebellum South possessed some eloquent examples of that art.

CHAPTER 22

Pericles and Tara

I

T WAS SUGGESTED in the last group of chapters that dissembling was the primary symbolic function of the white-columned architecture of the transmontane South, and of all that of the Piedmont except for a few houses that sprang directly from the influence of Arlington House, of Nicholas Biddle or of Thomas Jefferson. It was also suggested, however, in the short statement at the beginning of this part, that one of the elements in that architecture was a sensible adaptation to the southern continental climate. Before we bite into much more symbolism, it might be advisable to lay out a paragraph or two about that adaptation.

In the first decades of the nineteenth century the southern climate induced the growth of a distinctive architectural form. Even in Mississippi or Alabama the weather is, on occasion, colder than in, say, Ireland or England, and it is, for long stretches, much hotter. So the Deep South produced two houses, one inside the other, the larger for summer, the smaller for winter. The core structure could be heated against the cold. When the weather turned, the breeze could cool the verandahs and the balconies and the platforms. Where the ground was boggy, the whole assemblage was raised on a stilted foundation. Where there was genuine terra firma, the pillars stood upon the ground. This is the peripteral format, built with a row of columns on all sides.

Peripteral colonnades were fairly common in the South. They were probably first seen in Louisiana in the late eighteenth century, though we cannot be certain of such things. We can be much more certain of an assertion that leads us back again to symbolism: peripteral colonnades are not attributes of anything that can, with any degree of reverence for antiquity, be associated with Greek domestic architecture.

Greek houses were not built that way. In the Classical period, Greek houses were small, without exterior columns. They were more like the houses of Santa Fe or Albuquerque than those of Athens, Georgia, or Natchez, Mississippi. Fur-

337

thermore, Greek temple buildings did not carry hip or flat roofs; they characteristically emphasized the gable, which was repressed in the peripteral form of southern mansion so often and so confusingly labeled "Greek Revival." A quick mental comparison of the triangular pediment of the Parthenon with its prominent gable, rich with sculpture, will demonstrate the difference between it and either the hip-roofed peripteral southern mansion or the Louisiana raised cottage.

Very well, the rejoinder might be, concede that Greek houses did not have hip roofs, nor did they have columns all around. But Greek temples had columns all around (and besides, what has this to do with symbolism?). To which one can reply, if temples are fair game for reviving, then let them be revived, but those vaultlike temples the Greeks intended for the habitation of the gods, or for the maintenance of an impenetrable mystery, have nothing whatever to do with the perforated format of buildings intended for human habitation near the Gulf of Mexico whose function it is to be, and to appear to be, open (and that is the symbolic point!).

What was "revived" in the Deep South? We have described two revivals. The first rediscovery was the biloggial form Palladio gave Giorgio Cornaro, one loggia atop another, centered about the front door, under a pedimented (triangular) gable. This we have called a Jeffersonian Revival. So far as we can now tell, it had no precedents in Greece or in Rome. The British Palladians did not favor it; in America it appeared in the first Monticello and the first Classic façade for The Hermitage, and spread from there. Its political symbolism among admirers of Jefferson was clear enough, and it was easy to forget that nearly a century earlier it had appeared even before Mr. Jefferson in one or two instances in South Carolina (see Chapter Ten).

The second revival, also Palladian, mounted a grand temple-form portico on the front of a façade of almost any material—stone, brick, frame or log. In Grecian proportions, at Andalusia, Arlington and Berry Hill, it meant Whiggery. In its grand-slam, post-reconstructed-Hermitage form it was Roman, imperial and generally Jacksonian.

These were the styles available to migrant carpenter-builders moving about the middle South in the 1840's and 1850's, styles ready to compete or mate with the galleried cottage form of the Gulf and the Mississippi Valley. By that time, architects and clients of the South had read of Greece, and many possessed pattern-books that were in effect anthologies of Classical oddments. Henry Howard of Louisiana, that grand master of architectural gasconade, was perfectly capable of reaching into his steamer trunk for bits of Grecian costume to hang about the strange jumbled shapes he assembled for the last generation of antebellum sugar nabobs. But only a Greek who had the misfortune to live on under the orientalized despotism of the Seleucids would have recognized that sort of architecture. It is absurd for writers to tell us that men like Henry Howard were "inspired by Greek example." If they were inspired by anything, it was by the bulging purses of their suddenly rich clients.

Except for Millwood, Milford and a very few others, the last great houses built in the Deep South in the late 1850's were in no sense Classical. Despite their profusion of columns, they lacked order and coherence. They were bloated and deformed, encrusted with ornamental devices torn from one or another pattern-book, or purchased by the yard in papier-mâché. If "General Grant" is an apt term for the vulgar excesses of the 1870's, General Grant reached the South before the Civil War.

Not only the Greeks have suffered from the attribution to them of the worst excesses of the southern nouveaux riches; the promiscuous use of the term "Greek Revival" has obscured the wonderful variety of southern architecture under a rank undergrowth of literary foolishness. It is a pity that some of the great names of American intellectual history have offered aid and comfort to a process that has also obscured the intriguing symbolism that this architecture, freed of the debris, reveals.

A Mysterious Cult

LET US HEW away at the undergrowth, starting at the top, with that contributed by the magnificent Vernon Parrington. Even he was capable of error. It was Parrington who instructed us that the antebellum South was enthralled by what he called a "persuasive ideal of Greek democracy." This, he said, was what "lay back of Calhoun's defense of slavery . . . Espousing the ideal of democracy, he yielded to the seductions of a Greek republic." The relative scarcity of what could, with any precision, be called Greek Revival architecture in the South ought long ago to have led to a critical assessment of Parrington's thesis. Yet his "ideal of Greek democracy" has gained an extraordinary hold on writers about the Old South. Many people actually have been persuaded that, in the South before the Civil War, columned houses were temples to that cult.

Subsequent historians embellished Parrington's "ideal." Said Clement Eaton: "Calhoun cleverly harmonized a support of slavery with the deep democratic instinct of his constituents, or in the phrase of Vernon Parrington, he invoked the dream of Greek democracy." The phrase is, indeed, Parrington's, but the dream, unfortunately, cannot be shown to be Calhoun's.

Rollin Osterweiss also invoked the authority of Parrington for the vast influence in the South of a "cult" of Greek democracy which, he assured us, "called for the establishment of a free state based upon a slave proletariat after the manner of Pericles' Athens." He then stitched in a connection to architecture, by way of George Washington. The first President was, he said, "the contemporary symbol of Cincinnatus" and gave impetus to the "classic ideals of architecture" sponsored by "Thomas Jefferson, conditioned by Palladio."

So far so good. But Osterweiss went on to assert that Washington and Jeffer-

339

son were responsible for the spread of "the vogue for the Greek Revival . . . over the Upper South." In an image worthy of a romantic painter like Thomas Cole, he depicted Virginia political philosophers like Thomas Dew and George Fitzhugh taking delight "from the Corinthian porch of St. Paul's and the portico of the Planters' Hotel," and reached a peroration in a grand rhetorical question: "Were these not the very symbols of their political ideal—the Athenian democracy?"

The answer is: no, they were not! There is very, very little evidence that the "political ideal" of Dew, Fitzhugh or Calhoun was Athenian democracy. Parrington was imaginative but misleading, and too many other historians have followed his lead. They have labored mightily to associate the cool white clarity of Classic columns with another theme, valid enough in itself: that the South was in the grip of a "chivalric cult." (As we shall see, in Chapter Thirty, there were many literary people in America at this time, North and South, who were, indeed, immersed in a romantic medievalism. But the architectural expression of that "cult" was Gothic.)

Osterweiss could give no examples of "an evolving consciousness of 'Southernism' " heavily tinctured with "a devotion to a chivalric cult" which, somehow, also stressed the theme of Athenian democracy. He could not because there were none.* Instead of starting with Parrington, one should start with Calhoun. There are no references to Athenian democracy in his major work, *A Disquisition on Government*, and only the most scattered, unsystematic and insignificant references elsewhere. If Calhoun was persuaded by the ideal of a Greek democracy, he kept it quite secret.

What can be said of Calhoun can be said with equal truth of Fitzhugh and Dew: if Athenian democracy was their "political ideal," they scrupulously avoided mentioning it in their voluminous political writings. Lesser southern philosophers, pamphleteers and orators made passing references to Pericles' Athens, but not with much enthusiasm, and not systematically. From the outset of the American republic, in the North and in the South, a knowledge of the classics was a necessary part of the education of a statesman, but Bernard Bailyn, who knows this part of the story thoroughly, assures us that this did not result in any cults; the classics were "illustrative, not determinative, of thought."

Even the more classically educated generation that preceded Calhoun, Fitzhugh and Dew was no more enthralled by Greek precedent than they. Throughout the eighteenth and nineteenth centuries, before and after the Greek Revival, many classically influenced courthouses and state capitols were built in America. But

---

* *Classical ghosts visited Cambridge as well as New Haven, and billowed the curtains of the study of Dean Richard M. Gummere of Harvard. He wrote that despite frequent classical references in the debates on the Constitution, "Franklin's advice ultimately prevailed—that it was irrelevant to follow the example of 'those republics which contained the seeds of their own destruction.' " But then Gummere proceeds to say, without citation: "There must have been a haunting charm to them, for Calhoun used them as illustrations for his states' rights theory." Where? (Richard Mott Gummere,* The American Colonial Mind and the Classical Tradition *[Cambridge, Mass: Harvard University Press, 1963], p. 183.)*

Cade House,
Washington,
Georgia

*Courtesy of the Library of
Congress*

nearly all in the South are of Roman and Palladian derivation, not Greek. Many of them have been offered to support the Parrington-Osterweiss "cult" hypothesis, like the catalogues of classical names for towns and offices in such works as Howard Mumford Jones's history of American culture in the 1840's. The lists of names are interesting; they do show a desire to invest the process of government with dignity. But they do not suggest any intention to conduct that process according to Greek or, for that matter, Roman precedents. Since the cataloguers did their compilations, later scholars like Lewis Cohn-Haft have searched our political history for the actual use of classical procedures or precepts and found "very little." Translations of ancient words ("republic") were used, but "in novel meanings," not according to their "ancient usage."

American politicians of the first two generations had much to say about the utility of Greek or Roman precedent, and nearly all of it was negative. The Founding Fathers, certainly, gave no encouragement to any cult of Greek democracy. Charles Pinckney of South Carolina was emphatic that his "political situation" was "distinct from either the people of Greece or Rome or of any state we are acquainted with among the ancients." John Adams regarded Greek precedent to be "inadequate" to the "wants" of a nation as vast and diverse as the United States. James Madison regarded the Constitution as an appropriate "novelty in the political world," having "no model." Thomas Jefferson said that ancient society was "so different . . . from what it is now and with us, that I think little edification can be obtained" from classical political writing. Benjamin Rush was an extreme case, urging the abandonment of the study of the classics entirely.

Yet many guidebook writers still are true believers in the Parrington-Oster-

341

weiss cult. When great historians are so emphatic, it is hard for lesser mortals not to believe that Greek political ideas and Greek architecture set the tone for ante-bellum Southern life. Osterweiss, for instance, could persuade a multitude with his vision of a typical southern politician "who dreamed of Greek democracy" directing "the artillery of his flamboyant oratory from the heights of an imaginary Acropolis." His southern Acropolis is, indeed, imaginary, but not in the sense he suggests; one could find nineteenth-century versions of the Acropolis on the Dan-ube, on the Susquehanna, in Edinburgh, in St. Petersburg and at Potsdam, but search the South in vain for similar structures until 1897, when a plaster Parthenon was erected for the Nashville World's Fair, and you will find only Berry Hill, the citadel of a Unionist foe of slavery.*

The great plantation house as an appropriate expression of the slave system was (if anything classical) Roman, not Greek. Perhaps that is what Osterweiss was trying to tell us. After all, he did give us Cincinnatus, a Roman. Roman too were the other models of Washington's conduct, like Cato (by way of Addison's play).

Dr. Joel Abbott House, Washington, Georgia, 1797; enlarged by Robert Toombs, 1840–60
Courtesy of the Library of Congress

* *Perhaps an older example may be found upon the "Acropolis" of Palmyra, Virginia? The name suggests to Greek Revivalists a citadel clad all in white marble, glimmering in the southern sunlight upon its rocky outcrop, a mirage of Hellenic grandeur, something out of the motion-picture version of* The Man Who Would Be King. *But when one comes into its actual precincts, one finds an amiable red-brick courthouse with only the suggestion of an arcade of columns in its brickwork. It is the pup of Jefferson's pavilions at Charlottesville, but it would baffle the expectation of any ancient Athenian.*

Jefferson's models were Roman, rationalized and simplified by Palladio, as can be seen at a glance at the rotundas at the University of Virginia, at Monticello or at the ruins of Barboursville. His abomination of Greek architecture is clear enough, but he was not successful in propagating even a cult of Palladian architecture. Perhaps that was spoiled for him by Napoleon, who did propagate a cult of the Roman, and had few admirers anywhere in America—except, of course, Andrew Jackson.

In any case, despite the eloquence of Jefferson and the enormous skill of Benjamin Henry Latrobe, their architectural "cult" of Ideological Classicism was very slow in seeping out of the national capital; nearly a generation was to pass before it appeared in more than a very few instances in the South.

Some enthusiasm for things Hellenic did appear in those years, and there were a few literary references to a sentimentalized, slave-based, Athenian "democracy." Some towns in the South were renamed in sympathy for contemporary Greek insurrections against the Turks, but many more were renamed in the North. An architectural Greek Revival based on sympathy for contemporary struggles for freedom had a firmer ideological base in the North than in the South.

Greeks and Romans

IN THE SOUTH ITSELF, one could observe an obvious distinction between that handful of buildings based on Greek classicism and the multitude of distant derivations from Rome via Palladio, Jefferson and pattern-books. Jeffersonian elegance is difficult to emulate, and the clarity, symmetry and precision of the Greek architectural ideal do not look or feel the same as the bullying Roman style without Palladio or Jefferson to tame the propensity for excess, the restless piling of effect upon effect, the asymmetry, domes, attenuated columns and promiscuous orientalisms. Both Greece and Rome were slave-based societies, it is true. Yet so were all societies that could afford slaves, until very recent times. If one is searching for architectural expressions of forced servitude, one could find them more accessibly in the Gothic than in the Classic, for slavery in southern Europe and serfdom in northern Europe are very hard to distinguish in their effects. Yet no one has bothered to write a parallel exposition to that of Parrington and Osterweiss claiming the Gothic Revival to be symbolic of a cult of medieval serfdom.

Trying to make a Greek of Calhoun, a Parthenon of Monticello or of a Louisiana raised cottage, does not help us understand Southern architecture. There was very little Greek Revival architecture, but what there was was very important, if we read its symbolic intentions. Those intentions can be ascertained by assembling what we know about the clients of a fair sample of the important Greek Revival houses in the South. That was the task of Part Three.

Yet can we not try to understand the reasons why there did appear, throughout the South, screens of columns, barriers of columns, cages, indeed, of columns? Need we require of them that they be Greek or Roman or anything other than what they were to those who built them? And what was that? I can offer my own hypothesis, which will not please everybody, but it has the virtue of being compatible with what we have learned about the conditions of southern life before the War Between the States, and, perhaps, since.

Columns in Context

FROM TIME TO TIME, in newspaper descriptions of southern antebellum mansions, one encounters the phrase "forest of columns," an evocative image. One can imagine orderly rows of "counter-trees," repudiating the natural colors and curves of the forest. Strict and cool, they stand in measured succession. But their artifice is not uncontested. They are introduced at the end of long alleys of trees that actually grow, have roots in the soil and branches lifted to the sun. As we come closer to the house, we see nature at work, as well, on these columns, softening their lines, making their whiteness more gentle. Nature's agents are time and moisture, Spanish moss and vagrant tendrils of vine. White pillars, white and linear, contend against nature, asserting that man is dominant over time, and place, and temperature.

The columned house was a frontier expression that appeared at the leading edge of agriculture, as if the frontiersman, with a few good crops of cotton behind him, strode out from his log cabin and painted white the trees left standing about his clearing.

Tidewater South Carolina, Georgia and Virginia planters who could still afford to build new houses in the years between 1820 and 1860 already had their plantations; they did not need to construct new ones.* As a matter of fact, the seaboard planters' most eloquent apologist, William Gilmore Simms, found the Classic Revival offensive; glaring whiteness and cold evocations of stone offended against the southern light, he said, and the mountainous origins of the Greek style made it quite foreign to flat coastal Carolina terrain. But on the raw uplands, some planters may have selected that color and that harsh linearity *because* it offended against the southern landscape and southern light. Perhaps they wanted to defy their circumstances; perhaps they needed, psychologically, to bring stark white hard-edged forms into the midst of that lush green curvilinear landscape. Their affinity for whiteness and rectilinear forms can best be understood as a gesture of defiance against the land and climate, against troublesome work forces, against

---

As we have noted, there appears to be only one peripteral plantation house in South Carolina, Carolina Hall, near Florence; none in Virginia or North Carolina; and none even in the Georgia Tidewater. The Georgia Classic Revival is a late, upland phenomenon.

fluctuating prices, against uneasy conscience, against perpetual change of fortune and of place. Theirs was a gesture as bellicose as that of the West Indian planters of the seventeenth century who built fortress-houses.

The long oak alleys, now grown so romantic in those imaginations which have cleansed them of squalid slave cabins tucked behind the trees, would, if we let them, evoke for us images of other ceremonial entrances of similar intention. In China these oaks might be stone lions, stretching for leagues to warn of the power of the emperor whose palace awaited at the end of the awesome way. In the New South the house stands, withdrawn, until the visitor traverses a series of planted processions of trees and deliberate baffles of fencing. At the end, the real house is hidden. It lies within a screen of columns, which, as Alberti told the architects of the Renaissance, is one of the strongest walls men can devise.

When one reaches, ultimately, that house itself, one comes to the riddle wrapped in all these enigmas. The riddle is the real cult that dominated the life of the antebellum South, a cult whose holy place is a white cage, set apart from lascivious nature within all these planes of protection. That cult is so profound, and so ancient in its origins, that we have space here only to suggest it; it would take a very large volume to parse it out. It was no cult of Athenian democracy that animated these architectural shrines of a troubled, proud and passionate people. It was the cult of southern womanhood.

The stately reasoning of proslavery apologists like John C. Calhoun constituted an edifice of painstaking logic. But always, to the southern reasoning and to the southern architecture of this time, there clings a scent of desperation, an insistence on neatness of argument at fearful emotional expense. The planters were famous for their outbreaks of intemperate behavior. They had ready recourse to violence against their slaves, and it was also turned against each other. Though somewhat contained in the courtly protocols of dueling, it was always ready to erupt in tavern brawls. In the same way that they channeled their violence into the deadly punctilio of the duel, they built white cages to hold some portion of life within trim white rectilinearity. They made much of the rituals of daily behavior, of precision of political argument, and of a courtly relationship to white women.*

It was not merely the illusion of harmony and stability in the slave system, taken as a whole, that was expressed in the architecture of the "big house"; each such house expressed an anxious supremacy over the passions of each slave owner, and a supremacy over nature—including human nature—that was always tentative. For nature is so insistent that it will quickly overwhelm the intentions of any man. Vines and moss will take over, snakes will nest under the porch, the shadow side of man will break its way through. This is true everywhere, but in architecture it is nowhere so poignantly presented as in the antebellum South.

There has been much recent scholarship that puts in doubt how punctilious they were toward white women, even those of their own class, but this is no place to sort out the prevalence of southern masculine courtesy. I can only note respectfully that I have observed it, in some places, to this day.

CHAPTER 23

Elegance and Terror: The Wade Hamptons

ELEGANCE AND TERROR. Candlelight and silver; torchlight and severed heads. The hands that poured the claret had taken scalps, had whipped slaves, had trembled with avarice.

Wade Hampton was often called "Patriarch of the Hamptons of South Carolina." It would be more accurate to speak of them as the Hamptons of Virginia, North Carolina, South Carolina, Florida, Alabama, Mississippi, Tennessee, Kentucky and Louisiana, for Wade Hampton I and his son Wade Hampton II owned land in all those states. No other family presents, in three generations, so complete a picture of the westward progress of the plantation system. The Carters of Tennessee, partners in many speculations with men who were also partners of the first Wade Hampton, were, by comparison, small fry.

When Wade Hampton I visited the state legislature of Alabama, the members unanimously offered him "a seat within the bar of the house." When Wade II visited the Washington racecourse in Charleston, he "was hailed by a buzz of welcome everywhere he went and at one time with a loud acclamation as he passed along." The two occasions, apparently both demonstrations of esteem, were, however, not of quite the same character, because in Alabama and in South Carolina there was no one who believed the father and the son to be of the same character. The accolades had quite distinct resonances: Wade I was hated, but he had made himself the richest planter in the South. Wade II was thought by many to be a little soft financially, but he was immensely popular and thought to be the "complete model and specimen of the old time, outspoken, open handed Carolina Gentleman."

No one would have accused Wade I of openhandedness. It was the common judgment that "he not only mistreats his slaves, but stints them on food, overworks them, and keeps them almost naked." James Stuart, who reported that judgment, also said that as he passed one of Hampton's plantations, Houmas, on a riverboat en route from New Orleans to Baton Rouge, "I could have wished that he had been present, to hear the remarks made by the passengers in the boat generally on the severe and cruel treatment with which his numerous bands of slaves are treated; and that here, where people are obliged to speak with great caution, not one individual said a word on the subject, who did not express themselves in terms of commiseration for the unfortunate creatures subject to his tyranny."

The opinions of antislavery commentators were not unique: Edmund Ruffin, an eloquent apologist for slavery, endorsed Stuart's impression of Hampton, saying he was "glad" Stuart "exposed . . . some detestable cruelty of particular southern slaveholders—especially of the late Gen. Wade Hampton."

The passage of time, and of space, insulated Wade II, and his gentle generation, from the old tyrant who endowed them. Houmas, only one of the plantations inherited by the daughter of Wade I and her husband, John Smith Preston, was sold at the end of the 1850's for $1.5 million (about $11 million in 1985 wealth) after it had provided them with the bulk of the income they generously deployed in patronage of the arts and artists, including Hiram Powers, James De Veaux and William Scarborough. We have no description of the interiors of the slave cabins of Houmas, but we do have a view of the interior of the Prestons' mansion, which was located far from the indignities of Houmas, in Columbia, South Carolina, in 1851:

> Their house is a perfect curiosity shop with all their European things, bronzes, antique and modern, Etruscan vases, Herculanian dittos, lava ornaments, Swiss carvings, musical boxes, pictures, engravings and lastly carved German furniture and inlaid tables and bookcases.

The progeny of Wade Hampton I were members of the richest family in the South—richer even than their contemporary Adelicia Hayes Cheatham and her brood—and "patrician" they may have become. But the etymology of that word calls attention to their father, who had his own ways of attracting attention. In 1811 an army led by Wade I defeated five hundred rebellious slaves and killed sixty-six of their number in the battle at André's Plantation; the heads of twenty of them were ordered "strung aloft" on poles along the road south of New Orleans by way of a warning against any repetition. A month afterward the city of New Orleans provided a "splendid dinner . . . to General Hampton." Twelve "regular toasts" were followed by "a number of voluntary toasts . . . and the evening spent in mirth and songs."

Banqueting was a favorite recreation for planters, with and without occasion for celebration. At the Hamptons', the table of Wade I "was adorned, not only with dainties and dishes of substantial excellence, but with magnificent cups and vases of silver." Theodore Weld (a prejudiced witness) recorded some of the table talk. He says the old man, speaking at a dinner party, reported that he had tried feeding his slaves cottonseed mixed with corn. When he used one-half corn they "seemed to thrive tolerably well," but when the mix was altered to one-fourth corn, he declared "with an oath . . . they died like rotten sheep!" This was the master (according to the *Niles' Weekly Register*) of two thousand slaves on his Carolina and Louisiana plantations in 1826.*

A few years later Wade II and his brother-in-law commissioned sculptured marble heads of his family from Hiram Powers, and portrait heads from the painter James De Veaux. De Veaux, remembering the support given his artistic career by the wife of Wade I, "burst into tears" of gratitude. The Hamptons lived in a time when such contrasts were commonplace. We are impoverished by the failure of historians to tell us what we need to know about Mrs. Hampton. Judging by her children, she must have brought a remarkable tenacity—and decency—into the household of her husband.

The Founding Father

THE ASCENT TO RICHES of Wade Hampton I was breathtaking in its speed and scale. His father was a farmer who rented, for a share of his tobacco crop, a small farm from George Mason, in the portion of Virginia now overwhelmed by the suburbs of the District of Columbia. He removed first to Rowan County, North Carolina, and then to the borderland between North and South Carolina, in circumstances so obscure that we do not know in what state or in what year the first Wade was born. It was a brutal, toilsome and perilous life. It made men hard. Wade's father, mother and nephew were killed by Indians while he was still a boy. (This part of the story is much like those of Andrew Jackson, John C. Calhoun and Langdon Cheves, who sprang from the same frontier region—see Chapters Seventeen, Eighteen and Twenty-two).

Wade I commenced his career as an Indian trader. He acquired his first major "stake" through extorting the trade goods and store from a Loyalist merchant who had the misfortune to display his political sympathies to the independence forces while they were predominant, but was unable to escape because his ship ran aground. At that point Wade I favored independence. Before the British recaptured Charleston, where he was then plying his trade, the town was "mad . . . with the love of money and speculation . . . there were more fortunes made here in the year 1777 than perhaps ever were made in any year before . . . the orgy of speculations and profiteering that set in with the war" drove out "the old conservative merchants" and introduced "a new set of daring adventurers, who were willing to take great risks in the hope of making great gain."

_____

* *He violated a South Carolina statute "by privately bringing in negro slaves from North Carolina" during that state's brief effort to control intrastate commerce in slaves; Governor John Drayton reported Hampton's notorious slave-trafficking in a letter intended to explain to Thomas Jefferson why it would be difficult for Jefferson's son-in-law to export his slave crop through the Carolinas to the West.*

Wade Hampton I
*Courtesy of The Charleston
Museum, Charleston, S.C.*

Hampton was one of these daring adventurers. He added to profiteering as a merchant a brisk business as paymaster and provisioner to the independence forces. This phase came to an end in 1780, when the British, under Lord Cornwallis, seized the town. Hampton promptly swore himself to be "a true and faithful subject to His Majesty, the King of Great Britain," signed a congratulatory address to Cornwallis and commenced provisioning the British and Loyalists. A year later, however, as the British fortunes flagged, he rejoined the independence movement, fought bravely and put his considerable skills to work as an organizer of victory.

He did not neglect his own interests, however, retaining, as his own, slaves confiscated by the independence forces. He married, and moved after the war into the upcountry lands near Columbia that belonged to his wife's family. There he lived to the end of his days in a frame plantation house, Woodlands. Woodlands had a central block with a piazza or gallery across the front and two dependencies on each side. The gallery was low, apparently in one story, like those of the plantations of the West Indian emigrants to South Carolina a century earlier. Houmas, his western headquarters, was the characteristic Louisiana version of the West Indian cottage, with a hipped roof, columns all about, and a belvedere on the roof. It was quite simple and functional, like Wade I himself.

349

Wade Hampton was a true spiritual successor to the West Indian planters. (At one point he recommended that the United States take advantage of Britain's Napoleonic distractions to seize "some of the West India islands, any one or two of which will bring us wealth enough in a year or two to pay for a navy.") Unlike the planters of Barbados, however, his wealth did not come from agriculture alone. He applied West Indian principles to continental opportunities. He was widely believed to have sought and achieved election to the United States House of Representatives only to induce Congress to provide a compensation scheme for his speculations in western lands. The most noisome of these had required the wholesale bribery of the Georgia legislature and various Tennessee political figures in the Yazoo frauds. One day on the floor of the House he was confronted by John Randolph of Roanoke. "Shaking his long, lean finger at Mr. Hampton, he exclaimed, at the top of his voice, 'Mr. Speaker, I hope, sir, to see the day when a Yazoo claimant and a villain, will be synonymous terms.' " Hampton's western machinations were on such a vast scale, so complex, so intertwined with those of John C. Calhoun, Andrew Jackson and other famous men, that few people of his own time dared to attack him, and few today would try to unravel his affairs.

What can be readily learned about them can be summarized in this way:

In the mid-1780's Hampton had two patents in Alabama, one for 107,760 acres and the other of 131,160 acres, in association with John Sevier. Altogether, in the Muscle Shoals area, Hampton registered plats for more than 600,000 acres, and he later accumulated, and sold just in time, 900,000 acres. He and John Hall, a land-speculating doctor from Philadelphia, worked closely together: Hall acquired one million acres of Georgia pine barrens, and later claimed to be "processing nearly two million acres in Georgia, South Carolina and Kentucky."

Absalom Chappell wrote of his contemporary Hampton "in his proud meridian of manhood: . . . Behold him losing no time, after buying from the State, but with characteristic sagacity and celerity hastening to become a mighty seller of what he had bought, and in less than a year safely shifting off his enormous portion of the prey into other hands at a huge profit and putting the money in his pocket." Hampton outwitted and outpaced his rivals in transactions involving, in the late 1790's, 430,000 acres in Kentucky, 650,000 acres in Pennsylvania, 700,000 acres in North Carolina, 930,000 in Virginia, 2,300,000 in Georgia and 950,000 in South Carolina (numbers rounded).

He was also engaged, at the time, in ferry-, bridge-, ship- and road-building, and in extensive sales of merchandise and slaves.

Wade Hampton also bought land to hold, and it was as a proprietor of plantations worked by hundreds of slaves that he acquired his greatest wealth. His income was derived from sugar and from cotton. Unlike most of his fellows, he lived remotely, not in towns. His home in South Carolina was as isolated as that of an eighteenth-century West Indian planter, at a great distance from his neighbors, amid twelve thousand acres of cropland.

He was an exception—and he was not companionable. He could not "bear the system of collecting in villages . . . If he has a friend he says he don't want him a Near neighbor." He lacked charm, and distrusted the charming. The diarist Edward Hooker, in a generally admiring profile, spoke of him as "a great enemy to finery, and treats it with marked contempt . . . for the tinsel of Language he entertains a sovereign contempt . . . I should think him deficient in that tender and amiable sensibility which . . . makes us love our fellow creatures." General Winfield Scott, who served under him in 1811, and was crusty and abrupt himself, saw Hampton as "vigorous, prompt, sagacious, but of irritable nerves; consequently often harsh, and sometimes unjust; but followed in every instance, by the acknowledgment of wrong . . ." He did not appear to require, for his self-esteem, either to be consistently right or to be consistently approved; not only did he admit error to Winfield Scott, but after Randolph of Roanoke had sought to skewer him with that long, lean finger and the accusation of Yazoo fraud, he sidled over, quite ready for amicable parley.

His chilly capacity to proceed about his business unperturbed by obstacle, scruple or remonstrance brought him a third great fortune, to be heaped upon the mountain of his wealth. In 1811 he was living on a plantation in South Carolina which included, in a single field, 800 acres of corn and 1,600 acres of cotton. Other men might have rested, but he returned to military life and to western land acquisition simultaneously. His absentee holdings were to make him "the most extensive planter in the U.S."

He was given command of the American forces contending with the Spaniards in Florida and assigned to protect New Orleans from the threat of British invasion. A week after he put down the slave revolt at André's Plantation, he was "called away on business," which delayed the celebratory dinner we have earlier described. The business was the acquisition of Houmas Plantation for $300,000 (about $2 million in 1985 wealth). The terms were $100,000 cash, about the annual net profit of the place, and $50,000 per year for each of the four years in which it produced twice that much or more, net. In addition he acquired one 5,000-acre plantation in Mississippi and another of 2,500 acres. Houmas had about 31,000 acres, and another of his acquisitions, Houmas Point, contained about 900 acres of excellent sugar land.

While he was engaged in moving his regular troops across Georgia, the Augusta *Chronicle* reported that he was just as busy leading the march of slaves from South Carolina to serve his new Louisiana lands: "Brigadier General Wade Hampton and suit, Commander in Chief of the Western Army, preceded by a division of fifty ragged, meagre looking negro infantry. Should his excellency fail in obtaining laurels before Mobile [where the British were threatening to land] he will be able to make sugar at New Orleans."

Hampton was adept at making things—he was unafraid of technological change. He heard of Eli Whitney's gins and first pirated copies by purchasing the plans from an "ingenious young mechanic" who had "introduced himself into the apartment [where the gin was being shown] in women's apparel." Because the pirated plans were defective, he quickly importuned Whitney to sell him many gins direct, and drove them by water power as early as 1799. In that year he put in his first cotton crop, yielding $60,000. He nearly tripled his South Carolina production by 1807, to 1,500 bales.

Hampton's total sales from his South Carolina plantations in 1813 approached $60,000, and just before his death, in 1834, his Louisiana plantations brought $115,000 per year. This was at a time when free white agricultural workers in the United States averaged about fifty cents a day in wages.

In the year of his death,* this remarkable man was described as "plain . . . in his dress, and rather churlish." He had been the greatest planter in the Carolinas, and he was now also the largest sugar producer in Louisiana. Like many other old men, he "ran to cash," apparently associating liquidity with longevity. He offered "a commission of 25 or $30,000, as a dash," to agents who might, "in half joke & half earnest, throw out, now & then, a hint to some of their neighboring nabobs" that his Louisiana plantations might be for sale. No such transaction occurred until after his death, when the Prestons sold Houmas for five times what he had paid for it.

Millwood and Milford

IT IS SAID THAT Wade Hampton II destroyed the old man's will, which favored him, because he felt rich enough and wanted to share with his siblings. He had already received some assistance from his father (though not nearly enough in the eyes of his friends) and a plantation near Augusta, Georgia, from his father-in-law (who had also been his father's Charleston factor). He died in 1858 on one of his plantations in Mississippi. Though he was solvent, he left a half million dollars in debt, because of his generosity, it was said, in endorsing notes for other people.

After the death of Wade I, Woodlands, the lonely family seat, was left empty for a while; then it was remodeled and enlarged to become Millwood, a white-pillared palace for Wade II. But he was too gregarious to be happy there for much of the time, so he also bought a house in Charleston; his mother and his brother-in-law, John Preston, were already living in the village of Columbia, despite the contempt for such places expressed by Wade I.

We have already noted the gratitude of James De Veaux for the patronage of Mrs. Wade Hampton I. She, her son, her daughters and their husbands (with one exception) made a circle of generous and informed patrons who traveled widely in

---

* Aside from his vast landholdings, slaves, crops and merchandise, he left a bond worth $10,000, as well as $100,000 in the New Orleans branch of the Bank of the United States, $180,000 in the hands of his New York factor, $45,000 with his New Orleans factor, and nearly as much again with another factor (figures rounded).

Wade Hampton II
*From the Historic Columbia Foundation,
Columbia, S.C.*

Europe, but did not merely acquire, in the manner of too many Americans who inherit money. They sponsored the work of sculptors like De Veaux, painters, furniture makers and silversmiths. Like Haller Nutt, in Natchez, with whom they shared many political ideas, they sustained into the second generation the vigor of the first, but channeled some of its energy into a passionate desire to surround themselves not only with works of art (which was conventional enough) but with working artists (which was not). Wade Hampton II was often a partner in patronage with his brothers-in-law, John S. Preston and John L. Manning.

As we noted, the Hamptons of the second generation, including Wade II, Preston and Manning, were exceptions to many generalizations about southern planters; they had few counterparts, except, it happens, the great architectural patrons around Halifax, Virginia, and the Natchez group we will visit next. Their opinions and their business affairs were national in scope, and they built very distinguished houses. They were at home in cosmopolitan New Orleans or Philadelphia, which was still, in the 1840's, a lively place. They were atypical among southerners, even among rich southerners, politically, aesthetically and economically. In the 1850's they lost control of their region, and they lost their fortunes in the 1860's as a consequence.

It is true that they largely depended on absentee revenues. But they also took a determined part in the agricultural development of the upland Carolina region of their "home estates," and its politics. (We will come in a moment to their deter-

353

mined opposition to their political antagonist, whom they loathed personally, Wade II's other brother-in-law, James Henry Hammond.)

So much has been written about this group that it is strange how little is known about their relationships to their architects.*

The great fluted columns of Wade II's Millwood still stand near Columbia amid the charred ruins of the house, as they were left by General Sherman's troops. But though it was a very famous house, until recently we have not had even a clue as to its possible architect. That clue came from another Hampton house, Milford, the headquarters of Governor Manning. The two were probably quite similar in their central pavilions and in some of their details.

Until the 1970's a series of reclusive owners made an equal mystery of Milford. The Hamptons had long ago lost the place, and early-twentieth-century owners would not permit it to be visited or photographed. It stood, remote, at the end of a long red-dirt road near Sumter. It was always apart. Far from the clusters of houses around county seats where lived most of Manning's peers, it stood high on a knoll above an endless swamp, looking out over the tops of the trees below. Its entrance road led past a small stone temple, which served as a gatehouse, to set the tone for the great columned house.

Conjectural rendition of Millwood

Credit: William J. Keenan, II, AIA, Architect, in The Venturers: The Hampton, Harrison and Earle Families of Virginia, South Carolina and Texas, *by Virginia G. Meynard*

* *Robert Mills designed a majestic stone mansion for Wade I, but the old man could not be persuaded to abandon Woodlands or, one suspects, the money needed to fulfill Mills's designs.*

The isolation of Milford kept it from the fate of Millwood, for it was out of the main line of the movement of the Union armies in South Carolina until the very last day of the war; then, as a Union detachment seemed ready to loot the place, their commander, General Edward E. Potter, intervened after a conversation with Governor Manning, one of those wonderfully formal discourses of considerable length which are asserted by histories of the Civil War to be verbatim, though any stenographers must have been very busy at the time.

Governor John L. Manning

Collection of the South Carolina Historical Society

The house itself is an amazing transcript of its period, and beautiful besides. It is in excellent condition, the dark capitals appearing almost black above six massive white Corinthian columns. There are four very large rooms with fifteen-foot ceilings on the ground floor; a fifty-foot hall at the center opens back to a semicircular stairhall and a free-standing stair leading up to the second floor, where the ceilings are only a foot lower. By a shrewd deployment of mirrors and interior columns, the entire lower floor appears breezy and open, and the cornices richly complement the marble mantels and the gleaming hardware.

There is no other southern mansion that so fully presents what taste and restraint can do with large resources. Seen from the rear, the house has a late-eighteenth-century look, with two dependencies to the side, and the curve of the stairhall answers the smaller curves that provide niches for statuary. Milford* is much more elegant, more sculptured, than the blocky "Greek" of its country cousins.

There is no written record of its architect, but it certainly represented the most advanced fashion. It was started in May 1839, and the design of the sliding doors in the great double parlor is straight out of Minard Lafever's *Beauties of Modern Architecture* published in 1835. Lafever, like the Dakin brothers (see Chapter Sixteen), learned his trade in the office of Ithiel Town and, like them, once was in partnership with James Gallier. Lafever knew his market; doors like those, he said, "would eclipse every thing of the kind yet introduced." When Manning gave a set of drawings to his master carpenter, Nathaniel F. Potter, he was pleased; they suited his taste "in every respect" and "are much admired by those to whom I have shewn it."

Plans by whom? Not by Potter (to whom they have been erroneously attributed); Manning gave them to Potter, who provided the specifications. "Admired" by whom? Whose approbation would have pleased the proud and sophisticated Manning, this immensely rich man, living in such a remote place, with no peers but his wife's relatives? Where would he have gone for architect and for approval? Manning traveled often to the western plantations his wife had inherited (where the Dakins were working for his neighbors), to Philadelphia and New York, where having architectural plans "much admired" would give much pride.

In the early 1830's, Charleston was past its prime, but still very rich, still building enough grand structures to attract good architectural talent and still drawing part of that talent from Providence.†

It may have been this building boom of the early 1830's that attracted Potter (and his partner and brother, James) from their brick-making business in Providence to doing general contracting in South Carolina. They certainly knew Russell Warren (see Chapter Nine), who was in full career as a contractor and architect based in Providence, with major jobs, requiring brick, from New Bedford to Charleston. Potter, who was thirty-one at the time, with no architectural designs to his credit of which we have knowledge, corresponded with Manning from New York, where he may easily have encountered another likely participant in the assemblage of talent probably responsible for Milford: Charles F. Reichardt, a German-born architect who had been trained in the grand Classical manner and descended on Charleston at Christmas 1836.

It seems to me likely that those admirable plans came from the hand of

---

* *The Manning family spelled it Millford, as early correspondence indicates, but the other spelling is now so common as to have prescriptive right.*

† *Philadelphia was still the nation's scientific and cultural capital, but Manning was probably just far enough south to be beyond the range of its predominance of trade and cultural approbation. (See Chapter Seventeen for Philadelphia's influence in North, not South, Carolina.)*

Milford
Photos by Gene Waddell

357

Reichardt.* It is also likely that both the Potters and Warren participated in their execution. We know that Manning paid Warren for some plans, possibly working drawings for the house or for outbuildings.

A little detail may be useful here, because Milford is a masterpiece, and there has been vast confusion about those responsible for its design. Its plan is that of a villa, like those of the late eighteenth century in England or Germany, which formed a sort of vernacular tradition in Charleston, with the staircase placed in a rounded turret at the back of a large central hallway. Its scale, proportions, raked blocking course and Corinthian capitals are much like those of the Charleston Hotel. Gene Waddell, of the South Carolina Historical Society, recently blew the dust off the contract to build the hotel in 1838, and discovered that its contractors were the brothers Potter and its architect was Reichardt.†

Charleston's biographer of architects, Beatrice St. Julien Ravenel, tells us that Reichardt may well have been trained in Berlin by the great Karl Friedrich Schinkel (1781–1841). She relied, it seems, on a comment by a friend of Reichardt, Dr. John Beaufain Irving, who stated that the Charleston Theater was "constructed from designs by and under the immediate supervision of Mr. Reichardt—a gentleman I know well—an architect of considerable celebrity, a pupil of the celebrated Schinkel, in Prussia." Schinkel was a theater designer, theoretician and official architect for the huge neo-Greek monuments that celebrated the rise of Prussia after the Napoleonic Wars. His practice extended from the Crimea to Athens. It appears that its influence reached, as well, the sandhills of South Carolina.

Schinkel's Berlin Museum was under construction from 1823 onward, at the same time as the British Museum, both of a monumental Classicism. It does not take too much imagination to see their colonnades proceeding across the Atlantic, to be continued down the length of Reichardt's Charleston Hotel, then, after a jump, along the fifteen huge columns he placed across the Guard House front on Meeting Street, and then again continuing on a smaller scale, on his Vendue Range in the same city.

We know Reichardt was in New York by 1835, for in that year he shared in the award for designs for the huge prison known as the Tombs. The pattern-book-maker Minard Lafever was also a contestant; wherever we can trace Reichardt thereafter, we also seem to find Lafever's characteristic ornament.

Reichardt and Lafever knew each other's work, since both were among the

* The Hamptons, and Hampton in-law Governor Manning in particular, may have had an affinity for German Neoclassicism. As clues we have not only Sally Hampton's report of so much carved German furniture, and the governor's probable relationship to Reichardt; in 1853 he selected another German-trained architect, John R. Niernsee, to design the state capitol in Columbia.

† With two contracting brothers involved named Potter, bearing the same name as the Union general who had the dramatic conversation with the governor, we need not wonder that many historians have thought the architect was also named Potter, related somehow to the great Bishop Potter of New York.

founders of the New York chapter of the American Institution of Architects, Reichardt in the first cadre, in 1836, Lafever in the second, in 1837. In the years 1834 through 1836 New York enjoyed a building boom, which collapsed at the end of 1836. Then, apparently, Reichardt set forth to Charleston. We know little else about him, except that he seems immediately to have been received as a man of importance and had at least one connection with the horse-loving Hamptons: he designed a grandstand for the racecourse at Charleston's Hampton Park.*

Reichardt's known work in Charleston was, like much of Schinkel's, stage-craft. Façades were intended to be impressive, and they were. The Charleston Hotel was so important to the sense of drama that city was reacquiring, after two torpid decades without an important building, that after it burnt in 1838 it was completely rebuilt in 1839. It was so conspicuous that Wade Hampton II had to be aware of it. Potter was the master builder, transmitting designs for remodeling

The Charleston Hotel
Collection of the South Carolina Historical Society

* *Horse-breeding and horse-racing and the Greek Revival have had important associations, as we saw in discussing Nicholas Biddle and James Coles Bruce in Chapter Seventeen.*

old Wade's Woodlands into the Neoclassic palace called Millwood, adding its wings and a twelve-columned colonnade in the same year. Manning's house followed the next spring, while the team of Reichardt and the Potters was still available.

Reichardt seems to have been a restless man, for in 1840 he disappeared again. The best guess is that he went to the West Indies and Central America, for a decade later someone bearing his name, now back in Germany, published two books about travels there. But earnest bustling through the German archives, which I have stimulated a generation after an earlier search, has failed to produce any documents tying the mysterious architect either to Schinkel or to the Hamptons. A pity. He should have left us a volume of reflections on the taste of South Carolina.

The Hamptons at Mid-Century

IN CHAPTER TWENTY we encountered Adelicia Hayes Cheatham, a tigress who required armies and great banking houses to accommodate her determination that even a civil war would not disrupt the ordered pace of her affairs in the Louisiana delta country. Others were not so fortunate. John L. Manning confronted General Potter's troops on his own front porch just after he returned from "an extended tour throughout the West, under special commission" of the Confederate governor of South Carolina. His affairs were in hopeless disorder, and now a Yankee foraging party was there, in his front yard, having passed the little temple of a gatehouse, with fire in their eyes and dry tinder all about.

That the house, built by two Yankees named Potter, should be saved by another was one of the many ironies in the life of John Manning, a man ruined by a war he tried to prevent. Manning had been politically active as a Unionist before the conflict, like his friends and brothers-in-law John S. Preston and Wade Hampton II—and very unlike another brother-in-law, the fire-eating Secessionist senator James Henry Hammond.

Hammond was more in the mold of Wade Hampton I; he was, in the language of Carol Bleser, editor of his letters, "a tough son of a bitch. Having wed his wife for her wealth," says Bleser, he "proceeded to exploit her property to the fullest— hauling enormous amounts of muck up from the Savannah River to enrich the land . . . Although this grueling, dangerous, and unhealthy work was carried out by slaves, Hammond always took credit for supervising the work himself rather than employing overseers."

It was Hammond who, in March 1858, proclaimed on the floor of the United States Senate that "cotton is King" and also that "in all social systems there must be a class to do the menial duties . . . the drudgery . . . requiring a low order of intellect and but little skill." This was what he called the "mud-sill of society,"

James Henry Hammond
From the South Caroliniana Library,
University of South Carolina

and he was content that "the South . . . found a race adapted to that purpose . . . We use them for our purpose, and call them slaves."

He was a most unadmirable man. In 1846 Wade Hampton II threatened to horsewhip him if he returned to political life in Columbia, where he had engaged in bizarre intimacies with Hampton's four daughters, his nieces, none of whom were then over eighteen, and he stayed out of public life for fourteen years, until Hampton was on the brink of death. His wife finally left him when he refused to give up a Negro mistress, though he seems to have had little affection for the mistress either. But he was an energetic planter, who managed nearly twenty-two square miles of plantations, and there was no doubt whatever of his loyalty to the Confederacy. Half his estate was in Confederate bonds when he died in 1864, "old and crushed," according to his son.

The Hammond plantation, Redcliffe, stands in the center of Hammond's enriched land, on a hill amid landscaped grounds, looking down on the Savannah River, just inside South Carolina. It is a graceless barn of a place, as representative of the harsh, unapologetic, egocentric and querulous man who built it as is Milford of the stately and fastidious Manning.

Hammond had been an unrelenting and cruel father, a vicious husband, but somehow there was in him a quality of force and nasty persistence which made his career interesting. He was the fortune-hunting son of an itinerant Yankee school-master who became almost a parody of the bellicose and graceless upcountry planters who had come to rule the South. Redcliffe had a series of distinguished

361

Redcliffe
From The Hammonds of Redcliffe, *Oxford University Press*

Photograph of a wedding party at Redcliffe in 1897 that gives some
idea of the scale of the house
From The Hammonds of Redcliffe, *Oxford University Press*

subsequent owners, some of them his own descendants, but the stamp of James Henry Hammond is set hard upon it. Wayne Andrews said of it that it was "a pompous thing, but not completely uninspired, like the retreat of John C. Calhoun."*

Fortunately for posterity, Milford was saved by the intervention of General Potter, to remind us of the architectural taste and the great qualities of men like John L. Manning and courteous, quiet, kindly Wade II, who was so often said to be "the embodied spirit" or "finest flowering" of Carolina "blood and Carolina honor." We do not find it strange that the leader of the next generation, Wade III, became the most romantic of Robert E. Lee's generals, succeeding Jeb Stuart as commander of the Confederate Cavalry. Wade Hampton III was, like his father, a brave and intelligent man. He, too, opposed secession. He favored giving educated Negroes the vote in 1865, and after becoming governor in 1876 refused to ride the dark tide of white supremacy. Despite the opposition of his followers, he appointed Negroes to office. He went on to the United States Senate, where he served with sober wisdom and distinction.

Wade III emerged from a lost war, a lost fortune and a youth spent among plantation owners in a tight, apprehensive society that censored mails, sermons and newspapers, that feared dissent of any sort as an invitation to servile insurrection, that drove artists and writers from the state, and that moved with bitterness and braggadocio into a civil war. After a brilliant military career, he commenced a civil career as a compassionate, intelligent man who was always willing to learn, to move with the times and to resist the forces of hate. He was

> six feet in height, with deep chest, broad shoulders, narrow hips and powerful legs, his was a superb presence, and in the saddle he and his horse seemed one. His complexion, hair, and large blueish-grey eyes gave him the appearance of an old Saxon king. The call to arms naturally found him in the saddle at the head of the cavalry, where his genius for command, his quiet poise, dash and daring, endeared him to Lee, and to his men, and to all his people.

Claude Bowers, who penned that description in the 1920's, was so powerfully affected by this genuinely splendid figure that he carried his admiration of the man over into admiration for the system that Hampton had transcended, and had tried to redeem. Bowers' picture of the youth of Wade Hampton III offers us a picture of the Old South which makes it all seem so easy, so tranquil, so unremarkable that, believing it, we could fail to give Wade III his due.

The reference, while unkind, is appropriate. Hammond thought Calhoun a genius: "No man alive is equal to him." Calhoun's propositions, he thought, were "as clear as a sunbeam." Calhoun reciprocated, saying to Hammond, "I know no one better informed, than you are, on the great subject [slavery] that now agitates the country, or more capable of deciding what should be done." By this time, apparently, Calhoun was ready to endorse Hammond's view that slavery was "the greatest of all the great blessings which a kind providence has bestowed upon our glorious region."

Wade Hampton III
*Courtesy of The Charleston Museum,
Charleston, S.C.*

Wade Hampton was symbolical of the finest flowering of prewar Southern chivalry and aristocracy. Patrician by birth, instinct, training, his manner was democratic. Born in the Charleston town house of his mother, his boyhood was passed among the ancient oaks and rose gardens of Millwood . . . This stately house with its impressive columns was the seat of hospitality almost medieval in its magnificence . . . Great numbers of slaves, fat and contented, worked in house and field, grinning in the sunshine and warmly attached to an indulgent master.

It was not quite so. His old grandfather, after all, was still a brooding presence. The oaks and rose gardens—and the genteel life—were barely two decades old. What was remarkable about Wade Hampton II, and his even more remarkable son, was that they justified the descriptions "beau ideal," "finest flowering," "complete model and specimen" and "embodied spirit." They survived a rapacious patriarch and a cruel and crabbed system, and lived good lives, seeking to improve that system as best they could. We should compare Bowers' picture with the lamentable reality, and thus see how grand was the accomplishment of the southern gentleman at its best. To do this we should set him not against a dreamy romantic background that would have required little of him, but instead against the ugly and demeaning reality, which permitted only a few, like Wade Hampton III, to survive as whole men.

The Old South was far more diverse, economically and architecturally, than

Hollywood or hagiography has told us. Even within that diversity, even within groups that do not fit any stereotype, there was more diversity still. Lest it be thought for a moment that all Unionist diversifying planters built alike, we will now move westward across land that once composed the plantations of the Hampton family into Mississippi, where, upon the great river, those holdings abutted another set of huge possessions, those of the Nutt family of Natchez, with whom the Hamptons had much in common, except in architectural taste. The Hamptons were free to draw on New York or Rome for artistic talent. The Nutts looked to Philadelphia. But the Nutts shared with the Hamptons an insistence that the client have a powerful say in the process of creation.

CHAPTER 24

Natchez,
and the Nutts

NATCHEZ PERCHES on the east side of the Mississippi River, 2,500 nautical miles from its headwaters. A crow can travel half that distance between these two points, looking down at the coiling river, which seems in no hurry to come to terms with the sea. The Mississippi dominates a huge, temperate, fertile province, larger than all of Europe. Sometimes the river seems like a dragon or a great boa; capriciously it devours a plantation house, or an old French town, or a cornfield. Sometimes it seems instead like a warrior monarch, making alliances, gathering its confederate freshwater chiefs, the St. Croix, the Des Moines, the Missouri and the Ohio, the White, the Red, the Arkansas and the Platte, for the confrontation with the remorseless final saline world of the Gulf. Seen on the map it may appear less formidable, rather like the giant intestine of the continent, grinding and dissolving those substances it needs for nourishment, and carrying what it does not require to deposit in the sea.

For tens of thousands of years these digestive processes occurred very slowly in the great valley of America. Rivers and rain and wind did their work at their own pace. Mudflats were produced, extending for hundreds of miles. Gaining fresh deposits, they rose high enough to stand above the river most of the time—except when the river chose to flood. On these mudbanks, great cottonwood trees grew, and almost anything else would grow there after people had removed the trees. By 1820 vast fertile flatlands were planted in indigo and sugar and cotton. Their owners looked out with satisfaction from their perch high on the bluff at Natchez, itself a heap of fertile loess, a hundred miles in extent and a hundred feet in depth.

The Natchez Junto

SETTLERS PUT in their first crops on that loess escarpment because it was high enough to give safety from the erratic appetites of the river. It also provided humans with hope of breezy relief from plague-bearing mosquitoes that bred in the streams and swamps of the Mississippi and Louisiana flatlands. The French, arriving in the early sixteenth century, built a fort there many years before they dared do so upon the low-lying site that became New Orleans.*

Natchez began as a little French outpost, which became Spanish and then French again for reasons associated with European, not American, politics. By the end of its period of nominal Spanish rule it was already, like Mobile, in the grip of shrewd, driving Americans of English, Scottish and Irish descent, who made it their own colony. They actually ran up the American flag from time to time before the Louisiana Purchase legalized a de facto extension of the United States.

So it was that a very old European settlement entered the nineteenth century. Honeymooners like Andrew and Rachel Jackson, from the hinterland, would go to Natchez as Yankees would go to Boston, to learn what the great world was like. As the interior filled with people, Natchez and other old towns sustained their relationships to the eastern seaboard. And so, as we stand in its environs, preparing to look about its history, we are leaving the backcountry behind and joining again the main channel of our story.

By 1820 Natchez was the base for a prosperous band of scientist-planter-entrepreneurs who looked as much to Philadelphia as to New Orleans. They could afford to keep up their links with the eastern metropolis; in fact, they could not afford not to do so. Their capital requirements were huge, and Philadelphia, not New Orleans, was the banking center of America. No group of Americans ever cultivated and reaped so intensively and so continuously such expanses of fertile and well-watered land as these planters of Natchez. Virginia speculators such as William Byrd, King Carter and George Washington, and their successors such as Wade Hampton, the Halifax Whigs and the nabobs of the Nashville basin held title to larger premises, but they did not farm, nor intend to farm, many of them. The wheat kings of the Red River of the North had not enough consistent rain to farm either continuously or intensively, as they learned to their grief in the late 1880's. The huge ranches of Texas and New Mexico often could only offer drink to one head of their cattle per section.

The landholdings in Mississippi and Louisiana of the "Natchez Junto" spread north and south in the rich brown-black earth along the river and its innumerable

---

European settlers had been preceded on the bluff by the equally prudent Indians, whose tribal name the whites gave to the place. As often happened during the expansion of Europe into other continents, the natives were massacred first and then romanticized, in Chateaubriand's novel Les Natchez.

loops, leftovers and backwaters. After they had oligopolized their base on the loess hillocks around Natchez, they shifted capital (millions of dollars of capital in some cases) northward into the lowlands along the east side of the Mississippi, which were denied smaller farmers by the high cost of ditching and draining. Then they turned to the flat lowlands of Louisiana, across the way. By the 1850s a few Mississippi families, nearly all from Natchez, were cultivating 130,000 acres in Louisiana alone. Just in Concordia Parish, across from Natchez itself, and in Madison Parish, the Surgetts (alternatively spelled "Surgets") owned 8,000 acres. Upriver, in Adams County, Mississippi, they owned 7,150; in Wilkinson County as many or more, nearly all of which were under cultivation; to say nothing of 50,000 acres for speculation in Arkansas and, probably, shares in land syndicates in Illinois. They were not the richest of the group of a dozen or so of these landowners; their holdings are merely representative. So, it happens, were their politics; like most of the others, they were Whigs and opposed secession. With the others, the Surgetts were deeply engaged in precisely the sort of diversification into Midwestern corn and wheat lands that attracted the Halifax Whigs of Virginia. In Abraham Lincoln's home county in Illinois, for example, a syndicate represented by Nathaniel Ware of Natchez bought more than 21,000 acres as early as 1835 and 1836.

Classical Natchez

AT THE OUTSET, the traders and small planters who established themselves on the embankments above the Mississippi had reproduced there the architecture of the Caribbean lowlands; as late as 1808 the indefatigable English traveler Fortescue Coming told his diary he was "much struck with the similarity of Natchez to . . . West Indian towns, particularly St. John's, Antigua." But within four years Natchez, like Mobile, began to assume an eastern cast. In 1811 or 1812 the banker, lawyer and planter Lyman Harding engaged Levi Weeks to design and build Auburn, a large red-brick classical house with a giant portico. It was the first in the territory, boasted Weeks to a friend, to bear the stamp of the Palladian orders. Both Harding and Weeks were from Massachusetts, and Weeks brought more to the territory than an architectural education. He was a living link to Natchez' brief tenure as the capital of Aaron Burr's western empire. It was in Natchez that Burr gathered his forces for his final assault on New Orleans. It was there he heard of the defection of his ally, General James Wilkinson. Near Natchez he began his flight through the Mississippi wilderness, only to be betrayed again into the hands of the agents of the government of his archenemy, Thomas Jefferson.

Levi Weeks, the respectable Natchez architect, probably came to the place as a result of a recommendation from Burr himself. Weeks owed his life to Burr; he had good reason to take his recommendations. In 1800 he had been the defendant

The Elms, in Natchez. Built in 1782, in the "Caribbean" style
during the Spanish era.
Courtesy of Natchez Pilgrimage Tours

Auburn
Courtesy of the Mississippi Department of Archives and History

in a lurid trial, charged with the murder of a lady of his acquaintance. Burr, who was the leader of the Republicans, headed a defense team that also included Alexander Hamilton and Brockholst Livingston, the two most prominent Federalist attorneys in New York. Apparently this formidable array took the case in competitive solicitude for the interests of the artisan class, of which young Levi Weeks, then a poor carpenter, was thought to be a representative. After Burr got him off, Weeks led a vagrant's life until he headed for Natchez, which sheltered him as it had Burr, but for a much longer time.

Aaron Burr, the defender of Levi Weeks, was himself defended after his treason trial by Nicholas Biddle. But it was not through Weeks' timorous use of the orders that Biddle's more confident Classicism reached Natchez. He had a direct agent there, for banking and for architecture, a man as mysterious as Weeks, but one who became much richer: Levin Marshall.

He was a collateral Marshall, one of the Baltimore kin of the Chief Justice who presided over Aaron Burr's treason trial. He was, it seems, a handsome fellow, dashing, "of slight build . . . a dark, intense face, aquiline nose, thin lips with a slight hauteur." (How many of these Whiggish bankers had a slight—or more than slight—hauteur!) He was possessed of some means, for soon after he arrived in Mississippi, about 1823, he commenced buying land. We do not know how much he accumulated, but it certainly included nearly 9,000 acres in Louisiana and 2,500 in Adams County, around Natchez itself.

Marshall was, however, a banker first and a planter second. Apparently he was associated with Biddle in the New Orleans branch of the Second Bank of the United States, and then Biddle appointed him head of the Natchez branch. With Marshall one must constantly use the cautionary "apparently" because his descendants preside over a treasure of his papers, which they are loath to share and are said to be bowdlerizing. This may be because Marshall was what he was alleged to be, Biddle's paymaster for western politicians, including Henry Clay. It is unlikely to be just because he was also the proprietor of Natchez' best hotel, where the juleps were served with moss roses at the brim.

When Biddle began the remodeling of Andalusia, in 1834, Marshall followed suit, placing a clean Grecian house beside, and at right angles to, one of those Creole cottages which Fortescue Coming had noted.* The house was called Richmond, and the interior of the Greek portion is a splendid example of the more sedate period of that revival before it was engulfed by the exuberance of Minard Lafever and the Philadelphia and New York suppliers of ornament-by-the-yard. Still later, Marshall added a third house, this time a large, sober brick annex to the rear.

Marshall's chief contribution to Natchez was to show how to build Greek Revival houses of the lineage of Andalusia or Berry Hill. His was—and is—the

---

* An obvious parallel is the juxtaposition to a similar cottage of Hyde Hall (see Chapter Twelve).

Richmond
Courtesy of Natchez Pilgrimage Tours

only one in town. He was also (apparently) responsible for the Grecian design of two banks, one of which (in 1985 called the Britton and Koontz Bank) he dominated directly and the other (in 1985, the Commercial Bank) indirectly. Both bank buildings were under construction at about the same time as Richmond, and as other banks across the nation that felt the influence of Nicholas Biddle.

The inspiration for Richmond may have come from Philadelphia, but the most famous building in Natchez, and the most complete expression outside Philadelphia of Philadelphia's architectural skill, is Longwood, sometimes called "Nutt's Folly." It was constructed from Philadelphia millwork, roofing, stone, mantels, windows, doors, nails, lime, tin and flues, by a Philadelphia architect who supervised Philadelphia artisans and foremen. It was built for a man whose father and daughters were educated in Philadelphia. Father and son were perhaps the last legitimate intellectual successors to the great Philadelphia gentlemen-scientists of the early days of the Republic.* They were Doctors Rush and Haller Nutt.

---

* *New Orleans was even more of a Philadelphia town than Natchez. Its chief financial houses were manned by agents of New York and Philadelphia houses, and the influence of Philadelphia on Natchez was, to a considerable extent, mediated by New Orleans. We could have chosen to follow a New Orleans entrepreneur and his architect for these chapters, but the redemption of "Nutt's Folly" (from writers who underrate its importance as a monument to the Enlightenment) seemed nobler work.*

Britton and Koontz Bank (*above*) and Commercial Bank, Natchez

Photos by Ronald Miller, courtesy of the Historical Natchez Foundation

Rushford Nutt

RUSHFORD NUTT was one of that extraordinary circle of men illuminated by the Philadelphia Enlightenment in the last decades of the eighteenth century. His patronymic was the Danish "Canute"; many of the family, before and after this time, spelled it "Knutt." The first to leave records had come with the Danish invasions to Britain, before the time of Edward the Confessor. Their descendants joined the British invasions of America in the seventeenth century. Rushford was born in Northumberland County, Virginia, in 1781. Though his biographer avers that he "numbered among his friends both Benjamin Franklin and David Rittenhouse, for whom he named his first born son," a friendship with Franklin, who died in April 1790, seems too prodigious even for Nutt (though we know enough of Rush Nutt's puckishness to think it was probably he who allowed this thought to creep into the records).

David Rittenhouse lived six years longer than Franklin. The great astronomer was universally proclaimed as America's scientific genius. Why should not a young man who had been trained in science, among men who had sat at the feet of Rittenhouse, assert his aspirations for his own son by giving him such a name? (Rittenhouse Nutt disappointed his father.)

Benjamin Rush was the eulogist and anointed successor of Rittenhouse, in Philadelphia and in the American Philosophical Society. He began his medical education in Philadelphia and continued at Edinburgh. He was a chemist, an expert in public health and a pioneer student of mental illness, and, like Rittenhouse, vehemently opposed to slavery. He was thirty-four years older than Rushford Nutt, but they did become friends, and the older man was so potent a force in his life that Nutt acknowledged his intellectual paternity by shortening his first name to Rush. After completing his studies in medicine under Rush, he sustained throughout his life the kind of broad scientific curiosities that Rush had encouraged.

Most of Rush Nutt's writings have been lost, but we have some of their titles: they range across theology, natural history, agronomy and mechanics. He arrived in Philadelphia when the members of the Philosophical Society were engaged in sorting out the competitive claims of John Fitch and James Rumsey for primacy in steam locomotion. There was high excitement about steam engines in general, which Nutt later carried forward in his development of a successful steam cotton gin.

Glimpses of the character of Rush Nutt glint from the dour pages of a journal he kept when reconnoitering Natchez and while walking more than a thousand miles through the southwestern wilderness. He began his explorations alone, in the heat of the summer of 1805. He started at the Mississippi and walked all the way from Natchez through the hamlets of Nashville and Knoxville to Virginia. He kept precise notes of the customs of the Indians he encountered, their food, language and dance, their architecture and town planning, their hygienic and sanitation devices, the antiquity of their culture, and their likely future. He was particularly interested in medical details, but he was writing more like an anthropologist than a traveling doctor.

He was also a rogue. He took pleasure in confusing his contemporaries and laid traps for historians with considerable success. When he came to Natchez, he said, he found in a building near the wharf "gentlemen around a table striking small bodies with staffs while drinking a liquid of a fiery nature," and "the same catastrophe was presenting itself on the other side of the street." One subsequent writer has solemnly suggested that this "could have been a house where voodoo was being practiced"; indeed it could, but it is more likely that some gentlemen were drinking whiskey and having a game of billiards.

Another set of images of Rush Nutt emerges from a chance reference to him in a book about Americans traveling in Turkey thirty years later. In 1835 Nutt encountered that priggish snob John Lloyd Stephens, the travel writer, in Smyrna, on his way to Istanbul. He sized up Stephens quickly and gave a classic performance of the backwoods oaf before some migrant princelings and countlets whom Stephens was trying to assure that all Americans were not bumpkins. Nutt, colleague of Rittenhouse, the inventor, scientist and physician, persuaded Stephens that he "had passed all his life on the banks of the Mississippi" and had "a thorough contempt for the uses of society and everything like polish of manners." This performance was so effective that Stephens told posterity that Nutt "had never been even to New York before; was utterly ignorant of any language but his own; despised all foreigners, and detested their 'jabber.' " Actually, there is evidence that he knew Greek, Latin and Hebrew. He had founded one college; his father-in-law had founded another.

Stephens justly observed that Rush Nutt had "a strong, active and inquiring mind," though embarrassingly agricultural. Nutt had closely studied the cedars of Lebanon and the olive trees of the Garden of Gethsemane, and, according to Stephens, had sent "enormous boxes of earth and stones, to be shipped to America." Nutt's archaeological interest had been stimulated thirty years earlier in his travels through the Indian country of Mississippi and Tennessee, and he apparently kept it up.

It seems likely that Nutt embarked on that earlier exploration not out of cool scientific curiosity but as a way of breaking out of the intense intellectual endeavors of his youth, after the continuities of that life were broken. He left Philadelphia with his wife to practice medicine in Virginia, but his wife died soon thereafter, and almost immediately he went off to the West.

After his prolonged pilgrimage to primitivism, very much like those of Sam Houston of Texas and Henry Hastings Sibley of Minnesota in similar circumstances,* he gathered his goods and chattels together and moved to Jefferson

* Both these good frontiersmen and later governors chose to spend long periods living among the Indians.

County, Mississippi, north of Natchez, where he commenced the practice of medicine and the accumulation of land. There he continued the spread of Philadelphia learning, founding Oakland College and training a series of young men in medicine. About 1809 he married Eliza, the daughter of another physician-planter, David Ker.

Ker had been educated at Trinity College, Dublin, and studied medicine in Edinburgh, at about the same time as Benjamin Rush. He migrated first to North Carolina, where he was one of the founders of Chapel Hill College (now the University of North Carolina), and then moved again, to the frontier of Mississippi, where he became a planter and judge of the Mississippi Supreme Court. His son was also a physician and became a very rich planter and partner with the two Drs. Nutt and yet another doctor, Stephen Duncan, also a product of Pennsylvania medical and scientific training, whose young wife had died and who went to Mississippi for a fresh start, arriving at about the same time as Rush Nutt. (What was the attraction of Natchez to physicians who aspired to be planters? Another emigrant from Northern Ireland, Frederick Stanton, also trained as a doctor, became so rich as a planter that he could build Natchez' most famous Classical Revival house, Stanton Hall.)

This circle of scientists and physicians dominated the intellectual life of a city that was, for a time, the West and South's closest approximation to Philadelphia in the density and power of its civility. It had two of the South's best newspapers, and such an effective public and private school system that four fifths of its adult whites were literate. One (perhaps enthusiastic) historian, William Banks Taylor, said it was "a noteworthy literary center, a hub of scientific thought . . . the cradle of higher education in Mississippi, and a cultural mountain rising over a dusty plain of agrarian mediocrity."

A few observations of the accomplishments of the Drs. Nutt may give a sense of the intellectual vitality of this group. In the early 1830's upland cotton was suffering from one of its periodic blights. Rush Nutt set forth to the cotton-growing areas of the Middle East to find strains of the plant that might be resistant to the diseases that were wiping out the entire crops of many southern plantations. He left no record of the sources of his discoveries, but he may also have investigated cotton culture in Mexico. Later agronomists suggest that he combined Mexican and Egyptian strains to produce what became known as Petit Gulf or Nutt cotton, which forms the basis of most of the cotton seed now raised in the United States for upland planting. J. F. H. Claiborne, an early Mississippi historian, described it as being "very prolific with a long fine and strong staple and free from rot . . . vigorous stalk . . . numerous large white bolls . . . easily picked, yielding more than any other cotton."

Rush Nutt and his son Haller continued giving "all the work of a cultivated and highly scientific education to agriculture in all its bearings" (in the proud words of Haller's widow). They introduced the planting of field pea as a fertilizer. They pioneered the practice of "plowing in" corn stalks to return nutrients to the

375

soil, instead of burning off the stalks. Following the lead of their partner Francis Surgett, they adopted contour plowing to keep the heavy loess of their hilly plantations from washing downhill.

The two Drs. Nutt were most famous for being the first planters to make the Whitney cotton gin a widely useful machine. Experimenting, in the old Philadelphia fashion, with grates, saws and brushes, they tinkered with the machine until it separated waste cotton from marketable fibers and kept a steady rhythm to detach motes or false seed. Finally, in 1830, they were the first to power the whole apparatus with steam, bringing an engine from Pittsburgh that was large enough to drive two gins. Marie Logan, the chronicler of the region around Rodney, Mississippi (now a ghost town but once the center of the Nutts' plantations on the east side of the river), proudly tells us that their coupling of cotton gins to steam engines "created a new industry and a rich source of profit for the northern foundries; especially in Philadelphia, old Ben Franklin's town, and in Pittsburgh, the city from which the original engine came."

Rush Nutt's boiler displayed in the background of a cotton-ginning exhibit
Courtesy of Mississippi Agriculture and Forestry

Haller Nutt

Courtesy of the Pilgrimage
Garden Club, Natchez

Julia Nutt

Courtesy of the Pilgrimage
Garden Club, Natchez

Haller and Julia Nutt

THE NUTTS' OWN PROFITS rose over the decades, but with many frightful oscillations to mark the upward trend. Cotton prices were no more stable for them than for anyone else, though their high-quality product did bring at least a dollar per bale more than other cotton. Haller was educated at the University of Virginia and the medical school at the University of Kentucky. Like his father and Stephen Duncan, he relied on the perspective provided by his classical education (they all spoke and wrote Greek and Latin, and Haller, at least, could read and write Hebrew) to impart some serenity during the erratic progress of their fortunes during the 1830's and 1840's. Haller's scientific education let him experiment with machinery when times were flush—he was in correspondence with Denison Olmsted of Yale about lightning rods, and he tried a variety of innovations in farm machinery—but all else was put aside to focus on survival when, in 1847 and 1848, cotton went into one of its periodic times of glut, and the price dropped to less than half what it had been a few years earlier.

377

Research languished while Haller sweated to stay ahead of his creditors. His factors in New Orleans refused his draft in 1848 and foreclosed on Araby, one of his best plantations, in 1850, but within the year he was on his way up again, buying Winter Quarters, set among the Louisiana holdings of his wife's family, and, soon thereafter, Longwood, a property in the suburbs of Natchez, which she had long coveted. From then on, until the strangling of the cotton market by the Civil War, the experiments and planning of the Nutts paid off. New plantations were added, productivity on existing plantations was increased, northern diversification was pursued and new banking relationships were established in Natchez, New Orleans and Philadelphia.

Haller Nutt was frail but very tough. His letters and those of his wife, Julia, are full of references to his illnesses, which appear to have included recurrent malaria; at least in his final years, he was "partially blind and—quite delicate." These were the words of his wife, daughter of Louisiana and Mississippi frontiersmen. As we will see, she was a formidable lady, but it is time now to look at the designer she and her husband chose for their architectural adventures, who was certainly their match. Samual Sloan was America's fiercest architectural entrepreneur until the time of Daniel Burnham and Frank Lloyd Wright. Dogged Robert Mills and shrewd old Dr. William Thornton may have been strong, but Sam Sloan was a tiger.

CHAPTER 25

Samuel Sloan and the Octagon

N O ARCHITECT BEFORE Richard Morris Hunt and Henry Hobson Richardson was so fortunate in finding compatible clients as Samuel Sloan. He was a tiger, but with other tigers as clients he got along just fine.

Sloan was born in 1815, a year earlier than Haller Nutt, in Chester County, Pennsylvania, of a Protestant Irish family. He was apprenticed as a carpenter in Philadelphia and worked under the direction of the English architect John Haviland on the Eastern State Penitentiary, where he learned the rudiments of that ability to plan very large institutional buildings which was the staple of his professional career. It was a time of intense interest in prison reform, mental hospital reform, reform of medical care and the care of the deaf and blind, and architects were as much the beneficiaries of that interest as inmates. In the 1830's and early 1840's Sloan worked upward, as carpenter, foreman and then supervisor, on all these kinds of institutions. He was lucky to have met, while working on a hospital for the insane, the enormously energetic reformer Dr. Thomas Kirkbride; together they developed a system for housing the insane that later led to a string of large architectural commissions.

Sloan was still listed as a carpenter-builder in the late 1840's when he won a commission as designer, as well, of a new courthouse and jail for Delaware County, Pennsylvania. He won it over professionals as eminent as Nicholas Biddle's architect Thomas U. Walter. His means must have been fairly—shall we say—aggressive. That was certainly the word to describe his style of entry thereafter into residential architecture. It is also, it happens, an apt term for the first clients who made that entry possible.

379

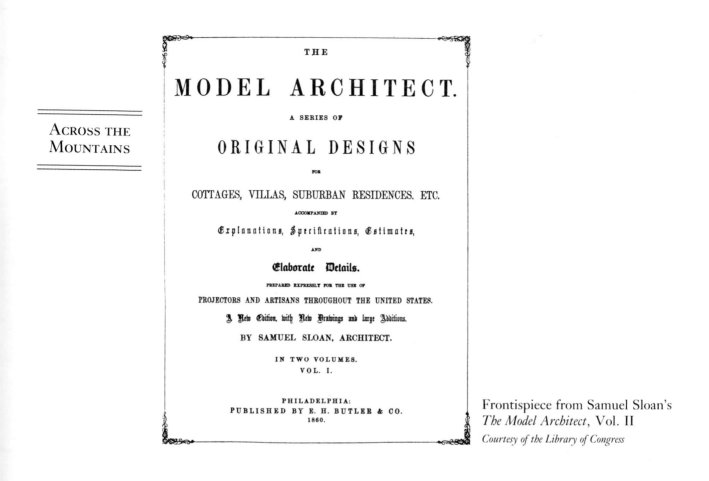

THE

MODEL ARCHITECT.

A SERIES OF

ORIGINAL DESIGNS

FOR

COTTAGES, VILLAS, SUBURBAN RESIDENCES. ETC.

ACCOMPANIED BY

Explanations, Specifications, Estimates,

AND

Elaborate Details.

PREPARED EXPRESSLY FOR THE USE OF

PROJECTORS AND ARTISANS THROUGHOUT THE UNITED STATES.

A New Edition, with New Drawings and large Additions.

BY SAMUEL SLOAN, ARCHITECT.

IN TWO VOLUMES.
VOL. I.

PHILADELPHIA:
PUBLISHED BY E. H. BUTLER & CO.
1860.

Frontispiece from Samuel Sloan's
The Model Architect, Vol. II
Courtesy of the Library of Congress

The Russian Connection

THOUGH RAILROAD MAGNATES like the Vanderbilts, the Goulds, the Ameses, and Henry Villard were to become clients from the 1880's onward, the first railroad fortunes to have an important impact on American architectural taste were those made in the 1850's along the Neva, not the Hudson, the Ohio or the Delaware.

To some extent this was because of personal animosity between Benjamin Henry Latrobe and the inventor Oliver Evans. The development of American railroads was retarded because Latrobe, the most celebrated engineer in the nation, was so angry at Evans (for reasons now obscure) that he was blinded to the advantages of Evans' proposals for steam locomotion. As early as 1805 Evans demonstrated an amphibious steam-powered wheeled vehicle in Philadelphia; Latrobe's derisive reports about such locomotive prototypes fueled the derision of others, and buttressed the case of canal and turnpike builders, who were eager to deny to railroaders the state and municipal subsidies they were seeking for themselves. Latrobe's role was ironic, since his son became a famous railroad engineer, largely responsible for the orderly growth of the Baltimore and Ohio, the first important American "road," which began operations—without steam locomotion —in 1827.

Soon after the B&O commenced business, however, it gained the services of a true master of the steam engine, the remarkable inventor and entrepreneur Ross Winans (1796–1877). He became its prime supplier of rolling stock, and after 1840 he built his own locomotive works. He was, like Rush Nutt, a tinkerer, but one who had a growing opportunity in an industry with an insatiable appetite for technological advance: his high-speed *Carroll of Carrollton* was a "splendid failure" in 1849.

Early in his career, Winans had manufactured the first American-built locomotive to compete successfully with the British in the international market, the *Columbus*, for the Leipzig and Dresden Railroad. He had also offered the Czar of Russia the B&O's prototype of a wind-driven rail car, and as engines were developed, the Czar sought to persuade him to come to Russia to build those necessary to create the Russian railroad system. His son Thomas (1820–1878) went instead, and became very rich indeed; when he returned to Baltimore he built a city house called Alexandroffsky and a country house called Crimea. Alexandroffsky survived until 1926. Miraculously, Crimea is still there, much as it was in 1860, at the center of the remaining two hundred of the thousand acres on which Thomas Winans and his French-Russian wife, and then their children, lived the lives of

Ross Winans, by Francis Lathrop
*Courtesy of the Maryland Historical Society,
Baltimore/Gift of Miss Elsie Celeste Hutton*

Crimea

Courtesy of the Peale Museum, Baltimore, Maryland

Russian aristocrats as late as the Russian Revolution of 1917, and even into the 1920's. The property was purchased by the city of Baltimore in 1940; the stone house, surrounded by verandahs* and set amid its outbuildings, serves as the headquarters for Leakin Park.

The chief partners of Thomas Winans in Russia, however, came not from Baltimore but Philadelphia, and returned there to make their marks architecturally. Under Nicholas Biddle's lead, Philadelphia was the first center of American railroad finance,† indeed the first cockpit of American industrialism. From the outset of invention and of production organized in a factory system, the region along the Delaware had provided a more lively welcome to skilled and enterprising "mechanics" than any other region of the country; it remained the center of invention in the 1840's, after the failure of Biddle's bank, a home of brash strivers who rode upward in society on steam railroads. As early as 1825 the ubiquitous William Strickland went off to Britain to catch up on the possibilities of rail travel, so undervalued by his mentor, Latrobe, and the Pennsylvania Society for the Promotion of Internal Improvements nurtured the careers of men like Andrew Eastwick and Joseph Harrison, Jr.

Perhaps that is where verandahs were born! They seem to be indigenous to the Crimea, though I have found no expert who professes to know if they were there before they appeared in America about 1740 (see Chapter Five).

† *Biddle often served as the intermediary for British lenders, who found debt instruments (bonds) more convincing forms of financing then the equity positions (stocks) being sold by dour Boston financiers, who saw debt instruments as somehow incompatible with the risks associated with the work ethic. After the fall of the Bank of the United States and the subsequent collapse of Biddle's own state bank around 1840, the center of finance did*

Both Eastwick and Harrison were machinists. Harrison was apprenticed at fifteen, became a foreman at twenty and went to work in 1835 for Eastwick, who had risen by the same stages earlier. Together they built their first steam engine, which was such a success that Harrison became a partner in 1839. In 1843 they went with Thomas Winans to St. Petersburg, with a contract in hand to build three million dollars' worth of rolling stock for the Czar. They developed their own manufacturing plants, with a labor force largely composed of serfs, supplying several hundred locomotives in the next twenty years for the Russian system. They began by making the equipment for the line between Moscow and St. Petersburg, which was pushed ahead by another engineering genius, George Whistler.

In 1849 or 1850 Eastwick returned to the United States, his pockets bulging with money, and Harrison followed two years later. Whistler died in Russia before the riches had been reaped, leaving his son, the artist James McNeill Whistler, with a czarist set of snobberies and a horror of poverty.

When Eastwick arrived back in Philadelphia, he announced to the world that he would show the town the kind of house a man as rich as a Russian nobleman would build. He found his match in Samuel Sloan. Sloan visited the proposed site, which had once been occupied by the botanical gardens of John Bartram, the early naturalist, and proceeded, unbidden by Eastwick, to draw up plans for a grand house. Eastwick, bemused, responded "in a pleasant and courteous way" that he already knew what he wanted and declined to examine Sloan's importunate proposal.

Sloan refused to be shaken off. Finally Eastwick looked the plans over and said what he disliked. That was enough for Sloan; he had learned what he needed to know. He gave Eastwick a big, bold design, a palace for a new millionaire-mechanic by an architect-mechanic. He also required us, at this point, to anticipate the discussion in Chapter Thirty of the American Picturesque. The taste of Haller Nutt, who is now our central figure and for whom this Philadelphia story is background, was not drawn to the Picturesque except as amusement; his central interest, as we shall see, was in Sloan's capacity to draw instead on that strain of Philadelphia rationalism which underlay much of the surface frippery of the Picturesque. But in order to bring Sloan into the story we must note, without elaboration, the kind of exoticisms he willingly provided to other clients on his way to Nutt.

Sloan gave Eastwick a house with the demeanor of an Italian villa of the sort that, in its asymmetry and informality, resisted the strictures of Palladio, and added ornamental details derived from the Romanesque, especially from that va-

---

shift to Boston, and with it shifted the balance of financing from debt to equity, for a period. In the 1850's the center of power shifted again, this time to New York, where debt and equity financing were handled by the same firms that acted as paymasters in railroad construction. Of these financier-contractors, the pioneering firm was Winslow, Lanier and Company, led by James F. D. Lanier, of whom more is to be told in Chapter Twenty-nine.

Eastwick's villa
Courtesy of the Library of Congress

riety known to the British as "Norman." He later explained that the simple,
massive forms, with their rounded arches, were only appropriate to a building
with very large proportions (and, therefore, to clients with very large wallets), and
he implied that clients like the all-conquering Eastwick were legitimate successors
to William of Normandy.

The newspapers pronounced that "this building made the architect's reputation." The site was the most prominent in the city; the design was clear and the
scale awesome. Within a year Sloan's office was at work on twenty-two buildings
in West Philadelphia, fourteen in the center of the city, six villas in New Jersey, a
"mansion" in Germantown, seven public schools, five commercial buildings and a
church.

Samuel Sloan took the Italianate villa, with its tower, rounded windows and
comfortable loggias. He gave it verandahs, enlarged its scale, arranged for it to
pivot about a grand central tower-hall, associated it with conquering Normans and

made it all the rage. Like so many of his ideas, however, the "suburban villa" was appropriated by Sloan from a much more skillful designer, John Notman (1810–65), a hard-drinking Scot who as early as 1829 had designed a Regency-Italianate house called Riverside across the Delaware in Burlington, New Jersey, for the eccentric Bishop George Washington Doane. We shall return to Notman in Chapter Thirty. Here we merely note his primacy and point out that the output of his career was scarcely greater than Sloan's for the year 1851 alone. Sloan was enormously prolific—he is credited with thirty-two hospitals for the insane, for example—and he was constantly at work making himself known to a larger public in a succession of books and by publishing a magazine which portrayed his own work.

In Philadelphia, James Eastwick made Sloan's reputation. Joseph Harrison sustained it. In 1855, amid the bustle of his other business, Sloan received the commission to build a mansion for Harrison on Rittenhouse Square. Harrison was more insistent than had been Eastwick on a Russian Palladian form, or perhaps one should say "Scottish," for it had been the Scot Charles Cameron who in the 1790's transferred the British Palladian style to the court of Catherine the Great. Nothing as ambitious as the great houses outside Edinburgh or St. Petersburg had been constructed in America in the eighteenth century. Now, on Rittenhouse Square, Cameron's style reappeared, with a slight Russian accent. There it was, on the scale of what Latrobe might have built in Philadelphia in the 1790's had his clients had the means, a great stone mansion with a central cube and two flankers,

Joseph Harrison, Jr., by
Thomas B. Read
*Courtesy of the Pennsylvania Academy of the
Fine Arts*

385

Residence of Joseph Harrison, Jr., Philadelphia

Courtesy of the Library of Congress

with rusticated stonework across the lower floor and plenty of linked round arched windows.

As befitted the mansion of an American mechanic, however, Harrison's house was mechanical-American inside, with steam heat (Harrison had learned a lot about steam), extensive interior plumbing and a complex ventilation scheme. At the same time, Harrison commissioned from Sloan a set of ten subsidiary dwellings along Locust Street, and at least two other row-house developments.*

By the mid-1850's, then, Sloan was the most celebrated architect in Philadelphia. He had progressed from Eastwick and Harrison to a succession of very rich clients including a Biddle or two, when Haller Nutt of Mississippi came to his door in 1858 or 1859.

---

* *Sloan's biographer, Harold Cooledge, tells us that "Harrison was deeply concerned with improving the living conditions of workmen and craftsmen in the Philadelphia area, and it was perhaps at his instigation that Sloan devoted so much of* The Architectural Review *[one of his publications] to a consideration of low-cost housing." It was in these experiments in low-cost housing that Sloan later made use of the octagon form developed for the Nutts at Longwood. (Harold N. Cooledge,* Samuel Sloan, 1815–1884, Architect, *p. 71.)*

A Touch of the Orient

SAMUEL SLOAN WAS READY to provide Haller Nutt with exactly the kind of exotic filigree the Romantic in Nutt wanted. And he could keep it to the superficial service of the kind of ruthlessly precise, scientific, geometric and mechanically ingenious structure that would appeal to the scientist in Nutt. They built together America's largest octagon, our grandest exercise in architectural geometry before the twentieth century. It was the most conspicuous survival in America of the rationalism of the French, British and Philadelphia Enlightenments. The true character of that house, which Nutt named after its plantation predecessor, Long-wood, has been obscured by its incidental Orientalisms. Its bulbiform dome and a few horseshoe arches have made it too easy for casual visitors and historians to dismiss it as an elaborate foolishness. It was not. It was a rational house.

Even its superficial Orientalism was associated in Nutt's case with science. He first encountered these forms on the expedition to the Middle East with his father, on which they sought out new strains of cotton (and encountered poor, credulous John Lloyd Stephens). Rush Nutt had gone there, it seems, out of the same scientific curiosity that led him to investigate the villages of the Indians in 1805, not only for cotton seed but for satisfaction of his speculations "about the world's origin."

His old mentor, Benjamin Rush, always expressed doubts about the literal truth of the biblical accounts, and Nutt's own skepticism had been heightened by his observations in the Mississippi Delta. He told Stephens (this time probably in truth) that after watching the depositing of soil on its floodplain by the Mississippi, he wanted to see the similar conditions along the Nile, and to answer what he regarded to be Bishop Usher's unscientific hypothesis that the Bible proved the world to be only six thousand years old. He was delighted to satisfy himself that the pyramids and the temples of Egypt were five thousand or more years old by checking the depth of the alluvial soil near them.

Thereafter his mind turned to Arabic and Turkish architecture, which to Americans of his day was as unknown as had been the Grecian when Nicholas Biddle ventured to the Aegean thirty years earlier. He brought home drawings of Oriental buildings, arabesques and Moorish palaces, we are told, suggesting that an interest in Middle Eastern architecture was fermenting within the Nutt family for twenty years before they read the books of, or met, Samuel Sloan.

Haller Nutt was thus an ideal client for Samuel Sloan. He was rich, and he was ready for an ingenious "mechanic" with a gift for Middle Eastern ornament but an underlying obsession with geometry. One could indulge in endless speculations about the structure of Sloan's psyche and its archetypal affinities. Geometry, of course, is also a conspicuous characteristic of Middle Eastern architecture, especially octagonal geometry. It seems better to restrain an impulse toward psychohistory and turn back, instead, into what we know of architectural history. The ground is not altogether stable, but it is less spongy than that which lies between us and the not-very-communicative Mr. Sloan.

John Notman's rendering of Alverthorpe, country seat of Joshua Fisher
Courtesy of the Atheneum of Philadelphia

That constant but unacknowledged source of ideas for Sloan, his competitor John Notman, had showed from the outset of his Philadelphia career a fondness for octagonal shapes, and his clients had received them with pleasure. A typical Notman octagon appeared on his grandest Philadelphia suburban villa, next to the high road in Jenkintown, as part of an assemblage he designed for Joshua Francis Fisher in 1850. Sloan did not thank Notman publicly for the tip. He had larger precedents to invoke, once his attention had been drawn to the pleasures of polygons with more than four sides. There was, of course, Vignola's famous pentagonal villa for the Farnese family at Caprarola, five 150-foot sides laid up around a rotunda sixty-five feet in diameter. Vignola needed no instruction from his contemporaries, Palladio or Serlio, for such concepts; polygonal seeds were floating everywhere in the air of the Renaissance.

Why were they still in the air in Philadelphia, three hundred years later? Why did Samuel Sloan and Haller Nutt come to such a quick understanding of the balance between ornament and structure? They seem to have hit it off right away, in their first meetings, which apparently occurred in 1858 when Nutt brought his daughters to Philadelphia to school.

Octagons, Oriental and Otherwise

ORNAMENT DID NOT upset the architectural mind of the nineteenth century. Less was not yet more, unless what was taken away was worse than what remained, or

Oriental Villa, front (*above*) and rear elevations
Courtesy of the Library of Congress

389

incompatible with it. Nor were Americans infatuated with ornament in the early nineteenth century. They merely delighted in its incidental pleasures. All sorts of curiosities appeared to please the eye without distracting the mind.

It is sometimes difficult for us, after the stridencies of late Victorian ornament and the countervailing astringencies of the "modern movement," to understand how much ornament could be enjoyed by people who were also devoted to what they called "common sense." Between 1830 and 1860 many clients and architects were able to enjoy ornamental cadenzas without forgetting what they thought to be the main theme of residential architecture: that a building must "work." It must be practical. It must serve its stated purpose. When practicality was achieved, then planners might play, might, so to speak, roller-skate along the verandah, slide down the banister, put a dome over the skylight, paint the pillars.

In 1852 Samuel Sloan drew a few arabesques on a plain Palladian villa among the designs in the first volume of his *Model Architect*. Though he called it "An Oriental Villa," he diffidently declared that "it would be folly to introduce the original pure style" or complete Oriental form because "no wise man will sacrifice his comfort in order to secure consistency in the appearance of his house with those that have been built in other countries, in other climates and perhaps for other purposes by people with different customs. Our style of living is totally unlike the East." If we were to ape their houses, rather than just enjoy their ornament, "we would certainly part with comfort." Comfort, he stresses, "is of the first importance."

In Volume Two, however, he let himself go. After a lengthy essay on the architecture of the Middle East, he produced another Oriental villa, richer in exotic detail and now spread upon an entirely new grid: an octagon. The octagon was becoming a symbol of practicality, of economy and convenience. It could carry the easy burden of ornamental fancy. He offered, he assured his readers, just a little parsley on the edge of a thoroughly common-sense roast. "Let every one arrange his dwelling so as to secure the greatest amount of convenience, and then exercise his judgement in decoration."

What was so "convenient" about the octagon? Why should we let ourselves be persuaded to skew all our rectilinear prejudices and accept the peculiar room shapes ordained by an octagonal container? Sloan's voice assumed the solemnity of organic architecture, a century before its time: "We hold that . . . each building is an independent being, and if it be consistent with itself both internally and externally, and to its purpose, then no fault can be found with it on that score."

This was what attracted Haller Nutt to Samuel Sloan: a grid of reason, conforming to the laws of nature, a grid upon which could be deployed some entertaining exoticisms to amaze the neighbors. While Sloan and Nutt were actually at work on Longwood, an outgrowth of the design in Volume Two, the Oriental villas depicted in subsequent editions conformed to each version of the house itself, as it developed by experiment. In 1861 Sloan assured his readers that

"An Oriental Villa—Design Forty-ninth" from *The Model Architect*, Vol. II. This
is the octagonal design the Nutts decided to build—with modifications.
Courtesy of the Library of Congress

"the choice of style . . . was less a matter of caprice than the natural growth of the
ground-plan."

Even the marvelous onion dome was an organic product, Sloan contended. It
surmounted a vast Latrobian central space occupying the center of the house, out
of which "all the principal rooms of the house may be entered . . . a medium for
light and ventilation." Such a huge light-well "naturally suggested the domed
observatory." After reason had divined what was "natural," he implied, it was
acceptable that "fancy dictated that the dome should be bulbiform—a remember-
ancer of Eastern magnificence which few will judge misplaced as it looms up
against the mellowed azure of a Southern sky." So much for the difficulties of
climate and culture.

The dome was not perceived by either architect or client to be at variance
with the essential geometry of the octagonal form. Nutt wrote Sloan in March

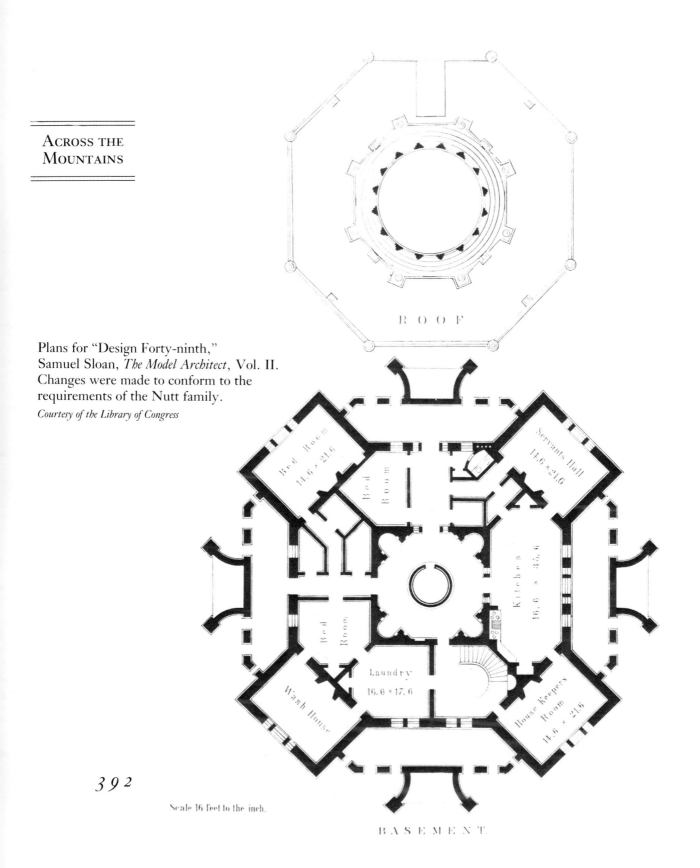

Plans for "Design Forty-ninth,"
Samuel Sloan, *The Model Architect*, Vol. II.
Changes were made to conform to the
requirements of the Nutt family.
Courtesy of the Library of Congress

ROOF

Bed Room
14.6 x 21.6

Bed
Room

Servants Hall
14.6 x 21.6

Kitchen
16.6 x 35.6

Bed
Room

Laundry
16.6 x 17.6

Wash House

House Keepers
Room
14.6 x 21.6

BASEMENT

Scale 16 feet to the inch.

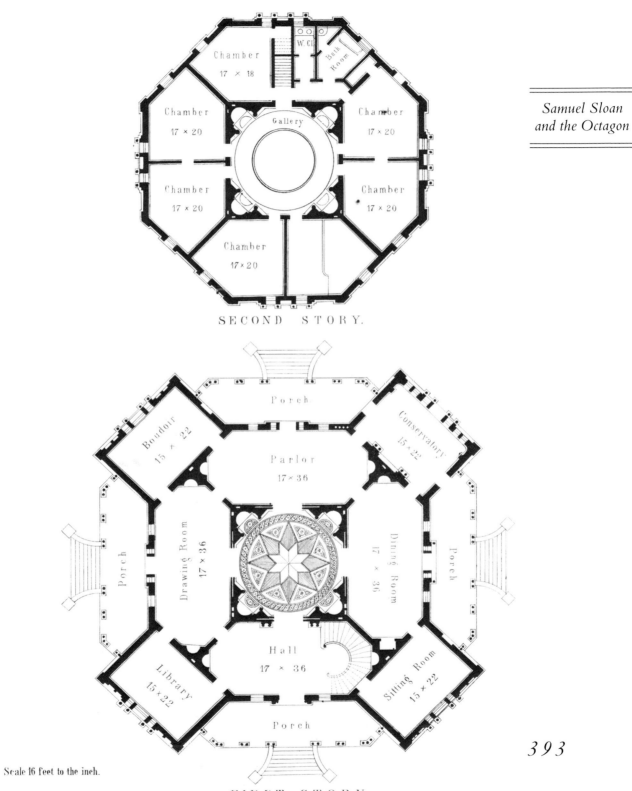

SECOND STORY.

Chamber
17 × 18

W. Cl.

Bath
Room

Chamber
17 × 20

Gallery

Chamber
17 × 20

Chamber
17 × 20

Chamber
17 × 20

Chamber
17 × 20

FIRST STORY.

Porch

Boudoir
15 × 22

Parlor
17 × 36

Conservatory
15 × 22

Porch

Drawing Room
17 × 36

Dining Room
17 × 36

Porch

Library
15 × 22

Hall
17 × 36

Sitting Room
15 × 22

Porch

Scale 16 feet to the inch.

393

1861 that the dome was complete and "it is creating much admiration now . . . I think after this the Octagon will be the style. So you must get up some other styles, or patterns on this style. Model them to be not so large or expensive." He apparently continued to think of the dome as a sort of billboard to call attention to the underlying form, which was composed of rings of rooms deployed around a central rotunda, and to have felt a sort of evangelical desire to propagate the cupolaed style. He asked for a "small model for Cupulo and Dome . . . so it could be taken to pieces . . . and not only used for my building but other work of the same sort." Two months later he told Sloan that they would make "the Octagon . . . the style," and asked for a large supply of lithographs of the house to distribute.

Octagons for All

SAMUEL SLOAN ANTICIPATED Haller Nutt's injunction to make accessible the results of their experiments to people of modest means. He published the results in the 1861 edition of his *Homestead Architecture*. In his patterns for clustered houses based on the floor plan of Longwood but substituting a service core for the rotunda, he rotated four "Clustered Cottages" around the center. Harold Cooledge, who has recently brought these plans to light, correctly notes that Sloan was not only anticipating Nutt but anticipating Frank Lloyd Wright as well; Wright's Suntop Homes, at Ardmore, near Philadelphia, were built along a similar plan in 1939.

Sloan and Wright were operating from the same social philosophy, one that comes out of a subtheme in the British Enlightenment. Both were delighted to accept large commissions from the very rich, but felt an obligation to make available to the many what they learned from experiments underwritten by their few "big" clients. The diffusion of architectural knowledge resulting from personal experiment was the theme announced in the first sentence of the book that almost certainly introduced the idea of the octagon to Samuel Sloan and to Haller Nutt in the first place. This was the 1848 edition of Orson Squire Fowler's *A Home for All, or, A New, Cheap, Convenient, and Superior Mode of Building:*

> To cheapen and improve human homes, and especially to bring comfortable dwellings within the reach of the poorer classes, is the object of this volume— an object of the highest practical utility to man.

Fowler was, like Rush and Haller Nutt, an amateur scientist, and like them he has been subjected to ridicule by people who lack his intelligence and questing spirit. Chief among those prone to disparage Fowler are those who substitute for his expansive qualities a slavish diligence that accumulates information without understanding, and can lead to advanced degrees in clotted triviality. Fowler has been derided for his architectural theories, his sexual theories and his psychological theories, often by people who neither have read them nor are aware of research in recent years that tells us that he was not far off in many of what once seemed his most outrageous hypotheses.*

To do justice by Fowler, we must accept him on his own terms, as a suggester, not a disposer; as a stimulus, not a final response. Fowler's interest in the interpenetration of the physical and psychological was expressed in a pioneering

The Octagon Cottage, from Orson S. Fowler's *The Octagon House, A Home for All*

From the Dover edition. Copyright © 1973 by Dover Publications, Inc.

* *As a psychologist, Fowler thought of himself as a counselor, not a clinician. It is true that he called phrenology a "science" of finding clues to character from the shape of the cranium. But science was not yet exalted to the heavens, at the right hand of medieval theology. Phrenology was a process that bore a prototypical relationship to research in our own time into left-hand, right-hand, and other locational aspects of the brain. Fowler and his classmate Henry Ward Beecher were both intrigued by the investigations of Johann Kaspar Spurzheim, a Viennese protopsychologist about whom they learned while at Amherst College. They were more enthusiastic than exact. The precision came later, in the 1860's, when Paul Broca, a French physician, explored the phenomenon he called "aphasia," or partial loss of speech through injury to the brain.*

Greater precision leading to scientific canonization came in 1981, when Roger Sperry won a Nobel Prize for work that showed that portions of the brain have specialized functions, a century and a half after people like Fowler were speculating about the correlation of behavior with specific areas of the brain. No one, least of all Fowler, would contend he deserves a posthumous Nobel Prize, but he deserves better than he has gotten. (I confess to admiring Fowler for some of the same reasons I admire General Ethan Allen Hitchcock's inquiries into the relationship of alchemy to psychology during the same period; they have been ridiculed by pedants who could not imagine the riches of understanding that lay just below the strata men such as Fowler and Hitchcock were mining. See Chapter Sixteen.)

set of sex manuals and health manuals, edited for a time by Walt Whitman. He was a passionate and effective advocate of vegetarianism. He urged the avoidance of alcohol and was unafraid to recommend eschewing conventions of Victorian dress that were unhealthy, like tight lacing of corsets. He was an effective marriage counselor and writer, and a thoroughly admirable man. He never pretended to be a trained architect. He was, as he put it, "a phrenologist, not a builder." He set out to give readers of his book on octagonal building what was "peculiar to this mode of building," but he urged them to go elsewhere for much else. They could get plans and specifications "common to this and other modes . . . from scientific works on the subject." Fowler the architectural experimenter is best observed in the spread of that form of cement construction he recommended called "pebble dash," to be laid within wooden forms to build houses that came as close as possible to the shape of a circle. The circle, and its polygonal approximations, he found often in nature; bees made hexagons, he noted, and he admired other crystalline configurations produced by insects.

Fowler's advocacy of octagons was even more successful than his advocacy of considered sexuality and of phrenology. Octagons appeared everywhere in the 1850's and 1860's. Octagonal schoolhouses followed his assertion that they made for "more sociability, better light and acoustics"; octagonal churches rediscovered the ancient understanding that congregations that faced each other, and abandoned basilican linearity, could "interchange . . . benevolent feelings"; octagonal barns produced the prototypes of railroad roundhouses; a spiritualist colony built an octagonal seance chamber; Californians built octagons; there is a cluster of octagonal houses in the St. Croix Valley, between Minnesota and Wisconsin, and there were 126 remaining octagons in New York State when I last counted them, in 1967.

Fowler was carried away by his enthusiasm for the organic origins of the octagon, as any person may be who makes his own discoveries. He was wrong in claiming that "the form as applied to domestic residences, is wholly original with the author." Like a good, practical American, he had found a scheme in nature and experimented with it, finding it could be "greatly improved upon . . . while planning and studying his own home."

We can take issue with the admirable Fowler, not on pedantic grounds but to assert the larger theme that a strain of scientific inquiry has led people, at many times and in many countries, to recommend round, hexagonal and octagonal forms for residences. They have often offered reasons of comfort and economy, when they give reasons at all.* They could also have given the reason that round and nearly round forms, like mandalas, are symbols of wholeness. (Church-builders have known that from the time of Justinian to that of Eero Saarinen.)

*The idea of octagonal homes "for all" had occurred to the "little masters" of the eighteenth century, who reduced the scale of huge French and British experiments in polygons for the rich, to cottages for the not-so-

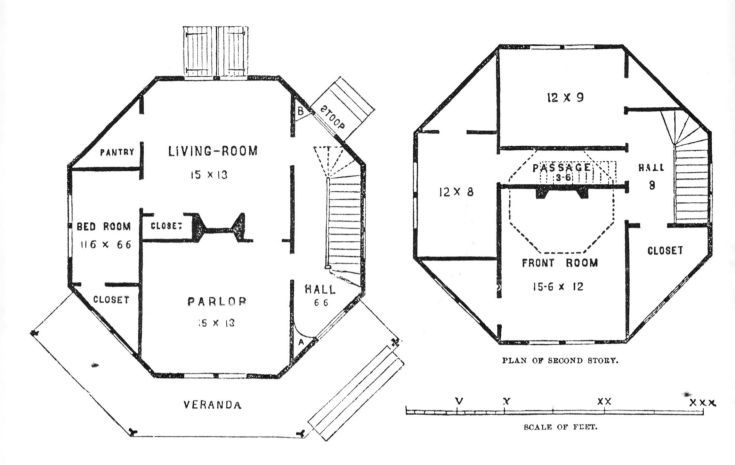

Plans of the first story (*left*) and second story of the octagon cottage. "The Octagon house of this size gives 137 more square feet on each floor than a square house of the same outside measurement . . ."

From the Dover edition of Orson S. Fowler's The Octagon House, A Home for All. *Copyright © 1973 by Dover Publications, Inc.*

rich. The theoretical exercises of men like Claude-Nicolas Ledoux (1736–1806) and Étienne-Louis Boullée (1728–99) were very much admired by Americans like Jefferson, and directly affected buildings for the University of Virginia. The Danish architect C. F. Hansen (1756–1845) built a circular country house not unlike a little round house on a island in Lake Windermere by one of the British "little masters," John Plaw (circa 1745–1820). Plaw included the house in his Rural Architecture *of 1785 and gave his reasons in his 1800 edition, that "the principles of symmetry and correspondence of parts" were as applicable to "Dwellings on a humble scale, and Cottages" as to mansions. In a reversal of the usual process of big teaching small, Frederick Hervey, the eccentric Earl of Bristol and Bishop of Derry, was so impressed by Plaw's little "perfectly circular" cottage, "which I saw upon an Island in the Westmoreland Lakes," that he "imitated it" on an enormous scale both at Ballyscullion, one of his Irish houses, in 1787, and again a decade later at Ickworth, in Suffolk.*

Waverly's octagonal hall
Photo by Roger G. Kennedy

Thomas Jefferson was encouraged to use the octagon by reading William Kent's *Designs of Inigo Jones* of 1727 and Robert Morris' *Select Architecture*, which was the source for his final elevation for Monticello.* First came an octagonal chapel for Williamsburg, around 1770. Monticello was a testing ground for octagonal rooms and octagonal pavilions, which went into the planning of Pantops, a house for his daughter Maria. When she died, he built, instead, the octagonal Poplar Forest as his summer retreat, into which he moved in 1809.

The Octagon, now headquarters of the American Institute of Architects in Washington, D.C., is actually a hexagon, but its plan, by Dr. Thornton, provides for a central rotunda. That scheme appeared even more clearly in Latrobe's competitive design offered the same client, Colonel John Tayloe. A geometric crystal around a rotunda is an important element in our story.

Palladian rotundas gave a series of architects, from Robert Adam to Thomas

---

* *Morris was one of that school of British writers in the middle of the eighteenth century, including William Halfpenny, Thomas Lightoler and John Carter, of whom John Plaw was also a member. They were the authors of a series of handbooks like the* Carpenters' Guides *of the American nineteenth century, which featured simplified versions of the geometrical experiments of a fertile period of invention that preceded the glacial Classicism of Napoleon. This was the period that nurtured the émigré architects who launched American architecture. (See Chapters Ten, Eleven and Fourteen.)*

Jefferson and Benjamin Henry Latrobe, the cue for a series of polygonal variations. Latrobe developed "light and air" shafts in a number of houses around Washington, and built, in Philadelphia, America's first large cylindrical building in the huge drum of the engine house of his waterworks in 1799.

The first expression of the octagon as the nucleus of a radial plan in Mississippi was not, in fact, Longwood, but Waverly, built near Columbus in 1852 by a cousin of Wade Hampton's, George Hampton Young. Young was a product of the long migration, from Virginia first to upcountry Georgia and then to Mississippi. The house is an H-plan, but instead of a great hall at the center, like that at Stratford, it has a huge octagonal airspace, thirty-five feet across and fifty-two feet high, drawing heat upward and letting light filter downward from windows in a "cupulo." Snowdoun, nearby, was built two years later, on a similar plan. It has lost its octagonal cupola, but there are many other houses in the Columbus area that show the same desire to build rooms concentrically around a central space, which serves for stairs, light and air. One of Fowler's own designs was erected at Horn Lake, Mississippi, and at the end of the nineteenth century Louis Sullivan turned back to the octagonal form for a group of cottages he built for himself and his friends on the shore of the Gulf in Ocean Springs.

Once again, however, we are ahead of ourselves. Architectural history did not receive very many large contributions from buildings in Mississippi and Louisiana between the time of Samuel Sloan and that of Louis Sullivan. The Civil War intervened, and the postbellum South was not a lively place architecturally. Its chief talents, like Louisiana's Henry Hobson Richardson, went off to the North. But before the lights went down they burned very bright, and at Longwood they illuminated more clearly than anywhere else in the South the interaction of a talented architect and a talented client.

CHAPTER 26

Building Longwood

THE COMPONENTS were in place:

There was Samuel Sloan, an architect unaccustomed to failure, fiercely ambitious, with a growing practice in the South. While he was working with Haller Nutt, at least two other residential clients, Colonel Ventress of Mississippi and John O. Thorn of Louisiana, arrived on his doorstep, and Bishop Leonidas Polk asked for plans for several small churches to be built in those two states. (The churches were not built because the bishop became otherwise occupied—as General Leonidas Polk, C.S.A. See also Chapter Twenty.)

There was Haller Nutt, his energy limited but his means apparently without limit, determined to build a great mansion using Philadelphia workmen, supplies and ideas, supervised by a Philadelphia architect, though his site lay 2,700 nautical miles from Philadelphia.

There was Mrs. Haller Nutt, the offspring of tough pioneers, and a woman with a will of her own.

Apparently all three shared a passionate interest in the rationalist implications of the octagonal form and a fascination with Oriental ornament.

Finally, there were the political and economic circumstances to which we have referred in general terms, now to be brought down to the specific circumstances of Haller Nutt himself. He was a very rich anti-Secessionist, trying to build a house using northern ideas and northern workmen in the teeth of convulsion in the South. Most of his poorer neighbors were becoming convinced by their political leaders to hate and fear the North. The most accessible targets for that resentment were the Natchez "southern Yankees," of whom Haller Nutt was, perhaps, the most conspicuous representative.

The Southern Yankees

ONE HISTORIAN HAS estimated that in 1860 Haller Nutt controlled twenty working plantations on 43,000 acres and owned 800 plantation slaves. He produced 3,500

400

Longwood
Courtesy of the Pilgrimage Garden Club/Natchez Pilgrimage Tours, Natchez, Miss.

bales of cotton annually and sugar of equal value. In addition he apparently had scattered northern investments and large cash balances with his bankers in Paris and London, which came from his direct sales of cotton and sugar in Europe. A chaos of financial reporting following his death and the Civil War leaves us with just enough evidence to conclude that he was at least as well diversified as his peers and relatives.

We know a little more of the affairs of others in his circle. We have caught a glimpse of their agricultural diversification in Ohio, Illinois and the states of the upper Mississippi, where the Natchez Junto* moved in parallel with the Halifax Whigs. Other diversification followed quite naturally. One half of the city's richest men were merchants, in constant commercial interchange with Cincinnati and St. Louis as well as New Orleans. Natchez was a lumber-milling center, and Haller Nutt found no difficulty in finding slave-artisans to manufacture the hundreds of thousands of bricks he required for Longwood. Natchez manufacturers and Natchez tradesmen were, generally speaking, Unionist in their interests; they

---

* *"Natchez Junto" was a political term for the early planter-merchant Federalists, but it is descriptive of the same people, and their sons, in their later Whig commercial role.*

required open navigation of the Mississippi for a ready supply of customers and goods.

Though much of the capital of the great planters of Natchez was tied up in slaves, they were no more trapped in the plantation economy than were their southside Virginia counterparts. To give two examples: Stephen Duncan owned shares in nineteen northern railroad companies, in the Atlantic Dock Company and in the Bank of New York. Edward MacGchee chose the iron industry for his diversification program. Land remained the favored investment vehicle, and one of the reasons for the antipathy of the poorer whites toward the nabobs who had oligopolized the lowlands along the Mississippi was that they also tied up, for speculation, enormous acreage in Arkansas and Texas. They had no need to sell, and denied access to smaller farmers. Conversely, one of the reasons for the large planters' Unionist sentiments was that they feared the loss of the assurance, provided by the federal Constitution, of the inviolability of contract and land tenure.

The tension between the big planters and the artisan class may explain Haller Nutt's difficulty in obtaining, unbroken, merchandise from the North. His shipments had to be passed through the hands of poorer southerners, who resented his use of northern artisans and, more generally, his economic power and the "airs" of his group of "southern Yankees." He and the other members of the Natchez Junto, including the other four doctors (Duncan, the Kers and Haller's father), were strong Union men, though they were owners, taken together, of five or six thousand slaves. Support for secession in Mississippi came largely from holders of very few slaves or those who owned no slaves at all. One of the most powerful motives for cutting Mississippi away from the Union was the desire to "get at" the rich oligopolists of Natchez, to tax them, to break their hold on land and credit, and to remove the burden of the mortgages they owned.

Haller Nutt named one of his sons after the great Unionist orator of the planter class, Seargent S. Prentiss, who in his speeches in Mississippi echoed the fears of an emerging Jacobinism expressed by George Washington Parke Custis. Nutt said of the backcountry Jacksonians of 1837 that their "disorganizing and revolutionary" ideas were like those of the Jacobin clubs "during the worst times of the French Revolution." Rush Nutt's father-in-law had proudly said in 1803 that there was not a single Jeffersonian in Adams County, and the term "Natchez Junto" was coined by the backcountry Republicans (who later became Jacksonians) to describe the group in Natchez who, they claimed, were "one and the same with the old Natchez Federalists."

Natchez and Adams County held off the backcountry through the elections of the early 1850's, when forty-one of Mississippi's fifty-nine counties voted for the Unionists against the Secessionists. Then the backcountry rallied, numbers told; the tide turned and ran swiftly out. Adams County still opposed the Ordinance of Secession in January 1861, but it had only a scattering of allies, and these came from other counties where the junto members had large holdings. Though

Adams did not stand outside the Confederacy, it is a fact that the Confederate flag never flew officially over Natchez.

As they lost control of Mississippi, the members of the junto became more and more disaffected from the course of events, and saw themselves increasingly as an isolated aristocratic remnant. This was already clear to an English visitor of the 1840's, Sir Charles Lyell, who reported that in Natchez, more than any other place in the United States, he met men of property who spoke as if they were beleaguered by "a rude, ignorant and coarse democracy." That was the democracy that took Mississippi out of the Union. It was led by some of the planter class, but in Natchez, as in Mobile, the predominant view among the great planters was Unionist.

Some of the Natchez Junto remained Unionist right through the war. Haller Nutt cried out against "this infernal Secession—the authors of which I have for 30 years condemned as the vilest traitors." David Hunt clung to his Ohio lands as "someday . . . our last asylum." Stephen Duncan sued the Richmond government for his wartime losses and, with Ayres Merrill, one of his neighbors, moved to New York. Levin Marshall broke with his son, who supported secession, and died in New York. Joseph Dunbar Shields remained, but refused to eat South Carolina rice, in protest against the Secessionist hotheads of that state. Benjamin Wailes and Frank Surgett opposed the war quietly and remained to observe its disasters.

Haller Nutt's will to build grew more stubborn during the two years before secession. Longwood would have been hard enough to build in peacetime, but there was a kind of madness in his dogged, bitter, passionate determination to build it in wartime, in the face of hostility of the Secessionists, and the sabotage of the rivermen, longshoremen and, one can easily suppose, local artisans. He was determined to win, not only in the midst of a sectional civil war but also in the presence of an ugly class conflict. It would be a mistake to prettify that conflict. Nor would it be wise to see either Nutt or Sloan as heroes of the Union cause. They were egocentric, ambitious, powerful men, with a determination to proceed against all odds, a determination fueled by a defiance of anything, or anybody, who stood in their way.

The Project Gets Under Way

OUR FIRST PIECE of written evidence of the relationship between Nutt and Sloan is a letter from the latter, responding to a Christmas Eve inquiry from Nutt about when Sloan planned to come to Natchez to lay out the house. It was January 11, 1860; Sloan said he planned to reach Natchez by the middle of the month. Apparently he got there, and departed again before February 3, when Nutt wrote him to apologize for his having been in bed all during Sloan's visit and to introduce his strong-minded wife to their correspondence:

I find on conversation with Mrs. Nutt that some of the views are entirely different from what we had understood before and for fear of producing other difficulties I wanted to write you so you would not go too far.

There were such small matters as her iron safe in the bedroom (best put it in a closet) and the dumbwaiter in the dining room (most objectionable; best put it in the pantry). And, of great importance to the way the house would function, "all agree" it was "objectionable" to put the kitchen in the basement. "I am afraid," added Nutt, "there is other points not well agreed upon." These were, presumably, practical matters, for he allowed that in regard to "architectural proportions and style . . . I feel sure that your taste is far better than Mrs. Nutt's and my own."

Nevertheless, he gave notice, then and there, that he, as well as his wife, had no intention of being a passive client: "I feel great interest in the Building and do destroy much of the pleasure attending it if I did not agree on the general arrangements."

That was on February 3. Nutt wrote again on the eighth with more suggestions, though he admitted being "somewhat fearful that my last might disconcert you." Mrs. Nutt insisted that the safe be in the bedroom itself; there were problems with the blind doors in the corner rooms, the difficulty of the dumbwaiter was unresolved, but, apprehensively, Nutt told Sloan to "use your own discretion and GO AHEAD."

Silence from Sloan.

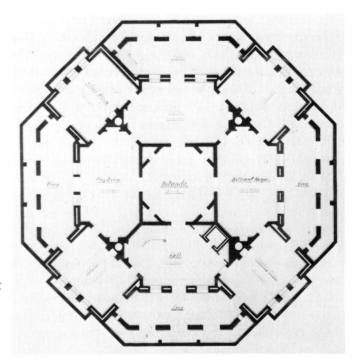

Actual plans of the basement (ground floor) built at Longwood. This is the only floor that was completed.

Courtesy of Natchez Pilgrimage Tours

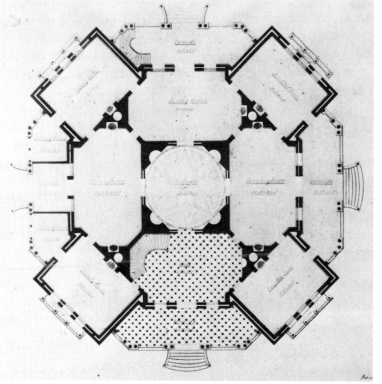

Principal floor of
Longwood, from
original plans
*Courtesy of Natchez
Pilgrimage Tours*

Was he letting his clients soak for a while, or was he offended? On February
21, Nutt had not had a reply and sent another letter urging Sloan to follow his
own plans. Sloan replied on the twenty-eighth, saying blandly that Nutt's suggestions for the building would not "interfere with the general plan," the magnitude
of which began to appear. Sloan proposed to prefabricate, in Philadelphia, window
frames, blinds, sashes and hinges, and then ship them by water down the Atlantic
Coast, around Florida, along the Gulf, and up the Mississippi—a distance as great
as if they were going to Yucatán. Nutt, he said, should start accumulating lumber.
They would at the outset require 100,000 feet of one-inch rough boards.

On the second of March Sloan wrote again, consoling Nutt: on the eighth the
windows were under way and the plans, in book form, were about to be mailed.
Sloan was sure "you yourself and Mrs. Nutt will be well pleased with it in every
detail." He suggested that local carpenters do the rough work, until Philadelphia
craftsmen came to carry out the complex design for the roof and then move on to
the interior. He would send out his assistant to supervise, for four dollars a day.
The assistant turned out to be Addison Hutton, who became, thereafter, Sloan's
partner. (In the 1870's, Hutton was the architect of what Talbot Hamlin called
the "swan song" of the Greek Revival, the Ridgeway branch of the Library Company in Philadelphia.)

405

Nutt wrote back on March 12 that the building "is attracting much attention and considerable stir among the mechanics and many a prophecy is brought up in regard to the result." The local "mechanics" might well be excited: Who would get the chance to work on such a huge and exotic project? And what about this northern architect? All the stir, said Nutt, "has excited in me, I must confess, a greater desire to have as perfect a building as we can plan and execute." Some of his neighbors, who may have intended more conventional houses, "are now inclined to hold back and see the result of mine." Some of this holding-back may have come from political prudence: the storm was building in the backwoods. South Carolina and the Mississippi legislatures were threatening secession if Mr. Lincoln, or Mr. Seward, or any other Republican, won the presidency.

Nutt persisted with some details: "Mrs. Nutt says she wd prefer the pivot blind." And something bigger than a detail: could there be a mistake about 100,000 feet of rough lumber—"100,000 feet is a large pile of lumber." No, replied Sloan; there wasn't any error. (Eventually they ordered three times that much.) Nutt asked Sloan to make another journey to Natchez, to be sure the building was adapted "to the locality," especially because, he said on March 24, at the pace "you are pushing ahead . . . We are driving things rapidly and have already made a large show towards a house." Perhaps Sloan should supply the lime from Philadelphia, a thousand bushels of it to be sent in kegs.

On March 29 Nutt felt it necessary to inform Sloan about the difficulty of putting Negro slaves to work in tandem with white artisans. The white mechanics, he wrote, were accustomed to work a fixed number of hours a day, a custom he could not pass on to his slaves. Nutt lamented that the only spare time they (the slaves) had was "at breakfast and in the middle of the day, some two hours or so."

On April 9 Sloan was ready to ship nails, gas pipe, water pipe, drain pipe, mantels and grates. By the twenty-first there were also the bay windows and door frames, brackets, cabinets, tin, nails, slate, door sills and stone chimney tops. Nutt had written on the fifth that he was "getting on pretty well with my work—but fear not as forward as you would like." He had made, in his slave-operated manufactory, 180,000 bricks and was getting ready to make 300,000 more. The hundreds of thousands of feet of finished lumber that he now knew to be needed would be hauled, he said, "with ten teams."

Early in May 1860 Nutt asked for two Philadelphia bricklayers; slaves could make bricks, apparently, but not lay them well enough for his standards. Sloan provided them, and a carpenter. Sloan himself visited Natchez between May and July. Afterward, he said he had arrived home on July 10, "safely . . . without stoppage," and immediately began "putting all the columns together." The letters between the two, after this visit, became friendly, almost affectionate. Sloan urged Nutt to return the visit: "I hope to see you pass into the office some morning before long."

But things were becoming difficult in Mississippi. Nutt wrote on July 16 that the frames and slate arrived "very much damaged." It was "the hottest weather ever known here" and he had "been a good deal sick since you were here." The bricklayers had left. On account of the delays at Longwood, Hutton had gone off to supervise another local job, a remodeling for Colonel Ventress of Woodville, Mississippi. Sloan replied on the thirtieth that Nutt's letter gave him "much uneasiness," because he knew the goods had been so well packed that they could not have been injured before they reached New Orleans for transshipment. They would have arrived intact unless harmed "by wilful acts."

By August things seemed to have quieted; Sloan recommended a change in the entrance and, having learned his lesson, asked Nutt to "talk over the matter" with Mrs. Nutt. The reply was that "Mrs. Nutt and I both agree that this change would be very unfortunate." Could not a decision be delayed until he and Mrs. Nutt came to Philadelphia in September? The presidential campaign was in full swing; the country was bitterly divided; the Secessionists were in full cry. On August 23, Nutt wrote that "something might happen to Mr. Hutton so I will be deprived of his supervision during the erection of my house"; he suggested that the head carpenter, apparently less vulnerable, be made fully cognizant of the architectural plans.

In November 1860 Abraham Lincoln was elected President, in a four-way race. Natchez, and the counties it dominated along the Mississippi River, voted for the Unionist, John Bell, but the state was carried by John C. Breckinridge, the

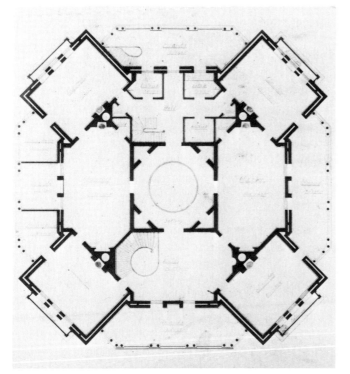

Second floor of Longwood, from original plans. Water to supply the bathroom was to be caught by gutters around the dome and attic roofs, piped down to the ground, then underground and up to a copper reservoir on top of the kitchen (a two-story building) and thence, by gravity, to the bathroom.
Courtesy of Natchez Pilgrimage Tours

407

candidate of the extreme southern Democrats. In December South Carolina seceded, followed by Mississippi, Florida, Alabama, Georgia and Louisiana in January 1861. On January 9 a ship attempting to supply Fort Sumter, in Charleston Harbor, was fired upon by the South Carolinians. The Confederate States of America were formed on February 4, a month before Lincoln was inaugurated in Washington. In April Fort Sumter fell to the South Carolina insurgents, and on May 13 Great Britain declared its neutrality. At Big Bethel, in June, and at Manassas, in July, were fought the first major battles of the American Civil War.

After Mississippi seceded, Addison Hutton, the Yankee who was a houseguest as well as a construction superintendent, became too much of a risk even for the Nutts. He left after overhearing Mrs. Nutt express her worries about his presence. The four carpenters followed him northward in March 1861. Nutt proudly sent Sloan a notice filed by them in the Natchez newspaper, which showed, he said, "that Philadelphia Mechanics have been south and well treated and not hanged." The four spoke of the "very liberal and uniformly kind treatment extended" during their "sojourn" with Mr. Nutt, and thanked the citizens of Natchez for their great courtesy "during the intense excitement through which we have just passed."

On May 5 Nutt wrote Sloan that there was danger sending out tinsmiths, saying that "affairs may grow more aggravating and possibly workmen from the North may be molested." A portion of this letter was censored by the Confederate authorities, and five days later Sloan wrote Nutt saying he had not heard from him, which led him "to believe that the mails are now interfered each way. The very thoughts of the condition of our country gives me pain."

On May 19 Nutt replied, as much for the eyes of the censors as for Sloan: "We do not feel much like taking the trouble of writing nowadays and paying postage on letters what are suppressed by the agents of those who issue the stamps." But, since the rain was coming in through his untinned roof, he asked Sloan to send the tinners after all, if he could find "sober, discrete men" who would "attend to their business."

This was the letter in which he rejoiced that the dome was complete and was exciting "much admiration." It was wartime. He was writing to an architect on the other side of the battle lines and he thought "after this the Octagon will be the style"!

On June 20, between the news of Big Bethel and the battle at Manassas, Sloan wrote, saying: "Much regret communications are cut off. We hope, however, they may soon resume." His letter was carried to Natchez by Mr. Volmer, a Philadelphia merchant who was on his way to Colonel Ventress' house to arrange for the delivery of furniture. The tinners, Sloan reported, "to my surprise . . . declined going in consequence of the state of the country." He allowed himself another expression of affection: "I hope you are all well and should be glad to see you."

A month later Sloan found another set of tinners, twin brothers, who "are quiet men and pay attention to nothing but their business." He actually thought of going to Natchez himself and taking his son, who had been ill, with him. Sloan apparently had little sense of the conditions along the lower Mississippi, for he opined that the "change might be much benefit" to his son. This letter was heavily censored on its way to Nutt.

Nutt's Philadelphia suppliers were making large advances to their suppliers and workmen. One of them began to worry about the likelihood that "as long as this war continues there will be no transmitting of goods to the South, nor of money to the North." He asked Nutt to explain to Colonel Ventress that mantels he had received from Sloan's shops could only have been injured by "downright carelessness or maliciousness on the part of those handling them" in the South.

In August 1861 Sloan still expected to visit Natchez, and told Nutt that Volmer, after returning to Philadelphia, had proclaimed Longwood "the greatest establishment he ever saw. . . . He told me he would not have missed it for 10,000 dollars. (I would not like to tempt him.)" Volmer, an earnest and somewhat obsequious soul, wrote Nutt that what he and Sloan were accomplishing had shown him that "if men only try and persevere, much can be accomplished." Others were equally eager to keep their lines open to Nutt. The doormaker, George J. Henkels, wrote on July 25, four days after the federal defeat at Manassas: "As soon as your house is ready and the communications is opened I can forward the doors . . . I do hope our intercourse will soon be renewed but God Only Knows what is to be done as the War spirit predominates here."

In New Orleans, solder for the tin roofs and gutters was sent along to Natchez by people who apparently thought Nutt to be an enthusiastic Confederate. They reported in August that the victory of Manassas was having a "most favorable effect" in Europe. They hoped "our Government may be acknowledged by the principal powers" and that "measures may be taken to break up the blockade."

In September Nutt told Sloan, "I now feel broken up as Mr. Smith has concluded to leave me and return to his family." Smith was apparently the last of the Philadelphia workmen. Despondently, Nutt wrote: "This is perhaps the last chance I may have of writing you until we have Peace." He asked Sloan to send him the plans of the basement, although, he said bitterly, they might be impounded by the local postal authorities "as contraband of War." But to Sloan the tone was still the same: "I hope you are well and that it may not be long before we can resume our accustomed friendly correspondence." In December Sloan wrote into the darkness, saying, "It has been rumored here that the men have been drove from the work at your house. . . . We have found it to be a fact that they have been drove from Col. Vantresses building . . . they barely escaped with their lives and without any cause whatever."

In the spring of 1862, the war in the South began in earnest. In February Fort Donelson, in Tennessee, fell to the Union forces after General Ulysses S. Grant demanded its unconditional surrender. In April Grant salvaged victory at Shiloh. New Orleans fell to a Union fleet led by Admiral David Farragut, and Natchez soon was lost to the Confederacy as well.

That spring two thousand bales of Haller Nutt's cotton were burnt by the Confederates, presumably to keep them out of the hands of the federal forces. In the fall the Confederates burned his cotton gin and sawmill at Winter Quarters. In the spring of 1863 the army of Grant, closing in on Vicksburg, upriver from Natchez, commandeered without compensation a huge supply of corn that Haller Nutt had grown at Winter Quarters and Evergreen. His wife estimated the total to be 64,000 bushels. She went on to say that "Mr. Nutt, being a strong Union man and already having suffered much from the Confederates, rather welcomed the advent of the Union army as about to receive friends. Accordingly the plantations . . . at the advent of this Army were like smiling gardens of Paradise."

At Longwood, construction stopped. Nutt's slaves boarded up the windows on the upper floors. Orders for furniture were canceled, and the family gathered in living quarters on the lower floor, which had been intended for a billiard room, wine cellar and playrooms (but not, of course, for that offensive kitchen).

Finally, on July 4, 1863, Vicksburg surrendered to Grant, and the Mississippi was open again, flowing "unvexed to the Sea." In October Samuel Sloan wrote that he had heard, at last, from Haller Nutt, having "thought of yourself and family thousands of times." Nutt's letter has been lost, but it apparently had asked for plans and proposed finishing Longwood. Sloan said he had not written because "the check to communication was near you and far distant from me."

The war itself seemed distant also, to Sloan. In 1863 his business was unusually "brisk," though in the first year of the war it had been "at a complete standstill . . . I did not make office rent." Now business was "in a very flourishing condition . . . We see no signs of War and in fact were it not for newspapers should not know such was the case. I have seen nothing of the Army, except some recruiting occasionally . . . With yourself I must say that I long to see this cruel war ended. We must hope for the best . . . Mrs. Sloan sends her kind regards to yourself and Mrs. Nutt and yet has hopes of seeing each of you again in Philadelphia."

The furniture man sent his regards and "hopes he may have the pleasure of furnishing the new house."

Things were not so blithe in the South. The Union troops did not discriminate neatly among the political sympathies of southern planters. The "gardens of Paradise" left in their path by Haller Nutt were destroyed. Farm implements, stock and household articles were either taken or broken. Julia Nutt wrote (in claims for damages, which she pursued until her death in 1897) that "Desolation, as the souvenir of some 50,000 to 80,000 men, reigned supreme." The Union forces stripped the landscape of wood to fuel the river fleet and set the unharvested fields afire. "The Army needed large quantities of both lumber and brick," said Mrs. Nutt, and took 200,000 feet "of the best quality Cypress" from the piles awaiting construction at Longwood. They also took, she alleged, the contents of Nutt's new brick kiln: 426,000 bricks.

Samuel Sloan had only limited knowledge of what was happening to his client. He wrote his last letter to Nutt on December 2, 1863, saying:

And am greatly pleased to hear from you but regret to learn of the destruction and havoc that has been made upon your properties . . . There is not a person here of your acquaintances but that sympathize amply for you and hope with you that this terrible War will soon end—we are all up to the eyes in business and have but little time to think of the terrible condition sections of the country have been plunged into and the horrible loss of life, all brought upon us by a very few politicians . . . Businesses of all kinds are moving rapidly and looking prosperous . . . Please write me again . . . as it seems like old times again to receive letters from that quarter.

It was not quite "like old times." On June 16, 1864, Julia Nutt buried Haller. He had visited Vicksburg "on private and public business" and caught pneumonia. According to his wife, "it was not Pneumonia that killed him. The doctor said it was not. It was his troubles. Three million dollars worth of property swept away; the labor of a life time gone; large debts incurred by the War . . . and his helpless wife with eight children and two other families looking to him for support . . . This crushed him and he died."

This was written in 1883. The federal government had not yet fully repaid Julia's losses. She made it clear that it could never truly do so. "You can give me back my money but you can never give me back my husband nor my children their father . . ."

In her account of the events following the death of Haller Nutt, she asserted that in 1863 she "had but one weeks provisions in my storerooms and no money. I had jewels"—she certainly did; their invoices are staggering—"but I could not sell them; I had dresses but I could not sell them. I had twenty-four cows and while I could keep them I sent my younger son, Prentiss"—Seargent Prentiss Nutt, the son named after the great Unionist orator—"to the Union Camp to sell milk." So she supported herself until the cows "were taken from me by U.S. soldiers," who took as well her remaining "sheep, cattle, wagons, mules, horses and harness, fencing, axes, and worst of all . . . the last and heaviest blow, $8,787 in cash" that was being held by one of Nutt's executors.

> Then came the dark and winter days of my life. I gathered wild weeds and fed my children on them and when winter came on we thanked God when we could get a little corn. My youngest child was but a baby and my oldest son, just sixteen . . . many a time and often in years since then have my children gone to bed half starved and we have lived on sour milk. The world did not know what was going on in my private household and therefore it could not pity us.

Afterwards

IN 1873 JULIA NUTT received from the United States government the sum of $56,368.25 in compensation for her wartime losses. She took it under protest, to

pay her debts. Over the next twenty-five years she kept up an unrelenting effort to recover more, pursuing Union commanders from Grant to General Alfred Ellet, who had commanded in Natchez, and whom she "found in Kansas." In 1882 an action by Congress awarded her $256,884.05 more, but the next year she was back again, with another accounting for $3,073,357.99 and "For the Life of Haller Nutt, HOW MUCH?" Prentiss Nutt, her son and attorney, continued the suit until the 1930's. Though he changed his name to S. Prentiss Knutt, his character retained a good share of her steely purpose and her unrelenting and bitter anger.

Julia continued to live in the only finished portion of Longwood, an apartment in the basement, for thirty-three years after Haller Nutt's death. By the early 1890's she must have been somewhat restored in fortune (or somewhat failing in her capacity to judge what it was), for she got estimates on finishing the place. No

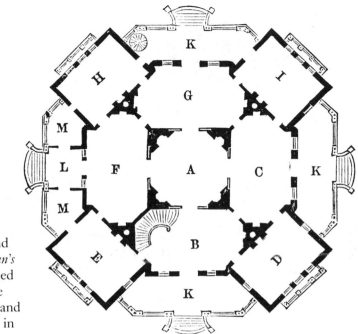

PRINCIPAL FLOOR

"Design I—Oriental Villa" and plans from Samuel Sloan, *Sloan's Homestead Architecture*, published in Philadelphia in 1861. These represent Longwood as built, and were run in *Godey's Ladies Book* in 1860.

Courtesy of the Library of Congress

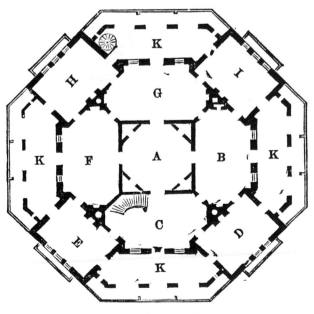

GROUND FLOOR

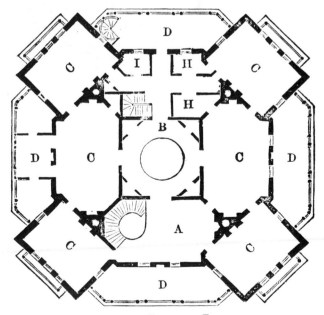

CHAMBER PLAN

work was actually performed; it was left the way Haller Nutt last saw it; the upstairs floors were gaunt brick shells. Julia's daughter, also named Julia, continued to live there until her death in 1932. The wooden parts of the house have since been painted (unfortunately in white, rather than the "oriental colors" Sloan specified, but that can be remedied) and the place sustained as a memorial to Haller and Julia Nutt. Longwood is best this way, with its geometry exposed, its great spaces left to speak clearly for the rationalist premises that commended the octagon form to the experimental mind of its builder.

It is inevitable, perhaps, that a house that displays certain superficial exoticisms should excite the desire of some writers to present it as a huge joke. It has been subjected to more fatuous architectural criticism, more demonstrations of writing from postcards rather than from the experience of spaces, than any other house in America. But it always was what Sloan proclaimed it to be, a clear-headed exercise in geometry, "essentially an x with trapezoidal spaces between the arms filled in with verandahs, so that the exterior assumes the shape of an octagon." Anyone who comes to it unprejudiced can feel the audacity of its cavernous testimonial to the Philadelphia Enlightenment, lightened, in turn, with a little superficial Oriental playfulness.

What of Samuel Sloan? What of all that "press of business" that kept him from thinking too much about other "sections of the country"? He continued a comfortable practice of architecture until the year of his death, 1884. He never recaptured the pace of that first year under the aegis of Andrew Eastwick, and his practice declined a little in the postwar years. But he continued to find plenty of clients in the South, including those for his last commission, the Governor's Mansion of North Carolina. He fell from favor in Philadelphia perhaps, as Harold Cooledge suggests, because his aggressiveness had alienated too many of his peers. The gentle Addison Hutton did very much better. And of course, Sloan was no match for the next generation of Philadelphians, led by that maker of marvels, Frank Furness.

Part V

PIVOT POINT

THE PLANTATIONS of the mid-Atlantic and of the West Indies were organized to serve and supply the European metropolis. Demand and command came from the power center. Americans, on the periphery of that system, felt its centripetal power indirectly, not so much from the east as from the south. Our South was the great source of cotton and then of sugar to Europe, and, in the first four decades of the nineteenth century, the great market for northern-grown food.

From the point of view of Britain, during fifty years after American independence, it was the American South, not the North, that was most important. The South supplied cotton to feed the mills, and the mills supplied work for the Midlands and riches for a new crop of millionaires called, at the time, "cottentots."

From 1800 onward, the manufacturers of the American North, especially those of the Brandywine Valley, contended for shares in the Atlantic machinery market with the roughest competitors Europe could put in the ring. It was considerably later before American finance was able to contend so mightily. Though American capital resources were becoming more and more sufficient to our own capital needs, our bankers did not rear themselves up to obtrude on the plans of European financiers in major international transactions until the nineteenth century was over.

Lenders and investors of the early nineteenth century, like Stephen Girard, Nicholas Biddle or John Jacob Astor, were, in Europe, objects of curiosity or of somewhat patronizing admiration. The tone was: "Not bad for beginners." The next generation, with which we are now concerned, loomed larger, but were still not true contenders for power on a world scale. Biddle was powerful enough to ordain that banks should be Grecian, or that Henry Hitchcock should be forced to pay his debts, or that the Halifax Whigs or the Natchez Junto should accommodate his wishes. Nonetheless, seen from a larger perspective, he appeared, even to his friends, to be important almost as much as an intermediary for the British as an actor in his own right.

415

As the clients of William Jay could testify in *1820*, and the clients of Charles Dakin learned twenty years later, it was the British bankers who held the ultimate power. C. J. Ingersoll proudly said of Nicholas Biddle that he was "praised and respected in Europe"; it seems likely that much of that respect and praise came in proportion to his ability to assure Europe of a continuous supply of cotton, through the management of a credit system that had many functions, but whose chief importance in international finance was to stabilize and increase that supply.

The accomplishments of finance capital in the early republic, and of industrial growth in the Philadelphia region and along the Merrimack, have been adequately chronicled. It was very likely that other centers of finance and industry would emerge in a country as rich as this in fertile land and fresh water, in fish and animals for food, in eager immigrants for labor, in the experience of tool-making and the accessibility of written sources of information, in virtual safety from invasion by hostile peoples possessing comparable technology, yet, at the same time, in ready communication with them to permit emulation. And other centers did emerge, slowly during the period covered by this book, then, soon after our part of the story ends, in a rush.

One of the greatest of these new centers of power began to emerge in the midwestern states that send their easy rivers down gradual slopes to the Great Lakes. In our final group of chapters we will describe the migration that settled that region, and the beginning of its financial independence.

We have already observed a parallel migration, a little farther south, composed largely of speculators and cultivators of the earth drawn by "cotton pull" or driven by the complex forces we have included in the term "tobacco push." In the nineteenth century one could not see along that central-states migration much stirring of independent financial power. That occurred instead in the states where slavery was forbidden, and even there it was not easy. At every step of the way, American finance sputtered and coughed, as its requirements exceeded what it could produce. At every stage that pump had to be primed with fresh European infusions and, as we have observed somewhat to our surprise, infusions as well from the surplus funds generated by the plantation economy of the South. But it needed assistance less and less to produce a flow of money equal to what was needed.

This part of our story begins rather humbly, in Indiana, as an ambitious young man leaves his bankrupt father's dry-goods store to learn the rudiments of international finance in the pursuit of stray pigs.

We are now back in the 1840's. Nicholas Biddle has fallen, but American banking is rising in importance in the world. Northern capitalism is already outweighing the plantation economy of the South, not, of course, as measured by the value of exports,* but as measured by political power and the capacity, through economic decisions, to move large masses of people about the landscape to serve its needs.

---

* The value of exports has been a handy standard for judging the relative importance of one or another crop in an economy chiefly engaged in crop production. That economy is now developing more industrial complications.

This shift of power can be clearly observed in Indiana. In its early years, Indianan bankers were adjuncts to the plantation economy; much of the pork they financed went to feed the growers of cotton. By the 1850's, though the plantations remained of immense importance, all eyes no longer turned southward. The North was an increasingly independent factor in the world economic system, and northern bankers were accumulating capital of their own, now requiring the favor of Europe only for large blocks of credit. The domestic economy was larger, more diverse and therefore increasingly free of the international system.

The South, dependent on that system more than any other section, was still the most important market for the food crops of the West. Nonetheless, by degrees, the West was beginning to cut itself away from the South, to tie itself, instead, to the rising power of the Mid-Atlantic and New England.

These shifts in alignment occurred as an increasing number of immigrants made their way westward along the Great Lakes and the National Pike. The compass of power swung even more decisively with the discovery of gold in California in 1848, which increased the independence of American capitalism generally, but affected the North and the central states more than the South. In the 1850's railroads completed the work begun by the turnpikes and canals; the South was isolated in her colonial economic status and her anachronistic system of forced labor.

The northern migration, in parallel to that we have described for the South, was, like the southern migration, destabilizing and enormous in scale. But the subsistence farms that were established as way stations on the northern route were not as exposed to the whims of international markets as the cotton plantations farther south, nor were northern farmers living amid the tensions of a labor system based on coercion. There was a greater degree of independence for the hog and corn and small-grain and dairy producers of the North than for the cotton planters of the South. And though conditions in northern cities were not idyllic, there was far greater vocational independence of choice for the poor northern worker than the poor southern slave, or the southern tenant who had no city at hand wherein to try his luck.

We are entered, therefore, into a different sort of emotional climate than that of the South, and a different context for architecture. Just before we turn north, however, across the Ohio River, with one family of southerners who made that choice with large consequences to the history of their country, we should pause to observe that along their route there was another of those pockets of uniqueness which explode under the feet of anyone who wishes to make generalizations about the antebellum South. Not very far from the ultimate destination of Thomas Jefferson's tragic nephews, not far from those "dark byways" chronicled by William Alexander Carothers, there was a region of slave-powered plantation life that was economically, socially and architecturally distinct from the rest of Kentucky and Tennessee. We will not examine it in any detail, but will merely note it as a region that belonged not quite to the South and not quite to the North.

Here were sunlit uplands luxuriant with tall grass bearing an abundant blue seed. Great herds of deer, elk and buffalo were feeding there. The settlers found just enough trees to give shelter, without so many as to require much clearing. Into this land, after much travail along the way, came some old friends of Thomas Jefferson. For them, stability meant the reassertion of old ways of building in this new country. Its fertility, and the high prices others would pay the first claimants to purchase shares in its fertility, provided them with the building funds to re-create in Kentucky their memories of Virginia. For them, the sage of Monticello served as mail-order architect.

But this little "New Virginia" was a sweet exception to the general rule, and we must save its description for another book. It lies in a byway, not on the high road to the West.

Let us pass over into Indiana, leaving the eighteenth century for the hastening nineteenth.

CHAPTER 27

Hellenism
in the North

As the balance of economic power shifted from the South to the North, or, rather, from the plantation economy to the North Atlantic manufacturing economy, architecture seemed to follow along. A close observer of Palladian forms might be led to think that Palladianism had an affinity for winners.

The southern system, dominant from South Carolina across Georgia, Alabama and Mississippi, made its last acquisitions in Arkansas and east Texas. It marked its control with white cages (or, if you prefer, peripterally columniated houses) and those large Roman-columned houses which we observed in Part Four, none of which bore much relationship either to the rising power of that revival of Greek forms initiated at Arlington House or to the Palladian architectural ideals of Thomas Jefferson.

The North, however, found in Arlington House its fit symbolic dwelling. A gable-roofed house with a pediment became the characteristic Classic Revival form of the westward progress of emigrants from the seaboard North. This was a sort of vernacular Palladianism, with a temple in the center, sometimes with the wings for which we can thank Palladio, sometimes just a white shoe-box Parthenon. Thousands of these temples for yeomen appeared from the coast of Maine to Port Townsend, on Puget Sound.

Arlington House was the nation's residential symbol of the triumph of the yeoman class. We need, on occasion, to be reminded that the Washington family was not noble; it was not even composed of gentry in the British sense; George Washington was not born to a manor but to his father's ironworks and small farm. He was "First in the Hearts of His Countrymen" in large measure because he steadfastly refused to assume Napoleonic or even Louis Philippean status. He was

419

George Washington,
by Gilbert Stuart

*Courtesy of the Library of
Congress*

representative of yeoman aspirations and, more importantly, of yeoman possibilities. That was his magic.

He was well aware of that. He stood in 1790 as he stands now before us, in the Gilbert Stuart portrait, clad in the sober black of the President of a republic of equals. His hand grasps no scepter, but is extended to clasp the hand of a visiting yeoman. This was the figure enshrined at Arlington, in a Grecian temple. The association was clear to everyone who shared the vision of Thomas Paine that Americans were the legitimate heirs of the republican virtues of ancient Greece, after a leap across the millennia and across the seas. "What Athens was in miniature, America will be in magnitude."

Ideological Classicism, too mild to be called a cult but making gratifying associations of architecture and yeomanry, received its charter from Benjamin Henry Latrobe, in his "Oration to the Society of Artists" in 1811. He told his audience, meeting in Philadelphia, that in that community he felt at home. It was a free city, where merchants were the clients of architecture. There, he said, men like Samuel H. Fox understood how to exercise a "mild but powerful influence" in the interest of a democratic Classicism like that of the Bank of Pennsylvania. Latrobe rejoiced that a new Greece was developing in the "woods of America," a land that like "Greece was free." "In Greece," he said, "every citizen felt himself an important . . . part of his republic."

Latrobe was an abolitionist and, if asked, would certainly have acknowledged the irony implicit in his use of the word "citizen." It is probably just as well that he was never given an opportunity to create a residential symbol for the kind of citizenship he envisaged, because he would then have had to grapple with the ambiguities that dogged George Washington Parke Custis. Custis' Irish farmhands —see Chapter Thirteen—could have risen in the world to qualify as citizens, and some did, but his slaves, as he acknowledged with anguish, could not. Yet Custis and George Hadfield did produce such a symbol at Arlington House, the symbolic residence of the classical yeoman. That symbol was obviously more credible in the North than in the South because in the North its ambiguities were less obvious.

(We should note here, because it becomes important in the next chapter, that Latrobe did not design any houses in what could be called a Greek Revival style. His was the residential Classicism of the 1790's, not that of the 1820's or 1830's. His Philadelphia and Washington houses were cubical, elegant and more like those

Decatur House,
by Benjamin Henry Latrobe
Credit: A property of the National Trust for Historic Preservation

4 2 1

of William Jay than like Arlington House or Berry Hill. They set the tone for others that displayed Philadelphia taste westward in the Ohio Valley. There they acquired, from other hands, porticoes and Grecian entablatures, but they remained cubical with low, hipped roofs, quite unlike the Parthenonic shape of Arlington and its successors. Latrobe supplied the language but not the examples for Hellenic yeomanry. His successors did that.)

George Hadfield's friend Ithiel Town reinforced the theme of Arlington House in his Bowers House, built in 1825 in Northampton, Massachusetts, and in a series of Grecian mansions, first in New England and then, following the route of northern migration, across New York and the lake states. After Arlington came sympathetic monuments to the Greeks themselves, who were at the moment giving their lives in their heroic fight for freedom from the Turks. Nicholas Biddle, at the same time, was putting his very considerable influence behind the Greek Revival as the architecture of finance.

Town was the most influential architect and engineer in America after the death of Latrobe. His Classicism was predominantly Greek, not Roman. It never went out of control, and it did not need to be grandiose to make its effects. It carried with ease, therefore, the democratic ideology of classic yeomanry.

Ithiel Town's Bowers House in Northampton, Massachusetts

Courtesy of the Northampton Historical Society, Northampton, Mass.

As the Yankees swept westward, they built many versions of Hadfield's and Town's models. The grandest, after the Bowers House, was Rose Hill (about 1835), on Seneca Lake, in western New York. The western reserve of Ohio and the towns of southern Michigan have scores of them. The Eli Cooley house in Racine, Wisconsin, was one of the finest, built for the mayor of the town about 1853. In the 1850's Minnesota was too busy surviving to afford the expense of porticoes, but when the German settlers of New Ulm in that state rebuilt their burnt-out town after the Sioux outbreak of 1862, Adolph Seiter reached all the way back to the models of Robert Morris and Palladio for an earnest little box of a house, with two diminutive flankers and a porch all the way across the front.

Though this form was popular, it was not undignified. Quite the contrary. The Arlington-Bowers form was popular because it was dignified. Americans of the last decades before the Civil War took pride in their accomplishments. They thought of themselves as fulfilling the best aspirations of Europe. They did not think it strange to inhabit temples to their own grand but common humanity.

This did not require a "cult of Greek democracy." Americans already had a cult of the Founding Father; the central temple section of his shrine was put in place by 1824, where no one could miss it. After that canny Yankee, Town,

Eli Cooley House (now the Kuehneman House)
Courtesy of Preservation-Racine, Inc.

showed how easy it was to write well-tempered variations on the theme, a multitude of others appeared.

We should do Thomas Jefferson all appropriate honor, but we need not claim too much influence for his architectural ideas. We have noted his essays in the form composed of a central temple with flankers.* But though Jefferson's Palladianism probably did reinforce the flankered Grecian of Arlington and of Ithiel Town, if one registers in the mind Jefferson's houses, then the white temple and flankers of New England and the Midwest, and then, finally, Arlington and the Bowers House, it is obvious that Jefferson's work is at the end of a light, delicate Palladian tradition, and that Arlington is the prototype of another, blockier and more straightforward, much more widely followed in the North.

Palladian Classicism was actually not very popular in the South, though Jefferson took pains to display it in theme-and-variation form at his university, and though for a little while, gentle biloggial houses, like Annfield and the first Hermitage, were seen where Jefferson's personal influence was strong. But from the 1840's until the War Between the States, the South wanted something else, something bolder, grander, more ostentatious than Palladianism could offer, even with a Grecian overlay.† In the years after Arlington House and the University of Virginia were finished, the South was moving away from the ideology of ennobled yeomanry, symbolized so confidently on Arlington Heights. The ennobled yeoman, on his templed hill, was replaced in southern mythology with the "cavalier who rode with Rupert," the "younger son of a great English family." Planters carpentered-up distinguished lineage out of wishes and out of confusions of names, amid a confusion of ideas. It had never been easy to stitch together the myth of yeomanry and the reality of human slavery. The strain and anxiety required by that effort had degenerated into a nasty junkerism by 1860.‡

---

* *Jefferson repeatedly experimented with something like this pattern, taken directly from Palladio or modified a little by Robert Morris. His first version of Monticello, right out of Morris and Palladio, included the biloggial portico we saw in its Tennessee variations in Chapter Twenty. Many historians have attributed to the twenty-two-year-old Jefferson a more attenuated but otherwise similar design for Brandon, in the Tidewater, in 1765, and to the mature Jefferson a tighter one, for the James Semple House in Williamsburg in 1780.*

† *Jefferson did not influence the Greek Revival of Nicholas Biddle and his clientele. Andulusia had no flankers. Girard College and Berry Hill were laid out, instead, as temple-compounds, quite un-Palladian in feeling, each unit separate, not juxtaposed according to Jefferson's or Palladio's sense of graduated functions, each unit getting smaller as it became less important.*

‡ *There are two or three examples of the Greek Revival style as we have described it in Louisiana, resulting from the training or the influence of the Dakin brothers, who learned from Town, but that appears to be all, in comparison to hundreds in the North. James Dakin's first known work was a splendid combination of Town's temple form and Latrobe's central rotunda form, in a house for J. W. Perry in Brooklyn, New York (1832). Neither he nor his brother Charles was asked to do anything like it after they moved south. The South liked cubes with verandahs better than it liked a Parthenonic gabled rectangle with two little temples at its sides. Dakin designed a house with Corinthian columns like the Bowers House for Mrs. Abigail Stark in New Orleans, in 1844, which was followed closely by Henry Howard's Woodlawn Plantation and Madewood Plantation, both of 1846. A vernacular version is the Bonner House, built in 1850 in Claiborne Parish in northwestern Louisiana.*

There was not quite the same discordance between eighteenth-century theory and nineteenth-century practice in the North. The factory system had its own ugliness; and there were many voices pointing out that the drilled squads of workers in huge buildings were not living like independent yeomen on templed hills. But where independent yeomen still thrived, where the memory of Arlington House was not yet bitter, where the factory system had not yet taken hold, there still flourished Ideological Classicism.

Even where the factory system was present, the myth was so powerful that the proprietors could, without apparent embarrassment, place temples above the mills, on green or only slightly sooty hills.* Perhaps there was some intent to compensate for the loss of a general "simplicity of the ancients." Perhaps there was only a blindness to the loss of the context within which the forms of Greece had originally come to America. All we know is that there were innumerable expressions of affinity to ancient Greece in public and private buildings across the North in the same years the factory system was spreading.

We also know that after Arlington House, with its peculiar reliquary "programme," the Greek Revival in the North was assiduously promoted by merchants and bankers who were simultaneously proclaiming affinity to Greece and to capitalism. They were not finicking about strict historical accuracy, rhetorically or architecturally—not much interested in archaeological replication; perhaps that is one reason why "the Greek style" was so adaptable to popular use. A gabled Parthenonic shape would do, with broad white boards laid up in the appropriate vertical positions to simulate columns—often with a fine sense of proportion. The same pine boards, laid horizontally, could suggest a Grecian entablature.

It is important to underline, again, that one does not say much more about the archaeological exactitude of what was revived in the Greek Revival style in the North when one calls it "Greek" than one does in applying this term south of the Mason-Dixon line. These were eclectic styles from the outset. What is sometimes called "Greek" owed as much to fifteenth-century Florence or sixteenth-century Rome or first-century (A.D.) Rome as to fifth-century (B.C.) Greece. It presents the touch of the Hellenistic Baroque and the British Baroque, of Vanbrugh, Adam and Soane, of Vitruvius, Palladio and Minard Lafever. A temple is buried in it somewhere, but beneath a great deal else.

* *I have not yet found any writing of the 1830's or 1840's about the relationship of the way the Acropolis in Athens looked down upon what were somewhat less sanitary conditions in the shops and warehouses, stretching to the docks of Piraeus, to the way mansions of New Bedford or Worcester or New Haven or Madison, Indiana, surveyed the works and docks below.*

CHAPTER 28

Solid Citizens
in Indiana

THE OHIO IS a respectable river. It is not spectacular, nor romantic in the way of the Hudson. It does not dash itself against Palisades; on its banks are no abrupt little mountains to store up legends and cascading kills, nor broad granite shoulders to be given white-framed hotels, like epaulets. The Ohio never supported a class of patroons, as did the Hudson, nor did it ever welcome whalers home. The Ohio was not like the St. Croix or the Mississippi, a lumber river of importance: it saw no rafts to match theirs, acres-wide, sent to build great cities.

The Ohio is a workaday river, a convenience river, the sort of stream one is tempted to take for granted. One cannot imagine Cleopatra lounging with Antony between Gallipolis, Ohio, and Cairo, Illinois, as one might imagine them at ease upon the swell of the Mississippi. On the Ohio they would be too much hooted at by tows* adjusting processions of barges. Barges not of Cleopatra's kind. Nor of Palladio's. The Ohio fills its barges not with queens or architects, not with heroes or persons of genius, but instead with pork and salt and sulfur, steel and coal and petroleum. It is a broad river, which can be accommodating because it is relatively free from rapids. When an automobile comes to the top of one of its bluffs, and begins a descent toward the riverbank, the pace naturally slackens, perhaps in sympathy with the stately progress of the vessels that pass across the windshield, so to speak, in their own insistent lassitude.

This deliberate river marked the northern boundary of the mid-Atlantic empire. The slave-driven, single-staple plantation system exhausted itself along the Ohio. And in the 1840's the little river ports on its northern shore were the setting

---

* I am instructed by my colleague John White that freshwater tugs are called tows, though they do as much shoving as pulling.

of a change in the life of that river valley, which ordained a much larger change in the life of the American nation.

The Old Southern Ohio

THE OHIO HAD BEEN a southern river in every sense. Latitude and temperature were confirmed by economics. Cairo, Illinois, is farther south than Richmond, Virginia. There is no point in the state of Delaware that is as far south as the town of Chesapeake in the state of Ohio. Anyone who has spent much time in Indiana can confirm by the sweat of his brow what the statistics tell us: it is considerably hotter there in the summer than it is on Barbados. Relative altitude also pointed the Ohio southward: its waters run downhill to the Gulf.

Until iron and the steam engine altered things, the compass needle in America's great central valley pointed firmly north and south. Then, with the coming of the railroad, the horizontal tug of iron rails became stronger and stronger, and swung the compass by ninety degrees.

At first the hiss of steam power had been a cheerful sound for the South. It was the sound made by the engines of riverboats. In 1811 the first steamboat appeared in New Orleans and set upon the Crescent City even more securely the crown of the Mississippi Valley. Nicholas Roosevelt and his wife (the daughter of Benjamin Henry Latrobe) had been right in naming the first steam-driven boat on the river after New Orleans. It was a crude vessel, but improvements in design after 1820 brought the average transportation cost of goods pushed upstream from New Orleans down from five dollars to twenty-five cents. The effects of steam technology were less dramatic when running with the current; downstream costs had only to come down from a dollar.

Boats may push against the current, but they do not make their own channels. Even steamboats must accommodate the landscape. The railroad defies it. Railroads bridge rivers, tunnel through mountains, flatten hills, embank their way across valleys.

The builders of the Erie Canal had altered the land about as much as boating people could, but they only showed the way to the railroads' invasion of the West. In the ceremony opening the canal, the catechist had asked by what means had the "waters of the Great Lakes . . . been diverted from their natural course?" And by whose authority? The answer, then, was by "the enterprise of the people of the State of New York." Soon it was not only the waters of the Great Lakes but the natural profusion of the whole interior region that was diverted from natural courses. In 1851 J. D. B. De Bow of New Orleans wrote that the railroads had "rolled back the mighty tide of the Mississippi and its ten thousand tributary streams until their mouth, practically and commercially, is more at New York and Boston than at New Orleans."

What did this change mean for the political and social outlook of the Ohio Valley, especially for its stance toward slavery and disunion? Picture books about

427

the young Lincoln have left us images of yeoman emigrants from Kentucky, Tennessee and the seaboard states that fed population through the central gaps of the Appalachians. But free and independent uplanders were not the only southerners to join the western emigration. Slaveowners came too. We recall how narrowly Edward Coles and his Quaker allies beat back a majority of the Illinois legislature intent on bringing another slave state into the Union. We have observed the enormous investments, and consequent power, of landowners from the South in the northwest territories. Not all of them were as cool to slavery as Easley, Willingham and the Natchez Junto.

Until the coming of the railroad, the Ohio Valley was still very much as Edward Coles found it, and left it, an offshoot of the slave system. The same proslavery, prosouthern majority that drove Coles from Illinois dominated the Indiana legislature in 1860. It took the power of a great governor, backed by a resourceful financier, to defy them and keep Indiana within Lincoln's Union.

Frederick Jackson Turner totted up the origins of the members of the Ohio legislature of 1822. Only 25 percent were from New England; 38 percent were from the Deep South. As late as 1850, after a substantial northern influx, only 11,000 of the roughly one million people in Indiana were natives of New England against 175,000 natives of the South. In Illinois 140,000 were from the South and only 37,000 from New England. Missouri was a slave state in 1860, many of whose slaveowners traveled widely in Iowa, the legislature of which was also probably still dominated by southerners as late as 1850. There were important enclaves of southern sympathy in the mining areas of southwestern Wisconsin and northwestern Illinois.

The struggle for dominance of the region was not fought out at these extremes. If it had been, the outcome would have been otherwise, for the northern immigrants were heavily outweighted at most vital points. It was the less predictable sympathies of the emigrants from New York, New Jersey and especially Pennsylvania that would determine where the West would rally. But those sympathies were solicited by an increasing number of neighbors who had no doubts whatever about their desire to live in a region unburdened with either the moral odium of slavery or the economic threat of competition from hardworking blacks. An aversion to both is clear from the political discourse of leaders of the northern cause, including Abraham Lincoln.

It was the railroad that brought the great flood of northern immigration into the Ohio Valley Empire in the 1850's—in the nick of time.

Railroad versus River

THE RAILROAD WENT westward in parallel to the Ohio. Then its progress was interrupted by the Mother of Waters. If it had been stopped there, the north-south axis of easy water transportation could have remained at least of equal potency to the east-west axis established by the rails.

New Orleans thus had a stake in permitting the mighty Mississippi to roll to the sea "unvexed" by railroad bridges. So had St. Louis. The Chamber of Commerce of that city, which presided over the junction of the Missouri and the Mississippi, saw the railroad reach the Mississippi, and most of its members wished to stop it there. Some railroad promoters were already active in the city, but a majority of the Chamber endorsed a resolution that any bridge over the river would be "unconstitutional, an obstruction to navigation, dangerous." They proclaimed "the duty of every western state, river city, and town to take immediate action to prevent the erection of such a structure."

The steamboaters did more than issue proclamations. A series of rivercraft had altercations with the piers of the first such bridge, near Rock Island. The ensuing lawsuits gave Abraham Lincoln, for the railroad company, the chance to remind the courtroom that east-west travel "has its rights as well as that of north and south."

The bridge at Rock Island stayed in place, and on a fine spring day in 1856, thirty-one years after the opening of the Erie Canal, cheers echoed from the banks of the Mississippi after the porter's call: "Passengers for Iowa keep their seats!" As journalist-historian Marquis Childs tells the story, when the last car of the first train to cross the Rock Island Bridge had reached the Iowa shore, "a mighty shout went up. 'We're over, we're over!' and Chicago said 'Yes, the Mississippi is practically no more.' "

Chicago spoke too soon. The rivers, chief among them the Mississippi, had not yet conceded defeat to the railroads. The contest between the two for mastery of the great valley of America was fought out in many places, including the drawing rooms of two houses, designed by the same architect, composed of the same materials and in the same style, on the river side of First Street in Madison, Indiana.

A Passionless Repose

THESE TWO HOUSES represent, in their grand way, a fairly common type along the river. They are descendants of those Middle Colony buildings we called "Wrenaissance" in Chapter Seven. In the border states along the Ohio River, as in Maryland, Virginia or New Jersey, they were often built of brick. As one runs one's eye across the northern architectural landscape, from Nantucket to Oregon, one sees white wooden cubes laid out like rows of dice, with openings in the place of five-spots. They are the northern wooden version of the brick cubes we see in Madison, and across the Middle Colonies and the Ohio Valley. Both are direct descendants of the Georgian, given an injection of elegance by Benjamin Henry

Shrewsbury House   *Copyright © Dan Carraco 1983*

Lanier House   *Courtesy of the Indiana Historical Society*

Latrobe in the 1790's (as we noted in the last chapter) and in the 1830's and 1840's made Grecian by the addition of thick bands of wood just below the roof, and sometimes porticoes. They were then called Greek Revival, though more often than not they had most un-Hellenic hipped roofs and cupolas.*

This was Ohio Valley Hellenism, which, as it spread northward and up the smaller tributaries of the Ohio itself, fused into the Arlington-Bowers model we have discussed. The lineage of the cubical style, of course, goes back to the severe Renaissance buildings in Pienza, Siena and Florence—see Chapter Eight. Francis Costigan, architect of Madison, Indiana, drew upon the experience of Leon Battista Alberti and Bernardo Rossellino, by way of Pieter Post in Holland, and Inigo Jones and Hugh May in England, as well as those provincial designers who chose to wrap themselves in the "style of Christopher Wren."

If this recital seems a little pedantic, it would not have seemed so to many of the Americans who wanted very much to think of themselves as the heirs of the Renaissance, and built accordingly. The genealogy of their architecture was almost as important to them, in the middle of the nineteenth century, as their own genealogy. They eagerly purchased designs for the structures the popular pattern-books informed them to be of ancient respectability. Some of them purchased family portraits at the same time.

From the region of the Chesapeake and the Delaware, the cubical style was carried westward by emigrants into the central states and reappeared along the Ohio. One can see our two splendid examples by walking down High Street (now prosaically renamed First Street) in Madison, parallel to Main Street. Down along the river, a block away, once stood docks and warehouses. A few blocks farther were lumber mills and slaughterhouses. They are gone now, but this was once a very busy scene. Madison was the largest town in the state for most of the 1840's.

As you walk west, crossing Poplar Street, the mansion of Captain Charles Lewis Shrewsbury appears on the left. Just past Elm Street, a block farther on, is the residence of James F. D. Lanier.

These houses were built to present qualities of great value in a raw, rough, uncertain and changeful time and place. This was not yet a place ready for the competing Picturesque, with its changefulness and engaging unpredictability, which we will be examining in Chapter Thirty. Men devoted to that style, like the architect Calvert Vaux, working in distant New York, did not think the Classical style accorded very well with "this locomotive age," but he did not understand. It was precisely what he called the "passionless repose" of the Classic, especially in its solid, cubical Philadelphia form, that commended it to men in frontier villages like Madison, men like Shrewsbury and Lanier. Here was another kind of looking

---

* The brick boxes of the Middle Colonies were composed into an art form first by Latrobe. (A surviving example of his work in this manner is the Decatur House on Lafayette Park, in Washington, D.C.) His example, as we have seen, was followed in hundreds of handsome instances in Baltimore and Philadelphia. It appeared occasionally in New England where the hand of Bulfinch, emulating Latrobe, was powerful enough to influence even the Yankees to build in brick.

back—but unlike either the exhausted fashions of the central states or the unconvincing antiquarianism of the twentieth century, here, along the Ohio, fundamentally familiar basic forms prevailed, around which clients encouraged a few inventions by their builders. We will see some examples of this invention in a moment.

Perhaps a certain loftiness was the basis for that repose, a well-earned capability for looking back, and down, on the places where the broiling and milling and sweating were done. The cupola on the roof of Lanier's house, visible from the river, holds an observatory twelve feet high and twelve feet in diameter. On that side, as well, is a grand portico, which is embellished like the cupola with vigorous Greek Revival ornament, freely developed from the pattern-books of Minard Lafever. The landward side of the house is more restrained, more in keeping with passionless repose. It implies the portico, subtly, with four brick pilasters, and it wears wrought iron like a winsome ribbon at the throat.

The Steadiest of American Types

THESE WERE THE HOUSES of solid citizens. At least, that is what those citizens wanted them to seem to be. The brick cube was very popular among that class of persons to whom a good, respectable appearance was essential to their gaining credit (literally and figuratively) from their fellow citizens. When one thinks of these houses, or of their clients, one is reminded of what Henry Adams said of the burghers of Philadelphia: "The . . . mind is not complex; it reasoned little and never talked; but in practical matters it was the steadiest of all American types; perhaps the most efficient; certainly the safest." Steady. Safe. Efficient. That was what one wanted to be perceived to be, especially if one needed to borrow a great deal of money. An impressive, reassuring façade was as important in Indiana in the nineteenth century as in Virginia or South Carolina in the eighteenth (see Chapter Eight).

Behind their similar façades were quite different men, but neither lived so steadily, so safely as their domiciles implied. Shrewsbury was a river man; Lanier a railroad man. Both were playing for high stakes. Sometimes they played against each other. Shrewsbury was a Confederate sympathizer; Lanier personally financed Indiana's adherence to the Union. Shrewsbury was the tough product of the Kanawha salt mines, and prospered while he and his numerous relatives provided the cohesion to assemble a series of "Associations," primitive trusts that held back production and held up prices from the late 1830's to the early 1850's. Lanier was the proud child of improvident Tidewater aristocrats; he rode back to respectability with the railroad. The railroad brought prices down; it opened the region to sources of salt outside western Virginia, it diverted the livestock and grain products of the Ohio Valley from the river system of the South toward the East. For Shrewsbury the metropolis was New Orleans, for Lanier it was New York.

Lanier House from the river
Copyright © Dan Carraco 1983

J. F. D. Lanier
Courtesy of the Indiana Historical Society

Charles Shrewsbury
Courtesy of Historic Madison, Inc.

433

Stairway and hall
in the Shrewsbury
House
Copyright © Dan Carraco
1983

Shrewsbury grew old and bitter in an Age of Steam and Steel. J. F. D. Lanier became its first important financier, the forerunner of the great Pierpont Morgan.

Lanier's house was under construction in 1843 and 1844, the years in which Charles Shrewsbury heeded his father-in-law's importunings to move the head-quarters of C. L. Shrewsbury and Company from Kanawha to Madison. It appears that John Woodburn, the father of Shrewsbury's wife, Ellen, had been trading with Louisville and New Orleans since he came to Indiana in 1818, while most of the state was still Indian territory. Woodburn kept building his steamboat business, while Shrewsbury and his brothers organized a series of oligopolies to control the production and pricing of western Virginia salt; the first brought thirty-five producers together under the umbrella of William Shrewsbury and Company as early as 1836. After Charles moved to Madison, Woodburn seems to have transferred control of his shipping operations to his sons-in-law and followed the pull of the South to become a planter in Mississippi in 1852.

Shrewsbury, looking down the street at Lanier's handsome new house, was by 1846 or 1847 rich enough to match it. Actually, what Shrewsbury apparently had in mind was not just matching but overmatching—doing what Lanier had done, but just a little better. The parlor of the Shrewsbury house has a ceiling height of sixteen feet; Lanier's was thirteen. The room itself is forty feet long; Lanier's was thirty. Lanier's circular staircase is tucked, demurely, into a wall; Shrewsbury's stands free, its hands on its hips, in the middle of the hallway. The ornament of Lanier's drawing room is restrained; Shrewsbury's is as rich, I think, as that of any other surviving house in America of the Greek Revival style, except Stanton Hall in Natchez. Francis Costigan gave both Lanier and Shrewsbury designs up to the ambitions of any Baltimore or Philadelphia merchant. For Shrewsbury he added the kind of Lafeverish ornament that was favored by the cotton nabobs of the upland South. They were, after all, Shrewsbury's customers, and in later military matters, his allies.

By 1850 the differences between Lanier and Shrewsbury were becoming clear, differences having to do with the contest between river and railroad, between North and South, and these two citizens of Madison grew apart. But they had established their wealth in a perfect symbiosis of their talents. Shrewsbury had supplied the salt and Lanier financed the ham on the hoof which had made Madison, during their youth, a close competitor to Cincinnati as chief supplier of pork products to the ravenous plantations of the South.

CHAPTER 29

Salt Pork,
Railroads and War

REPEATEDLY IN AMERICAN HISTORY the livestock and mining frontiers have preceded the agricultural frontier. We are prone to forget the origins of the name "Cowpens" in South Carolina, and to regard the mining of bog iron by seventeenth-century Virginia planters as *infra dig*. We do not often look at the flat contours of our present cornbelt and recall that, economically, the Midwest once had many of the characteristics of the Rocky Mountain West. Its chief attraction for the first western railroads was not its farmland but the lead mines around Galena, Illinois, and then the copper mines of upper Michigan. Daniel Drew, the pious fraud who later waxed so rich in railroads, learned his methods as the proprietor of the Bull's Head Tavern, a drovers' rendezvous on the Long Trail from the Scioto Valley of Ohio to New York. Corn, the first and most reliable crop of the pioneers of Indiana and Illinois, was fed to hogs, and hundreds of thousands of hogs were driven down their own "Long Trail," from Indiana through the Saluda Gap to feed the South. Others were floated to market. Abraham Lincoln knew the importance of river navigation firsthand because his father raised hogs, and those hogs which could not be walked to market were carried there in boats after they were turned into pork. The future President was a renowned hog-slaughterer. He was so good at that bloody work that he gained the right to accompany barge-loads of salt-cured pork from southern Indiana to New Orleans, where he learned important lessons about slavery.

Lincoln did not need to go far from home, however, to encounter the intermediaries between his southern customers and his hog-raising neighbors. Hogs prowled the woods, and drovers prowled after them. When a herd was found, agents for southern plantations bought them with notes drawn on banks; the first local bankers were those who were willing to advance cash against these notes.

(Thomas Lincoln, Abraham's father, sold more than one hundred hogs this way in 1830.)

This pattern of hog financing had interesting political consequences. Bankers tended to be Whigs. The routes taken by the drovers mapped out not only the lines of later turnpikes and railroads but also the ganglia of Whig power; voting patterns and livestock patterns, then and now, have much in common.

Among the Whigs of Indiana and Illinois were two young men who earned enough by storekeeping and hog-slaughtering to sustain their studies in the law. Abraham Lincoln turned from the law to politics and gained the presidency. James Lanier turned from the law back toward the hog business (but at a high, abstract financial level) and became so proficient that he, as much as the more celebrated Jay Cooke, financed the success of the Lincoln presidency.

In the 1840's Lanier's home town, Madison, Indiana, sustained four large packing plants, one of which slaughtered 43,000 hogs in one year. Hogs were important in Madison; Henry Ward Beecher, it is said, was once so fully engaged in theological discourse with the town's leading matron (probably Mrs. James Lanier) that it was only at the vestibule of the church that he noted she had been followed there by a family of pet pigs. It was on the occasion of that visit that he stood at the Grecian door on the river side of Lanier's house, looked out upon the violets "that begemmed the terrace" and "impulsively expressed the desire to lie down and roll among the darlings of the spring." (Anyone who has seen a pig among violets knows how tempting is its example.)

The doorway and the violets owed much to pigs. By 1847 James Lanier lived in his solid, respectable house as the master of the inland triangular trade. He had learned how to buy, at a discount, the hog paper given local bankers by drovers. Then he would travel to its place of issuance, New Orleans, redeem it in full at maturity, buy cotton paper at a discount from the always capital-short New Orleans bankers, present it for payment in full at maturity at its place of issue, New York, and with the proceeds, return to Indiana to start over again. We know how he went about this, because he enjoyed describing it after he had progressed in the next decade to financing a million dollars a day in railroad bonds and negotiating for his country's credit with the Rothschilds.

He recalled, as well, in his remarkable memoirs that buying hog paper did not require as much cash as reputation. James Lanier could not always give cash. Sometimes all he had to give were his own notes. Let us see how the son of a bankrupt gentleman-storekeeper came to have the cash and the credit.

James F. D. Lanier

WE SAW THEM FIRST in Chapter Twenty-one, that "sallow planter and his lady" at the "rear of a long cavalcade" of pioneers going west, away from exhausted soils and exhausted hopes. They had "bidden adieu to the scenes of their youth and

437

undertaken the long and painful pilgrimage through the wilderness." For some, like Jefferson's nephews, the pilgrimage ended in murder and suicide. Others, like General Nathan Whitfield of Gaineswood (see Chapter Sixteen), lived to see family portraits taken down from the pegs driven into log walls and rehung from the freshly painted cornices of a mansion.*

PIVOT POINT

The experience of James Lanier was something like Whitfield's, but he started lower and rose higher. His boyhood experience was full of shame. When he became a man, and very rich, he was at pains to recall the early history of his family in America, before the "long and painful pilgrimage." The elderly George Washington Parke Custis had assured him that the Laniers and the Washingtons were in several ways related. He was proud to tell of his own achievements, to redeem the intervening dark.

Lanier said of himself, "I strove to be respected." He had a first name, James, but he seldom encouraged its use after he was free of the summons that had called him, at the age of ten or twelve, from the storeroom of the dry-goods store where he learned "how to be respectful and obliging to all." His boyhood was spent in one forced move after another, in the train of a grandfather whose pretensions to the status of "planter" went unfulfilled, and of an improvident father. His father lost what remained of their inheritance, tried shopkeeping and died bankrupt.

J. F. D. Lanier grew up to keep his pride quiet, to take only measured risks and always to calculate the consequences of action on reputation. He had bitter memories of pretension, improvidence and defeat. "I was diligent, . . . and made it a point to be punctual in every duty and appointment." In that way the world would know that he was not the sort of man to follow his father into bankruptcy. "It was my purpose in life to respect scrupulously the rights of others, but always to be firm in the assertion of my own." Respect was not the reward of the soft or the changeable; to earn it one required "rigid adherence" to a "plan of life," watchfulness and "fidelity in every engagement."

George Washington died in 1799, with the old century and the old way of life. James F. D. Lanier was born in the next year. His grandfather had fought in William Washington's cavalry during the Revolutionary War and joined the westering of the 1780's. He first tried Nashville, where he shared quarters with Andrew Jackson. Nashville did not work out, and he removed to Bourbon County, Kentucky, where his son and grandson joined him. Bourbon County did not work out either. The grandfather resolved to try Pendleton County. The father lost what was left of the property he had brought west in one of those shadowy title suits in which Jackson lost his second fortune. His son learned a lesson; Jackson the lawyer had survived Jackson the speculator.

After Bourbon County, the familiar story began again. The children were packed into wagons with a slave or two (probably those too old to be readily sold),

---

* *The standard of living of westerners nearly always dropped below whatever it had been in the East, and often stayed low for many years before it rose again. The hope, and the general experience, was that it would rise much higher, if not in the first generation, then in the next.*

some silver and linens, and on they went, to the north this time, away from Jackson's route down the Natchez Trace toward New Orleans. They crossed the Ohio, gave up their last two slaves and settled for a while in Preble County, Ohio. The father did no better there, despite the friendship of the governor of the territory, William Henry Harrison. In declining health and spirits, he moved again, to the hamlet of Madison, Indiana, where after a last try to extricate himself from debt by becoming a dry-goods dealer, he died insolvent in 1820. His son resolved "never to allow my liabilities to exceed my means" and to wipe out the mark against the family's good name. Later he was able to tot up his father's debts and pay them all.

The magnificent white-columned house that he built, twenty years after that,

Engraving of the Lanier House
Courtesy of the Indiana Department of Natural Resources

looked down High Street to the crumbling walls of the little building that had been the family's dry-goods store and home. Later still, after he had become the nation's most important financier of railroads, he remembered his grandfather and father, and paid his emotional debts to them as well. In his memoirs he told his children that his father had served in the War of 1812, commanding a stockade "situated on a narrow neck of land separating the waters flowing into Lake Erie from those flowing into the Gulf of Mexico, and named in honor of General Wayne and in commemoration of his celebrated northwestern campaign in which my grandfather served." Upon the site grew the city of Fort Wayne, a "center of a vast system of railroads," said Lanier (who had financed nearly all of them), and the center, too, of his successful speculations in land. "The very ground which my father and grandfather periled their lives to wrest from savage tribes, I have labored long and earnestly . . . to improve and enrich by the arts of peace, and thus to complete their work."*

George Washington had warned that the Spaniards, downstream on the Mississippi, would "hold out lures" to the people of the West; separated by range after range of mountains from the seaboard, the westerners might, he said, dissolve their ties with the eastern states at "the touch of a feather" unless held by stronger bonds than a few ribbons of road through the Appalachian passes. The real threat that the West might be detached from the Union, however, did not come from the Spaniards but from the South. As Lanier looked back on his life, he rejoiced that he had helped to knit the West and the North together "through the instrumentality of the railway." The Ohio Valley had been "brought within easy distance of Eastern markets," and also brought within reach of emigrants from the North, of Unionist sentiments.

The rush of that population into the region not only altered its political orientation but quickly increased land values.† J. F. D. Lanier, watchful and never over his head, built a few dollars earned as a storekeeper into a snug fortune earned as a lawyer, and that fortune into a fund to buy land, a stake in a bank, control of a bigger bank, through the banks a great deal of hog paper, more real estate and finally, railroad stock.

Lanier and the Railroads

ALONG THE WAY, James Lanier had learned the virtues of knowing more than his neighbors about a necessary but intricate craft. As clerk of the Indiana House of Representatives, he "became master of the rules and modes of conducting business." Not only was he useful to those who "found themselves in positions of embarrassment from want of familiarity" but he was also able to be useful to

---

George Whistler, railroad engineer and father of the painter, was born at Fort Wayne in the year of James Lanier's birth.

†*It is interesting to note the parallel between Henry Hitchcock's Alabama and James Lanier's Indi-*

himself. He promoted the Indiana Turnpike and then the state's first railroad. His knowledge of the legislature and of the real-estate market permitted him (for the first but not the last time) to assure foreign investors of his "usefulness." The capital of his first bank "was almost wholly borrowed from abroad."

What distinguished Lanier, all his life, from most of his competitors was a prudent boldness. He had an eerie sense of balance, a capacity to walk to the edge of the possible and not an inch farther. He was ever mindful of his father's fall from grace. Though his bank participated hugely in the up-rush of speculative values, he never stretched too far. In what he called "the terrible catastrophe of 1837 . . . nearly every bank in the Western and South-western States failed, with the exception of that of Indiana." His bank, though it was slow in paying its interest, stayed solvent.

That happy outcome was by no means assured in the midst of the panic, when the people of Indiana chose James Lanier to persuade the Secretary of the Treasury of their solvency. Lanier filled his saddle bags with $80,000 in gold—this man who had only recently been earning $3.50 a day—and made the long and dangerous ride alone to Washington. The Secretary correctly inferred that any bank with that much specie available, and with that sort of manager, could be trusted with the government's deposits. The Secretary's decision in those dark days was "much to our convenience and advantage."

Lanier's personal credit was established. Thereafter he built it. He borrowed to buy hog paper—and borrowed to buy railroad paper. More important, he was learning how to persuade others to buy railroad paper. One could sell foreigners almost anything once, but to keep their confidence, ah! that was the thing. From his triangular transactions he had developed an eye for credits, "without the loss, I believe, of a single dollar in any transaction." In 1849 "the subject of railroad construction began to excite general attention." A year later the excitement was settling down, and Lanier "felt the time had at last come when railroads could be

ana. Alabama functioned as a colony to produce a single crop, exposed to the whims of British (and later New York) commodity and financial markets. Indiana's bankers, led by Lanier, diversified their agricultural base, generated and reinvested capital and, with the instructive exception of the 1830's, kept their loans in balance with their internal capacity. Indiana, again led by Lanier, built railroads that tied the state into a transcontinental agricultural and industrial system, while Alabama's roads were a feeder system for cotton shipment, only slightly exploiting the vast forest, mineral and water-power potential of that state.

Here are the statistics showing the population of the two states in the first half of the nineteenth century (in thousands):

Year	Alabama	Indiana
1800	1	6
1810	9	25
1820	128	147
1830	310	343
1840	591	686
1850	772	988
1860	964	1,350

safely undertaken as renumerative investments." Then he put something more important than an $80,000 sack of gold in his saddlebags. He put there his reputation as the resuscitator first of the almost defunct bank and then of the almost defunct Madison and Indianapolis Railroad.

In New York he formed a partnership with Richard H. Winslow to sell railroad securities. According to the *American Railroad Journal*, "Mr. Lanier brought with him the first Western railroad bond ever offered" in the New York market.

At that moment Indiana had 139 of the West's 655 miles of railroad lines. New Orleans was still "the sole port of export." Winslow and Lanier had seen what the rivers could do, and now they set out to persuade the public what the rails could do. "In newspaper articles and pamphlets . . . in great numbers" and by personal persuasion, they built public confidence. "We were without competitors for a business we had created, and consequently made money very rapidly." They sold bonds and stock, and "coupled contracts for the purchase, at a large commission, of rails." They frequently undertook, for their own account (meaning with their own credit), an entire issue, and as often earned a second or third commission for paying out the interest due on the bonds. During the next six years, 10,724 miles of line were constructed, and, said Lanier with pardonable pride, "with all the important lines we were, in one way or another, connected."

A substantial amount of this business was done with foreign investors, with whom Lanier's Indiana performance had produced warm recollections, quite unlike their general experience with American "internal improvements." State banks were generally in default on the debts incurred to British investors. Sydney Smith of the *Edinburgh Review* said he never met an American at dinner "without feeling a disposition to seize and divide him—to allot his beaver to one sufferer and his coat to another—to appropriate his pocket handkerchief to an orphan and to comfort the widow with his silver watch . . . How such a man can set himself down at an English table without feeling that he owes two or three pounds to every man in the company, I am at a loss to conceive." The wrath of the Rothschilds was stated with greater gravity: "You may tell your government," James Rothschild, their Paris patriarch, had said to an American emissary, "that you have seen the man who is at the head of the finances of Europe, and he has told you that they cannot borrow a dollar, not a dollar!"

As early as 1847 James Lanier was in the offices of that formidable figure in Paris, as well as those of the London Rothschilds and their allies, the house of Hope & Co. in Amsterdam. Somehow he persuaded them to look more kindly on Indiana securities, and in the next five or six years Winslow and Lanier often negotiated "a million of bonds," meaning railroad bonds, in a day, often to people who had previously felt as did Smith and James Rothschild.

Though, like Nicholas Biddle, Winslow and Lanier were vastly overweighted by the great European financiers, the wealth they accumulated went to create an ever-enlarging pool of capital available in America for American projects; that pool was far more significant by the time they withdrew from railroad financing than it had been, while Biddle was trying to prop up the price of cotton. Their withdrawal occurred before the panic of 1857. Winslow's health began to fail in 1854. Lanier did not like the smell of the financial winds. He announced he did not wish to stay in the railroad-financing business without his partner, who, he said "had, above all men I ever knew, the faculty of inspiring others with the zeal and confidence which he himself felt." What a pair they must have been!

Lanier was inspiring enough on his own. In 1857 the second panic in twenty years forced "many of our most valuable enterprises into bankruptcy." Lanier did not walk away. To him "it devolved naturally upon parties who had been instrumental" in selling the securities of these enterprises "to find means to raise them from their depressed condition." Especially did he feel this responsibility toward the Pittsburgh, Fort Wayne and Chicago, "a company with which I had been early identified [serving cities with which his father and grandfather had been even earlier identified] and for whose good name . . . I was most solicitous." The story of the "raising" of that road is too complex to recount in detail here, but the other shareholders made it clear that it was largely due to "the good name and financial strength of Mr. Lanier, joined to his well-known prudence and caution" which "tended to inspire great confidence."

Over and over again, it was that capacity to "inspire . . . confidence," and his willingness to put his own credit on the line, which enabled Lanier to rescue enterprises to which he felt a commitment. He was not a chilly man; at the outset of his career he had been a good trial lawyer, but his passionate advocacy of each of his clients left him emotionally shattered. "Success or defeat . . . gave me more pleasure or pain" than it did his clients, he said. "I found the labor and anxiety of my profession too much for my strength, which led me to give it up" and retire to the world of financial abstraction. He had his commitments and he acted on them. He could not have sold bonds to others, in the early days of Winslow and Lanier, if he had not been willing to guarantee payment personally of the obligations in which he asked others to believe.

The time came when, despite the accumulation of private fortunes in the United States that could be invested in securities of railroads or of governments, the divided nation spent its capital in a civil war, and the government of the United States itself exhausted the still limited pool of domestic credit. It was the master of the reassuring manner and the reassuring performance, James Lanier, who then went to the Rothschilds and other European bankers on behalf of President Lincoln to persuade them of the likely survival of that government. But his most daring extension of credit was to his home state, in its worst extremity.

Lanier and Public Credit

JAMES LANIER WAS proud of having made it possible for the railroads to carry a great wave of people out of the northern states to overcome the southern predominance of the Ohio Valley. Still, in 1860, Indiana, cut off by the swamps of northwestern Ohio from the main emigrant routes, remained more deeply southern in its sympathies than either Illinois or Ohio. Lanier had supported the candidacy of Indiana-born Abraham Lincoln, but their home state was divided among the party of Lincoln, the Douglas Democrats and outright Secessionists like Charles Shrewsbury. By the second year of the Civil War, the balance had tipped heavily toward the South; the 1862 election returned a legislature "bitterly opposed to the War . . . determined to take the State out of the Union ranks."

The strength of Confederate sentiment was made even clearer in the summer of 1863, when southern forces under General John Hunt Morgan found the Ohio River steamboat operators had gathered an appropriate number of steamboats at Brandenburg, Kentucky, for his convenience. He transported his troops across the river to invade Indiana. They had a series of easy victories over the militia and found easy financial support: the millers of the old state capital, Corydon, oversubscribed Morgan's requisitions of cash. One of his men later described his two-week campaign through the state as an "enjoyable time."

It was not as enjoyable as it would have been had not Lincoln's governor of Indiana, Oliver P. Morton, put down a clever Secessionist conspiracy by the legislature between the 1862 elections and Morgan's Raid. Aside from the steamboat operators (Charles Shrewsbury among them?) and those compliant millers of Corydon, the state was not prepared to join the Confederacy when Morgan appeared.

The plot that Governor Morton defeated was to cut off funds with which he could pay the militia. After the 1862 elections, the governor and the Unionist members of the legislature, knowing they were in a minority, withdrew, leaving the legislature without a quorum, and essentially inoperative for the next two years. Then Lanier wrote Morton saying he would underwrite the war effort. He did so to the tune of $400,000 of unsecured general credit "to equip and put promptly into the field" Indiana's first six infantry regiments.

The next step by the Secessionists was to try to break the credit of the Unionist administration, in part to assure their friends in Europe of the general insolvency of the Lincoln government. There were eager listeners in London. William Ewart Gladstone, whom the Prince Consort called "the real leader of the House of Commons," was readying himself for the prime ministry. Gladstone pronounced that "Jefferson Davis and the other leaders of the South have made an army; they are making, it appears, a navy; and they have made what is more than either, they have made a nation." These sentiments came naturally to the son of that vehement anti-abolitionist John Gladstone, head of the West India Association and owner of 2,183 slaves. British bankers and manufacturers, said the London *Times*, were "partners with the Southern planter." Those bankers were quite ready to accommodate Mr. Davis' new "nation" if it could prove itself "a stronger credit" than Mr. Lincoln's embattled Union.

Once again Lanier was ready to put himself, his reputation and his personal credit behind the Morton and Lincoln Administrations. He offered to pay the interest on the state's debt, personally. The state's fiscal agent, John C. Walker, a Confederate sympathizer, had possession of the creditors' list and denied it to the governor and Lanier, but they "procured" the list somehow, and Lanier thereafter made the payments, advancing $640,000 of his own funds over the next two years.

The 1864 elections were fiercely contested; Lincoln and his Secretary of War saw to it that every Indiana soldier not immediately needed on the picket lines was sent home to vote, and all hospitalized Indiana soldiers were sent to be repaired—and to vote—in Indiana hospitals. Morton, Lanier and Lincoln won, barely.

Oliver Morton went on to the United States Senate. Lanier was, apparently, content to go back to his business. He was, he said, "a business man from taste as well as from habit," but he made at least two trips to Europe "to reassure European capitalists as to the soundness of U.S. government bonds," once in 1865 and again in 1868.

Francis Costigan

WHAT OF THE ARCHITECT of the Shrewsbury and Lanier houses? We are back now in the murk. American history has not been generous in supplying us with information about artists, unless, like George Whistler's son James, and Samuel Sloan, they took great pains to publicize themselves (see Chapter Twenty-five). Francis Costigan is a shadowy figure who has left us not a word of autobiography. We do have his signature, inscribed in silver on an insert in the newel post of James Lanier's house. This is not a book that sets out to present a catalogue of the works of any of the architects we discuss, but the temptation is strong to risk a little pedantry in order to do better by Francis Costigan, who has so far had to be content to have a productive lifetime compressed within the space of a few newspaper columns, one unpublished master's thesis and some painfully inaccurate paragraphs in magazines of local history.

Costigan was born in Washington, D.C., on March 4, 1810, and died of tuberculosis on April 18, 1865. He was reputed to have been apprenticed in Philadelphia, and in 1835 he was a carpenter and a builder with a store on Frederick Street in Baltimore. It seems likely that the Panic of 1837 drove him westward, for he purchased property and baptized his child in Madison in 1838. His first commission in Madison was probably started in that year, a cubical, wooden, vaguely Grecian house, which still exists on West Main Street. For this house, which has elements that recur in Costigan's later known work, and which was built while he was known to be in Madison, his client, Jacob Shuh, had also been trained as a carpenter. Shuh had built up a steam-operated wood-carding and linseed business, but was bankrupted when a flash flood piled up behind the abutments of James Lanier's new railroad (one man's fortune is another man's grief) and swept down and destroyed his mill, wiping him out. Shuh disappeared from history.

445

House designed by Costigan for Jacob Shuh, now the Whitsitt House
Courtesy of the Indiana Historical Society

Costigan may have designed the Roman Catholic church where his eldest son and namesake was baptized. St. Michael's was built after his arrival in Madison, from stone taken from James Lanier's railway cut. The style is plain, but the shallow plastered vault of the ceiling of the sanctuary echoes, though faintly, the elegance of Latrobe's cathedral in Baltimore.

Costigan was certainly the architect of a double house on Vine Street, half of which was his own residence. It has two fine Classic Revival doorways and a double parlor that presage his experiments with making dramatic a basically simple space, which he carried to whimsical conclusions in the house he designed for himself a decade later.

Costigan had been working his way up through church records from plain "Francis Costigan" to "Mr. Francis Costigan" for two years by the time James Lanier was ready for an architect to build him a proper mansion. Costigan had demonstrated his skill; Lanier was no man to speculate on an unknown, even one from Baltimore. Shrewsbury had Lanier's example before him both as to style and as to architect. Costigan, on the other hand, had in Shrewsbury a man of more brilliant hue than Lanier, and he gave him a more brilliant house. Costigan seems to have known the work of the Dakin brothers, or to have been proceeding on very sympathetic lines a decade or more after their work in Mobile and Louisville, for he drew on the closest grand structure in the Grecian mode, James Dakin's Bank of Louisville (built in 1834, Hellenic probably by subtle or not-so-subtle suggestion of Nicholas Biddle), for Shrewsbury's skyline. He also took themes from the Dakins' old partner, Minard Lafever, on which he wrote his own cadenzas. On the river side of Shrewsbury's house he provided columns at the doorway, of his own peculiar lotuslike order. He used them again in the wonderful little house he designed and built for himself in 1852.

There Costigan set out an exercise in deception for effect. The lotus columns

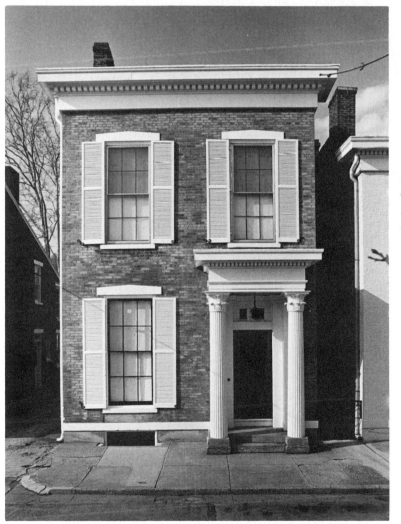

Francis Costigan's own house in Madison

*Copyright © Dan Carraco
1983*

447

Doorway of Francis Costigan's house

Copyright © Dan Carraco 1983

at the door were a hint that one has to look closely to catch him breaking all the rules, breaking them very subtly. He owned two adjacent lots on 408 West Third Street, but chose to use just one of them to work out some games with interior space in a house just over twenty-one feet wide. The entrance, set into an unprepossessing two-windows-up-and-door-and-window-below brick façade, is very subtly detailed in a free Grecian manner. He used again his "Costigan order," and the subtle elaboration of the entry, though very small in scale, suggests something of the drama inside. The front door is a curved pocket door, which admits the visitor into a tiny vestibule. The abrupt front stairway rises to a second-floor landing so small that it has a rotating gate which prevents the unwary from falling down the back stairs after achieving the front, and vice versa.

This dexterity is necessary because Costigan wanted to provide an awesome double parlor in a dimunitive house, packing all the illusion he could into one room. The visitor enters the parlor at a diagonal, on the curve suggested by the front door, and the space opens out with a shock: it is thirty-four feet long, seventeen broad and has a fourteen-foot ceiling. That is about all there is in the house: one grand illusion, with a closet and a tiny kitchen downstairs and two

The Kentucky Blind Asylum in Louisville
Courtesy of the Photographic Archives, Ekstrom Library, University of Louisville

small bedrooms above. Costigan could do as much with his architectural credit as Lanier could with his financial credit; each had little to work with, and each kept his promises.

Local folk memory attributes to Costigan two other large houses, long ago demolished, in the same neighborhood as those of Shrewsbury and Lanier.* Some details might corroborate attributing to him the Grecian elements of the Marsh-Jackson house on Telegraph Hill, either before or after it was Gothicized. He was more certainly the designer and builder of the recently destroyed Madison Hotel, of ninety rooms, and a succession of very large, very handsome and very complex institutional buildings in Indiana and Kentucky.

Costigan's hand has been seen by some in the Madison Baptist Church, across Vine Street from his double house, in part because he used a similar order in the Indiana Blind Asylum, which he designed in 1851, in Indianapolis. The church was completed after Costigan had followed the railroad prosperity and the prospect of more institutional commissions from Madison to Indianapolis, where he

* *Known as the McKee and Godman houses.*

449

produced not only the Blind Asylum but also the Hospital for the Insane and the Deaf and Dumb Asylum. In 1855 he designed the Kentucky Blind Asylum in Louisville.

He must have been known as a competent and experienced designer of houses for the "new men" of the Ohio river ports. He certainly had succeeded in giving them solid, steady appearances—by "them" I refer to both the men and the houses —and this must have been quite satisfactory, in the light of the highly unsteady circumstances in which all such "new men" live. Now he was engaged to put a classical face on institutional buildings that at once organized philanthropy into efficient units and removed it from the notice of many citizens in whose households, or neighborhoods, the unfortunate had previously languished.

These very large hospitals and asylums were in many ways like the factories of the time—a very large subject and one heatedly debated by many historians. There are few things that are safe to say about it, but among those safe things may be that they were reflections of a general enthusiasm for reform in the care of the handicapped, physically or mentally, and for prison reform, and that a classical façade for such buildings (like a classical façade and a cubical—"solid"—form for domestic buildings in a frontier community) could be seen as an attempt at compensation. Classical asylums were wrapped in a consoling style, cut as propriety dictated, which may have offered some solace to the feelings of guilt and anxiety that people felt when "putting their relatives away."

But this is much too ambitious a subject for us to attempt to cover in a book which is mostly about the clients for domestic architecture. Here we must be content to note that Costigan's work, like John Notman's and John Haviland's (see Chapters Twenty-five and Thirty), is genuinely distinguished as architecture. (Even Sloan's admirers could not make much of a case for his as works of art.) They are immense in scale—the Kentucky Hospital is far larger, and better designed, than most of the state capitols of the time—and they display both engineering ingenuity and a kind of soberly playful use of classic devices on a grand scale.

In 1931 the Indiana *Construction Recorder*'s "Wash Tub" columnist (anonymous, to our loss) noted that one Orval Williamson had made a folio of ten plates on Costigan's Blind Asylum. The folio, he said, was "beautifully rendered . . . full-flavored like eighteenth-century work." To achieve the exactitude he wanted in those renderings, Mr. Williamson "pulled out a plumb": measuring Costigan's work, he found the most careful use of entasis (subtle swellings of verticals to satisfy the distortions of visual perspective) which had gone unnoticed in measuring buildings in Greece itself until Sir John Pennethorne did so at almost exactly the same time Costigan was beginning his set of public buildings. It appeared, said the "Wash Tub," that Costigan knew not only his Stuart and Revett but also his Pennethorne, which the "Wash Tub," of course, knew as well. If that were not enough to establish the "Tub's" credentials, the writer went on report that

Costigan's Blind Institute was wrecked in 1931 to make way for the gardens of a plaza containing a modern version [the World War I Memorial Plaza] of a tomb erected in Halicarnassus to Mausolus, king of Caria, by his filthy-rich, disconsolate widow, Artemisia. When the tomb was gone, Artemisia jumped in the river.

It is a pity we have no more words on Costigan by this wholly sympathetic critic. For while he was at work on his public buildings, Costigan built a hotel in Indianapolis, called the Bates House, which gave him further opportunity to display his freedom from literal Classicism. It was a free Grecian structure, but had a strange set of Gothicoid little columns where an orthodox Greek Revival architect would have given us a replica of a Lysicrates lantern. Even odder was the Oriental House, which he built for himself, to make a new start as a hotelkeeper. (He quickly abandoned hotelkeeping and went back to architecture.) Its Italianate shape and wholly original ornament led the way to the most peculiar of his mid-century compositions, the Hasselman House in Indianapolis, for which his sole

Costigan's drawing for the Hasselman House in Indianapolis
Courtesy of the Indiana Historical Society

known surviving drawing still exists in the Indiana Historical Society. For it he invented a strange flower motif with a much enlarged pistil, which, said the Indianapolis *News* without a smile in 1921, "does not represent any of the natural American flora," though one botanist "surmised" it might have to do with a passionflower.*

There were, it seems, other Indianapolis houses that, like the Hasselman House, have been lost to us, upon which Costigan might have lavished more botany, more passion and perhaps even some ornithology. The Oliver Tousey House at 709 N. Illinois was identified as housing the Gatling Gun Club in 1958. It, too, was designed by Costigan, according to one recollection, though not to others.

The Wallace Residence, on the corner of Fletcher Avenue and Irving Street, was "a sorry looking sight" in 1921, but in 1945 another writer remembered that it had ornament resembling the Hasselman botanical wonders. Costigan may have built for himself, and inhabited when he was not a hotelkeeper, a house described as the "Costigan-Abrams-Hendricks" house at Meridian and North Street. A Scots carpenter from Dumfries, James White, who later became mayor of Indianapolis, worked for Costigan in Madison and Indianapolis and said he had helped Costigan lay the joists for that house. The Groves House on the southwest corner of Meridian and North has also been attributed to Costigan, and it is possible that it could have justified another newspaper report, this time of 1929, that "there are old residences in Indianapolis where he has used conventionalized figures of birds of no known species." Or, as is the case with so much reporting on Costigan, is somebody confused, this time mixing birds with flowers?

We are unlikely to know, for though there are wispy reports of exquisite Costigan drawings, and the increasing appreciation for his work in Madison is drawing attention to it, there seems to be little more to be learned about his designs, most of which have been destroyed, or his character. We know that he died in 1865, and that he was buried in Greenlawn Cemetery. The loss of Indiana's most important architect in the nineteenth century went unreported in the local press because it was overshadowed by that of Abraham Lincoln.

---

* *The Hasselman House went down to make way for the Indianapolis Athletic Club. The enlarged pistil also appeared on the interior columns of the post office; Costigan was the contractor for that building, and redesigned parts of it; there is no evidence elsewhere that Ammi B. Young, its designer, was a lover of passionflowers, so this must have been Costigan's idea.*

452

CHAPTER 30

The American Picturesque

Now, THOUGH IT REQUIRES a little backtracking, it is time that we note, alongside the mansions and the sober little boxes and cubes of the American Classical vernacular, a more animated companion. It was the American Picturesque, which has been remarkably patient in awaiting its turn upon these pages. It has been there all along, receiving an occasional pat on the head, but not until the decade just before the Civil War was it strong enough to set the skylines of whole villages to dancing.

Subsequent scholars have tamed its antic motion and composed its jolly jumble into subcategories like the Gothic Revival or the Italian Revival or the Norman Revival. Yet, as the competition for the design of the Smithsonian Institution demonstrated in 1846, the architects of the Picturesque were unperturbed by purism. They were willing to hang window moldings and skylines "to suit," upon a number of stock floor plans, which made for informal living and beguiling crannies. The coat often was the same, however they may have changed neckties or the color of a pocket handkerchief.

What counted in the Picturesque was the general effect. Cultivated persons, softened in sensibilities and intrepid in taste, knew just how to feel when presented with a scene in a landscape painting or a landscape design. They had been instructed that architecture should seem to have "movement," rising and falling, approaching and receding, the way natural scenery seems to have movement when one passes it in a boat—on the River Wye or on the Susquehanna—or in a railway carriage. The Picturesque landscape designer knew that though engineering and horticulture might be science, they were to be deployed for emotional effect; he sought to engineer the emotions through the deployment of plants, of paints and of buildings.

453

Small environments were created on canvas, long before Mark Rothko painted ambience. Devotees of the Picturesque then proceeded to bring architecture into their endeavors, and included buildings as part of landscape, to enhance their effects. It would be a mistake, however, to think of them as doing so only in a sort of *fin de siècle* desire for experience, to swoon about in the psychedelia of natural stimuli. These artists are not mere aesthetes. They were born into an earnest and reforming generation. Architects, like painters and landscape designers, did not doubt the ability of man to make his environment, and thereby to improve himself. An elevating painting,* an ennobling landscape or an exalting environment could do a lot of good. Deploying skillful people to create pictures in three dimensions was to join in the work of improvement. Many Americans, even hard-bitten old Samuel Sloan, saw Art in moral terms. They were seeking to use architecture, as others had used art and horticulture, to tame men as well as nature.

Sam Sloan was willing to offer his clients any style of architecture they wanted. Some of them wanted the Picturesque; some clients always had. While our attention has been given largely to the Classical tradition in America, and to its origins in Palladio and the Dutch and English classicists (Part One) as it came to dominate American taste (Part Three) even in attenuated and adulterated form (Part Four), there always was another strain in American taste and psychology, just as there always was in European taste. It was not quite eradicated, not was it underground. It was always present, insisting that there was much to be said for the Middle Ages, for a little cheerful disorder, for the colors of earth, for asymmetry and indirection.

All the great architects who have done their turn in these pages tried their hand at this—shall we say anticlassical?—way of building, or if they did not, powerful persons among their contemporaries did. And in Minnesota, in 1862, another of their number showed how a man who might have been Haller Nutt's boon companion, but of another turn of mind, could be prompted to repudiate the architecture of reason and of subtle geometric experiment and turn, instead, to a wholehearted architecture of feeling and effect (oh, I know there will still be people who think Longwood is a Picturesque structure, too, but I have done my best to scotch that idea).

In Part Two we saw Classicism struggling against the persistence of late medieval forms, and pointed out that in a cold climate, where a merchant wished to store his merchandise above his living quarters, it made good sense to put the

---

* *The pictorial origins of the Picturesque were romantic landscapes. Reaching into the backgrounds of portraits by Titian (1477–1576), painters of the next century, Claude Lorrain (1600–82), Nicolas Poussin (1594–1665) and Salvator Rosa (1615–73) selected certain elements and then enlarged them, to create languid, elegiac landscapes, full of earthy greens and browns, under skies of alarming blue. These pictures contributed to architecture oddments of buildings which peeped out from the underbrush, or were descried in the haze upon a hill. The buildings that were not depicted in ruins were often seen as towered farmhouses, with rounded arches. These were villas of the imagination, seen as they might have been during the tranquil centuries of Roman rule, or as one could see them (by squinting a good deal) in the seventeenth-century Italian landscape.*

warehouse in the attic under a steep snow-shedding roof, and then, when one got rich, to ornament that triangular warehouse front with crockets and finials, with ogival curves or crow-steps or any other device that said "prosperous merchant" just as eloquently as a Palladian villa might carry a coat of arms in its pediment.

Snow falls not only on the rich. Steep roofs are desirable also for the poor. and cottages in all wood-building countries have ornamented the place where the steep roof stops and shelters the wall. Folk architecture anticipated the eighteenth- and nineteenth-century fashions in the Picturesque with carven tracery along eaves in playful imitation of nature, simulated wooden vines blending mankind's creations with nature's. These practices persisted in the Old and then the New World while Classicism was at its most earnest, calling attention to gables for other reasons than those associated with commerce. The structures upon which these folk traditions kept their strength also tended to sprawl informally, and the pleasures of such informality were periodically rediscovered by the self-conscious and artistic.

In Chapter Six we noted a group of transitional architectural forms between the fortified farmhouse and the vulnerable cottage or the open-armed Palladian villa. Among these was the cross-plan squire's house, which was common enough in England to be the model for the Washington family's Sulgrave, and reappeared in America at such places as Bacon's Castle, around 1660, and the Iron Monger's House. It was also, it seems, the form chosen by the Custis family for its Williams-burg headquarters, for in Chapter Four we observed General John Hartwell Cocke stating that he "copied from" that "well-remembered old six-chimney house" as well as from Bacon's Castle when in 1803 he began building Bremo Recess.

These forms were indeed well-remembered. They did not need to be revived; they were as continuous as those for building churches in the Gothic. (Such congregations as that of Trinity Church, in New York, started with Gothic in the seventeenth century and continuously rebuilt in Gothic through the nineteenth.)

The same thing had happened in England; while Inigo Jones was instructing the court of Charles I about the Palladian Renaissance, his strong-minded contemporary Sir Charles Cavendish was showing at Bolsover in Derbyshire, in 1612, that he preferred castles when they were no longer needed. All the great names of British Classicism, recited in Chapter Seven, except some of the rather humorless Palladians led by Lord Burlington, made forays into castle-building as part of a generally nostalgic relief from too much Classical order. A century after Bolsover, John Vanbrugh created a series of little castles; so did his partner Nicholas Hawksmoor, who designed Gothic buildings for Oxford University. So too did Robert Adam, whose castles are sometimes Gothic outside and Pompeiian within. Sir Christopher Wren designed Gothic churches, though he disliked doing so; Burlington's partner William Kent first tried his hand at the Gothic at Hampton Court, then at Gloucester Cathedral. Finally at Stow (as the enthusiastic Gothicist Robert Walpole exclaimed) Kent came to see nature as a garden.

That was the point. The English and then the Americans believed that nature could be cultivated, but some of them wanted it cultivated to appear more natural than when left to itself. Gardens, said the Picturesque landscapers, should be natural. Away with Frenchified, Baroque parterres! Demobilize their regiments of classical statuary! Soften all edges! Shroud all extremities! Let nature sweep all before her!

PIVOT POINT

Sweeping in behind nature, in the eighteenth century, came all manner of exoticism. It is entirely possible that the early mixing of Chinese and Gothic motifs occurred because the discovery of Chinese gardens by British and American travelers in the eighteenth century encouraged a new informality in gardening. The Chinese had set little pavilions in their gardens, and soon little Gothic temples (in Britain) or gazebos (in the provinces) began to appear. Thomas Jefferson and George Mason of Gunston Hall both used Chinese themes and a few pointed arches on the garden sides of their houses or in their gardens themselves.

The façades of their houses which faced the world, on the other hand, remained as severely Classical as the entrance front of Mount Vernon. George Washington kept his comfortable verandah to the rear. But that amazing man and his Virginia neighbors were experimenting with the Picturesque in their gardens because they were very sensitive to painting, to pictures. Painters passed along to these amateur architects an attitude toward the relationship of structure and landscape. The artist selected exactly those bushes and hillsides, copses and dales, flocks, herds and rivulets, towers, bays and walls he wanted. And so did landscape designers like Washington and Jefferson.

Washington was, it seems, the first American collector of landscape painting.

Sedgeley
Courtesy of the New-York Historical Society, New York City

He could not afford Gainsborough. He was a bit too old for Constable, or for the advent of the American Picturesque. But the walls of Mount Vernon were hung with landscape paintings he ordered. We are left to wonder what architecture he might have ordered had he been a decade younger when he returned home from his presidency, if he had lived as late into the Picturesque era as Thomas Jefferson.

There was something more intense than cool aesthetic pleasure expressed among those Americans of Jefferson's generation who built Picturesque houses. Antiquity is, as Palladio knew, comforting. Just a few generations of antiquity can be so; it takes the imagination of a man like Nicholas Biddle to feel oneself very close to Pericles. So romantics who leap shorter spans of time choose less ancient affinities. (This is quite a different phenomenon from the dogged clinging to the past among destabilized planters that we observed in Chapter Three. The Picturesque is not the architecture of alienation; it is something much more cheerful than that. It is closer to an architecture of association, as we shall see.)

It was not long after their revolution that Americans showed signs of wanting to demonstrate that everything was not new, that their new habitations had been within the landscape, not just lately dumped upon it. Houses could be made to look older than they were, acquiring the comfortable quality of antiquity. Probably that is why Cocke selected one well-remembered transition form, the cross-plan, in 1803; it was a link to the Middle Ages. Almost certainly that was why, four years earlier, the shady William Crammond had sought to buy instant respectability by commissioning Latrobe to design another transition form, the corner-turreted reduction of a form like Colbeck. His vaguely medieval house was called Sedgeley. It had the same rough configuration as Mulberry, or those plantation houses which William Jay found when he landed to take up his exile upon Mauritius (see Chapter Eleven).

There was apparently enough appetite for the Picturesque in the 1820's so that William Jay, reduced to building speculative houses to suit the popular taste, thought it wise to offer a Gothic villa (see Chapter Eleven), and by the 1830's many Americans had discovered the style. Some were reading those British novelists like Thomas Love Peacock and Horace Walpole, who had passed from a love of verdure to a love of compost, soliciting delicious gloom by sojourning in a "venerable family-mansion in a highly picturesque state of semi-dilapidation." Few, however, were so enraptured by the glories of dilapidation that they built ruins *de novo*, as did British lovers of the Picturesque.

By the 1840's there was in America equal enthusiasm for the Gothic and for the Picturesque in its more businesslike Italianate format, with comfortable rounded arches, rather than prickles and pinnacles, crockets and finials. Style was now transatlantic, and America was no longer a generation behind British fashion.* Travel was easier, and there were more people rich enough to travel, rich

---

* *The lead into the Italianate was given by the Prince Regent's architect, the protean John Nash. Nash imparted to the Picturesque a new set of contours when at Cronkhill in 1802 he produced an Italian villa out of*

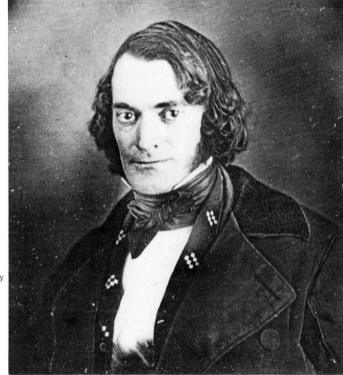

Andrew Jackson Downing
Frederick Law Olmstead Papers, courtesy of George B. Tatum

enough to buy architectural fashion-books, rich enough to be a little bored with the Classical.

It was not just that the Classical had been around for so long that clients were tiring of it; architects were uncertain they could squeeze many more variations out of its exhausted themes. James Dakin told the commissioners for the Louisiana State Capitol that he recommended the Picturesque in its Gothic guise, instead, because another exercise in "the Grecian or Roman order of architecture . . . would unavoidably appear to be a mere copy of some other Edifice already erected and often repeated in every city and town of our country."

The concept of one architect copying another brings us back again to Samuel Sloan and his unacknowledged mentor, John Notman—see Chapter Twenty-five. Notman, like any other architect of his time, could work in either the Classic or

---

a landscape by Claude. He showed the way to the Scottish horticulturist John Claudius Loudon (1783–1843), who became the first popular advocate of the Picturesque in Britain and America. Loudon began with an Encyclopedia of Agriculture, *in 1825, and proceeded to produce one on plants, in 1829, before publishing his enormously influential* Encyclopedia of Cottage, Farm and Villa Architecture and Furniture *in 1833. Nash had built, and Loudon written, just in time to catch the eyes of a growing class of suburban gentlemen of America.*

the Picturesque, but when he came to America from Edinburgh, he came as an evangelist for the latter.*

Edinburgh had grown classically first, in the hands of the brothers Adam and their successors. Then during its boom years, the 1820's, it turned to the Picturesque. The boom ended in bust, Edinburgh went bankrupt, and in 1833 Notman emigrated to the United States. He brought with him the seeds of the Scottish Picturesque and planted them almost immediately in the landscape design for Philadelphia's Laurel Hill Cemetery, which made his reputation.

Notman found reinforcement from his association with the equally passionate anticlassicists in New York, among whom was Calvert Vaux, whose views about the "passionless repose" of the Greek Revival we heard in Chapter Twenty-eight, and who thought as much in musical as in pictorial terms.† This circle of architects, literary men and horticulturalists had as their chief "composer" (that was his word for himself, by which he meant designer) Alexander Jackson Davis. Their publisher of "sheet music" for the public (to pursue Davis' metaphor) was the landscapist, architect and prolific author Andrew Jackson Downing.

The Psychology of the Picturesque

THESE MEN USED metaphors drawn from all the senses to encourage their clients to look at architecture in a new way, to see it, feel it, hear it, smell it, as it implied qualities about themselves that they wished to impart to the world. Throughout this book we have talked about the desire of the people who built houses to create an impression of character. In the 1830's this process of choosing style for effect became fully conscious in the generation of Orson Fowler (see Chapter Twenty-five); it was made articulate by architects as interested in psychology as in bricks or mortar.

Downing was their leader, the friend of Notman and the partner of Vaux. He spoke of "the expression of every house, as well as every face in the country." For the villa he said, "Whatever gives to the villa its best and truest expression of human sympathy and affection confers on it its highest and most lasting character of beauty." He was a horticulturalist who came to architecture through landscape. He spent his life working with living things, composing plants and trees for effect. He thought of houses as having the qualities of living things. Houses, he knew,

---

He had been trained by James Playfair, who was building Italianate villas in the suburbs of Edinburgh in the 1820's. Our evangelical friend John Claudius Loudon was there also. In Playfair's office was G. L. Meason, who made the Italianate the logical outcome of British associations of landscape painting, landscape design and architecture as landscape, in a book called On the Landscape Architecture of the Great Painters of Italy, *published in 1828.*

†*A propensity that continued in the Picturesque tradition through the time of Louis Sullivan.*

459

have faces. On their faces they have expressions. Smile, and people will think you are pleasant. Snarl, and they will not. Said Downing, in "the expression of every house" one can see "a spirit of frankness or reserve, a spirit of miserly care or kind hospitality, a spirit of meanness or generosity, a spirit of system or disorder, a spirit of peace or discord . . ."

PIVOT POINT

The Picturesque of Downing, however, could not be worn as a mask to misrepresent what lay behind it. It was to be used only by those prepared to make that "outward form . . . express our best ideal of life." We must select a true architecture. We must not erect a lie, for we will be found out if our house "is foreign to [our] habits, education, tastes and manners." We must not seem to be "wearing a court costume of some foreign ambassador." If, out of ambition, we build ourselves a castle, "unless there is something of the castle in the man . . . the real castle . . . [will be likely] to dwarf him to the stature of a mouse."

Among the Picturesque variations, Downing said, the Italianate, with the "tower and the campanile . . . every feature . . . indicates originality, boldness, energy, and variety of character." He is speaking of us! answered a chorus of

Andrew Jackson Downing's own house
Courtesy of the Library of Congress

Americans. Very well, replied Downing, then take to the suburbs and act accordingly. Remember, the conscience of the Picturesque will be watching, and if it find "a pretentious, shallow man in such a habitation" it will pronounce him to be a "jackdaw in the eagle's nest!" *

The advocates of the Picturesque, then, called for thoughtful men to take to the suburbs, where a villa might be placed amid "land . . . laid out as a pleasure ground . . . with a view to recreation and enjoyment, more than profit." † Downing suggested the Italian Picturesque to a person "of elegant culture and variety of accomplishment," such as a "retired citizen or man of the world." The style, he said, "expresses not wholly the spirit of country life nor of town life, but something . . . a mingling of both." Samuel Sloan, catching on rapidly, solicited for his version of the Italianate "a man of wealth, who wishes in a quiet way to enjoy his wealth. It speaks of him as a person of educated and refined tastes, who can appreciate the beautiful both in art and nature; who, accustomed to all the ease and luxury of a city life, is now enjoying the more pure and elevating pleasures of the country." The scores of Italianate villas that sprang up, from Detroit to Richmond, from Maine to Lake Washington, Mississippi, all implicitly wore large placards reading NO JACKDAWS HERE!

No one has yet stuck pins in the map to mark out the locations of all the Italianate villas of America,‡ but my impression is that the Italianate villa was predominantly a style associated with the new industrial managers of the Delaware Valley, the suburbs of New York, and the central and northern regions that were in active trade relations with these people. The architects chiefly associated with the style, Davis, Downing, Vaux, John Notman and Samuel Sloan, found nearly all their clients in those areas.§

Why was this so? These villas do not seem to have appealed so much to literary or artistic men as to active or recently retired factory managers, of the sort Thomas Cochran masterfully describes in his *Frontiers of Change*. We cannot reconstruct the individual motivations of them all, but we can let our imaginations play on the implications of this passage from a letter from Downing to Davis, now in New York's Metropolitan Museum of Art:

* Downing was willing to warn his countrymen against pretentiousness, but he would have no obsequiousness either. Cottages of the British fashion were, he said, "too inconsiderable" for our successful men, too "humble for the proper pride of republicans." We should be bold enough for villas.

† That required more than de Toqueville's famous "modest competence." It required, and manifested, riches, riches on the scale of those Washington Irving would slyly attribute to himself as he mock-mournfully complained: "I beat all the gentlemen farmers in my neighborhood, for I can manage to raise my vegetables and fruits at very little more than twice the market price." (Vernon Parrington, Main Currents in American Thought, vol. 1, p. 207.)

‡ In the way Wilbur Zelinsky put dots across the map of Georgia to locate Greek Revival houses. Zelinsky proved some interesting points about the relationship of that style to the urban, new-rich cotton planters of the Piedmont (see Chapter Twenty-two).

§ Henry William Cleaveland carried the style with him to California, remaining, like Notman, in touch with Downing and Vaux.

The American Picturesque

461

The bell turret . . . which stands where the buttress did before, helps the composition wonderfully—I would hang a bell in it and have a handle in the dining room. This bell would be very useful if the family wanted to call the proprietor from the manufacturing village below where he would be nearly all the time—and I think it would be in keeping for the owner of manufactures as maintaining the proper connection between residence and the dependencies— as de Tocqueville says that the great manufacturer is the feudal lord of modern times.

The villa style may have been so attractive to industrial managers because it was associated with the town, with the place of business. It was, of course, suburban, but, as that name implies, "under the sign of the city." It was not pretentious, but it was proud. It was, finally, to be constructed in materials and given colors that would hold up well in the polluted air of urbanizing America. It was as if the owner could smile with satisfaction on the smoke of his chimneys, without too much apprehension for the hues of his stucco. The same feelings were not so likely to be found within the white-temple owner next door. There, perhaps, lurked what was left of a real country gentleman, a squire whose acres were becoming occupied by the apparatus of improvement and progress.

Still, though the Italian villa style later may have become the chosen instrument of manufacturing proprietors, great and not-so-great, it did not begin, in America, with them. John Notman commenced his residential practice, and then introduced the villa, with more exotic clients.

Dunn and Doane

NATHAN DUNN WAS a China trader who spent a dozen years in the Orient and assembled there an enormous collection of Chinese sculpture and painting. He also acquired an affinity for Chinese landscape and architecture. Notman gave him a Chinese landscape and a "cottage" with a slight Chinese accent at Mount Holly, New Jersey, in 1837–38. Three years later Dunn had Notman design a museum for his collection, more than two hundred feet long, at Hyde Park Corner in London. The museum was entered through a copy of a Chinese summer house.

Near Mount Holly was Burlington, the residence of the very rich and very eccentric Bishop George Washington Doane, who once, it is said, had himself packaged as freight and shipped to New York to offer a lecture. He was a good hymn-writer ("Fling Out the Banner, Let It Float") and, in his own time, regarded as the model of a High Church bishop. He was, more to our purpose, a superb client for architects. He commissioned Richard Upjohn to produce one of America's most beautiful churches, St. Mary's, Burlington. He also gave Notman the opportunity to instate as an American art form the Italianate Picturesque, with a Scottish burr. Notman designed Doane's well-publicized villa called Riverside in 1839, and Doane was the first of many clients in the Princeton and Philadelphia

Riverside
Courtesy of the Burlington County Historical Society,
Burlington, New Jersey

Bishop George Washington Doane
Courtesy of the Historical Society
of Pennsylvania

463

regions to commission Picturesque Italian villas from Notman. The least scathed of them now serves as the Faculty Club at Princeton University.

Notman was a frequent loser to Sloan in the infighting for commissions in the Philadelphia area. From the outset, however, his designs reached a public beyond that area in the publications of Downing, who, though he worked closely with Davis, regarded Notman as a welcome ally, not as a dangerous competitor, in the battle against the Classic Revivals in the cause of the Picturesque.

Chivalry

THIS CHAPTER HAS BEEN as tortuous in its time scheme as a Gothic novel, and its characters, though real, as improbable. We are now ready to present the culmination of all these tales, in a great Picturesque house with ornamented gables, a floor plan distantly reminiscent of the old cross-plan, based on a design by Downing which owed a great deal to the instruction of Notman. It was the creation of a literary gentleman, and he would not wish us to enter his front door until we go back, one last time, to literature.

In the years before the Civil War, the Picturesque was often seen as the architecture of chivalry, and there was an association between the architecture of chivalry and the literature of chivalry that lasted until chivalry died, face down in the mud, in the lines before Petersburg in 1865.

James Renwick, Sr., an engineer and father of a third paladin of the style, very early made that association. Renwick, Sr., had made a walking tour of England in the company of his good friend Washington Irving in 1815. He had already recommended to Columbia University that it rebuild itself in the Gothic; he and Irving confirmed their prejudices by on-the-spot inspections of the ancient monuments of Britain, sketching as they went.

Sir Walter Scott populated those monuments, from Kenilworth to Land's End, with imaginary garrisons—the names of his characters are far more familiar than the names history gives to those who actually built them—and he was then building his own castle, in the Gothic style, at Abbotsford. It was to become a four-star "worth a journey" attraction to all the "bold" but "refined," "original" but "tasteful" people of America who could afford the voyage. If my uncomputerized hunch is correct, these tended to be a somewhat more literary crowd than the industrial managers who were drawn to the Italianate version of the Picturesque. After they returned, many emulated the contours of Abbotsford, though none could afford to emulate its genuinely baronial scale.

Irving made a Dutch-Gothic amalgam for himself at Sunnyside.* James Fen-

---

* *Irving was a friend and fellow traveler, as well, of William Jay's kinsman, the cotton-broker turned preacher Robert Bolton, who, with Irving's encouragement, built a Downingesque miniature of Abbotsford (but still a very large house) in Pelham, New York.*

Abbotsford
Courtesy of the British Tourist Authority

imore Cooper returned from Abbotsford to Gothicize his ancestral hall at Cooperstown, New York—see Chapter Twelve. Robert Gilmor of Baltimore, whom
we met a little earlier, made the pilgrimage to Abbotsford after his graduation
from Harvard in 1828. He returned to commission Davis to build Glen Ellen,
surrounded by two thousand acres of grounds for "recreation . . . not for profit,"
as he could afford to do. When he retired, he added a brand new Gothic ruin.*

* *His father was a Scottish trader who was a confidant of Nicholas Biddle's, and grew so rich and shrewd
that Latrobe used him as an example of the sort of man who could not be pushed around as some of his Baltimore
clients sought to push Latrobe.*

Glen Ellen, the castle at Loch Raven
Courtesy of the Peale Museum, Baltimore, Md.

Glen Ellen and Notman's villas were among a score or more designs that the books of Andrew Jackson Downing put at the disposal of Americans of literary tastes. Many of them did have the qualifications he recommended: sufficient if not ample means, boldness and originality. Among those who qualified on every count was William Gates LeDuc.

466

CHAPTER 31

Minnesota Gothic

The Place

WHEN WILLIAM GATES LEDUC first went there in 1850, Minnesota was at the edge of things. To find him we must find it, at the end of the reach of the Old Northwest, only partially included in the original domain of the United States, known merely for its interminable mosquito-ridden swamps, its furs and its bad weather. The upper Mississippi River had been of so little interest to the British in the Colonial period that they omitted it from the territory covered by the Quebec Act. Lord Ashburton, as late as 1842, thought the salient of land between the Pigeon River and Lake Superior (an arrowhead later found to be largely composed of iron ores) was of "little importance" to either the United States or Great Britain, and abandoned it to Daniel Webster for map-making convenience.

The source of the Mississippi lies within what has always been a frontier—a borderland. Before men came into the region, two frontiers intersected there, as they intersect today. One straggles vaguely north and south, green against brown as the pinelands strike the prairie. The empire of the pine was the St. Lawrence watershed, extending into central Minnesota and an area covering the northern curlings of the Mississippi. Between it and the open grassland there was an intermediate zone of hardwood clumps, which ended on the shore of the vast dry lake bed that has become the Red River Valley, where the wind has to contend with only a few bedraggled cottonwoods.

East and west lies another ancient transition zone, between the deep brown soil of the central valley and the rock, swamp and muskeg of the arctic littoral. In northern Minnesota farms and pastures abandon their effort, leaving the scene to wolves, moose and migrating birds. It was not until the middle of the nineteenth century that the agricultural frontier was recognized to lie as far north as that— Prairie du Chien, in southwestern Wisconsin, was believed to be the farthest

467

possible outpost of farmers. Though the country was gentle in contour and well provided with water, it was also cold, distant and exposed to a vicious wind, and few were willing to predict that it would be hospitable to masses of settlers.

The People

AT THE BEGINNING of the sixteenth century, streams of explorers, exploiters and settlers went out of Europe into the Americas, Africa and Australia. There they created new Europes in which the aborigines were either assimilated, penned into reservations or eradicated. To the middle of North America, after it had been crossed by exploration from the east and the south, there came a rush of land-hungry farmers. They devoured the area in chunks. The census statistics show a surprisingly orderly pattern of occupation, state by state, decade by decade. The great surges came in sequence:

	1800	1810	1820	1830	1840	1850	1860
OHIO	45,000	231,000					
INDIANA		24,000	147,000				
ILLINOIS			55,000	157,000			
WISCONSIN					31,000	305,000	
MINNESOTA						6,000	169,000

That tide of emigration was not, of course, composed of identical droplets. In fact, its coloration was remarkably different in Wisconsin and Minnesota from what it had been in Illinois or especially in Indiana. Architecturally, however, by 1850 the qualities of the South and the North were already coming together to compose the beginnings of a western style. A few galleried cottages appeared as far north as Frontenac, Minnesota, showing that plantation owners had gone that far to hunt, despite the chill. The most elaborate of these cottages, St. Hubert's Lodge, was built in 1856 by Israel Garrard, the son of a governor of Kentucky.

Cottages like St. Hubert's Lodge were part of a galleried vernacular community that had been established by the advance of Europe across the Atlantic into the Caribbean and the Gulf, and up the Mississippi, where it had met another advancing column of invasion out of the St. Lawrence, up the Great Lakes, south along the ancient portage route of the St. Croix, to the great river itself. Both the southern and northern prongs of this advance, as they joined in Minnesota, were under the command of the French. French soldiers settled into the region, not bothering to conquer it. As they enjoyed its fruits of fur and fish and freedom from the inhibitions of the central administration in Paris, they built galleried houses. St. Louis, the capital of the inland empire under both the French and their Anglo-American successors, saw the fullest development of a double-galleried

St. Hubert's Lodge, Frontenac, Minnesota
Courtesy of Frontenac State Park

*Minnesota
Gothic*

style appropriate to a continental, rather than a Caribbean, climate: stone mansions arose there, built by great fur-trading families like John Jacob Astor's partners, the Chouteaux.

By the time the galleried style reached Minnesota, it was no longer southern. It had become western. Even former New Englanders attached two floors of "porches," or verandahs, to their white-painted frame houses along the St. Croix. An older, and persistently southern, vernacular appeared in red-brick houses, which composed whole towns like Galena, Illinois, and portions of river ports as far north as Red Wing, Minnesota. But the true southern influence petered out as settlement pressed into the subarctic regions of Minnesota and Wisconsin.

The northernmost expression of southern sentiment was felt in Minnesota during the tenure of Willis A. Gorman as President Franklin Pierce's territorial governor of Minnesota. One morning in 1853, Gorman, who had been a Kentucky legislator and a proslavery congressman from Indiana, appeared at the offices of a Democratic newspaper in St. Paul, whose editor, Thomas M. Newson,* had had the temerity to print an antislavery editorial. Tapping the gold head of his cane in the palm of his hand, Gorman proclaimed, "Well, sir, by God, sir, you have ruined the Democratic party, sir!" Unfolding the leaves of a "great book," he proceeded to give Newson a lecture on the virtues of slavery.

Gorman would have been quite at home in the settlements around the lead mines in northwestern Illinois or southwestern Wisconsin; in St. Paul he had little

* *The editor grew to be a major in the Civil War and a historian.*

469

effect, and on the issue of slavery would have been hopelessly outvoted by the Yankee majorities then accumulating in the Wisconsin and Minnesota legislatures. New England settlement had swept into northern Illinois and Indiana and flooded into the region of the pines and oak-openings as far west as the Mississippi and the Minnesota. Yankees had been pulled there by cheap land, pushed out of their homes by the pressure of unemployable populations and by a sort of latter-day enclosure movement. In Vermont, especially, sheep-raising had been consolidated into the hands of a few large producers.

The railroad, of course, made the passage easier, but even before Yankee migrations took to the rails, a newer New England was rising in the West. Both the senators and all but two of the representatives Wisconsin sent to the Forty-second Congress were from northern New England. In Wisconsin's Constitutional Convention, in 1846, half the forty-two members of New England birth were from Vermont alone. Another thirty percent came from New York, where their home counties had a heavy New England base. Only ten were from all the states of the south and south central sections, according to the computations of Frederick Jackson Turner. Turner did not carry his detailed inquiry into emigration into Minnesota, but my own checking of biographies of prominent local figures listed by such writers as Major Newson leads to the view that Minnesota in 1860 had a population derived from very much the same sources as Wisconsin's a decade earlier; a quick check of these figures against those for Indiana, in Chapter Twenty-eight, shows that Minnesota's North-South nativity distribution (where its citizens were born) was almost the polar opposite of Indiana's.

There were architectural and political consequences of these demographics. The Classic Revival in architecture reached Wisconsin and Minnesota along the northern emigration route, as it was expiring in the older states. Towns like Racine and Kenosha, Taylors Falls and St. Croix Falls, grew into clusters of white houses with classical trim, some with porticoes set over their doorways. These rectangular, gabled houses, nearly always of white-painted wood, are not at all like the brick cubes, most often with hipped roofs, favored in towns of southern derivation, though the architectural products of the Yankee strain of settlement and those marking the emigration from the South and the Middle Atlantic states were affected, of course, by the architecture of the alluvial culture that preceded them. That culture was French, and it looked for cultural guidance to St. Louis and then, further on, to New Orleans, where many of the chief citizens dwelt in galleried houses.

The northern emigrants also carried with them a much broader sympathy for the Picturesque than could be found in the South. This is a little odd, on the face of it, for it was in the South that the cult of chivalry flourished, with its jousting and its juleps, its ladies fair and its double standard, its propensity for plumes and poses. But the Gothic is, after all, a northern style—steep roofs shed snow; castles look best perched upon crags along the Hudson, not on loess hillocks beside bayous. The Picturesque in America added verandahs before it did in England,

470

but even with a verandah a Gothic Revival house of stone can be very hot in summer.*

In any case, in the farthest reaches of the Old Northwest, little Picturesque cottages, the white shoe-box houses of New England and the brick cubes of Maryland and Virginia, acquired the galleries of the interior alluvial culture as they settled comfortably into what we now call the Middle West. From the perspective of Boston, that region was, I suppose, ultima Thule.

William Gates LeDuc

WILLIAM GATES LeDUC was sure it was not to remain so. He believed that the sons of New England were the truest Americans, Americans the truest humans, and Minnesota the place to which the best of New England must emigrate.

It was one of his proudest recollections that he acclerated that emigration by a series of promotion stunts culminating with the presentation of a bull bison to the New York Crystal Palace Exhibition of 1853. The adventures of the bison and its custodian on the streets of the city attracted much attention to his display of the natural riches of the territory of Minnesota. He believed that attention (and the convenience provided by the railroads he also promoted) led to "the movement of immigration . . . a large proportion" of which was composed of "men and women educated in the common and high school, speaking our language, familiar with our forms of government, exemplary in their morals, with sound minds and sound bodies." He was grateful for "the editorial approval of Horace Greeley," which he eagerly solicited. It was Greeley who endorsed the view that "no part of the West is receiving a more intelligent or valuable class of immigrants than Minnesota. The climate is the delight of the New Englander . . ."

LeDuc's chauvinism, redeemed by his good humor, had interesting consequences, most of which appeared after the Civil War and therefore are properly beyond our scope. But he is an irresistible character, and three short stories from that period of his life may be related here, because they bear upon his efforts to make American agriculture, especially that of remote, chilly Minnesota, self-sufficient.

He did not approve of the propensity of Americans to import gastronomic delicacies such as wine, tea and, appropriately enough for a scion of the West Indies trade, sugar. The blueberry bogs of northern Minnesota might seem a most unprepossessing place to compete with Burgundy and Bordeaux, but not to a man of LeDuc's temper. He tried to persuade his countrymen to switch to blueberry wine during the 1850's. They disappointed him.

Twenty years later, as commissioner of agriculture under President Hayes,

---

* There were a few Gothic Revival cottages built in the South, especially in the Tombigbee watershed, where the Waverley novels had a devoted following.

he tried again, this time to encourage domestic production of tea and sweeteners. The tea importers' lobby tried to make him out to be a fool, stimulating the press to barrage him with "abuse and ridicule." He persisted. His first real encouragement came from a Scottish teagrower who was passing through Washington on his way to plantations in India. He told LeDuc he was on the right track, and LeDuc responded by asking his help in reconnoitering the devastated South to find "the proper place for a government tea-garden."

The search produced an appropriate site in South Carolina at Sommerville, one of the burnt-out plantations belonging to Henry Middleton, an "unconverted rebel" of the family that had also lost the buildings at Middleton Place to the depredations of General William T. Sherman.

It happened that LeDuc's business card carried his title, General. When he called on Middleton in Charleston, to try to purchase Sommerville, he had the ill luck to present that card. Fortunately it did not say what kind of general he was—he had been quartermaster to Sherman. Middleton was chilly enough, saying he had no land to sell to any Yankee general. LeDuc responded with elaborate courtesy, noting that Middletons had signed the Declaration of Independence and that

William Gates LeDuc

Haas Brothers photo, courtesy of the Minnesota Historical Society

LeDuc was representing the government that the Declaration established, not the army. He noted as well that "the South, ruined by the war, is relying on one crop, cotton, and getting poorer" while LeDuc was trying to "turn the twelve million dollars we are now sending abroad to other farmers into the hands of southern farmers."

Middleton relented. He would sell no land, as he had said. But he would lease it for twenty years—for a dollar. LeDuc paid the dollar; he had it cast specially as a presidential silver medal with a head of George Washington on one side and a suitable inscription on the other.

LeDuc had two other opportunities to treat with southern planters, in association with his quest for American self-sufficiency and agricultural progress. After the Civil War, Louisiana sugar planters, who were accustomed to organizing their production with regiments of slaves and were capital-short, complained they could not raise crops with free laborers, and in 1878 or 1879 a delegation came to visit LeDuc, led by Duncan Kenner, master of Belle Helene plantation and formerly minister plenipotentiary of the Confederate government to the states of Europe. Very courteously LeDuc welcomed them. He gave them some samples of corn-sugar sorghum to taste and exhorted them to experiment with enlarging their single-crop cane production by growing corn for sorghum. "We are importing between one and two million dollars worth of sugar annually, raised by farmers of other countries," he told them; we should grow our own. He had learned that even in Minnesota, good sweeteners could be made from corn syrup. LeDuc, more than any other American, developed the beet-sugar industry, though he had to acknowledge in his old age that his country was still importing sugar, instead of using a product "made at home where it should be."

The career of William Gates LeDuc also included wartime service as attorney for William G. Harding, master of Belle Grove, the only house in Middle Tennessee that could compete with Adelicia Franklin's Belmont. The contretemps occurred while Mrs. Franklin (by then Mrs. Acklen) was engaged in her profitable prestidigitation with the cotton crops of 1863 and 1864 (see Chapter Twenty). LeDuc was one of the commanders of the Union forces occupying Nashville. Harding was beleaguered by Union supporters who coveted the three hundred Angora goats, the herds of bison, elk, deer and especially the fine horses Harding kept in the paddocks and pastures around his house.

LeDuc was outraged at the intention of the provost marshal to pillage the place. He was a lawyer and accepted Harding as a private client, drawing up a declaration that the master of Belle Grove had been "a loyal citizen since the time General Buell . . . advanced and took possession of Nashville." The region could "ill afford to lose either the products or the example of the farmer who remains quietly at home in the steady and peaceful pursuit of his vocation." Surely, when "the rebel army is driven from the state" the government would wish other farmers (even, perhaps, those without bison, elk, deer or Angora goats) to "return to their homes and remain peacefully on their farms."

The provost marshal relented. Harding offered to pay LeDuc for his services as attorney, but it seemed more appropriate for him merely to make a gift of two Angoras of opposite sexes, which were sent to Ohio and kept for LeDuc's return from military service. They produced a "flock of sixteen beautiful, white, long silky-haired goats."

LeDuc hoped for a new kind of livestock, to be grown on Minnesota's farms, which could produce the material for native cloths.* But though Angoras are beautiful, they are not easily domesticated. And they are ravenous. On LeDuc's farm at Hastings they "refused to be satisfied with the grass of my pasture," and destroyed the trees of his orchard. They were lent to a farmer who wished to use them for the service for which nature designed them—clearing brush, a task now performed by a mechanical "brush-hog." They did that well, it seems, but they also multiplied, and ate everything else available. The farmer presented them back to LeDuc, who turned them over "to a Swede, who, I suppose, ate them."

Enough of these preliminaries. Let us start with William Gates LeDuc, at his beginning.

This was a variation of the dream of his predecessor G. W. P. Custis, chief advocate of the creation of a U.S. Agricultural Commission. Custis had high hopes for his sheep and for the homespun cloth to be made of native wool—see Chapter Thirteen.

CHAPTER 32

The Career of
William Gates LeDuc

THE WEST INDIES, which have figured so prominently in our tale, must, of course, reappear in this final chapter. William Gates LeDuc took his last name from his grandfather, a refugee from the slave revolts in the French islands, who came to Connecticut and married into an old Yankee family. We would know more about him had not his wife destroyed his papers, fearing that more knowledge might induce other members of the family to seek to recover his lost possessions in the islands—two of her brothers had died in the West Indies trade.

Other French and West Indian refugees had created a little colony they called "Gallipolis" on the Ohio River, and the LeDucs joined them, settling twenty miles farther north, in Wilkesville, where William was born in 1823. He was named for an uncle who had fought beside James Lanier's father (see Chapter Twenty-nine) in William Henry Harrison's 1812 campaign.

While the West Indian grandfather had sufficient resources to build a "brick box" with a center hall in Wilkesville, his son, William's father, brought his family up in a "dog trot" log cabin deeper in the wilderness, in Amesville, Ohio. William was taken to Lancaster for schooling, where he became a friend of William Tecumseh Sherman, whose middle name marked the triumph of William Henry Harrison over the Indians. (Sherman was known as "Cump" to LeDuc, then and later during his service in the Civil War.)

Though he started life in a log cabin, William G. LeDuc had no intention of being a horny-handed son of toil. That sort of life "was not attractive to my parents or to any of their children." Agriculture was one thing; drudgery was another. LeDuc aspired to be able to afford scientific agriculture, in the high-minded, gentlemanly way of G. W. P. Custis or Nicholas Biddle. He saw cultivated fields *475*

as a gentleman might, as Andrew Jackson Downing did, "as a pleasure ground
. . . with a view to recreation and enjoyment, more than profit." Of course, such
a stately view of things required that one become rich.

PIVOT POINT

Very early, then, William LeDuc set himself to rise above the level of subsistence farming. After his schooling in Lancaster, he worked long enough as a
farmer, school-book salesman, storekeeper and itinerant teacher (in rural Mississippi) to pay for his entry into Kenyon College* and for enough legal studies to be
admitted to the bar—though not in Ohio. He charmed the authorities there, and
they acknowledged that he had, as he said, "read law." But they perceived that he
had read only enough of it to "practice in a new territory."

That is what he wanted, anyway. After exploring Tennessee, Missouri, Iowa
and Illinois, he asked a cousin: "Where shall I go, John? I want to be on the
frontier somewhere," and took that cousin's advice to head up the Mississippi to
Minnesota Territory, in 1850.

He set himself up as a lawyer. As did James Lanier, LeDuc discerned a special
opportunity associated with a territorial legislature. Lanier had found a dearth of
expertise in legislative procedure. In the capital of Minnesota, a village many
people still called Pig's Eye, LeDuc noted dearths not only of people who could
write but also of things to write with and on. He opened a stationery shop and
then a bookstore. (His books were more often sold for prizes in card games among
the legislature than for the delectation of persons who, like LeDuc, could read and
write Greek—or English.) Next he brought in a limited line of pianos, and issued
an "Annual," in which he chronicled local events and enjoyed "giving names to
some localities," like the Minnesota River, which had previously been drably
named for his friend Joseph R. Brown (who did not seem to mind.)

He and Brown were fellow entrepreneurs. Major Thomas Newson, the young
editor Willis Gorman had tried to terrorize, described LeDuc as "a tall, quick,
active man, with positive convictions, fertile in expedients, with a restless brain
and unbounded energy." By the 1850's LeDuc could afford a little frame house in
Pig's Eye—or, as it was renamed, St. Paul—with some Gothic trim and a yard
"for recreation and pleasure." There he and Brown hatched a hundred expedients.
They got a legislative charter to put Mississippi River water in barrels to sell to
the people of St. Paul. LeDuc's crucial role in the development of the modern
typewriter (which has to be relegated here to a footnote because it is debatable and
had its impact after the Civil War) may have begun at this time.† Certainly it was
in the 1850's that Brown began tinkering with a steam automobile. He actually
produced what he called a "steam-wagon," which looked something like a steam-
roller. It ran a little distance and then reposed, rusting, upon the prairie.

* At Kenyon the most important building had been completed in 1829 in the "English Gothic." The Gothic
was popular in Ohio very early and enjoyed a continuing run along the Ohio and Mississippi for fifty years.

† LeDuc was very proud that he introduced to the government service, and thus to all bureaucracies, the
use of the typewriter. That much is beyond dispute. He may also have made a critically important suggestion for

LeDuc's interest in prairie agriculture only developed, apparently, when he had become sufficiently comfortable not to fear having to be a farmer. In 1853 he also conveyed to New York, along with the bison, the seeds grown by "a small colony of Yankees who had settled on some fertile lands a few miles above the junction of the St. Croix with the Mississippi."* They had demonstrated that wheat, among other crops, could be grown "with great success and profit" even in Minnesota.

This was no small discovery. It was contrary to the prejudices of those who believed the prairie good only for the browsing of animals. A hundred thousand emigrants proved that little colony of Yankees to be right, then two hundred thousand, then more. About 1880 a group of English agriculturalists called upon LeDuc in Washington, on their way to explore the headwaters of the flood of wheat which had so poured into the English market from the American Midwest that it was a prime cause of the British agricultural depression of the 1870's. (That depression can be graphed quite precisely, because the fall in the price of British-grown grain kept pace with the decline in the frequency of the building of English country houses.)

Haller Nutt and William Gates LeDuc both started houses on the brink of the Civil War. LeDuc was luckier. He lived to complete his, and to enjoy it until his death in 1917.

The resources that went into it were derived from its setting, one of the town-sites that LeDuc promoted and exploited.† He and a group of friends were always plotting a new town-site, each more glamorous than the last. Major Newson joined in the game: "Everybody went into the business . . . procuring acres and laying

---

the design of the modern typewriter, though there is no more acrimonious subject of dispute among historians of technology than the origin of that machine. We are told that his interest in the invention of a typewriter dated back to 1850. In 1867 he visited the saintly tinkerer Christopher Latham Sholes in Milwaukee. Sholes was working with Carlos Glidden on a book-paging machine. Glidden's real interest was in a mechanical spader to replace a plow, and not in typewriters, but he is said by some to be the hero of the occasion, rather than LeDuc. Perhaps it was the search for a spader that took LeDuc, an irrepressible agricultural experimenter, to Milwaukee. In any case, somebody suggested to Sholes that "a machine be made that will write letters and words and not figures only." Some authors say it was a chance remark by Glidden. LeDuc said it was his idea, and on other matters LeDuc (who, in his eighty-fourth year, wrote his memoirs on the Remington machine that was the outcome of all this) was a remarkably precise and accurate witness.

* Those Yankee colonists were experimenting on lands occupied by the Sioux and Chippewa. It was never altogether clear which, for the Indians were constantly at war with each other. LeDuc himself witnessed a skirmish between the two tribes in the streets of St. Paul.

† He tried his hand repeatedly at promoting railroads as well, but without conspicuous success. Soon after he arrived in St. Paul, he drew a charter for the first Minnesota railroad, the Lake Superior and Mississippi Road (to run north and south, as had Lanier's from Lake Michigan to the Ohio). After the war, he organized the Hastings, Minnesota and Red River of the North Railroad, to run east and west, with the new axis of transportation. He also tried mining in Utah, and his milling ventures made him, it is said, the first to market flour from Minnesota spring wheat. Neither railroads nor milling nor mining made him very rich, however. It was real-estate speculation that kept him going.

them out into cities . . . On paper these cities (there were no towns) looked elegantly . . . with their court house squares, and parks, and churches, and school houses and steamboats, and railroad trains, and though their lots were located in marshes and in many cases in water, yet that, unknown to the purchasers, did not prevent the ignorant from buying, and so the wave rolled on, gaining force and carrying with it good honest men, as well as bad men and robbers."

In January 1857 St. Paul had a population of six thousand; by October it had nearly ten thousand. In the previous year LeDuc had consolidated holdings in the town-site of Hastings, a few miles down the Mississippi, which he had, in part, acquired in payment of a legal fee for protecting one speculator against another. Lots were going very well. So was his flour mill, and his legal business, and his stationery business with its sidelines in books and pianos. So were all the civilizing influences that he brought to the frontier.

Then in 1857, "all of a sudden, like lightning from a clear sky, a great financial wave broke over the country, and down went almost everybody, especially those who had dealt extensively in real estate. They became land-poor."

LeDuc survived, barely, though many of his friends, including the bankers of St. Paul, went bankrupt. Their paper promises were valueless. The economy returned to barter as what little gold or silver there had been in circulation "was seized and hoarded up." It was a grim time. Those who had escaped from the drudgery of farming found little comfort in a newspaperman's injunction that they should cease their speculations in real estate and "turn their attention to the cultivation of the soil."

William LeDuc was ever hopeful, though, ever resourceful, and he began when his fortunes were low to plan for a country villa that would be appropriate for himself when the time came again for him to be "a retired gentleman of cultivated tastes." In 1855 the editor of the St. Anthony *Express** had lamented the "striking want" of houses expressing such tastes. Fortunately, Mrs. William G. LeDuc was on hand to set a better tone, assisted by one of Andrew Jackson Downing's books from her husband's bookstore.

Mrs. LeDuc, like Mrs. Haller Nutt, was a strong-minded lady. William had met her at Kenyon, the seat of Ohio Gothicism. She liked the plan of the Gothic villa that was Downing's frontispiece and traced it, against a window to reverse it, on the back side of the paper (she had lived long enough in Minnesota to want all the light she could get in the dining room, which Downing, unaccountably, had put on the north side.)

Minnesota's economy improved from 1858 to 1861, and the LeDucs were ready to start their house. Then the South Carolina militia fired on Fort Sumter. LeDuc's responsibilities to the nation were clear to him. He was a skilled storekeeper and lawyer; if men like Lanier, in their sixties, could finance the war, men

---

St. Anthony was the next town upriver from Fort Snelling, which, in turn, was just upriver from St. Paul. St. Anthony became Minneapolis somewhat later.

Mary LeDuc
Courtesy of the Minnesota Historical Society

in their forties, like LeDuc, could manage it. LeDuc sold his mills, hired an overseer for his farmlands, packed off his family to their relatives in Ohio and volunteered for the Quartermaster Corps. He also selected contractors to get to work on his house. Like so many others, he thought the war would soon be over.

Though the contractors began clearing the site in 1862, neither their work nor the war went well. The Union forces in the West had been frustrated in their efforts to take Vicksburg, and their forces in the East had been defeated at Fredericksburg with terrible losses. Back in Minnesota, 1862 had been the year of the great Sioux outbreak. The Indians had burnt out New Ulm, not far up the Minnesota River, and driven back the frontier a hundred miles. They came very close to Hastings; venturing onto the prairie from LeDuc's building site was perilous. In January 1863 LeDuc, at the front, learned that his contractor at Hastings had disappeared. His wife, Mary, told the children, "Our house will have to stand over until Papa is out of the army." LeDuc refused to acquiesce: he was filling his evenings, as the rain beat upon his tent and he dried out his boots, with thoughts of "Calliero Silks, dressy trinkets" for his wife, "furniture and China and Carpets and lastly Books and Pictures for our new house that is to be as we hope . . . a house we will have or try to have when . . . the war is over." In February 1863 he asked "Fighting Joe" Hooker, his commander, for thirty days to straighten things out at home.

He found a new supervisor, a young master carpenter named Eric Cogshall, *479*

Gothic villa by Andrew Jackson Downing   *Courtesy of the Library of Congress*

and after LeDuc went back to war, Cogshall took over. He had LeDuc's plans checked with a second architect and concluded that he would have to act as the real architect himself: "no mechanic could build from them unless he went altogether upon his own judgement." (Downing had provided only a sketch of the plan and elevation.) On his instructions, and on payment of $20 from LeDuc, a new set of plans was drawn and construction started. LeDuc was dreaming of silks and books and pictures; Mary reported herself sitting and sewing and thinking "of the happiness we will enjoy when we are once more in our own house." And what a house! "As the children say, do you suppose anybody ever thought more of having a pretty house—'with a tower,' adds Willie."

In September LeDuc gave his commanding general good reason to be glad his quartermaster was a man who could not only dream but act. "Fighting Joe" had led his Union forces in a characteristically dashing raid into the heart of Confederate Tennessee. They had seized Chattanooga, but now, with winter coming on, fifty thousand of them sat there trapped, low on rations and isolated, for the Rebel troops held the heights on both sides of the river, which was the only route over which their supplies could reach them through the mountainous and flooded terrain. Nobody but LeDuc, apparently, knew how to build and navigate a riverboat powerful enough to work its way upstream against the mountain current.

LeDuc himself reported his experience was a little sketchy: "I had once owned a fourth interest in a steamboat, and fooled away considerable money and time on her." But he took over the construction of a 150-foot scow with a steam engine compiled of parts from local factories, rescued the boat from a flood, fired the

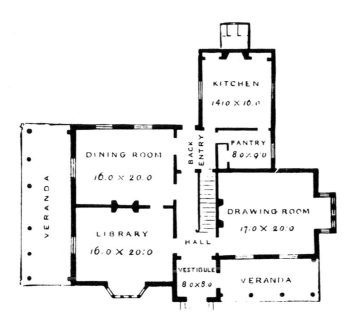

Plan of Downing's Gothic villa
Courtesy of the Library of Congress

army's pilot "as he was ignorant of river boats or navigation, could not steer, and knew nothing of . . . signals," and himself took the wheel on the first crazy journey upriver, in a black night. Navigation depended not so much on maritime experience as on his knowledge of "Southern patois" and of the complex politics of Tennessee soldiers (some of whom fought for each side). When watchfires were

LeDuc House under
construction

*Courtesy of the Minnesota
Historical Society*

spotted, he would call out, and by sorting out the speech patterns of the answers he was able to find his goal.

Forty thousand rations and 39,000 pounds of forage were landed in the morning, to provide for an army which had "half a breakfast ration" left and which had made three days' rations of four cakes of hard bread and a quarter pound of pork. "The soldiers," LeDuc reported, "were jubilant, and cheering 'The Cracker line open . . . three cheers for the Cracker line' as if we had won another victory; and we had." They went on to seize the heights of Lookout Mountain in the "Battle Above the Clouds," fighting on full rations and a sense that nothing was impossible.

In Minnesota, however, things had not gone so well. Though LeDuc's old real-estate partner, General Henry Hastings Sibley, had driven the Sioux across the Red River into Dakota Territory, strikes and shortages of everything from ox-teams to shingles had driven up prices in Minnesota even beyond the rocketing pace of national inflation, and the unanticipated costs were also driving up LeDuc's anxieties. He knew Cogshall had done wonders. The young man, though barely literate, had developed everything necessary for specifications, with little aid from the apparently distracted or inept local architects; he had kept on going, he told LeDuc, despite the fact that he had "never had as unplesant a job in my life and the house has been built without masons or stone cutters." The walls and roof of the house were in place. Somehow LeDuc had to find the money.

Unlike Haller Nutt, LeDuc had no reserves stashed away in Paris or London, and no reserves behind him. He hoped "some lots can be sold" (the frontiersman's first hope) and "that the wheat crop will turn out well" (the second). Mary knew what was coming: "I will not go into debt to anyone," she wrote. "I am going to be careful and spend as little as I can."

LeDuc responded that "I will have to borrow . . . and rely upon a good crop of wheat to pay it. You may be sure I don't like to do it at all but see nothing else for it unless I stop the house & that [he said in the same tones as Haller Nutt] is not good policy." Mary was "anxious and troubled about our expenses and the borrowing of Money in Hastings," but she was not one to flag in the race so late. She gave her assent: "It can't be helped now. If we could only be together there all these cares would be lighter." LeDuc, in the middle of the battles for Tennessee, reached out for her hand, saying, "All the use I have for what money I earn is for yourself and the children first, the home secondly, and my own expenses." And then, as Nutt had done, he turned his face to the wind and went ahead: "It will take everything to push forward the house as fast as I desire & then to furnish it properly . . . Money is nothing, enjoyment of life is everything. Money only is accessory."

Cogshall traded the use of some of LeDuc's land for a lime-kiln to supply the lime he needed; he traded more land for labor, which was short in wartime. Wages escalated. Logs lay unmilled in the north, because a drought in the summer of 1863 meant that rafts could not be floated down the shallow rivers to the mills. The "ornamented shingles" LeDuc had wanted were even scarcer than lumber, and Cogshall wrote advising him to settle for plain ones because "it is quite a job to ornamint so large a roof and I think shingles ornaminted is to[o] Dutchy." So much for "Rhineland Gothic"!

A few things other than "Dutchy" shingles had to be simplified. Haller Nutt's marble fireplaces from France never reached him; William LeDuc's were never ordered. He used pine, painted to simulate marble, instead. But he insisted on brass chandeliers fitted for gas, though it was nearly forty years before they could be used; LeDuc was always ahead of his time.

Some of the people in Hastings and Ohio had heard rumors of war profiteering, well justified with regard to many suppliers to the army, but not, it happens, to LeDuc. One of the workers on the house, Jim Rutliff, passed along to LeDuc (somewhat tactlessly, it seems) the yarn that "when me and Cog was shingling to tower, I heard one fellow say to another passing by—Look them towers! if you want to see what kind of houses Uncle Sam can build." LeDuc told Mary he thought he might "dress up and put on airs and pass for a very rich person with funds in some secret bank . . . It is a national misfortune that smartness should be considered preferable & more desirable than honesty but so it is."

Mary replied in good humor, knowing her husband well. From her temporary quarters in Ohio, among relatives she did not respect, she wrote: "Aunt Sally is like the man in Hastings . . . She asked Mother, if you were not getting rich." He was not, but they kept going. Mary, by now, was fully committed, debts or not. "I hope and pray our house may be finished, so we can go back. I will keep boarders—anything!"

In 1864 things went better for the Union cause, and for the finances of the LeDucs. The wheat crop was good, and so were land sales, as the population of Hastings increased. LeDuc reported the good news: "This and the rents for this year ought to enable us to finish off the house properly without going into debt. Especially if we could sell some more property." Perhaps the war would end quickly, he wrote in April, and "if I get out of the service we can live in tents this summer how would you like that? Camp life in Minnesota—We could move about when we liked and take our house with us." As it turned out, they actually had a real masonry house, with a tower, a little unfinished, perhaps, but nonetheless worth it all.

Like Longwood, LeDuc's villa was very ambitious; like Longwood it was the expression of cosmopolitan taste on a frontier. The house was three stories high, with a taller tower, all of limestone, with carved verge-boards, crockets and finials, drip-moldings and leaded glass.

Upon LeDuc's release from the Army, he, his wife and their three children had a fire-lighting ceremony in "the house we built to be happy in." For LeDuc, scholar and gentleman, that was a house with plenty of books. At the top of the tower, where Pliny the Elder had prescribed for Roman gentlemen a place to rest and admire the view, LeDuc kept a little room furnished with a chair, a table and bookshelves. Downstairs in the parlor, in the evenings, his family would read their favorite authors, Charles Dickens and Sir Walter Scott. They performed them as

LeDuc House

Courtesy of the Minnesota Historical Society

well. Once in his schooldays in Ohio, LeDuc had played "an old Castilian" soldier to "Cump" Sherman's Pizarro; now he played Dickens' Captain Cuttle, "complete with a hook for one hand."

He also played host to President Hayes in September 1878. The presidential party arrived at the station of LeDuc's little Hastings & Dakota Railroad and remained for three hours at his Picturesque villa in the suburbs. This was perhaps the high point of LeDuc's later life. His wife died in 1904. His income diminished in the long depression that afflicted Minnesota after 1896. His sense of drama and his equally well-developed sense of humor saw him through the rough patches, and his final years were spent in comfort, as the result of a bequest from the widow of his old friend General Daniel Butterfield. LeDuc died of pneumonia at the age of ninety-four, as the United States was entering the First World War, in the bedroom of the house that brought the grand Picturesque manner to the extremity of the Old Northwest.

Once when the Swedish novelist Fredrika Bremer was traveling with Andrew Jackson Downing on the Hudson, they spied a large gray stone Gothic house upon the shore. "Do you see—a castle!" "Ah!" she replied, "but it is a very young castle!"

LeDuc House today
Photo by Dick Bancroft

If Downing and Bremer had been upon a little tributary of the Mississippi in 1900, they might have seen LeDuc's castle on its shore, and it would not have seemed so young. There it was, amid its great old trees, cloaked in ivy, a little seedy, perhaps, but a part of its landscape. Up in the tower the old man might have been writing on his Remington of a life of "originality," "boldness," "energy" and "variety." There he was, the perfect client of the Picturesque, "a person of educated and refined tastes, who could appreciate the beautiful both in art and in nature."

In that house General William Gates LeDuc, lawyer, railroad and town-site promoter, agronomist, engineer, enthusiast for domestic teas, sugars, goats, rice and manufactures, developer of steam cars and typewriters, storekeeper, farmer and miller, had found some repose. There he enjoyed for nearly fifty years "the pure and elevating pleasures of the country."

Afterword

WE ARE AT THE END of our journey. This book would have become too heavy for you to carry about in a briefcase, and much too thick for the glove compartment, if we had followed our story much beyond the first half of the nineteenth century. The Civil War is a natural stopping place. Though it is never true that history stops at any point, or starts at another, there is no other decade in our national life that divides what preceded it from what followed as dramatically as the 1860's.

So we will stop there. We have looked over into the next period, of course, in order to carry some of our characters to their own ends, but only as we stand in one pasture, looking across to another. We have also stopped at the frontier of American architecture, about 1860. American building styles went farther, but not in continuous movement; they had to leap across the sea of grass and the great American desert to the places beyond, to California and Oregon, Washington and Hawaii. In 1860 the kind of architecture we have been describing had not penetrated the vast interior space of the continent. Most of that interior space was very high and very dry; it was mountain and desert then thought to be difficult to bring under the plow, and was often marked on maps as "Indian Country," lying west of a line drawn from Duluth, on Lake Superior, skewering Minnesota and then angling south-southwest across the plains of Iowa to the Missouri, following the river until it turned away eastward, then southward to the Gulf, crossing on the way the indomitable rivers of the plains.

We have come a long way from the valley of the Po and the tame little Brenta, where we first observed an architect and his clients erecting residential personae as they moved amid the mysteries of the psychology of money and the psychology of architecture.

These mysteries hover over the stories told in these pages, stories of gain and loss and survival, stories of people using money and materials to create their habitations, living as well as they could, leaving architectural history to be written by others. At the end of many biographies we came at last to Haller Nutt, James F. D. Lanier and William Gates LeDuc, and their womenfolk.

As I have reflected on these three careers, I have sensed yet another mystery beyond the facts. The lives of each of these people flowed into the maelstrom of our Civil War, drawn by a pull I do not profess to understand. It is as if all of them enacted some larger part of the American story than their own lives, larger even than their own class or section, as if all were led to behave in the way they did by the sheer suction of that enormous, whirling, fiery torment.

America had been a nation of villages and farms and little cities. Away from them, the men were drawn into the war. When it was over, those who survived went back to their women in an altered America. Some things had been speeded up. Some things had died. Some joinings, some embraces, some sweet words, some honesties across a table could never, now, find their way into memory because they remained unconsummated. And, people being what they are, murders by the hundred thousand took the place of murders *seriatim*. Some deadly injuries of spite and a multitude of vicious possibilities added fuel to the fire of war. A myriad of small unrelated stories of love and hate were consolidated into a single, enormous horror.

Into the cauldron, into the refiner's fire, into the blacksmith's flame went the materials of the first America, to make the materials for the second.

Bibliography

Ackerman, James S. "The Geopolitics of Venetian Architecture in the Time of Titian." In *Titian, His World and His Legacy,* edited by David Rosand. New York: Columbia University Press, 1982.

Adams, William Howard, ed. *The Eye of Thomas Jefferson.* Washington: National Gallery of Art, 1976.

Adler, Michael H. *The Writing Machine.* London: Allen & Unwin, 1973.

Agar, Herbert. *The Price of Union.* Boston: Houghton-Mifflin, 1950.

American Heritage Atlas of American History. New York: American Heritage, 1966.

Andrews, Wayne. *Pride of the South. A Social History of Southern Architecture.* New York: Atheneum, 1979.

Baltimore City Directory. Baltimore: R. L. Polk & Company, 1835.

Battles and Leaders of the Civil War, Being for the Most Part Contributions by Union and Confederate Officers. New York: Century Company, 1884–88. Reprint. New York: T. Yoseloff, 1956.

Bleser, Carol. *The Hammonds of Redcliffe.* New York: Oxford University Press, 1981.

Bolton, Henry Carrington, and Reginald Pelham Bolton. *The Family of Bolton in England and America, 1100–1894, A Study in Genealogy.* New Haven: Private printing (Tuttle, Morehouse and Taylor Press), 1895.

Boorstin, Daniel. *The Lost World of Thomas Jefferson.* New York: Holt, 1948.

Bowers, Claude G. *The Tragic Era: The Revolution After Lincoln.* Cambridge, Mass.: Houghton-Mifflin, 1929.

———. *The Young Jefferson, 1743–1780.* Boston: Houghton-Mifflin, 1945.

Brantley, William Henderson. *Banking in Alabama, 1816–1860.* Birmingham, Ala.: n.p., 1961.

———. "Henry Hitchcock of Mobile." *Alabama Review,* vol. V, no. 1 (January 1952).

Braudel, Fernand. *The Mediterranean and the Mediterranean World in the Age of Philip II.* New York: Harper and Row, 1972.

Bridenbaugh, Carl. *Peter Harrison, First American Architect.* Chapel Hill, N.C.: Institute of Early America, 1949.

———, and Roberta Bridenbaugh. *No Peace Beyond the Line: The English in the Caribbean, 1624–1690.* New York: Oxford University Press, 1972.

Bridwell, Ronald Edward. *The South's Wealthiest Planter: Wade Hampton I of South Carolina, 1754–1835.* Ph.D. dissertation, University of South Carolina, 1980 (Ann Arbor, Mich.: University Microfilms, 1980).

Brookings, Jean A. "A Historic Mansion." *Minnesota History*, vol. 37 (March 1961).

Buisseret, David. *Historic Architecture of the Caribbean*. London: Heinemann, 1980.

Bull, Henry De S. "Ashley Hall." *South Carolina Historical Magazine*, vol. 53 (April 1952).

Burns, Lee. *Early Architects and Builders of Indiana*. Publications of the Indiana Historical Society (Indianapolis), vol. 2, no. 3, 1935.

Caldwell, Mary F. *Tennessee: The Dangerous Example—Watauga to 1894*. Nashville: Aurora Publishers, 1974.

————. *Tennessee: The Volunteer State, 1769–1923*. Chicago: Richtext Press, 1968.

Calhoun, John C. "A Disquisition on Government." *Speeches of John C. Calhoun*. New York: Harper and Brothers, 1843.

Carman, Harry J., and Harold C. Syrett. *A History of the American People*. New York: Knopf, 1952.

Carmer, Carl L. *The Hudson*. New York: Holt, Rinehart, and Winston, 1974.

Carson, Gary, et al. "Impermanent Architecture in the Southern American Colonies." *Winterthur Portfolio*, Vol. 16 (1981), pp. 135 ff.

Carter Archives. Compiled by Pollyanna Creekmore and Muriel C. Spoden. Nashville: Tennessee Historical Commission, Tennessee Department of Conservation, 1974.

Carter, Edward C., II, et al., ed. *The Journals of Benjamin Henry Latrobe, 1799–1820: From Philadelphia to New Orleans*. New Haven: Maryland Historical Society/Yale University Press, 1980.

Chambers, D. S. *The Imperial Age of Venice: 1380–1580*. London: Thames and Hudson, 1970.

Charlottesville, Virginia. Alderman Library, University of Virginia. "Articles of Agreement of the Albemarle Iron Works," December 28, 1770.

Childs, Marquis. *Mighty Mississippi*. New York: Ticknor & Fields, 1982.

Churchill, Winston. *History of the English-Speaking Peoples*. New York: Bantam Books, 1963.

Claiborne, John Francis Hamtramck. *Mississippi as a Province, Territory and State*. Baton Rouge, La.: Louisiana State University Press, 1964.

Cochran, Thomas. *Frontiers of Change: Early Industrialization in America*. New York: Oxford University Press, 1981.

————, and William Miller. *A Social History of Industrialization*. New York: Harper Torchbooks, 1961.

Cohn-Haft, Lewis. "The Founding Fathers and Antiquity: A Selection Passion." In *The Survival of Antiquity*. Northampton, Mass.: Smith College Studies in History, 1980.

Coleman, Martha J. "Milestones in Indiana." *Indianapolis Star*, November 17, 1940.

Coming, Fortescue. *Sketches of a Tour*. Pittsburgh: 1810.

Commager, Henry S. *The Empire of Reason*. New York: Oxford, 1982.

Cooledge, Harold N. *Samuel Sloan, 1815–1884, Architect*. Ph.D. dissertation, University of Pennsylvania, 1963 (Ann Arbor, Mich.: University Microfilms, 1963).

Cottman, George S. *The James F. D. Lanier Home: An Indiana Memorial*. Indianapolis: W. B. Burford, 1927.

Crawford, E. T., Jr. "Salt-Pioneer Chemical Industry of the Kanawha Valley." *Industrial and Engineering Chemistry*, vol. 27, nos. 10, 11 and 12 (October–December 1935).

Crook, J. Maurdant. *Victorian Architecture: A Visual Anthology*. Reprint. New York: Johnson Reprint Corporation, 1971.

Dalcho, Frederick. *An Historical Account of the Protestant Episcopal Church in South Carolina*. Charleston: E. Thayer, 1820. Reprint. New York: Arno Press, 1972.

Daniel, Jere R. *Experiment in Republicanism: New Hampshire Politics and the American Revolution, 1741–1794*. Cambridge, Mass.: Harvard University Press, 1970.

Davis, David Brion. *The Problem of Slavery in the Age of Revolution, 1770–1823*. Ithaca, N.Y.: Cornell University Press, 1975.

Davis, Iseley and Evangeline Davis. *Charleston, Houses and Gardens*. Charleston, S.C.: Preservation Society of Charleston, 1975.

Davis, Terence. *The Gothick Taste*. Newton Abbot, England: David and Charles, 1974.

Dayton, Ruth Woods. *Pioneers and Their Homes on Upper Kanawha*. Charleston, W.V.: West Virginia Publishing Company, 1947.

De Gruyter, Julius Allan. *The Kanawha Spectator* (Charleston, W.V.), 1976.

Dictionary of American Biography. Johnson, ed. New York: Scribners, 1929.

Downing, Andrew Jackson. *The Architecture of Country Houses*. New York: D. Appleton, 1850. Reprint. New York: Dover, 1969.

Downing, Antoinette Forrester. *Early Homes of Rhode Island*. Garrett and Massie, Richmond, Va.: 1937.

Drinnon, Richard. *Facing West: The Metaphysics of Indian-Hating and Empire-Building*. Minneapolis: University of Minnesota Press, 1980.

Dunn, Richard S. *Sugar and Slaves: The Rise of the Planter Class in the English West Indies, 1624–1713*. Chapel Hill, N.C.: University of North Carolina Press, 1972.

Eaton, Clement. *The Freedom-of-Thought Struggle in the Old South*. New York: Harper and Row, 1964.

———. *The Mind of the Old South*. Baton Rouge, La.: Louisiana State University Press, 1967.

Eberlein, Harold Donaldson, and Cortlandt van Dyke Hubbard. *Historic Houses of the Hudson Valley*. New York: Architectural Book Publishing Company, 1942.

Edmunds, Pocahontas Wight. *History of Halifax*. Private printing, 1977.

Elliot, William. *The Washington Guide*. Washington: S. A. Elliott, 1826.

Evans, Eli N. *The Provincials: A Personal History of Jews in the South*. New York: Atheneum, 1976.

Fairbairn, Charlotte Judd. *The Washington Homes of Jefferson County, West Virginia*. Ranson, W.V.: Whitney & White.

Farrington, Joseph. *Diary of Joseph Farrington*. London: 1923.

Flanders, Ralph Betts. *Plantation Slavery in Georgia*. Chapel Hill, N.C.: University of North Carolina Press, 1933.

Fogel, Robert William, and Stanley L. Engerman. *Time on the Cross: The Economics of American Negro Slavery*. Boston: Little, Brown, 1974.

Foley, Mary Mix. *The American House*. New York: Harper and Row, 1980.

Fowler, Orson Squire. *A Home for All, or, A New, Cheap, Convenient, and Superior Mode of Building*. New York: Fowler & Wells, 1848. Reprint: *The Octagon House, A Home for All*. New York: Dover, 1973.

Freehling, William W. *Prelude to Civil War: The Nullification Controversy in South Carolina, 1816–1836*. New York: Harper and Row, 1965.

Garden Club of Virginia. *Homes and Gardens in Old Virginia*. Edited by Frances Archer Christian and Susanne Williams Massie. Garrett and Massie, Richmond, Virginia: 1962.

Gastil, Raymond D. *Cultural Regions of the United States*. Seattle: University of Washington Press, 1975.

Gates, Paul W. "Southern Investments in Northern Lands Before the Civil War." *Journal of Southern History*, Vol. 5 (May 1939), pp. 155 ff.

Genovese, Eugene D. *From Rebellion to Revolution: Afro-American Slave Revolts in the Making of the Modern World.* Baton Rouge, La.: Louisiana State University Press, 1979.

Gilchrist, Agnes A. "Girard College: An Example of the Layman's Influence on Architecture." *Journal of the Society of Architectural Historians*, vol. 16. no. 2 (May 1957).

Girouard, Mark. *Life in the English Country House.* New Haven: Yale University Press, 1978.

Goodfellow, G. L. M. "George Hadfield." *Architectural Review*, vol. 138, no. 821 (July 1965).

Goodfriend, Joyce. "Burghers and Blacks." *New York History*, vol. 59 (April 1978).

Gosner, Pamela. *Caribbean Georgian: The Great and Small Houses of the West Indies.* Washington: Three Continents Press, 1982.

Govan, Thomas Payne. *Nicholas Biddle, Nationalist and Public Banker, 1786–1844.* Chicago: University of Chicago Press, 1959.

Gowans, Alan. *Images of American Living: Four Centuries of Architecture and Furniture as Cultural Expression.* New York: Harper and Row, 1976.

Green, Jack P. "Society and Economy in the British Caribbean During the Seventeenth and Eighteenth Centuries." *American Historical Review*, vol. 79 (December 1974), pp. 1499–1517.

Gregorie, Anne King. *History of Sumter County, South Carolina.* Sumter, S.C.: Library Board of Sumter County, 1954.

Greiff, Constance M. *John Notman, Architect, 1810–1865.* Philadelphia: The Athenaeum of Philadelphia, 1979.

Hamlin, Talbot Faulkner. *Benjamin Henry Latrobe.* New York: Oxford University Press, 1955.

————. *Greek Revival Architecture in America.* New York: Oxford University Press, 1944. Reprint. New York: Dover, 1975.

Hardesty, John. *West Virginia Counties.* (Richwood, W.V.), 1973.

Herndon, George Melvin. *William Tatham, 1752–1819: American Versatile.* Johnson City, Tenn.: East Tennessee State University Press, 1973.

Hersey, George L. "Godey's Choice." *Journal of the Society of Architectural Historians*, vol. 18, no. 10 (1959).

————. "Thomas U. Walter and the University at Lewisburg." *Journal of the Society of Architectural Historians*, vol. 16, no. 1 (1957).

Hindle, Brooke. *Emulation and Invention.* New York: New York University Press, 1981.

Howarth, David, et al. *The Men-of-War.* Alexandria, Va.: Time-Life, 1978.

Hunsberger, George S. "The Architectural Career of George Hadfield." *Records of the Columbia Historical Society*, volume 51–2 (1955).

Hunte, George. *Barbados.* New York: Hastings House, 1974.

J. F. D. Lanier State Memorial. Indianapolis: Indiana Dept. of Natural Resources, 1971.

James, Dorris Clayton. *Antebellum Natchez.* Baton Rouge, La.: Louisiana State University Press, 1968.

Kane, Harnett T. *Natchez on the Mississippi.* New York: Morrow, 1974.

Kaufmann, Emil. *Architecture in the Age of Reason: Baroque and Post-Baroque in England, Italy, and France.* New York: Dover, 1968.

Kennedy, Roger. *American Churches.* New York: Stewart, Tabori and Chang, 1982.

Kennedy, Roger. *Men on the Moving Frontier*. Palo Alto, Calif.: American West Publishing Company, 1969.

Kimball, Sidney Fiske. *American Domestic Architecture*. New York: AMS Press, 1970.

———. *Domestic Architecture of the American Colonies and of the Early Republic*. New York: Dover, 1966.

———. *Thomas Jefferson, Architect*. New York: Da Capo Press, 1968.

Klapthor, Margaret, and Howard Morrison. *George Washington: A Figure Upon the Stage*. Washington: Smithsonian Institution Press, 1982.

Knight, Ralph. "The Miraculous Steamboat." *Saturday Evening Post*. vol. 234, no. 25 (June 24, 1961).

Kreger, Janet L. "Construction of a Wilderness Mansion." Unpublished manuscript, available through the Minnesota Historical Society.

LaFever, Minard. *The Beauties of Modern Architecture*. New York: Appleton, 1835.

Laidley, William Sydney. *History of Charleston and Kanawha County, West Virginia and Representative Citizens*. Chicago: Richmond-Arnold Publishing Company, 1911.

Landy, Jacob. *The Architecture of Minard LaFever*. New York: Columbia University Press, 1970.

Lane, Mills. *The People of Georgia: An Illustrated Social History*. Savannah, Ga.: Beehive Press, 1975.

Lanier, James. *Memoirs*. Private printing. Available from the Indiana Historical Society, Indianapolis, Indiana.

LeDuc, William Gates. *Recollections of a Civil War Quartermaster*. St. Paul: North Central Publishing Company, 1963.

Lerski, Hanna H. *William Jay*. Lanham, Md.: University Press of America, 1983.

Lethbridge, Francis D. "The Federal City as Client." *American Institute of Architects Journal*, vol. 45 (May 1965).

Lewis, Henry N. *More Taste than Prudence: A Study of John Evans Johnson (1815–1870)*. Chapel Hill, N.C.: Borderer Press, 1983.

Liscombe, R. W. *William Wilkins, 1778–1839*. New York: Cambridge University Press, 1980.

Little-Stokes, Ruth. "The North Carolina Porch." In *Carolina Dwelling: Towards Preservation of Place, in Celebration of the North Carolina Vernacular Landscape*, edited by Doug Swaim. Raleigh, N.C.: North Carolina State University Press, 1978.

Logan, Marie T. *Mississippi–Louisiana Border Country: A History of Rodney, Mississippi, St. Joseph, Louisiana, and Environs*. Baton Rouge, La.: Claitor's, 1970.

Long, Edward. *History of Jamaica*. London: T. Lowndes, 1774.

Lord, Walter. *The Dawn's Early Light*. New York: Norton, 1972.

Malone, Dumas. *Jefferson and His Time, Volume 6: The Sage of Monticello*. Boston: Little, Brown, 1981.

McAdams, Ina May Ogletree. *The Building of "Longwood."* Austin, Texas: published by author, 1972.

McGehee, Millie. "Auburn in Natchez." *Antiques*, March 1977.

Merk, Frederick. *History of the Westward Movement*. New York: Knopf, 1978.

Merrill, Boynton. *Jefferson's Nephews: A Frontier Tragedy*. Princeton, N.J.: Princeton University Press, 1976.

Meyers, Marvin. *The Jacksonian Persuasion: Politics and Belief*. Stanford, Calif.: Stanford University Press, 1957.

Meynard, Virginia G. *The Venturers: The Hampton, Harrison and Earle Families of Virginia, South Carolina and Texas.* Easley, S.C.: Southern Historical Press, 1981.

Middleton, Robin and David Watkin. *Neoclassical and Nineteenth-Century Architecture.* New York: Abrams, 1980.

Miller, John Chester. *The Wolf by the Ears: Thomas Jefferson and Slavery.* New York: Macmillan, 1977.

Moltke-Hansen, David, ed. *Art in the Lives of South Carolinians: Nineteenth-Century Chapters.* Charleston, S.C.: Carolina Art Association, 1979.

Morison, Samuel Eliot. *The Maritime History of Massachusetts: 1783–1860.* Boston: Houghton-Mifflin, 1961.

Morrison, Hugh. *Early American Architecture from the First Colonial Settlements to the National Period.* New York: Oxford University Press, 1952.

Mosby, Marijida Waldron. "Salt Industry in the Kanawha Valley." Master's thesis, University of Kentucky, 1950.

Mozingo, Todd R. "Francis Costigan." Master's thesis, University of Virginia, 1975.

Nash, Gary B. *The Urban Crucible: Social Change, Political Consciousness, and the Origins of the American Revolution.* Cambridge, Mass.: Harvard University Press, 1979.

Nelligan, Murray. "The Building of Arlington House." *Journal of the Society of Architectural Historians,* vol. 10, no. 2 (May 1951).

Newson, Thomas McLean. *Pen Pictures of St. Paul, Minnesota, and Biographical Sketches of Old Settlers, from the Earliest Settlements of the City, up to and Including the Year 1857.* St. Paul: published by author, 1886.

Newton, Roger Hale. *Town and Davis, Architects.* New York: Columbia University Press, 1942.

Nichols, Frederick Doveton. *The Architecture of Georgia.* Savannah, Ga.: Beehive Press, 1976.

———. "The House that Chainstores Built." *Virginia History,* vol. 17.

North, Douglas C. *The Economic Growth of the United States, 1790–1860.* Englewood Cliffs, N.J.: Prentice-Hall, 1961.

Nutt, Merle C. *The Nutt Family Through the Years, 1635–1973.* Phoenix: published by author, 1973.

Osterweiss, Rollin G. *Romanticism and Nationalism in the Old South.* New Haven: Yale University Press, 1949.

Palladio, Andrea. *The Four Books on Architecture.* Reprint. New York: Dover, 1965.

Parrington, Vernon L. *Main Currents in American Thought.* New York: Harcourt Brace and Co., 1927–30.

Parry, Albert. *Whistler's Father.* Indianapolis: Bobbs-Merrill, 1939.

Parry, John H. *The Age of Reconnaissance: Discovery, Exploration and Settlement, 1450 to 1650.* New York: Praeger, 1969.

Perkins, Edwin J. *The Economy of Colonial America.* New York: Columbia University Press, 1980.

Pickens, Buford. "Mr. Jefferson as Revolutionary Architect." *Journal of the Society of Architectural Historians,* vol. 34, no. 4 (December 1975).

Pierson, William H., Jr. *American Buildings and Their Architects.* Vol. 2. Garden City, New York: Doubleday, 1980.

Proctor, John Clagett, ed. *Washington, Past and Present: A History.* New York: Lewis Historical Publishing Company, 1930.

Rasmussen, Steen Eiler. *Towns and Buildings Described in Drawings and Words*. Cambridge, Mass.: MIT Press. Revised Danish edition, 1949.

Ravenel, Beatrice St. Julien. *Architects of Charleston*. Charleston, S.C.: Carolina Art Association, 1945.

Redmill, John. "Grange Park Transformed." *Country Life*, May 15, 1975.

Remini, Robert V. *Andrew Jackson and the Bank War: A Study in the Growth of Presidential Power*. New York: Norton, 1967.

————. *Era of Good Feelings*. Arlington Heights, Ill.: AHM, 1979.

Restak, Richard M. "The Brain." *Wilson Quarterly*, Summer 1982.

Reynolds, Helen Wilkinson. *Dutch Houses in the Hudson Valley Before 1776*. New York: Dover, 1965.

Reynolds, James. *Andrea Palladio and the Winged Device, A Panorama Painted in Prose and Pictures Setting Forth the Far-Flung Influence of Andrea Palladio, Architect of Vicenza, Italy, 1518–1580, on Architecture All Over the World, From His Own Era to the Present Day*. New York: Creative Age Press, 1948.

Robertson, Ross M., and Gary M. Walton. *History of the American Economy*, 4th Edition. New York: Harcourt Brace Jovanovich, 1979.

Rogin, Michael Paul. *Fathers and Children*. New York: Knopf, 1975.

Root, Edward W. *Philip Hooker: A Contribution to the Study of the Renaissance in America*. New York: Scribner's, 1929.

Sandburg, Carl. *Abraham Lincoln: The Prairie Years*. New York: Harcourt Brace, 1926.

Scherrer, Anton. "Francis Costigan." *Journal of the Society of Architectural Historians*, vol. 17, no. 1.

Schlesinger, Arthur, Jr. *The Age of Jackson*. Boston: Little, Brown, 1945.

Scully, Arthur, Jr. *James Dakin, Architect: His Career in New York and the South*. Baton Rouge, La.: Louisiana State University Press, 1973.

Sheridan, Richard B. "Planter and Historian: The Career of William Beckford of Jamaica and England, 1744–1799." *Jamaica Historical Review*, vol. 4 (1964).

Sitterson, J. Carlyle. *Sugar Country: The Cane Sugar Industry in the South, 1753–1950*. Lexington, Ky.: University of Kentucky Press, 1953.

Sketch of the Life of J. F. D. Lanier. Printed for the use of his family only. New York: 1870–71. Available from the Indiana Historical Society, Indianapolis, Indiana.

Sloan, Samuel. *The Model Architect: A Series of Original Designs for Cottages, Villas, Suburban Residences, etc., Accompanied by Explanations, Specifications, Estimates, and Elaborate Details Prepared Expressly for the Use of Projectors and Artisans Throughout the United States*. Philadelphia: E. H. Butler, 1852.

————. *Sloan's Homestead Architecture: Containing Forty Designs for Villas, Cottages and Farmhouses, With Essays on Style, Contruction, Landscape Gardening, Furniture*. Philadelphia: Lippincott, 1861.

Smith, Henry Nash. *Virgin Land: The American West as Symbol and Myth*. Cambridge, Mass.: Harvard University Press, 1950.

Smith, Joseph Frazer. *White Pillars: Early Life and Architecture of the Lower Mississippi Valley Country*. New York: William Helburn, 1941.

Smith, Samuel D., ed. *Summary of Archaeological Explorations at the Carter House*. Nashville: Tennessee Department of Conservation, 1979.

Spencer, Donald S. "Edward Coles: Virginia Gentleman in Frontier Politics." *Journal of the Illinois State Historical Society*, vol. 61, no. 2 (Summer 1968).

Stanton, Phoebe B. *The Gothic Revival and American Church Architecture*. Baltimore: Johns Hopkins University Press, 1968.

Stealey, John Edmund. "The Salt Industry of the Great Kanawha Valley of Virginia: A Study in Ante-Bellum Internal Commerce." Ph.D. Dissertation, West Virginia University, 1970.

Steinberg, Sheila, and Cathleen McGuigan. *Rhode Island: An Historical Guide.* Providence, R.I.: Rhode Island Bicentennial Foundation, 1976.

Stephens, John Lloyd. *Incidents of Travel in Greece, Turkey, Russia and Poland*. New York: Harper and Brothers, 1838.

Stoney, Samuel Gaillard, et al. *Plantations of the Carolina Low Country*. Charleston, S.C.: Carolina Art Association, 1938.

The Story of the Typewriter. New York: Herkimer, 1923.

Stroup, Roger. "Up-Country Patrons." In *Art in the Lives of South Carolinians*, edited by David Moltke-Hansen. Charleston, S.C.: Carolina Art Association, 1979.

Stubbs, Thomas M. "Milford." Unpublished. Collection of the South Carolina Historical Association.

Summerson, Sir John Newenham. *The Classical Language of Architecture*. Cambridge, Mass.: MIT Press, 1963.

Swaim, Doug, ed. *Carolina Dwelling: Towards Preservation of Place, in Celebration of the North Carolina Vernacular Landscape*. Raleigh, N.C.: North Carolina State University Press, 1978.

Swierenga, Robert P. *Pioneers and Profits: Land Speculation on the Iowa Frontier*. Iowa City, Iowa: University of Iowa Press, 1968.

Tatum, George B. *Andrew Jackson Downing: Arbiter of American Taste*. Ph.D. dissertation, Princeton University, 1949 (Ann Arbor, Mich.: University Microfilms, 1949).

Taylor, William Banks. *King Cotton and Old Glory: Natchez in the Age of Sectional Controversy and Civil War*. Hattiesburg, Miss.: Taylor, 1977.

Taylor, William Robert. *Cavalier and Yankee*. New York: Braziller, 1961.

Temin, Peter. *The Jacksonian Economy*. New York: Norton, 1969.

"Trace Church Builder." Madison (Indiana) *Courier*, October 11, 1935.

Trumbull, John. *Autobiography of Colonel John Trumbull*. Edited by Theodore Sizer. New Haven: Yale University Press, 1953.

Turner, Frederick Jackson. *The United States, 1830–1850: The Nation and Its Sections*. New York: Norton, 1965.

U.S., Department of Agriculture. *Century of Service*. Washington: U.S. Government Printing Office, 1963.

U.S., Department of the Interior, "Shuh-Leininger-Holstein-Whitsitt House," Historic American Buildings Survey, 1978.

United States Works Projects Administration. *Guide to Virginia*. Washington: U.S. Government Printing Office, 1940.

Vaux, Calvert. *Villas and Cottages*. New York: Harper, 1857. Reprint. New York: Dover, 1970.

Veblen, Thorstein. *The Portable Veblen*. Edited by Max Lerner. New York: Viking Press, 1948.

Verey, David. *Gloucestershire, Volume 2: The Vale and The Forest of Dean*. New York: Penguin, 1980.

Verlinden, Charles. "Medieval Slavers." In *Economy, Society and Government in Medieval Italy*, edited by David Herlihy, Robert S. Lopez and Vsevolod Slessarev. Kent, Ohio: Kent State University Press, 1969.

Vidal, Gore. *Burr: A Novel.* New York: Random House, 1973.

Waddell, Gene. "The Introduction of Greek Revival Architecture to Charleston." In *Art in the Lives of South Carolinians*, edited by David Moltke-Hansen. Charleston, S.C.: Carolina Art Association, 1979.

———. "Robert Mills' Fireproof Building." *South Carolina Historical Magazine*, vol. 80, no. 2 (April 1979).

Walker, John. "Maria Cosway." Unpublished manuscript.

Wallace, Anthony F. C. *Rockdale: The Growth of an American Village in the Early Industrial Revolution.* New York: Knopf, 1978.

Wallace, David Duncan. *The History of South Carolina.* New York: American Historical Society, 1934.

Waltman, Henry G. *Livestock and Poultry in Frontier Indiana.* Washington: Smithsonian Institution Press, 1977.

Walton, Gary M., and James F. Shepherd. *The Economic Rise of Early America.* Cambridge, England: Cambridge University Press, 1979.

Wardin, Albert W., Jr. *Belmont Mansion.* Nashville: Historic Belmont Association, 1981.

"The Wash Tub." *The Construction Recorder* (Indianapolis), vol. 13, no. 11, June 6, 1931.

Waterman, Thomas T. "Some Early Buildings of Barbados." *Journal of the Barbados Museum and Historical Society*, vol. 13, nos. 3 and 4 (1946).

———, and Francis B. Johnston. *Early Architecture of North Carolina.* Chapel Hill, N.C.: University of North Carolina Press, 1941.

Watkin, David. *Thomas Hope and the Neo-Classical Ideal.* London: Transatlantic Press, 1970.

Weaver, Herbert. *Mississippi Farmers, 1850–1860.* Gloucester, Mass.: P. Smith, 1968.

Webster, Richard. *Philadelphia Preserved: Catalog of the Historic American Buildings Survey.* Philadelphia: Temple University Press, 1976.

White, John H., Jr. *American Locomotives: An Engineering History, 1830–1880.* Baltimore: Johns Hopkins Press, 1968.

Williams, Eric. *Capitalism and Slavery.* New York: Capricorn Books, 1966.

Wilson, Samuel, Jr. "Architecture of Early Sugar Plantations," in *Green Fields*, Lafayette, La.: University of Southwestern Louisiana Press, 1980.

Wright, Louis B. *The First Gentlemen of Virginia.* Charlottesville, Va.: University Press of Virginia, 1964.

———. *South Carolina: A Bicentennial History.* New York: Norton, 1976.

Yarnall, Elizabeth Biddle. *Addison Hutton: Quaker Architect, 1834–1916.* Philadelphia: Art Alliance Press, 1974.

Young, James Sterling. *The Washington Community.* New York: Columbia University Press, 1966.

Zelinsky, Wilbur. "The Greek Revival House in Georgia." *Journal of the Society of Architectural Historians*, vol. 13, no. 2 (May 1954).

Notes

PART I. *The Atlantic Progression*

PAGE

3 "the watchful eye": This description of sugar-making comes from an elegant catalogue prepared for an exhibit: *Green Fields* (Lafayette, La.: University of Southwestern Louisiana Press, 1980).

3 "stillness of death": Ibid., p. 3.

3 "If a Boyler" . . . "that stuck between": Richard S. Dunn. *Sugar and Slaves*, pp. 194–95.

CHAPTER 2. *Palladio and the Plantations*

16 "Face dark": James Reynolds, *Andrea Palladio and the Winged Device*, p. xvi.

16 "The fire": Ibid., p. 119

17 "Soon I shall quit Venice": Ibid., p. 51.

21 In the center of the sixteenth century: James S. Ackerman, "The Geopolitics of Venetian Architecture in the Time of Titian," pp. 41ff. The slumbering Venetian mainland may seem safe enough, but it is dangerous to try for any unequivocal statements about the degree of continuity, or change, in the habits of Venetian agriculturalists in the sixteenth century. Professors James S. Ackerman and Douglas Lewis are the kindliest of men, and patient. They have both tried to help me get things right; they disagree with each other on some matters of interpretation, but I think they would agree that an excellent bibliography of differing views on the matter can be found in footnotes 11 through 22 of Ackerman's article cited above.

21 "My father . . . did not": D. S. Chambers, *The Imperial Age of Venice: 1380–1580*, p. 77.

26 Palladio was quite explicit: Andrea Palladio, *The Four Books on Architecture*, p. 53.

26 black slaves on Cyprus: Charles Verlinden, "Medieval Slavers."

27 "sugar was almost certainly": Fernand Braudel, *The Mediterranean and the Mediterranean World in the Age of Philip II*, pp. 154–55.

27 It was Genoa, not Venice: Gary M. Walton and James F. Shepherd. *The Economic Rise of Early America*, p. 14; Dunn, op. cit., p. 60.

CHAPTER 3. *Sugar, Slaves and Architecture*

32 In the seventeenth century, Barbados had a population: Dunn, op. cit., p. 88.

33 "a grand, gloomy pile": Ibid., pp. 195–96.

33 The ruins of Stokes Hall: David Buisseret, *Historic Architecture of the Caribbean*, p. 14.

499

34   "thought to be the noblest": Edward Long, *History of Jamaica*, vol. 2, p. 6.

36   "the finest British Colonial dwellings": Thomas T. Waterman, "Some Early Buildings of Barbados," p. 141.

37   "bungalows structured of wood": Dunn, op. cit., p. 291.

38   "large enough to hold sixty chairs": Ibid., p. 217.

38   "It was the custom in Jamaica": Ibid., pp. 293–94.

39   "neither cool" . . . "so low": Ibid., pp. 291–93.

39   "coming from a cold country": Dr. Sloane, a contemporary witness, quoted in ibid., pp. 285–86.

39   "a race between quick riches": Ibid., p. 333.

39   "carbuncled faces": Ibid., p. 335.

39   Yet they were very rich: Ibid., pp. 46, 59.

40   William Beckford: Richard B. Sheridan, "Planter and Historian: The Career of William Beckford of Jamaica and England, 1744–1799," pp. 38–40.

42   "it is but of late": Edward Long, quoted in Pamela Gosner, *Caribbean Georgian*, p. 135.

42   "not unusual to see": Ibid.

CHAPTER 4. *Dutch Colonial*

49   painted over the intervening drab: I am indebted to Gene Waddell for this information; the first house so repainted was Alice Huger Smith's at 69 Church Street.

49   "Medieval towns had heretofore": Alan Gowans, *Images of American Living: Four Centuries of Architecture and Furniture as Cultural Expression*, pp. 52–53.

52   "The trade of the world": David Howarth et al., *The Men-of-War*, p. 6.

53   planters and merchants: Carl and Roberta Bridenbaugh, *No Peace Beyond the Line: The English in the Caribbean, 1624–1690*, p. 67.

53   New Amsterdam slave trading: Joyce Goodfriend, "Burghers and Blacks," p. 125.

54   "carpenters, joiners": George Hunte, *Barbados*, p. 45.

56   "had as good right": Samuel Gaillard Stoney et al., *Plantations of the Carolina Low Country*, p. 47.

58   North Chacan plantation: Ibid., p. 45.

58   "copied from . . . the well-remembered": "The Richmond Planter," 1844, quoted in Garden Club of Virginia, *Homes and Gardens in Old Virginia*, p. 121.

59   Ashley Hall: Henry De S. Bull, "Ashley Hall," pp. 61ff.

CHAPTER 5. *The Caribbean Cottage*

62   Van Cortlandt's slaves: Goodfriend, op. cit., p. 132.

63   Mount Gulian and slave labor: Described in Harold Donaldson Eberlein and Cortlandt van Dyke Hubbard, *Historic Houses of the Hudson Valley*, p. 48.

67   "Mr. Livingston has": Helen Wilkinson Reynolds, *Dutch Houses in the Hudson Valley Before 1776*, p. 15.

67   "groups of men": Ibid.

67   "in the long run . . . meant": Gowans, op. cit., p. 62.

68   "What a great convenience": Samuel Wilson, Jr., "Architecture of Early Sugar Plantations," pp. 62–63.

69   descriptions of Port Royal: Dunn, op. cit., p. 299.

69   open "piazzas": Gene Waddell, unpublished letter, April 28, 1982.

69   Middleburg and Oakland: Stoney, op. cit., pp. 48, 52, 62; see also Gene Waddell, unpublished letter, April 28, 1982.

69   North Carolina houses: Ruth Little-Stokes, "The North Carolina Porch," pp. 104ff; Thomas T. Waterman and Francis B. Johnston, *Early Architecture of North Carolina*, p. 183.

70   Orphan House: Frederick Doveton Nichols, *The Architecture of Georgia*, p. 27; and Mary Mix Foley, *The American House*, pp. 67–70.

70   Hager and Saucier: Foley, op. cit., pp. 67–70.

72   impermanent houses: Gary Carson et al., "Impermanent Architecture in the Southern American Colonies," pp. 135ff.

PART II. *Going Ashore to Stay Ashore*

CHAPTER 6. *Transitional Architecture Ashore*

78   "Some two years since": J. Carlyle Sitterson, *Sugar Country: The Cane Sugar Industry in the South, 1753–1950*, pp. 38–40.

82   The South Carolina historian Samuel Stoney tells us: Stoney, op. cit., p. 34.

87   "a belated Elizabethan": Louis B. Wright, *The First Gentlemen of Virginia*, p. 212.

CHAPTER 7. *Anglo-Dutch Provincial*

94   "Homegrown patricians": Carson et al., op. cit., pp. 135ff.

97   "carpentering, bricklaying": Goodfriend, op. cit., p. 131.

98   "wearing the gold chain": Eberlein and Hubbard, op. cit., p. 13.

103   "pomps and vanities": Jere R. Daniel, *Experiment in Republicanism: New Hampshire Politics and the American Revolution, 1741–1794*, p. 34.

103   "sprung from such ancestors": Ibid., p. 3.

104   "a field of battle": Ibid.

104   "Governor Wentworth's compliments": Ibid., p. 4.

106   "The place of my residence": Ibid., p. 3.

106   "a dock of masts always ready": Ibid., p. 12.

106   "a Lilliputian Wentworth House": John Wentworth quoted in Carl Bridenbaugh, *Peter Harrison, First American Architect*, p. 141.

108   "Mobbish turn": Gary B. Nash, *The Urban Crucible*, p. 273.

110   "Mr. Harrison": Hugh Morrison, *Early American Architecture from the First Colonial Settlements to the National Period*, p. 451.

CHAPTER 8. *Home and Land*

115   "American pioneering spirit": Thorstein Veblen, *The Portable Veblen*, p. 400.

116   "did not farm for profit": Mark Girouard, *Life in the English Country House*, p. 2.

118   "belonged to trading families": Wright, op. cit., p. 47.

120   Hugh Morrison assures us: Morrison, op. cit., p. 424.

CHAPTER 9. *Yankees and West Indians*

127   "The contrast in lifestyle": Dunn, op. cit., pp. 337ff.

130   "very ill conditioned": Ibid., p. 50.

130   "It pleased the Lord": Ibid., p. 336.

130   "By the 1680's": Ibid., pp. 336–37.

141   "had never been an important": Samuel Eliot Morison, *The Maritime History of Massachusetts: 1783–1860*, p. 32.

Chapter 10. *Charleston*

145   "ample and fragrant blossoms": Iseley and Evangeline Davis, *Charleston, Houses and Gardens*, n.p.

145   "adorn successively and perfume": Ibid.

145   "best repute for cooking": Ibid.

147   During its golden age: Edwin J. Perkins, *The Economy of Colonial America*, p. 153.

147   Eli Evans . . . has found: Eli N. Evans, *The Provincials: A Personal History of Jews in the South*, pp. 50ff.

147   Sir Alexander Cumming: Louis B. Wright, *South Carolina: A Bicentennial History*, p. 56.

148   "the first community": Quoted in Eli Evans, op. cit., p. 51.

150   "Gallic": Stoney, op. cit., p. 55.

151   encouraged Thomas Waterman . . . to suggest: Thomas T. Waterman, "Some Early Buildings of Barbados," p. 148.

153   "almost Asiatic splendor": Wayne Andrews, *Pride of the South: A Social History of Southern Architecture*, p. 62.

153   "the grandest hall": Iseley and Evangeline Davis, op, cit., n.p.

154   "They looked to the Augustan London": Wright, *South Carolina: A Bicentennial History*, p. 103.

154   "the citizens of South Carolina": Perkins, op. cit., p. 95.

155   "the most miserable": Wright, *South Carolina: A Bicentennial History*, p. 19.

155   "many a man": David Duncan Wallace, *The History of South Carolina*, p. 46.

Chapter 11. *Savannah: William Jay and Robert Mills*

163   "whipped off": Henry Carrington Bolton and Reginald Pelham Bolton, *The Family of Bolton in England and America, 1100–1894, A Study in Genealogy*, p. 275.

163   "You shall instruct my negroes": Ibid.

168   "temporary pavillion of great extent": The quotation comes from a newspaper file available at the Georgia Historical Society in Savannah, in an article on Scarbrough which I found difficult to date.

174   "The Bank was saved": Peter Temin, *The Jacksonian Economy*, p. 48.

174   "Men went to bed rich": Bolton and Bolton, op. cit.

175   "better advantages": Frederick Dalcho, *An Historical Account of the Protestant Episcopal Church in South Carolina*, p. 214.

175   He left to his son: Will of William Mason Smith, Charleston County *Will Book* (available through the South Carolina Historical Society, Charleston), p. 814.

176   "more common for the inhabitant": Dalcho, op. cit., pp. 215–16.

176   He found some work: David Verey, *Gloucestershire, Volume 2: The Vale and the Forest of Dean*, pp. 151, 471; and Nichols, op. cit., p. 48.

176   the indefatigable researches of Hanna Lerski: Hanna H. Lerski, *William Jay*.

176   "a large share of wit": Ibid., p. 279.

177   "several very ambitious-looking dwellings": Nichols, op. cit., p. 34.

178   "gentlemen not professional men": Beatrice St. Julien Ravenel, *Architects of Charleston*, p. 121.

CHAPTER 12. *An Upcountry Boomtown*

184 "After Alexander of Macedon": Carl L. Carmer, *The Hudson*, p. 222.

184 "By whose authority": Ibid., p. 220.

185 "As seen from the river": Edward W. Root, *Philip Hooker: A Contribution to the Study of the Renaissance in America*, p. 15.

186 "more Dutch than decent": Root, op. cit., p. 12.

186 "one of the . . . churches": Ibid., p. 14.

189 an admiring portrait: Gore Vidal, *Burr: A Novel*, references throughout.

189 "there was not a trace": Robert V. Remini, *Era of Good Feelings*, p. 333.

190 "the grubbiest school": Ibid.

190 "executed his duties": Root, op. cit., p. 27.

192 "afforded peculiarly favorable": *Dictionary of American Biography* (New York: Scribners, 1930), vol. IV, p. 151.

195 "two of the finest rooms": Root, op. cit., p. 196.

195 "mercifully spared": Ibid.

PART III. *The Classic Period*

200 "beyond" Philip Hooker was "the wilderness": Root, op. cit., p. 9.

CHAPTER 13. *Speculators, Stagecraft and Statecraft*

202 "greatest commercial emporium": John Clagett Proctor, ed., *Washington: Past and Present*, p. 689.

202 Thornton predicted a population: James Sterling Young, *The Washington Community*, p. 23.

203 "Two unfinished stark white citadels": Ibid., pp. 41–42.

203 "This embryo capital": Ibid.

203 "in America": *Records of the Columbia Historical Society, 1973–1974*, pp. 35ff., translated by David J. Brandenberg and Millicent H. Brandenberg, available through the Columbia Historical Society, Washington, D.C.

203 Washington lands: Murray Nelligan, "Old Arlington: The Story of the Lee Mansion National Memorial" (unpublished but available at Arlington House).

205 "a house that any one might see": Edward C. Carter, II, ed., *The Journals of Benjamin Henry Latrobe, 1799–1820: From Philadelphia to New Orleans*, p. 71, footnote 13.

205 Godfrey Vigne and Frances Trollope: Nelligan, "Old Arlington," p. 149. Further information on Hadfield can be found in Edward C. Carter, II, ed., *The Journals of Benjamin Henry Latrobe, 1799–1820: From Philadelphia to New Orleans*, p. 72, fn. 16; in a letter sent by Hadfield to Thomas Jefferson in the *Jefferson Papers*, volume 222, op. 39775, Library of Congress; from the files of the *Daily National Intelligencer* (Washington, D.C.), especially February 13, 1826, which contains an obituary of Hadfield; in Claude Bowers' treatment of Maria Cosway in *The Young Jefferson, 1743–1789*. I also obtained a great deal of information about Hadfield from conversations with John Walker and Margaret Davis, who are working to develop biographical material on both George and Maria Cosway Hadfield.

209 "We enrich a friend": Nelligan, "Old Arlington," p. 94.

209 "the plough and the loom": Ibid., p. 95.

209 "not discernible in the woods": Ibid., p. 106.

209 "This may be the last time": Nelligan, "Old Arlington," p. 128.

210   "the right of opinion": Ibid.

210   "the little men": Ibid., p. 155.

210   "the unhappy error": Ibid., p. 221.

210   "If Mr. Custis": Ibid.

210   "the mightiest serpent": Ibid., pp. 156–74.

210   "refuge for the poor Africans": Ibid., p. 155.

210   "rich, full-toned voice": Ibid., p. 64.

210   "selfish, dictatorial": Ibid., p. 440.

211   "I can anticipate": Ibid., p. 441.

212   "Grandmother always spoiled": Ibid., p. 37.

212   "ready submission": Ibid., pp. 325, 42–43.

213   "that ridiculous figure Custis": Ibid., pp. 181, 410.

214   "Your father": Ibid., p. 405.

214   references to the stage: Margaret Klapthor and Howard Morrison, *George Washington: A Figure Upon the Stage*, p. 124.

214   designer of Arlington House: The best piece on Hadfield is by G. L. M. Goodfellow, "George Hadfield." Other good sources are George S. Hunsberger, "The Architectural Career of George Hadfield," and Francis D. Lethbridge, "The Federal City as Client." Lethbridge provides us with a brief, tantalizing bit of autobiography by Hadfield, located in William Elliot's *The Washington Guide*, pp. 15–24. Specifically, the question of Hadfield's authorship of the wings as well as the central portion of Arlington House is settled by Murray Nelligan, in "The Building of Arlington House," pp. 11–15.

215   his sister Maria: John Walker, in his manuscript "Maria Cosway," has compiled the most complete information available on Maria Cosway and has, in the process, disposed of many myths about her. I am indebted to him for the use of much of the material in this paragraph and what follows. His book is not, at this writing, in print, so I include no page references. For Charles' shrewdness, Walker gives an example from the correspondence of Sir Horace Mann.

215   The youth of George and Maria Hadfield: Walker's work, ibid., supersedes Claude Bowers' references to this phase of Maria's life. Walker had access to Maria's own autobiographical letter, now in the Victoria and Albert Museum. See Bowers, *The Young Jefferson: 1743–1780*, pp. 447ff.

215   "ambitious, proud and restless": The description is taken from the envious painter James Northcote's sketch of Cosway, offered by Walker.

216   The relationship of Maria, Jefferson and di Paoli: Walker has considered and presented the evidence about the concurrent affair with di Paoli, and presented the correspondence that powerfully suggests di Paoli's paternity.

217   Benjamin West's opinion of Hadfield's skills was cited in George S. Hunsberger, "The Architectural Career of George Hadfield," p. 46.

217   Hadfield was blackballed: Joseph Farrington, *Diary of Joseph Farrington*, p. 85; see also Francis D. Lethbridge, "The Federal City as Client," pp. 25–26.

218   five hundred dollars and a building lot: Lethbridge, op. cit., pp. 25–26.

218   "plainly to be seen": Ibid.; see also Hunsberger, op. cit., pp. 51ff.

218   "offered an adequate sum": Lethbridge, op. cit., p. 26.

218   "This most admirable artist": John Trumbull, *Autobiography of Colonel John Trumbull*, pp. 177–78.

218   "driving to ruin": Talbot Faulkner Hamlin, *Benjamin Henry Latrobe*, p. 324.

218   "I have long since learned": Hunsberger, op. cit., p. 54.

218   "In losing the prospect": Hamlin, op. cit., p. 286.

219   "much respected in Washington": Hunsberger, op. cit., pp. 60, 64.

CHAPTER 14. *Classic in Context*

222 "simplicity of the ancients": Colen Campbell, quoted in Emil Kaufmann, *Architecture in the Age of Reason: Baroque and Post-Baroque in England, Italy, and France*, p. 4.

222 "Noble simplicity": David Watkin, *Thomas Hope and the Neo-Classical Ideal*, p. 155.

223 "In the fine age of the arts": Ibid., p. 157.

223 "The Greek Revival": Sir John Newenham Summerson, *The Classical Language of Architecture*, pp. 38–39.

223 "man in America": Talbot Hamlin, *Greek Revival Architecture in America*, pp. 318–19.

225 Henry Drummond: My information on Drummond and Grange Park is largely based on two splendid articles, one by John Redmill entitled "Grange Park Transformed," and the other by J. Maurdant Crook in *Victorian Architecture: A Visual Anthology*, pp. 220ff.

225 Grange Park was commenced: The date of Grange Park is sometimes given as 1804, but David Watkin confirms to me by letter that we should stick to 1809, which is given by R. W. Liscombe in *William Wilkins, 1778–1839*.

226 "a good family house": Crook, op. cit.

227 "sunshine on the buildings": Robin Middleton and David Watkin, *Neoclassical and Nineteenth-Century Architecture*, p. 48.

228 "The ruling temper of his mind": Records of the Columbian Institute for February 1826, available at the Columbia Historical Society, Washington, D.C.

229 "an Architect of respectable standing": Roger Hale Newton, *Town and Davis, Architects*, p. 50. Authorities differ on Hadfield's death date, but the contemporary *Daily National Intelligencer* says it was the fifth, not the seventh, of February.

229 "trio of domestic buildings": Ibid.

230 "From the days": Hamlin, *Benjamin Henry Latrobe*, p. 4.

233 "I have changed the taste": Ibid.. p. 148.

234 "Your fondness for Gothic architecture": Ibid., p. 345.

235 "changed the taste": Ibid., p. 148

CHAPTER 15. *Nicholas Biddle*

236 "was not I think happy": Thomas Payne Govan, *Nicholas Biddle, Nationalist and Public Banker, 1786–1844*, p. 4.

236 "sensitive about his": Ibid., pp. 12–13.

236 "knowledge . . . is doubly valuable": Ibid., pp. 4, 6, 15–16.

236 "a very extraordinary": Ibid., p. 10.

237 "his personal contribution": Ibid., pp. 1–4, 10, 36.

237 "these wretches": Ibid., pp. 16–18.

237 "Orator, in the classical style": Ibid.

238 "a kind of American triumph": Ibid., pp. 14, 15, 20.

241 "simplicity and purity": Agnes A. Gilchrist, "Girard College: An Example of the Layman's Influence on Architecture," pp. 22ff.

241 "plain brick": Ibid. For more on Girard College, see George L. Hersey, "Thomas U. Walter and the University at Lewisburg"; Richard Webster, *Philadelphia Preserved: Catalog of the Historic American Buildings Survey*, p. 285; Talbot Hamlin, *Greek Revival Architecture in America*, p. 83; and Govan, op. cit., p. 406.

243 "licked his hands": Govan, op. cit., pp. 406–407.

244 "I prefer my last letter": Govan, op. cit., pp. 81–82.

245 "that the promise is good": Ibid., p. 280.

246   "vulgar misdemeanors": Ibid., p. 409.
247   "unfit to lead": Ibid., p. 348.
247   "busy, active, and anxious": Ibid., p. 412.
247   "at his country seat": Ibid.
247   "a handsome building": Ibid., p. 397.

CHAPTER 16. *Mobile and Yankee Classicism*

248   "people of color": William H. Brantley, "Henry Hitchcock of Mobile," p. 4.
248   "as a traveler walked": Joseph Frazer Smith, *White Pillars*, p. 137.
249   "our city": Brantley, "Henry Hitchcock of Mobile," p. 16.
250   "this is the only fruit": Ibid., p. 14.
250   "stoic fortitude": Ibid., p. 23.
251   "too much my pride": Ibid.
251   "fell on his knees": Ibid., p. 24.
253   "wonderful energy": Ibid., p. 8*n*.
253   "General Jackson could not be supported": Ibid., p. 15*n*.
256   "no sales of cotton": *Niles' Weekly Register*, May 6, 1837.
257   "the largest concourse": Mobile *Advertiser*, August 12, 1839.

CHAPTER 17. *The Halifax Whigs*

261   "virtually became a member": Govan, op. cit., p. 43.
262   "spent some time in Philadelphia": Sidney Fiske Kimball, *Domestic Architecture of the American Colonies and of the Early Republic*, p. 183.
262   a tired hypocrite: For a view of Coles friendly to Jefferson, see Dumas Malone, *Jefferson and His Time, Volume 6: The Sage of Monticello*, pp. 320, 325–26. For a not-so-friendly view of the relationship, see John Chester Miller, *The Wolf by the Ears: Thomas Jefferson and Slavery*, pp. 167, 205–208.
263   "extremely obnoxious man": Donald S. Spencer, "Edward Coles: Virginia Gentleman in Frontier Politics," pp. 150ff.
263   "stiff little Virginia aristocrat": Ibid.
263   an almost successful coup: Ibid.
263   shadowy architect: Henry N. Lewis, *More Taste than Prudence: A Study of John Evans Johnson.* This is the only source of accurate information about him for me to cite. I am indebted to Dr. Lewis for reference to the horse-breeding father.
264   "one of those rare beings": Winston Churchill, *History of the English-Speaking Peoples*, p. 286.
264   "sat often at table": These accounts of the Bruces at Berry Hill are drawn from an excellent article by Kenneth Cook and Faye Royster Tuck in the Halifax, Virginia, *Record-Advertiser* on March 28, 1974, from which comes the quotation from Marshall's letter to his mother, and from one on July 17, 1980, as well as the South Boston, Virginia, *News and Record-Advertiser* of September 20–25, 1973.
264   "astonished to learn": Ibid.
265   "our great national sin": *Illinois Intelligencer*, December 10, 1822.
265   Andrew Jackson: Marie T. Logan, *Mississippi-Louisiana Border Country*, p. 15. She quotes various authorities, including Sparks.
265   "blasts of public frenzy": See newspaper accounts by Cook and Tuck, mentioned above.
265   "the disturbances now existing": James S. Easley, letter to J. P. Casaday, May 9, 1861, *Letter Book*, Easley Manuscripts, University of Virginia Library.

265 "Do you think a Virginian": James S. Easley, letter to S. Noble, April 20, 1861, Easley Manuscripts, University of Virginia Library.

266 more than half the stock: Frederick Jackson Turner, *The United States, 1830–1850: The Nation and Its Sections*, pp. 177–78.

266 the real-estate investments of southerners: Paul W. Gates, "Southern Investments in Northern Lands Before the Civil War," pp. 155ff.

266 "Easley was his favorite partner": Pocahontas Wight Edmunds, *History of Halifax.*

267 southern "mania" for northern land: Gates, op. cit., pp. 155ff.

268 "We are truly happy": James S. Easley and Willingham, letter to Hoyt Sherman, May 12, 1865, quoted in Robert P. Swierenga, *Pioneers and Profits: Land Speculation on the Iowa Frontier*, p. 175.

268 "Hold on to my western lands": Ibid., p. 179. For Easley's postwar operations, see pp. 175–79.

271 "the omphalos was Philadelphia": Catherine Bishir, quoted in Doug Swaim, ed., *Carolina Dwelling*, p. 87.

PART IV. *Across the Mountains*

CHAPTER 18. *Orpheus Observed*

277 "Everything . . . looks perennial": Charleston *Courier*, May 31, 1843.

279 became rich very quickly: Michael Zuckerman, who may not agree with my speculations about esthetic history, has suggested in letters the possibility that the success of the Tennessee group, in particular, arose from their marginality amid the political equipoise of the time.

280 conservative and chary of change: For the other side of the case, for Jackson as precursor to Franklin D. Roosevelt, see Arthur Schlesinger, Jr., *The Age of Jackson.*

282 "only two houses": Henry Nash Smith, *Virgin Land: The American West as Symbol and Myth*, p. 25.

282 "not less than one thousand": Ibid.

284 "substantial, independent yeomanry": Ibid., p. 134.

285 "agricultural labor": Ibid., p. 144.

287 "culture productive of": Boynton Merrill, *Jefferson's Nephews: A Frontier Tragedy*, p. 45.

288 "worn out": Ibid.

288 "washed away the earth": Ibid., p. 47.

288 "Tobacco planters gave up": United States Works Projects Administration, *Guide to Virginia*, p. 62.

288 "men are raised": Miller, op. cit., p. 241.

288 "beyond the mountains": Ibid., pp. 240–41.

288 "I consider a woman": Ibid., p. 251.

CHAPTER 19. *The Carter Mansion*

292 between 1775 and 1800: Samuel D. Smith, ed., *Summary of Archaeological Explorations at the Carter House.*

292 "extraordinary great hall": Hamlin, *Greek Revival Architecture in America*, p. 236.

293 Salmon's book: For the use of Salmon in Virginia, see Waterman and Johnston, op. cit., references under *Palladio Londinensis* on p. 450.

296 Corotoman: Ibid., p. 110.

297 John Carter of Tennessee: I am indebted to John F. Hackett for some of the archival research

that follows, including the appraisal of Carter's wealth. There is a vast cache of documentary evidence assembled by Pollyanna Creekmore and Muriel C. Spoden for the Tennessee Historical Commission and the Tennessee Department of Conservation, dated May 1974 (now available through the Tennessee Department of Conservation, Division of Parks and Recreation, Nashville, Tennessee); the loss of records mentioned here appears in a letter on p. 830.

298   "he was a kinsman of Robert": *Dictionary of American Biography*, vol. 3, p. 539.

298   Tennessee historians: Mary F. Caldwell, *Tennessee: The Volunteer State, 1769–1923*, vol. 2, p. 86; Creekmore and Spoden, op. cit., p. 853.

299   emerges into history: Creekmore and Spoden, op. cit., p. 852.

299   Amherst County: Charlottesville, Va., "Articles of Agreement of the Albemarle Iron Works," ibid., p. 823. The Amherst County, Virginia, *Deed Book* for October 1765 lists a John Carter as "planter," but this is probably John son of Charles, son of Thomas. The Virginia *Gazette* for February 1765 gives Edward Carter as the family representative in the winding-up of the business of Carter and Trent. (He would have been older than John of Tennessee.)

299   Blenheim: United States Works Projects Administration, op. cit., p. 627; Garden Club of Virginia, op. cit., pp. 388ff. The details are not crucial to our story, but should be rechecked against primary sources for other purposes.

299   "by reason of his eminence": *Dictionary of American Biography*, vol. 3, p. 539.

299   In 1769: George Melvin Herndon, *William Tatham, 1752–1819: American Versatile*.

300   "Virginia people" were "insisting": Creekmore and Spoden, op. cit., p. 824.

300   goodwill among the Indians: Ibid., p. 825.

300   "to fight the English": Ibid.

301   "an irregular squatters association": Frederick Merk, *History of the Westward Movement*, p. 85.

301   "a dangerous example": Mary F. Caldwell, op. cit., pp. 365–66.

301   "many persons of distinction": Ibid.

302   "in every respect": Ibid.

302   "The property of the Tories": Colonel G. W. Sevier, quoted in Creekmore and Spoden, op. cit., pp. 326–27.

302   a quarter of all the slaves: Ibid., p. 875.

303   "Have [you] any knowledge": Ibid., pp. 831–32.

CHAPTER 20. *The Legitimate Succession*

307   "to make a country": Michael Paul Rogin, *Fathers and Children*, p. 76.

307   "expressed doubts": Ibid., p. 91.

308   "ruinous" expansions: Marvin Meyers, *The Jacksonian Persuasion: Politics and Belief*, p. 28.

311   "housing of a very proud": Joseph Frazer Smith, op. cit., p. 73.

312   "Here lies the dust": Ibid., p. 72.

318   "the largest single stones": Albert W. Wardin, Jr., *Belmont Mansion*, p. 25.

318   "The marbles and pictures": Ibid., p. 27.

CHAPTER 21. *Cotton Pull*

320   "The Southern states": Vernon L. Parrington, *Main Currents in American Thought*, p. 80.

321   "white-columned plantation houses": Wright, *South Carolina: A Bicentennial History*, p. 151.

322   "Great Britain will lose": Douglas C. North, *The Economic Growth of the United States, 1790–1860*, p. 22.

322   "peddling traffic": Eric Williams, *Capitalism and Slavery*, p. 128.

322   "disseverence of the United States": Ibid.

325 "The British . . . demand": William Henderson Brantley, *Banking in Alabama, 1816–1860*, vol. 1, p. 346.

325 "long trains of cars": Mills Lane, *The People of Georgia: An Illustrated Social History*, p. 154.

326 "a kind of cotton insanity": Ibid.

326 "cotton manufacturers from Manchester": Ibid., p. 153.

326 "On deck, a few gentlemen": Ibid., p. 154.

326 Along the Carolina coast: David Moltke-Hansen, ed., *Art in the Lives of South Carolinians: Nineteenth-Century Chapters*, p. b-13.

327 "worn-out, sad, exhausted": Lane, op. cit., p. 161.

327 "deserted plantations": Ibid.

327 "many gangs of slaves": Ibid., p. 164.

327 "Lord, Lord, Howell": Ibid., p. 161.

327 "men in constant motion": Meyers, op. cit., pp. 31–33.

328 "We are just allowed": William Robert Taylor, *Cavalier and Yankee*, pp. 207, 223.

331 "where all is peace": Miller, op. cit., p. 105.

331 "all the whites": Ibid., p. 218.

331 "nothing portends more calamity and mischief": Ibid., p. 217.

331 "throw so many wild Tigers": Ibid., p. 135.

331 that information was shared: Eugene D. Genovese, *From Rebellion to Revolution: Afro-American Slave Revolts in the Making of the Modern World*.

332 "Guiana averaged": Ibid., p. 33.

333 "exciting these very people": Richard Drinnon, *Facing West*, pp. 90, 97. See also Rogin, op. cit., pp. 27–28; Walter Lord, *The Dawn's Early Light*, pp. 44–45.

333 "a Negro, not an Indian": Rogin, op. cit., pp. 194–95

334 "allow no terms to the Indians": Ibid., p. 238.

335 "like the weak": William H. Freehling, *Prelude to Civil War: The Nullification Controversy in South Carolina, 1816–1836*, p. 127; and Robert W. Fogel and Stanley L. Engerman, *Time on the Cross: The Economics of American Negro Slavery*, pp. 33–34.

CHAPTER 22. *Pericles and Tara*

339 "persuasive ideal": Parrington, op. cit., pp. 69ff., esp. 78–81.

339 "Calhoun cleverly harmonized": Clement Eaton, *The Freedom-of-Thought Struggle in the Old South*, pp. 155–56.

339 "called for the establishment": Rollin G. Osterweiss, *Romanticism and Nationalism in the Old South*, pp. 108–109.

340 "an evolving consciousness": Ibid., p. 206.

340 "illustrative, not determinative": Lewis Cohn-Haft, "The Founding Fathers and Antiquity: A Selection Passion," p. 139.

341 "very little": Ibid., p. 148.

341 The Founding Fathers: Charles Pinckney, John Adams, James Madison, Thomas Jefferson and Benjamin Rush, all quoted in ibid., pp. 151–53.

344 William Gilmore Simms: Gene Waddell, "The Introduction of Greek Revival Architecture to Charleston."

CHAPTER 23. *Elegance and Terror: The Wade Hamptons*

346 Hamptons of Virginia . . . : Ronald Edward Bridwell, *The South's Wealthiest Planter: Wade Hampton I of South Carolina, 1754–1835*, p. 756. Here and hereafter, I rely upon what is by far

the best work written on the Hamptons, this exemplary but as yet unpublished Ph.D. dissertation for the University of South Carolina. See also Roger Stroup, "Up-Country Patrons."

346 "a seat within the bar": Robert Stroup, "Up-Country Patrons," p. 2.

346 "was hailed by a buzz of welcome": Ibid.

346 "complete model and specimen": Ibid.

346 "he not only mistreats his slaves": Bridwell, op. cit., p. 772.

347 "glad" Stuart "exposed": Ibid.

347 "Their house is a perfect curiosity shop": Stroup, op. cit., p. 9.

347 "strung aloft": Ibid., p. 577.

347 "splendid dinner": Bridwell, op. cit., pp. 578, 756.

348 "seemed to thrive": Ibid., pp. 424, 771, 772–73.

348 "burst into tears": Stroup, op. cit., p. 5.

348 "mad . . . with the love of money": Bridwell, op. cit., pp. 76, 77, 80, 91.

349 "a true and faithful subject": Ibid., pp. 117–18, 125.

350 "some of the West India islands": Ibid., p. 501.

350 "Shaking his long, lean finger": Ibid., p. 280.

350 "processing nearly two million"; Ibid., p. 316.

350 "in his proud meridian": Ibid., p. 324.

351 "bear the system": Ibid., p. 384.

351 "a great enemy to finery": Ibid., p. 383.

351 "vigorous, prompt, sagacious": Ibid., p. 503.

351 "the most extensive planter": Ibid., pp. 386–87.

351 "called away on business": Ibid., pp. 388, 391.

351 "Brigadier General Wade Hampton": Ibid., p. 394.

351 "ingenious young mechanic": Ibid., pp. 406ff.

352 "plain . . . in his dress": Ibid., p. 768.

352 "a commission of 25": Ibid.

352 the old man's will: Waddell, "The Introduction of Greek Revival Architecture to Charleston," p. 2. See also Bridwell, op. cit., p. 780.

354 Robert Mills: Mills's design for Hampton is located at the South Carolina Historical Society.

355 conversation with Governor Manning: Edward E. Potter, quoted in the Manning-Potter "transcript," which appears in the *Sumter Watchman and Southern* as one of a series of weekly installments by the Reverend W. W. Mood, commencing July 8, 1886.

356 "would eclipse every thing": Minard Lafever, *The Beauties of Modern Architecture*, p. 94.

356 "in every respect": John L. Manning, letter of May 22, 1839, quoted in Thomas M. Stubbs, "Milford."

356 Potter, who provided the specifications: Potter's specifications appear in the *Newsletter of the Victorian Society*, Winter 1973–74, vol. 5, no. 7.

358 Beatrice St. Julien Ravenel: *Architects of Charleston*.

358 "constructed from designs": Dr. Irving's statement appeared in the Charleston *Daily Courier* on April 16, 1870, and was reprinted in the *South Carolina Historical Magazine*, vol. 53, p. 41. I am indebted to Gene Waddell of the South Carolina Historical Society for this attribution.

358 Reichardt and Lafever: Ravenel, op. cit.

360 Neoclassic palace: For Millwood, the best information (until Waddell and Martz publish their research on the topic) is to be found in Anne King Gregorie's *History of Sumter County*. See also the Charleston *Courier*, September 27, 1844.

360 "an extended tour throughout the West": Stubbs, op. cit.

360 "a tough son of a bitch": Carol Bleser, *The Hammonds of Redcliffe*, pp. 7–8.

360 "cotton is King": Ibid., p. 40. Hammond's speech to the U.S. Senate was delivered on March 4, 1858.

361   He was a most unadmirable man: For a good, temperate, brief account of Hammond's life, see ibid., pp. 7ff., 32–33.

363   "a pompous thing": Wayne Andrews, op. cit., p. 107.

363   "six feet in height": Claude G. Bowers, *The Tragic Era: The Revolution After Lincoln*, pp. 508–509.

364   "Wade Hampton was symbolical": Ibid.

CHAPTER 24. *Natchez, and the Nutts*

368   the Surgetts: Herbert Weaver, *Mississippi Farmers, 1850–1860*, p. 108.

368   Nathaniel Ware: Paul W. Gates, op. cit., p. 160.

368   "much struck with the similarity": Fortescue Coming, *Sketches of a Tour*, p. 293.

368   Harding and Weeks: Millie McGehee, "Auburn in Natchez," pp. 546ff.

368   Aaron Burr's western empire: For Aaron Burr in Natchez, see Harnett T. Kane, *Natchez on the Mississippi*, pp. 29ff., not a very sympathetic account. For one more persuasive to me, see Gore Vidal's *Burr: A Novel*, pp. 382ff., or better still, see any one of the standard biographies of Burr.

370   a defense team: Vidal puts the account of this trial in the mouth of Washington Irving (*Burr*, pp. 153–54), a pretty conceit, but his account does square with the court records.

370   Levin Marshall: What little we know of Marshall can be found in Kane, op. cit., pp. 190ff., and some passing references to his landholdings in Weaver, op. cit., pp. 108, 109, 118, 119.

370   "of slight build": Kane, op. cit., p. 191.

373   "Canute": Merle C. Nutt, *The Nutt Family Through the Years, 1635–1973*, pp. 4ff.

373   "numbered among his friends": Ibid., p. 86.

373   America's scientific genius: Daniel Boorstin, *The Lost World of Thomas Jefferson*, p. 13.

373   Benjamin Rush: Ibid., pp. 14–15.

373   John Fitch and James Rumsey: Brooke Hindle, *Emulation and Invention*, pp. 25ff.

373   Nutt's journal: Portions of Nutt's journal are reprinted in Logan, op. cit., pp. 27ff.; larger portions are accessible from the Park Service, and the Huntington Library has a list of some of his writings.

374   "could have been a house": Logan, op. cit., p. 30, fn. 77.

374   "had passed all his life": John Lloyd Stephens, *Incidents of Travel in Greece, Turkey, Russia, and Poland*, pp. 203ff.

374   "a strong, active": Ibid., pp. 204–205.

375   "a noteworthy literary center": William Banks Taylor, *King Cotton and Old Glory: Natchez in the Age of Sectional Controversy and Civil War*, pp. 7–8.

375   to find strains: John Francis Hamtramck Claiborne, *Mississippi as a Province, Territory and State*, pp. 141–42. See also Logan, op. cit., pp. 44–45, and Kane, op. cit., pp. 288ff.

375   "very prolific": Claiborne, op. cit., p. 141.

375   "all the work": Ina May Ogletree McAdams, *The Building of "Longwood,"* pp. 110ff.

376   "created a new industry": Logan, op. cit., p. 46.

378   "partially blind": McAdams, op. cit., pp. 110ff. For Nutt's character, I will offer many examples in the correspondence cited.

CHAPTER 25. *Samuel Sloan and the Octagon*

381   Ross Winans: John H. White, Jr., *American Locomotives: An Engineering History, 1830–1880*, p. 22, appendix A. I have been unable to find very complete coverage of the two Winans, though

they appear in standard histories of the B&O, and their antics are nicely summarized in White, op. cit., pp. 22ff. The Russian adventures are reported in Albert Parry, *Whistler's Father*, pp. 25–29, 37–38, 155–57, 159 and 284 especially, though the whole book is worth reading. For biographical summaries and dates, I have used White's exemplary appendix A.

383 "in a pleasant and courteous way": Harold N. Cooledge, *Samuel Sloan, 1815–1884, Architect.* For this account I am indebted to Cooledge's discovery of an unidentified newspaper clipping, cited on p. 51. Sloan's description appears in several editions of his *Model Architect.*

385 a hard-drinking Scot: Constance M. Greiff, *John Notman, Architect, 1860–1865,* esp. pp. 63ff.

386 Harrison commissioned from Sloan: Cooledge, op. cit., pp. 68ff.

387 expressed doubts: Boorstin, op. cit., pp. 112ff.

387 the pyramids: Kane, op. cit., p. 289.

390 "An Oriental Villa": Samuel Sloan, *The Model Architect,* vol. 1. pp. 76–77.

390 "Let every one": Ibid., vol. 2, pp. 71–73.

391 "the choice of style": Samuel Sloan, *Sloan's Homestead Architecture,* design no. 1. This is also the design that appeared in *Godey's Ladies' Book* of 1860.

394 "it is creating much admiration": Haller Nutt, letter to Samuel Sloan, March 20, 1861. All letters mentioned in this and the following chapters can be found (unless otherwise noted) in McAdams, op. cit.

394 "the Octagon . . . the style": Haller Nutt, letter to Samuel Sloan, May 19, 1861.

394 "To cheapen and improve': Orson Squire Fowler, *A Home for All, or, A New, Cheap, Convenient, and Superior Mode of Building,* p. 3.

394 psychological theories: For a good summary of current locational theories for the brain, see Richard M. Restak, "The Brain."

396 "more sociability": Carmer, op. cit., pp. 272ff. Carmer lived in a famous octagon in Irvington, New York.

396 "the form as applied": Fowler, op. cit., preface.

396 reasons of comfort and economy: Steen Eiler Rasmussen, *Towns and Buildings Described in Drawings and Words;* p. 139; and Emil Kaufmann, *Architecture in the Age of Reason: Baroque and Post-Baroque in England, Italy, and France,* pp. 62ff.

398 Thomas Jefferson was encouraged: William Howard Adams, ed., *The Eye of Thomas Jefferson,* pp. 19, 274, 275, 278.

398 Latrobe's competitive design: Hamlin, *Benjamin Henry Latrobe,* pp. 104–105.

CHAPTER 26. *Building Longwood*

400 Colonel Ventress . . . and John O. Thorn: There are constant references to Ventress in the Sloan-Nutt correspondence. Thorn appears in Sloan to Nutt, March 31, 1860, and Bishop Polk in a letter dated July 16, 1860. All letters mentioned in this chapter (unless otherwise noted) can be found in McAdams, op. cit.

400 "southern Yankees": William Robert Taylor, op. cit., p. 10.

401 bankers in Paris and London: Cooledge, op. cit. I am indebted to Harold Cooledge for the information that Nutt dealt directly with French and British buyers and had bank accounts there, information based upon his study of unpublished correspondence and records in the Nutt papers in the Huntington Library.

401 One half of the city's richest men: William Robert Taylor, op. cit., p. 12.

402 Stephen Duncan . . . Edward MacGehee: Ibid., pp. 16–17.

402 The tension between the big planters and the artisan class: William Robert Taylor, ibid., does an excellent job of summarizing this material and gives a good list of scholarly references. See especially pp. 16ff. and his notes.

402   Seargent S. Prentiss: Quoted in ibid., p. 22.

402   "disorganizing and revolutionary": Ibid., p. 27.

403   the Confederate flag never flew: Ibid., pp. 39, 43.

403   "this infernal Secession" and "someday . . . our last": Ibid., pp. 45, 46; and Kane, op. cit., pp. 190ff.

405   "swan song": Hamlin, *Greek Revival Architecture in America*, p. 63.

408   He left after overhearing: Elizabeth Biddle Yarnall, *Addison Hutton, Quaker Architect, 1834–1916*, p. 33.

410   His wife estimated: Julia Nutt's 1883 deposition against the U.S. government is reprinted in full in McAdams, op. cit.

410   boarded up: Kane, op. cit., pp. 290–91.

414   "essentially an X": Samuel Sloan quoted in George L. Hersey, "Godey's Choice," p. 108.

Part V. *Pivot Point*

416   "praised and respected": Turner, op. cit., p. 109.

Chapter 27. *Hellenism in the North*

420   "What Athens was": Henry S. Commager, *The Empire of Reason*, p. 26.

420   "Oration to the Society": Hamlin, *Benjamin Henry Latrobe*, pp. 318–19; see also Alan Gowans, *Images of American Living: Four Centuries of Architecture and Furniture as Cultural Expression*, pp. 261–62.

425   eclectic styles: Summerson, op. cit., p. 42.

Chapter 28. *Solid Citizens in Indiana*

427   "waters of the Great Lakes": Carmer, op. cit., pp. 219–20.

427   "rolled back the mighty tide": Quoted in Harry J. Carman and Harold C. Syrett, *A History of the American People*, vol. 2, p. 142.

428   Frederick Jackson Turner totted up: Turner, op. cit., pp. 269–76.

429   "unconstitutional, an obstruction": Carl Sandburg, *Abraham Lincoln: The Prairie Years*, vol. 2, p. 39.

429   "has its rights": Ibid., p. 38.

429   "a mighty shout": Marquis Childs, *Mighty Mississippi*, p. 96.

431   "this locomotive age": Calvert Vaux, *Villas and Cottages*, p. 45.

432   "The . . . mind is not complex": Henry Adams, *The Education of Henry Adams*, as quoted in Raymond D. Gastil, *Cultural Regions of the United States*, p. 171.

435   Shrewsbury grew old: As to Charles Shrewsbury himself, there is very little information outside of church records and local memories, upon which I have relied, but which cannot be rechecked by other scholars. For the Shrewsbury clan, and the Kanawha salt business, I am grateful for the assistance of Professor Emory Kemp of West Virginia University, and to the following sources: E. T. Crawford, Jr., "Salt—Pioneer Chemical Industry of the Kanawha Valley"; Marijida Waldron Mosby, "Salt Industry in the Kanawha Valley"; John Edmund Stealey, "The Salt Industry of the Great Kanawha Valley of Virginia: A Study in Ante-Bellum Internal Commerce"; Ruth Woods Dayton, *Pioneers and Their Homes on Upper Kanawha*; William Sydney Laidley, *History of Charleston and Kanawha County*; Julius Allan De Gruyter,

The *Kanawha Spectator;* John Hardesty, *West Virginia Counties;* and Kanawha County court records.

435 John Woodburn: In 1982, while this chapter was being composed, a sheaf of typed notes was found in the Madison-Jefferson County Library, dated April 22, 1927, with the notation "Irvington," which was where one Shrewsbury daughter, Mary Shrewsbury Wyatt, and her daughter, Eleanor Wyatt Wood, were living on that date. They appear to be family reminiscences, and I have taken the material in this paragraph from those notes.

CHAPTER 29. *Salt Pork, Railroads and War*

436 Hogs prowled: Henry G. Waltman, *Livestock and Poultry in Frontier Indiana.*

437 Bankers tended to be Whigs: Turner, op. cit., p. 303.

437 "that begemmed the terrace": George S. Cottman, *The James F. D. Lanier Memorial Home: An Indiana Memorial,* pp. 16, 19. 20.

437 he enjoyed describing it: James Lanier, *Memoirs.*

438 "I was diligent": Ibid., pp. 6, 11.

438 Jackson the speculator: Ibid., pp. 6, 7.

439 his father's debts: Ibid., pp. 7, 8, 11.

440 "situated on a narrow neck": Ibid., pp. 7–8.

440 "hold out lures": Ibid., pp. 9–10.

440 "through the instrumentality of the railway": Ibid., p. 8.

440 "became master": Ibid., p. 12.

441 "the terrible catastrophe": Ibid., pp. 13–14.

441 "much to our convenience": Ibid., p. 16.

441 "the subject of railroad construction": Ibid., pp. 17–18.

442 "Mr. Lanier brought with him": *American Railroad Journal,* March 2, 1861.

442 "In newspaper articles": Lanier, op. cit., pp. 17, 19, 20.

442 "without feeling a disposition": Thomas C. Cochran and William Miller, *A Social History of Industrialization,* pp. 48–49.

442 "You may tell your government": Ibid.

442 in Paris: Martha J. Coleman, "Milestones in Indiana."

442 "a million of bonds": Lanier, op. cit., p. 19.

443 "had, above all men": Ibid.

443 "many of our most valuable": Ibid., pp. 24, 28.

443 "Success or defeat": Ibid., p. 11.

443 guarantee payment personally: *American Railroad Journal,* March 2, 1861.

444 deeply southern . . . "bitterly opposed": Lanier, op. cit., pp. 32–33.

444 "to equip and put promptly": Cottman, op. cit., p. 8.

444 "the real leader": *Encyclopaedia Britannica,* 11th edition (London: 1911), vol. 12, p. 69.

444 "Jefferson Davis": Eric Williams, op. cit., pp. 176–77.

444 John Gladstone: Ibid., pp. 89–90.

444 "partners with the Southern": Ibid., pp. 176–77.

444 offered to pay: Cottman, op. cit., pp. 16–20, and Lanier, op. cit., pp. 32–35. Cottman's account of these transactions is confirmed by Lanier, though he omits the first $400,000. More details are given in O. P. Morton, "Message to the General Assembly of Indiana," January 6, 1865, which can be found in the Indiana Historical Society Archives.

445 "a business man": Lanier, op. cit., p. 37; mention of his European expeditions may be found in the *National Cyclopedia of American Biography* (New York: James T. White & Co., 1898), vol. 23, p. 199.

445 Francis Costigan: There is no published biography of Costigan. The newspaper accounts of his work are a litter of errors, but there is a good unpublished master's thesis, "Francis Costigan," by Todd R. Mozingo of the University of Virginia (1975), available from Historic Madison, Inc., which does very well in sorting out what was known by 1975.

445 Frederick Street in Baltimore: *Baltimore City Directory*.

445 purchased property: Jefferson County *Deed Book* P, p. 179, November 13, 1838.

445 baptized his child: St. Michael's Church baptismal records, Madison, 1838.

445 Jacob Shuh: U.S., Department of the Interior, "Shuh-Leininger-Holstein-Whitsitt House," pp. 3, 7, 12.

446 St. Michael's: "Trace Church Builder."

446 Vine Street: Jefferson County *Deed Book* P, p. 179, November 13, 1838.

446 "Mr. Francis Costigan": "Trace Church Builder."

447 James Dakin's Bank: Arthur Scully, Jr., *James Dakin, Architect: His Career in New York and the South*, pp. 26ff.

449 Local folk memory: Mozingo, op. cit., p. 41.

449 Madison Hotel: Cottman, op. cit., p. 14.

449 Costigan's hand: Mozingo, pp. 68ff., and Anton Scherrer, "Francis Costigan," pp. 30–33. Scherrer is accurate for these, which I have confirmed with contemporary and later newspaper accounts, but is otherwise as sprinkled with errors as is almost everything else written about Costigan. Elsewhere, Costigan has been credited with Ammi B. Young's Post Office in Indianapolis, later the Fletcher Bank, and with James Renwick's Odd Fellows Hall. The Odd Fellows *Annual Communication* of July 1853 takes care of the latter, and the National Archives, Records Group 121, Entry 26, Box 114, the former.

450 "beautifully rendered": "The Wash Tub."

451 "Costigan's Blind Institute": Ibid.

451 the Oriental House: The Oriental House was included in Costigan's will, so it seems that this attribution is correct, though it appears in a wildly inaccurate statement of his work in Berry R. Sulgrove, *History of Indianapolis and Marion County* (Philadelphia, 1884). We are told of the will in Lee Burns, *Early Architects and Builders of Indiana*, which is generally correct but misattributes Renwick's Odd Fellows Hall to Costigan.

452 "does not represent": Indianapolis *News*, April 9, 1921. Scherrer tells us that the "surmise" was by Dr. Alembert W. Brayton. Scherrer (op cit., note 5) says that "to my knowledge, nobody in Indianapolis ever had the temerity to question Dr. Brayton's opinions."

452 "a sorry looking": Indianapolis *News*, April 9, 1921.

452 botanical wonders: Anton Scherrer, article in Indianapolis *Times*, October 10, 1945.

452 A Scots carpenter: T. V. Krull, article in Indianapolis *Star*, vertical file of Historic Madison, Inc., date mutilated, but presumably of the 1930's.

452 "there are old residences": Claude J. Hammond, article in Shelbyville *Democrat*, November 4, 1929, quoted in *Indiana Biography* series, vol. 4, p. 1. Like articles about Lanier and Costigan in *Outdoor Indiana*, it is a nest of errors.

452 his work in Madison: Mozingo, op. cit., attributes to Costigan the Claypool House "to the south of the Hasselman residence," but gives no documentation, and the John A. Bridgeland House in Richmond, Indiana, citing the Richmond *Democrat* of October 20, 1964. But Costigan scholars have had bad luck with newspapers.

CHAPTER 30. *The American Picturesque*

457 "venerable family-mansion": Terence Davis, *The Gothick Taste*, p. 22.

458 "the Grecian or Roman": Scully, op. cit., p. 128.

459   in musical . . . terms: An admirable summary of what Alexander Jackson Davis meant by "composing" is found in William H. Pierson, Jr.'s, *American Buildings and Their Architects*, vol. 2, pp. 270ff.

459   "the expression of every house": Andrew Jackson Downing, *The Architecture of Country Houses*, pp. 260–61.

461   "jackdaw": Ibid., p. 263, and also Pierson, op. cit., p. 297.

461   "of elegant culture": Downing, op. cit., p. 286.

461   "a man of wealth": Sloan, *Sloan's Homestead Architecture*, p. 32.

462   "The bell turret": Available through the Metropolitan Museum of Art's Prints and Drawings Division.

462   Mount Holly: Greiff, op. cit., pp. 66ff., 80ff.

462   St. Mary's: Phoebe B. Stanton, *The Gothic Revival and American Church Architecture*, pp. 31ff., 73ff.

CHAPTER 31. *Minnesota Gothic*

467   "little importance": *American Heritage Atlas of American History*, p. 158.

468   explorers, exploiters and settlers: This description first appeared twenty years ago in my *Men on the Moving Frontier*, now out of print.

469   "Well, sir": Thomas McLean Newson, *Pen Pictures of St. Paul, Minnesota, and Biographical Sketches of Old Settlers, from the Earliest Settlements of the City, up to and Including the Year 1857*, p. 208.

470   In Vermont: Turner, op. cit., p. 266.

470   Only ten: Ibid., p. 273.

471   sons of New England: Much of what we have to say of William Gates LeDuc can be in his own words, thanks to the North Central Publishing Company of St. Paul, which in 1963 published his *Recollections of a Civil War Quartermaster*, one of the most entertaining of American autobiographies. It met with disgracefully crabbed and uncomprehending reviews from local historians. See pp. 42ff. and 53 for references to Yankee immigrants and bison at the Crystal Palace.

471   "no part of the West": *Daily National Intelligencer*, January 31, 1857.

471   blueberry wine: LeDuc, op. cit., p. 148.

472   "abuse and ridicule": Ibid., p. 151.

472   "the proper place": Ibid., pp. 149ff.

473   Louisiana sugar planters: Ibid., pp. 158–61; U.S., Department of Agriculture, *Century of Service*, p. 21.

473   "a loyal citizen": LeDuc, op. cit., pp. 139ff.

CHAPTER 32. *The Career of William Gates LeDuc*

475   "was not attractive": LeDuc, op. cit., p. 22.

476   "Where shall I go?": Ibid., p. 29.

476   "giving names": Ibid., p. 36.

476   "a tall, quick": Newson, op. cit., p. 222.

476   development of the modern typewriter: Among innumerable possible sources of information about the early typewriter, I have used Michael H. Adler, *The Writing Machine*, p. 138. (Adler spells LeDuc "LeDue.") See also *The Story of the Typewriter*, p. 36; Augustine V. Gardner's introduction to LeDuc, op. cit., p. x.

477   "a small colony of Yankees": LeDuc, op. cit., pp. 43, 53ff.

477   English agriculturalists: Ibid., p. 156.

477   "Everybody went into the business": Newson, op. cit., p. 666.

478   "all of a sudden": Ibid., pp. 675–76.

478   "striking want": Jean A. Brookings, "A Historic Mansion," p. 192.

478   to reverse it: Ibid., p. 193.

479   "Our house will have to stand": Mary LeDuc, letter dated January 1, 1863, located in Minnesota Historical Society Archives.

479   "Calliero Silks": William LeDuc, letter to Mary LeDuc, December 17, 1862, Minnesota Historical Society Archives.

480   "no mechanic": Eric Cogshall, letter to William LeDuc, April 14, 1863, Minnesota Historical Society Archives.

480   "of the happiness": Mary LeDuc, letter to William LeDuc, April 12, 1863, Minnesota Historical Society Archives.

480   "I had once owned": *Battles and Leaders of the Civil War, Being for the Most Part Contributions by Union and Confederate Officers*, vol. 3, pp. 676ff.; more details are to be found in Ralph Knight, "The Miraculous Steamboat."

482   "never had as unplesant a job": Eric Cogshall, letter to William LeDuc, November 8, 1863, Minnesota Historical Society Archives.

482   "some lots": William Gates LeDuc, diary, March 4, vol. 243, Minnesota Historical Society Archives.

482   "I will not go into debt": Janet L. Kreger, "Construction of a Wilderness Mansion," p. 18.

482   "I will have to borrow": William LeDuc, letter to Mary LeDuc, May 13, 1863, Minnesota Historical Society Archives.

482   "anxious and troubled": Mary LeDuc, letter to William LeDuc, May 20, 1863, Minnesota Historical Society Archives.

482   "All the use I have": William LeDuc, letter to Mary LeDuc, August 12, 1863, Minnesota Historical Society Archives.

482   "it is quite a job": Brookings, op. cit., pp. 195ff.

483   "when me and Cog was shingling": Kreger, op. cit., p. 21.

483   "dress up and put on airs": William LeDuc, letter to Mary LeDuc, December 30, 1863, Minnesota Historical Society Archives.

483   "Aunt Sally": Mary LeDuc, letter to William LeDuc, May 31, 1863, Minnesota Historical Society Archives.

483   "This and the rents": William LeDuc, letter to Mary LeDuc, April 28, 1863, Minnesota Historical Society Archives.

483   "if I get out": William LeDuc, letter to Mary LeDuc, March 23, 1864, Minnesota Historical Society Archives.

483   "the house we built": Brookings, op. cit., p. 198.

484   "an old Castilian": William Gates LeDuc, *Recollections of a Civil War Quartermaster*, p. 11.

484   "complete with a hook": Brookings, op. cit., p. 200.

485   "Do you see": Andrew Jackson Downing, op. cit., p. 262.

Index

About the Author

Since 1979 ROGER G. KENNEDY has been director of the National Museum of American History at the Smithsonian Institution. Prior to his appointment at the Smithsonian, he was vice president of financial affairs for the Ford Foundation and also vice president for the arts of that foundation. A former banker who currently serves as director of and/or consultant to a number of international financial and industrial organizations, he is also the author of the highly acclaimed book *American Churches*, published in 1982.